Gangs in America's Communities

Second Edition

SAGE was founded in 1965 by Sara Miller McCune to support the dissemination of usable knowledge by publishing innovative and high-quality research and teaching content. Today, we publish more than 750 journals, including those of more than 300 learned societies, more than 800 new books per year, and a growing range of library products including archives, data, case studies, reports, conference highlights, and video. SAGE remains majority-owned by our founder, and after Sara's lifetime will become owned by a charitable trust that secures our continued independence.

Los Angeles | London | Washington DC | New Delhi | Singapore | Boston

Gangs in America's Communities

Second Edition

James C. Howell
National Gang Center

Elizabeth Griffiths
Rutgers University

Los Angeles | London | New Delhi
Singapore | Washington DC | Boston

Los Angeles | London | New Delhi
Singapore | Washington DC | Boston

FOR INFORMATION:

SAGE Publications, Inc.
2455 Teller Road
Thousand Oaks, California 91320
E-mail: order@sagepub.com

SAGE Publications Ltd.
1 Oliver's Yard
55 City Road
London EC1Y 1SP
United Kingdom

SAGE Publications India Pvt. Ltd.
B 1/I 1 Mohan Cooperative Industrial Area
Mathura Road, New Delhi 110 044
India

SAGE Publications Asia-Pacific Pte. Ltd.
3 Church Street
#10-04 Samsung Hub
Singapore 049483

Copyright © 2016 by SAGE Publications, Inc.

Printed in the United States of America

Cataloging-in-publication data is available from the Library of Congress.

ISBN 978-1-4833-7972-2

This book is printed on acid-free paper.

Acquisitions Editor: Jerry Westby
Editorial Assistant: Laura Kirkhuff
Production Editor: Olivia Weber-Stenis
Copy Editor: Matthew Connor Sullivan
Typesetter: C&M Digitals (P) Ltd.
Proofreader: Sally Jaskold
Indexer: Jeanne R. Busemeyer
Cover Designer: Anupama Krishnan
Marketing Manager: Terra Schultz

SUSTAINABLE FORESTRY INITIATIVE
Certified Chain of Custody
Promoting Sustainable Forestry
www.sfiprogram.org
SFI-01268
SFI label applies to text stock

15 16 17 18 19 10 9 8 7 6 5 4 3 2 1

Brief Contents

Detailed Contents

Preface

Street gangs can be perplexing, and fighting them is often considered a futile exercise. The two main purposes of this book are, first, to demonstrate that the essential features of street gangs can be understood despite their highly varied and sometimes enigmatic public presence, and second, that some gang prevention, control strategies, and programs are effective, in contradiction of widespread proclamations that nothing works.

Street gangs are not well understood largely because they are typically shrouded in myths (some of which they create themselves), folklore, urban legends, media exaggerations, popular misconceptions, and international intrigue. Taking a historical approach to the emergence of gangs in the United States, this book uncovers their origins and traces their development, first, in the Northeast region of the United States; next, in the Midwest; then, in the West region; and last, in the Southern region. The authors analyze the key historical events that produced waves of gang growth in the respective regions. These trends are brought up to date with 14 years of annual national survey data showing a marked increase in gang activity since the beginning of the new millennium. The book also examines gang trends along the U.S.–Mexico border and in Central America, along with an assessment of the threat of such highly publicized gangs as Mara Salvatrucha (MS-13) and 18th Street (M-18), and prison gangs such as the Mexican Mafia.

American gang history also serves as an excellent backdrop for reviews of myths about gangs, theories of gang formation, and various ways of defining and classifying gangs. Gangs emerged in the United States in a rainbow of colors, beginning with the White ones, reflecting both outside immigration and internal racial/ethnic and territorial conflicts. Understanding the history of evolving gangs in America also engenders a stark realization that gang joining is typically a logical choice for powerless and marginalized youth who have been relegated to the fringes of society. Social and economic conditions in inner-city areas, organized crime, and deviancy centers foster widespread criminal activity where ganging together for safety is an understandable response.

The text explains how youngsters who are making the transition from childhood to adolescence form new gangs. These *starter gangs* often emerge somewhat spontaneously by authority-rejecting children and adolescents who have been alienated from families and schools. Finding themselves spending a great deal of time on the street, youth may form gangs with other socially marginalized adolescents and look to each other for protection and street socialization. Although most youths who join are on average in a gang for less than a year, some of these gangs increase their criminal activity, especially when conflict with other street groups solidifies them, becoming a formidable force in the streets. Girls often are active participants in youth gangs, and they commit very similar crimes to boys. Interestingly, research on younger gangs shows that the most criminally active ones tend to be gender balanced.

To be sure, there is a harsh, cold reality about street gangs in major cities that we ignore at our own peril. Many of these gangs incubated in the most poverty-stricken zones of very large American cities begin as the youngest cliques or sets of well-established gangs, in systematic age-graded succession. These gangs can dominate inner-city streets and create a feudal-like territory that often leads to ongoing gang wars for turf, dominance, and physical prowess—typically in very small gang *set spaces*.

Cities with populations in excess of 100,000 persons are home to the overwhelming majority of dangerous gangs representing the bulk of gang members in the entire country, and particularly older, more violent gangs with mainly young adult participants. Two-thirds of these cities consistently experience large numbers of gang-related homicides and other gang-related violence, mayhem, intimidation, and pervasive fear. Case studies illustrate that cities have gang-problem histories much like individuals' careers in crime. The authors and colleagues have identified common gang-history patterns among groups of cities across 14 years of annual national survey data. Very large cities with long histories of gang problems tend to display relatively stable patterns of serious gang presence; in contrast, small cities, towns, and counties fluctuate in presence and seriousness of gang activity. In these smaller places, gangs can emerge and dissolve more readily. Regional patterns show that while chronic gang presence characterizes city-wide patterns in all parts of the country, chronic gang cities are most common in the West, whereas emerging and variable gang cities are more likely to be found in the Northeast, and contracting gang cities are more characteristic of the Midwest. In terms of gang-related violence, only a very small proportion of homicides in very large Southern cities are associated with gangs; by contrast, approximately three-quarters of very large cities in other parts of the country report that, on average, one-fifth to one-half of their annual homicides are gang-related. Both characteristics of place and features of the gangs themselves contribute to serious gang problems in American cities.

Preventing gangs from forming and eliminating established gangs altogether is virtually impossible, when they are rooted in the cracks of our society. But the exceedingly good news is that gang crime can be reduced—even among some of the worst gangs—and communities can be made safe from the social destruction that follows in their wake. Although there is no quick fix, no magic bullet, several steps can be taken to bring measurable relief. But to expect dramatic results would be naïve, given the community conditions in which gangs thrive and that well-established street gangs place unusual demands on their members including an oath of loyalty, a code of secrecy, penalties for violating gang behavioral codes, and unequivocal promises of protection.

The main implication is that communities must organize themselves better than the gangs and present a more formidable front. Once communities make a commitment to this end, they are in an excellent position to undertake strategic planning toward overcoming the gangs. Each community needs to assess its own gang activity, prepare a strategic plan that fits its specific gang problem, and develop a continuum of programs and activities that parallels youths' gang involvement over time. *Prevention* programs are needed to target children and early adolescents at risk of gang involvement to reduce the number of youths who join gangs. *Intervention* programs and strategies are needed to provide necessary sanctions and services for slightly older youth who are actively involved in gangs to separate them from gangs. And law enforcement *suppression* strategies are needed to target the most violent gangs and older, criminally active gang members. Each of these components helps make the others more effective, provided that evidence-based services and strategies are incorporated in the continuum. The final chapters provide ample examples of these and link readers to online resources for more detailed information. Students and community stakeholders should then have the capacity to use these electronic resources to assess gang problems and actively assist or guide the mapping of a strategic plan in a given neighborhood or community.

Acknowledgments

Most important, the authors are grateful to Jerry Westby, Publisher, and Laura Kirkhuff, Editorial Assistant, Criminology & Criminal Justice, at SAGE Publications for expertly shepherding the development and production of this book. In addition, the authors are indebted to SAGE's adopters and other reviewers of the first edition of this book who kindly provided valuable comments on original chapters:

Ed Bowman, Lock Haven University of Pennsylvania

Clare Choak, University of Greenwich, Avery Hill

Michael Fischer, Norfolk State University

Frederick Hawley, Western Carolina University

Jorja Leap, University of California, Los Angeles

Roger Neal McIntyre Jr., Valdosta State University

Chris Messer, Colorado State University–Pueblo

Shannon Reid, University of North Carolina at Charlotte

Julie Schnobrich-Davis, Central Connecticut State University

These insightful reviews identified several areas of needed improvement. Four major themes in these critiques follow, each of which is addressed in the present volume. First, broader coverage of various scholars' research on girls' roles in gangs and services for them is provided. Second, prison gangs are discussed in much more detail, particularly their relationships with counterpart street gangs. Third, case studies of cities' gang problem histories are provided in Chapters 7 and 8. Fourth, U.S. gang history is expanded beyond New York City, Chicago, and Los Angeles—the major epicenters.

Howell's Personal Acknowledgments

I owe a special debt of gratitude to my gang mentor, Walter B. Miller (deceased), whom I came to know during his pioneering multi-city gang studies in the late 1970s with support from the federal Office of Juvenile Justice and Delinquency Prevention, where I was Director of Research. An anthropologist by training, Dr. Miller stimulated my interest in gangs and convinced me of the value of an historical perspective for understanding modern-day gangs. I also was very fortunate in benefitting from associations with other early eminent gang scholars and program developers early in my career, including Ron Huff, Malcolm Klein, Joan Moore, Jim Short, Irving Spergel (deceased), and Diego Vigil. I later had the distinct pleasure of working collaboratively with several colleagues at the National Gang Center[1] (Meena Harris, Trelles D'Alemberte, John Moore, Steve Ray, Arlen Egley, Ron Doyle, Becky Panebianco, and Javier Camacho), and on gang projects with many others across the years, including Becky Block, Richard Block, Beth Bjerregaard, Jim Burch, Steven Chalmers, David Curry, Scott Decker, Finn Esbensen, David Farrington, Mark Fleisher, Adrienne Freng, Amanda Gilman, Barry Glick, Victor Gonzalez, Rachel Gordon, Beth Griffiths, David Hawkins, Karl Hill, Megan Howell, Lori Hughes, David Huizinga, Errika Fearby Jones, Candice Kane, Barbara Tatem Kelley, Marv Krohn, Alan Lizotte, Billy Lassiter, Rolf Loeber, Jim Lynch, Ron Mangum, Cheryl Maxson, John Moore, Andrew Papachristos, Becky Petersen, Dana Peterson, David Pyrooz, Terrance Taylor, Terry Thornberry, George Tita, Deborah Weisel, Susan Whitten, John Wilson, and Phelan Wyrick.

This second edition has been greatly expanded and improved with the addition of Elizabeth Griffiths as co-author. Beth's pioneering gang research adds a vitally important dimension to this book, particularly her nationwide analysis of cities' histories of gang activity, a line of research that is new to criminology and the gang field. Beth also enriches this book with intriguing descriptions of cities' gang problem trajectories over a 14-year period. Working with her on this second edition is a highlight of my professional career.

In addition, this book is greatly enriched by Megan Q. Howell's recent research on gang members' presence in the North Carolina juvenile justice system. Her pioneering research spotlights gang members' relatively greater representation with each level of system penetration; the sizeable representation of gang members among offenders with serious, violent, and chronic histories; the risk and treatment need profiles of these groups; and statewide gang prevention and treatment programming. Megan's research helps fill a huge void in knowledge of gang members' juvenile justice system careers, from filed court complaints to secure confinement and research-based interventions.

As is the case with any researcher's book, this one draws on other research that I have published in the recent past, in particular the following works:

Egley, A., Jr., & Howell, J. C. (2011). *Highlights of the 2009 National Youth Gang Survey*. Washington, DC: Office of Juvenile Justice and Delinquency Prevention.

Egley, A. E., & Howell, J. C. (2012). *Highlights of the 2010 National Youth Gang Survey*. Washington, DC: Office of Juvenile Justice and Delinquency Prevention.

Egley, A. Jr., & Howell, J. C. (2013). *Highlights of the 2011 National Youth Gang Survey*. Washington, DC: U.S. Department of Justice, Office of Juvenile Justice and Delinquency Prevention.

Howell, J. C. (2007). Menacing or mimicking? Realities of youth gangs. *The Juvenile and Family Court Journal, 58,* 9–20.

Howell, J. C. (2013). Why is gang membership prevention important? In T. R. Simon, N. M. Ritter, & R. R. Mahendra (Eds.), *Changing course: Preventing gang membership* (pp. 7–18). Washington, DC: National Center for Injury Prevention and Control, Centers for Disease Control and Prevention, U.S. Department of Health and Human Services, and National Institute of Justice, Office of Justice Programs, U.S. Department of Justice.

Howell, J. C., & Egley, A., Jr. (2005). Moving risk factors into developmental theories of gang membership. *Youth Violence and Juvenile Justice, 3,* 334–354.

Howell, J. C., Egley, A., Jr., Tita, G., & Griffiths, E. (2011). *U.S. gang problem trends and seriousness.* Tallahassee, FL: Institute for Intergovernmental Research, National Gang Center.

Howell, J. C., & Young, M. A. (2013). What works to curb U.S. street gang violence? *The Criminologist, 38*(1), 39–43.

Petersen, R. D., & Howell, J. C. (2013). Program approaches for girls in gangs: Female specific or gender neutral? *Criminal Justice Review, 38,* 491–509.

I gratefully acknowledge these publishers for my use of material in this book.

Griffiths's Personal Acknowledgments

I would like to express sincere appreciation for the various scholars who have directly influenced my intellectual development, including Rosemary Gartner, Augustine Brannigan, George Tita, Bob Agnew, Anthony Doob, Julian Tanner, Bill McCarthy, Al Blumstein, Daniel Nagin, Jacqueline Cohen, A.R. Gillis, and Jody Miller, among others. I am also indebted to Buddy Howell for including me in a project that led to the OJJDP publication *U.S. Gang Problem Trends and Seriousness, 1996–2009,* and that ultimately led to my involvement in this book. Buddy is the preeminent expert on gangs and gang formation, and I am very fortunate to have had this chance to work with him. Finally, thanks also go to Jerry Westby and Laura Kirkhuff at SAGE Publications for facilitating my participation in the second edition.

NOTE

1. The National Gang Center was supported by Cooperative Agreement No. 2010-GP-BX-K076, awarded by the Bureau of Justice Assistance, and Grant No. 2007-JV-FX-0008 and Cooperative Agreement No. 2011-MU-MU-K001, awarded by the Office of Juvenile Justice and Delinquency Prevention, Office of Justice Programs. The opinions, findings, and conclusions or recommendations expressed in this publication are those of the author and do not necessarily reflect the views of the U.S. Department of Justice.

CHAPTER 1

History of Gangs in the United States

◈ Introduction

This chapter traces the emergence and growth of youth or street gangs in the United States.[1] We take a regional approach following Howell (2015), for three reasons. First, Howell's detailed historical account shows that gang emergence displays a regional pattern of development, beginning with the Northeast, followed by the Midwest, next, in the West, and lastly, in the Southern regions of the United States. Second, a few very large cities stand out in each of the four regions for rapid development of gang problems within their urban centers, particularly in New York City, Chicago, and Los Angeles. In time, each of these cities would serve as springboards for within-region diffusion of gang culture. Third, taking a regional approach helps to isolate key conditions and events underlying the emergence of gangs and fueling their expansion. In this sense, a regional perspective has some comparative benefits. Therefore, this book examines social and historical events associated with the emergence and expansion of gang activity (see Howell, 2015, for extensive documentation of these developments and a theoretical description of the observed patterns).

According to Sante (1991), the history of street gangs in the United States began with their emergence on the East Coast around 1783, as the American Revolution ended. These gangs emerged in rapidly growing eastern U.S. cities, out of the conditions created in large part by multiple waves of large-scale immigration and urban overcrowding. This chapter examines the emergence of gang activity in four major U.S. regions, as classified by the U.S. Census Bureau: Northeast, Midwest, West, and South. The purpose of this regional focus is to develop a better understanding of the origins of gang activity and to examine common influences on gangs themselves. Miller (1966/2011, p. 247) delineated criteria for identifying the "urban adolescent street gang" that are useful in guiding our historical review of gangs: (1) recurrent congregation; (2) at one or more locations outside their homes; (3) with affiliation based on self-defined inclusion criteria; (4) with subgroup delineations on the basis of age, authority, roles, prestige, or cliques; and (5) involvement in a versatile repertoire of activities with "hanging," mating, and recreational and illegal activity of central importance.

◈ Street Gang Emergence in the Northeast

New York City's Ellis Island was the initial main port of entry to the United States. A small number of Dutch immigrants first arrived in the early 1600s, taking Manhattan Island from the indigenous people who lived, hunted, and fished there. Three large groups of early immigrants populated the Northeast. The first immigrants came mainly from England and English territories, and a much smaller number comprised Dutch, German, Swedish, and Scandinavian peoples (Pincus & Ehrlich, 1999). Immediately following the American Revolution, English Protestants were the first large immigrant group, representing more than 80% of residents up to 1800. In the second large wave, commencing around 1865, approximately 11 million immigrants arrived from mainly northern and western regions of Europe, especially Great Britain, Germany, and Scandinavia (Denmark, Norway, Sweden). The third group of immigrants, from countries of southern and eastern Europe—the Poles, Italians, Austrians, and many others—another 11 million or so, arrived from 1890 to 1930. Largely consisting of low-skilled, low-wage laborers, not unexpectedly, the two large immigrant surges overwhelmed the housing and welfare capacity of the young Northeastern and Midwestern cities, contributing directly to slum conditions and the accompanying crime problems, gangs included. Street gangs also emerged, beginning in Chicago, from similar conditions of social disorganization following large-scale population movement into the Midwest. The West and South regions experienced a distinctively different immigration pattern. We begin chronologically, with the Northeast region.

The Lower East Side of the city—particularly around the Five Points—later fell victim to rapid Irish immigration and ensuing political, economic, and social disorganization (Riis, 1902/1969). Bourgois (2003) also identifies Irish and Italian immigrants as early European settlers in East Harlem. Virtually all of the Puerto Ricans arrived there much later, mainly in the two decades following World War II.

Street gangs on the East Coast developed in three phases. The first phase began after the American Revolution. These gang-like groups were not seasoned criminals—only youth fighting over local turf. The beginning of serious ganging in New York City, the second phase, commenced a few years later, around 1820, after immigration began to pick up (Pincus & Ehrlich, 1999). A third wave of gang activity ensued in the 1930s and 1940s after Latino and Black populations began to arrive in large numbers. Soon, according to Gannon (1967), the initial all-White New York gangs now were largely Puerto Rican or Black.

First Period of New York City Gang Growth: 1783–1860s

The first gang with a definite, acknowledged leadership—named the Forty Thieves and made up largely of local thieves, pickpockets, and thugs—formed around 1826 in the back room of Rosanna Peers's greengrocery, located in the Five Points district (Haskins, 1974). The second gang that formed in the area, the Kerryonians, named themselves after the county in Ireland from which they originated. Other gangs soon formed in a nearby area known as the Bowery. Battles between the Bowery Boys and Five Points gangs and the supporting gangs they had spawned (claiming more than 1,000 members each) were legendary. On occasion, out-manned police summoned both the National Guard and the regular army to quell the fights. A 2002 movie, *Gangs of New York*, vividly depicted these gangs, albeit with some exaggerations and distortions in "a blood-soaked vision of American history" (Gilfoyle, 2003, p. 621). A third cluster of gangs operated along the docks and shipyards on the East Side River of Manhattan (Asbury, 1927; Haskins, 1974). These gangs, largely composed of adolescents, were skilled at pirating cargo on the ships and docks. Occasionally, they battled nearby gangs and were far more violent than either the Five Points or Bowery Boys gangs.

Gangs in Boston, comprising White Catholic and predominantly Irish youth, with a few Italians, were first reported in the 1840s, likely having evolved from the fighting street corner groups (W. Miller, 1966/2011). Also, Adamson (2000) reports that Philadelphia's *Public Ledger* identified nearly 50 White gangs in the City of Brotherly Love between 1840 and 1870. Although these gangs persisted for some time, they were neither as well organized nor as ferocious as the New York City gangs. This assessment would change, within just a couple of decades.

Second Period of New York City Gang Growth: 1860–1930s

Gangs' growing strength was demonstrated in the Civil War draft riots precipitated by young Irish street gangs. First staged in 1863, these riots were in opposition to a federal law (the Conscription Act) that gave President Lincoln the power to draft American citizens (men ages 20 and 45) into war (Haskins, 1974). Although a clause exempted persons who paid the U.S. government $300, this option was not available to residents of Five Points and the Bowery. Two gangs led the protest, involving at least 50,000 mobsters. The riot turned into a racist event. At least 18 Black men were lynched, and as many as 70 of them "vanished without a trace" (Sante, 1991, p. 351).

For 20 years following the Civil War, corruption was rampant in New York City. Haskins (1974) pinpoints a governmental and political organization, Tammany Hall, at the center of much of the corruption—even aiding and abetting gang activity. Needless to say, gang membership grew enormously during this period. Another 8.8 million immigrants reached the United States in the late 1800s and early 1900s—the Poles, Italians, Austrians, and other nationalities (Pincus & Ehrlich, 1999), worsening the slum conditions and leading to the permanency of tenement houses (Riis, 1902/1969). As families bettered themselves economically, they would move to more suitable communities. In turn, newer immigrants would occupy the lower rung in society that advancing families vacated. This pattern of ethnic invasion and succession continued into the 20th century.

Gangs and other criminal groups responded to conditions of social and physical disorder, forging their own stronghold in New York City. The gangs rapidly expanded as slum conditions grew worse, and in 1916, according to Haskins (1974), police launched the first U.S. war on gangs. Police beat and arrested untold numbers of gang members, and criminal courts imprisoned more than 200 of their most important leaders. But the gangs survived, for they already were rooted in the cracks of the urban slum setting.

Third Period of New York City Gang Growth: 1930s–1980s

Beginning in the 1930s, the most intensive gang activity in New York City shifted from downtown (Manhattan) to both northern (Harlem and the Bronx) and southeastern (Brooklyn) locations in the metropolitan area. German and Irish Catholics already populated the northern areas of the city, and rural southern Italians arrived at the turn of the century, to face ethnic hostility from English Americans and the Irish in particular. Gangs were visible in East Harlem and that area soon would be a gang hot spot, although when they formed there is uncertain. Bourgois (2003) suggests that White gangs quite likely emerged there by the early 1900s, growing out of ethnic Irish and Italian clashes. Soon more Blacks would arrive, in the Great Migration of Blacks from the rural South northward between 1910 and 1930, making up 14% of New York City's population by the end of that period. By the time of World War II, Harlem was one of the first Black ghettos in America, and "the area could not have been riper for the sprouting of street gangs" (Haskins, 1974, p. 80).

More fighting gangs took root after the arrival of Latinos (from Central America, South America, and the Caribbean) in the 1930s and 1940s, who settled in areas of New York City populated by European Americans—particularly in East Harlem, the South Bronx, and Brooklyn. Bourgois (2003) describes how the largest new group of immigrants, 1.5 million largely impoverished Puerto Ricans seeking jobs in the U.S. factories, fled "sugar cane fields, shantytowns, and highland villages [only] to be confined to New York City tenements and later to high-rise public housing projects in the two decades following World War II" (p. 51). Three-way race riots commenced in the 1940s among Italian Americans, Puerto Ricans, and Blacks in Harlem. Ethnic invasion and succession was a key precipitating factor. With the massive influx of Puerto Ricans, East Harlem turned Latino, and soon came to be known as *El Barrio*, or as Spanish Harlem.

In Manhattan, adolescent gang fights between the Jets of European extraction and the Puerto Rican Sharks were featured in Leonard Bernstein's classic musical *West Side Story*. By then, gang members were primarily non-White (Black, Mexican American, and Latino), as early White European gangs had all but disappeared as a result of assimilation into mainstream American society. The new gangs were more organized, better armed, and often involved in drug activity (Haskins, 1974). Following another wave of Black migration beginning in the 1950s, some Black gangs were very prevalent in East Harlem and other segregated communities in New York City, bringing their total to 800,000 (Haskins, 1974). In the mid-1950s, the first high-rise public housing project in the United States was built there for several thousand poor Puerto Rican and Black families in a "slum clearance" initiative. More serious gang fights followed as the common residence brought them together in frequent and direct contact.

Up to the 1970s, a mixture of youth gangs remained in both the northern and southern areas of New York City. The 1970s and 1980s brought another large wave of migrants to the United States, around 7 million people (Pincus & Ehrlich, 1999). M. Sullivan (1993) relays that during the 1980s, many of the new immigrants into Brooklyn were Asian and non–Puerto Rican Latinos, especially Dominicans, followed by Central and South Americans. The newer Hispanic groups began to succeed Puerto Ricans. "In fact, by the late 1990s, Hispanics had replaced Blacks as the largest minority group in the city" (Lobo, Flores, & Salvo, 2002, p. 704). In the southernmost sections—Brooklyn, the South Bronx, and Chinatown—a variety of gangs had emerged (M. Sullivan, 1993).

Modern-Day Eastern Gangs

In the 1990s, urban renewal, slum clearances, and ethnic migration pitted gangs of Black, Puerto Rican, and Euro-American youth against each other in battles in New York City to dominate changing neighborhoods and to establish and maintain their turf and honor (Schneider, 1999). But New York City was no longer the epicenter of serious street gang activity in the Northeast. In the meantime, gang activity grew more serious in Philadelphia (W. Miller, 1982/1992). For more than a decade leading up to 1980, Philadelphia ranked third (behind Los Angeles and Chicago) in the average number of gang-related homicides of all U.S. cities. Boston ranked fifth, but gang activity was evident in 37 cities around Boston by the early 1970s (W. Miller, 1974b). Following the growth of Black gangs in Philadelphia to about 100 violent gangs by the late 1960s, police reported about 40 gang-related killings each year in the mid-1970s (W. Miller, 1975). For a time, broadcast media dubbed the city the "youth gang capital" of the nation (Ness, 2010, p. 32). By 1980, authorities in Long Island, in nearby New Jersey (Newark and Jersey City); eastward on Long Island; northward in Albany, Cambridge, Hartford, New Haven, and Springfield; westward in Pittsburgh; and southward in Baltimore also reported gang activity—expanding the scope of gang activity in all directions within the region (W. Miller, 1982/1992, pp. 157–159). In time, gang activity in this region expanded within other states, particularly Massachusetts, New Jersey, and Connecticut. From 1996 to 2009, almost half (45%) of the 45 large Northeast gang problem cities (with populations greater than 50,000) were classified as "chronic" gang cities (Chapter 7).

The development of prison gangs in the Northeast region contributed to the expansion of street gang activity, although this region was not the first to see these emerge—the West and Midwest led the way, as we shall see. The strong influence of prison gangs in this region would come much later. Nevertheless, Pennsylvania was among the first half-dozen states in the United States to report prison gangs, composed of members of the city's Black street gangs (Camp & Camp, 1985). Later in this chapter, we review the extent of prison gang activity in the United States, and assess the impact of these organizations on street gangs.

Street Gang Emergence in the Midwest

Chicago emerged as an industrial hub between the Civil War and the end of the 19th century after its officials recruited a massive labor force from the peasantry of southern and eastern Europe. Gangs that flourished in Chicago grew mainly from the same immigrant groups that populated the early serious street gangs of New York City. In his 1927 book, Thrasher plotted on a map of the city the location of the 1,313 early gangs (with some 25,000 members) that he found in Chicago in the 1920s. This exercise revealed Chicago's "gangland" in "interstitial areas," zones of the city lying between the commercial central city and residential neighborhoods. In that zone, characterized by social disorganization, gangs representative of a wide variety of White ethnic groups emerged and thrived. Thrasher viewed the gang as an interstitial element in the framework of society, and gangland as an interstitial region in the layout of the city.

First Period of Chicago Gang Growth: 1860s–1920

Chicago's street gangs developed among children of White immigrants along ethnic lines, mainly Polish, Irish, and Italian (Thrasher, 1927/2000). Merely nascent gangs at first, by the 1860s more menacing Irish gangs had clubrooms in the basements of saloons. By the 1880s, large Irish gangs (e.g., the Dukies and the Shielders) were prevalent and terrorizing the German, Jewish, and Polish immigrants who settled there. They also fought constantly among themselves, but they occasionally united to battle nearby Black gangs. The Black immigrants had arrived following the U.S. Civil War, to escape the misery of Jim Crow laws and the sharecropper's life in the Southern states. But serious Black gangs likely did not appear until the 1920s, following the bloody Chicago riot of 1919, precipitated by the death of a Black youth who had been swimming in Lake Michigan (Tuttle, 1996; Voogd, 2008). After drifting into an area demarcated for Whites, he was either stoned to death or drowned. Police never arrested the White man who led the attack.

Second Period of Chicago Gang Growth: 1920–1940s

Mexican American and Black gangs became prominent in the second period of Chicago gang growth, though "the impact of Black street gangs on the Black community was minimal, at best, prior to the 1940s" (Perkins, 1987, 25). None of the Chicago gangs that Thrasher (1927/2000) classified in the 1920s was of Mexican descent, and only 7% (63 gangs) were Black. This rapidly changed, beginning in the 1940s, after massive migration of both groups into Chicago. The first major wave of Mexican migration occurred during the years 1919 to 1939, seeking to take advantage of new employment opportunities (Arredondo, 2004; McWilliams, 1943). Soon, Mexican immigrants spread into two Chicago communities that had long been settled by the Irish, Germans, Czechs, and Poles (Pilsen and Little Village), wherein Spergel (2007) suggests Mexican American gangs grew to join the ranks of the most violent gangs in the city. Several small Mexican American gangs formed in Chicago during the 1930s, a second-generation product of marginalization, youth conflict, and defiance (Diamond, 2009). More such gangs formed following the 1943 Chicago zoot suit riot (explained below), instigated by numerous attacks on Mexican American youth by White and Black youths, directly stimulating the formation of gangs in self-defense (McWilliams, 1943).

Between 1910 and 1930, during the Great Migration of more than a million Blacks from the rural South to the urban North for jobs, Chicago gained almost 200,000 Black residents (Marks, 1985; B. Miller, 2008), giving the city a very large Black population—along with New York City, Cleveland, Detroit, Philadelphia, and other Northeast and Midwest cities. Perkins (1987) directly attributes the race riot of 1919 to gang formation—in which Black males united to confront hostile White gang members who were terrorizing the Black community. Black gangs formed to counter the aggressive White youth, but these relatively unorganized Black gangs were no match for the well-organized, all-White gangs that were based in athletic clubs that provided ready participants when conflicts emerged.

Third Period of Chicago Gang Growth: 1940s–1980s

The Chicago Black population grew enormously from 1940 onward (B. Miller, 2008). Most of the immigrant Blacks in Chicago were forced to settle in the area known as the Black Belt (a 30-block stretch of dilapidated housing along State Street on the south side), where abject poverty soon was concentrated. To alleviate the housing shortage and better the lives of poor city residents, from 1955 to 1968, the Chicago Housing Authority (CHA) constructed in that area more than 20,000 low-income family apartments (virtually all of which were in high-rise buildings), the best known of which are Governor Henry Horner Homes, Cabrini Green, and Robert Taylor Homes (RTH). The latter complex, the largest of the three, consisted of 28 sixteen-story buildings in uniform groups of two and three along a two-mile stretch from the industrial area near downtown into the heart of the Black ghetto on the south and west sides of Chicago (Venkatesh, 2002, 2008). Gangs grew stronger in the buildings, and also in several instances took control of them, literally turning them into high-rise forts. Gang wars erupted, largely over drug-trafficking turf, and Chicago's Black gang problem "exploded" in the 1960s, a period of increased gang "expansion and turbulence" in Chicago (Perkins, 1987, p. 74). Venkatesh (2008) notes, "Most remarkably, law enforcement officials deemed Robert Taylor Homes too dangerous to patrol" (p. 36).

As an illicit economy began to emerge in the 1970s, gangs based in RTH were able to exert greater control over residents' income-generating opportunities (Venkatesh, 1996). The gangs not only controlled drug distribution within their respective territories in RTH, but also facilitated the resale of stolen car parts for tenants in their area, and they sometimes provided protection for women who were using their apartments as brothels. On occasion, the gangs provided financial resources for necessities such as building repairs and upkeep. For some residents, involvement in illicit economic enterprises the gangs facilitated became their main livelihood. In some instances, gangs actually came to serve as *de facto* police, providing safety from outsiders. Because gangs provided some relief to residents in the form of safety and financial resources for necessities, most residents reluctantly tolerated the increased violence associated with gang involvement in drug trafficking (Venkatesh, 1996, 2002). In an unusual gesture of appreciation, the extremely violent gangs sponsored picnics for residents.

Partly in response to what Diamond (2009) tags as growing racial and ethnic violence, Black, Puerto Rican, and Mexican American gangs proliferated in the late 1950s. Racial unrest also contributed to rapid gang growth in Chicago.

> The Civil Rights Movement was advocating nonviolence, racial pride, and unity. But Black students who were having nonviolent demonstrations in the South had little influence on Black street gang members [in Chicago] who were having their own distinctly more violent demonstrations. (Perkins, 1987, p. 29)

The rise of the Black Panthers instilled Black pride, and their demise stirred resentment and anger toward White police and governance. Diamond (2009) describes how the Black gangs that were prevalent in Chicago in the 1960s were immersed in a street culture that promoted racial empowerment and racial unity. The youth subculture supplied distinctive gang clothing, hairstyles, music, and other symbols including clenched fists, the symbolic Black Power gesture.

By 1960, the Mexican migration into Chicago had reached 56,000, prompting residents to dub the city the "Mexico of the Midwest." In the mid-1970s, Latino gangs, Black gangs, and Caucasian gangs in Illinois prisons formed loose alliances, the largest of which were the People and the Folk. The remaining gangs were independents and were not aligned with either of these groups. Until recent years, these alliances were respectfully maintained on Chicago's streets, and the People and the Folk were strong rivals. "Now, although street gangs still align themselves with the People and the Folk, law enforcement agencies all seem to agree that these alliances mean little" (Chicago Crime Commission, 2006, p. 11). Nevertheless, Cureton (2009) explains, "the Chicago style of gangsterism stretches to Gary, Indiana, and Milwaukee, Wisconsin, where alliances are fragile enough to promote interracial mistrust and solid enough to fuel feuds lasting for decades" (p. 354). The period of Chicago's White ethnic gangs' dominance came to an end soon after Thrasher's research in the late 1920s was completed, however. As J. Moore (1998) explains, "The gangs of the 1920s were largely a one-generation immigrant ghetto phenomenon" (p. 68).

Modern-Day Midwest Gangs

Chicago remains the epicenter of gang activity in the Midwest. "Chicago gangs tend to be larger in size, more organizationally sophisticated, and more heavily involved in large-scale drug dealing than gangs in other cities" (Papachristos, Hureau, & Braga, 2013, p. 422). By 2006, 19 gang turfs were scattered around Chicago, throughout Cook County (Chicago Crime Commission, 2006, p. 119). Next, gangs began emerging in the larger region surrounding Chicago on the north, west, and south sides. Notably, the Chicago gang culture soon spread to nearby cities, south to Gary, Indiana, southeast to Columbia, Ohio, and north to Milwaukee, Wisconsin (Cureton, 2009; Huff, 1993). In time, other cities in the surrounding Great Lakes Basin[2] reported large numbers of gang homicides, particularly Green Bay, Wisconsin; South Bend, Indiana; Grand Rapids, Michigan; Akron and Toledo, Ohio; and Buffalo and Rochester, New York (Howell, Egley, et al., 2011). A total of 16 Midwest cities with populations greater than 100,000 have reported persistent violent gang activity over the past 14 years in the National Youth Gang Survey—approximately 40% of total annual homicides are gang-related. Taken as a whole, these cities form a large hot spot of gang violence in the Great Lakes Basin. From 1996 to 2009, two-thirds (67%) of the 95 large Midwest gang-problem cities (with populations greater than 50,000) were classified as "chronic" gang cities (Chapter 7).

Much of the span of gang activity in the Great Lakes Basin is attributable to the enormous growth of gangs in Chicago and in Illinois prisons. In 1969, Mayor Richard J. Daley declared "war on gangs" that moved gang leadership from the streets of Chicago to state prisons (Hagedorn, 2006). Gang leaders soon were able to swell their ranks from inside prison through active recruitment efforts among unaffiliated inmates. By the mid-1980s, Illinois had the largest number of gangs and gang members in prison of all U.S. states (Camp & Camp, 1985). The gang alliances came to be called *supergangs* or *gang nations*. Though largely fictive, these alliances contributed to young people's hopelessness, despair, and proclivity for violence that was carried back to the streets (Diamond, 2009; Hagedorn, 2006; Venkatesh, 2002). Though unsubstantiated, People and Folk alliances took credit for the major street conflicts that took place in Chicago in the 1980s (Perkins, 1987).

◈ Street Gang Emergence in the West Region

The emergence of street gangs in the West region pre-dates settlement of the area, and historical events that led to gang formation therein date back to the 16th century, when people of Indian, Spanish, Mexican, and Anglo backgrounds inhabited a broad region that was then northern Mexico and is currently the American Southwest, encompassing parts of present-day Arizona, Colorado, Nevada, New Mexico, and Utah. The first gangs there grew out of later Mexican immigration. Gang precursor groups are said to have first appeared there as early as the 1890s (Redfield, 1941; Rubel, 1965). Widely recognized experts on Mexican American gang origins (J. Moore, 1978, 1991; Vigil, 1990, 1998) suggest that the precursor of urban gangs in the West region was a unique Mexican "male cohorting tradition," *palomilla* (meaning literally, flock of doves). With this custom of regular association, small groups of boys and young men commonly developed solidarity and evolved into more gang-like forms called *pandilla* and *banda* (a more tightly knit group; Paz, 1961/1990). The first Mexican American gang members, reported in El Paso, were called *Pachucos* (a Mexican-Spanish word for a young Mexican living in El Paso, and belonging to a *banda*). Actually, the first Mexican American gang in the United States was reported in the Mexican section of El Paso in 1924 (R. E. Dickerson, cited in Thrasher, 1927/2000, p. 139). Gang culture moved along the continuous westward migration route to Los Angeles. Seemingly coalesced under urban social pressures associated with impeded or blocked social and cultural assimilation, the first Mexican Los Angeles gangs, which Bogardus called *boy gangs* in 1926, clearly were patterned after the *pandilla, banda*, and *pachuco* (Bogardus, 1926; J. Moore, 1978; Vigil, 1990, 1998).

Mexican migration to the United States increased sharply during the Mexican Revolution (1910–1920), facilitated by Mexico's new rail system, and the labor needs of the West, Southwest, and the

Midwest. Telles and Ortiz (2008) relay that these three factors combined to draw 700,000 legal Mexican immigrants to the United States from 1911 to 1930. The trail from Mexico to Los Angeles soon became a well-travelled road, with a multi-generation tradition of migration to and from Mexico and the United States. Although the original inhabitants of Los Angeles were native Mexicans, Anglos came along and displaced them in the late 19th century, and segregated incoming Mexicans in barrios along the eastern margin of the town center (Vigil, 2014). In large part, social and cultural angst was based in the ironic situation that Mexican immigrants faced. Under the 1848 Treaty of Guadalupe Hidalgo, the Mexican government ceded a large southwestern region to the United States. Mexican citizens in the area we now know as California, Nevada, Utah, Arizona, and Texas, and residents in parts of New Mexico and Colorado became naturalized U.S. citizens. Yet, when they later migrated from Mexico, they were treated as foreigners, and told to go back home. But that region *was* their homeland before U.S. annexation.

First Period of Los Angeles Gang Growth: 1890s–1920s

J. Moore (1993) asserts that the Mexican American gangs in the barrios (neighborhoods) of East Los Angeles typically formed in adolescent friendship groups in the 1930s and 1940s. The first bona fide Chicano gang crystallized in *El Hoyo Marvilla*[3] (in Belvedere, East Los Angeles, Boyle Heights area) in the 1930s (J. Moore, 1991, p. 27). J. Moore (1993) and Vigil (1993) both believe conflict with groups of youth in other barrios, school officials, police, and other authorities solidified them as highly visible groups. This intense bonding to barrios and gangs is unique to Los Angeles and other southwestern cities. Vigil and Long (1990) explain, "Each new wave of immigrants has settled in or near existing barrios and created new ones, [providing] a new generation of poorly schooled and partially acculturated youths from which the gangs draw their membership" (p. 56). Thus, isolationism and stigmatization were major contributing factors to gang growth and expansion.

Second Period of Los Angeles Gang Growth: 1940s–1950s

Mexican migration into the United States accelerated again, beginning in the early 1950s, bringing what Telles and Ortiz (2008) pinpoint as almost 1.4 million more persons by 1980. The Mexican-origin population in the United States grew from 2.5 million to 8.7 million during this period. The Los Angeles area received the most Mexican immigrants. Indeed, "Los Angeles has long been the Latino 'capital' of the U.S., housing more people of Mexican descent than most cities in Mexico" (J. Moore & Vigil, 1993, p. 27).

Two social events led to the expansion of Mexican American gangs in the West: the Sleepy Lagoon murder and the zoot suit riots. Sleepy Lagoon was a popular swimming hole in what is now East Los Angeles. A Mexican youngster was killed there in 1942, and members of the 38th Street Mexican American gang were arrested and charged with murder by the Los Angeles Police Department. Unfortunately, the criminal trial resembled a "kangaroo court," in which five of the Mexican gang members were convicted and sentenced to prison.

> Mexican street gangs changed forever because of these convictions. The jail sentences also acted as a glue to unite the Mexican community in a common cause, a fight against class distinction based on prejudice and racism, a fight against the establishment. (Al Valdez, 2007, p. 98)

The 38th Street gang members' cause continued in prison, and other gang members especially held them in high esteem as martyrs.

The zoot suit riots had a similar unifying effect for Mexican Americans and fueled gang recruitment. Zoot suits were a fashionable clothing trend in the late 1920s and popularized in the nightclubs of Harlem. The exaggerated zoot suit included an oversized jacket with wide lapels and shoulders, and baggy pants that narrowed at the ankles, typically accompanied by a wide-brimmed hat. The style traveled west and south into Mexico and California via the El Paso Mexican street gang population. Soon, the Anglo community, the police, and the media began to view the zoot suiters as a savage group that presumably had attacked vulnerable White women and was also said to be responsible for several local homicides. Vigil (2002) elaborates that military personnel on leave and citizen mobs chased and beat anyone wearing a zoot suit—Mexican American and Black youth alike—during a five-day riotous period. Without any doubt, the zoot suit riots solidified and served as a catalyst for expansion of Mexican American gangs in the West and Southwest. Other similar anti-Mexican riots followed in the summer of 1943, in San Diego, Philadelphia, Chicago, Detroit, Harlem, and many other cities (McWilliams, 1948/1990).

Third Period of Los Angeles Gang Growth: 1950s–1980s

In the third stage, the development of Black gangs in Los Angeles follows a pattern that resembles the emergence of Black gangs in Chicago. As in Chicago, Harrison (1999) shows a pattern of south-to-north Black migration in the 1950s, 1960s, and 1970s. Cureton (2009) is certain that this development subsequently fueled the growth of Black gangs in Los Angeles. Southern Blacks had come there looking for a better life with employment in factories. Instead, institutional inequality (in housing, education, and employment) and restrictive housing covenants legalized in the 1920s rendered much of Los Angeles off-limits to most minorities (Alonso, 2004; Cureton, 2009). Black residents challenged these covenants, leading to violent clashes between White social clubs and clusters of Black youth. Cureton (2009) explains, "Fear of attack from Whites was widespread and this intimidation led to the early formation of Black social street clubs aimed at protecting Black youths against persistent White violence directed at the Black community" (p. 664).

Alonso (2004) documents Black gang formation in Los Angeles principally in two phases: in the late 1940s and in the 1970s. He and other observers contend that Black Los Angeles gangs formed in the late 1940s as a defensive response to White violence in the schools. Vigil (2002) reports the first racial gang wars to have occurred "at Manual Arts High in 1946, at Canoga Park High in 1947, and at John Adams Junior High in 1949" (p. 68). Quite likely, many of these Black gangs and others initially formed in the marginal areas of communities, typically close to Whites, which permitted the Black gangs to draw more members. In the second phase, the effects of residential segregation (particularly in public housing projects), police brutality, and racially motivated violence in the aftermath of the 1960s civil rights conflicts "created a breeding ground for gang formation in the early 1970s" (Alonso, 2004, p. 659).

Thus, it is not surprising that the gangs that grew in the 1950s and 1960s were far more serious gangs than the earlier ones. Vigil (1988) explains that beginning as early as 1940, low-income housing projects helped to curb social problems for impoverished Los Angeles families, but these large-scale settlements also contributed to gang growth among Black and Mexican youths alike. Five such Mexican American housing projects in East Los Angeles have become barrios in their own right. But Black gangs appear to have evolved principally out of Black–White racial conflicts. Cureton (2009) attributes the

Black civil rights movement (1955 to 1965) to an underclass-specific, socially disorganized, and isolated Black community. Alonso (2004) explains that events of the 1960s were the last chapter of the political, social, and civil rights movement, a turning point away from the development of positive Black identity in the city. According to Davis (2006), a major contributing factor was that poverty and high unemployment rates were most prevalent among Black youth.

More frequent street conflicts increased the wide variety of street groups, and also expanded the base of Black gangs into two camps, Crips and Bloods. Crips wore blue clothing; the Bloods chose red. Both the Bloods and the Crips drew large memberships in the public housing projects built in the 1950s. Av. Valdez (2007) reports Blacks made up nearly 95% of the membership of these two gangs, whose presence, according to Alonso (2004), quickly spread into other areas of South Los Angeles, including Compton and Inglewood. "Crip identity took over the streets of South L.A. and swept Southside schools in an epidemic of gang shootings and street fights by 1972," first involving 18 Black gangs, that multiplied to 60 by 1978 and to 270 throughout Los Angeles County by the 1990s (p. 669).

Mexican American gangs also steadily grew in number during this period, fueled by three historical developments: the Vietnam War, the War on Poverty, and the Mexican American movement of the 1960s and 1970s (Acuna, 1981). Vigil (1990) contends that the Vietnam War depleted the barrios of a generation of positive role models. The ending of the War on Poverty eliminated jobs and increased marginalization. In the meantime, major demographic shifts occurred throughout the greater Los Angeles area as another surge of Mexican immigrants that arrived in the 1960s joined the other Latino groups that began migrating to Los Angeles in the late 1970s. These first-generation residents have replaced heretofore Black and third-generation Latino ghettos and barrios, respectively (Vigil, 1990).

San Francisco evidenced gang activity as early as the 1960s, and these nascent gangs were mainly African American and Asian with a mixture of Mexican gangs later into the early 1990s (Joe, 1994; W. Miller, 1975; Waldorf, 1993; Waldorf & Lauderback, 1993). The alluring Los Angeles gang culture soon began to draw the attention of youth in nearby communities and cities. The Bloods became particularly strong in the Black communities in South Central Los Angeles—especially in places on its periphery such as Compton—and in outlying communities such as Pacoima, Pasadena, and Pomona (Alonso, 2004; Vigil, 2002). By 1972, Vigil (2002) reports there were 18 Crips and Bloods gangs in Los Angeles, and these were the largest of the more than 500 active gangs in the city in the 1970s. By the end 1970s, according to W. Miller (1982/1992), street gangs had emerged in most populated areas across California.

Modern-Day Western Gangs

The number of Black gangs in Los Angeles increased from just 60 in 1978 to at least 270 by the 1990s (Alonso, 2004). In fact, by the 1980s, Black gangs had become "a major street force" (Vigil, 2002, p. xvi), and some Bloods and Crips gangs were involved in crack dealing and consumption in the ghettos of South Central Los Angeles (Cockburn & St. Clair, 1998). An epidemic of gang homicides followed (Hutson, Anglin, Kyriacou, Hart, & Spears, 1995) This development expanded the visibility of both Black and Mexican American street gangs and quickly drew media interest (Reeves & Campbell, 1994) and police attention (U.S. General Accounting Office, 1996). Today, many West Coast Black street gang members affiliate themselves with the Bloods or Crips (Al Valdez, 2007). Many other gangs and naïve youth across America mimic them and adopt their symbols and other elements of their gang culture. This diffusion of gang culture is equally pronounced—if not more so—among Mexican American gangs (Martinez, Rodriguez, & Rodriguez, 1998; Vigil, 2002).

Los Angeles remains the epicenter of Western region gang activity. From 2001 to 2008, almost half of all homicides in Los Angeles were gang-related, compared to about 14% elsewhere in California (Tita & Abrahamse, 2010). Interestingly, Tita and Abrahamse found that Los Angeles appears to serve as an "early warning" agent with respect to upturns in gang violence across the state. "Gang violence begins to increase (and peak) earlier in Los Angeles than in the remainder of the state" (p. 28). In addition, Los Angeles has produced four gang forms that have gained national prominence in the past two decades: (1) the traditional Black Bloods and Crips; (2) a mixture of prison gangs; (3) the highly publicized Mexican American 18th Street and Salvadorian Mara Salvatrucha gangs, both of which are viewed by the media and federal agencies to be transnational gangs; and (4) Asian gangs.

Los Angeles gang culture produced two gangs that have been called *transnational gangs*, and no other street gangs exceed them in generating widespread public fear. These are the notorious 18th Street Mexican American gang and Mara Salvatrucha, a Salvadorian Los Angeles gang. (These gangs are discussed in more detail in Chapter 8.) The West region is also known for its Asian gangs that grew there in the 1990s and first decade of the 21st century among Filipinos, Koreans, Samoans, and Central Americans, creating a veritable "rainbow of gangs" (Vigil, 2002). Among the Asian groups, the Vietnamese gangs seem to have drawn the most attention, because of their territorial style, avoidance of monikers, and fluid structure (incessant changing membership).

A total of 45 Western cities with populations greater than 100,000 reported persistent violent gang activity during the period 1996–2009 in the National Youth Gang Survey (of which 38 are in the state of California)—each of which reported about 40% of total annual homicides as gang-related (Howell et al., 2011). The California cities in this group include Los Angeles, Oxnard, Pasadena, Pomona, Riverside, Salinas, San Bernardino, San Diego, San Francisco, San Jose, and Santa Ana. Overall, almost 9 out of 10 (87%) of the Western region's 162 gang problem cities with populations larger than 50,000 were classified as "chronic" gang cities during the period 1996–2009 (Chapter 7, this volume). This proportion is higher than in any other region.

◈ Street Gang Emergence in the South

The broad South region emerged much later than other regions as an important gang territory, for reasons that are not well understood. The following are most plausible (see Howell, 2015, for supporting information). First, the South was not engulfed by the waves of White ethnic immigrants from Europe that came to the East Coast from 1783 to 1860. Second, the South remained an agricultural region until after World War II. Third, Black–White youth conflict was minimized with the "Great Migration" of more than a million Blacks from the rural South northward between 1910 and 1930. Fourth, Southern culture was deeply religious in its early history—"the most solidly Protestant population of its size in the Western Hemisphere" (Woodward, 1951, p. 449). Fifth, the Southern states largely were bypassed by the Mexicans who migrated mainly to the Midwest and Western regions. Sixth, Southern cities have always been virtually devoid of public parks where youth conflicts could be staged.

First Period of Southern Gang Emergence: 1920s–1970s

Although most of the early Mexican migration northward leapfrogged Texas, nascent gangs quite likely formed in San Antonio in the 1920s, growing out of the *palomilla* groups of youths in migrating families, as did gangs in El Paso. For many decades, it appears that San Antonio was the only large city in the South that experienced gang activity, but it may have been too isolated geographically to extend its gang influence through the youth subculture (Telles & Ortiz, 2008).

With the exception of San Antonio, W. Miller (1982/1992) concludes that gang activity likely did not emerge in the Southern states prior to the 1970s. Toward the end of that decade, only six southern cities reported gang activity—Dallas, Texas; Durham, North Carolina; Fort Worth, Texas; New Orleans, Louisiana; Miami, Florida; and San Antonio, Texas. Among these cities, only Miami and San Antonio were considered to have a moderately serious gang problem at that time (W. Miller, 1975). Actually, Dallas and Fort Worth reported a greater problem with disruptive local groups than gangs in the 1970s.

Second Period of Southern Gang Growth: 1970s–1990s

San Antonio's gang problem was first identified as a serious one (along with Miami) in W. Miller's (1975) first multi-city gang study. Before the end of the 20th century, W. Miller's (1982/1992) research shows that the South region matched the other major regions in the prevalence of gang activity. Several Southern states saw sharp increases in the number of new gang counties by 1995: Florida (23%), South Carolina (15%), Alabama (12%), and Texas (8%). From the 1970s through 1995, the South region led the nation in the number of new gang cities, a 32% increase, versus increases of 26% in the Midwest, 6% in the Northeast, and 3% in the West.

Because of its historically pluralistic population, Miami was insulated from Southern culture and racial conflicts with White youth were practically nonexistent (personal communication, J. Camacho, April 23, 2014). Miami officials first recognized gang activity in the mid-1980s according to annual reports of the Dade County District Attorney (1988). Based on references to gangs in the testimony of Dade County witnesses, within a three-year period (1984–1987), it appeared that the number of active gangs increased from 36 gangs to more than 70. Distinguishing features of Miami gangs also changed significantly, from neighborhood play groups to gangs with older members who had become involved in more serious and violent crimes, including drug trafficking, firearm use, and associated violence. These developments reflected the reality that Miami was becoming a central port for drug trafficking into the United States. In time, street-based gangs intermingled with organized drug trafficking groups.

Modern-Day Southern Gangs

It comes as a surprise that Houston was not a major gang center in the South before the first decade of the new millennium—given that its western border is shared with Mexico. However, massive Mexican migration to the East, Midwest, and West largely bypassed Houston. Based on interviews with Houston agency representatives, the city had a "borderline" gang problem in 1980 (W. Miller, 1982/1992). The first gangs to form there likely were barrio gangs much like the Mexican American gangs in Los Angeles. In one expert's view (De León, 2001), Mexican immigrants into Houston maintained their barrio/cultural identity for many years, and that identification intensified, providing the basis for frequent gang fights. By the mid-1990s, gang-related homicides were commonplace there. From 1996 to 2009, only about 20% of homicides in the city were gang-related (Howell, Egley, et al., 2011).

In concert with Houston, Miami currently anchors Deep South gang activity, along with New Orleans and Atlanta to a lesser extent. Miami officials acknowledged a significant gang problem in 1980, but with few gang-related homicides at that time (W. Miller, 1982/1992). Much like other very large cities, Miami has seen steady growth of gang violence, such that about 20% of homicides in the city were gang-related in the recent past (Howell, Egley, et al., 2011). In 1980, New Orleans agency representatives reported a relatively serious problem with youth groups other than gangs (W. Miller, 1982/1992). However, in the period 1996–2006, 4 in 10 homicides in New Orleans were gang-related (Howell, Egley, et al., 2011). Gangs appear to have been incubated in public housing projects that housed large numbers of Blacks in Atlanta: "With constant exposure to crime and criminals, many children fell into the pit of gangs, drug dealing, stealing and worse" (Atlanta Public Housing Authority, 2010, p. 34). Atlanta police reported about 20% of homicides in the city as gang-related from 1996 to 2009. A total of 12 broader South cities with populations greater than 100,000 have reported persistent violent gang activity over the past 14 years in the National Youth Gang Survey—accounting for approximately 40% (or more) of total annual homicides as gang-related (Howell, Egley, et al., 2011).

◈ Another Wave of Immigrant Groups

The Immigration and Nationality Act of 1965 ended the national quotas on foreigners in the United States. This led to a shift in immigration to the states, from European origins to Central and South America and Asia (Bankston, 1998). The next 25 years brought in many groups of Asians (Cambodians, Filipinos, Koreans, Samoans, Thais, Vietnamese, and others) and Latin Americans (Colombians, Cubans, Dominicans, Ecuadorians, Mexicans, Panamanians, Puerto Ricans, and others) (W. Miller, 2001)—altogether about 16.6 million people of all nationalities (Pincus & Ehrlich, 1999). Native American gangs also would emerge much later (Bell & Lim, 2005; Major, Egley, Howell, Mendenhall, & Armstrong, 2004). By the late 1980s, the children of many American-born or Americanized parents among the new immigrants, dubbed "the new second generation" of the post-1960s immigrant groups (principally Asian and Latin Americans), had reached adolescence or young adulthood (Portes & Rumbaut, 2005; Portes & Zhou, 1993), and some of them joined gangs. Studies show that because of the successful assimilation of early European migrant groups into American society, gangs virtually disappeared by the third generation (Telles & Ortiz, 2008; Waters, 1999). Telles and Ortiz did not find this to be the case with Mexican Americans. With each generation, familiarity with the gang lifestyle increased and thus gang involvement grew, at least through the fourth generation.

◈ The Institutionalization of Street Gangs

For purposes of contrast, it is important to keep in mind that the early European White ethnic gangs did not become fully institutionalized anywhere. In Chicago, J. Moore (1998) observed that "the gangs of the 1920s were largely a one-generation immigrant ghetto phenomenon" (p. 68). So it was in the Northeast as well. Most White immigrant gang youth matured out of gangs as their families moved out of downtown in northeast and Midwest cities, into areas of second settlement, and assimilated into mainstream American society and into the adult labor force. By 1975, the majority of American gangs were no longer White youth of European stock (W. Miller, 1975). What is it, then, that distinguishes White, Black, Mexican American, and Latino gangs in particular that have persisted in one form or another for almost a century?

The social adaptation process began once European White ethnics arrived in the United States, in their struggles to assimilate into the dominant American society. Immigrant families felt "marginalized" between their society of origin and the dominant American culture to which they had migrated (Vigil, 2002, 2006). Once children and adolescents experienced this discomfort, gangs emerged as a group that provided relief on an ongoing basis. Having been left out of mainstream society because of language, education, cultural, and economic barriers, this situation left them with few options or resources to develop socially. Naturally, they drew comfort from places where they were not marginalized, often in the streets and in gangs. In this way, gangs helped immigrant youth adapt to tribulations from social disorganization. For example, Whyte (1943b) discovered that gang turfs "were not *disorganized*, but rather *differently* organized and that street corner groups provided a clear and *organized* response to the disruption of formal social institutions" (pp. 7–8). Similarly, in *The Social Order of the Slum*, Suttles (1968) also observed mechanisms by which street gangs contributed to a "skeletal" frame of order in the world of street corner gangs. These included social interactions on the streets and relational patterns such as modes of dress, dating rituals, public interaction, and familial patterns. In this context, gangs organized youths' behavior.

W. Miller (1974) identified three prominent goals of street gangs: territorial defense, maintenance of personal and collective honor, and achieving prestige by besting one's peers. Adamson (2000) coined the term *defensive localism* to describe a variety of functions that gangs provide in communities that include securing living space, upholding group honor, policing of neighborhoods, and the provision of economic, social, employment, welfare, and recreational services. Racial conflicts across America served to expand gangs' role to the protection of minority groups to which they belonged.

After mutual acceptance, membership is consummated in a ceremony that Vigil (2004) has likened to a religious baptism in the sense of turning away from past life and turning toward the gang for the life course. At the individual level, a need for protection is the main reason youth give when asked why they joined a gang (Esbensen, Deschenes, & Winfree, 1999). They want to feel safe and respected, but they want to be an integral part of the social scene. At the group level, age-graded gang structure in Mexican American gangs ensures that there is a place for everyone, even the youngest members. It allows for gang regeneration with the inclusion of each new generation; and it additionally provides the social arena for youngsters to learn and demonstrate important gang customs among themselves (Vigil, 1993).

In Chicago and Los Angeles, Mexican American street gangs clearly were integrated in the everyday life of many Mexican communities. For Mexican American gangs, a large measure of integration or cohesiveness comes from the tradition of linking the gang name with neighborhood or barrio of residence—with *mi barrio* (my neighborhood) becoming synonymous with my gang (Vigil, 1993).

Mexican American gang traditions are perpetuated in the barrios of East Los Angeles through four distinct processes: kinship, alliance in fights, extensions of barrio boundaries, and forming branches (J. Moore, Vigil, & Garcia, 1983). First, without exception, gang membership is extended to relatives who live outside the barrio. For Mexican American gang boys, a *homeboy* (fellow gang member) is the equivalent of a *carnal* (blood) brother. In addition, the gang takes on kin-like characteristics, especially mutual obligations among gang members. Second, because fighting is the defining characteristic of barrio gangs—particularly with another gang—boys from other barrios became allies in fights. Third, gang boundaries often extend into other barrios when members of multiple gangs live within them. Twenty cliques of the *Hoya Marvilla* gang were formed across a several decades through these methods (J. Moore, 1991; Vigil, 2007). The *El Hoya Marvilla* and White Fence gangs—now nearly 80 years old— are testament to this process of gang perpetuation.

At the group level, Decker (1996) delineated a "cycle of violence" process that often accounts for gang cohesion and cyclical gang conflicts that wax and wane and sometimes extend over a number of years (C. Block & Block, 1993). The process begins with a loosely organized gang. Members have loose bonds to the gang. This state is common and may last a long time. However, collective identification of threat from a rival gang (through rumors, symbolic shows of force, cruising, and mythic violence) quickly expands the number of participants and increases cohesion. Next, a mobilizing event occurs or is rumored and sometimes involves violence—or the threat of it. This development serves to mobilize gang activity and the group becomes more alert and cohesive. A violent incident against the threatening group occurs, followed by rapid de-escalation. Later, violent retaliation by the opposing gang occurs. Papachristos's (2009) Chicago research revealed a similar process, finding that "gangs are not groups of murderers per se, but rather embedded social networks in which violence ricochets back and forth . . . [and] what begins as a single murder soon generates a dozen more as it diffuses through these murder networks" (p. 76). These events become, in effect, "dominance contests" in which "violence spreads through a process of social contagion that is fueled by normative and behavioral precepts of the code of the street" (p. 81). In other words, violence is contagious on the streets and perpetuates intergang conflicts that sometimes are re-kindled for decades.

The Unique Contribution of Prison Gangs to Street Gang Institutionalization

Briefly, prison gangs originated to provide protection to gang members from members of other hostile gangs inside prisons. The most widely accepted definition of a prison gang is

> an organization which operates within the prison system as a self-perpetuating criminally oriented entity, consisting of a select group of inmates who have established an organized chain of command and are governed by an established code of conduct. (Lyman, 1989, p. 48)

The American Correctional Association (ACA) adopted in 1993 the more inclusive term *security threat groups* (STGs), defined as "two or more inmates, acting together, who pose a threat to the security or safety of staff/inmates, and/or to the orderly management of the facility/system" (ACA, 1993, p. 1). In time, the term STG virtually supplanted usage of prison gang terminology.

As U.S. prison populations began to grow in the 1950s (Justice Policy Institute, 2000), prison gangs were formed by inmates for protection from rival gang members. A sharp upturn in confinement in state prisons and local jails commenced in 1970 (338,029) and increased to 1,965,667 in 2000, for almost a six-fold increase over the three decades. With the accelerated growth in numbers of inmates, racial-ethnic conflicts prompted formation of prison gangs. In a mid-1980s survey of all state and federal prisons, facility administrators in 33 states indicated that they had gangs in their prisons (Camp & Camp, 1985). Having been formed to provide protection inside prisons from rival street gang members, the prison gangs were "an extension of an identical organization imported from the streets" (Jacobs, 1974, p. 397). Two states stand out for sheer strength and statewide influence of their prison gangs: California and Illinois.

California has been dubbed the "mother" of major prison gangs because six major prison gangs were active in the state's prisons by 1984, and these without doubt contributed directly to the growth of gang activity throughout the state and to some extent in the West region. Gang suppression legislation, coupled with the state's indeterminate sentence provision and its "Three Strikes and You're Out" law, served to increase confinement of street gang members (Schlosser, 1998). In turn, growing conflicts and assaults between northern and southern California gang inmates led to the formation of *Sureños* and *Norteños* networks, and a rivalry that produced many gang wars, both in prisons and on the streets (National Alliance of Gang Investigators' Associations, 2009). Rival southern California Hispanic street gangs thus were enemies with anyone from northern California, and vice versa. In time, this rivalry would unite the respective clusters of gangs in jails and state prisons. By the mid-1990s, the California prison system was said to be full of warring gangs, members of the Crips, Bloods, Mexican Mafia, and Black Guerrilla Family, to name a few.

In Chicago, massive incarceration of gang members followed Mayor Daley's 1969 gang war. Prison administrators inadvertently strengthened the gangs by using them to help maintain control of prisons, thus allowing them "to consolidate, form alliances, and grow in number and strength" (Venkatesh, 2002, p. 133). The Illinois prison gangs were "reorganized at a level of sophistication that dwarfed the type of structures that had developed in the streets" (Perkins, 1987, p. 17). By the mid-1970s, Latino, African American, and Caucasian gangs in Chicago and elsewhere across the state had merged into two major coalitions in Illinois prisons, the "People" and the "Folks," by inmates who were seeking protection through coalition building (Chicago Crime Commission, 2006). They soon took control of older inmate organizations by guile and targeted violence, and became the strongest force within the prisons. Once members were freed from prisons, they quickly moved to battle, over-power, and subsume the weaker street corner groups (Cureton, 2009). By the mid-1980s, Illinois had the largest number of gangs and gang members in prison of all U.S. states (Camp & Camp, 1985). Across Illinois, Department of Corrections' officials estimated that some 5,300 inmates were active gang members in 1984, constituting 34% of all inmates (Camp & Camp, 1985, pp. 134–135). Some of the Chicago gang leaders formed organizational networks both inside and outside prisons that linked inmates with others in jails and on the streets in illegal enterprises, creating what came to be called *webs*, *supergangs*, or *gang nations* (Venkatesh, 2002, p. 134). "But significantly, and unlike past inmate groups, the gangs maintained their ties to the streets" (Hagedorn, 2006, p. 203). People and Folk alliances accounted for the major street conflicts that took place in Chicago in the 1980s (Perkins, 1987). Under these coalitions, gang conflicts were far more serious because they involved multiple gangs on occasion.

In a 2009 survey of Directors of Security in the 53 U.S. prison systems (federal and state), 19% of all inmates were classified as gang members, half of whom belonged to gangs prior to imprisonment, and, interestingly, half of them joined gangs after entering prison (Winterdyk & Ruddell, 2010). Just 12% of all federal and state prison inmates were members of prison gangs in 2003, thus the 19% figure in 2009 represents a substantial increase in just seven years—reflecting the growing strength of prison gangs. Of course, estimates are far higher in states with a history of major street gang activity such as in Illinois prisons. By the mid-1980s, Illinois had the largest number of gang members in prison of all states, and the largest proportion of gang-involved inmates (34%) (Camp & Camp, 1985; see Sundt, Castellano, & Briggs, 2008, for more recent estimates).

The Texas Fusion Center's prison gang threat assessment matrix incorporates 10 factors that are important in determining the threat posed by each gang (shown within In Focus 1.1). Each factor is rated using a weighted, point-based system that generates a composite score. This score provides a metric of the overall threat level of each gang. The most significant gangs are classified as Tier 1, with other significant gangs classified as Tier 2 and Tier 3.

IN FOCUS 1.1
GANG THREAT TIERS

Relationship With Cartels: This factor examines the extent to which a gang is connected to Mexico-based drug cartels. A gang may be assessed as having no relationship, a temporary or short-term association, or a long-term business venture or exclusive relationship.

Transnational Criminal Activity: This factor considers whether a gang has transnational criminal connections, as well as whether the gang's criminal activity has spread into the transnational realm.

Level of Criminal Activity: This factor rates the type and frequency of crimes perpetrated by the gang. Crimes are rated on a scale covering a range of offenses, from misdemeanors to felonies.

Level of Violence: This factor assesses the overall level of violence perpetrated by the gang in its criminal activity. It ranges from generally nonviolent offenses, such as money laundering, to crimes involving extreme violence, such as torture and murder.

Prevalence Throughout Texas: This factor determines the extent to which a gang is active throughout the state. The geographic reach of some gangs is limited to specific cities or regions of Texas, while others are widespread across the state.

Relationship With Other Gangs: This factor examines the nature of a gang's alliances and influence with other gangs. This may include limited and temporary contact or formal alliances, whereas some gangs exercise direct oversight over other gangs.

Total Strength: This factor assesses the known size of the gang, measured by the number of individuals confirmed by law enforcement and criminal justice agencies to be members of the gang. This number is almost always an underrepresentation of the true size of the gang, as many members are unknown to law enforcement.

Statewide Organizational Effectiveness: This factor examines the gang's effectiveness in organizing members under its leadership across the state.

Juvenile Membership: This factor considers the extent to which the gang recruits juveniles and is active in schools, as gang recruitment of juveniles is considered a unique threat.

Threat to Law Enforcement: This factor considers the extent to which the gang represents a threat to law enforcement. Some gang members may only use violence to resist arrest or to flee from law enforcement, while others may actively target officers.

Source: Texas Fusion Center, 2013, p. 10

As of 2014, the Tier 1 gangs in Texas are Tango Blast and Tango cliques, Texas Syndicate, Texas Mexican Mafia, and Barrio Azteca (Joint Crime Information Center, 2014). "These organizations pose the greatest gang threat to Texas due to their relationships with Mexican cartels, large membership numbers, high levels of transnational criminal activity, and organizational effectiveness" (p. 11).

Importantly, Texas Fusion Center intelligence reveals that prison and street gangs are now increasingly working together for financial gain—even with rival gangs in large operations, some of which are with traditional drug trafficking organizations.

 ## Concluding Observations

Important differences in the history of gang emergence are apparent in the four major U.S. gang regions. First, the timing has differed. Serious gangs first emerged on the East Coast in the 1820s, led by New York City. A half-century passed before gangs emerged in the Midwest (Chicago), while West (Los Angeles) regions saw significant gang development a full century later than New York City. The South would not experience significant gang problems for another half-century, in the 1970s. Second, the racial or ethnic composition of gangs in each region varied over time. In both New York and Chicago, the earliest gangs arose in concert with external migration of European origins—the traditional classic ethnics of the period from 1783 to 1860 (particularly German, French, British, Scandinavian). Other groups of White ethnics soon arrived during 1880 to 1920—mainly Irish, Italians, Jews, and Poles—and the second-generation youth were most susceptible to gang involvement. The latter nationalities almost exclusively populated the early serious street gangs of New York and Chicago. Gangs in the Western region formed in the Mexican American *barrios*. Black gangs formed there following large-scale Black migration from the Southern region in the 1950s, 1960s, and 1970s. For both of these peoples, gangs were largely a by-product of macrohistorical (racism and repression) and macrostructural (immigration and ghetto/barrio living) processes (Krohn, Schmidt, Lizotte, & Baldwin, 2011). Gang emergence was delayed in the Southern region because conditions that led to gang formation and growth in the Eastern, Midwestern, and Western region were largely absent in the South, or present on a much smaller scale. A new wave of immigrants, principally Asians and Latinos, was welcomed into the United States in the mid-1990s by less restrictive immigration policies.

Street gangs are now well institutionalized in the United States. Youth gang problems in the United States grew dramatically between the 1970s and the 1990s, with the prevalence of gangs reaching unprecedented levels in the mid-1990s (W. Miller, 2001). By the mid-1990s, all 50 states and the District of Columbia, and 40% of local law enforcement agencies nationwide reported youth gang problems (Egley & Howell, 2013). Prison gangs now have stronger relationships with street gangs than ever before, mutually engaged in criminal enterprises on an ongoing basis in many states.

DISCUSSION TOPICS

1. Why do street gangs exist? What explanations does history suggest?

2. What roles did racial/ethnic conflict, organized crime, and political corruption play in the development of street gangs? Which of these factors was more important in each region?

3. Why is the South region so different in its street gang history?

4. Why was high-rise public housing such an important contributor to street gang problems?

5. How are prison gangs linked with street gangs?

RECOMMENDATIONS FOR FURTHER READING

Conditions That Give Rise to Gangs

Adamson, C. (1998). Tribute, turf, honor and the American street gang: Patterns of continuity and change since 1820. *Theoretical Criminology, 2,* 57–84.

Adamson, C. (2000). Defensive localism in white and black: A comparative history of European-American and African-American youth gangs. *Ethnic and Racial Studies, 23,* 272–298.

Alonso, A. A. (2004). Racialized identities and the formation of black gangs in Los Angeles. *Urban Geography, 25,* 658–674.

Anbinder, T. (2001). *Five points.* New York: Free Press.

Bernard, W. (1949). *Jailbait.* New York: Greenberg.

Davis, M. (2006). *City of quartz: Excavating the future in Los Angeles* (2nd ed.). New York: Verso.

Diamond, A. J. (2009). *Mean streets: Chicago youths and the everyday struggle for empowerment in the multiracial city, 1908–1969.* Berkley: University of California Press.

Freng, A., & Taylor, T. J. (2013). Race and ethnicity: What are their roles in gang membership? In T. R. Simon, N. M. Ritter, & R. R. Mahendra (Eds.), *Changing course: Preventing gang membership* (pp. 135–149). Washington, DC: U.S. Department of Justice, U.S. Department of Health and Human Services.

Hagedorn, J. M. (2006). Race, not space: A revisionist history of gangs in Chicago. *Journal of Black History, 91,* 194-208.

Hayden, T. (2005). *Street wars: Gangs and the future of violence.* New York: New Press.

Howell, J. C. (1998). *Youth gangs: An overview* (Juvenile Justice Bulletin. Youth Gang Series). Washington, DC: U.S. Department of Justice, Office of Juvenile Justice and Delinquency Prevention.

Howell, J. C., & Moore, J. P. (2010). *History of street gangs in the United States* (National Gang Center Bulletin No. 4). Tallahassee, FL: Institute for Intergovernmental Research, National Gang Center.

McWilliams, C. (1943, June). Zoot-suit riots. *New Republic, 108,* 818–820.

McWilliams, C. (1948/1990). *North from Mexico: The Spanish-Speaking people of the United States.* (Rev. ed.). New York: Greenwood.

Perkins, U. E. (1987). *Explosion of Chicago's Black street gangs: 1900 to the present.* Chicago: Third World Press.

Riis, J. A. (1892). *Children of the poor.* New York: Charles Scribner's Sons.

Riis, J. A. (1902/1969). *The battle with the slum.* Montclair, NJ: Paterson Smith.

Ro, R. (1996). *Gangsta: Merchandizing the rhymes of violence.* New York: St. Martin's Press.

Short, J. F., Jr., & Hughes, L. A. (Eds.). (2006). *Studying youth gangs.* Lanham, MD: AltaMira Press.

West, C. (1993). *Race matters.* Boston: Beacon.

Northeast Gang History

Bourgois, P. (2003). *In search of respect: Selling crack in El Barrio* (2nd ed.). New York: Cambridge University Press.

Brotherton, D. C., & Barrios, L. (2004). *The Almighty Latin King and Queen Nation: Street politics and the transformation of a New York City Gang.* New York: Columbia University Press.

Haskins, J. (1974). *Street gangs: Yesterday and today.* Wayne, PA: Hastings Books.

Riis, J. A. (1902/1969). *The battle with the slum.* Montclair, NJ: Paterson Smith.

Sante, L. (1991). *Low life: Lures and snares of old New York.* New York: Vintage Books.

Tita, G. E., Cohen, J., & Engberg, J. (2005). An ecological study of the location of gang "set space." *Social Problems, 52,* 272–299.

Midwest Gang History

Arredondo, G. F. (2004). Navigating ethno-racial currents: Mexicans in Chicago, 1919–1939. *Journal of Urban History, 30,* 399–427.

Block, C. R., & Block, R. (1993). Street gang crime in Chicago. *Research in Brief.* Washington, DC: U.S. Department of Justice, National Institute of Justice.

Block, C. R., Christakos, A., Jacob, A., & Przybylski, R. (1996). *Street gangs and crime: Patterns and trends in Chicago.* Chicago: Illinois Criminal Justice Information Authority.

Chicago Crime Commission. (1995). *Gangs: Public enemy number one, 75 years of fighting crime in Chicagoland.* Chicago: Author.

Cureton, S. R. (2009). Something wicked this way comes: A historical account of Black gangsterism offers wisdom and warning for Black leadership. *Journal of Black Studies, 40,* 347–361.

Dawley, D. (1992). *A nation of lords: The autobiography of the vice lords* (2nd ed.). Prospect Heights, IL: Waveland Press.

Diamond, A. J. (2009). *Mean streets: Chicago youths and the everyday struggle for empowerment in the multiracial city, 1908–1969.* Berkley: University of California Press.

Hagedorn, J. M. (2006). Race, not space: A revisionist history of gangs in Chicago. *Journal of Black History, 91,* 194-208.

Huff, C. R. (1993). Gangs in the United States. In A. Goldstein & C. R. Huff (Eds.), *The gang intervention handbook* (pp. 3–20). Champaign, IL: Research Press.

Keiser, R. L. (1969). *The Vice Lords: Warriors of the street.* New York: Holt, Rinehart & Winston.

Lombardo, R. M. (1994). The social organization of organized crime in Chicago. *Journal of Contemporary Criminal Justice, 10,* 290–313.

Lombardo, R. M. (2002). The Black Hand: Terror by letter in Chicago. *Journal of Contemporary Criminal Justice, 18,* 394–409.

Monti, D. J. (1993). Gangs in more- and less-settled communities. In S. Cummings & D. J. Monti (Eds.), *Gangs: The origins and impact of contemporary youth gangs in the United States* (pp. 219–253). Albany: State University of New York Press.

Perkins, U. E. (1987). *Explosion of Chicago's Black street gangs: 1900 to the present.* Chicago: Third World Press.

Tapia, M. (2014). Latino street gang emergence in the Midwest: Strategic franchising or natural migration? *Crime & Delinquency, 60,* 592–618.

Venkatesh, S. A. (2000). *American project: The rise and fall of a modern ghetto.* Cambridge, MA: Harvard University Press.

Western Gang History

Alonso, A. A. (2004). Racialized identities and the formation of black gangs in Los Angeles. *Urban Geography, 25,* 658–674.

Davis, M. (2006). *City of quartz: Excavating the future in Los Angeles* (2nd ed.). New York: Verso.

Durán, R. J. (2012). *Gang life in two cities: An insider's journey.* Chichester, NY: Columbia University Press.

Martinez, R., Rodriguez, J., & Rodriguez, L. (1998). *East Side stories: Gang life in East L.A.* New York: PowerHouse.

Moore, J. W. (1978). *Homeboys: Gangs, drugs and prison in the barrios of Los Angeles.* Philadelphia: Temple University Press.

Moore, J. W. (1991). *Going down to the barrio: Homeboys and homegirls in change.* Philadelphia: Temple University Press.

Quicker, J. C. (1983). *Seven decades of gangs.* Sacramento, CA: California Commission on Crime Control and Violence Prevention.

Valdez, Al. (2007). *Gangs: A guide to understanding street gangs* (5th ed.). San Clemente, CA: LawTech.

Valdez, Al, & Enriquez, R. (2011). *Urban street terrorism: The Mexican Mafia and the Surenos.* Santa Ana, CA: Police and Fire.

Vigil, J. D. (2002). *A rainbow of gangs: Street cultures in the mega-city.* Austin: University of Texas Press.

Vigil, J. D. (2007). *The projects: Gang and non-gang families in East Los Angeles.* Thousand Oaks, CA: Sage.

Vigil, J. D. (2014). Cholo! The migratory origins of Chicano gangs in Los Angeles. In J. M. Hazen & D. Rodgers (Eds.), *Global gangs: Street violence across the world* (pp. 49–64). Minneapolis: University of Minnesota.

NOTES

1. A much-abbreviated history of gangs in the United States is presented in this chapter. For a detailed nationwide history and extensive analysis of gang emergence, development, and institutionalization, see Howell, 2015.
2. The Great Lakes region of North America includes the eight U.S. states of Illinois, Indiana, Michigan, Minnesota, western New York, Ohio, and Wisconsin; and parts of several Canadian provinces on the north banks of the Great Lakes.
3. Meaning *Que Maravilla*! Translated "what a marvel" or "what a wonderful city."

CHAPTER 2

Myths and Realities of Youth Gangs

◈ Introduction

Because of their criminal activities and deliberate efforts to control the streets, gangs can engender enormous fear in community adults and youth (Lane & Meeker, 2000, 2003). But two groups in particular have a tendency to exaggerate the nature and seriousness of gangs: the broadcast media and the gangs themselves (Esbensen & Tusinski, 2007; Howell, 2007; Thompson, Young, & Burns, 2000). J. Moore (1993) explains,

> Most typically, [the media stereotype] is that gangs are composed of late-adolescent males, who are violent, drug- and alcohol-soaked, sexually hyperactive, unpredictable, confrontational, drug-dealing criminals . . . They are demonic, and all the worse for being in a group. (p. 28)

In many communities, when gangs are enshrouded in images such as this, the determination of appropriate community responses can be thwarted.

This chapter presents several popular gang myths along with research that substantiates realities that contradict the myths, or at least brings them into serious question. Technically speaking, *myths* refer to beliefs that are strongly held and convenient to believe but are based on little actual information; they are not necessarily false (T. Bernard, 1992). Beliefs that are unequivocally false are properly labeled *fallacies*. Although useful, such a clear-cut distinction often cannot be made in reference to gangs because, depending on how they are defined, at least one exception may be found to every myth, thus the more inclusive term is used herein.

Felson (2006) argues that the gangs themselves complicate community action by creating myths as part of what he calls their *big gang theory*. The process often transpires as follows: Youths sometimes feel that they need protection on the streets in their communities. The gang provides this service. However, few youth of the younger gangs are nasty enough to be particularly effective in protecting youths. Hence, they need to appear more dangerous than they actually are to provide maximum protection. Felson observed that gangs use a ploy found in nature to maximize the protection they seek to provide. To scare off threatening predators, some harmless animals and insects will mimic a more dangerous member of their species. In turn, predators learn to avoid all species—both harmless and dangerous—that look alike. For example, Felson notes that the coral snake, an extremely dangerous viper, is mimicked by the scarlet king snake, which is often called the *false coral snake* because of its similar colors and patterns. Although the latter snake is not venomous at all, it scares off potential predators by virtue of its appearance.

Felson (2006) suggests that gangs use the same strategy, providing signals for local gang members for making their gangs resemble truly dangerous big city gangs. These standardized signals or symbols typically consist of hand signs, colors, graffiti, clothes, and language content. Gang members can display these scary signals at will to create a more menacing image. Employing a famous gang name will help them intimidate others. Once enough people believe their overblown dangerous image, it becomes accepted as reality.

◆ Consideration of Key Myths About Gangs

Misrepresentations of gangs in the print media have been well documented in four analyses covering articles published over the past four decades (Best & Hutchinson, 1996; Esbensen & Tusinski, 2007; W. Miller 1974a; Thompson et al., 2000). As Bjerregaard (2003) notes, legislators also sometimes foster overreactions to gangs with very broad laws that prescribe severe penalties for any type of gang involvement. Almost invariably, though, newspaper accounts, popular magazine articles, and electronic media broadcasts on youth gangs contain at least one myth or fallacy. First, the leading newsweeklies and most major newspapers consider "gangs" to be a monolithic phenomenon and do not describe the diversity among distinctively different types of gangs, such as prison gangs versus drug gangs and youth gangs. Second, the demographic image of gang members as exclusively males and racial or ethnic minorities is perpetuated. Third, news outlets portray gangs as an urban problem that has spread to new areas, as part of a conspiracy to establish satellite sects across the country. Fourth, most gangs are characterized as hierarchical organizations with established leaders and operating rules. Fifth, the pervasiveness of violence is exaggerated. And the members themselves are prone to overstatements, for example, always claiming they were victorious in fights (Klein, 1995; Al Valdez, 2007).

Myth 1: Most Gangs Have a Formal Organization

A key premise of the big gang theory is that modern-day gangs are highly organized and function in a ruthless manner much like organized crime groups or drug cartels. A main reason why a gang appears to be more menacing than a mere collection or group of lawbreakers is that the term *gang* implies that its members are organized, commit crimes in groups, and are thus resolutely committed to violence and mayhem (McCorkle & Miethe, 2002).

Reality

A few street gangs have evolved into highly organized, entrepreneurial adult criminal organizations (Coughlin & Venkatesh, 2003; Papachristos, 2001, 2004). However, studies in a growing number of cities show that gangs are far less organized than expected. "Gangs," says Klein (1995), "are not committees, ball teams, task forces, production teams, or research teams . . . They do not gather to achieve a common, agreed-upon end" (p. 80). In fact, very few youth gangs could meet the essential criteria for classification as "organized crime" (Decker, Bynum, & Weisel, 1998; Klein, 1995). As Klein notes (2004),

> Organized crime groups such as drug cartels must have strong leadership, codes of loyalty, severe sanctions for failure to abide by these codes, and a level of entrepreneurial expertise that enables them to accumulate and invest proceeds from drug sales. (pp. 57–59)

Such criminal gangs and organized crime networks are often highly structured.

IN FOCUS 2.1
CITIES THAT HAVE GANGS WITH LOW LEVELS OF ORGANIZATION

- Chicago, Illinois (Decker et al., 1998)
- Denver, Colorado (Esbensen, Huizinga, & Weiher, 1993)
- Detroit, Michigan (Bynum & Varano, 2003)
- Cleveland and Columbus, Ohio (Huff, 1989, 1996, 1998; J. Miller, 2001)
- Kansas City, Missouri (Fleisher, 1998)
- Milwaukee, Wisconsin (Hagedorn, 1988)
- Las Vegas and Reno, Nevada (McCorkle & Miethe, 2002; Miethe & McCorkle, 1997)
- Los Angeles, California (J. Moore, 1978, 1991; Vigil, 1988, 2002)
- New York, New York (Kontos, Brotherton, & Barrios, 2003; M. Sullivan, 2006)
- Phoenix, Arizona (Zatz, 1987; Zatz & Portillos, 2000)
- San Diego, California (Decker et al., 1998; Sanders, 1994)
- San Francisco, California (Waldorf, 1993)
- Seattle, Washington (Fleisher, 1995)
- St. Louis, Missouri (Decker & Curry, 2000; Decker & Van Winkle, 1996; Monti, 1993)
- Washington, DC (McGuire, 2007)

In the most definitive study of the extent of gang organization conducted to date, Decker and colleagues (1998) compared two gangs in Chicago with two San Diego gangs; police had described all four gangs as the most highly organized gangs in these cities. The researchers found that the Chicago Gangster Disciples were far more organized than either the Latin Kings from Chicago or the two San Diego gangs, but that none of the gangs exhibited the extremely high level of organization attributed to them by law enforcement. In another example, according to the FBI's (2009) intelligence reports, MS-13 was a predominant gang in Washington, DC. McGuire (2007) found only small cliques of MS-13 in that city.

In contrast, street gangs are generally loosely organized groups that are constantly changing—consolidating, reorganizing, and splintering (Katz & Jackson-Jacobs, 2004; Monti, 1993; Weisel, 2002a, 2002b). Chapters 3 and 8 reference various street gang structures, and none of these resembles a corporate structure; typically there is only an informal division of labor with "shot callers" who play a key leadership role, and these may change from one gang activity to another. Tita, Cohen, and Engberg (2005) contend that gangs' public image and reputations are very large, yet their set spaces are very small, typically much smaller than neighborhoods or even census tracts—even, as R. Block (2000) notes, for very violent Chicago gangs.

Myth 2: Gangs of the Same Name Are Connected

This myth—that big city gangs spawn small local gangs of the same name—is a key premise of the big gang theory and broadcast media presentations. Local gangs that call themselves Crips and Bloods, for example, are assumed affiliated with parent gangs of the same names in distant cities.

Reality

The common notion that local gangs are affiliated with big city gangs persists because of the similarity of their names and symbols, which mimicry or imitation explain. An analogy helps reveal the reality of the situation. Local Little League baseball teams may appear to be affiliated with major league baseball teams because of similar names and uniforms, but there is no connection between local youth teams and professional baseball clubs. So it is with gangs; there rarely is any connection whatsoever between local gangs and big city gangs known by the same names. The reality is that local gangs often "cut and paste" bits of Hollywood images of gangs and big-city gang lore into their local versions of gangs (Starbuck, Howell, & Lindquist, 2001). And, they often do a poor job of this copying—perhaps using the wrong colors, distorting the original gang's symbols, and so on. To illustrate the point, Fleisher (1998) documents a gang of youth in Kansas City who said they were affiliated with the Chicago Folks gang, but when asked about the nature of their affiliation, they couldn't explain it. They said that they just liked to draw the Folks' pitchfork symbol.

Local gangs also like to create the impression that they are composed of numerous "sets" or cliques and, as Felson (2006) suggests, to promote a nastier image. Rather than one big gang with many branches, most communities have several small gangs (discussed in Chapter 3), and even though some of them may use a common name, there rarely is any connection between them. Notable exceptions are the Chicago-based Gangster Disciples (FBI, 2009) and both 18th Street and Mara Salvatrucha, Los Angeles–based gangs with connections to *maras* (gangs) they enhanced in Central America (Cruz, 2010), as discussed in Chapter 8.

Myth 3: Our Gangs Came From Somewhere Else

Gang migration refers to the movement of gang members from one geographic area to another (Maxson, 1998), and the gang migration myth presumes that street gangs migrate across the country to establish satellite sets. The most predominant myth is that they likely came to the local city or town to set up a drug-trafficking operation. The story of migrating, cocaine-trafficking street gangs became widely accepted, and it was elaborated to embrace the notion that Southern California and Chicago gangs formed alliances in their respective regions and expanded across the United States, radiating out from the areas where they originated—up the West Coast to Vancouver; to Chicago, Kansas City, and Denver in the Midwest; and to the East Coast (United States Attorney General, 1989). Readers may have seen arrows superimposed on national maps to illustrate the supposed movement of gangs across the country to set up branch operations.

Reality

Mapped gang movement routes describe exceptions rather than the rule. Klein (1995, 2004) asserts that most youth gang problems are homegrown, and gang *members* rather than *gangs* themselves tend to migrate. When families move, their gang-involved offspring usually move with them. This reality explains most so-called gang migration. More consistent with the reality, Maxson (1998) notes that gang networks and connections generally extend not more than 100 miles from the city of origin, and rarely further. Of course, there are exceptions. Fleisher (1995) found that some Compton and Hover Crips from Los Angeles moved north to Seattle, Washington, and set up drug-trafficking gangs there. Other instances are noted elsewhere in this book. The National Alliance of Gang Investigators' Associations (2005) contends that a few gangs do have the capacity to expand into other regions, but McGuire (2007) along with Van Gemert, Peterson, and Lien (2008) debunk the notion of international migration of gangs. However, W. Miller (2001) claims some gang member migration occurred in conjunction with the enormous U.S. population shift during the 1980s and 1990s from metropolitan to suburban and rural areas. Maxson's (1998) research shows that the most common reason—in more than half the instances—behind the migration of gang members is social considerations, including family moves to improve the quality of life and to be near relatives and friends.

Myth 4: The Mara Salvatrucha (MS-13) and 18th Street (M-18) Gangs Are Spreading Across the United States

As Central American gang expert Cruz (2010) explains, the word *mara* in the Salvadoran vernacular commonly refers to any group of people, and is widely synonymous with *folks* and also is slang for *gang*. *Trucha* is a slang word meaning "stay alert." The term *maras* is used to denote Central American gangs. These gangs originated in El Salvador in the 1960s, born in poor neighborhoods and dysfunctional families—conditions of multiple-marginality (Cruz, 2014). Mexican immigrants formed 18th Street under similar conditions in Los Angeles barrios (Vigil, 1988, 2006) because a local gang, Clanton Street, rejected all youths who could not prove 100% Mexican ancestry. Soon, MS-13 and 18th Street battled for territorial and identity allegiances of Mexican American, Salvadoran, and youth of other nationalities in Los Angeles (Cruz, 2014). This war continued in El Salvador as deported immigrants, including prison inmates, were returned from Los Angeles to their native country.

The FBI (2008) has asserted that MS-13 is operating in 42 U.S. states, and that both it and the 18th Street gang is active in 20 states (cited in Franco, 2010, p. 2). According to the FBI (2011) these gangs spread from the Los Angeles area and Central America to other communities across the United States, particularly Atlanta, Dallas, Washington, DC, and New York metropolitan areas. The FBI (2009) estimates membership of 18th Street "at 30,000 to 50,000" in the U.S. and Central America while the MS-13 gang "is estimated to have 30,000 to 50,000 members and associate members worldwide, 8,000 to 10,000 of whom reside in the United States" (pp. 23, 26).

Reality

The large estimates of membership in these two gangs cannot be verified. For one thing, common immigration patterns cannot be separated from gang-related activity in these numbers. In addition, Franco (2010) relays that various estimates of the membership of these two gangs "are difficult to corroborate" (p. 8). The Washington Office on Latin America (WOLA) conducted a brief evaluation and analysis of the characteristics, both local and transnational, of Central American gangs in the Washington, DC, area (McGuire, 2007). This study revealed that 18th Street, at that time, did not "have a strong presence in the DC area," but that Mara Salvatrucha "does have a presence in the Washington area" (pp. 1–2). Although the WOLA research found that "the evidence supports the argument that [these] gangs are not a major public security issue in the Washington D.C. area," the study concluded that "Central American gangs do affect specific communities in a serious way, however, and they need to be addressed" (p. 40). Similar research to determine the actual presence of these gangs has not been conducted in other regions of the United States. Chapter 8 addresses the extent to which these gangs are transnational in scope and dangerous.

Myth 5: Gangs, Drugs, and Violence Are Inexorably Linked

This myth is another product of the big gang theory that imaginative gang inmates told to researchers in the late 1980s. Their tales and the subsequent media accounts vividly described violent money-making gangs that intended to wipe out local drug dealers as they presumably marched across the country. The gangs-drugs-violence myth soon was revived again in the broadcast media (K. Johnson, 2006). In sum, the gangs-drugs-violence myth ties together three big gang theory components—(1) migrating gangs, (2) gang drug trafficking, and (3) the inevitable violence—wherever migrating gangs take their drug operations, either locally or to other cities.

Reality

The gangs-drugs-violence myth is a complex one that must be dissected in parts. The migrating gang notion is a key to the first part; the second one is gang control of drug trafficking; the third part is the related violence.

As explained previously, in clarifying the fourth myth, the migrating-gang myth has been refuted in two independent national surveys of law enforcement: in Maxson's (1998) work and by respondents in the National Youth Gang Survey (detailed in Chapter 8). Law enforcement officers do not view migrating gangs as the predominant factor contributing to gang violence. They claim that drug involvement and intergang conflicts are far more important factors.

Coughlin and Venkatesh (2003) state, "The consensus appears to be that drug trafficking is usually a secondary interest compared to identity construction, protecting neighborhood territory, and recreation" (p. 44). It may come as a surprise to many readers to learn that, although street gang members often are actively involved in drug sales, gang research confirms that *few street gangs control drug distribution operations.* While research does indicate that some drug distribution operations are managed by former youth gangs that transformed themselves into drug gangs or by drug gangs initially formed as such, further studies show most drug-trafficking operations are managed by adult drug cartels or syndicates (Eddy, Sabogal, & Walden, 1988). J. Fagan and Chin (1989) note active street level groups include drug "crews" and "posses," while Klein and Maxson (1994) and J. Moore (1993) add traditional narcotics operatives. The groups may also include new adult criminal organizations formed in some cities to service the growing drug market.

Important distinctions between youthful street gangs and drug gangs (cartels or syndicates) are shown in Table 2.1. Drug gangs are very common. For example, Braga, Kennedy, and Tita's (2002) assessment of homicide incidents in Baltimore identified some 325 drug-trafficking groups, but few of them were youth gangs. However, gang member involvement at the level of street sales brings gangs into

Table 2.1   Common Differences Between Street Gangs and Drug Gangs

Street Gangs	Drug Gangs
Versatile ("cafeteria-style") crime	Crime focused on drug business
Larger structures	Smaller structures
Less cohesive	More cohesive
Looser leadership	More centralized leadership
Ill-defined roles	Market-defined roles
Code of loyalty	Requirement of loyalty
Residential territories	Sales market territories
Members may sell drugs	Members do sell drugs
Intergang rivalries	Competition controlled
Younger on average, but wider age range	Older on average, but narrower age range

Source: OUP Material: *The American Street Gang* by Malcolm W. Klein (1995), Table 4.4 from p. 132. Reprinted with permission from Oxford University Press.

the mix, because their members very often use drugs and need to procure them. As Av. Valdez and Sifaneck (2004) assert, the gang collectively encourages this and sometimes provides protection for its drug-selling members even though the gang itself may not benefit from the sales.

Another important question surrounds the violence connection, whether street gang involvement in the drug business typically leads to violence comparable to strictly drug gangs and the associated drug wars among cartels (Eddy et al., 1988; Gugliotta & Leen 1989; Leinwald, 2007). The reality is that it sometimes does, but as discussed in Chapter 8, youth gang-related violence mainly emanates from other conflicts. As for homicides, studies in eight cities have shown that gangs account for a large share but the correlation between gang-related homicides and drug trafficking is actually very weak in the following cities:

- Baltimore, Maryland (Braga et al., 2002)
- Boston, Massachusetts (Kennedy, Piehl, & Braga, 1996)
- Chicago, Illinois (C. Block & Block, 1993; C. Block, Christakos, Jacob, & Przybylski, 1996; Curry & Spergel, 1988)
- Indianapolis, Indiana (McGarrell & Chermak, 2003)
- Los Angeles, California (Hutson et al., 1995; Klein, Maxson, & Cunningham, 1991)
- Minneapolis, Minnesota (Kennedy & Braga, 1998)
- St. Louis, Missouri (Decker & Van Winkle, 1996; Rosenfeld, Bray, & Egley, 1999)
- Stockton, California (Braga et al., 2002)

Street gang wars over market control sometimes produce a large number of homicides. Block and colleagues (1996) report one set of ongoing gang drug wars in Chicago that involved two "brother" gangs, the Black Gangster Disciples and the Black Disciples; in another case, the Black P. Stones committed a substantial number of homicides in the course of their push to reestablish themselves in the drug market. But as Tita and his colleagues observe regarding the gangs-drugs-homicides intersection in Los Angeles, "even in situations where gangs, drugs, and homicides coincided, the motivation for those homicides was much more likely to stem from an argument over quantity/quality of the drugs, payment, or robbery of a drug dealer or customer than from two groups fighting for market control" (Tita, Riley, Ridgeway, et al., 2003, pp. 5, 36).

Myth 6: A "Wanna-Be" Is a "Gonna-Be"

This myth speaks to the inevitability of becoming an actual gang member once a youth begins to display some affinity to gang culture. If a youth associates with gang members and toys with gang lifestyles, then joining is virtually presumed in accordance with this myth.

Reality

This assumption is misleading. Youth who associate with a gang do not necessarily become members. In a St. Louis study of middle school students across the city, Curry, Decker, and Egley (2002) found more than half of the surveyed youngsters who reported never having been in a gang said they had engaged in at least one kind of gang involvement. More than a third of them had gang members as friends, nearly one-third had worn gang colors, nearly one-quarter had hung out with gang members, and one-fifth had flashed gang signs. In another study of a Florida sample of nearly 10,000 middle school students, Eitle, Gunkel, and Gundy (2004) reported only 5% of the sample self-reported having joined a gang, but half of the non-gang youths engaged in one or more behaviors that suggested "gang orientations": They had flashed gang signs, worn gang colors on purpose, drank alcohol or gotten high with gang members, or hung out with gang members. Girls sometimes have continuous associations with gangs, but never join, as Av. Valdez, Cepeda, and Kaplan's (2009) multiyear San Antonio study illustrated.

Myth 7: Children Are Joining Gangs at Younger and Younger Ages

No other gang myth is repeated in broadcast media more often than this one. The youngest reported gang member is said to be four years of age.[1]

Reality

In the first city-wide gang study, Thrasher (1927/2000) classified 18 children under age 10 as gang members, although they were associated with what he called *child gangs* or play groups. Technically speaking, then, for a child to join a "gang" is nothing new. In the modern era, quite likely only children who are born into gangs (referred to as *blessed in*) by virtue of intergenerational traditions are actually bona fide gang members below age 10. Below this age, few children are sufficiently exposed to gangs (although Kotlowitz [1992] notes exceptions in Chicago public housing); and adolescents prefer not to hang out with children. As discussed in Chapter 3, gang joining typically begins during the transition from elementary school to middle school. It is at this point that children first experience some freedom from adult supervision, experience exposure to gangs, and are sufficiently alienated from parents and school to find them inviting.

Myth 8: Gang Members Spend Most of Their Time Planning or Committing Crimes

A popular notion about gangs is that they constantly and indiscriminately perpetrate violence. Bjerregaard (2003) explains how the media frequently "use narratives to help convey the danger associated with gang activities frequently relying on stories of drive-by shootings that killed innocent victims" (p. 175).

Reality

Klein (1995) summarized gang life as being

> a very dull life. For the most part, gang members do very little—sleep, get up late, hang around, brag a lot, eat again, drink, hang around some more. It's a boring life; the only thing that is equally boring is being a researcher watching gang members. (p. 11)

Esbensen (2000) concurs: "For the majority of the time, gang youth engage in the same activities as other youth—sleeping, attending school, hanging out, and working odd jobs. Only a fraction of their time is dedicated to gang activity" (p. 2). W. Miller's (1966) well-trained street workers intensively observed seven gangs over a two-year period and recorded some 54,000 behavioral sequences in 60 categories. Among these, only 3% related to assaultive behavior.

In addition, Maxson and Klein (1990) show that failure to distinguish *gang-motivated* crime from *gang-related* crime greatly exaggerates the extent of planned gang crime. The former term applies to crimes committed on behalf of the gang or in furtherance of a gang function; the latter term—the more general measure—requires only that a gang member was involved regardless of the type of crime or circumstances surrounding it.

Myth 9: Gangs Often Have Highly Unusual Initiation Rites

This popular myth holds that to become a full-fledged member, without exception, youths who join a gang must participate in an initiation ritual, and perhaps commit a serious violent act against a stranger, chosen at random (Best & Hutchinson, 1996).

Reality

Vigil (2004) asserts that gang initiations often require initiates to endure a character test in what are called *beat-downs* or *jump-ins*. But requiring inductees to victimize innocent members of the public is extremely rare. There are several versions of ritual-associated myths, which periodically circulate on the Internet in the form of "urban legends." For example, Fernandez (1998) recounts the flickered-headlights myth, which refers to a legend that gang members must drive after dark with their headlights turned off in order to choose victims. According to this myth, if an approaching motorist flashes his or her head lights at the gang members' car (presumably in a friendly attempt to alert the driver that the lights are off), the gangsters must chase down and kill the motorist. Saunders (2011) identifies another media-induced hysteria that gangs from Mexico are robbing women in Walmart parking lots. Each of these urban legends and many others are nothing but hoaxes that are quickly debunked by law enforcement and skeptical observers.

Myth 10: Most Youths Are Pressured to Join Gangs

A commonly held notion about gang involvement is that youths are surely pressured to join gangs. Otherwise, why would youngsters become involved in these terrible groups?

Reality

As unlikely as it may seem, many youths who join very much *want* to belong to gangs, because gangs often are at the center of appealing social action—parties, hanging out, music, dancing, drugs, and opportunities to participate in social activities with members of the opposite sex. Other adolescents often look up to gang members because of their rebellious and defiant demeanor. For example, Wiist, Jackson, and Jackson's (1996) survey of Houston middle school students revealed that the classmates whom they looked up to as peer leaders did not have the qualities one might expect: 1 in 4 had beaten or punched another person, and nearly 2 in 10 had been in a gang fight.

Social interaction and a need for protection are main reasons that youths give when asked why they joined a gang. They want to feel safe and secure, and they want to be an integral part of the social scene. They may seek support that their own parents and family do not provide. The pressures they may feel to join the gang are usually associated with family relations and normal peer influences, or come from gang members who warn them that they may be without protection if they do not join—particularly in correctional institutions. Most youths can manage these circumstances without reprisal from other gang members (Decker & Kempf-Leonard, 1991).

The gang-joining process is generally similar to the manner in which most of us would go about joining an organization. It is a gradual process that may consume multiple years. A youngster typically begins hanging out with gang members at age 12 or 13 (even younger in some instances), and joins the gang between age 13 and 15—typically taking from six months to a year or two from the time of initial associations (Decker & Van Winkle, 1996; Esbensen & Huizinga, 1993; Huff, 1996, 1998; Vigil, 1993). But many associates never join.

> I guess we were all looking for a feeling of being wanted, so we went and did it. We were all fighting and what have you. Then they handed us a can of spray paint and some baggies and we were on our way. —Anonymous member of the Ganzas gang (in J. Moore, 1991, p. 34)

Myth 11: Adults Recruit Adolescents to Join Gangs

It is widely believed that adult gang members apply pressure to children and adolescents to join gangs. Legislators and media reports often presume that sinister adult gang operatives are using their stealth to draw younger and younger victims into their clutches, often around schools, much like pedophiles. The illogic of this presumption is never explored in such broadcasts. A corollary view is that adult gangs recruit youngsters to act as runners in their lucrative drug trade. Because of these concerns, some state anti-gang laws include enhanced penalties for adults who recruit children into gangs.

"We started it, me and Pelona and Maggie and India, just hanging around together and meeting at each other's house. More girls started coming over and then the boys started naming us 'honey-drippers' 'cause we used to have this record . . . we used to play over and over." — Anonymous female member of the White Fence gang (in J. Moore, 1991, p. 29)

Reality

Almost without exception, other youngsters recruit gang members. Although youths commonly report ordinary peer pressure (from friends who are in the gang and siblings), the reality is that the adult gang members' recruitment of youth is extremely rare. Just as children and adolescents are recruited into cliques, friendship groups, and gangs by peers who are members or interested in joining themselves, it typically is similar aged peers who exercise the most influence. Gangs sometimes apply peer pressure on recruits in the course of gang expansion (J. Moore et al., 1983). To be sure, and as Fleisher and Decker (2001) confirm, prison gangs actively recruit new members through threats, force, and protection offers; Sheley and Wright (1995) believe this likely occurs more often than reported in juvenile correctional facilities as well. Moreover, very few gang studies have documented the use of juveniles in drug running; the best example is likely Bynum and Varano's (2003) Detroit study. Interestingly, Hagedorn (1994) found Milwaukee's older gang members actually refused to allow juveniles to get involved in the drug trade, because of the dangers involved. More common, it seems, is the use of coercion by older gang members, "pressing younger dudes into taking the fall" when arrested (personal communication, Deborah Weisel, January 21, 2009).

Myth 12: Once Kids Join a Gang, They're Pretty Much Lost for Good

Gang involvement is seen as a permanent condition; once youths join a gang, there is no turning back. The grip of the gang is said to be permanent. This myth has its origins in the mystique of dominating gangs, first promulgated in the romantic movie *West Side Story*, with the claim, "Once you're a Jet, you're a Jet all the way, From your first cigarette to your last dying day" and also in the "blood in; blood out" credo.

Reality

Gang involvement is rarely a permanent status. Field studies, community youth interviews, and surveys of students find that "for many youth, actual membership in the gang is a short-term fling" (J. Moore, 2007b, p. x). Excluding cities with a large number of intergenerational gangs, multiple studies conclude approximately half of the youngsters who claim membership in a gang typically leave it within a year. In Rochester, New York, Krohn and Thornberry (2008) found half of the boys (50%) and two-thirds of the girls report being a gang member for one year or less; and only 22% of the boys and 5% of the girls remained members for three or four years. In Pittsburgh, R. A. Gordon and colleagues (2004) determined almost half (48%) of the boys were gang members for only one year, and just 25% for up to two years. Seattle researchers Hill, Liu, and Hawkins (2001) reported that 31% belonged for longer than a year, but only 1% belonged for five years. In Denver, Esbensen and Huizinga (1993) indicate 67% were a member for just one year, and only 3% belonged for all four years. Interestingly, most (60%) of the active Denver gang members "indicated that they would like not to be a gang member and expected to leave the gang in the future" (p. 582). Nationwide data collected by Bjerregaard (2010) also show that gang involvement is "a transient phenomenon" among teenagers.

Adolescence is a time of changing peer relations and fleeting allegiances to both friends (Warr, 2002) and gangs (Decker & Curry, 2000; Fleisher, 1998). Involvement in a variety of peer groups is common during the adolescent period. However, multiyear and intergenerational gang membership is far more common in cities with long-standing gang problems, such as Chicago (Horowitz, 1983) and Los Angeles (J. Moore, 1978).

> I'd dress my kids in gang clothes. I thought they were so cute. I thought I was so smart. I dropped out of school and there I was, a baby mamma with two kids in Florencia-13 clothes.
>
> —Joanna (in Leap, 2012, pp. 61–62)

Other studies in traditional gang cities also found that gang membership was a relatively temporary experience for the majority of gang-involved youths (Hagedorn, 1998; Klein, 1971; Short & Strodtbeck, 1965/1974; Vigil, 1988; Yablonsky, 1967). Prison gangs are a different matter, to be sure. Fleisher (1995) notes the "blood in; blood out" credo is shared among prison gangs, including the Mexican Mafia, La Nuestra Familia, Texas Syndicate, and Mexicanemi. Other gangs have death penalty offenses, which "include but are not limited to: stealing drugs or drug money for personal use, testifying in open court against another member, failing to kill someone after being directed to do it, or betraying gang loyalty" (p. 141).

Myth 13: The Gang's Here for Good

It is commonly believed that once gangs appear, they become a permanent fixture in communities. As J. Moore suggests (1993), this notion seems to be based on the view that gangs thrive only "in inner-city neighborhoods where they dominate, intimidate, and prey upon" innocent citizens (p. 28).

Reality

Howell and Egley (2005a) report national survey data showing that in cities with populations under 50,000, gang problems regularly wax and wane. In smaller areas with populations under 25,000, only 10% of the localities reported persistent gang problems. Having a gang problem is certainly not a permanent condition in sparsely populated areas. Moreover, in these smaller areas, gang problems are, comparatively speaking, relatively minor in terms of size (e.g., number of gangs and gang members) and impact on the community. Hence, Howell (2006) asserts the probability of permanent gang problems is far greater in the nation's large cities than in the smaller ones and in rural counties—although experiencing gangs forever once they appear is not by any means a certainty, even in large cities (discussed further in Chapter 7).

Myth 14: Gang Members Are a New Wave of Super Predators

John DiIulio (1995a, 1995b) coined the term *super predator* to call public attention to what he characterized as a "new breed" of offenders, "kids that have absolutely no respect for human life and no sense of the future . . . These are stone-cold predators!" (1995b, p. 23). Elsewhere, DiIulio and coauthors have described these young people as "radically impulsive, brutally remorseless youngsters . . . who murder, assault, rob, burglarize, deal deadly drugs, join gun-toting gangs, and create serious [linked] disorders" (Bennett, DiIulio, & Waters, 1996, p. 27). DiIulio (1995b) warned that juvenile super predators would be "flooding the nation's streets," coming "at us in waves over the next 20 years . . . Time is running out" (p. 25). DiIulio (1995b, 1997) and J. Wilson (1995) predicted a new "wave" of juvenile violence to occur between about 1995 and 2010, which they based in part on a projected increase in the under-18 population. The sharp increase in adolescent and young adult homicides in the late 1980s and early 1990s (Blumstein, 1995a, 1995b) was tied to the presumed new wave of juvenile super predators, and attributable partly to drug-trafficking gangs that presumably grew to profit from the so-called crack cocaine epidemic. Several popular magazines featured stories on the predicted crime wave, and many depicted on their covers young Black thugs—often gang members—holding handguns. Stories that played to readers' fears were common. The dire warnings of a coming generation of super predators supported what Esbensen and Tusinski (2007) assert was a helpless feeling that the young minority gang-involved offenders were beyond redemption.

Reality

None of these assumptions proved to be correct. The new wave of super predators never arrived. Several researchers have debunked this myth and the associated doomsday projections; the anticipated increase in juvenile violence was vastly exaggerated (Howell, Lipsey, & Wilson, 2014). A new wave of minority super predators did not develop, nor did a general wave of juvenile violence occur. Rather than super predators, public policy analysts and the research communities attribute the dramatic growth in homicide largely to the availability of firearms—primarily handguns, the involvement of young people in illicit drug markets, and an increase in gang homicide (C. Block & Block, 1993; Cook & Laub, 1998; Howell, 1999).

M. Fishman (1978) first discovered *crime reporting waves*, which begin as crime themes that journalists develop, often from police sources, in the process of gathering information, organizing it, and selecting news to be presented to the public. Journalists routinely rely on one another for newsworthy crime trends. Fishman noted how additional media outlets ran a story after seeing the initial attention that it garnered, and how the original story was embellished as it was repeated in another locality. In this manner, a crime theme spreads throughout a community of news organizations, as one media outlet after another repeats the story. Hence, a crime reporting wave may develop as the story is recounted, added on, and often embellished.

In another example, an experienced gang researcher tested the veracity of a broadcast warning of a coming wave of gang activity in New York City. The media stories concentrated on large gangs that presumably were present in New York City, Los Angeles, and Chicago: Bloods, Crips, Latin Kings, and Netas. J. Sullivan (2006) explains, "The nationally famous gangs finally came to New York City in 1997, at least in name" (p. 22). Furthermore, "Many stories were told of the rituals supposedly associated with Blood membership" (p. 30). In the most widely circulated version, induction into the Bloods gang required recruits to commit random violent acts, such as slashing the face of a total stranger with a razor. In an embellished claim, the slashing victim had to be a family member, including one's mother. The crescendo of this hysteria was reached on Halloween, 1997: "As the day approached, rumors circulated throughout New York City that Halloween would be a day of a massive Blood initiation" (p. 30). Alas, "the mass slayings never occurred. The hysteria subsided, and the media lost interest" (p. 31). Data that Sullivan collected in the three neighborhood areas proved that nothing happened in the way of a surge in gang activity, only a spike in media reports.

Myth 15: Gangs Were Actively Involved in the Crack Cocaine Epidemic

Skolnick (1989, 1990) interviewed imprisoned members of the California Crips and Bloods in the late 1980s. The gang members said they were transforming themselves into formal criminal organizations to profit from the "crack cocaine epidemic." They also claimed they were expanding their criminal operations across the country. The California gang members' story influenced public perceptions of gangs via broadcast media in several ways. The myth of formal organization is particularly important. The notion that gangs were becoming huge powerful criminal organizations—much like highly structured corporations—became widely accepted. A national conference concluded that "it is well known that gang members are key players in the illegal drug trade," and that "there is clear evidence . . . that the demand for drugs, especially crack cocaine, has led to the migration of Los Angeles gang members across the country" (Bryant, 1989, pp. 2–3). The threat drug-trafficking youth gangs represented to the nation seemed apparent. "The fierce circle of drugs, profits, and violence threatens the freedom and public safety of citizens from coast to coast. It holds in its grip large jurisdictions and small ones, urban areas and rural ones" (T. Donahue, in Bryant, 1989, p. 1). Representatives in other levels of the federal government immediately began promoting this assumption (Hayeslip, 1989; U.S. General Accounting Office, 1989; United States Attorney General, 1989).

Because the growth in youth gun violence in the period from the mid-1980s to the early 1990s coincided with the so-called crack cocaine epidemic, a couple of researchers suggested that these developments were related and could involve gang members. Blumstein and Rosenfeld (1999) stated the assumed connection:

> As the crack epidemic spread in the mid- and late-1980s, so did the danger around inner city drug markets, driving up the incentive for more kids to arm themselves in an increasingly threatening environment. That environment also became a prime recruiting ground for urban street gangs. (p. 162).

Reality

It is difficult to find convincing empirical evidence of a nationwide crack cocaine epidemic in the scholarly literature (for convincing evidence to the contrary, see Hartman & Golub, 1999; Reeves & Campbell, 1994). Only a few cities appear to have experienced such widespread cocaine use to qualify as an "epidemic," principally in Los Angeles, Oakland, New York City, Detroit, Miami, and Washington, DC (Reeves & Campbell, 1994, p. 160). Street gangs' involvement was very limited. There is evidence that some Los Angeles Crips and Bloods gangs were involved in large-scale cocaine trafficking (Cockburn & St. Clair, 1998). However, more extensive research showed that street gang involvement in cocaine drug trafficking in California was overstated (Klein et al., 1991; Maxson, 1998; Maxson, Woods, & Klein, 1996). In general, empirical support for Blumstein and Rosenfeld's (1999) hypothesis is not convincing. In two studies these widely respected scholars cite, Cork (1999) and Grogger and Willis (1998) attempted to show a causal connection between youth violence and a presumed crack cocaine epidemic, but actual crack use could not be distinguished from other more widespread means of ingesting cocaine (Golub & Johnson, 1997), and neither of these studies empirically established the expected connection directly to gangs.

The crack cocaine phenomenon was not as widespread as Blumstein and Rosenfeld presumed; it was limited to a few cities. Moreover, Ousey and Lee (2004) note that "different drug 'epidemics' have hit different cities at different points in time"; hence, Blumstein and Rosenfeld's hypothesis does not universally apply. In reality, drug distribution and related drug wars are overwhelmingly the province of adult criminal organizations and cartels (Eddy et al., 1988; Gugliotta & Leen, 1989; Klein, 2004), not street gangs that are without the financial backing and access to banks for money laundering that adult organized crime groups enjoy. Researchers have long doubted that gangs composed largely of adolescents could manage interstate drug-trafficking operations (Howell & Decker, 1999). There are a few exceptions, of course, and Pittsburgh and Detroit are two of these, in which gang involvement in drug trafficking was extensive (see Chapter 8). But the most authoritative sources are in agreement that the so-called crack cocaine epidemic was an instrumental part of the Reagan administration's "war on drugs" (Brownstein, 1996; Reeves & Campbell, 1994).

Myth 16: Zero Tolerance of Gang Behaviors Will Eliminate Gangs From Schools

Calls for increased law enforcement presence in schools commenced in the late 1980s with the Reagan administration's policy of aggressive enforcement of antidrug laws. By 1993, *zero-tolerance* (ZT) policies were adopted by school boards across the country, often broadened to include not only drugs and weapons but also tobacco use and school disruption. In 1994, President Clinton signed the Gun-Free Schools Act into law (Public Law 103-227) that mandates an expulsion of one calendar year for possession of a weapon and referral of students who violate the law to the criminal or juvenile justice system. By the late 1990s, at least three-fourths of all schools reporting to the National Center for Education Statistics said that they had ZT policies in place for various student offenses, including bringing firearms or other weapons to school; gang activity; alcohol, drug, and tobacco offenses; and physical attacks or fighting (Skiba & Peterson, 1999). These policies specify predetermined mandatory consequences or punishments for specific offenses. In the school setting, ZT is a disciplinary policy that sends this message by punishing all offenses severely, no matter how minor, and suspension from school is the most common punishment. There is no room for discretion. ZT policies are also called *one strike and you're out* policies. These policies are based on deterrence philosophy, and they originally targeted drug use, gang involvement, and gun possession.

Reality

To enforce school-based ZT policies, armed police are increasingly placed in schools, the end result of which appears mainly to send more children to juvenile courts for minor forms of misbehavior that should have been addressed as disciplinary matters (Figure 2.1). A Texas study of nearly 1 million Texas public secondary school students shocked the public in finding that among students who were followed for more than six years beginning in 2000, nearly 60% were suspended or expelled from school (Fabelo et al., 2011). It turns out that only 3% of the total disciplinary actions were in response to conduct for which state law mandated suspensions and expulsions; virtually all were made at the discretion of school officials, presumably in response to violations of local schools' conduct codes.

This research pinpoints a highly controversial performance issue, one that has surrounded the placement of law enforcement officers in schools from the beginning: the prospect of widening the net of the juvenile justice system over minor offenders. ZT policies have had the effect of clogging juvenile justice systems with low-risk offenders, and school resource officers are viewed as key players in this undesirable outcome. Many public schools "have turned into feeder schools for the juvenile and criminal justice systems" (Advancement Project, 2005, p. 11). The Civil Rights Division of the U.S. Department of Justice recently filed a lawsuit charging that Meridian, Mississippi, officials are running

Figure 2.1   Schoolhouse Zero Tolerance

Source: Skiba, R.J. and Peterson, R. (1999). The dark side of zero tolerance: Can punishment lead to safe schools? *Phi Delta Kappan, 80,* pp. 372-376. Illustration by Joseph E. Lee. Reprinted by permission.

a "school-to-prison pipeline" in violation of the constitutional rights of students who are wrongfully reported to law enforcement for minor disobedience by public schools.

Zero-tolerance policies can have a cumulative effect, as follows:

- The "difficult schools" with ZT policies can increase future delinquency by imposing more severe sanctions (Kaplan & Damphouse, 1997).

- Suspension and expulsions from school often mean that students are removed from adult supervision and, in turn, experience more exposure to delinquent peers, which can lead to delinquency onset (Hemphill, Toumborou, Herrenkohl, McMorris, & Catalano, 2006).

- Delinquency involvement can increase gang membership and court referral (Esbensen & Huizinga, 1993; Hill, Howell, Hawkins, & Battin-Pearson, 1999; Thornberry, Krohn, et al., 2003).

- Teenagers who experience juvenile justice system intervention are substantially more likely than their peers to become members of a gang (Bernburg, Krohn, & Rivera, 2006).

Myth 17: Sole Reliance on Law Enforcement Will Wipe Out Gangs

Because gangs are commonly believed to have come from somewhere else, it is presumed that law enforcement agencies can turn them away at the city or county borders, or remove all of them from the area by arrest, prosecution, and confinement. This deterrence strategy is called *gang suppression.*

Reality

When used as a single strategy, gang suppression tactics do not have a history of success. The Los Angeles Police Department (LAPD) has long been a leader in the use of these tactics. The most notorious gang sweep, Operation Hammer, was an LAPD Community Resources Against Street Hoodlums (CRASH) unit operation (Klein, 1995). It started in South Central Los Angeles in 1988, when a force of a thousand police officers swept through the area on a Friday night and again on Saturday, arresting presumed gang members on a wide variety of offenses, including existing warrants, new traffic citations, curfew violations, illegal gang-related behaviors, and observed criminal activities. All of the 1,453 people arrested were taken to a mobile booking operation adjacent to the Los Angeles Memorial Coliseum.

Most of the arrested youths were released without charges. Slightly more than half were gang members. There were only 60 felony arrests, and charges were filed on only 32 of them. As Klein (1995) describes it, "This remarkably inefficient process was repeated many times, although with smaller forces—more typically one hundred or two hundred officers" (p. 162). Incredibly, the Rampart CRASH officers, who were fiercely involved in fighting gangs, came to act like gang members themselves. Leinwand (2000) describes how the CRASH officers wore special tattoos and pledged their loyalty to the anti-gang unit with a code of silence. They protected their turf by intimidating Rampart-area gang members with unprovoked beatings and threats. Rafael Perez, an officer in the Rampart Division who was arrested in 1998 for stealing cocaine from a police warehouse, provided testimony for CRASH officers' arrests when he implicated 70 officers in a variety of illegal activities: planting evidence, intimidating witnesses, beating suspects, giving false testimony, selling drugs, and covering up unjustified shootings.

The Operation Hammer incident illustrates how it is unfair and unrealistic to expect that law enforcement can succeed in extinguishing street gangs by the use of gang suppression tactics. Street gangs are a product of U.S. history and are homegrown.

Myth 18: Nothing Works With Gangs

There is a tendency to believe that the gang problem is too complex to be solved, or that prior attempts have been misguided and ineffective.

Reality

In the words of the renowned meta-analyst when speaking about juvenile delinquency, Lipsey (1995) stated,

> [I]t is no longer constructive for researchers, practitioners, and policymakers to argue about whether delinquency treatment and related rehabilitative approaches "work," as if that were a question that could be answered with a simple "yes" or "no." As a generality, treatment clearly works. (p. 78)

So it is with the gang field. It is no longer constructive to say that nothing works strictly because a blue-ribbon program that consistently shows large reductions does not exist. On occasion, even homegrown programs can outperform blueprint juvenile delinquency programs (Lipsey & Howell, 2012). More than a dozen gang programs show measurable reductions in some form of gang-related behavior; others show either reductions in risk factors or protective benefits. In the gang world, it would be unrealistic to expect large reductions in gang-related crime because of the intractability of gangs, given that they are anchored in cracks in societies and gang members often suffer from multiple-marginality in key sectors of their lives. The larger issue is what works, for whom, and under what circumstances?

However, Klein and Maxson (2006) overlooked several programs that have demonstrated scientific evidence of effectiveness with gangs or gang members (which are reviewed in Chapters 9 and 10). One of the effective gang programs (the Comprehensive Gang Prevention, Intervention, and Suppression Program) demonstrated crime reductions in controlled studies in five cities (Chapter 10), specifically contradicting Klein and Maxson's critique of this particular program. A highly reliable meta-analysis of comprehensive gang programs by Hodgkinson and colleagues (2009) also revealed other gang programs that were effective, though published after Klein and Maxson's review in 2006. It should also be recognized that programs that have proven effective in reducing gang violence have not produced particularly large reductions, though statistically significant.

◈ Concluding Observations

Gang problems are often difficult to assess, and gangs are often shrouded in myths, which can lead to ineffective community responses. For example, if it is believed that local gangs migrated from distant cities such as Los Angeles or Chicago, officials may assume that the newly arrived gang members can be driven out. If they and their families are established residents of the city, however, this approach is unlikely to work.

In the 1980s and 1990s, myths and stereotypes about gangs and gang members contributed to moral panic in America. In this state of moral panic, political and social leaders suddenly define a specific group of people as a major threat to our values and behavioral standards. A "war on gangs" was declared. The LAPD's Operation Hammer is a reminder of the futility of singular suppression strategies, particularly street sweeps.

The myths and stereotypes, coupled with a lack of research to address their validity, contribute to our lack of ability to address the gang problem effectively. The first responsible step in every community that suspects it has a gang problem is an objective, interagency, and communitywide assessment to determine if in fact a gang problem exists, and if so, to identify the dimensions of the problem. Every effort must be made to discard preconceived notions in this assessment because many of these are based on gang myths.

DISCUSSION TOPICS

1. From your perspective, what is the most surprising gang myth?

2. Review several newspaper or magazine articles on gangs and see how many myths you can identify.

3. Why are gang myths so popular, and who benefits from gang myths besides broadcast media?

4. How can gang myths be countered?

5. Dissect the so-called crack cocaine epidemic. Did it actually happen? Why was it promoted? What role did politics play in promoting it? Why is it still considered by many criminologists to have happened?

RECOMMENDATIONS FOR FURTHER READING

Street Gang Involvement in Drug Distribution Operations

Esbensen, F., Peterson, D., Freng, A., & Taylor, T. J. (2002). Initiation of drug use, drug sales, and violent offending among a sample of gang and nongang youth. In C. R. Huff (Ed.), *Gangs in America III* (pp. 37–50). Thousand Oaks, CA: Sage.

Gugliotta, G., & Leen, J. (1989). *Kings of cocaine*. New York: Simon & Schuster.

Howell, J. C., & Decker, S. H. (1999). *The youth gangs, drugs, and violence connection* (Juvenile Justice Bulletin. Youth Gang Series). Washington, DC: Office of Juvenile Justice and Delinquency Prevention.

Howell, J. C., & Gleason, D. K. (1999). *Youth gang drug trafficking* (Juvenile Justice Bulletin. Youth Gang Series). Washington, DC: U.S. Department of Justice, Office of Juvenile Justice and Delinquency Prevention.

Huff, C. R. (1989). Youth gangs and public policy. *Crime and Delinquency, 35,* 524–537.

Klein, M. W., Maxson, C. L., & Cunningham, L. C. (1991). Crack, street gangs, and violence. *Criminology, 29,* 623–650.

Levitt, S. D., & Venkatesh, S. A. (2001). Growing up in the projects: The economic lives of a cohort of men who came of age in Chicago public housing. *American Economic Review, 91,* 79–84.

Papachristos, A. V. (2005). Gang world. *Foreign Policy, 147*(March–April), 48–55.

Sanchez-Jankowski, M. S. (1991). *Islands in the street: Gangs and American urban society.* Berkeley: University of California Press.

Taylor, C. S. (1990a). *Dangerous society.* East Lansing: Michigan State University Press.

Taylor, C. S. (1990b). Gang imperialism. In C. R. Huff (Ed.), *Gangs in America* (pp. 103–115). Newbury Park, CA: Sage.

Venkatesh, S. A. (1996). The gang and the community. In C. R. Huff (Ed.), *Gangs in America* (2nd ed., pp. 241–256). Thousand Oaks, CA: Sage.

Venkatesh, S. A. (2008). *Gang leader for a day: A rogue sociologist takes to the streets.* New York: Penguin Press.

How Gang Members Spend Their Time

Hughes, L. A., & Short, J. F. (2005). Disputes involving gang members: Micro-social contexts. *Criminology, 43,* 43–76.

Klein, M. W. (2004). *Gang cop: The words and ways of Officer Paco Domingo.* Walnut Creek, CA: AltaMira Press.

Miller, W. B. (1958). Lower class culture as a generating milieu of gang delinquency. *Journal of Social Issues, 14,* 5–19.

Miller, W. B. (1966). Violent crimes in city gangs. *The Annals of the American Academy of Political and Social Science, 364,* 96–112.

Short, J. F., Jr., & Strodtbeck, F. L. (1965/1974). *Group process and gang delinquency.* Chicago: University of Chicago.

Spergel, I. A. (1995). *The youth gang problem.* New York: Oxford University Press.

Length of Gang Membership Period

Bendixen, M., Endresen, I. M., & Olweus, D. (2006). Joining and leaving gangs: Selection and facilitation effects on self-reported antisocial behaviour in early adolescence. *European Journal of Criminology, 3,* 85–114.

Esbensen, F., & Huizinga, D. (1993). Gangs, drugs, and delinquency in a survey of urban youth. *Criminology, 31,* 565–589.

Gilman, A. B., Hill, K. G., Hawkins, J. D., Howell, J. C., & Kosterman, R. (2014). The developmental dynamics of joining a gang in adolescence: Patterns and predictors of gang membership. *Journal of Research on Adolescence, 24,* 204–219.

Gordon, R. A., Lahey, B. B., Kawai, E., Loeber, R., Stouthamer-Loeber, M., & Farrington, D. P. (2004). Antisocial behavior and youth gang membership: Selection and socialization. *Criminology, 42,* 55–88.

Pyrooz, D. C., Decker, S. H., & Webb, V. J. (2014). The ties that bind: Desistance from gangs. *Crime and Delinquency, 60,* 491–516.

Pyrooz, D. C., Sweeten, G., & Piquero, A. R. (2013). Continuity and change in gang membership and gang embeddedness. *Journal of Research in Crime and Delinquency, 50,* 239–271.

Thornberry, T. P., Krohn, M. D., Lizotte, A. J., Smith, C. A., & Tobin, K. (2003). *Gangs and delinquency in developmental perspective.* New York: Cambridge University Press.

Moral Panic

Esbensen, F., & Tusinski, K. (2007). Youth gangs in the print media. *Journal of Criminal Justice and Popular Culture, 14,* 21–38.

Geis, G. (2002). Ganging up on gangs: Anti-loitering and public nuisance laws. In C.R. Huff (Ed.), *Gangs in America III* (pp. 257–270). Thousand Oaks, CA: Sage.

Howell, J. C. (2007). Menacing or mimicking? Realities of youth gangs. *The Juvenile and Family Court Journal, 58,* 9–20.

Jackson, P. G., & Rudman, C. (1993). Moral panic and the response to gangs in California. In S. Cummings & D. Monti (Eds.), *Gangs* (pp. 257–275). Albany: State University of New York Press.

McCorkle, R. C., & Miethe, T. D. (2002). *Panic: The social construction of the street gang problem.* Upper Saddle River, NJ: Prentice Hall.

St. Cyr, J. L. (2003). The folk devil reacts: Gangs and moral panic. *Criminal Justice Review, 28,* 26–45.

Thompson, C., Young, R. L., & Burns, R. (2000). Representing gangs in the news: Media constructions of criminal gangs. *Sociological Spectrum, 20,* 409–432.

Welch, M., Price, E. A., & Yankey, N. (2002). Moral panic over youth violence: Wilding and the manufacture of menace in the media. *Youth & Society, 34,* 3–30.

White, R. (2008). Disputed definitions and fluid identities: The limitations of social profiling in relation to ethnic youth gangs. *Youth Justice, 8,* 149–161.

Zatz, M. S. (1987). Chicano youth gangs and crime: The creation of moral panic. *Contemporary Crises, 11,* 129–158.

NOTE

1. Among thousands of print and broadcast reports of very young gang members over a decade (A. Egley, personal communication, February 24, 2011).

CHAPTER 3

Defining Gangs and Gang Members

◈ Introduction

There is no single, universally accepted definition of a *gang* or a *gang member*. In fact, neither gang researchers nor law enforcement agencies can agree on a common definition, and as Spergel and Bobrowski (1989) report, a concerted national effort in the 1980s failed to reach a consensus between researchers and practitioners on what constitutes a gang, a gang member, or a gang incident. Thus, federal, state, and local jurisdictions in the United States tend to develop their own definitions. W. Miller (1982/1992) explains, "In general, police departments in large cities apply the term quite narrowly, police in smaller cities and towns less narrowly, most media writers more broadly, and most distressed local citizens very broadly" (p. 17). Nevertheless, rather explicit definitions of both gangs and gang members are essential for effective communitywide strategic planning. Reaching agreement on these matters is no small feat. As seen in Chapter 2, no other deviant group is shrouded in more mythic and misleading attributes than gangs.

Europeans are sometimes critical of American criminologists for the difficulties associated with defining gangs universally and, in turn, for the discordant findings that sometimes occur (Hallsworth & Young, 2008; Pitts, 2008). However, researchers should not be dismayed given that gang members themselves have difficulty defining their gangs (Fleisher, 1998). When R. Petersen (2004) asked bona fide female gang members confined in a youth correctional facility to explain the difference between a gang and a peer group, "the majority of the young women in this study did not know how to respond . . . and most did not believe that major differences existed" (p. 30). In addition, observers may often fail to appreciate the diversity of gangs in the United States, and in other parts of the world as well.

This chapter first addresses the matter of defining gangs, and next explores ways to define gang members. The last section examines the demographics of gangs and gang members in the United States.

◆ Defining Gangs

Early Gang Definitions

In 1898, educator Henry D. Sheldon conducted the first student survey that collected information on gang involvement. In Sheldon's survey of 2,508 students in five cities in different U.S. regions, children and adolescents themselves voluntarily provided written descriptions about organizations in which they participated. Sheldon noted that some of the students' organizations, which he categorized as "predatory," included organized *fighting gangs* (a term the students freely used to describe small groups that fought between schools or sections of a town or city) along with bands of robbers, hunting clubs, play armies, and other amusements.[1] Several of the predatory sorts of gangs in which the young students participated dabbled in property crimes and some fighting. For the most part, these were child-dominated play groups—although a few of them persisted throughout the teenage years, with the typical boys who claimed involvement in predatory groups aged 10 to 13. Sheldon (1898) explained the "predatory organization" as "the typical association of small boys. After 12 years of age boys transfer their interest from these loose predatory bands to more definitely constructed athletic clubs" (p. 428).

In the early 1900s, the interests of professional groups—including psychologists, sociologists, and youth workers—turned to the grouping behavior of very young boys. An intense interest in this matter developed and remained for almost half a century due to the emerging notion that child and adolescent grouping might well be instinctive. Several reports described the juvenile and amateur gangs. In fact, so many reports were published on "boy life" that a bibliography, written by R. T. Veal in 1919, contained as many as 2,000 references to works that appeared in print during the last decade of the 19th century and up to 1918.

Early research investigated organized gaming among children, and such young groups were often considered to be "gangs of boys," which often were loosely defined. Scott (1904–05) considered groups containing less than five boys to be too small to constitute a gang (these he called *chums*). His Springfield, Massachusetts, survey included boys ages 10 to 18 and revealed that 68% belonged to a group—which Scott referenced as a *gang*. Among these youngsters, two-thirds said that their gang had secrets, although this often was nothing more than a distinctive whistle or call-out. One-half of the group members said that their gang had some sort of unspecified initiation.

Other early 20th-century groups of children and juveniles evidenced a considerable degree of organization, many of which rightfully could be considered gangs. In 1912, at least 66 gangs were revealed in Puffer's extensive interviews and observations of boys under his direction as principal of a Massachusetts industrial school for wayward youth. These gangs usually had names—"the Hicks Street Fellows, The Bleachery Gang, Morse Hollow Athletic Club, Warf Rats, Crooks, Liners, Egmen, Dowser Glums" (Puffer, 1912, p. 30). Typically ages 10 to 16, the members tended to gather daily, often on a street corner, and they expressed a sense of ownership of that area along with their clubroom tents or camps. Puffer attributed a social purpose to the gatherings: "Boys from bad, broken, or inefficient homes are forced to provide their own social life, and the gang is their one instinctive reaction to their social environment" (p. 28). Two-thirds of the young groups Puffer studied had a leader, and most gangs had some form of initiation, "to test the new fellow's grit and strengthen his spirit of loyalty" (p. 35). These gangs also were typically governed by rules, particularly around snitching and lying on one another, and standing by each other in trouble. Although many of the gangs to which Puffer's juvenile reformatory inmates belonged were comparable to play groups, a number of the participating youths were involved in mischievous deeds, fighting, stealing, and some criminal activities.

Apparently, then, some gangs at least were pretty thoroughly bad. On the other hand, some gangs proved to be almost as thoroughly good. Their members were real boys, but on the whole the gang was helping them to become worthy citizens and upright men. (p. 12)

In the course of his research, Puffer is presumed to have provided the earliest gang definition:

The gang is, in short, a little social organism . . . with a life of its own which is beyond the lives of its several members. It is the earliest manifestation . . . of that strange group-forming instinct, without which a beehive, an ant hill and human society would be alike impossible. (p. 38)

Puffer also characterized gangs as "for the boy one of three primary social groups [which include] the family, the neighborhood, and the play group; but for the normal boy the play group is the gang" (p. 7). While Puffer attributed gangs' existence to lack of parental supervision, it is nevertheless apparent that the prevailing view of that era—that boys and adolescents have an instinctive "grouping" tendency, sometimes leading to prolonged ganging together (Spaulding, 1948)—influenced Puffer's views. In particular, Puffer believed that boys begin to develop "the gang-forming instinct" about the age of 10 (p. 72).

Similarly, Thrasher (1927/2000) defined the gang as

an interstitial group originally formed spontaneously, and then integrated through conflict. It is characterized by the following types of behavior: meeting face to face, milling, movement through space as a unit, conflict and planning. The result of this collective behavior is the development of tradition, unreflective internal structure, esprit de corps, solidarity, morale, group awareness, and attachment to a local territory. (pp. 18–19)

Thrasher's study was so comprehensive and widely respected that half a century would pass before more specific gang definitions were developed. It also is important to note that several recent studies confirm the importance—if not the universality—of conflict for gang formation and identity.

Well, at that time [ours] was not [seen] as a gang. It was just a meeting of youngsters in the streets. . . . It was just that you go out and you hang out in the playground or in the street and talk. —Anonymous male member of the Hoya Maravilla gang (in J. Moore, 1991, p. 26)

Various scholars have developed detailed criteria for the term *gang*, particularly the following:

Gangs are groups whose members meet together with some regularity, over time, on the basis of group-defined criteria of membership and group-defined organizational characteristics; that is, gangs are non-adult-sponsored, self-determining groups that demonstrate continuity over time. (Short, 1996, p. 3)

[A gang is] any denotable adolescent group of youngsters who a) are generally perceived as a distinct aggregation by others in the neighborhood, b) recognize themselves as a denotable group (almost invariably with a group name), and c) have been involved in a sufficient number of delinquent incidents to call forth a consistently negative response from neighborhood residents and/or law enforcement agencies. (Klein, 1971, p. 13)

A youth gang is a self-formed association of peers united by mutual interests with identifiable leadership and internal organization who act collectively or as individuals to achieve specific purposes, including the conduct of illegal activity and control of a particular territory, facility, or enterprise. (W. Miller, 1982/1992, p. 21)

A collective of youths—most likely young adults (16 and over)—that has a discernible organizational structure, whose members recurrently interact and congregate in particular areas or neighborhoods, use collective and individual symbols for identification purposes, and engage predominantly in acts of violence (including threats and intimidation) and drug-related crimes. (Oehme, 1997, p. 67)

The two latter definitions were generated empirically, in a multicity U.S. survey and in a statewide North Carolina study, respectively. Oehme's definition reflects specific offenses in which local gangs were involved. Indeed, for law enforcement, gang definitions are usually described in the context of criminal activity. For example, the Chicago Police Department (Chicago Crime Commission, 1995) asserts that gang characteristics consist of a gang name and recognizable symbols, a geographic territory, a regular meeting pattern, and an organized, continuous course of criminality.

Currently, federal law defines the term *gang* as

an ongoing group, club, organization, or association of five or more persons: (A) that has as one of its primary purposes the commission of one or more of the criminal offenses . . . (B) the members of which engage, or have engaged within the past five years, in a continuing series of offenses . . . and (C) the activities of which affect interstate or foreign commerce. (18 USC § 521[a])

Concurrent to the definition, current federal law describes the term *gang crime* as

(1) A federal felony involving a controlled substance . . . for which the maximum penalty is not less than five years. (2) A federal felony crime of violence that has as an element the use or attempted use of physical force against the person of another. (3) A conspiracy to commit an offense described in paragraph (1) or (2). (18 USC § 521[c])

Also, current federal law describes the term *gang member* as

a person who: (1) Participates in a criminal street gang with knowledge that its members engage in or have engaged in a continuing series of offenses . . . (2) Intends to promote or further the felonious activities of the criminal street gang or maintain or increase his or her position in the gang. (3) Has been convicted within the past five years for: (A) An offense described in subsection (c). (B) A state offense . . . (C) Any federal or state felony offense that by its nature involves a substantial risk that physical force against the person of another may be used in the course of committing the offense. (D) A conspiracy to commit an offense described in subparagraph (A), (B), or (C). (18 USC § 521[d])

State law applies outside of federal jurisdiction. The National Gang Center (2013a) identifies that 42 states and Washington, DC, have legislation that defines *gang*. Every definition includes criminal/illegal activity or behavior.

Thirty-five states refer to a gang as an "organization, association, or group," 33 states define a gang as consisting of three or more persons, and 26 states include a common name, identifying sign, or symbol as identifiers of gangs in their definitions. The following is the authors' synthesis of these criteria in a composite gang definition as reflected in state statutes: A gang is an organization, association, or group consisting of three or more persons that is involved in criminal/illegal activity or behavior, and has a common name, identifying sign, or symbol as identifiers. However, this definition lacks the specificity that is needed for classification of youth gangs.

The National Gang Center (2013a) reveals that 14 states have legislation that defines a *gang member*. Only six states have a list of criteria, some of which a person must meet to be considered a gang member. Of those, five states require that a person must meet at least two criteria to be considered a gang member, such as self-admission of gang membership and having been identified as a gang member by law enforcement. Self-identification as a gang member has proven to be the most robust indicator (Curry, 2000; Esbensen, Winfree, He, & Taylor, 2001; Matsuda, Esbensen, & Carson, 2012).

Considerable research has identified definitional elements that law enforcement respondents (and other agency representatives) view as important gang characteristics of a gang (Miller, 1982/1992; Needle & Stapleton, 1983; Spergel & Curry, 1993): (1) "has a name," (2) "commits crimes together," (3) "has a leader or several leaders," (4) "hangs out together," (5) "displays or wears common colors or other insignia," and (6) "claims a turf or territory." The 1998 National Youth Gang Survey asked respondents to rank order six gang characteristics (National Youth Gang Center, 2000). "Commits crimes together" clearly was the most important criterion, and the next most popular characteristic was "has a name." Overall, respondents used all six criteria though in varying combinations. Students are also quite adept in recognizing gangs, while most often employing three criteria: (1) having a name, (2) spending time with other members of the gang, and (3) wearing clothing or other items to identify their gang membership (Howell & Lynch, 2000).

A review of research on the variety of gangs and gang members follows.

Typologies of Gang Members and Gang Structures

In 1927, Thrasher first characterized the members of the typical gang as resembling three concentric circles, with the core members (the power structure consisting of the leader and his lieutenants) forming the inner circle, the full-time members or regulars in the second ring, and an outside ring composed of occasional members or hangers-on.

Later, Klein (1971) and Spergel (1990) described gangs or alliances among them as either "vertically" or "horizontally" structured. Gangs structured vertically imply a hierarchy that differentiates between leaders and followers or age groups who move from one level to another as they become older or otherwise earn higher status in the gang. Gangs structured horizontally have no such hierarchy. Rather, these gangs consist of social networks that might or might not be allied with other gangs (Fleisher, 2002, 2006b).

In between these gang forms, researchers have further differentiated gang structures. For example, Vigil (1988) classified Hispanic gang members as regular members, peripheral members, temporary members (who typically join the gang later and remain a part of it for a shorter length of time), and situational members (who join in gang party activities but avoid the more violent activities whenever possible). In Chicago, Hutchison and Kyle (1993) described Hispanic gangs in the city as having chapters (with each gang containing subgroups differentiated by age, typically between pee-wees, juniors, and seniors), and evidencing an intergenerational pattern. Tita, Riley, Ridgeway, and colleagues (2003) clearly differentiate gang leaders from other members:

> Most gangs have some sort of hierarchy that includes "shot callers," or leaders who tend to be older and more isolated from day-to-day activity of the gang; "shooters," or those most likely to commit an attack against another gang; and "active soldiers," or those most likely to associate with a gang but not necessarily involved in attacking rivals. Most gang members are in the latter group. (p. 12)

In the mid-1960s, New York City Youth Board's street workers classified more than 200 New York City street gangs (containing an estimated 3,100 boys) as corner groups, social groups, conflict groups, and "the thoroughly delinquent and pathological group" (Gannon, 1967, p. 121). Nearly 9 out of 10 street workers agreed that distinctions between "core" and "peripheral" membership was valid, and approximately half of them indicated that the gangs typically had "a significant relationship to some older or other group," mainly an older group (p. 122).

Many gangs have no clear age-differentiated structure. Because of this diversity, several widely respected gang researchers have cautioned the field about over-defining and categorizing gangs in a potentially misleading way (Bookin-Weiner & Horowitz, 1983; Curry & Spergel, 1992; Horowitz, 1990; Short, 2006; Sarnecki, 2001; J. Sullivan, 2006), particularly if a given definition happens to reify certain gangs by attributing real features to their essential fictive existence. A few gang researchers "have shown how network analysis can transform perceptions of a 'gang problem' from a fuzzy inkblot into a comprehensive blueprint by producing a highly detailed and visual way of looking at a specific gang situation" (Papachristos, 2005b, p. 645). Shifting membership and an intermittent existence characterize many gangs, especially those with younger members. Outside gang territories in major gang problem cities, perhaps gangs should be viewed as social networks rather than as bounded "organizations" (Fleisher, 2006b; Papachristos, 2005b). Youth drift in and out of these groups, and as Fleisher (1998) reminds us, even members may be unable to name all current members.

Two contrasting gang structures follow. The Fremont Hustlers gang was a haphazardly assembled social unit composed of deviant adolescents who shared social and economic needs and the propensity for resolving those needs in a similar way (Fleisher, 1998, p. 264).

- First, Fremont gang kids did not use the term *member*; rather, the closest expression was "down with Fremont."
- Second, the kids didn't talk about how their gang was structured and operated.
- Third, the membership boundary was open; Freemont Hustlers had no written set of rules, no membership requirements, and no leader or hierarchy.
- Rather, the gang was a loosely assembled collection of girls and boys, several of whom were previously members of other Kansas City gangs.

In contrast, larger gangs in many cities are composed of age-differentiated segments, each bearing a name. "The fundamental building block of gangs remains the age-graded set or clique of local youngsters" (Monti, 1993, p. 10). These are the building blocks of the Eighteenth Street Gang in Los Angeles (LA) that once had an estimated membership of 20,000 (Vigil, 2002). It "has been less completely defined by territorial boundaries than by its population, which is more dispersed socially, with cliques and affiliates radiating in all directions from its place of origin" (Vigil, 2014, p. 53). Early on, Mexican American gangs in each neighborhood were organized into two or three age-graded cliques, with new younger cliques constantly forming. For example, since the 1940s, Cuatro Flats gang in Pico Gardens in East LA has consisted of 14 cliques or *klikas*, typically starting with 13- and 14-year old members and often lasting until they are 20 or 21 years old (Vigil, 2007, p. 65). Pico Gardens (P.G.) is the current clique, having been established in 1989. The original one was the Apacaches (1945–1955), followed by Continentals (1962–1965), Sinners (1965–1970), Enanos (1968–1975), Peacemakers (1968–1975), Penguins (1969–1976), Chicos (1970–1977), Termites (1970–1975), Dukes (1973–1979), Night Owls (1974–1980), Pico Stoners (1983–1986), Countdowns (1987–1990), and Chicos (1989–1993). Recent cliques are more ethnically mixed. "Because of the barrio's location near downtown L.A., the clique draws from other ethnic groups, primarily Central Americans and Vietnamese [and some Black members], in making up a gang of mostly Mexican Americans" (p. 72).

A Spectrum of Gangs and Other Groups

"Everyone belongs to a gang—the LAPD and the Bloods and Crips and even the . . . Boy Scouts; there's no differences. We all the same."—Darius (in Leap, 2012, p. 81)

Developing a gang definition that captures the younger gangs, yet excludes adult criminal organizations that are not considered youthful street groups, is challenging. To complicate this matter, multiple terms are used interchangeably in defining gangs—*youth gang, street gang, criminal street gang*, and *gang*—and whether or not each of these terms refers to a common problem in practical applications is not clear. Because the focus of this book encompasses both gangs comprising children and adolescents as well as older gangs populated by young adults, the two terms most commonly used in the gang research literature are employed: *youth gangs* or *street gangs*. *Youth gang* is a useful term for drawing attention to the younger gangs—and an important target for prevention and early intervention initiatives. The *street gang* term makes a point of emphasis, denoting older gangs that have a presence on city streets and commit characteristically urban crimes, especially assault, robbery, gun crimes, and murder. This term also applies to some "crews" and "posses" that are specialized groups engaged in predatory crimes or drug trafficking (W. Miller, 1982/1992). Many of these appear to be bona fide street gangs who are given an alternative name in the interest of denying a "gang problem."

In the interest of inclusiveness with respect to street presence, it is important, however, to avoid over-identification of street gangs with adult organized crime groups. A number of state legislatures have modeled their gang definitions after California's gang law that defines a *criminal street gang* as "any ongoing organization, association, or group of three or more people, whether formal or informal, having as one of its primary activities the commission of criminal acts" (Street Terrorism Enforcement and Prevention Act, 1988, California Penal Code sec. 186.22[f]). This definition encompasses adult criminal enterprises (organized crime) that typically are not considered to be street gangs. Interestingly, there is no widely accepted definition of organized crime.

W. Miller (1982/1992), an anthropologist, remains the only researcher to have attempted to empirically categorize an identifiable law-violating youth group across multiple cities. Based on his 26-city study, he identified 20 such groups, of which three were gangs: turf gangs, gain-oriented gangs (typically "extended networks"), and fighting gangs. The 17 remaining law-violating youth groups included burglary rings, established predatory cliques, robbery bands, extortion cliques, drug-dealing cliques and networks, assaultive affiliation cliques, and others.

At the other end of the spectrum, it is important to distinguish between actual young gangs and small groups of youngsters who commit delinquent acts in concert. Unsupervised peer groups are small groups (typically three to four members) of adolescents who are highly transitory and not well organized (Warr, 1996, 2002). Short (1996) points out that many of these groups are involved in occasional delinquent behavior but lack a commitment to a criminal orientation. Hence, they may be considered as only "troublesome" and not of great concern as a threat to society. These adolescent groups lack the size, formal organization, and permanence of youth gangs, and their delinquency typically is not as frequent, serious, or violent.

The most important point to keep in mind in any attempt to define youth gangs is that such groups are not necessarily an integral feature of the experiences of young people during adolescence. R. M. Gordon (1994) offers an age-graded continuum of social and criminal groups to view gangs, anchored at one end by childhood play groups and at the other by adult criminal organizations. The following groups are represented along this continuum:

- *Childhood play groups*—harmless groups of children that exist in every neighborhood.

- *Troublesome youth groups*—youths who hang out together in shopping malls and other places and may be involved in minor forms of delinquency.

- *Youth subculture groups*—groups with special interests, such as "goths," "straight edgers," and "anarchists," that are not gangs. (Goths are not known for criminal involvement, but some members of other youth subcultures have histories of criminal activity [Arciaga, 2001].)

- *Delinquent groups*—small clusters of friends who band together to commit delinquent acts such as burglaries.

- *Taggers*—graffiti vandals. (Taggers are often called gang members, but they typically do nothing more than engage in graffiti contests.)

- *School-based youth gangs*—groups of adolescents that may function as gangs only at school and may not be involved in delinquent activity, although most members are involved.

- *Street-based youth gangs*—semi-structured groups of adolescents and young adults who engage in delinquent and criminal behavior.

- *Prison gangs*—groups of adults who engage in criminal activity primarily for economic reasons.

The Texas Department of Public Safety (Texas Fusion Center, 2013, p. 19) has documented four gang organization structures among prison gangs across the state. Each of these gangs has street extensions or counterparts—which are reflected in the gang structures.

Paramilitary models include a hierarchical structure with clear distinction between ranks, which often include military titles such as general, captain, lieutenant, sergeant, and soldier. Senior leaders are able to issue orders to subordinates that are generally carried out as instructed. Gangs using this model include Texas Mexican Mafia and Barrio Azteca.

Regional cell models are composed of several cells that are part of the same organization, but that act generally independent of one another at an operational level. Each cell may have a strict internal hierarchy similar to a paramilitary model, though between cells there is little coordinated command and control. Texas Syndicate is an example of a Texas gang with a regional cell model.

Cliques of gangs tend to adopt a common culture and identity, but have few tangible connections to each other. Each clique may have a senior member who acts as a leader, and larger cliques may have a more structured hierarchy. In some cases, cliques of the same gang may work in opposition to each other. Examples of clique-based gangs are Bloods, Crips, and Mara Salvatrucha (MS-13).

Loose affiliation gangs have relaxed membership requirements and little to no detectable leadership hierarchy. This model tends to be the most dynamic, allowing for rapid growth while simultaneously limiting the extent to which groups of members can be effectively managed. Tango Blast is an example of a Texas gang with a loose affiliation model.

The Mexican Mafia's paramilitary structure that connects its prison gangs to the street gang counterparts and enables it to control local drug trafficking typically consists of a crew chief, a crew of gang members in the target area (a street crew that operates much like a local franchise), and workers comprised of Mexican Mafia or other Sureno street gang members (Al Valdez & Enriquez, 2011).

Some of the Illinois prison gangs formed organizational networks that linked inmates with others in jails and on the streets in illegal enterprises, creating what came to be called *webs*, *supergangs*, or *gang nations* such as the Black Kings Nation (Hagedorn, 2006; Venkatesh, 2000).

Figure 3.1 illustrates the overlap of delinquent groups, criminal groups, youth gangs, street gangs, and prison gangs.

Most gang-problem cities will have a mixture of adult and adolescent gangs. Based on his multiyear study of the epidemiology of violence and drugs among 26 Mexican American gangs on the south and west sides of San Antonio, Av. Valdez (2003) constructed a useful typology of four distinct gang types, the main features of which are sketched here from Valdez's detailed descriptions and illustrations with actual gangs observed in his long-term study.

Figure 3.1   Overlapping Gangs With Other Groups

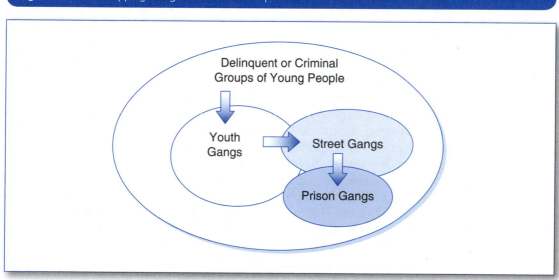

- *Criminal adult dependent* (4 gangs). "In these gangs, adults provided access to illegal drugs, weapons, drug-dealing networks, and national and international (Mexican) markets for stolen merchandise" (p. 21). Adults also provide protection against rival gangs and adult criminals. Drug dealing (particularly heroin) is the primary source of illegal income for these gangs. Violence was not uncommon among them, and it typically revolved around business transactions.

- *Criminal non-adult dependent* (5 gangs). Although this type of gang is similar to the criminal adult dependent gangs in its centralized organizational structure, it differs from those gangs in being more loosely knit with a flexible leadership structure, and it is less influenced by adults. These gangs also tend to be more territorially based than the first type, and members are involved more often in personal fights within the gang and with rival gang members.

- *Barrio-territorial* (12 gangs). These gangs, which constitute the majority of the gangs in Valdez's study, are younger than others and tend to operate independently of any adult gang influence and devoid of any centralized organizational structure. These are located in a variety of neighborhoods on the south and west sides of San Antonio, ranging from those with single-family homes to public housing units. Criminal activities tend to be less gang directed and more individual based, and include drug dealing auto theft, burglary, robbery, and other less serious crimes.

- *Transitional* (5 gangs). The remaining five gangs fit into this category. They are smaller than others and semi-organized with a loose leadership structure, often centered on a charismatic leader. These gangs are often formed along residential lines, such as living in the same building, in subareas of public housing projects, or in particular neighborhoods. Partying with drugs and alcohol are common activities. Criminal activities usually are individually based and include drug dealing, auto theft, and burglaries. School-based gangs are a subset of these smaller, less structured gangs. These gangs are formed and maintained in the junior high and high schools.

Gang Subculture

A distinctive gang subculture often distinguishes street gangs. A *sub*culture can form when two national cultures are brought into close physical contact. Incomplete adaptation or assimilation of the two cultures can produce a subculture. This process may take several generations. Once well developed, the subculture provides the "ought-to" values and "blueprints for action" norms that "often substitute for the voids left by conventional social control institutions" (Vigil, 2014, p. 59).

The Mexican American *cholo* subculture in the Western United States is an excellent example of how a subculture develops. From the mid-19th century, Mexican immigrants had been culturally marginalized between their society of origin and the dominant American culture to which they had migrated—or within which native Mexicans had become enveloped following U.S. annexation of their land. As the result, a *cholo* (a derivative of the Spanish *solo*, meaning "alone") subculture emerged, an American product (Vigil, 2014). *Cholo* youth, the poorest of the poor marginalized immigrants, could not fully assimilate into Anglo culture or develop a unique identity incorporating aspects of both Anglo and Latino culture (Horowitz, 1983; Lopez & Brummett, 2003; Lopez, Wishard, Gallimore, & Rivera, 2006; Vigil, 1988, 1990). Vigil (1988) documents the *cholo* style as further developed in the 1930s and 1940s when the second generation was under intense conflict: It grew out of "the effects of racism, the persistent cycle of underclass involvement with little chance of social mobility, and the general malaise engendered by problems with getting jobs and staying in school" (p. 39). The *cholo* term came "to refer primarily to the gang-oriented street style of dress and of walking and talking" (Moore, 1991, p. 153).

Synonymous with development of the *cholo* subculture, Vigil (1988) shows how a street gang subculture emerged, made up of elements or fragments of past Mexican culture. This youth gang subculture "is a response to the pressures of street life and serves to give barrio youth a source of familial support, goals and directives, and sanctions and guides" (p. 2). It provides a social structure and a cultural values system—norms, goals, and behavioral expectations—and together with age-graded cohorts, these undergird formidable street gangs. In this way, the youth gang subculture functions to socialize and acculturate barrio youth. "The pressures and anxiety of urban poverty, of the struggle toward a better life, and of overcoming feelings of ethnic and racial inferiority made immigrant cultural adaptation problematic. Such an experience often resulted in gangs" (p. 4). After decades of continuous migration, social isolation, prejudice, and discrimination, the Mexican American youth gang subculture became so pervasive that all Mexican immigrant youth are compelled to come to terms with it—even though most of them never join. The children in families that suffer the most acute poverty and limited social mobility opportunities are the youths who come to be "most intensely involved" in gangs (p. 5). Vigil (2002) elaborates:

> What established gangs in the neighborhood have to offer is nurture, protection, friendship, emotional support, and other ministrations for unattended, un-chaperoned resident youths. In other words, street socialization fills the voids left by inadequate parenting and schooling, especially inadequate familial care and supervision. This street-based process molds the youth to conform to the ways of the street. (p. 10)

Being a *cholo* allows such youth to assert a Latino identity, take pride in it, and avoid "being *enbacheado* (Anglicized)" (Vigil, 1988, p. 42). In other words, these street youth shaped their own *cholo* subculture. Thus, Vigil concludes that the *cholo* subculture "has become an institutionalized entity that provides many poor, barrio youths with human support networks and a source of personal ego identity that are unavailable to them elsewhere" (p. 39). "Street socialization refers to the main arena where youth learn the routines and rhythms of the street subculture of gangs" (Vigil, 2014, p. 56).

Ritual and symbolic representation

In the Southwest, Mexican American gangs have a unique subculture that is rich in ceremonial ritual and symbolic representations expressed in Mexican language, specific clothing styles, hair styles, tattoos, and graffiti. With the passage of time, each successive generation contributed features to the gang culture, including a distinctive speech form and a style of dress. Sanders (1994) details the clothing:

> A uniform consisting of a Pendleton shirt, buttoned at the top over a white T-shirt, a hair net over short hair combed straight back, a bandanna tied around the head pulled down just above the eyes, dark sun glasses, a hat, and baggy khaki pants makes up the outward cholo style. (p. 129)

Arciaga, Sakamoto, and Jones (2010) observe a simpler style in this era: the khaki pants, white T-shirt, and plaid shirt. This style of dress remains common with many gangs around the United States, and because of its youth subculture foundation, Mexican American gang culture is remarkably uniform across the United States.

Baseball caps and clothing of a professional sports team are also commonly worn to signify identification with that team's reputation, not actual endorsement. Baggy clothing (and sometimes particular brands) is another gang trademark—once worn only by gang members—but this also is a popular style in general adolescent subculture.

> Gang members wear gang colors and symbols on many items: shirts, bandanas, jewelry, sports clothing, hats (including altering or writing graffiti on the insides of hats), hairbands, shoe-laces, belts, belt buckles, and specific shoe brands whose names or logos have a specific meaning to the gang. (p. 11)

Walker and Schmidt (1996) note how students would carry their clothes in bags so that they could change into conforming colors as they cross gang boundaries. Of course, tattoos are widely used in all gang cultures across the United States, typically to show one's level of commitment to a gang.

There are multiple forms of graffiti, only one of which is the gang type, as shown in Table 3.1. Gangs of all origins employ graffiti for various motives—to mark turf, threaten violence, boast achievements, honor the slain, and to insult or taunt other gangs. Klein (1995) reports that graffiti not only is useful in establishing gang identity, but also may be used as a symbolic form of gang conflict. Hutchison and Kyle (1993) add that some individual "taggers" and "tagger groups" have become conflict-oriented gangs as a result of conflict over graffiti.

Nicknames, tattoos, and places are uniformly used in the Mexican gang culture. Fellow gang members create and assign nicknames to signify acceptance, with which tattoos containing one's nickname and barrio confirm. Vigil (1988) asserts that public tattoos in the form of *placas*—literally meaning plaques, public tattoos, and also graffiti—on walls and fences publicize a person's affiliation and commitment. Furthermore, gang graffiti is informative in educating the viewer about gangs that are active in the community, denoting their boundaries, their symbols, the names or monikers of members, and other messages, and is also a way to claim territorial dominance in communications intended for members of other gangs to see. Hutchison (1993) explains that traditional Mexican American gangs did not adopt particular colors in the early 1990s, except, according to Al Valdez (2007), in California where northern Mexican American gangs identify with red and southern ones favor blue.

According to Al Valdez (2007), gang graffiti is often called the *gangland's newspaper*. Thus,

> the analysis of gang graffiti may also be used to learn about the structure of the gangs, conflicts and alliances between particular street gangs, and possible linkages among street gangs . . . Regardless of the particular region of the country, the content of gang graffiti is generally consistent; it is designed to convey specific messages about group identity, gang allegiances, and individual membership. (Hutchison, 1993, pp. 138, 163)

Another consistency Al Valdez identifies is the practice of insulting or challenging another gang by using a "puto-out," that is, crossing out or writing over the name or symbol of that gang. But, there are also some interesting differences in gang graffiti between Mexican American gangs in Chicago and LA. This, Hutchison (1993) points out, is proof that LA gangs did not migrate to Chicago. Each Chicago gang has a specific symbol; LA gangs do not. LA gangs have specific lettering styles; Chicago gangs do not. LA gang graffiti identifies the gang's barrio; this is not so in Chicago. Certain elements of gang

Table 3.1   Types of Graffiti and Associated Motives

Type of Graffiti	Features	Motives
Gang[a]	Gang name or symbol, including hand signs Gang member names, nicknames, or sometimes a roll-call list of members Numbers: code in gang graffiti, with a number representing the corresponding letter in the alphabet (e.g., 13 = M, for the Mexican Mafia) or a penal or police radio code Distinctive, stylized alphabets: bubble letters, block letters, backward letters, and Old English script Key visible locations Enemy names and symbols or allies' names	To mark turf To threaten violence To boast of achievements To honor the slain To insult or taunt other gangs
Common Tagger[b]	High-volume, accessible locations High-visibility, hard-to-reach locations May be stylized but simple name, nickname tag, or symbols: single-line writing of a name usually known as a *tag*, whereas slightly more complex tags, including those with two colors or bubble letters, known as *throw-ups* Tenacious (keeps retagging)	Notoriety or prestige Defiance of authority
Artistic Tagger	Colorful and complex pictures known as *masterpieces* or *pieces*	Artistic Prestige or recognition
Conventional Graffiti	Spontaneous Sporadic episodes or isolated incidents Malicious or vindictive	Play Rite of passage Excitement Impulse Anger Boredom Resentment Failure Despair
Ideological	Offensive content or symbols Racial, ethnic, or religious slurs Specific targets, such as synagogues Highly legible Slogans	Anger Hate Political Hostility Defiance

[a]Copycat grafts look like gang graffiti and may be the work of gang wannabes or youths seeking excitement.

[b]*Tagbangers*, a derivative of tagging crews and gangs, are characterized by competition with other crews. Therefore crossed-out tags are features of their graffiti.

Source: Weisel, 2004, p. 9.

culture have been incorporated into the general adolescent subculture in LA, but not in Chicago. Hutchison contends that this is because the Chicago barrios were settled much later. He asks, does this imply that the Mexican American gang culture in Chicago will someday become integrated?

In addition to identity signified via clothing, Arciaga and colleagues (2010) discuss how gang members use hand signs to show affiliation to their set, show disrespect to rivals, challenge rivals, and provoke confrontations. To a gang member, a hand sign is a nonverbal form of communication that can lead to violence. It follows that many gangs have their own hand signs. To throw a hand sign at a rival gang member is considered an insult or a challenge, called *set tripping*, and is often the catalyst for gang-related violence.

Gang graffiti may also reveal an incident of importance and who did it. Fallen comrades are often memorialized with the RIP (Rest in Peace) message. "Unfortunately, graffiti can be the prelude to gang violence. Monitoring graffiti in the schools, neighborhoods, and homes can be a good indicator to show rising tensions between individual gang members and rival gangs" (Al Valdez, 2007, p. 77).

Expressions of conformity, again, include symbolic ways of dressing and other displays of gang affiliation. Thus, prohibited behaviors and consequences include disrespecting one's gang colors, fighting members of one's own gang, ratting out a member of one's own gang, running from a fight, and pretending to be a member of a rival gang (Decker & Van Winkle, 1996). The consequences can include demotion in gang rank and violent beatings.

Key Elements of Gang Definitions

Bjerregaard (2002b) catalogued various gang definitions in the literature according to the key definitional criteria of gangs that are found in them. These criteria are intended "to verify or confirm that an individual is a member of a traditional street 'gang' and not just a group of friends or individuals that hang out together" (p. 37). Bjerregaard's review is updated in Table 3.2 to add several recent definitions, in accordance with Bjerregaard's original framework. The most common features of gangs in the 23 cited gang definitions follow.

Criminal activity

The bottom row of Table 3.2 shows the total number of gang definitions that incorporate each of the seven key characteristics. The most common element for defining gangs is involvement in criminal activity or commitment to a criminal orientation—cited in three-fourths (18) of the 23 listed definitions. Law enforcement and legislative definitions emphatically emphasize this criterion for classifying gangs. The major source of state and law enforcement definitions is the previously cited California Street Terrorism Enforcement and Prevention Act. However, consideration of this factor separates gang researchers into two camps. In one camp are those who contend that gang definitions should not incorporate this element. These advocates argue that the inclusion of criminal behavior in the gang definition presents a tautology for researchers who wish to investigate and explain delinquent and criminal behavior by looking at the individual's gang membership (Bjerregaard, 2002b). In the opposing camp are those who contend that, in the absence of this criterion, gang definitions could envelop nongang groups such as boy scouts, girl scouts, and private school students. Advocates in both camps make valid points. However, when a gang definition is used to help communities assess gang activity that represents a threat to their safety, it certainly should include the criminal behavior criterion, because it is precisely criminally active gangs that must be identified in this practical application.

Table 3.2   Key Elements of Gang Definitions

Researchers	Name/ Identity	Leadership	Colors/ Dress/ Symbols	Territory/ Turf	Meetings/ Continuous Association	Organized	Criminal Activity
Thrasher, 1927/2000				X	X	X	
B. Cohen, 1969	X	X		X		X	
Klein, 1971	X						X
Cartwright et al., 1975					X	X	X
W. Miller, 1982/1992		X		X	X	X	X
Johnstone, 1981		X	X	X		X	X
Spergel, 1984	X	X		X		X	X
Hagedorn, 1988	X			X			
Spergel, 1995			X		X	X	X
Short, 1996					X	X	
Howell & Lynch, 2000	X		X	X	X		X
J. Moore, 1991				X		X	X
Huff, 1993	X		X	X	X		X
Chicago Crime Commission, 1995		X		X		X	X
Nat'l Drug Intelligence Center, 2008	X		X				X
Decker & Van Winkle, 1996			X	X			
Oehme, 1997			X	X	X	X	X
Curry & Decker, 2003					X		X

(Continued)

Table 3.2 (Continued)

Researchers	Name/ Identity	Leadership	Colors/ Dress/ Symbols	Territory/ Turf	Meetings/ Continuous Association	Organized	Criminal Activity
CA Council on Criminal Justice, 1989	X			X	X		X
CA STEP Act, 1998	X		X			X	X
Esbensen, Winfree, et al., 2001		X	X			X	X
Esbensen et al., 2008	X						X
Federal Law 18 USC § 521(a)					X	X	X
Total	10	6	9	13	11	14	18

Source: Modified from Bjerregaard, 2002b, p. 34.

Organizational structure

The organizational structure of the gang is the second most frequently specified aspect of gangs, in nearly two-thirds (14) of the 23 definitions. Early gang research placed an emphasis on the frequency of association in specifying the gang's organizational structure (Huff, 1993; W. Miller, 1982/1992; Oehme, 1997). Having identifiable leadership is another indicator of organizational structure of the gang. In addition, a hierarchy of membership is sometimes present. The key issue here, and as Weisel (2002) contends, is whether a "continuous organizational structure is present" (p. 185). Esbensen, Winfree, and colleagues (2001) discovered that members of gangs that were somewhat "organized" (i.e., had initiation rites, established leaders, and symbols or colors) self-reported higher rates of delinquency and involvement in more serious delinquent acts than other youths. Several studies show that better organized gangs are more actively involved in criminal activity (Bjerregaard, 2002a; Decker, Katz, & Webb, 2008; Egley & Howell, 2010; Esbensen, Winfree, et al., 2001; Pyrooz, Fox, Katz, & Decker, 2012). Initiation into Mexican American gangs in LA is called *put on*, meaning the same thing as *jumped in* Black gangs (Leap, 2012). Once a fully accepted member—after "putting in work"—homies are "strapped" with a gun.

> You look up, you're strapped and you're already a gangbanger. Before I got in, the picture of the gang is beautiful, but once I got it, these guys wanna make you a killa. —Kenny (in Leap, 2012, p. 126)

Territory or turf

The third most common defining characteristic of gangs is claiming a turf or specific location in the neighborhood (13 of 23 definitions). Identification with a particular territory is another form of symbolism that helps identify groups as gangs, although this indicator has been used less in recent years because of the growing mobility of gangs—owing mainly to suburban sprawl, more widespread use of automobiles, and expanding highway networks. However, a cautionary note should be issued here. Territory or turf claiming has not diminished in large cities where most bona fide street gang members reside and gangs remain institutionalized. For example, in territories of both Black and Mexican American gangs in LA, "every neighborhood has a tattoo" (Leap, 2012, p. 109). And violent gangs in large cities typically have well-defined turfs or "set spaces." For example, researchers mapped the locations of 13 criminal street gangs in the East LA area where Chicano gangs first formed (Brantingham, Tita, Short, & Reid, 2012). Intergang conflicts there are ongoing, predominantly clustered along the boundaries between gangs' respective set spaces.

It is a curious thing that gang definitions do not place more emphasis on named gangs as an identification criterion, particularly given the intertwined status-providing function of gangs and individual identity needs of alienated youth (Vigil, 2004). This is an important matter in the case of Hispanic gangs, because the gang name is often linked with neighborhood or barrio of residence, and what Vigil (1993) calls the youth's "'psycho-spatial identity' with their territory or 'turf'" (p. 98), with *mi barrio* (my neighborhood) becoming synonymous with *my gang*.

A European gang definition

The Eurogang Network definition was developed by consensus among participating scholars for the purpose of researching European gangs: "A youth gang, or troublesome youth group, is any durable, street-oriented youth group whose involvement in illegal activity is part of its group identity" (Esbensen et al., 2008, p. 117). The absence of a gang name criterion in the Eurogang definition may explain why it has not applied well to Hispanic/Latino gangs in the United States (p. 129).

This definition incorporates five indicators. Klein and Maxson (2006) explain:

1. Durable is a bit ambiguous, but at least an existence over several months can be used as a guideline . . . The durability refers to the group.

2. Street-oriented implies spending a lot of group time outside home, work, and school—often on streets, in malls, in parks, in cars and so on.

3. Youth can be ambiguous. Most street gangs are more adolescent than adult, but some include members in their 20s and even 30s.

4. Illegal activity generally means delinquent or criminal, not just bothersome.

5. Identity refers to the group, not the individual self-image. (p. 4)

In Klein and Maxson's view, these "are the minimal necessary and sufficient elements to recognize a street gang" (p. 4). This broad gang definition—currently applied in multiple Eurogang studies, in collaboration with the Eurogang Research Network—has caused some consternation among European scholars. Deuchar (2009) explains why: "The word gang is a highly contested term, and the criteria for classifying someone as a gang member are debatable [and also because] some people in deprived communities may regard their peer networks simply as 'friendship groups'" or other similar terms (p. 10). Hallsworth and Young (2008), R. White (2008), and Pitts (2008) object to the characterization of youth groups in the United Kingdom as "gangs" because of the bad example that American media have set in overuse of this arguably pejorative term, and also owing to the reservations of other European scholars. This point may well be valid because the Eurogang Research Network's gang definition seriously over-classified American gangs in a multi-city U.S. study, in which only 38% of the youth classified as gang members considered their group to be a gang (Esbensen et al., 2008). In particular, two-thirds of Black youth classified as gang members viewed their group as a gang, versus less than half of Mexican American gang members and only 15% of White gang members. Esbensen and colleagues suggested that "the Eurogang Network definition may be capturing something more unique to Black gangs than to other racial/ethnic groups, or that youths of different racial/ethnic backgrounds may perceive the word 'gang' differently" (p. 129). In another analysis that compared the validity of the Eurogang definition in classifying youth as gang members with the proven valid self-identification method, the Eurogang definition seriously over-classified American youth as gang members by more than two times (36% versus 15%) (Matsuda et al., 2012).

A Recommended Gang Definition for Practical Purposes

To guide local assessments of gang problems (see Chapter 10 for details on this activity), communities need a more practical definition. Practitioners would have difficulty applying the Eurogang definition—particularly in making a determination as to whether or not involvement in illegal activity *is part of its group identity* because delinquent activity is normative among adolescents. It also is unfortunate that the Eurogang Network definition encompasses troublesome youth groups because, as Thrasher (1927/2000) asserted, this definitional element may erroneously mark groups as "gangs" that have not reached the tipping point of becoming a bona fide gang.

As an alternative, the following criteria for classifying groups as youth gangs take into account practical application of gang definitions in community assessments (Howell, 2013b). This definition has been disseminated by the Centers for Disease Control and the National Institute of Justice (Simon, Ritter, & Mahendra, 2013).

The group has five or more members.

Thirty states and Washington, DC, define a gang as consisting of three or more persons (National Gang Center, 2009). Federal law (18 USC § 521[a]) specifies that a *criminal street gang* must have five or more members to qualify as a gang. The federal standard of five or more members is preferred because this helps identify bona fide gangs that are not small delinquent cliques. This higher standard of five members is consistent with research on group offending and will help exclude small friendship groups that happen to be involved in delinquency, typically three to four members (Warr, 1996, 2002).

Members share an identity, typically linked to a name and often other symbols.

These features are covered in two key characteristics of gangs (Table 3.2): name/identity and colors/dress/symbols. Having a gang name helps distinguish gangs from the many other law-violating youth groups. Bjerregaard (2002b) believes this to be the most potent criterion of the symbolic aspects of gangs. The inclusion of a name requirement also should help community stakeholders distinguish gangs from other delinquent groups. Indeed, the two main criteria students use nationwide to identify gangs are having a name and time spent with other gang members (Howell & Lynch, 2000).

Members view themselves as a gang and are recognized by others as a gang.

This definitional element recognizes the importance of establishing affiliation with bona fide gangs, which have crossed the tipping point from a delinquent group. Hence, the use of this criterion ensures that groups designated as gangs will not be merely troublesome youth groups, because approximately 9 out of 10 youngsters who self-identify themselves as a gang member are members of gangs that are involved in delinquent activity (Esbensen, Peterson, Taylor, & Freng, 2010).

The group associates continuously, evidences some organization, and has some permanence.

This criterion contains two common characteristics of gangs (continuous association and having some degree of organization, Table 3.2) and the addition of the "permanence" element serves to distinguish gangs that exhibit persistence over time. There is no empirical basis for a specified period. Several months seems reasonable, as the Eurogang Network suggests. Furthermore, Howell and Egley (2005a) find that transitory or emerging gangs are far less likely to present a public safety threat to the community.

The group is involved in an elevated level of criminal activity.

Two-thirds of the definitions in Table 3.2 include this element, because it addresses public safety. The inclusion of this definitional element is based on Krohn and Thornberry's (2008) research showing delinquency rates are higher among gang members than other youth.

These criteria can be used in community-wide assessments of gang activity (see Chapter 9 for the assessment process). Communities that develop or otherwise adopt their own definitions will find that this leads to better understanding of local gangs, more targeted programming, and greater success in reducing gang crime.

◈ Defining Gang Members

Defining gang members is surprisingly complex. Most important, several levels of gang membership are conceivable. Many youth who associate with gang members on occasion never join. This group of associates, or affiliates, may be quite large (Curry et al., 2002; Eitle et al., 2004). Other studies in traditional gang cities also report that youth typically are members of gangs for relatively short periods of time (Krohn & Thornberry, 2008; Hagedorn, 1988; Klein, 1971; Short & Strodtbeck, 1965/1974; Vigil, 1988; Yablonsky, 1967). In their Denver gang research, Esbensen and Huizinga (1993) concluded, "It appears that the majority of gang members are peripheral or transitory members who drift in and out of the gang" (p. 582).

Chapter 9 describes how very young gangs form, referred to as *starter gangs* (which can be distinguished from a pre-gang in Chapter 1, or Hoyt's [1920] *embryo gang*). The youngest gangs—with members approximately ages 10 to 13—are formed in small groups of rejected, alienated, and aggressive children (Craig, Vitaro, Gagnon, & Tremblay, 2002). Debarbieux and Baya (2008) delve even deeper, showing how the groups of children that form gangs are more likely to attend "difficult" schools characterized by high student victimization rates, self-reported violence, poor student–teacher relations, and harsh punishments for minor behavior.

A common approach for reducing the complexities associated with determining gang involvement, and to reduce errors of false identification, is to ask respondents to self-identify gang membership (Esbensen, Winfree, et al., 2001; Winfree, Fuller, Vigil, & Mays, 1992). However, Rennison and Melde (2009) caution that "this method relies on the respondent's interpretation or perception of what constitutes a gang" (p. 495). As Howell and Lynch (2000) assert and noted previously, students most often employ three criteria: (1) having a name, (2) spending time with other members of the gang, and (3) wearing clothing or other items to identify their gang membership.

In an ingenious study, Esbensen, Winfree, and colleagues (2001) examined the impact of varying definitions of gang membership on the prevalence of gang members:

> Five types of gang members were created. The first two types were identified by use of single items: "Have you ever been a gang member?" and "Are you now in a gang?" Three increasingly restrictive definitions of gang membership were then created. The third type, "delinquent gang" member, included respondents who indicated that their gang was involved in at least one of the following illegal activities: getting in fights with other gangs; stealing things; robbing other people; stealing cars; selling marijuana; selling other illegal drugs; or damaging property. The fourth type, "organized gang" member, included delinquent gang members who also indicated that their gang had some level of organization. Specifically, the survey respondents were asked whether the following described their gang: "There are initiation rites; the gang has established leaders; the gang has symbols or colors." The last characteristic used to determine gang membership was an indicator of whether individuals considered themselves to be "core" or "peripheral" gang members. The impact of definitional criteria on the prevalence of youth gang membership is quite pronounced. Depending on which of the five different definitions of gang member is used, anywhere from 2% to 17% of the sample would be regarded as involved in a gang. Almost 17% of the respondents indicated that they had ever belonged to a gang . . . [but] as the definition of "gang" became more restrictive, the number of youths reporting involvement decreased: 7.9% reported belonging to a "delinquent gang"; 4.6% were in "organized delinquent gangs"; and only 2.3% were "core" members of an "organized delinquent gang." (Esbensen et al., 2010, p. 77)

Based on this study, Esbensen and colleagues (2010) conclude that a single-item self-identification definition of gang membership ("Are you now in a gang?") is a highly reliable indicator; the term *gang* "connotes something unique and distinguishable" (p. 78). "The vast majority (89%) of youths who indicated that they were currently in a gang also indicated that their gang was involved in delinquent activity" (p. 78).

Esbensen and colleagues (2008) applied a similar funneling approach with the Eurogang Network's gang definition in a multi-city American survey of almost 1,500 youths. They first restricted their gang sample to those respondents who indicated the following:

They had a group of friends with whom they spent time and who were aged 12–25; the group had been around for more than three months and hung out in public places; and, importantly, members of the group believed it was okay to do illegal things, and they reported committing illegal acts together. (p. 123)

Only 7.6% of the sample met all four of the criteria and thus were classified as bona fide gang members. Esbensen and colleagues (2008) also reported that exploratory analyses on this group's involvement in juvenile delinquency showed substantive differences in rates of involvement in violent crimes among active gang members of different racial/ethnic backgrounds.

In an earlier survey of nearly 6,000 eighth graders in 11 cities with known gang problems, 9% were currently gang members and 17% said they had belonged to a gang at some point in their lives (Esbensen & Deschenes, 1998; Esbensen et al., 2010). However, this percentage varied from 4% to 15% depending on location (see Table 3.3). Most of this variation is undoubtedly linked to city-size and seriousness of gang problems. Gang membership is even greater among representative samples of youth in high-risk areas of large cities, according to studies in Seattle (15%), Denver (17%), Pittsburgh (24%), and Rochester, NY (32%) (Hill et al., 1999; Lahey, Gordon, Loeber, Stouthamer-Loeber, & Farrington, 1999; Thornberry, Krohn, Lizotte, Smith, & Tobin, 2003).

Table 3.3 Prevalence of Gang Membership in 11 Locations

Location	Percentage of Youth Who Are Gang Members
Milwaukee, Wisconsin	15.4%
Phoenix, Arizona	12.6%
Omaha, Nebraska	11.4%
Las Cruces, New Mexico	11.0%
Kansas City, Missouri	10.1%
Orlando, Florida	9.6%
Philadelphia, Pennsylvania	7.7%
Torrance, California	6.3%
Providence, Rhode Island	6.0%
Pocatello, Idaho	5.6%
Will County, Oregon	3.8%

Source: Esbensen et al., 2010, p. 74.

◈ Demographic Characteristics of U.S. Gangs and Gang Members

We now turn to an examination of demographic characteristics of gangs and gang members, beginning with national data on the number of gang members and gangs, followed by gang member characteristics: age, race and ethnicity, and gender.

National Data on Gang Members

In the only national survey of students that asked about their gang involvement, in the late 1990s, almost 6% of boys and 3% of girls said they were gang members (Gottfredson & Gottfredson, 2001). In a nationwide youth sample, the National Longitudinal Survey of Youth, 8% of respondents reported that they were gang members by their early 20s, and membership peaked at age 15 (Pyrooz, 2014b). But these national data underestimate gang membership in gang problem cities according to studies in Seattle (15%), Denver (17%), Pittsburgh (24%), and Rochester, NY (32%) (Hill et al., 1999; Esbensen & Huizinga, 1993; Lahey et al., 1999; Thornberry et al., 2003).

Recent data indicate that nearly half of high school students report that there are students at their school who consider themselves to be part of a gang, and one-fifth of students in grades 6–12 report that gangs are present in their school (National Center on Addiction and Substance Abuse, 2010; Robers, Zhang, & Truman, 2012).

National Data on the Number of Gangs and Associated Members

The National Youth Gang Survey of law enforcement agencies provides data on gangs and their memberships nationwide. Overall, nearly one-third of cities, towns, and rural counties in this country reported gang problems in 2011 (Egley & Howell, 2013).

The number and size of gang memberships vary directly with population sizes of gang problem areas.

- The rural counties and small cities, towns, and villages (with 50,000 or fewer populations) typically report three or fewer gangs with less than 30 total members.

- In the second category, larger cities (with populations greater than 50,000) typically report about 10 gangs with about 150 total members.

- Cities with populations between 100,000 and 250,000 typically report about 20 gangs and about 400 members.

- Cities with populations greater than 250,000 typically report more than 30 gangs and more than 1,000 total members. (Egley, 2005)

Across these population groups, localities that report a persistent gang problem have far more gangs and gang members. For example, in Egley, O'Donnell, and Howell's (2009) National Youth Gang Survey (NYGS), respondents who consistently reported gang problems from 2002 to 2008 estimated 15 gangs and 250 members. In contrast, the respondents who inconsistently reported gang problems in this period averaged only six gangs and 74 members.

Age of Gang Members

Youth gangs have always been an adolescent phenomenon. Most studies show that a large majority of youths who join gangs do so at very early ages, typically between ages 11 and 15, with ages 14 to 16 the peak for gang involvement. In the National Longitudinal Youth Survey (NLYS), age 13 was the modal age for onset of gang involvement (Pyrooz, 2014b). Interestingly, the NLYS data that Pyrooz analyzed show that approximately 17% to 20% of the gang members joined in early adulthood. Esbensen and colleagues' (2008) multi-city sample of students drawn from known gang-problem areas illustrates this progression, finding 7% joined by age 12, 9% were members at age 13, and 16% were members at age 14 and older.

The ages of typical street gang members are older. NYGS respondents are asked in alternate years to provide information on the ages of members of all gangs in their respective jurisdictions. Figure 3.2 shows the relative proportion of juvenile and adult gang members on which respondents are able to provide information. Law enforcement representatives have always said that half or more of all members of gangs with a street presence are adults, from 50% in 1996 to 59% in 2008. However, as Barrows and Huff (2009) and also Howell, Moore, and Egley (2002) assert, to some extent, this increasing proportion of adults also reflects the parallel increase in gang intelligence systems. Absent regular purging

Figure 3.2   Age of Gang Members: 1996 to 2008

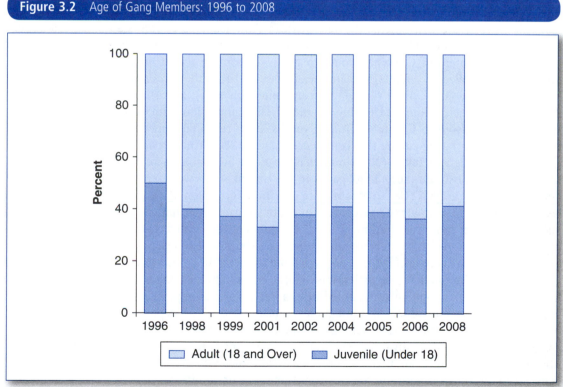

Source: National Gang Center 2014 online survey analysis.

of these databases—which Barrows and Huff contend is seldom done—young gang members age in the database with the passage of time.

Race and Ethnicity of Gang Members

In a comprehensive review of race and ethnicity of gang members, Freng and Taylor (2013) lamented, "The roles of race and ethnicity in gang membership are becoming increasingly complicated" in the United States (p. 136). This has not always been the case. As discussed in Chapter 1, early in U.S. history, gang members were largely Caucasians of various European origins, and it was not until the 1950s that scholars began to note the changed racial/ethnic composition of youth gangs. Most White European ethnics assimilated into mainstream American society, and along with that, a smaller proportion of these peoples' children joined gangs. Mexican American or Latino, African American, Asian, and other nationalities became predominant members with successive periods of immigration and internal migration. As Vigil (2002) observes, the offspring of these groups are overrepresented in inner-city areas in which concentrated disadvantage and social disorganization disproportionately give rise to gang activity.

Freng and Taylor's (2013) three noteworthy observations follow. First, gang members are not solely minorities; Whites are involved at higher levels than previously thought. In a 1995 survey of middle-aged students in 11 diverse cities in the United States, Esbensen and Lynskey (2001) found that Caucasian youth were almost as likely to claim gang membership as any other race/ethnicity. Overall, 31% of the gang members were African American, 25% were Caucasian, 25% were Hispanic, and 20% were of other race/ethnicities. This is the first multisite study to document the growing involvement of Caucasian youth in gangs. In a more recent multi-city student survey, Esbensen and colleagues' (2008) research team observed that the racial/ethnic proportions were relatively even for Caucasians (7.3%), African Americans (8%), and Hispanics (9%), but larger (13%) for multiracial groups (reflecting the increased immigration from outside the United States after 1995, discussed in Chapter 1). White youths likely resumed gang participation with widespread diffusion of gang culture that commenced in the 1980s (Chapter 4).

Second, Freng and Taylor (2013) note that gangs are becoming increasingly racially or ethnically mixed. Almost half (46%) of all gangs in the United States were reported to be multiethnic/multiracial in the 1996 NYGS. To obtain more specific information on this matter, the 1998 survey asked recipients to estimate the percentage of youth gangs in their jurisdiction with "a significant mixture of two or more racial/ethnic groups." Respondents estimated that more than one-third of their youth gangs met this criterion. Interestingly, Starbuck and colleagues (2001) found the largest proportion of this type of *hybrid gang* was reported in small cities, towns, and villages (54% of all gangs), and the smallest proportion was in large cities (32%). Owing to the historical immigration patterns and population shifts noted in Chapter 1, various regions and many localities show distinctive proportions of racial/ethnic groups. For example, Vigil reports that in LA, Mexicans, Blacks, Vietnamese, and Salvadorians are the predominant membership groups. Kontos and colleagues (2003) and M. Sullivan (1993) find a different mixture in New York City, where Puerto Ricans, non–Puerto Rican Latinos (especially Dominicans), followed by Central and South Americans, Mexican Americans, and African Americans predominate. In a nationwide youth survey, the National Longitudinal Study of Adolescent Health, the percentages of gang-involved youth within each race/ethnicity were American Indian/Alaskan Native (15%), Hispanic or Latino/a (8%),

Black or African American (6%), Asian (5%), White (3%), and other (8%) (Glesmann, Krisberg, & Marchionna, 2009).

Third, Freng and Taylor (2013) note that gang membership is often portrayed, especially by the media, as strictly a minority issue affecting the barrios and slums of the United States. To be sure, males and racial/ethnic minorities are disproportionately involved in gangs, and the reasons are clear, both empirically (Chapter 1) and theoretically (Chapters 3 and 4). Esbensen and Carson (2012) note the transition around 1950 when gang membership shifted from nationalities (White national or ethnic minorities, e.g., Irish, Italian, Polish, and Jewish) to racial/ethnic representation (Caucasian, African American, Puerto Rican, or Hispanic). And homogeneity of gang membership is high among racial/ethnic groups (Esbensen et al., 2008). More than two-thirds (72%) of White gang members and Black gang members (73%) indicated that most or all of their gang members were of the same race/ethnicity. In contrast, 90% of Hispanic gang members made this claim. It is also noteworthy that only 55% of the multiracial gang members indicated that they had a meeting place of their own, versus 67% of White gang members and 75% of Black and Hispanic gang members. Hence, territoriality appears to be more characteristic of Black and Hispanic youths than of the White and multiracial gang youths, and especially for Hispanic youth, in keeping with their barrio and cultural history. In addition, when asked about allowing others into their territory, Esbensen and associates found 68% of White gang members and 50% of the multiracial gang members said that they did, compared with only 40% of Hispanic gang members and just 20% of Black gang youth.

According to the 2011 NYGS, 46% of gang members nationwide are Hispanic/Latino, 35% are African American/Black, slightly more than 12% are White, and 7% are of other race/ethnicities.[2] There are large discrepancies between these figures and the proportions of racial/ethnic groups that are represented in self-report student surveys and law enforcement surveys. The largest discrepancy is for Whites and other racial/ethnic groups versus Hispanic/Latinos and Blacks. These four groups are about equally represented in self-report samples. These large discrepancies are not easy to explain other than the widespread over-representation of minority groups in the juvenile (Snyder & Sickmund, 2006) and criminal justice systems (Tonry, 2009). Another plausible explanation is that more law enforcement officers are deployed in inner-city areas where gang-involved Hispanic/Latino and African American youth are more visible.

The most noteworthy trend observed in Figure 3.3 is the greater representation of Hispanic/Latino gang members relative to the proportions of Black and White gang members in the NYGS. The proportion of Hispanic/Latino gang members only increased from 45% of all gang members in 1996 to 50% in 2008. However, this increase proved of greater significance when coupled with the drop in the proportion of Blacks from just under 36% to slightly less than 32%. Together, these changes mean that the differential between Hispanic/Latino and Black representation doubled from 9% in 1996 to 18% in 2008. This increase is partially explained by the fact that Latino immigrants make up the majority of the growth of foreign-born people who were living in the United States in 2005. And as Vigil (2008) reminds us, second-generation Hispanic/Latino youth are at high risk of gang involvement.

Immigrants are a large and growing segment of the U.S. population (Vericker, Pergamit, Macomber, & Kuehn, 2009). In the past 25 years, the United States has experienced a 150% increase in the foreign-born population, such that more than 35 million foreign-born people were living in the States in 2005. Latino immigrants make up the majority of this growth, and 53% of the foreign-born persons emigrated from Latin America. As a result of this increase in the foreign-born population, the share of all U.S.-born children with at least one immigrant parent has more than tripled. Currently, about 2 in 10 children are growing up in immigrant families.

| Figure 3.3 | Race/Ethnicity of Gang Members: 1996 to 2008 |

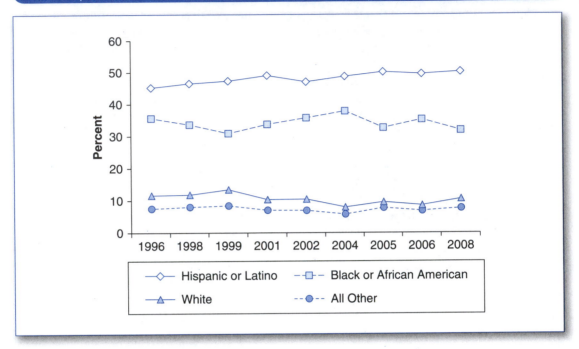

Source: National Gang Center 2014 online survey analysis.

Gender

Law enforcement agencies consistently report a far greater percentage of male gang members versus female gang members. A typical finding from law enforcement surveys is about 10% female membership, but this estimation is an acknowledged under-count, explained briefly below and in more detail in Chapter 6. Hughes (2005) underscores the enormous discrepancy between this source and self-report survey data: "Although female youth are shown to be relatively underrepresented in gangs and gang activity, they self-report gang membership at a rate up to 4½ times higher (20% to 46%) than typically indicated in surveys of law enforcement" (p. 100). Two factors appear to account for most of this discrepancy. First, law enforcement officers mainly observe older gang members (girls drop out earlier than boys), and, second, a smaller proportion of female gang members is actively involved in violent activity, particularly firearm possession and use. From a public safety perspective, the most important consideration is the accuracy of law enforcement classification of gang-related violence.

In sum, research on demographic characteristics, including NYGC results reported here, underscores the diversity of youth gang members. Presumptions can be very misleading. Two discoveries in recent studies seem especially important. First, most communities can be expected to have gang members that represent a variety of racial/ethnic backgrounds. Second, expect to find more female gang members than in the past. In addition, male-dominated gangs—or somewhat gender-balanced gangs—are more likely to be found than independent female gangs.

◈ Concluding Observations

Debates surrounding definitions of gangs and identification of gang members will continue indefinitely. There are numerous dimensions along which gangs can be classified. Gangs constitute a complex group phenomenon, and there is considerable variation in them from one locality to another:

> No two gangs are alike, and they change constantly in membership, structure, and behavior; new gangs are formed and old ones fade away or merge with others. They do not sit still to be examined under a microscope, or by any other method devised by researchers. When we study them, whether by observation, interviews, administering questionnaires and other research instruments, or by arrest rates, the best we can hope for are snapshots at a given time or over a period of time. (Short & Hughes, 2009, p. 406)

Knowledgeable law enforcement officials are particularly adept at enumerating older gang members and more established gangs and, no doubt, under-count young gangs and gang members. Everyone has difficulty recognizing and counting these. But the reason for law enforcement's limitation is that the youngest gangs and gang members may not yet be actively involved in criminal activity. In addition, many of the criminal acts of young gang members are not yet carried out in concert and in the streets. "Commits crimes together" is ranked the most important criterion for defining gangs among national samples of law enforcement—in large cities, suburban counties, small cities, towns, and villages, and also in rural counties (Howell, Egley, & Gleason, 2002). Hence, as discussed in Chapter 8, NYGS data show that law enforcement representatives' estimates of the number of gang members and gangs correlate with homicides.

That gang researchers disagree on the key elements of gang and gang members is not inconsequential. However, it is of utmost importance that stakeholders in neighborhoods, communities, and cities agree on a practical definition for the assessment of their own gang problem. If not, the danger is present that stakeholders may characterize their local gang problem in terms of images of big city gangs that may not apply. Most statutory gang definitions are too broad to be of practical value in gang prevention and intervention initiatives. A practical definition is offered here that local stakeholders can modify for the purposes of their assessment.

DISCUSSION TOPICS

1. Why are gangs so difficult to define and classify?

2. Why do police departments in large cities have a tendency to apply the term very narrowly, police in smaller cities and towns more broadly, most broadcast media very broadly, and most distressed local citizens perhaps most broadly of all?

3. How do myths about gangs factor into these tendencies?

4. Class exercise: Assume that your neighborhood or community is concerned about a potential gang problem. Construct a gang definition that you would take to a community meeting to guide discussion of the problem.

5. After reading the Decker and Kempf-Leonard (1991) article, test the acceptability of your definition from Exercise 4 in discussions with local stakeholders such as police, school officials, parents, court staff, social workers, middle and high school students, and others.

RECOMMENDATIONS FOR FURTHER READING

Peak Ages for Gang Involvement

Battin, S. R., Hill, K. G., Abbott, R. D., Catalano, R. F., & Hawkins, J. D. (1998). The contribution of gang membership to delinquency beyond delinquent friends. *Criminology, 36,* 93–115.

Bushway, S. D., Krohn, M. D., Lizotte, A. J., Phillips, M. D., & Schmidt, N. M. (2013). Are risky youth less protectable as they age? The dynamics of protection during adolescence and young adulthood. *Justice Quarterly, 30,* 84–116.

Esbensen, F., & Winfree, L. T. (1998). Race and gender differences between gang and non-gang youths: Results from a multi-site survey. *Justice Quarterly, 15,* 505–526.

Gilman, A. B., Hill, K. G., Hawkins, J. D., Howell, J. C., & Kosterman, R. (2014). The developmental dynamics of joining a gang in adolescence: Patterns and predictors of gang membership. *Journal of Research on Adolescence, 24,* 204–219.

Gottfredson, G. D., & Gottfredson, D. C. (2001). *Gang problems and gang programs in a national sample of schools.* Ellicott City, MD: Gottfredson Associates.

Hill, K. G., Lui, C., & Hawkins, J. D. (2001). *Early precursors of gang membership: A study of Seattle youth* (Juvenile Justice Bulletin. Youth Gang Series). Washington, DC: U.S. Department of Justice, Office of Juvenile Justice and Delinquency Prevention.

Lahey, B. B., Gordon, R. A., Loeber, R., Stouthamer-Loeber, M., & Farrington, D. P. (1999). Boys who join gangs: A prospective study of predictors of first gang entry. *Journal of Abnormal Child Psychology, 27,* 261–276.

Pyrooz, D. (2014). "From your first cigarette to your last dying day": The patterning of gang membership in the life-course. *Journal of Quantitative Criminology, 30,* 349–372.

Defining Gangs

Ball, R. A., & Curry, G. D. (1995). The logic of definition in criminology: Purposes and methods for defining "gangs." *Criminology, 33,* 225–245.

Bookin-Weiner, H., & Horowitz, R. (1983). The end of the gang: Fact or fiction? *Criminology, 21,* 585–602.

Esbensen, F., Brick, B. T., Melde, C., Tusinski, K., & Taylor, T. J. (2008). The role of race and ethnicity in gang membership. In F. V. Genert, D. Peterson, & I. Lien (Eds.), *Street gangs, migration and ethnicity* (pp. 117–139). Portland, OR: Willan.

Esbensen, F., & Maxson, C. E. (2012). *Youth gangs in international perspective: Results from the Eurogang Program of Research.* New York: Springer.

Esbensen, F., Winfree, L. T., He, N., & Taylor, T. J. (2001). Youth gangs and definitional issues: When is a gang a gang, and why does it matter? *Crime and Delinquency, 47,* 105–130.

Horowitz, R. (1990). Sociological perspectives on gangs: Conflicting definitions and concepts. In R. Huff (Ed.), *Gangs in America* (pp. 37–54). Newbury Park, CA: Sage.

Howell, J. C. (2013). Why is gang membership prevention important? In T. R. Simon, N. M. Ritter, & R. R. Mahendra (Eds.), *Changing course: Preventing gang membership* (pp. 7–18). Washington, DC: National Center for Injury Prevention and Control, Centers for Disease Control and Prevention, U.S. Department of Health and Human Services, and National Institute of Justice, Office of Justice Programs, U.S. Department of Justice.

Klein, M. W. (1995). *The American street gang.* New York: Oxford University Press.

Matsuda, K. N., Esbensen, F., & Carson, D. C. (2012). Putting the "gang" in "Eurogang": Characteristics of delinquent youth groups by different definitional approaches. In F. Esbensen & C. L. Maxson (Eds.), *Youth gangs in international perspective: Results from the Eurogang program of research* (pp. 17–33). New York: Springer.

Race and Ethnicity of Gang Members

Esbensen, F., Brick, B. T., Melde, C., Tusinski, K., & Taylor, T. J. (2008). The role of race and ethnicity in gang membership. In F. V. Genert, D. Peterson, & I. Lien (Eds.), *Street gangs, migration and ethnicity* (pp. 117–139). Portland, OR: Willan.

Esbensen, F. A., & Carson, D. C. (2012). Who are the gangsters? An examination of the age, race/ethnicity, sex, and immigration status of self-reported gang members in a seven-city study of American youth. *Journal of Contemporary Criminal Justice, 28*(4), 465–481.

Freng, A., & Taylor, T. J. (2013). Race and ethnicity: What are their roles in gang membership? In T.R. Simon, N. M. Ritter, & R. R. Mahendra (Eds.). *Changing course: Preventing gang membership* (pp. 135–149). Washington, DC: U.S. Department of Justice, U.S. Department of Health and Human Services.

Glesmann, C., Krisberg, B., & Marchionna, S. (2009). *Youth in gangs: Who is at risk? Focus.* Oakland, CA: National Council on Crime and Delinquency.

Krohn, M. D., Schmidt, N. M., Lizotte, A. J., & Baldwin, J. M. (2011). The impact of multiple marginality on gang membership and delinquent behavior for Hispanic, African American, and White male adolescents. *Journal of Contemporary Criminal Justice, 27,* 18–42.

Pyrooz, D. (2014). "From your first cigarette to your last dying day": The patterning of gang membership in the life-course. *Journal of Quantitative Criminology, 30,* 349–372.

Vigil, J. D. (2002). *A rainbow of gangs: Street cultures in the mega-city.* Austin: University of Texas Press.

Zatz, M. S., & Portillos, E. L. (2000). Voices from the barrio: Chicano/a gangs, families, and communities. *Criminology, 38,* 369–401.

Diversity Among Gangs

Cohen, B. (1969). The delinquency of gangs and spontaneous groups. In T. Sellin & M. E. Wolfgang (Eds.), *Delinquency: Selected studies* (pp. 61–111). New York: John Wiley & Sons.

Covey, H. C. (2010). *Street gangs throughout the world.* Springfield, IL: Charles C Thomas.

Cummings, L. L. (1994). Fighting by the rules: Women street fighters in Chihuahua, Mexico. *Sex Roles, 30,* 189–198.

Cummings, S. (1993). Anatomy of a wilding gang. In S. Cummings & D. J. Monti (Eds.), *Gangs* (pp. 49–74). Albany: State University of New York Press.

Cummings, S., & Monti, D. J. (Eds.). (1993). *Gangs: The origins and impact of contemporary youth gangs in the United States.* Albany: State University of New York Press.

Decker, S. H., & Pyrooz, D. C. (2010). Gang violence worldwide: Context, culture, and country. *Small Arms Survey, 5,* 129–155.

Decker, S. H., & Weerman, F. E. (Eds.). (2005). *European street gangs and troublesome youth groups.* Lanham, MD: AltaMira Press.

Esbensen, F. A., & Carson, D. C. (2012). Who are the gangsters? An examination of the age, race/ethnicity, sex, and immigration status of self-reported gang members in a seven-city study of American youth. *Journal of Contemporary Criminal Justice, 28*(4), 465–481.

Gannon, T. M. (1967). Dimensions of current gang delinquency. *Journal of Research in Crime and Delinquency, 4,* 119–131.

Howell, J. C., Moore, J. P., & Egley, A., Jr. (2002). The changing boundaries of youth gangs. In C. R. Huff (Ed.), *Gangs in America* (3rd ed., pp. 3–18). Thousand Oaks, CA: Sage.

Klein, M. W. (1995). *The American street gang.* New York: Oxford University Press.

Leap, J. (2012). *Jumped in: What gangs taught me about violence, drugs, love, and redemption.* Boston: Beacon Press.

Miller, W. B. (1974a). American youth gangs: Fact and fantasy. In L. Rainwater (Ed.), *Deviance and liberty: A survey of modern perspectives on deviant behavior* (pp. 262–273). Chicago: Aldine.

Miller, W. B. (1974b). American youth gangs: Past and present. In A. Blumberg (Ed.), *Current perspectives on criminal behavior* (pp. 410–420). New York: Knopf.

Morash, M. (1983). Gangs, groups, and delinquency. *British Journal of Criminology, 23,* 309–335.

Short, J. F., Jr. (2006). Why study gangs? An intellectual journey. In J. F. Short & L. A. Hughes (Eds.), *Studying youth gangs* (pp. 1–14). Lanham, MD: AltaMira Press.

Spergel, I. A. (1964). *Racketville, Slumtown and Haulberg: An exploratory study of delinquent subcultures.* Chicago: University of Chicago Press.

Spergel, I. A. (1990). Youth gangs: Continuity and change. In M. Tonry & N. Morris (Eds.), *Crime and justice: A review of research* (Vol. 12, pp. 171–275). Chicago: University of Chicago.

Starbuck, D., Howell, J. C., & Lindquist, D. J. (2001). *Into the millennium: Hybrids and other modern gangs* (Juvenile Justice Bulletin Youth Gang Series). Washington, DC: U.S. Department of Justice, Office of Juvenile Justice and Delinquency Prevention.

Sullivan, M. L. (2005). Maybe we shouldn't study "gangs": Does reification obscure youth violence? *Journal of Contemporary Criminal Justice, 21,* 170–190.

Valdez, Al. (2007). *Gangs: A guide to understanding street gangs* (5th ed.). San Clemente, CA: LawTech.

Van Gemert, F., Peterson, D., & Lien, I.-L. (Eds.). (2008). *Street gangs, migration and ethnicity.* Portland, OR: Willan Publishing.

Vigil, J. D. (2002). *A rainbow of gangs: Street cultures in the mega-city.* Austin: University of Texas Press.

Walker-Barnes, C. J., & Mason, C. A. (2001). Ethnic differences in the effect of parenting on gang involvement and gang delinquency: A longitudinal, hierarchical linear modeling perspective. *Child Development, 72,* 1814–1831.

NOTES

1. Based on the students' descriptions, Sheldon (1898) classified the organizations in which they participated into seven categories: (1) secret clubs, (2) predatory organizations, (3) social clubs, (4) personal development associations, (5) philanthropic associations, (6) athletic clubs, and (7) organizations for the promotion of literacy, artistic, and music training.

2. http://www.nationalgangcenter.gov/Survey-Analysis/Demographics

CHAPTER 4

General Macro-Level Theories and Modern-Day Applications

◈ Introduction

This chapter reviews theories that provide explanations for the existence of gangs. Given that gangs are rooted in societal and community conditions, the most relevant theories should tie gang existence to those historical and environmental conditions, or at least place a premium on those economic, social, and political contexts. This is the lens through which gang theories are examined in this chapter, beginning with the earliest theories and then advancing to more recent ones. This arrangement is intended to give readers a sense of the generation of gang theories that match to some degree the historical evolution of the gangs that theories purport to explain (Table 4.1).

Macro-level, or *ecological*, theories concern themselves with characteristics of delimited geographical areas—neighborhoods, communities, census tracts, cities, counties, states, and nations—that are related to crime (Pratt & Cullen, 2005). These theories "seek to explain why certain characteristics of ecological areas, but not others, account for the distribution of crime" (p. 373). Particular attention is given to social disorganization theory because it is the backbone of gang theorizing. Prior to the new millennium, gang theory construction had been at a standstill for 40 years—since Cloward and Ohlin's (1960) strain theory/differential opportunity theory. Social disorganization theory is discussed in some detail, including Papachristos and Kirk's (2006) important extension of it to account for gang violence. Developmental theories that account for why youths join gangs focused on individuals, such as interactional theory and multiple marginalization theory, are considered in Chapter 5.

Table 4.1   Main Theories With Implications for Existence of Gangs

Theory	Primary Scholar(s)
Social disorganization	Burgess, 1925; Morenoff et al., 2001; Park, 1936a, 1936b; Park & Burgess, 1921, 1925; Papachristos & Kirk, 2006; Sampson & Laub, 1993, 2005; Shaw & McKay, 1942, 1969; Shaw et al., 1929; Thrasher, 1927/2000
Reaction formation	A. Cohen, 1955
Cultural norms of the lower class	W. Miller, 1958
Strain/differential opportunity	Cloward & Ohlin, 1960; Agnew, 2005
Subculture of violence	Wolfgang & Ferracuti, 1967
Routine activities/opportunity	Cohen & Felson, 1979; Felson & Cohen, 1980
Underclass	W. Wilson, 1987, 1999
Social conflict	Alonso, 2004; E. Anderson, 1998; Cureton, 2009; Currie, 1998; Pastor, Sadd, & Hipp, 2001

◈ The Chicago School and Development of the Social Disorganization Perspective

Given the rapid immigration and widespread concentration of poverty in the first large U.S. cities, it is no surprise that social scientists first focused their attention on urban social problems. A group of scholars in the University of Chicago's Department of Sociology is universally recognized for having ushered into the field of sociology a strong emphasis on the study of urban areas, using both quantitative and qualitative methodologies in urban studies. The term *Chicago school* referred to that collection of faculty and graduate students during the period from around 1915 to 1930–1935. Bursik and Grasmick (1993) report that the discipline of sociology was first established as a department at the University of Chicago in 1892, and except for strain theory, early delinquency theories originated at the University of Chicago, and the first gang theories grew out of this tradition.

Under the direction of Robert Park, the Chicago school researchers accomplished what Dimitriadis (2006) says "is to this day the most systematic and comprehensive study of a single urban center" (p. 345). This was no easy task: documenting, describing, and explaining urban life during a time of rapid growth and transition in the period between World War I and the Depression. Like New York City and other large urban centers, Chicago was undergoing "an unprecedented economic and cultural revolution that presented both dangers and opportunities—a point underscored by Robert Park time and again" (p. 338). Park brought a conception of the city and communities not simply as a geographical phenomenon but as a kind of social organism. In 1921, Park explained, "Sociology, speaking strictly, is a point of view and a method for investigating the processes by which individuals are inducted into and induced to cooperate in some sort of permanent corporate existence which we call society" (p. 20).

Burgess's (1925) concentric zones theory describes the manner in which a city grows outward from the central business district to the suburbs. Of particular interest to Park and Burgess (1921) was the area immediately surrounding the central business district, known as the zone of transition, consisting of "ghettos" and "slums" located between the downtown financial and shopping center and the working-class homes. Hence, Park and Burgess constructed maps as a primary means of analyzing social life in the city. Their work drew colleagues' attention to the often disorganized transition zone.

As Burgess (1925) explains, this zone typically attracted real estate developers who bought large parcels of land in hopes of later growth outward from the central city. In the meantime, these speculators were not inclined to spend much money on property upkeep. It was natural for new immigrant groups to settle in these less expensive housing areas. The zone was also considered transitional in the sense that Bursik and Grasmick (1993) suggest is "a tendency for the centralization of populations into a geographic area to be followed by a period of decentralization during which these groups attempt to move into adjacent neighborhoods" (p. 8). Park (1936a, 1936b) referred to this normal process as *invasion* and *succession*, and he argued that a city's development and growth could best be understood according to these processes. Hence, Park and Burgess observed that this zone was characterized by high rates of residential mobility, deteriorated housing, abandoned buildings, and crime—characteristics that are associated with *social disorganization* within the zone.

These conditions of social disorganization were illuminated in a variety of studies: *The Polish Peasant in Europe and America* (Thomas & Znaniecki, 1927); *The Unadjusted Girl* (Thomas, 1923); *The City* (Park & Burgess, 1925); *The Ghetto* (Wirth, 1928); *The Hobo* (N. Anderson, 1926); *Suicide* (Cavan, 1927); *The Gang* (Thrasher, 1927/2000); *Gold Coast and Slum* (Zorbaugh, 1929); *The Taxi Dance Hall* (Cressey, 1932); *The Jack Roller* (Shaw, 1930); and *Street Corner Society* (Whyte, 1943b). Among these studies, widely applauded particularly for their richness of description and connection to human context, Park and Burgess's (1925) study proved to be a landmark one for having mapped the location of a wide variety of social problems and attendant social disorganization.

The application of social disorganization theory to crime and gangs grew specifically on Shaw and McKay's (1942, 1969) mapping of tens of thousands of the residences of male adolescents referred to the Cook County (Chicago) Juvenile Court from 1900 through 1965. Two very important conclusions immediately emerged from this massive database. First, as Bursik and Grasmick (1993) explain, "The relative distribution of delinquency rates remained fairly stable among Chicago's neighborhoods between 1900 and 1933 despite dramatic changes in the ethnic and racial composition of these neighborhoods" (p. 31).

Second, Shaw and McKay discovered that delinquency rates correlated negatively with the distance from the central business district. This finding provided the foundation for their seminal contribution to social disorganization theory, which Bursik and Grasmick (1993) describe as follows: "that the patterns of neighborhood delinquency rates were related to the same ecological processes that gave rise to the socioeconomic structure of urban areas" (p. 33).

Next, having been influenced by Park and Burgess's discovery that economically deprived neighborhoods tended to have high population turnover, and that poor neighborhoods tended to be characterized by racial and ethnic heterogeneity, Shaw and McKay "argued that these characteristics made it very difficult for the neighborhood to achieve the common social organization goal of its residents, a situation they called social disorganization" (Bursik & Grasmick, 1993, p. 33). Thomas and Znaniecki (1927) had earlier defined social disorganization as "a decrease of the influence of existing rules of behavior upon individual members of the group" (p. 2). It appears that this definition influenced Thrasher's research perspective and helped him explain the existence of youth gangs.

Thrasher's Contributions to Social Disorganization Theory

The development of gang theories has been uneven because gang theorists rarely pay attention to available findings in elaborating new theory (Hardman, 1967). Social disorganization theory is an exception. Thrasher made major contributions to the social disorganization theory of the Chicago school, of which he was a vital part. Clearly, his gang research was influenced by the pioneering studies of Park, Burgess, Thomas, and Znaniecki, and other colleagues of that time and place—with whom he "was in constant dialogue" (Dimitriadis, 2006, p. 336). First, Thrasher (1927/2000) describes the gangs' physical locations. This focus is, of course, a hallmark of the Chicago school studies: "There is nothing fresh or clean to greet the eye; everywhere [one sees] unpainted, ramshackle buildings, blackened and besmirched with the smoke of industry. In this sort of habitat the gang seems to flourish best" (p. 9). In addition, "Gangland represents a geographically and socially interstitial area in the city," in the slums and ghettos (p. 6). He further noted that "these regions of conflict are like a frontier [and] like a 'no man's land,' lawless, godless, wild" (p. 1).

Thrasher is said to have studied an astonishing total of 1,313 gangs. Short (2006), however, describes Thrasher's enumerated gangs as "legendary." Solomon Kobrin, a long-time associate of Shaw and McKay, told colleagues that the precise (1,313) number of studied gangs was an in-joke played on Thrasher by his graduate assistants, and that it was actually the house number of a nearby brothel.

Regardless of an exact number, Thrasher (1927/2000) himself emphatically states the value of this work: "Probably the most significant concept of [his] study is the term interstitial—that is pertaining to spaces that intervene between one thing and another" (p. 6). He adds more interpretation of the meaning of the term *interstitial*:

> In nature foreign matter tends to collect and cake in every crack, crevice, and cranny—interstices. There are also fissures and breaks in the structure of social organization. The gang may be regarded as an interstitial element in the framework of society, and gangland as an interstitial region in the layout of the city where unfettered ganging occurs. (p. 6)

Therefore, the gang is "an interstitial group [i.e., between childhood and adulthood] providing interstitial activities for its members" (p. 12). Thrasher even superimposed his "gangland" map over Park's concentric zone model to demonstrate the location of gangland as virtually confined within the parallel circular boundaries of Burgess's (1925) zone in transition.

In his further contextualization of gangs, Thrasher (1927/2000) connected ganging in relation to five community conditions: (1) community disorganization, (2) ineffective families, (3) poor-quality schooling, (4) association with undesirable peers, and (5) lack of leisure-time guidance. First, with respect to community disorganization, he contended that gangs form and flourish in communities in which normally directing and controlling customs and institutions fail to function efficiently and effectively. Contributing conditions included poverty, deteriorating neighborhoods, disintegration of family life, ineffective religion, lack of opportunity for wholesome recreation, inefficient schools, corruption and indifference in local politics, and unemployment. "All of these factors enter into the picture of the moral and economic frontier, and, coupled with deterioration in housing, sanitation, and other conditions of life in the slum, give the impression of general disorganization and decay" (p. 12). These conditions, Thrasher argued, resulted in the breakdown of social control because of the weakening of social institutions, particularly family life, education, and religion. Youths exposed to these conditions enjoyed "an unusual freedom from restrictions of the type imposed by the normal controlling agencies in the better residential areas of the city" (p. 170). In Thrasher's view, this freedom from normal social controls allows ganging to occur.

In addition, Thrasher (1927/2000) observed that immigration dynamics contribute significantly to community disorganization. Rapid immigration, he argued, created a "chaotic milieu" that lessened parental controls on their children. "Stated in another way, the problem is one of too quick and too superficial Americanization of the children of the immigrant. The more rapid this type of assimilation, the more rapid will be the disintegration of family control" (p. 170). It became impossible to maintain family discipline in this context "because of the lack of tradition in the American community to support it, and the constant coming and going out (immigrant succession) . . . In this sense, then, the gang becomes a problem of community organization" (p. 170).

Thrasher's (1927/2000) second contextual factor that explains ganging (or prepares youths for gang life) is ineffective families. By this, he refers to "any condition of family life which promotes the gang by stimulating the boy to find the satisfaction of his wishes outside the plan and organization of family activities" (p. 170). As noted, Thrasher found that immigration dynamics undermined parental control and nourishment of children. He also called attention to other sources of family deficiencies—including poverty and antisocial parents—contributing to neglect, and ignorance of proper childrearing practices or immorality, "but their general effect is the same: the family fails to hold the boy's interest, neglects him, or actually forces him into the street" by alienating him from family life (p. 170).

The quality of schooling that youngsters received in Chicago was the third key factor in preparing youths for gang life in Thrasher's view. In particular, the educational process during school hours did not interest future gang members; thus they resorted to truancy. In addition, the compulsory education law permitted youth to drop out at age 14, but they were prohibited from taking employment before age 16. Lastly, the lack of school extracurricular activities that supplemented the work of other agencies (during and after school hours) freed youths from adult supervision. As Thrasher (1927/2000) noted, "it often happens that boys expelled either as individuals or as a group from some formal organization are drawn together to form a gang" (p. 11).

Association with delinquent peers is Thrasher's (1927/2000) fourth contextual factor. Intimate "grouping" had long been viewed as a normal social tendency, especially among children and adolescents, beginning about the age of 10, according to early observers such as Puffer (1912) and Spaulding (1948). Although this tendency is no longer viewed as an innate trait, gang scholars still put plenty of currency into Thrasher's notion that, at the individual level, boys—gang and nongang alike—from an early age are influenced enormously by relations with their peers, and problem associations are often formed when the above conditions "give the boy an opportunity to roam about and choose his associates and his amusements for himself" (p. 171).

Thrasher's (1927/2000) fifth negative factor that contributes to conditions favorable to ganging is the lack of proper guidance for boys during leisure-time activities: "The common assumption that the problem of boy delinquency will be solved by the multiplication of playgrounds and social areas is entirely erroneous" (p. 171). Rather, it is guidance on the part of trained parents, teachers, and recreational leaders who can organize and direct wholesome activities that was largely absent in gangland. Freeing the boy from ordinary controls allows gangs to form.

It is readily apparent that Thrasher not only saw multiple factors that account for gang involvement, but also that the interaction of these factors increases the potency of them. Dimitriadis (2006) calls this perspective Thrasher's *situation complex*, his recognition that the collection of community, family, school, and peer factors form "a web of influences that could not be understood in isolation from, but only in relation to each other" (p. 338). This is the strength of Thrasher's *contextualization* of ganging, which he ties directly to immigration in a "matrix of gang development," to wit: "It seems impossible to control one factor without dealing with the others, so closely are they interwoven, and in most cases they are inseparable from the general problem of immigrant adjustment" (Thrasher, 1927/2000, p. 491). Bourgois (2003) notes that Thrasher devoted the last 15 years of his life to applying his theory to juvenile delinquency in Italian Harlem with great academic success, through his institute at New York University.

In sum, Thrasher's (1927/2000) gang social disorganization theory developed from the premise that youth gangs were rooted in the struggles of ethnic groups to establish themselves or maintain their standing in urban social systems—if only what J. Moore (1998) calls a *toehold*. Thrasher contended that his theory applied not only in Chicago but also in New York City, Boston, Minneapolis, Cleveland, Los Angeles, New Orleans, Denver, and San Francisco. The key element of his theory—and the Chicago school in general—was the weakening of social controls in the fabric of key institutions and social structural weaknesses, particularly in families, schools, communities, and religious institutions. It can be said that the lasting legacy of Thrasher's gang theory is that, in the tradition of the Chicago school, it cast a spotlight on "the processes by which gangs influence and are influenced by their physical environment . . . the human element" (Hughes, 2007, p. 44).

A key limitation of Thrasher's (1927/2000) gang social disorganization theory is its focus on the development of gangs in lower-class areas while ignoring the presence of gangs in suburban and working- and middle-class areas. But gangs had not yet been reported in these areas; these groups were far more prevalent in inner-city areas. Both Hughes (2007) and Short (1998) assert that critiques of Thrasher's theory also have noted the near absence of a focus on group processes and their relationship to individual and collective behavior. Other critics have been less charitable, including Becker (1999), who characterizes the Chicago school as promoting an "eclectic" mix of sociological approaches rather than an actual "unified school of thought." Subsequent development and testing of the theory would dispel this notion.

◈ Application of Social Disorganization Theory to Gangs

For nearly a century, social disorganization theory has endured as an explanation of crime and the existence of gangs, despite many academic challengers (J. Moore, 1998; Pizarro & McGloin, 2006). Numerous studies have found that gang behaviors and gangs themselves are more likely to be concentrated in poor and disorganized cities and communities (Curry & Spergel, 1988; Short & Strodtbeck, 1965/1974; Vigil, 1988, 2002).

Interestingly, the very survival of social disorganization theory may owe to an early Chicago school study, which found that gangs could provide at least a semblance of order in some "disorganized" communities. According to Papachristos (2004), Whyte's (1943b) *Street Corner Society* research demonstrated that gang turfs "were not *dis*organized, but rather *differently* organized and that 'street corner groups' provided a clear and *organized* response to the disruption of formal social institutions" (pp. 7–8). Similarly, in his discovery of *The Social Order of the Slum*, Suttles (1968) observed mechanisms by which street gangs contributed to a "skeletal" frame of order in the world of street corner gangs. These included social interactions on the streets and relational patterns such as modes of dress, dating rituals, public interaction, and familial patterns. Along with others' contributions, Whyte's and Suttles's studies appear to have prompted a significant modification of social disorganization theory, the identification of social networks that can bring order to otherwise disorganized communities. In this context, gangs organized youths' behavior, a point made emphatically by Whyte (1943a): "In other words, the boy's behavior is not un-organized; it is organized—by the gang" (p. 38).

The central thesis of social disorganization theory, according to Shaw and McKay (1942, 1969), is that ethnic heterogeneity, low socioeconomic status, and residential mobility reduce the capacity of community residents to control crime. Prevailing thought, for which there is growing research support, is that these structural disadvantages in communities make it difficult for residents to develop informal social control and mutual trust or social cohesion, both of which constitute Sampson and colleagues' (1997) concept of collective efficacy[1] and thus can reduce crime and violence in communities. Several studies, most notably Bursik and Grasmick (1993), suggest that where collective efficacy is lacking, the diminished private, parochial, and public forms of social control permit gangs to flourish. Furthermore, leading researchers such as Papachristos and Kirk (2006) find the principles of collective efficacy also apply to the control of gang crime. Short and Hughes (2010) suggest that "the extent to which detached workers—and other therapeutic or change agents and programs—develop social capital and collective efficacy among gang members and communities is, we believe, an important missing ingredient in arguments concerning their effectiveness" (p. 133).

Shaw and McKay (1931, 1942) specified three mechanisms by which social disorganization theory accounts for gang existence: neighborhood population mobility, ethnic heterogeneity, and poverty. They viewed mobility and population heterogeneity as disruptive influences on community institutions and networks, but these effects would vary according to, first, the rate of immigration, and second, the similarities between the newly arriving immigrants and the established residents of a neighborhood. As Papachristos and Kirk (2006) explain, these factors disrupt the normative foundation that supports effective social control, thereby contributing to a state of social disorganization.

> The extension of social disorganization theory to gang behaviors is straightforward: Gangs arise either to take the place of weak social institutions in socially disorganized areas, or because weak social institutions fail to thwart the advent of unconventional value systems that often characterize street gangs. (p. 64)

In this statement, Papachristos and Kirk offer two interpretations of social disorganization theory. The first is that gangs fill a void created by weak social institutions, as Thrasher suggested. Second, Papachristos and Kirk posit that the weakened social institutions allow destructive social organisms to flourish, including gangs. Each of these interpretations nicely fits the theory.

Key variables were specified in the next iteration of social disorganization theory, and the addition of neighborhood social control would remedy its blind spot to ganging outside of inner-city areas. These additions were explicitly codified and tested by Papachristos and Kirk (2006) in an apropos Chicago study. These scholars identified key crime-producing structural features of neighborhoods that had previously received substantial research support: concentrated disadvantage, residential instability, and immigrant concentration (Figure 4.1). Their explication of social disorganization theory also incorporated collective efficacy and social control as key social processes in neighborhoods. Their test of

Figure 4.1   Causal Model of Social Disorganization Theory Applied to Gang Behavior (Homicide)

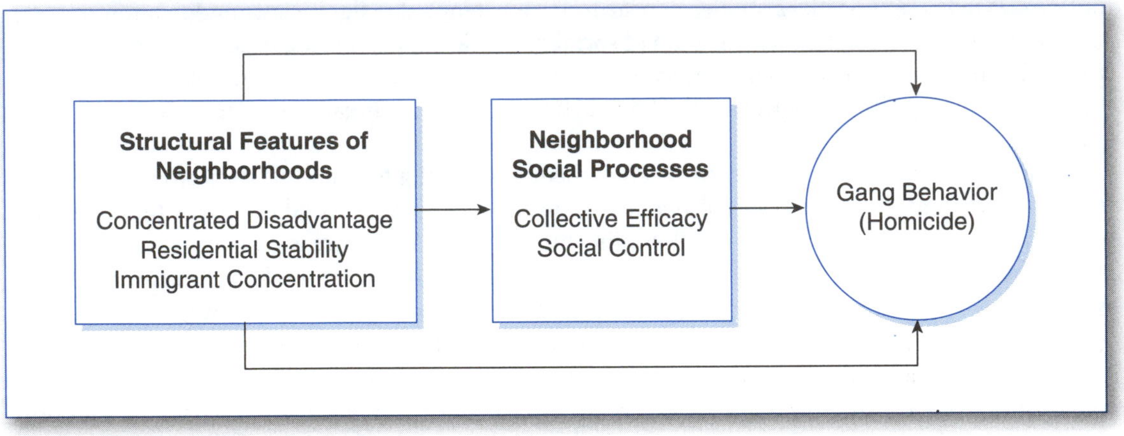

Source: Papachristos & Kirk, 2006, p. 68.

whether or not social disorganization theory predicted gang homicide encompassed the entire city of Chicago (847 census tracts combined into 343 neighborhood clusters).

Papachristos and Kirk (2006) found that the social disorganization theory predicted gang homicide, but not nongang homicide: "The neighborhoods with a high level of general violence are not necessarily the same neighborhoods that have high levels of gang violence" (p. 80). However, the researchers found that "collective efficacy operates similarly on violent gang behavior as it does on other forms of violent behavior" (p. 75) in mediating the effects of concentrated disadvantage. In addition, Papachristos and Kirk found that greater immigrant concentration was related to Hispanic homicides but not Black homicides.

Other gang studies have produced findings that also support social disorganization theory although not without exceptions. In an Arizona study, Katz and Schnebly (2011) found that some disadvantaged areas produce gangs while others do not. This study examined the relationship between neighborhood structure, violent crime, and concentrations of gang members at the neighborhood level. The researchers used official police gang lists, police crime data, and two waves of decennial census data (that characterized the socioeconomic and demographic conditions) on 93 neighborhoods in Mesa, Arizona. Two research questions were addressed: (1) How well do neighborhood-level structural conditions account for variability in gang member concentrations (gang member rates based on the police gang lists)? (2) What impact, if any, do levels of crime or community conditions have on the concentration of gang members in a given neighborhood? The study revealed that neighborhoods characterized by relatively high levels of economic deprivation and social or familial disadvantage indeed tend to have higher rates of gang membership. However, this study produced two surprising findings. First, "neighborhoods with high concentrations of gang members were not necessarily those with comparatively high levels of officially recorded violence" (p. 23). This anomaly could be a result of underreporting of gang crime. Second, "concentrations of gang members within neighborhoods was not significantly related to population density" (p. 23). This finding, according to W. Miller (1982/1992, pp. 75–76), could be attributed to the shifting of previous inner-city slums and ghettos to ring-city or suburban areas.

Independent St. Louis studies produced contrasting outcomes. First, in a study of gang formation in five geographic regions in the city, Monti (1993) observed that "gangs can be found in a variety of communities [and they] may be more prevalent in areas that are characterized as 'unsettled' [but] gangs can arise in communities with substantial strength and a varied organizational base" (p. 249). For example, Monti found that gangs formed in north St. Louis and adjacent suburbs in conjunction with migration of Black residents across the metropolitan area. "The emergence of youth gangs in this case . . . is better explained as an expression of community reorganization than disorganization" (p. 250).

In the second St. Louis study, Rosenfeld and fellow researchers (1999) examined gang homicides between 1985 and 1995 in St. Louis (in 588 census block groups composing the entire city), and found few differences between neighborhoods that had high levels of gang and nongang homicide. Both gang and nongang homicide tended "to cluster in areas with high levels of disadvantage and large concentrations of African-American residents" (p. 510). All three homicide types examined in the study—gang-affiliated, gang-motivated, and nongang youth homicides—also were concentrated in racially isolated, disadvantaged neighborhoods with moderate levels of instability, but gang-motivated events exhibited a somewhat distinctive spatial patterning, related to turf battles or retaliatory motives.

In the only test to date of social disorganization theory's ability to account for gang activity at the national level, Pyrooz and colleagues (2010) examined the effects of economic disadvantage and racial and ethnic heterogeneity on gang membership in the 100 largest U.S. cities using National Youth Gang Survey (NYGS) data. In contrast with macro-level gang studies Jackson (1991) and Wells and Weisheit (2001) conducted, asking only whether a city had a gang problem, this study analyzed gang membership rates (and changes in the number of gang members). The key finding from this research is that both economic disadvantage and racial and ethnic heterogeneity—two key cornerstones of social disorganization theory—exhibit independent, additive, and multiplicative effects on gang membership rates as reported in the NYGS. However, the results indicated that the effect of heterogeneity was twice as great as that of economic disadvantage. In cities with high heterogeneity, disadvantage had a larger effect. Conversely, the effect of disadvantage was modest in cities with low heterogeneity. Pyrooz and colleagues (2010) emphasize the main implication for gang research, that heterogeneity and disadvantage work together to produce higher levels of gang membership—in the 100 largest cities.

It is important to keep in mind that social disorganization theory was based on Chicago populations, and thus applies mainly to cities with large urban populations. The discordant findings in several studies suggest that even when communities are characterized by concentrated disadvantage, residential instability, and immigrant concentration, one can find different patterns of criminal gang activity and nongang crime. "The diverse findings . . . may be the result of a common problem in empirically oriented gang research: data are often aggregated in units that are too large to capture localized gang phenomena" (Tita, Cohen, & Engberg, 2005, p. 275). Long-term intergang wars can also explain these variations. Examples of the former case are plentiful in gang literature (W. Miller, 1974b, 1982/1992), with the Crips versus Bloods and MS-13 versus Eighteenth Street in Los Angeles serving as a good example of long-term gang battles. In Chicago, an ongoing conflict involved two "brother" gangs, the Black Gangster Disciples and the Black Disciples, which C. Block and colleagues (1996) report resulted in 45 homicides over an eight-year period. Each of these feuds likely was driven simultaneously by macro-level (e.g., social disorganization) and micro-level (e.g., drug wars) factors.

Moreover, "it is unknown whether neighborhood social processes operate in a similar way across different types of disadvantaged neighborhoods. It is possible that some social processes are unique to economically depressed areas" (Kingston, Huizinga, & Elliott, 2009, p. 53). This could be attributable to the condition that most studies lack a sufficiently large sample of disadvantaged neighborhoods to test these kinds of neighborhood-specific hypotheses. This situation is particularly evident in studies that have tested gang phenomena. Findings that are consistent at the national level often are not at the neighborhood or community level. Cities and communities have their own social, economic, and gang histories, which appears to account for disparate findings seen in several of these studies. Nevertheless, Papachristos (2004) notes social disorganization theories encounter two main problems in their application to gangs. First, as seen in the work of Whyte (1943b) and Suttles (1968), social disorganization theories do not account for the development of gangs in more stable, lower-class, and non-ghetto neighborhoods. Second, social disorganization theories do not account for social and demographic changes that do not fit within the original social disorganization paradigm. The key condition is the "underclass," which has not experienced the same ethnic succession as seen among European White ethnics. A related limitation is that factors other than the variables that comprise social disorganization theories may be important in accounting for gang presence in communities.

◈ An Explanation of Gang Origins, Expansion, and Violence

In Chapter 1, we provided an historical account of gang emergence and institutionalization in large cities. In what follows, we extend that explanation further by considering macro-level factors that contributed to gang origins, expansion, and associated violence. The initial emergence of street gangs in the United States can be explained by a series of social and historical events and urban conditions. This chapter organizes the key factors in five stages, with their unfolding beginning with the pre-gang era (at the time of the American Revolution), and extending more than two centuries, to 2012. These events and conditions have a foundation in social disorganization theory (Shaw & Mckay, 1931, 1942). By and large, these clusters or stages of factors account for the main periods of gang emergence and growth in three of the four major U.S. regions, though less so in the Southern region because several of these factors either did not apply or played out less intensively therein. For one thing, Southern cities were not overwhelmed with waves of immigrants either from Europe or other U.S. regions. The rather large group of Mexican immigrants has been assimilated in the Southern region without major violent incidents. Another case in point, the use of large-scale public housing has been somewhat more limited in the South region. However, both New Orleans and Atlanta had early high-rise public housing projects in which large numbers of poor Black residents were placed—first the Techwood Homes were built in Atlanta in the 1930s, followed by the Magnolia Projects in New Orleans in the 1940s. Gangs appear to have incubated in these settings, though not for some time.

Stage 1

Ideal conditions had been set for gang formation in Northeast cities following rapid population immigration from Europe to the United States following the American Revolution. This massive influx overwhelmed cities of destination as immigrant concentrations quickly exhausted available resources, creating social disorder. The first gangs comprised Irish men and adolescents who banded together to forge a wedge of safety and resource accumulation in the social disorder and widespread violence in the slums of New York City, Boston, and Philadelphia. Inevitably, it seemed, gangs developed out of three conditions that large-scale immigration produced: immigrant concentration in slums, residential instability, and extreme levels of poverty and other concentrated disadvantages. In other words, gangs formed to take the place of weak social institutions in socially disorganized areas.

Stage 2

In the second stage, family disorganization, low neighborhood control, and youth alienation were three products of social disorganization. Under these conditions, the socialization of children and adolescents slipped from the grasp of parents. Hence many youths failed to make an adequate social and cultural transition from family, to school, and to work. The term *multiple marginality* captures the process through which young people are left out of mainstream society because of language, education, cultural, and economic barriers in schools, neighborhoods, and communities. Immigrant youth felt alienated from families and schools. "Often, they seek a place where they are not marginalized—and find it in the streets" (Vigil, 2002, p. 7).

Stage 3

In this third stage, youth gangs formed, undergirded by the youth subculture that helped fill the gap between childhood and adulthood by providing values, customs, behavioral expectations, and the like for youth during the adolescent period. Two examples are instructive. In Mexican American culture, the *palomilla* custom of male friendship groups bridged the transition from childhood to adulthood for young males (Rubel, 1965). Later, along the migration trail, the first Mexican American gang members, called *Pachucos* (a Mexican-Spanish word for a young Mexican living in the United States, especially one of low social status who belongs to a more tightly knit group, a street gang, a *banda*), were reported in El Paso (McWilliams, 1948/1990). At the end of the first major migration trail, in Los Angeles, Mexican American gang members were called *zoot-suiters*, after a fashionable clothing trend in the youth subculture, and more generally, *Chicanos* (meaning second generation immigrants). In Chicago, youth identities became particularly well formed during the 1940s and 1950s, emerging from racial unrest and contributing to rapid gang growth (Diamond, 2009). Fighting gang subcultures pitted Blacks, Puerto Ricans, and Mexican American youth against one another along neighborhood boundaries, and gang members were at the forefront of racial conflicts. These conflicts emanated from Social Athletic Clubs, the foundation of White subculture that provided a pathway to success in patronage jobs, as firefighters, policemen, and the like, but these youth were almost without exception the instigators of youth conflicts.

Mostly Black and also Mexican American youth were integrated into gangs by the youth subculture's gangsta rap music, notably artists known as Tupac Shakur, Eazy E., The Game, Eminem, Ice Cube, 50 Cent, Dr. Dre, Jay Z, Snopp Dog, and Lil Wayne; also, Notorious B.I.G., Niggaz With Attitude (N.W.A.), Ricky Ross, Trick Daddy, and Young Jeezy (Hagedorn, 2008; Kubrin & Nielson, 2014, Nielson, 2012; Quinn, 2005). Historically, rap lyrics promoted prosocial values, but that changed with gangsta rap. Without doubt, gangsta rap strengthened the desire of youth to become part of a gang subculture that was portrayed by the rappers as a glamorous and rewarding lifestyle (Hagedorn, 2008, pp. 93–111). Stated succinctly, hip-hop youth culture intertwined with gangsta rap was widely embraced by gangs, and in their broader sphere of influence in youth subculture, as examples of "resistance identities" of youth (Bradley & DuBois, 2011).

Stage 4

Four factors were particularly important in this fourth stage of gang expansion and dangerousness: public housing projects, prison population growth, gun availability, and drug trafficking. The establishment of large public housing projects in major cities—particularly high-rise units that housed thousands of poor families in New York City, Chicago, and lower-level buildings in Los Angeles, virtually all of which were racial-ethnic minorities—had the unintended effect of strengthening gangs. In effect, these buildings provided a base of operations for gangs, an area that they could easily control, serving as *de facto* police (Popkin et al., 2000). In an ironic twist, gangs provided some relief to hyper-ghettoized residents in the form of safety from outsiders, and financial resources for necessities such as building repairs and upkeep. In exchange, most residents tolerated the increased violence associated with gang involvement in drug trafficking (Venkatesh, 1996, 2000).

As a direct consequence of the nearly sixfold increase in the number of imprisoned persons over the three decades from 1970 to 2000 (Justice Policy Institute, 2000), prison gangs grew enormously in response to inmates pleas for protection from rival gang members. Beginning in the late 1970s and early 1980s, gang members returning from prison to ghetto streets found few legitimate work opportunities, but plentiful opportunities to sell drugs, including marijuana, cocaine, and heroin (J. Moore, 1993). This continuing massive flow of returning inmates remains a major contributor to local gang violence, and involvement in drug trafficking has become more prominent in recent years. Most law enforcement agencies nationwide contend that returning inmates is the most predominant influence on local gang violence (Egley & Howell, 2013). Generally speaking, the growing availability of firearms among urban gangs has helped solidify their position in the streets.

> "Gang banging is not a lifestyle. It's a death style. Straight up." —Lil Monster, former Eight Tray Crip (in Goldman, Giles, & Hogg, 2014, p. 1)

Drug trafficking is the single most important factor that law enforcement identifies as influencing local gang violence (Egley & Howell, 2013). Pittsburgh is an excellent city example of street gang involvement in drug trafficking (see Chapter 8), along with the two major gang problem cities, Chicago (Venkatesh, 2008) and Los Angeles (Cockburn & St. Clair, 1998), each of which saw extensive gang participation in drug distribution in the 1980s. In general, cities that reported early onset of gang problems reported widespread gang involvement in drug trafficking (Howell, Egley, et al., 2002). Collaboration among prison gangs, street gangs, and adult criminal organizations is reported to be common in several states, particularly in Texas, according to the Joint Crime Information Center (2014).

Stage 5

In the fifth stage, more street gangs became more solidified and prominent, and prison gangs evolved. In concert with these developments, more violent gang activity ensued characteristic of "street gangs," keeping in mind that this term denotes gangs with older members that often commit more common urban crimes, especially assault, robbery, gun crimes, and murder. The significance of street gangs as a public safety matter was underscored in a Chicago Crime Commission (1995) report, *Gangs: Public Enemy Number One*. In 2007, Los Angeles Mayor Antonio Villaraigosa and Police Chief William Bratton released a list of the city's most dangerous gangs, promising to go after them with teams of police, federal agents, probation officers, and prosecutors—a modern-day war on gangs.

Following Chicago Mayor Daley's 1969 gang war and the large-scale incarceration of Chicago's Black gang members, Illinois prison administrators inadvertently strengthened prison gangs by using them to help maintain control of prisons, thus allowing them "to consolidate, form alliances, and grow in number and strength" (Venkatesh, 2000, p. 133). This "was perhaps the most important factor in their institutionalization" (Hagedorn, 2006, p. 203). Some of the gang leaders formed organizational networks both inside and outside prisons that linked inmates with others in jails and on the streets in illegal enterprises, creating what came to be called "webs," "supergangs" or "gang nations" such as the Black Kings Nation (Venkatesh, 2000, p. 134; see also Hagedorn, 2006; Spergel, 1990). By the mid-1980s, Latino, African American, and Caucasian gangs in Chicago and elsewhere across Illinois had merged for protection into two major coalitions in the state's prisons, the "People" (El Rukns, Vice Lords, Latin Kings, and others) and the "Folks" (Black Gangster Disciples, Latin Disciples, Spanish Cobras, and others). When gang members are released from custody, they often return to their neighborhoods of origin and renew old associations in their original street gang. Having done time and handled it successfully, they earned "rep" on the streets, particularly from fellow gang members and antagonists. If they resume prior criminal activity, the contacts made in the prison system will become more important.

Concentrations of gang violence in certain communities or neighborhoods of major gang cities have been well documented—particularly in Chicago (C. Block & Block, 1993) and Los Angeles (Hutson et al., 1995; Tita & Abrahamse, 2010). From 1987 to 1990, the four largest Chicago street gangs were also the most criminally active (C. Block & Block, 1993). They accounted for 69% of all street gang–motivated crimes and 56% of all street gang–motivated homicides. Hot spots of gang violence are set spaces and borders of gang territories. California researchers mapped the locations of 13 criminal street gangs in the East Los Angeles area where Chicano gangs first formed (Brantingham et al., 2012). As expected, ongoing intergang conflicts predominantly clustered along the boundaries between gangs' respective set spaces. Overall, more than 1,000 violent crimes (assault with a deadly weapon, attempted homicide, and homicide) occurred in the relatively small study area in a three-year period, 1999–2002. Sets of two of the very early gangs in that area, Cuatro Flats and White Fence gangs—presently in existence for nearly eight decades—accounted for much of the violence (Vigil, 2007). In 1996, at the height of gang violence in Chicago, R. Block's (2000) study showed that multiple-gang activity was observed in just 5% of the more than 25,000 grid squares citywide; however, "these squares accounted for 23.0% of the assaults and 44.3% of all drug-related incidents " (p. 379). Other research suggests that racial/ethnic transition in nearby tracts tends to elevate intergroup violence by both Black and Latino groups (Hipp et al., 2009).

An important caveat must be made regarding racial/ethnic involvement in gangs. As the gang history (Chapter 1) shows, the first gangs in the United States were White European ethnics. Following the immigration of people of color—particularly Blacks and Mexicans—gang members' color changed to black and brown, and with subsequent immigration, to a veritable "rainbow" of colors (Vigil, 2002). As noted in a study using data from the National Neighborhood Crime Study to examine the racial-spatial dynamic of violence, R. Peterson and Krivo's (2009; see also 2010) research on neighborhood crime rates in 2000 found that "proximity to more disadvantaged areas and especially to racially privileged (heavily white) areas is particularly critical in accounting for the large and visible inequality in violence found across neighborhoods of different colors" (p. 105). To be sure, there is a racial-spatial divide that channels life chances, opportunities, context, and outcomes in ways that make race matter through the life course—including, though not limited to, neighborhood context and involvement in youth/street gangs. Immigrant concentration appears to be less important than proximity to other hostile immigrant groups and conflict with dominant local groups (Griffiths & Chavez, 2004). Still, the influence of race and ethnicity on gang involvement is likely indirect. Readers are reminded that a key finding of early ecological studies in Chicago was that crime rates remained fairly stable in disorganized neighborhoods despite drastic changes in the ethnic and racial composition of those areas. So it is with gangs, there and elsewhere.

Other Macro-Level Theories

Three other macro-level theories are reviewed very briefly in this section. Our main purpose is to draw attention to societal-level theories that have currency for developing a fuller understanding of extreme deviance such as gangs and gang-related violence.

Underclass Theory

Auletta (1982) first used the *underclass* term to promote his characterization of socially dysfunctional behaviors among extremely poor minorities in New York City. W. Wilson (1987) then used the same term to capture the experiences of a highly disadvantaged African American population living in inner-city Chicago. Underclass theory proposes that in inner-city Black communities, the social impact of deindustrialization has been exacerbated by the departure of middle-class and working-class residents (W. Wilson, 1987, 1999). According to J. Moore (1998), those people who were able to relocate "were the beneficiaries of affirmative action in jobs and anti-segregation in housing" (p. 76). A distinguishable social class (the underclass) was created by a new set of demographic, technological, and economic conditions that had reduced the demand for low-skilled workers—permanently locking them out of the labor market and slicing off upward mobility routes that had been available to earlier generations. In her critique of this underclass theory, J. Moore (1998) argues that there are exceptions to disappearance of urban jobs for the lowest rungs of workers. "It should be noted that deindustrialization is not the only story: low-wage manufacturing—which, however is largely staffed with immigrant labor—has burgeoned in many cities, and, in addition, there has been growth of low-wage service jobs" (p. 76). Therefore, she prefers the term *economic restructuring* (the replacement of manufacturing work with service jobs) over underclass theory. As seen in Chapter 1, and as J. Moore and Pinderhughes (1993) assert, the underclass explanation was not applicable to the experience of the Mexican immigrant population in Los Angeles, or to other populations in several cities across the United States.

Routine Activities (Opportunity) Theory

Whereas purely macro-level theories attempt to explain why certain places heighten criminal motivations or gang activity, the routine activities theory (also called *opportunities theory*) (L. Cohen & Felson, 1979; Felson & Cohen, 1980) assumes that criminal propensity is present and intends to account for the opportunities that motivated offenders have to victimize other people or property. These opportunities consist of attractive or suitable targets (e.g., vulnerable persons with money, unlocked automobiles) and a lack of capable guardians. It is the convergence of motivated offenders, suitable targets, and lack of capable guardians in time and place that accounts for the nonrandom distribution of crime and violence in this theory. Wikstrom and Treiber's (2009) situational theory of violence suggests that certain persistent forms of violence may be driven by habitual processes, which occur in a setting that the actor regularly takes part in and which consistently present opportunities or frictions conducive to violence, and few deterrents. Examples include

> gang violence, which occurs in specific geographic areas (territories), presents regular opportunities and frictions (via the presence of fellow gang members, rival gang members and those "transgressing" on gang "turf") and few controls (is regulated by the rules of gang membership). (p. 89)

Indeed, such gang settings tend to become familiar for regular members, thus automating expected responses.

Griffiths and Chavez (2004) extend routine activities, or opportunity theory, in suggesting that certain other community characteristics may increase criminal opportunities. "For instance . . . increases in criminal facilitators (for example, guns), and demographic changes (for example, increases in young males who become involved in gangs) may explain large changes in crime and violence over a relatively short time" (p. 945). Griffiths and Chavez suggest that "neighborhoods may demonstrate differences in quantity and lethal violence, not only between one another at any given time, but also within their own boundaries over time. That is, they may have distinct trajectories" (p. 943). Following Clarke (1995), Griffiths and Chavez (2004) call attention to increases in guns and increases in young males who join gangs as "facilitators" that "may explain large changes in crime and violence over a relatively short time" (p. 945). In other words, such changes "need not, counter to the expectations of social disorganization theory, accompany structural or demographic changes in neighborhoods" (p. 945).

Griffiths and Chavez (2004) demonstrate in their space and time analysis that gun homicide trends from 1980 to 1995 were volatile in the most violent communities—in which social disorganization theory would predict stable high rates. Moreover, they extend routine activities/opportunity theory in finding some "high and increasing street gun communities" that surrounded the most violent ones. This finding, they suggest, provides "tentative support for the proposition that facilitators, such as guns, increase homicide victimization by bringing together victims and offenders in time and space, but that these opportunities diminish as one moves farther from the violent core" (p. 970). Without question, the same observation applies to street gangs.

Conflict Theory

The history of street gangs discussed in Chapter 1 provides a plethora of conflict examples. In New York City, after 1840, gang warfare replicated ethnic conflict in the climate of economic restructuring and intense competition for jobs. By the 1940s, three-way race riots involved Italian Americans, Puerto Ricans, and African Americans in East Harlem. In the 1990s, post–World War II urban renewal, slum clearances, and ethnic migration pitted gangs of African American, Puerto Rican, and Euro-American youth against each other in battles in New York City to dominate changing neighborhoods.

Chicago's early history saw large Irish gangs terrorizing the German, Jewish, and Polish immigrants who settled there from the 1870s to the 1890s. The reigning Irish gang, Ragen's Colts, attacked both Mexican American and Black youth, in marking the racialized boundaries of "their" space. The race riot of 1919, in which Black males united to confront hostile White gang members who were terrorizing the Black community, also contributed directly to gang formation. Partly in response to growing racial and ethnic violence, Black, Puerto Rican, and Mexican American gangs alike proliferated in the late 1950s.

In Los Angeles, physical and cultural marginalization (Vigil, 1988, 2002, 2008) gave rise to street gangs of Mexican origin, and two interracial events in the 1940s proved pivotal in the growth of Mexican American gangs in the West: the Sleepy Lagoon murder and the zoot suit riots. Later, both Alonso (2004) and Cureton (2009) suggest the Black civil rights movement (1955 to 1965) produced an underclass-specific, socially disorganized, and isolated Black community. Several gang historians show that the resurgence of new emerging street groups in Chicago and Los Angeles coincided with the political, social, and civil rights movements, particularly the Black Panther Party and the U.S. Organization (both of which were racially motivated entities) (Alonso, 2004; Cureton, 2009; Diamond, 2001). According to Alonso (2004), "Racialization and disenfranchisement of Black youth in specific geographic locales was a driving force behind initial gang formation" in Los Angeles (p. 669).

In each of these three cities, public housing isolated and ghettoized large numbers of Blacks and Mexican Americans and served to incubate more gangs with greater capacities for violence. From his study comparing Chicago with several European cities, Wacquant (2007) tells us that a form of *neo-apartheid* characterizes major American cities, Chicago in particular—the most racially segregated of all American cities, he claims—that produced the *hyper-ghetto*, in which there are no governing rules and regulations. The victims experience what Wacquant calls *advanced marginality*, which may account for a variety of violent social conflicts, gang violence included.

These examples of ganging as a consequence of ethnic and racial conflict amidst extreme disadvantage and dislocation from the labor market are consistent with conflict theorists' views of the origins of crime being rooted in social inequality. Moreover, the reciprocal effects of gang involvement and disadvantage are heightened by the heavy hand of law enforcement (and mass incarceration more broadly) encompassing nearly entire communities (Brunson, 2007; Clear, 2009; Wacquant, 2001). The subsequent effects of a criminal record on labor force participation (Pager, 2003), family formation (Lopoo & Western, 2005), and child welfare (Wakefield & Wildeman, 2013) tend to reinforce criminal opportunities, as legitimate opportunities wane.

◈ Concluding Observations

This chapter has drawn attention to macro-level theories of crime and gang-related indicators. Social disorganization theory has received substantial empirical support. The central thesis of this theory is that ethnic heterogeneity, low socioeconomic status, and residential mobility reduce the capacity of community residents to control crime. Three earlier reviews of research that tested social disorganization theory suggested a modest relationship between neighborhood structural disadvantage and delinquency, violence, and other child, adolescent, and adult behaviors (Bursik & Grasmick, 1993; Sampson et al., 2002; Sampson & Groves, 1989).

A more systematic and inclusive review indicates that the strength of the evidence in favor of social disorganization theory as an explanation of crime is more robust when compared with other ecological theories of crime. This observation comes from Pratt and Cullen's (2005) systematic review (employing meta-analysis) of more than 200 studies of ecological correlates of crime. "Concentrated neighborhood disadvantage" (most commonly measured in terms of racial heterogeneity, poverty, and family disruption) proved to be the strongest and most consistent predictor of crime. "Across all studies, social disorganization and resource/economic deprivation theories receive strong empirical support; anomie/strain, social support/social altruism, and routine activity theories receive moderate support; and deterrence/rational choice and subcultural theories receive weak support" (p. 373). In examining the strength and stability of macro-level predictors, Pratt and Cullen's systematic review revealed that just five of these scored high on *both strength of effects and stability* across studies: (1) percent non-White, (2) percent Black, (3) poverty, (4) family disruption, and (5) the effect of incarceration on crime rates. Unemployment, low firearms ownership, collective efficacy, religion, and unsupervised peer groups are other variables that scored *high on strength of effects*. Racial heterogeneity and residential mobility were among six variables that showed *moderate strength of effects and stability* across studies (along with household activity ratio, social support/altruism, inequality, and urbanism).

The second noteworthy observation is that support for social disorganization theory as an explanation of gang membership and gang violence is substantial. Several studies reviewed in this chapter suggest a relationship that is conditioned on the features of the supporting research, such as samples, research methods, and level of analysis (individual, micro, and macro). Arguably most important, Pyrooz and colleagues (2010) demonstrated the generalizable effects of economic disadvantage and racial and ethnic heterogeneity on gang membership rates, in the 100 largest U.S. cities with National Youth Gang Survey data. Other city-level studies showed strong relationships between social disorganization and gang violence in multiple-year data, in Chicago and in St. Louis. Coupling these results with Pyrooz and colleagues' (2010) national analysis provides additional support for social disorganization theory as an explanation of gang presence and associated violence.

However, even social disorganization theory is inadequate to account for the variability in cities' gang activity trajectories and distinctive gang homicide trajectory patterns (discussed in Chapter 7). As Griffiths and Chavez (2004) note, "Overall, there is little theoretical work on how [temporal changes in violence] may manifest over time and across space in urban areas" (p. 946). In Chapter 8, we incorporate community-level mediators, including aspects of the socioeconomic structure (increased unemployment), and increases in criminal facilitators (street gun usage) to help account for gang-related homicide trends. This research suggests that neighborhoods experiencing homicide increases along with growing street gun weaponry might also be spaces that experience drug markets or gang activity. Indeed, the highest-rate homicide neighborhoods in Chicago were located within the turfs of the notorious Vice Lords or the Black Gangster Disciples.

With these theories in mind, we presented in this chapter several macrohistorical (e.g., racism and riots) and macrostructural (e.g., immigration and ghetto/barrio living) events and conditions that largely account for gang formation, expansion, and associated violence. We organized key factors in five stages. In Stage 1, conditions of social disorganization in cities led to family disorganization, low neighborhood control, and youth alienation in Stage 2. In turn, these indicators of social disorganization fueled the formation of youth subcultures, aggression, group conflicts, and youth gangs in Stage 3. Next, social policies of public housing (especially high-rise buildings), enormous prison population expansion, gun availability, and drug trafficking opportunities in Stage 4 led, in turn, to more formidable street and prison gangs, and increased and more lethal gang violence in Stage 5.

DISCUSSION TOPICS

1. How did the early social disorganization theories provide a foundation for later theories?

2. Is social disorganization theory still relevant to modern-day gangs? Why or why not?

3. How much of modern-day gang activity does each of the most relevant macro-level theories explain? Arrange them in a pie chart with social disorganization theory and justify the relative proportion.

4. Critique the authors' five-stage theory of gang formation, expansion, and associated violence. Strengths? Weaknesses?

5. Can the most popular gang theories explain *hot spots* and *set space* influences on gang violence?

RECOMMENDATIONS FOR FURTHER READING

Collective Efficacy

Bursik, R. J., Jr., & Grasmick, H. G. (1993). *Neighborhoods and crime: The dimensions of effective community control.* New York: Lexington.

Morenoff, J. D., Sampson, R. J., & Raudenbush, S. W. (2001). Neighborhood inequality, collective efficacy, and the spatial dynamics of urban violence. *Criminology, 39,* 517–559.

Papachristos, A. V., & Kirk, D. S. (2006). Neighborhood effects on street gang behavior. In J. F. Short & L. A. Hughes (Eds.), *Studying youth gangs* (pp. 63–84). Lanham, MD: AltaMira Press.

Sampson, R. J. (2002). The community. In J. Petersilia & J. Q. Wilson (Eds.), *Crime: Public policies for crime control* (pp. 225–252). Oakland, CA: Institute for Contemporary Studies Press.

Short, J. F., Jr., & Hughes, L. A. (2010). Promoting research integrity in community-based intervention research. In R. J. Chaskin (Ed.), *Youth gangs and community intervention: Research, practice, and evidence* (pp. 127–151). New York: Columbia University Press.

Tita, G. E., Riley, K. J., & Greenwood, P. (2005). *Reducing gun violence: Operation Ceasefire in Los Angeles.* Washington, DC: National Institute of Justice.

Conflict Theory

Alonso, A. A. (2004). Racialized identities and the formation of black gangs in Los Angeles. *Urban Geography, 25,* 658–674.

Arredondo, G. F. (2004). Navigating ethno-racial currents: Mexicans in Chicago, 1919–1939. *Journal of Urban History, 30,* 399–427.

Cureton, S. R. (2009). Something wicked this way comes: A historical account of Black gangsterism offers wisdom and warning for African American leadership. *Journal of Black Studies, 40,* 347–361.

Currie, E. (1998). *Crime and punishment in America.* New York: Henry Holt.

Diamond, A. J. (2009). *Mean streets: Chicago youths and the everyday struggle for empowerment in the multiracial city, 1908–1969.* Berkley: University of California Press.

Gurr, T. R. (1989). *Violence in America.* Newbury Park, CA: Sage.

Hagedorn, J. M. (2006). Race, not space: A revisionist history of gangs in Chicago. *Journal of African American History, 91,* 194–208.

Hawkins, D. F. (2011). Things fall apart: Revisiting race and ethnic differences in criminal violence amidst a crime drop. *Race and Justice, 1,* 3–48.

West, C. (1993). *Race matters.* Boston: Beacon.

Wilson, W. J. (1987). *The truly disadvantaged: The underclass and public policy.* Chicago: University of Chicago Press.

Social Disorganization and Gang Activity

Curry, G. D., & Spergel, I. A. (1988). Gang homicide, delinquency and community. *Criminology, 26,* 381–405.

Griffiths, E., & Chavez, J. M. (2004). Communities, street guns and homicide trajectories in Chicago, 1980–1995: Merging methods for examining homicide trends across space and time. *Criminology, 42,* 941–975.

Hipp, J. R., Tita, G. E., & Boggess, L. N. (2009). Intergroup and intragroup violence: Is violent crime an expression of group conflict or social disorganization? *Criminology, 47,* 521–564.

Krohn, M. D., Schmidt, N. M., Lizotte, A. J., & Baldwin, J. M. (2011). The impact of multiple marginality on gang membership and delinquent behavior for Hispanic, African American, and White male adolescents. *Journal of Contemporary Criminal Justice, 27,* 18–42.

Mares, D. (2010). Social disorganization and gang homicides in Chicago: A neighborhood level comparison of disaggregated homicides. *Youth Violence and Juvenile Justice, 8,* 38–57.

Monti, D. J. (1993). Gangs in more- and less-settled communities. In S. Cummings & D. J. Monti (Eds.), *Gangs: The origins and impact of contemporary youth gangs in the United States* (pp. 219–253). Albany: State University of New York Press.

Moore, J. W. (1978). *Homeboys: Gangs, drugs and prison in the barrios of Los Angeles.* Philadelphia: Temple University Press.

Papachristos, A. V., & Kirk, D. S. (2006). Neighborhood effects on street gang behavior. In J. F. Short & L. A. Hughes (Eds.), *Studying youth gangs* (pp. 63–84). Lanham, MD: AltaMira Press.

Pyrooz, D. C., Fox, A. M., & Decker, S. H. (2010). Racial and ethnic heterogeneity, economic disadvantage, and gangs: A macro-level study of gang membership in urban America. *Justice Quarterly, 14,* 1–26.

Shaw, C. R., & McKay, H. D. (1969). *Juvenile delinquency and urban areas* (2nd ed.). Chicago: University of Chicago Press.

Suttles, G. D. (1968). *The social order of the slum: Ethnicity and territory in the inner city.* Chicago: University of Chicago Press.

Whyte, W. F. (1943a). Social organization in the slums. *The American Sociological Review, 8,* 34–39.

Whyte, W. (1943b). *Street corner society: The social structure of an Italian slum.* Chicago: University of Chicago Press.

NOTE

1. The term *collective efficacy* (informal social control and social cohesion) was created to describe this dimension of community disorganization (Sampson & Laub, 1997; Sampson, Raudenbush, & Earls, 1997). According to Sampson and colleagues (1997), "Collective efficacy refers to the process of activating or converting social ties to achieve any number of collective goals, such as public order or the control of crime" (p. 919). More specifically, "It is the linkage of mutual trust and the shared will to intervene for the public good that captures the neighborhood context of what [these schol term *collective efficacy*" (Sampson, Morenoff, & Gannon-Rowley, 2002, p. 457). Sampson and colleagues (1997) suggest this form of community or neighhood organization refers to cooperative efforts in defining, monitoring, and condemning undesirable behaviors that occur within a community. Examples include a willingness to intervene in such everyday situations as graffiti spray painting, truant children hanging out on a street corner, a fight in front of one's house, and a disrespectful child.

CHAPTER 5

Micro-Level Theories

Gang Involvement as a Developmental Pathway

◈ Introduction

The theories reviewed in Chapter 4 help explain the existence of gangs. In this chapter, the focus is on individuals and how they become involved in gangs. Like other adolescent problem behaviors, gang involvement develops gradually over time, and life-course development theories (Elder, 1985, 1997) best illuminate this process. Two technical terms that are used in this chapter require some explanation. First, a *developmental pathway* refers to patterned sequences of behaviors, such as patterns of delinquency from less serious problem behaviors to more serious offenses, or from minor delinquency to gang involvement, and in turn to serious property and violent crimes. Second, *trajectories* refer to larger classes or groups of individuals who differ in a behavioral trait or crime pattern over time, such as early onset versus late onset of delinquency. Both developmental pathways that include gang membership and gang members as a trajectory group are the focus of our attention in this chapter.

◈ Developmental Theories

Developmental theories have achieved widespread acceptance because these explain onset, escalation, course maintenance, de-escalation, and desistance in individuals' delinquent and criminal careers (Howell et al., 2014). Overall, the percentage of youth involved in delinquency increases from late childhood (ages 7–12) to middle adolescence (ages 13–16) where it peaks, and the down-slope of the age-crime curve represents the decrease in criminal activities from late adolescence (ages 17–19) into early adulthood (ages 20–25) (Loeber, Farrington, Howell, & Hoeve, 2012). Taken together, these four groups correspond with the bell shape of the age-crime curve or trajectory (Farrington, Loeber, & Jolliffe,

2008). However, high-risk/high-rate (e.g., the most prolific) offenders dominate among juveniles and young adults (Macleod, Groves, & Farrington, 2012). So it is with gang members: They too join in late childhood, become increasingly active in middle adolescence, and generally desist from gang activity in late adolescence. But there is unevenness in this general pattern; some youth join gangs at a very early age, and others, a bit later. Some youth remain involved for a short period of time; others, longer. We begin with consideration of broader developmental pathways to serious and violent behavior because gang involvement is embedded within delinquency careers.

To fully grasp the nature of gang members' careers, it is useful to first consider how gang involvement grows out of a juvenile delinquency pathway. Almost invariably, youths who join a gang had previously been involved in delinquent behavior. From this perspective, gang joining is a stepping stone in a longer pathway of delinquency involvement that spans the period from childhood to adolescence and into adulthood. In Focus 5.1 provides an example of the timing of gang membership relative to other problem behaviors in the oldest sample of Pittsburgh youth.

IN FOCUS 5.1
PITTSBURGH YOUTH STUDY: AGE OF ONSET OF PROBLEM AND CRIMINAL BEHAVIORS

Behavior (mean age in parentheses)

alcohol use (12.0)

serious theft (13.1)

tobacco use (13.2)

serious violence (14.6)

gang membership (15.4)

hard drug use (15.6)

marijuana use (15.7)

drug dealing (16.2)

gun carrying (17.3)

Source: Loeber, Farrington, Stouthamer-Loeber, White, & Wei, 2008, p. 150 (oldest cohort).

Developmental Delinquency Pathways

Loeber and colleagues (1997, 1999) discovered three main but overlapping pathways in the development of delinquency from childhood to adolescence (Figure 5.1). These are the authority conflict pathway, the covert pathway, and the overt pathway. The authority conflict pathway consists of pre-delinquent offenses, the covert pathway consists of concealing and serious property offenses, and

Figure 5.1   Developmental Pathways to Serious and Violent Behavior

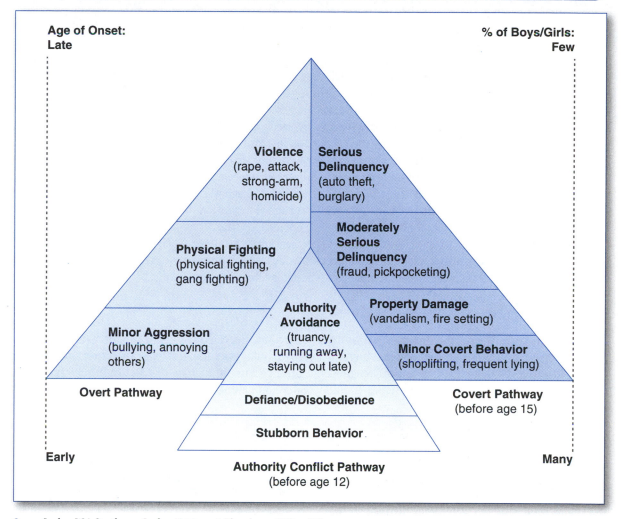

Source: Loeber, Wei, Stouthamer-Loeber, Huizinga, & Thornberry, 1999, p. 247.

the overt pathway consists of violent offenses. Loeber's pathways model has four important dimensions. First, the model shows an orderly progression over time from less serious to more serious offenses and delinquent behaviors—in actual behaviors that were charted by the research team. Second, the progressively narrowing width of the triangles in this figure illustrates the decreasing proportion of youth (from *many* to *few*) involved in particular problem behaviors and delinquent offenses. Third, the model shows the general age of onset (from *early* to *late*). Fourth, the pathways are hierarchical in that those who have advanced to the most serious behavior in each of the pathways usually have displayed persistent problem behaviors characteristic of the earlier stages in each pathway.

Problem behavior typically begins in the authority conflict pathway with stubborn behavior, followed by defiance or disobedience, then truancy, running away, or staying out late. Persistent offenders then typically move into either the overt pathway or the covert pathway. The first stage of the covert pathway is minor concealed behavior (shoplifting, frequent lying); this is followed by property damage (vandalism, fire setting) and then moderately serious (fraud, pickpocketing) and serious delinquency (auto theft, burglary). The first stage of the overt pathway is minor aggression (bullying, annoying others); physical fighting follows (often including gang fighting) and then more serious violence (rape, physical attacks, and strong-arm robbery). Thus, gang involvement (gang fighting) is an intermediate step in the overt pathway.

With age, Loeber, Burke, and Pardini (2009) reported a large proportion of Pittsburgh Youth Study boys progressed on two or three pathways, indicative of an increasing variety of behaviors over time. In particular, boys who were escalating in the overt pathway were more likely to progress in the covert pathway. This model also accounted for the self-reported high-rate offenders and court-reported delinquents. Kelley, Loeber, Keenan, and DeLamatre (1997) and Loeber and colleagues' (1999) validated the model on delinquents in Denver and Rochester samples, while Tolan and Gorman-Smith (1998) confirmed it in a Chicago study and in a nationally representative sample of adolescents (the National Youth Survey). The pathways model has also been largely replicated for girls (Gorman-Smith & Loeber, 2005; Loeber, Slot, & Stouthamer-Loeber, 2007), and this developmental model clearly illustrates how gang involvement is intertwined with other delinquent behavior, most prominently indicated by frequent gang fighting.

Developmental Theories

Several other developmental theories of delinquency have received empirical support (see Table 5.1). While few of these address co-offending, each of them holds potential for application to an individual's involvement in gangs. This is a challenging enterprise because numerous risk factors of relevance have been revealed in longitudinal studies, in multiple developmental domains, and with potentially varying influence across age levels.

Life-course–persistent and adolescence-limited offenders

Moffitt (1993) identified two main groups of offenders in the childhood and adolescent period: life-course–persistent offenders and adolescence-limited offenders. Life-course–persistent offenders begin offending in childhood, and adolescence-limited offenders begin their offending later. According to Moffitt, four characteristics distinguish life-course–persistent offenders: (1) early onset of offending, (2) active offending during adolescence, (3) escalation of offense seriousness, and (4) persistence in crime in adulthood. However, in the Rochester Youth Development Study, eight groups with diverging patterns of juvenile offending were observed, prompting Thornberry (2005) to conclude that "offending can start earlier or later, but onset is not distinctly divided into neat patterns of *early starters* and *late starters*" (p. 160). Our preference is to use the term *stable* when referring to multi-year gang members, and to use *serious, violent, and chronic* when referring to offenders who persist and advance to the highest levels in Loeber's serious property and violence pathways.

Life-course developmental theory

The key construct in Sampson and Laub's (1993, 2005) developmental theory is age-graded informal social control, particularly the strength of bonding to family, peers, schools, and later adult social

Table 5.1 Leading Life-Course Developmental Theories

Theory	Primary Scholar(s)
Age-graded informal social control	Sampson & Laub, 1993, 2005
Coercion/early onset model	Patterson et al., 1991
Developmental pathways/theory	Loeber, 1996; Loeber et al., 2007
Life-course–persistent and adolescence-limited offenders	Moffitt, 1993
Integrated cognitive antisocial potential (ICAP) theory	Farrington, 2003, 2005, 2006
Integrative multilayered control	LeBlanc, 1993
Interactional	Thornberry, 1987, 2005; Thornberry & Krohn, 2001; Thornberry, Krohn, et al., 2003; Thornberry, Lizotte, et al., 2003
Multiple marginalization	Vigil, 2002, 2006, 2008
Social development model	Catalano & Hawkins, 1996
Strain/differential opportunity	Cloward & Ohlin, 1960; Agnew, 2005
A unified theory of gang involvement	Wood & Alleyne, 2010

institutions (marriage and jobs). This theory received some research support by viewing gang membership as a turning point in the life course (Melde & Esbensen, 2011), finding that gang membership tends to impact attitudes, emotions, and behavior in a negative manner consistent with Sampson and Laub's (2005) turning point framework. The authors suggest that gang interventions can be most effective if they provide youth with means of building social capital, such as improved relationships with prosocial peer networks, school officials, and their families.

"To me it was my life, my one and only way . . . They were like my brothers and sisters. I mean, at that time, that's the only thing I had. It was them and my grandparents." —Anonymous male member of the Hoya Maravilla gang (in J. Moore, 1991, pp. 76–77)

Interactional theory

Thornberry and Krohn's encompassing interactional theory (Thornberry, 2005; Thornberry & Krohn, 2001, 2005; Thornberry, Krohn, et al., 2003) accounts for patterns of *onset, course length and shape*, and *desistance*. A key premise is that risk factors for gang membership are found in several interacting domains, including individual, family, peer, school, and neighborhood, and that different domains are more influential at different developmental stages in childhood and adolescence. In the initial test of this theory, school bonding and association with antisocial peers had significant effects on the odds of gang membership later in adolescence (Thornberry, Krohn, et al., 2003). The interactional feature of this theory is important. For example, delinquency involvement may worsen family life, which may weaken parental controls and in turn increase the likelihood of gang joining.

Multiple marginality theory

Vigil's (2002, 2006, 2008) theoretical explanation for Mexican American gang membership is that the social, cultural, ecological, and economical "marginalization" of youth that these and other immigrant people face in the United States create conditions that undermine traditional social control institutions, particularly family and school—as seen in Chapter 1. Vigil suggested that these extreme forces—macrohistorical (racism and repression) and macrostructural (immigration and ghetto/barrio living)—combine to strain and undermine social control and bonds with the family and school and also diminish respect for law enforcement. Having been left out of mainstream society because of language, education, cultural, structural, and economic barriers, this situation

> relegates these urban youths to the margins of society in practically every sense. This positioning leaves them with few options or resources to better their lives. Often, they seek a place where they are not marginalized—and find it in the streets. (2002, p. 7)

Because the complexity of Vigil's theory presents unusual measurement challenges, particularly the macrohistorical and macrostructural factors, researchers have only partially tested it to date. Nevertheless, Freng and Esbensen (2007) and Krohn, Schmidt, and colleagues (2011) generally found support for Vigil's theory for explaining current gang membership. More extensive validation of Vigil's theory should be forthcoming as the measurement issues are resolved. Without doubt, Telles and Ortiz's (2008) and Waters (1999) multi-intergenerational studies demonstrated that gang involvement is most pronounced among Mexican American youth in the second generation of migrants. Studies also show, because of the successful assimilation of early European migrant groups into American society, that gangs had virtually disappeared by the third generation (Telles & Ortiz, 2008; Waters, 1999). Assimilation of Mexican American and Black peoples into American society has not progressed so smoothly.

> "It was the most important thing in my life at that time. There was nothing that came even close to it except maybe my own personal family. But even then…my gang life was my one love." —Anonymous male member of the Hoya Maravilla gang (in J. Moore, 1991, p. 77)

Social development model

The social development model (Catalano & Hawkins, 1996) specifies hypotheses regarding the relationships among risk and protective factors in the etiology of both prosocial and antisocial behaviors. This model has been adapted to gang involvement (Gilman, Hill, Hawkins, Howell, & Kosterman, 2014). Briefly, "the theory hypothesizes two parallel, but distinct developmental pathways, one reflecting prosocial opportunities, involvement, rewards, bonding, and beliefs and the other reflecting antisocial opportunities, involvement, rewards, bonding, and beliefs" (p. 207). Gilman, Hill, Hawkins, and colleagues (2014) demonstrated the relevance of this developmental theory to adolescent gang membership in finding that neighborhood and peer antisocial environments and gang exposure (living with a gang member) strongly predicted gang joining. Unexpectedly, this research also showed that the effects of risk and protective factors did not vary with age, through age 19. The study authors suggest that this finding may be owing to the multiple studies showing that gang members are distinctively different from ordinary delinquents in that they possess more risk factors and generally experience them in multiple developmental domains during childhood and early adolescence, thereby generating enduring effects (Esbensen et al., 2010; Hill et al., 1999; Thornberry, Krohn, et al., 2003). Similarly, R. A. Gordon and colleagues (2014) found that developmental, familial, and contextual risk factors generalize across combinations of criminal activity, that is, the pairing of extreme violence with drug selling or combining drug selling and serious theft.

◈ Location of Gang Membership in Developmental Pathways

This section highlights research on the importance of the gang membership stage in the formation of youngsters' criminal pathways. The first studies to examine delinquency offending patterns among gang members along a developmental pathway before, during, and after boys are active gang members were conducted in Rochester, New York (Thornberry, Krohn, et al., 1993), Denver, Colorado (Esbensen & Huizinga, 1993), Pittsburgh, Pennsylvania (R. A. Gordon et al., 2004, 2014), and Seattle, Washington (Hill, Chung, Guo, & Hawkins, 2002; Krohn & Thornberry). This pattern has also been found in Canada (Gatti et al., 2005; Haviland & Nagin, 2005; Haviland, Nagin, Rosenbaum, & Tremblay, 2008) and Norway (Bendixen, Endresen, & Olweus, 2006).

In sum, evidence is plentiful in a number of longitudinal studies that youth gangs facilitate or promote increased involvement in delinquency, violence, drug use, and carrying a weapon (Krohn & Thornberry, 2008). In comparison with non-members, both short-term and stable gang members (multi-year participation) have significantly higher rates of self-reported crime in the Rochester gang study. Huizinga (2010) finds that multi-year gang members (two or more years) in Denver represented only 8% of the youth yet they committed 71% of all serious crimes. Thornberry (1998) notes the finding that gang involvement increases youths' criminality as "one of the most robust and consistent observations in criminological research" (p. 147).

R. A. Gordon and colleagues' (2014) recent analysis of Pittsburgh Youth Study data has filled an important gap in this line of research: the extent to which gang membership is associated with *simultaneous* engagement in *multiple* criminal behaviors. This research extended prior longitudinal studies by showing that gang-involved youth were especially likely to combine multiple types of crimes, particularly in two combinations (serious violence and drug selling; and serious violence, drug selling, and serious theft), and these multiple patterns of criminal activity were most elevated during periods of active gang participation. In fact, the increase was enormous, four to five times higher during waves of active gang membership than during waves before or after gang membership up to age 28.

Gang membership also affects the life trajectory of youth. In a national sample, youth who joined gangs were 30% less likely to graduate from high school and 58% less likely to earn a four-year degree than their matched peers (Pyrooz, 2014a). Arnett (2000) drew attention to this period of "emerging adulthood"—approximately 18–25 years of age when people have emerged out of adolescence but have not established themselves as young adults. Even in short periods of engagement, gang membership disrupts this process of becoming well-adjusted adults. Krohn, Ward, and colleagues (2011) found that gang membership was related to precocious transitions into adulthood that then predicted disrupted family relationships, economic instability, and criminal behaviors at the age of 30 years. Gilman, Hill, and Hawkins (2014) found that the effects of gang membership extended well into adulthood (age 33). Compared to their nongang peers, for those who reported joining a gang in adolescence, gang membership predicted lower rates of high school graduation, poor general health, depression, drug abuse or dependence, self-reported crime, official felony conviction, and incarceration in adulthood.

Figure 5.2 classifies individuals according to their gang membership over time (i.e., trajectory groups), from ages 10 to 23 in respondents to the National Longitudinal Survey of Youth 1997 (NLSY), a nationally representative sample of 8,984 persons. Pyrooz (2014b) identifies four main trajectory groups: adolescence limited (33%), late adolescence (26%), adult onset (17%), and early adolescence only (14%). The two remaining groups are not of sufficient size for practical significance: early persistent (6%, 43 individuals nationwide) and late persistent (4%, only 29 persons).

One might call these trajectory groups *age-gang membership curves*, analogous to the *age-crime curve* described earlier. The modal age of gang membership in this sample is 15. The first two trajectory groups, composing the majority (59%) of gang members in the age-member curves, show patterns of

Figure 5.2   Distinct Trajectories of Gang Membership in the Life Course

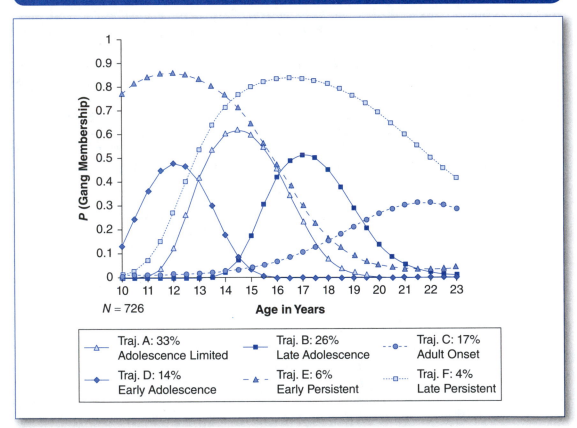

Source: Pyrooz, 2014b, p. 360

gang membership consistently reported in several longitudinal studies, in Denver, Montreal, Pittsburgh, Rochester, Seattle, and in the multi-city GREAT samples: a sharp increase in gang joining in late childhood or early adolescence, a peak in membership around ages 14–17, and a sharp decline thereafter, forming the classic bell curve. What is unique in this analysis is the sizeable group of (largely) adult onset members, making up 17% of the sample. Discounting that about one-third of this group had joined by age 17, this still is a substantively important group from a developmental standpoint. Past gang studies have not searched for persons who join gangs in adulthood. Thus, Pyrooz's research fills a gap with respect to the shape of age-gang member trajectories. However, broad surveys of young adults such as the NLSY may not be representative of members of gangs that are responsible for most of the violence associated with these because those gang members are not distributed evenly across the United States. Rather, those participants are concentrated in several respects, particularly in urban areas, and further, within specific neighborhoods and communities of large cities. To illustrate the discrepancy that can occur, looking at race/ethnicity, in Pyrooz's analysis of the NLSY data, the predominant racial/ethnic group is White persons. However, serious gang violence across the United States overwhelmingly involves members of color, both as victims and as perpetrators (Howell, 1999; Maxson, 1999).

◈ A Developmental Model of Gang Involvement

A central question is this: Why are some youth at high risk of joining a gang? There are two equally important perspectives on this matter. As Reckless, Dinitz, and Murray (1956) noted in the juvenile delinquency field, two sets of forces are at work. The first set is called *pulls*, or gang attractions, and an opposite set of forces is called *pushes*, or risk factors that may propel youth toward gangs. The latter set is the main focus of this chapter.

Perceived Benefits of Joining a Gang: Gang Attractions

Early gang research suggested that gang joining is a somewhat natural process. Thrasher (1927/2000) initially viewed the typical gang member as a rather well-adjusted American boy seeking an outlet for normal adolescent drives for adventure and expression. More recent gang studies have refuted this romanticized view of what gangs offer young candidates. A male gang leader expressed succinctly the main attractions of the gang in response to a question posed to him in the course of an interview. Hardman (1969) asked him what additional questions might be included in the interviews of other gang members to obtain a better understanding of the reasons why youths join gangs. He replied (quoted verbatim here):

> Ask them about feelin's of not bein' wanted at home; ask them about feelin' left out; ask them about the gang makin' up for some of these things they didn't get at home, y'know; ask them about the gang makin' them feel important, wanted, needed. Ask them about the feelin' of security that it gives you, always knowin' you got the guys backin' you up. Ask them about the feelin' of importance that they get from bein' in the gang. (p. 179)

Vigil (2002) helps further illustrate the attraction of gang membership as follows:

> What established gangs in the neighborhood have to offer is nurture, protection, friendship, emotional support, and other ministrations for unattended, un-chaperoned resident youths. In

other words, street socialization fills the voids left by inadequate parenting and schooling, especially inadequate familial care and supervision. This street-based process molds the youth to conform to the ways of the street. (p. 10)

In an 11-city study, Esbensen and colleagues (1999) compiled the following reasons youth reported for joining a gang, in the order of descending importance:

- For protection
- For fun
- For respect
- For money
- Because a friend was in the gang

Of these reasons, most studies relay that youth commonly join gangs for the safety they believe the gang provides, particularly in urban areas. Gangs are often at the center of appealing social action, including hanging out, music, drugs, and opportunities to socialize with members of the opposite sex. In other words, the gang may be appealing because it meets a youth's social needs. Decker and Van Winkle (1996) found youth also reported, albeit far less frequently, more instrumental reasons for joining a gang such as drug selling or making money. J. Moore's (1978) and Vigil's (1988) early ethnographic studies noted the strong influence of friends and family members who already are part of the gang, especially for Mexican American youth. More recent student surveys also show the importance of family ties for all racial/ethnic groups (Gilman, Hill, Hawkins, et al., 2014; D. Peterson, Taylor, & Esbensen, 2004). In many cases, youth view the gang as a surrogate family.

"We are not just Bloods, this is my blood. They are my family."—Ronny (in Leap, 2012, p. 71)

IN FOCUS 5.2
SAN DIEGO MEXICAN AMERICAN GANGS

The San Diego Mexican American gangs Sanders (1994) studied had a strong social orientation, focused on action events, status, and "kicking back." Action consisted of risk-taking activities. Status ensued from belonging to a gang that was feared or respected by other gangs in the community. Kicking back meant hanging out with other members, partying, drinking, and taking drugs. Although heavy drug users, they rarely were involved in trafficking (pp. 137–138).

These gangs were organized around cliques and barrios. A given barrio might have one or more gangs, although typically only one. Each gang consisted of age-grade cliques, each of which had one or more informal leaders. Sanders (1994) characterized these gangs as having more of the *influential* leader model of organization than the *horizontal* structure commonly found among Chicano gangs in Los Angeles. Strong solidarity grounded in the barrio identity held each gang and clique within it together. The continued existence of barrios gave stability to even inactive gangs.

Unlike the Black gangs described by Jankowski (1991) and Keiser (1969), the San Diego Black gangs (Crips and Bloods) that Sanders (1994) studied were not highly organized, but very large and divided into allied branches. Each of the branch territories was made up of sets. Their lack of organization was related in part to the fact that their territories were large, according to Sanders, because of their money-making enterprises. Each gang was made up of hardcore, affiliate, and fringe members. Because of the age cohorts, leadership structure, and limited number of hardcore members, these gangs were constantly in flux.

Sanders (1994) suggests that gangs ebb and flow from inactive neighborhood street groups to active fighting gangs with the incorporation of each new cohort of members. "As a new age cohort of boys comes into the gang, the level of activity rises. After a time, they either make their names, become more aware of the risks they are taking, or become cowed by the police or other gangs. When this occurs, the gang's activity subsides" (p. 61).

Source: Based on Sanders, 1994.

Romantic interests are another factor. Many female adolescents are attracted to gang life through their boyfriends. One study placed the research spotlight on San Antonio, Texas, girls who never joined the gang (Petersen & Valdez, 2004, 2005; Av. Valdez, 2007). They began hanging out with gang boys in childhood, just before age 12, and at the time of the study, 40% reported having a boyfriend in a gang, and 80% said they had a good friend in a male gang. Gang associations led to the girls' involvement in delinquent and criminal activities, including holding drugs (55%), selling drugs (31%), and holding weapons (27%).

Relationship of Risk Factors to Gang Involvement

Recent youth gang research has produced four seminal findings with respect to the impact of risk factors on the likelihood of gang membership. First, Howell and Egley (2005b) emphasize that risk factors for gang membership span all five of the risk factor domains (family, peer group, school, individual characteristics, and community conditions). Generally speaking, research-supported risk factors for gang joining apply alike for minorities versus non-minorities and for girls and boys. However, females evidence certain unique risk factors that are discussed in Chapter 6.

Second, risk factors have a cumulative impact; that is, the greater the number of risk factors the youth experience, the greater the likelihood of gang involvement. In a Seattle study, children under the age of 12 who evidenced as many as 7 of 19 measured risk factors were 13 times more likely to join a gang than children with none or only one risk factor (Hill et al., 1999). Esbensen and colleagues (2010) found a similar exponential relationship in a multiple-city survey beyond the accumulation of six of the particular risk factors measured in that study. As youth accumulated more of these risk factors, they were more likely to become involved with gangs as opposed to violence (52% of gang members experienced 11 or more risk factors, compared with 36% of violent offenders).

Third, the presence of risk factors in multiple developmental domains and the interaction of these appears to further enhance the likelihood of gang membership. Rochester researchers, Thornberry, Krohn, and colleagues (2003), examined seven risk factor domains, including (1) area characteristics, (2) family sociodemographic characteristics, (3) parent–child relations, (4) school, (5) peers, (6) individual characteristics, and (7) early delinquency. A majority (61%) of the boys and 40% of the girls who had elevated scores in all seven risk factor domains were gang members. This study finds that the *interaction* of risk factors across domains produces the greatest risk of gang membership.

Fourth, general delinquency, violence, and gang involvement appear to share a common set of risk factors (Esbensen et al., 2010).

◈ A Delinquency and Gang Theory

Howell & Egley (2005b) extended the age span of Thornberry and colleagues' (Thornberry, 2005; Thornberry, Krohn, et al., 2003) gang membership theory downward, so that the developmental model presented here (see Figure 5.3) encompasses antecedents of gang membership from birth through adolescence. This extension may prove beneficial because, as Loeber and colleagues (2009) note, about equal numbers of risk factors associated with early disruptive and delinquent behaviors begin very early, at or close to birth, and in the elementary school years, with fewer first appearing during the middle and high school years. "Thus, the most salient risk window of children's exposure to risk factors is prior to adolescence" (p. 301).

Thornberry and colleagues' theoretical model specifies four distinct developmental stages in the pathway to delinquency and gang involvement—preschool, school entry, childhood, and adolescence—and these are displayed in Figure 5.3. This discussion and Figure 5.3 also include attractions of the gang, or perceived benefits of joining, although this has not been conceptualized in research as a risk factor; it could be included, because gang attractions clearly elevate youths' risk for joining. The discussion that follows focuses on risk factor research that supports Thornberry and colleagues' theoretical model as it applies to delinquency and gang membership.

◈ A Review of Risk and Protective Factors for Gang Involvement

Studies do not agree on the most important risk factors for gang membership because of different criteria employed in researching these. Three credible lists of such risk factors have been generated. First, Howell and Egley's (2005b) review is detailed in the discussion in the next section. Second, Klein and Maxson's (2006) compilation was drawn predominantly from cross-sectional studies (14 of the 20 studies they reviewed are in this category). The cross-sectional studies measure both risk factors and outcomes at the same time, hence the causal ordering cannot be determined with certainty; what appears to be a predictor could well be an outcome of gang involvement. Third, Huizinga and Lovegrove (2009) compiled a short list of research-supported risk factors from an analysis of a number of longitudinal studies. This list was limited to factors that proved especially strong in at least two longitudinal study sites. This method is sound, but the drawback is that only 11 of more than 50 scientifically established risk factors in longitudinal studies met Huizinga and Lovegrove's stringent criteria. Research clearly shows that youth who have numerous risk factors in multiple domains are most likely to join gangs. In addition, research has established that the prevalence of risk factors varies among study sites (which explains, in large part, the dissimilar lists from one longitudinal study to another). Reliance on a very

Figure 5.3   Delinquency and Gang Theory

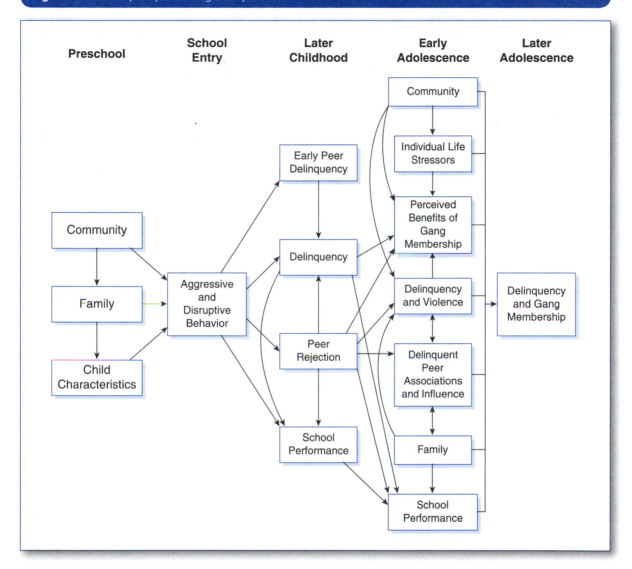

narrow list such as that generated by Huizinga and Lovegrove's stringent criteria could have the unintended consequence of overlooking important factors that have not been well researched. For example, high rates of school suspensions and truancy and other punitive school policies that have become more widespread in the past decade or more are potent risk factors in North Carolina cities (Graves et al., 2010; Weisel & Howell, 2007) and in France (Debarbieux & Baya, 2008), but these factors are not yet on any lists of research-based gang risk factors because of their newness and the practical orientation of the school-related research.[1] Therefore, for strategic-planning purposes, each community should examine a broad array of research–supported risk factors, and practical ones as well, to identify those that apply to a given community. Because the risk research has been conducted with a variety of racial and ethnic samples, there is every expectation that the research-supported risk factors apply across predominant racial/ethnic groups. Risk factors for girls are discussed at length in Chapter 6. Briefly, even though important gender differences have been discovered in recent years, there is considerable evidence of gender similarity in risk-factor predictors.

Table 5.2 contains risk factors for juvenile delinquency and gang involvement—almost all of which emanate from longitudinal quantitative studies. The risk factors for delinquency were identified in two national Office of Juvenile Justice and Delinquency Prevention (OJJDP) study groups, one on child delinquents (Loeber & Farrington, 2001), another on serious and violent juvenile offenders (Loeber & Farrington, 1998), and those published lists are updated here. The purpose for integrating them is to promote a holistic approach to delinquency and gang involvement. Note that the risk factors shown in Table 5.2 are organized by age level and that risk factors for gang involvement (almost all of which also predict general delinquency) are noted with an asterisk. Indeed, delinquency almost invariably precedes gang joining. Therefore, the theoretical model proposed here integrates developmental processes for delinquency involvement with gang membership. This developmental process is more likely to occur in disorganized communities where families, schools, and religious institutions are structurally weak, ineffective, and possibly alienating.

The Preschool Stage

In this first developmental stage, child characteristics and community and family deficits produce aggressive and disruptive behavior disorders by the time of school entry (Kalb & Loeber, 2003) and, in turn, according to Loeber and Farrington (2001), delinquency and school performance problems in later childhood. At birth—or beginning in the prenatal period for some infants—the family of procreation is the central influence on infants and children. During the preschool years, and especially in the elementary school period and onward, the array of risk factors expands, as some children are exposed to negative peer influences outside the home. Vaughn and colleagues (2009) describe a "severely impaired subgroup" (9.3%) of children identified in their analysis of data collected on a nationally represented cohort of more than 17,000 children drawn from approximately 1,000 kindergartner programs and collected by the National Center for Education Statistics.

Loeber and Farrington (2001) identify important family variables in the preschool stage that include low parental education (social capital) and a host of family problems, including what Pogarsky, Lizotte, and Thornberry (2003) found as a broken home, parental criminality, poor family or child management, abuse and neglect, serious marital discord, and young motherhood. Keenan (2001) along with Loeber and Farrington (2001) contend that pivotal child characteristics during the preschool period include a difficult temperament and impulsivity, typically described as aggressive, inattentive, and sensation-seeking behaviors.

The School Entry Stage

Kalb and Loeber (2003) identify products of dysfunctional families as early childhood aggression and disruptive behaviors, including stubbornness, defiance and disobedience, and truancy after school entry. This is particularly true in disadvantaged communities. Harsh parenting, according to Hipwell and colleagues (2007, 2008), is a key factor at this stage for girls, leading to conduct problems. Aggressive and disruptive behaviors are likely to be followed by rejection by prosocial peers, thus opening the door to

Table 5.2 Risk Factors for Delinquency, Violence, and Gang Involvement

Risk Factors Measured at Approximately Ages 0–2

Individual

- Conduct disorders (authority conflict/rebellious/stubborn/disruptive/antisocial)*
- Difficult temperament
- Hyperactive (impulsive, attention problems)*

Family

- Family poverty/low family socioeconomic status*
- Family violence (child maltreatment, partner violence, conflict)
- Having a teenage mother
- Maternal drug, alcohol, and tobacco use during pregnancy
- Parental criminality
- Parental psychiatric disorder
- Parental substance abuse
- Poor parent–child relations or communication
- Pregnancy and delivery complications

Risk Factors Measured at Approximately Ages 3–5

Individual

- Conduct disorders (authority conflict/rebellious/stubborn/disruptive/antisocial)*
- Lack of guilt and empathy*
- Low intelligence quotient
- Physical violence/aggression*

Family

- Family violence (child maltreatment, partner violence, conflict)
- Parental psychiatric disorder
- Parental use of physical punishment/harsh and/or erratic discipline practices

Risk Factors Measured at Approximately Ages 6–11

Individual

- Antisocial/delinquent beliefs*
- Lack of guilt and empathy*
- Early and persistent noncompliant behavior
- Early onset of aggression/violence*
- Few social ties (involved in social activities, popularity)
- General delinquency involvement*
- High alcohol/drug use*
- Hyperactive (impulsive, attention problems)*
- Low intelligence quotient
- Low perceived likelihood of being caught
- Medical/physical condition

(Continued)

Table 5.2 (Continued)

- Mental health problems*
- Physical violence/aggression*
- Poor refusal skills*
- Victimization and exposure to violence

Family

- Abusive parents
- Antisocial parents
- Broken home/changes in caretaker*
- Family poverty/low family socioeconomic status*
- Family violence (child maltreatment, partner violence, conflict)
- High parental stress/maternal depression
- Parent proviolent attitudes*
- Parental use of physical punishment/harsh and/or erratic discipline practices
- Poor parental supervision (control, monitoring, and child management)*
- Poor parent-child relations or communication
- Sibling antisocial behavior*
- Lived with a gang member*

School

- Bullying
- Chronic absenteeism
- Frequent school transitions
- Frequent truancy/absences/suspensions, expelled from school, dropping out of school*
- Identified as learning disabled*
- Low academic aspirations*
- Low achievement in school*
- Low school attachment/bonding/motivation/commitment to school*
- Old for grade/repeated a grade
- Poor student–teacher relations
- Poorly defined rules and expectations for appropriate conduct
- Poorly organized and functioning schools/inadequate school climate/negative labeling by teachers*

Community

- Availability of firearms*
- Economic deprivation/poverty/residence in a disadvantaged neighborhood*
- Exposure to firearm violence
- Neighborhood antisocial environment*
- Feeling unsafe in the neighborhood*
- Low neighborhood attachment*
- Neighborhood youth in trouble*

Peer

- Association with antisocial/aggressive/delinquent peers; high peer delinquency*
- Peer antisocial environment*
- Association with antisocial peers in the past year*
- Peer alcohol/drug use
- Peer rejection*

Risk Factors Measured at Approximately Ages 12–19

Individual

- Antisocial/delinquent beliefs*
- Lack of guilt and empathy*
- Early dating/sexual activity/fatherhood*
- Few social ties (involved in social activities, popularity)
- General delinquency involvement*
- High alcohol/drug use*
- High drug dealing
- Illegal gun ownership/carrying
- Life stressors*
- Makes excuses for delinquent behavior (neutralization)*
- Mental health problems*
- Physical violence/aggression*
- Violent victimization*

Family

- Antisocial parents
- Broken home/changes in caretaker*
- Delinquent/gang-involved siblings*
- Living with a gang member*
- Family history of problem behavior/criminal involvement
- Family poverty/low family socioeconomic status*
- Family violence (child maltreatment, partner violence, conflict)
- Having a teenage mother
- High parental stress/maternal depression
- Lack of orderly and structured activities within the family
- Living in a small house
- Low attachment to child/adolescent*
- Low parent education*
- Parental use of physical punishment/harsh and/or erratic discipline practices
- Poor parental supervision (control, monitoring, and child management)*
- Poor parent-child relations or communication
- Lived with a gang member*

(Continued)

Table 5.2 (Continued)

School

- Bullying
- Frequent school transitions
- Low academic aspirations*
- Low math achievement test scores (males)*
- Low parent college expectations for child*
- Low school attachment/bonding/motivation/commitment to school*
- Poor school attitude/performance, academic failure*
- Poorly organized and functioning schools/unsupportive and unsafe school climate/negative labeling by teachers*

Community

- Availability and use of drugs in the neighborhood*
- Availability of firearms*
- Community disorganization*
- Economic deprivation/poverty/residence in a disadvantaged neighborhood*
- Exposure to violence and racial prejudice
- Neighborhood antisocial environment*
- Feeling unsafe in the neighborhood*
- High-crime neighborhood*
- Low neighborhood attachment*
- Neighborhood physical disorder
- Neighborhood youth in trouble*
- Antisocial neighborhood*

Peer

- Association with antisocial/aggressive/delinquent peers, high peer delinquency*
- Association with antisocial peers in the past year*
- Association with gang-involved peers/relatives*

* Risk factors for gang membership

Sources: National Gang Center, OJJDP Strategic Planning Tool (2014 update).

antisocial or deviant peer influences, which predict delinquent activity in later childhood and early adolescence. The link between physical aggression in childhood and violence in adolescence is particularly strong (Brame, Nagin, & Tremblay, 2001; Broidy et al., 2003).

It is important to note that most disruptive children do not become child delinquents, nor do most child delinquents engage in delinquency in adolescence. Loeber and Farrington (2001) report one-fourth to one-third of the disruptive children at school entry are at risk of becoming child delinquents, and about a third of all child delinquents later become serious, violent, and chronic offenders. However, as Thornberry and Krohn (2001) explain, "the earlier the onset, the greater the continuity" (p. 297). Compared with late-onset delinquents, Wasserman and Seracini (2001) suggest child delinquents tend to come from dysfunctional families with one or more of the following characteristics: family disruption (especially a succession of different caregivers), parental antisocial behavior, parental substance abuse, mother's depression, and child abuse and neglect.

Loeber, Farrington, Stouthamer-Loeber, and colleagues (2003) indicated families with a harsh child punishment profile are overrepresented in such disadvantaged neighborhoods, and serious delinquency tends to occur more quickly in youngsters residing in these communities. Taken together, concentrated disadvantage at the community level, family problems, and certain child characteristics lead to early childhood problems (aggression and disruptive behavior), and each of these four conditions, in turn, increases the likelihood of delinquency in childhood and gang membership in adolescence.

The Later Childhood Stage

In the third developmental stage, later childhood, other risk factors (explanatory variables) that prepare children for gang membership begin to come into play. Children who are involved in delinquency, violence, and drug use at an early age are at higher risk for gang membership than other youngsters (Craig et al., 2002). Hipwell and colleagues (2005) contend that girls are more prone to earlier alcohol use than boys, and greater physical aggression was associated with early alcohol use. More than one-third of the child delinquents in Krohn, Thornberry, Rivera, and Le Blanc's (2001) Montreal and Rochester samples became involved in crimes of a more serious and violent nature during adolescence, *including* gang fights. Thornberry and Krohn (2001) conclude, "In brief, very early onset offending is brought about by the *combination and interaction* of structural, individual, and parental influences" (p. 295).

Coie and Dodge (1998) link peer rejection in childhood to a tendency for greater susceptibility from the influence of deviant peers, including more aggressive youths. Aggressive and antisocial youths begin to affiliate with one another in childhood and Cairns and Cairns (1994) suggest this pattern of aggressive friendships may continue through adolescence. A Montreal study led by Craig (2002) suggests displays of aggression in delinquent acts at age 10 or perhaps younger may be a key factor leading to gang involvement. Peers rated gang members as significantly more aggressive than nongang members at ages 10 to 14. Warr (2002) identifies the negative consequence of delinquent peer associates as one of the most enduring findings in empirical delinquency studies. Lacourse and colleagues (2006) find associations with delinquent peers increase delinquency and the likelihood and frequency of physical aggression and violence, which in turn increases the likelihood of gang membership in early adolescence.

School-related variables that lead to gang involvement, according to studies led by Craig (2002) and Hill (1999), include low achievement in elementary school, low school attachment, and having been identified as learning disabled. Factors that weaken the student–school bond (commitment to school) in the later childhood stage contribute to delinquency and gang membership. Poor school performance (poor grades and test scores) in childhood is likely to result from prosocial peer rejection, child delinquency, and family problems.

The Early Adolescence Stage

The remainder of this developmental model incorporates only risk factors that predict gang involvement. Children who are on a trajectory of worsening antisocial behavior are more likely to join gangs during adolescence, and they tend to have more problems than nongang members (Esbensen et al., 2010; Howell & Egley, 2005b). Esbensen and Huizinga (1993) suggest gang entry might be thought of as the next developmental step in escalating delinquent behavior—a product of risk factors that accumulate from birth through childhood and onward.

Community or Neighborhood Risk Factors. "Communities too have careers in delinquency" (Short, 1996, p. 224). As discussed in Chapter 1, the key conditions that gave rise to early gangs in U.S. history are urban slums, social disorganization, and concentrated disadvantage. As children grow older and venture outward from their families, they are more and more influenced by community conditions. The key factors include residence in a disadvantaged neighborhood, lots of neighborhood youth in trouble, and a ready availability and use of firearms and drugs. Bingenheimer, Brennan, and Earls (2005) claim exposure to firearm violence approximately doubles the probability that an exposed adolescent will perpetrate serious violence over the next two years. Other undesirable community conditions include feeling unsafe in the neighborhood and low neighborhood attachment. All of these are conditions in which gangs and violence tend to thrive.

Family Risk Factors. Studies show that both family structure and poor quality of interactions and interrelationships among family members are important risk factors for gang membership. With respect to family structure, a broken home (absence of either or both biological parents) and multiple family transitions or caretaker changes are important predictors of gang membership.

Several family interactions and interrelationships predict gang membership. In Hill and fellow researchers' (1999) study, the most negative arrangement was one biological parent and other adults in the home. One of the most prominent risk factors is poor parental supervision (including control, monitoring, or management of family matters). These factors suggest the importance of well-structured family activities. Other family conditions compromise parental capacity to carry out their child development responsibilities, including low parent education, family poverty, low family socioeconomic status, pro-violent attitudes, and child maltreatment (abuse or neglect). Living with a gang member is a key risk factor for gang joining (Gilman, Hill, Hawkins, et al., 2014).

> "I'd dress my kids in gang clothes—I thought they were so cute. I dropped out of school and there I was, a baby mama with two kids in [gang] clothes." —Joanna (in Leap, 2012, pp. 59–60)

School Risk Factors. Most studies of risk factors for juvenile delinquency and gang membership have examined only one segment of the school–student relationship: satisfactory academic performance. The low achievement of children is one side of the coin; poor-quality (poorly functioning) and unsafe schools is the other side (G. Gottfredson, 2013; Lyons & Drew, 2006). Thornberry and Krohn's team (2003) concluded that poor school performance on math tests predicts gang membership for males, as well as low attachment to teachers. Hill and colleagues (1999), and also Le Blanc and Lanctot (1998), found future gang members perform poorly in elementary school, and they have a low degree of commitment to and involvement in school. A contemporary indicator of poor-quality schools is zero tolerance policies that produce high suspension, expulsion, and dropout rates. In addition to alienating students from schools and teachers, thus weakening the student–school bond, zero tolerance policies release many youths from adult supervision during the day and after school, which Vigil (2002) suggests potentially exposes them to deviant influences on the streets and a higher likelihood of gang involvement themselves. Modern-day studies of school experiences now include (a) measures of "school climate" (G. Gottfredson, Gottfredson, Payne, & Gottfredson, 2005), (b) identification of "difficult" schools (typically characterized by higher levels of student victimization, sanctions, and poor student-teacher relations) (Debarbieux & Baya, 2008), and (c) weak student "connectedness" to schools (Resnick, Ireland, & Borowsky, 2004). Debarbieux and Baya's (2008) study of "difficult" schools found that the percentage of students who were gang members doubled in them.

"Gang participation is much greater in schools perceived by students to be unsafe" (G. Gottfredson, 2013, p. 91). In a survey of more than 10,000 junior high and high school students nationwide, Alvarez and Bachman (1997) uncovered the key school-related situations that make students fearful of assault both at school and while going to and from school: Recent victimization experiences, the presence of a violent subculture at the school (e.g., gang presence and attacks on teachers), and availability of drugs/alcohol were related to fear in both contexts. Vigil (1993) concurs that students who feel vulnerable at school may seek protection in the gang.

Peer Risk Factors. Based on their Montreal study, Lacourse and colleagues (2006) conclude that being part of a deviant peer group is associated with the onset, persistence, and aggravation of conduct problem symptoms during adolescence. Thornberry and Krohn's team (2003) identified association with peers who engage in delinquency as one of the strongest risk factors for gang membership, particularly for boys. Moreover, both Craig and colleagues (2002) and Lahey and colleagues (1999) found association with aggressive peers—whether or not they are involved in delinquency—during adolescence as a strong predictor of gang joining. Lacourse, Nagin, Tremblay, Vitaro, and Claes's (2003) Montreal study produced similar findings. Furthermore, rejection by prosocial peers (being unpopular) seems to be a key factor that pushes children into affiliations with delinquent groups and gangs (Haviland & Nagin, 2005; Thornberry, Krohn, et al., 2003).

Individual Risk Factors. A variety of individual risk factors increase risk of gang joining. Children who are child victims of abuse or neglect are more likely to join gangs (Fleisher, 1998; J. Miller, 2001; Thornberry, Krohn, et al., 2003). Mental health problems also increase risk for gang joining. Influential early theorizing about gang members held that violent gang members were so impaired mentally and socially that they should be classified as "sociopathic" (Yablonsky, 1967). Psychopathic symptoms can be misleading because the group dynamics of gangs often promotes psychopathic traits, particularly *locura* (acting extremely crazy) in Mexican American members (Vigil, 1988). To be sure, sociopathic traits include serious psychological disorders. Goldstein and Glick (1994, p. 20) summarize the common features of sociopaths:

- Aggressive, reckless, cruel to others, impulsive, manipulative, superficial, callous, irresponsible, cunning, and self assured
- Fails to learn by experience, is unable to form meaningful relationships, is chronically antisocial, and is unresponsive to punishment
- Is unable to experience guilt, is self-centered, and lacks a moral sense
- Is unreliable, untruthful, shameless, shows poor judgment, and is highly egocentric
- Is unable to show empathy or genuine concern for others, manipulates others
- Is loveless and guiltless

The most representative study of gang members to date contradicted Yablonsky's supposition of widespread sociopathic traits (Av. Valdez, Kaplan, & Codina, 2000). This representative San Antonio study drew a large sample of members of 26 gangs (160 male gang members between 14 and 25 years old), and was randomly drawn by catchment area, gang types, and gang membership status. Only a very small proportion (4%) of the sample of gang members was classified as "sociopaths" in individual screens using the Hare Psychopathy Checklist (Hare, Hart, & Harpur, 1991). Nevertheless, 4 out of 10 gang members were assessed as possibly having serious psychological problems with the potential for a sociopathic diagnosis.

> "I admired [gang] people, growin' up, and some of them were . . . killers and gangsters, but they all had this persona about them, and I would think, Damn, I wanna be just like that when I grow up." —Ronny (in Leap, 2012, p. 98)

However, prevalence rates are much higher among older gang members, particularly for those who have been victimized. For example, in a recent psychological assessment of identified gang members among a sample of serious and violent offenders ages 14–17 in two cities' juvenile justice systems (Philadelphia and Phoenix), Dmitrieva and colleagues (2014) reported a greater prevalence of sociopathic traits in this study sample (comprising only serious and violent juvenile offenders) than revealed above in Valdez's representative community sample. In addition, a British study identified very high incidence of serious psychiatric problems among older gang members, ages 18 to 34 (Coid et al., 2013). One in four gang members suffered from psychosis, 60% had high anxiety, 85% were diagnosed with an antisocial personality disorder, and more than half were dependent on drugs or alcohol. In addition, traumatization and fear of further violence was exceptionally prevalent in these older gang members.

Protective Factors

Juvenile delinquency and gang involvement are common outcomes of the relative preponderance of risk factors over *promotive* factors. Stouthamer-Loeber, Loeber, Wei, Farrington, and Wikstrom (2002) describe promotive factors as not only serving to buffer individuals from negative effects of risk factors (the common conceptualization of protective factors), but also promoting conventional social behavior and desistance. In extremely high-risk conditions, people need more than a simple majority of protective factors to overcome multiple risk factors (Stouthamer-Loeber, Loeber, Stallings, & Lacourse, 2008). Moreover, Stouthamer-Loeber and fellow researchers (2002) note the condition of considerable exposure to risk domains paired with the relative absence of protective domains "dramatically increases the risk of later persistent serious offending" (p. 120).

Bushway, Krohn, Lizotte, Phillips, and Schmidt (2013) found several factors that could protect adolescents across a decade (from age 13 to age 23) who were engaged in violent acts (consisting of attacking someone with a weapon, other assault, gang fighting, throwing objects at a person or persons, robbery, and rape). Protective factors were identified for four violence prevalence trajectory groups and two gang fighting prevalence trajectory groups. Total cumulative protection across all domains proved to be most helpful for those at risk, especially in the family (parental support, parent partner status) and individual domains (educational aspirations, self-esteem, academic achievement, and group conventional behavior) for those at risk for involvement in violent acts. "Keeping adolescents focused on school, feeling good about themselves, and involved with conventional peers all seem to be productive avenues for protecting our youth" (p. 22). Parents still mattered for violence incidence, even in mid to late adolescence, by age 23. According to Stouthamer-Loeber and associates (2008), the strongest protective factors for desistance from overall serious offenses are parents' good supervision, the youth's high-perceived likelihood of getting caught when delinquent, and low parental stress.

Protective factors for gang involvement and related violence must be validated in longitudinal studies. Just two such studies have been conducted to date. The first study found research support for protective factors in the major developmental domains from the 5th to 12th grades: prosocial family, school, neighborhood, peer environments, and individual characteristics (Gilman, Hill, Hawkins, et al., 2014). Positive family and school environments appeared to operate through other domains, mainly peer and neighborhood. In the family context, not living with a gang member was a key protective factor. Interestingly, these protective factors did not lose potency with age. However, early intervention may be particularly beneficial in preventing female gang onset because girls virtually ceased joining gangs by age 15, though boys continued to join gangs through age 19.

Research in the Rochester Youth Developmental study (Krohn et al., 2014) finds that, from mid-adolescence onward, six of the protective factors interacted with the chronic violence trajectory to reduce violence incidence (including gang fighting and gun carrying): (1) cumulative protection across domains, (2) cumulative protection in the family domain, (3) educational aspirations and (4) self-esteem in the individual domain, and (5) parental supervision and (6) parent partner status in the family domain. Thus of central importance is increasing the level of positive feelings youth have for themselves and their parents, and empowering parents to better supervise teenagers' behavior and choice of friends.

◈ Apex of Gang Member Criminal Activity

Keeping in mind the age-gang membership curve, we next profile youths who maintain an active course of gang activity for an extended period of time, thus expanding the peak in the age-gang membership curve by delaying desistance. Most youths who join gangs have already been involved in delinquency and drug use. Once in the gang, they are quite likely to become more actively involved in delinquency, drug use, and violence (Thornberry, 1998; Krohn & Thornberry, 2008). Invariably, longitudinal gang studies show that members are far more actively involved in criminal activity during the period of active gang membership than either periods before or after (Krohn & Thornberry, 2008). But is this elevated criminal activity composed of serious property and violent crime as the Loeber pathways model suggests? Yes, in both community and juvenile justice system samples.

Among the Pittsburgh young men, two particular sets of criminal activities (i.e., drug selling and violence; drug selling, theft, and violence) were most elevated when youth were in gangs (R. A. Gordon et al., 2014). In sum, this research suggests that gang involvement can propel high-risk delinquents who have begun a career in crime to new heights. In parallel with this research, the Rochester study suggested that the gang culture of violence introduces members to even more dangerous enterprises. "Gang members carry guns to protect themselves and their turf from rival gangs, who, in turn, must arm" (Lizotte, Krohn, Howell, Tobin, & Howard, 2000, p. 830). Then, in late adolescence, involvement in serious drug trafficking, which may be independent of gang involvement, is a much stronger factor explaining hidden gun carrying—typically after gang involvement has ended. In two large statewide multiyear samples of adjudicated serious and violent juvenile offenders, gang members were about three times more likely than other offenders to be chronic serious property and violent juvenile delinquents (Baglivio, Jackowski, Greenwald, & Howell, 2014; M. Howell & Lassiter, 2011).

◈ Long-Term Impact of Gangs on Participants

For the gang to have devastating consequences, it need not be a large formal gang. Even low levels of gang organization have important consequences for involvement in crime and victimization (Decker et al., 2008; Esbensen, Winfree, et al., 2001; T. Taylor, 2008). Various forms of violent victimization are associated with gang joining (T. Taylor, 2008; T. Taylor, Freng, Esbensen, & Peterson, 2008). What the available research shows most clearly is that a constellation of risky behaviors, gang fights included, elevates one's risk of violent victimization,[2] and as Melde (2009) notes, for both genders. These risky behaviors include participating in gang or group fights, carrying a weapon, committing serious assault, selling drugs, and associating with delinquent peers. In addition, studies led by Esbensen (2010) and D. Peterson (2004) conclude that violent victimization rates are higher for gang members than they are for their nongang counterparts.

Thornberry, Krohn, and colleagues (2003) found that gang involvement has a way of limiting youngsters' life chances, particularly if they remain active in the gang for several years. Over and above embedding its members in criminal activity, the gang acts as a powerful social network in constraining the behavior of members, limiting access to prosocial networks, and cutting members off from conventional pursuits. Thornberry and colleagues found that gang involvement tends to produce precocious, off-time, and unsuccessful transitions that bring disorder to the life course in a cascading series of difficulties, including school dropout, early pregnancy or early impregnation, teen motherhood, and unstable employment. Long-term gang membership also leads to negative life-course transitions in adulthood for males, engagement in street crime, and, in turn, being arrested as an adult (Krohn, Ward, et al., 2011), as well as abusing their own children as a long-term result of the "gang way of life" (Augustyn et al., 2014).

Gilman and colleagues (2014) extended this line of research, finding that the effects of gang membership cascaded into three broad areas of adult functioning (up to age 33): illegal behavior, educational and occupational attainment, and physical and mental health. Compared with those who had never joined a gang, yet were actively involved in delinquency, those who reported joining a gang in adolescence were (at age 27, 30, or 33 years) nearly three times as likely to report committing a crime in the preceding year, almost four times more likely to report receiving income from illegal sources, nearly three times more likely to meet the criteria for drug abuse or dependence in the preceding year, and more than two times more likely to have spent time incarcerated in the preceding year. By comparing gang members with other delinquents, this research underscores the additional negative consequences of gang involvement. In another long-term follow-up of offending careers of Pittsburgh youth (up to age 29), gang membership was among the strongest predictors of convictions for homicide (Loeber & Farrington, 2011).

Juvenile and criminal justice system careers of gang members begin at an early age. Recent research shows that the deeper the level of juvenile justice system penetration, the greater the likelihood of gang involvement (M. Howell & Lassiter, 2011). 7% of all juveniles against whom delinquent complaints are filed, 13% of juveniles adjudicated delinquent, 21% of juveniles admitted to short-term detention, and 38% of juveniles committed to secure residential facilities. In addition, Gilman and colleagues (2014) and Benda, Corwyn, and Toombs (2001) find that adolescent gang membership is a strong predictor of entry into the correctional system for adults. A statewide Florida analysis also showed that serious, violent, and chronic juvenile offenders are almost four times more likely to indicate gang association than other offenders (Baglivio et al., 2014). The strongest research-supported risk factors for recidivism among gang members who had been adjudicated delinquent are frequency of violent assaults, degree of gang embeddedness, low self-control, and frequency of associations with fellow gang members (Howell et al., 2014, p. 155).

◈ Desistance From Gang Membership

The down slope of the age-gang member curve represents the desistance process (Decker, Pyrooz, & Moule, 2014). Findings from longitudinal studies in Denver, Pittsburgh, Rochester, Seattle, and a multisite GREAT sample indicate that active gang membership periods are relatively brief. However, there is considerable variability:

- The majority of gang members remained involved with gangs for one year or less (48% to 69%).

- Declining percentages reported two (17% to 48%), three (6% to 27%), and four or more (3% to 5%) years of gang membership among sites (Pyrooz et al., 2013, p. 244).

It is noteworthy that up to one in four (27%) gang members in the five studies remain active for at least three years. More embedded members remain active for a longer period of time. In particular, *gang embeddedness* refers to duration youth in gangs, as indicated by frequent routine contacts, participation in important gang activities, and perceived higher social status from gang participation (Pyrooz et al., 2013). The explanation for the gradual down-slope is that desistance does not occur abruptly. In one study, gang embeddedness was associated with slowing the rate of desistance from gang membership over the full five-year study period. Gang members with low levels of embeddedness leave the gang quickly, crossing a 50% threshold in six months after the baseline interview, whereas high levels of embeddedness delay similar reductions for about two years (Pyrooz et al., 2013). In the largest study of gang desisters, a total of 1,185 youth who left their gang (Carson et al., 2013), young members typically became disillusioned with gang life and then decided to simply drift away from gangs in adolescence, typically "without fanfare or consequences" (p. 529). There are exceptions, to be sure, several of which Carson and colleagues document. Where gangs are fully institutionalized in communities, members cannot easily leave their gangs. "Even after relinquishing their gang member status, [youths] may still associate with members of the gang; these are their neighbors, friends, and family members, after all" (Peterson, 2012, p. 82). In the words of an older gangster,

"You never leave the neighborhood—you just stop participatin'. I guess I'm like an alumni. I graduated. But I still check in with my old homies. We visit." —Kenny (in Leap, 2012, p. 148)

◈ Concluding Observations

The goal of this chapter was to show how youth become involved in gangs. Developmental models help to map the offense-based pathway to gang involvement. The developmental framework, in a simplified manner, depicts key stepping-stones in the gang member pathway. Future theoretical work needs to incorporate these research-supported risk factors. Gang involvement is a key stage in the formation of youngsters' criminal pathway, and gang membership also has a way of limiting youngsters' life chances, that extends far beyond the period of active gang participation. Over and above embedding its members in criminal activity, in Rochester, New York, the gang acts as a powerful social network in constraining the behavior of members, limiting access to prosocial networks, and cutting members off from conventional pursuits. These effects of the gang tend to produce precocious, off-time, and unsuccessful transitions that bring disorder to the life course in a cascading series of difficulties, including school dropout, early pregnancy or early impregnation, teen motherhood, and unstable employment. In addition, the gang "way of life" leads to poor general health, depression, drug abuse, child maltreatment, continued criminality, arrests, and incarceration in adulthood.

Several tentative conclusions can be drawn about studies to date on risk factors for gang membership. First, a caveat is in order. Only a relatively small number of longitudinal studies have investigated these, and as Krohn and Thornberry (2008) note, still fewer of them have used a common set of risk factors. Consequently, there are few replicated results. In addition, it must be emphasized that, as in the case of many other problem behaviors,

> gang membership does not seem to be a product of a few central risk factors; none exerts a massive impact on the likelihood of being a gang member. But, the accumulation of risk is strongly related to the chances of becoming a gang member. Gang members have multiple deficits in multiple developmental domains, each of which contributes in a small but statistically significant way to the chances of becoming a gang member. (p. 138)

Over the long term, fulfilling the developmental needs of children is a goal of great importance for reducing gang involvement. These developmental needs span the individual, family, school, peer, and neighborhood domains. The likelihood of joining a gang is far greater when multiple risk factors are present, and even more so when risk is present across all five of the developmental domains (Hill et al., 1999; Thornberry, Krohn, et al., 2003). In the most detailed risk study to date, examining the relative influence of risk factors from childhood to adulthood in a representative Seattle sample (Gilman, Hill, Hawkins, et al., 2014), the strongest predictors of joining a gang are living with a gang member, antisocial neighborhood, and antisocial peer environments. School factors apply more strongly earlier in the developmental process, in early childhood, particularly low academic achievement, school marginalization, and suspension from school.

Future gang members share several of the same risk factors seen in future serious and violent adolescent offenders, including association with delinquent peers, drug and alcohol use, school problems, and family problems. Thus, a continuum of responses consisting of age-appropriate services is needed to develop risk factors and service needs as they emerge with age. Gang involvement should routinely be assessed at each stage of juvenile justice and criminal justice system processing. Recommended procedures are detailed in Chapter 10.

DISCUSSION TOPICS

1. What are the key propositions of developmental or life-course theories?

2. How does Loeber's pathways model explain continued progression from less serious to more serious delinquent offenses?

3. Which theories best account for youths who advance to the top of Loeber's pathways model, that is, become serious (property), violent, and chronic offenders?

4. What factors best explain the bell-shaped age-gang membership curves?

5. Why does gang membership have long-reaching negative effects across the life course?

6. What are some of the common misperceptions about gang involvement, persistence, and desistence that are debunked, based on your reading of this chapter?

RECOMMENDATIONS FOR FURTHER READING

Gang Attractions

Decker, S. H., & Curry, G. D. (2000). Addressing key features of gang membership: Measuring the involvement of young members. *Journal of Criminal Justice, 28,* 473–482.

Decker, S. H., & Van Winkle, B. (1996). *Life in the gang: Family, friends, and violence.* New York: Cambridge University Press.

Melde, C., Taylor, T. J., & Esbensen, F. (2009). "I got your back": An examination of the protective function of gang membership in adolescence. *Criminology, 47,* 565–594.

Thornberry, T. P., Krohn, M. D., Lizotte, A. J., Smith, C. A., & Tobin, K. (2003). *Gangs and delinquency in developmental perspective.* New York: Cambridge University Press.

Tobin, K. (2008). *Gangs: An individual and group perspective.* Upper Saddle River, NJ: Prentice Hall.

Vigil, J. D. (1993). The established gang. In S. Cummings & D. J. Monti (Eds.), *Gangs: The origins and impact of contemporary youth gangs in the United States* (pp. 95–112). Albany: State University of New York Press.

Developmental and Life Course Theories and Processes

Alleyne, E., & Wood, J. L. (2012). Gang membership: The psychological evidence. In F. Esbensen & C. L. Maxson (Eds.), *Youth gangs in international perspective: Results from the Eurogang Program of Research* (pp. 151–168). New York: Springer.

Alleyne, E., & Wood, J. L. (2014). Gang involvement: Social and environmental factors. *Crime & Delinquency, 60,* 547–568.

Caspi, A., Lahey, B. B., & Moffitt, T. E. (2003). *The causes of conduct disorder and serious juvenile delinquency.* London: Guilford Press.

Farrington, D. P. (2003). Developmental and life-course criminology: Key theoretical and empirical issues—the 2002 Sutherland Award Address. *Criminology, 41,* 221–255.

Farrington, D. P. (2006). Building developmental and life-course theories of offending. In F. T. Cullen, J. P. Wright, & K. R. Blevins (Eds.), *Taking stock: The status of criminological theory* (pp. 335–364). New Brunswick, NJ: Transaction Publishing.

Gilman, A. B., Hill, K. G., & Hawkins, J. D. (2014). The long-term consequences of adolescent gang membership on adult functioning. *American Journal of Public Health, 104,* 938–945.

Gilman, A. B., Hill, K. G., Hawkins, J. D., Howell, J. C., & Kosterman, R. (2014). The developmental dynamics of joining a gang in adolescence: Patterns and predictors of gang membership. *Journal of Research on Adolescence, 24,* 204–219.

Hawkins, J. D. (Ed.). (1996). *Delinquency and crime: Current theories.* New York: Cambridge University Press.

Melde, C., & Esbensen, F. (2011). Gang membership as a turning point in the life course. *Criminology, 49,* 513–552.

Patterson, G. R., Capaldi, D., & Bank, L. (1991). An early starter model for predicting delinquency. In D. J. Pepler & K. H. Rubin (Eds.), *The development and treatment of childhood aggression* (pp. 139–168). Hillsdale, NJ: Lawrence Erlbaum.

Pyrooz, D. (2014). "From your first cigarette to your last dying day": The patterning of gang membership in the life-course. *Journal of Quantitative Criminology, 30,* 349–372

Thornberry, T. P. (Ed.). (1997). *Developmental theories of crime and delinquency.* New Brunswick, NJ: Transaction Publishing.

Risk Factors That Predict Gang Membership

Coid, J. W., Ullrich, S., Keers, R., Bebbington, P., & DeStavola, B. L. (2013). Gang membership, violence, and psychiatric morbidity. *American Journal of Psychiatry, 170,* 985993.

Dmitrieva, J., Gibson, L., Steinberg, L., Piquero, A., & Fagan, J. (2014). Predictors and consequences of gang membership: Comparing gang members, gang leaders, and non-gang-affiliated adjudicated youth. *Journal of Research on Adolescence, 24,* 220–234.

Gebo, E., & Sullivan, C. J. (2014). A statewide comparison of gang and non-gang youth in public high schools. *Youth Violence and Juvenile Justice, 12,* 191–208.

Gilman, A. B., Hill, K. G., Hawkins, J. D., Howell, J. C., & Kosterman, R. (2014). The developmental dynamics of joining a gang in adolescence: Patterns and predictors of gang membership. *Journal of Research on Adolescence, 24,* 204–219.

Glesmann, C., Krisberg, B., & Marchionna, S. (2009). *Youth in gangs: Who is at risk? Focus.* Oakland, CA: National Council on Crime and Delinquency.

Gordon, R. A., Rowe, H. L., Pardini, D., Loeber, R., White, H. R., & Farrington, D. (2014). Serious delinquency and gang participation: Combining and specializing in drug selling, theft and violence. *Journal of Research on Adolescence, 24,* 235–251.

Howell, J. C., & Egley, A., Jr. (2005). Moving risk factors into developmental theories of gang membership. *Youth Violence and Juvenile Justice, 3,* 334–354.

Yiu, H. L., & Gottfredson, G. D. (2014). Gang participation. *Crime & Delinquency, 60,* 619–642.

Protective Factors Against Gang Membership

Bjerregaard, B., & Smith, C. (1993). Gender differences in gang participation, delinquency, and substance use. *Journal of Quantitative Criminology, 9,* 329–355.

Bushway, S. D., Krohn, M. D., Lizotte, A. J., Phillips, M. D., & Schmidt, N. M. (2013). Are risky youth less protectable as they age? The dynamics of protection during adolescence and young adulthood. *Justice Quarterly, 30,* 84–116.

Hill, K. G., Howell, J. C., Hawkins, J. D., & Battin-Pearson, S. R. (1999). Childhood risk factors for adolescent gang membership: Results from the Seattle Social Development Project. *Journal of Research in Crime and Delinquency, 36,* 300–322.

Krohn, M. D., Lizotte, A. J., Bushway, S. D., Schmidt, N. M., & Phillips, M. D. (2014). Shelter during the storm: A search for factors that protect at-risk adolescents from violence. *Crime & Delinquency, 60,* 379–401.

Li, X., Stanton, B., Pack, R., Harris, C., Cottrell, L., & Burns, J. (2002). Risk and protective factors associated with gang involvement among urban African American adolescents. *Youth and Society, 34,* 172–194.

Maxson, C. L., Whitlock, M., & Klein, M. W. (1998). Vulnerability to street gang membership: Implications for prevention. *Social Service Review, 72*(1), 70–91.

Thornberry, T. P., Krohn, M. D., Lizotte, A. J., Smith, C. A., & Tobin, K. (2003). *Gangs and delinquency in developmental perspective.* New York: Cambridge University Press.

Interactional Theory

Krohn, M. D., Ward, J. T., Thornberry, T. P., Lizotte, A., & Chu, R. (2011). The cascading effects of adolescent gang involvement across the life course. *Criminology, 49,* 991–1028.

Thornberry, T. P. (1987). Toward an interactional theory of delinquency. *Criminology, 25*(4), 863–891.

Thornberry, T. P., & Krohn, M. D. (2001). The development of delinquency: An interactional perspective. In S. O. White (Ed.), *Handbook of youth and justice* (pp. 289–305). New York: Plenum.

Thornberry, T. P., Krohn, M. D., Lizotte, A. J., Smith, C. A., & Tobin, K. (2003). *Gangs and delinquency in developmental perspective.* New York: Cambridge University Press.

Multiple Marginality

Deuchar, R. (2009). *Gangs, marginalised youth and social capital.* Sterling, VA: Trentham Books.

Freng, A., & Esbensen, F. (2007). Race and gang affiliation: An example of multiple marginality. *Justice Quarterly, 24,* 600–628.

Krohn, M. D., Schmidt, N. M., Lizotte, A. J., & Baldwin, J. M. (2011). The impact of multiple marginality on gang membership and delinquent behavior for Hispanic, African American, and White male adolescents. *Journal of Contemporary Criminal Justice, 27,* 18–42.

Valdez, Av. (2007). *Mexican American girls and gang violence: Beyond risk.* New York: Palgrave Macmillan.

Vigil, J. D. (2006). A multiple marginality framework of gangs. In A. Egley, C. L. Maxson, J. Miller, & M. W. Klein (Eds.), *The modern gang reader* (3rd ed., pp. 20–29). Los Angeles: Roxbury.

Vigil, J. D. (2008). Mexican migrants in gangs: A second-generation history. In F. van Gemert, D. Peterson, & I.-L. Lien (Eds.), *Street gangs, migration and ethnicity* (pp. 49-62). Portland, OR: Willan Publishing.

Vigil, J. D. (2010a). *Gang redux: A balanced anti-gang strategy.* Long Grove, IL: Waveland Press.

Vigil, J. D. (2010b). Multiple marginality and human development: Applying research insights for gang prevention and intervention. In R. J. Chaskin (Ed.), *Youth Gangs and Community Intervention: Research, Practice, and Evidence* (pp. 155–174). New York: Columbia University Press.

Gang Involvement Increases Delinquent and Violent Behavior

Bendixen, M., Endresen, I. M., & Olweus, D. (2006). Joining and leaving gangs: Selection and facilitation effects on self-reported antisocial behaviour in early adolescence. *European Journal of Criminology, 3,* 85–114.

Dishion, T. J., Veronneau, M. H., & Myers, M. W. (2010). Cascading peer dynamics underlying the progression from problem behavior to violence in early to late adolescence. *Development and Psychopathology, 22,* 603–619.

Gatti, U., Tremblay, R. E., Vitaro, F., & McDuff, P. (2005). Youth gangs, delinquency and drug use: A test of selection, facilitation, and enhancement hypotheses. *Journal of Child Psychology and Psychiatry, 46,* 1178–1190.

Gilman, A. B., Hill, K. G., & Hawkins, J. D. (2014). The long-term consequences of adolescent gang membership on adult functioning. *American Journal of Public Health, 104,* 938–945.

Gordon, R. A., Lahey, B. B., Kawai, E., Loeber, R., Stouthamer-Loeber, M., & Farrington, D. P. (2004). Antisocial behavior and youth gang membership: Selection and socialization. *Criminology, 42,* 55–88.

Haviland, A. M., & Nagin, D. S. (2005). Causal inferences with group based trajectory models. *Psychometrika, 70,* 1–22.

Haviland, A. M., Nagin, D. S., Rosenbaum, P. R., & Tremblay, R. E. (2008). Combining group-based trajectory modeling and propensity score matching for causal inferences in nonexperimental longitudinal data. *Developmental Psychology, 44,* 422–436.

Krohn, M. D., & Thornberry, T. P. (2008). Longitudinal perspectives on adolescent street gangs. In A. Liberman (Ed.), *The long view of crime: A synthesis of longitudinal research* (pp. 128–160). New York: Springer.

Krohn, M. D., Ward, J. T., Thornberry, T. P., Lizotte, A., & Chu, R. (2011). The cascading effects of adolescent gang involvement across the life course. *Criminology, 49,* 991–1028.

Melde, C., & Rennison, C. M. (2008). The effect of gang perpetrated crime on the likelihood of victim injury. *American Journal of Criminal Justice, 33,* 234–251.

Thornberry, T. P., Lizotte, A. J., Krohn, M. D., Smith, C. A., & Porter, P. K. (2003). Causes and consequences of delinquency: Findings from the Rochester Youth Development Study. In T. P. Thornberry & M. D. Krohn (Eds.), *Taking stock of delinquency: An overview of findings from contemporary longitudinal studies* (pp. 11–46). New York: Kluwer Academic/Plenum Publishers.

Gang Involvement and Outcomes Over the Life Course

Augustyn, M. B., Thornberry, T. P., & Krohn, M. D. (2014). Gang membership and pathways to maladaptive parenting. *Journal of Research on Adolescence, 24,* 252–267.

Gilman, A. B., Hill, K. G., & Hawkins, J. D. (2014). The long-term consequences of adolescent gang membership on adult functioning. *American Journal of Public Health, 104,* 938–945.

Gilman, A. B., Hill, K. G., Hawkins, J. D., Howell, J. C., & Kosterman, R. (2014). The developmental dynamics of joining a gang in adolescence: Patterns and predictors of gang membership. *Journal of Research on Adolescence, 24,* 204–219.

Gordon, R. A., Rowe, H. L., Pardini, D., Loeber, R., White, H. R., & Farrington, D. (2014). Serious delinquency and gang participation: Combining and specializing in drug selling, theft and violence. *Journal of Research on Adolescence, 24,* 235–251.

Krohn, M. D., Ward, J. T., Thornberry, T. P., Lizotte, A., & Chu, R. (2011). The cascading effects of adolescent gang involvement across the life course. *Criminology, 49,* 991–1028.

Lizotte, A. J., Krohn, M. D., Howell, J. C., Tobin, K., & Howard, G. J. (2000). Factors influencing gun carrying among young urban males over the adolescent-young adult life course. *Criminology, 38,* 811–834.

Desistance

Carson, D. C., Peterson, D., & Esbensen, F. (2013). Youth gang desistance: An examination of the effect of different operational definitions of desistance on the motivations, methods, and consequences associated with leaving the gang. *Criminal Justice Review, 38,* 510–534.

Gilman, A. B., Hill, K. G., & Hawkins, J. D. (2014). The long-term consequences of adolescent gang membership on adult functioning, *American Journal of Public Health, 104,* 938–945.

Krohn, M. D., Ward, J. T., Thornberry, T. P., Lizotte, A., & Chu, R. (2011). The cascading effects of adolescent gang involvement across the life course. *Criminology, 49,* 991–1028.

Pyrooz, D. C., Decker, S. H., & Webb, V. J. (2014). The ties that bind: Desistance from gangs. *Crime and Delinquency, 60,* 491–516.

Pyrooz, D. C., Sweeten, G., & Piquero, A. R. (2013). Continuity and change in gang membership and gang embeddedness. *Journal of Research in Crime and Delinquency, 50,* 239–271.

Sweeten, G., Pyrooz, D. C., & Piquero, A. R. (2013). Disengaging from gangs and desistance from crime. *Justice Quarterly, 30,* 469–500.

NOTES

1. Reports of research of this sort are classified as grey literature because they were not published in traditional professional journals or books.
2. Including receiving injuries from an assault or robbery (e.g., being attacked by someone with a weapon or by someone trying to seriously hurt or kill them). Injuries were considered serious if they involved a cut or bleeding, being knocked unconscious, or hospitalization.

CHAPTER 6

Girls and Gangs

◈ Introduction

Girls have been active participants in U.S. gangs since the late 19th century (Asbury, 1927). The early street gangs in New York City typically had female auxiliaries comparable to what Sante (1991) describes as the "farm leagues for boys" in which males advanced to street-level battles.[1] Female gangsters who had ties with the older Five Points gangs helped by serving as lookouts and decoys. Younger members of some of the female gangs acted independently at times, hiring themselves out as errand runners, lookouts, or spies in brothels.

A couple of women are renowned in Asbury's (1927) historical accounts of early gangs for their fighting ability, Hell-Cat Maggie and Battle Annie. Both were active in male gangs in the 1850s. Hell-Cat Maggie fought along the Bowery gang's front line in many of the great battles. Distinguished by her filed teeth and artificial nails constructed of brass, "When Hell-Cat Maggie screeched her battle cry and rushed biting and clawing into the midst of a mass of opposing gangsters, even the most stout-hearted blanched and fled" (p. 30). Battle Annie and other females often positioned themselves on the outskirts of the gang battles, "their arms filled with reserve ammunition, their keen eyes watching for a break in the enemy's defense and always ready to lend a hand or tooth in the fray" (p. 29).

The preceding introduction encapsulates typical early characterizations of female gangs as auxiliaries to male gangs, as tomboys, or as sex objects, and these images, until recently, dominated the literature on female gang members. J. Moore and Hagedorn (2001) explain, "Even when describing female gang members as tomboys, researchers emphasized that the females' motivations were focused on males" (p. 1). Bowker (1978b) adds that as auxiliaries to male gangs, it is assumed that females were much like a "little sisters" group to them. These authors suggest, "In retrospect, the early skepticism about whether female gangs were 'real gangs' seems odd. It seems to have been based on a very narrow view of what a gang really is. Gangs—male and female alike—differ greatly from one another" (p. 2).

◈ Females in Early Gang Studies

Pioneering research on female crime involvement in the 1970s set off a firestorm in criminology and specifically in the gang arena. Adler (1975a, 1975b) contended that some important differences in the organization of female gangs and in members' behavior occurred in the period from 1945 to 1975. The key change, she argued, was the evolution from predominantly auxiliary status—as weapon and drug carriers, lookouts, and girlfriends—to greater autonomy and independent activity. Adler contended that the women's liberation movement fostered a nationwide female crime wave in the 1970s. This claim has been soundly discredited. Rather, Chesney-Lind (1993, 1999) insists that what occurred was a "surge of media interest" in crimes committed by females in that period, particularly slanted stories that stereotyped females as "liberated crooks."

Chesney-Lind (1999) noted a second "media crime wave" of the same sort reported in newspaper and magazine articles published in the 1990s. In "the first crime wave, the liberated 'female crook' was a white political activist, a 'terrorist,' a drug using hippie" (p. 309). In the second crime wave, the "demonized woman is African American or Hispanic, and she is a violent teenager" (p. 309). She is often also presumed to be a gang member (Esbensen & Tusinski, 2007). Based on her meticulous review of the evidence, Chesney-Lind's (1999) assessment is that "in both instances, there was some small amount of truth in the image found in the articles. [But] girls and women have always engaged in more violent behavior than the stereotype of women supports" (p. 309).

Several seminal female gang studies undertaken in the late 1970s and 1980s moved research on female gangsters beyond the auxiliary role, including research on Chicano, Black, Puerto Rican, and other race/ethnicity female gang members. Studies of Mexican American gangs or gang members were carried out in Los Angeles (Harris, 1988; J. Moore, 1991; J. Moore & Long, 1987; Quicker, 1983a) and in Chicago (Horowitz, 1983), and on Puerto Ricans in New York City (Campbell, 1984/1991, 1987). Studies of Black female gangs or gang members were conducted in Philadelphia (Brown, 1977, 1999), Los Angeles (Bowker, 1978a; Bowker & Klein, 1983), and in Boston (W. Miller, 1973, 1966/2011). These diverse studies supported two general themes: first, that girls exhibited some independence from boys, and second, that there was a tendency to engage in fighting and more serious criminal activity.

By and large,

> by the mid-seventies descriptions of girl gang roles and activities were less likely to be restricted to the traditionally female (subordinate) role. Gang girls were more often depicted as being actively involved in conflict situations, which, in the past, were believed to be male-dominated; e.g., gang feuds, individual and gang fights. (Fishman, 1999, p. 67)

Interestingly, Campbell's participant observation research (1984/1991, 1990, 1999) drew the most attention with respect to these two themes. Campbell's 1984 book *The Girls in the Gang: A Report From New York City* was pivotal. What is particularly remarkable is that her subjects consisted of only three female gang members (two of whom were Puerto Rican) from four different gangs (one woman was a member of two gangs). Yet Campbell's presentation of their compelling life histories ranked on a par with the early Chicago school studies. Make no mistake—despite the fact that the girls' gangs were auxiliaries to male gangs, these were criminally active women, involved in selling drugs, intergang warfare, organized crime, prostitution, domestic violence, and a variety of property crimes. More important, Campbell insisted that gang girls simply had not been studied as assiduously as boys.

> Instead they had been stereotyped as promiscuous sex objects—segregated in "ladies auxiliary" gangs—or as socially maladjusted tomboys, vainly trying to be "one of the boys." The stereotypes appeared in the social work literature and were strongly imbedded in much of the [gang] research literature. (J. Moore & Hagedorn, 1996, p. 205)

◈ Modern-Day Studies of Female Gang Members

Joan Moore's Los Angeles study (1991) led the way in modern-day studies of female gang involvement. Moore had returned to the barrios of East Los Angeles to see what had changed, if anything, in the Mexican American gangs that she described in her earlier (1978) widely acclaimed study. For her follow-up study, Moore chose two quite large gangs, White Fence and Hoyo Maravilla, that were among those she first studied in the 1970s. These gangs operated within two neighborhoods, Boyle Heights and Maravilla, and both of these large gangs had been in existence for 45 years when Moore returned. Because she was interested in gang behaviors of both females and males, Moore oversampled cliques within the two chosen gangs. She then randomly selected samples of 51 female and 106 male members for intensive study. They were interviewed in 1986–1987. Moore's research is arguably the most important female gang study of the 20th century, for the rigor of her research design, the methodology she used (blending ethnographic and quantitative methods), and her discoveries on female gang involvement. Her research reveals the striking evolution of female gangs to a greater independent status and also the more active criminal involvement of female gang members.

Moore (1991) made several important discoveries in comparing female gang members of the 1970s with those of the 1950s through intensive interviews. First, more of the gang members were female than expected. Although gang cliques with female participants were oversampled, it was surprising that about one-third of the total membership of both very large gangs was female (p. 136). Second, there were more independent female cliques in the 1970s than in the 1950s—particularly in the Hoyo Maravilla gang. Third, the newer female cliques had more rowdy girls who fought, drank, or used drugs heavily. A surprisingly large proportion (80%) of the women defined themselves as *loco*—compared with 65% of men—although few women admitted to *muy loco* behaviors (p. 63). As a young woman recalled,

> "I mean things didn't really matter. I mean nobody could explain anything. First we would just go and do it. We wouldn't even think, you know . . . And then we would go and get in trouble and we'd think about it later on." —Anonymous White Fence female gang member (in J. Moore, 1991, p. 63)

Moore's findings soon were substantiated in other studies of females in a variety of locations across the United States. First, a series of longitudinal studies of male and female gang members revealed extensive female participation in gangs, as Moore's research had suggested. The first such premier studies were the Denver Youth Survey, the Seattle Social Development Project, and the Rochester Youth Development Study. These were the first major longitudinal studies of random samples of high-risk youth in which sub-studies of gang members were embedded, and the first large-scale U.S. studies to include representative samples of girls. The self-report measure of gang involvement used in these three studies revealed that gang members in large urban samples of adolescents were nearly as likely to be females as males. The Denver Youth Survey found that females constituted between 20% and 46% of the gang members during a four-year study period, and 18% of the boys and 9% of the girls self-identified themselves as gang members (Esbensen & Huizinga, 1993; Esbensen et al., 1993). More startling, in the Rochester Youth Development Study, a *larger* proportion of female (22%) than male (18%) adolescents self-reported gang membership up to age 15 (Bjerregaard & Smith, 1993). In both study sites, female gang members evidenced a higher prevalence rate for delinquency involvement than both nongang girls and nongang delinquent boys, and a higher incidence rate for all types of offenses than for nongang boys in Denver and Rochester. The Seattle longitudinal study was the first to establish risk factors for gang membership in longitudinal studies (Hill et al., 1999). Gilman and colleagues' (2014) recent research examined risk and protective factors for girls' and boys' gang involvement from early adolescence into adulthood, finding similarity in the influence of these factors across genders.

Next, J. Miller's (2001, 2014) studies of female gang members in St. Louis, Missouri, and Columbus, Ohio, made three important contributions. First, her research described family and neighborhood contexts of gang involvement. Second, the serious family problems girls faced (particularly violence and drug use) pushed them to seek emotional and social support elsewhere. Lastly, Miller joined others in documenting the strong influence that gang-involved family members have on girls' decision to join (following J. Moore, 1991).

Most recently, Peterson's series of female gang member studies drawing on the two multicity databases of the Gang Resistance Education and Training (GREAT) project has yielded valuable insights on girls' gang involvement in the early-adolescent period—most notably the extensive gender composition of the gangs in which females participate (Peterson, Miller, & Esbensen, 2001; Peterson & Morgan, 2014; Peterson et al., 2004). This latter topic is discussed below. In addition, Peterson (2012) puts in perspective girls' gang involvement—first, that nationwide, girls' presence and contribution to gangs is significant. Second, girls' gang activities bring much harm to themselves and society. Third, a better understanding of girls' motivations and risk factors for involvement can inform prevention and intervention initiatives.

◈ Level of Female Gang Involvement and Seriousness of Crimes

Several important discoveries have been made over the past decade or more regarding the level of female gang involvement and seriousness of crimes (Bjerregaard, 2002a). First, female involvement in gangs promotes delinquency involvement at a higher level than if females associate with highly delinquent peers who are not gang members. Thus, gang membership facilitates delinquency over and above the effect of delinquent peers for females as well as males (Battin-Pearson, Thornberry, Hawkins, & Krohn, 1998). Comparing the 15-year-old girls who are gang members with nonmembers who are in the highest quartile of delinquent peers shows that the female gang members in Rochester still self-report significantly more involvement in general delinquency, violent delinquency, drug selling, and drug use. Gang involvement has the same facilitating effect for girls as for boys, and Rochester, Thornberry, Krohn, and colleagues (2003) suggest this effect is particularly strong with respect to violent delinquency and drug selling.

Second, gang members of both sexes are significantly more likely to have participated in delinquency, including serious delinquency and substance abuse, and to have committed these acts at much higher frequencies than same-sex nonmembers. Thus, gang membership promotes delinquency and substance use across both sexes (Krohn & Thornberry, 2008; Thornberry, Krohn et al., 2003).

Third, delinquency among girl gang members, just as among boys, is higher than among opposite-sex nongang members (Deschenes & Esbensen, 1999; J. Miller & Decker, 2001). For example, a multi-city survey of eighth graders undertaken in the mid-1990s found that delinquency among girl gang members is up to five times higher than among boys who are not members of gangs (Esbensen & Winfree, 1998).

Fourth, female gang members commit similar crimes to those male gang members commit, but both Bjerregaard (2002a) and Haymoz and Gatti (2010) conclude that a smaller proportion of girls participate in serious, violent offenses. However, studies vary somewhat with regard to the types of crimes committed; that is, some indicate that girls commit less violent crimes than boys, while others show no difference. But the most consistent finding is that, among early adolescents, girl gang members commit crimes that are similar to those by boys, including assault, robbery, and gang fights (Esbensen et al., 2010), although smaller proportions of girls are involved (Bjerregaard, 2002a). Interestingly, Bjerregaard found that within organized gangs, larger proportions of girls than boys were involved in some offenses.

Fifth, Bjerregaard (2002a) suggests that female gang members are becoming more extensively involved in the more serious and violent offenses. In the Rochester study, 29% of females in the sample were gang members at some point during the middle and high school period, and they accounted for virtually all of the entire sample of females' serious delinquencies (88%), for nearly two-thirds (64%) of all female violent offenses, and for almost 8 out of 10 female drug sales (Thornberry, Krohn, et al., 2003). A multi-city survey found that more than 90% of both male and female gang members reported having engaged in one or more violent acts in the previous 12 months (Table 6.1). The researchers demonstrated that 75% of female gang members reported being involved in gang fights, and 37% had attacked someone with a weapon (Esbensen et al., 2010). Ness (2010) observed another common situation in some cities when a gang sister or group of them is victimized—or rolled on—by others.

◈ The Question of Increasing Female Gang Involvement

Although the question of increasing female gang involvement cannot be answered with certainty, the limited available evidence suggests that this is the case (Peterson, 2012). Only one nationally representative annual survey gauges female gang membership—the National Youth Gang Survey; however, the respondents in this survey are law enforcement agencies, which typically estimate that only about 10% of the gang members they observe are female.[2] This relatively low estimate should come as no surprise because girls who join gangs tend to leave them at an earlier age than boys and hence have less street presence than boys. Related to this point, law enforcement seems to pay less attention to very young gang members because their attention is properly focused on older more serious and violent gang members. In a national school survey, Gottfredson and Gottfredson (2001) found gang joining among boys peaked at the 10th grade, but two years earlier for girls, at the eighth grade.

Nevertheless, the proportion of females among active gang members is undoubtedly larger than in the past century. In the 1997 National Longitudinal Survey of Youth, male versus female

Table 6.1   Gang Member's Annual Prevalence and Individual Offending Rates (IORs) by Sex

	Male		Female	
Violent Act	**Prevalence (%)**	**IOR (mean)**	**Prevalence (%)**	**IOR (mean)**
Hit someone	79	7.5[a]	78	6.6
Attacked someone with a weapon	53[a]	5.2	37	4.3
Robbed someone	33[a]	6.0	15	5.2
Participated in a gang fight	81	6.6	75	5.9
Shot at someone	35[a]	4.6	21	4.1
General violence	94	19.6[a]	94	14.2
Serious violence	85	14.0[a]	81	9.8

[a] $p < .05$, gang boys versus gang girls; chi-square test for prevalence; t-test for IOR

Source: Esbensen et al., 2010, p. 84.

differences in the proportion who joined gangs was not as large as previous research had suggested. Snyder and Sickmund (2006) report the male-to-female ratio in this national sample was approximately 2:1 (11% of males versus 6% of females). This greater discrepancy than seen in recent surveys in multiple cities with gang problems is likely attributable to sampling. As seen in Chapter 3, much higher proportions of youths join gangs in cities with a history of gang activity. For example, in a multi-city sample drawn in gang problem cities, Esbensen and colleagues (2008) found almost equal proportions of boys (9%) and girls (8%) self-reported gang membership. Also, Black and Hispanic boys have only slightly higher gang membership rates (10.2% each) than girls. By comparison, in known gang problem areas, surveys of students and other adolescent samples show that approximately one-third of all gang members are female (Bjerregaard, 2002a). In another study, Gottfredson and Gottfredson's (2001) nationwide student survey, 35% of the self-identified gang members were girls.

◈ The Importance of Gang Gender Composition

Only in the past 15 years has widespread attention been given to the gender composition of the gangs in which females participate (Curry, 1998; Peterson et al., 2001). Several studies indicate that mixed gender gangs are quite common. Student respondents in Esbensen and fellow researchers' (2008) multi-city student sample of male and female gang youths, mostly ages 12 to 15, classified the members of their gang as predominantly gender balanced (54% male and 46% female), regardless of racial/ethnic composition.[3] Only 10% of the boys and 4% of the girls said their gang was same gender. These findings are consistent with several other studies that show considerable gender-mixed gang activity.

The greater mix in female gangs would prove to have noteworthy implications for involvement in criminal activity. Peterson, Miller, and Esbensen (2001), found that females in all- or majority-female gangs exhibited the lowest delinquency rates, and females in majority-male gangs exhibited the highest delinquency rates (including higher rates than males in all-male gangs). In general, these studies suggest that criminal activity and violence tend to increase as the proportion of males in the gang increases. Why this is so is not well understood. It is worth noting that in Giordano's (1978) and Warr's (1996, 2002) studies of peer influence on delinquency, the cross-sex groups of delinquents have higher rates. In particular, Warr (1996) found in an analysis of national data that, unlike males, delinquent offenses reported by females are significantly more likely to occur in mixed-sex groups. In 2007, Haynie, Steffensmeier, and Bell's national study confirmed this, finding that "among females, the odds of engaging in violence are greatest when adolescent girls are enmeshed in a highly violent friendship network comprised of a greater proportion of male friends" (p. 249).

Several studies strongly suggest that girls are more likely to be involved in serious offenses when they are members of more organized gangs (Bjerregaard, 2002a). In reference to gangs in general, research on Esbensen and fellow researchers' (2001) multi-city sample of students found that members of gangs that are somewhat "organized" (i.e., have initiation rites, symbols or colors, established leaders, specific rules, and engage in illegal activities) self-report higher rates of delinquency and involvement in more serious delinquent acts than other youths. There may well be few differences between male and female gangs in this regard. In fact, Esbensen and colleagues (1999) note that, if anything, the gangs in which girls were involved were slightly more organized than those to which boys belonged. Equally important, Decker, Katz, and Webb's (2008) Arizona study found that the more organized the gang (having initiation rites, established leaders, and symbols or colors), the more likely members were to be involved in violent offenses, drug sales, and violent victimizations—even at low levels of organization.

According to reports of self-nominated gang members in a study conducted in California, Illinois, Louisiana, and New Jersey, both male and female members of young gangs considered their gangs to be relatively well organized; in one report on this study, Bjerregaard (2002b) found more females reported "having larger gangs, a gang name, a leader, regular meetings, a turf, and special clothing" (p. 91). Once she applied the "organized" requirement to self-identified gang involvement in this multi-state sample, Bjerregaard (2002b) found that

> female prevalence rates of gang delinquency are similar to or higher than those reported by the males . . . This finding is contrary to much of the prior research which reported that females were less likely to be involved in both criminal offenses and that females sometimes acted as inhibitors to such offenses occurring. (Campbell, 1990; Fishman, 1995; Klein, 1995) (p. 93)

Nevertheless, girls are significantly less likely to be gang-involved serious, violent, and chronic juvenile offenders (Baglivio et al., 2014), and girls' violent acts seldom involve firearms or result in death.

◈ Female Associates of Gang Members: Risks and Re-Victimization

A San Antonio study of girls who associated regularly with gang members (Av. Valdez, 2007) in the Mexican barrios on the West Side of San Antonio, in the area of eight public housing projects where some of the city's poorest families live, provides a unique perspective on gang risks and re-victimization. Valdez chose to move his research spotlight off the gangs themselves and onto 150 randomly selected girls who associated with male gang members but never joined their gangs.[4] Because gangs were ever-present in the West Side barrios, hanging out with gang members became "a daily routine in the lives of many of these adolescent females" (p. 3).

Valdez discovered that girls in these neighborhoods who were continuously exposed to high-risk situations and dangers unwittingly place themselves "beyond risk" (or at extreme risk) for violent victimization, practically assuring multiple and extremely problematic outcomes. "Their involvement in risky behavior—such as the perpetration of physical fights, early onset of sexual behavior, substance use, and/or other delinquent behavior—is characteristic of growing up in these environments" (p. 3). Valdez isolated the major risk factors that elevated risk for the girls he studied.

First, the family context was extremely detrimental for the females who would later be gang associates. The use of drugs and alcohol, violent acts, and criminal behavior were "normalized" within the family context of the girls in his study, and 8 out of 10 of the girls had a family member who used drugs. More than 6 out of 10 had someone in the house with a drinking problem, typically the father. Many of the young women felt the impact of family violence in their everyday lives. More than 7 out of 10 of them had family members involved in criminal activity. More than half of them had witnessed their parents physically fighting in the home.

Second, peer relationships increased the girls' risk for violent victimization, particularly their gangs' associations. Each of the female gang associates was "distinctly integrated into the male gangs through their relationships with the male gang members" (p. 87). The girls typically first associated with the gang members before age 12. When interviewed by Valdez, 43% said they currently had a boyfriend in a gang, and 81% said they had a good friend in a gang. The longer the duration of gang affiliation, the greater the girls' participation in male-gang delinquent activities. Not surprisingly, "the data indicate that many of the girls had a history of incarceration that occurred after they became affiliated with the gang" (p. 86).

Third, individual exposure to risky behaviors including delinquency, violence (particularly physical fights), substance use, and sexual relations was extensive among the female gang associates. Based on his exhaustive study, Valdez (2007) developed the following typology to categorize nongang females:

- *Girlfriends* are defined as a type of female gang associate who is a current steady partner of a male gang member. Relationships range from being a male gang member's "main chick" or *santita* (saint) to the teenage mother of his child. This type of female is least involved in everyday gang activities, and to some extent these girls are shielded from male gang members (e.g., not sexually harassed), out of respect.

- *Hoodrats* are a more complex type of female gang associate. Although often (but not necessarily) she is sexually promiscuous, she is often seen hanging out and partying with the guys and generally is a heavy polydrug and alcohol user. Male gang members often refer to this type of female as *bitch*, *shank*, *player*, and *whore*. She normally does not develop an emotional relationship with any of the boys, yet among the four female types, she is most actively involved in everyday gang activities.

- *Good girls* include childhood friends of many of the male gang members, often having attended the same schools, and having parents who interact with each other. In time, these relationships came to be based on mutual respect. Males characterize these females as "nice girls." Compared with the other types of female gang associates, this type tends to have conventional lifestyles, very infrequent involvement in criminal activities, and also limited involvement in everyday gang activities.

- *Relatives* refer to girls who are close relatives to gang members, typically sisters and cousins. These kinship ties afforded this female type special status within the social network. For example, if one of these girls were dating a gang member, she would be given special status as his main chick and also as a homeboy's sister or cousin. This type of female gang associate also has limited involvement in everyday gang activities.

All types of girls in Valdez's typology were involved in physical street fights, ranging from pushing and shoving to more violent attacks that often resulted in injuries. Hoodrats were most actively involved in everyday gang activities and were "more likely to participate in illegal activities in association with male gang members" (p. 98). Some of the Hoodrats were involved in more serious activities such as drug dealing and weapon sales, but often independently of the male gang. In addition, by virtue of their association with a particular male gang, tensions were created with other girls associated with rival gangs. Valdez observed that the female gang associates in the barrios on the West Side of San Antonio "are continuously exposed to high-risk situations and dangers, which are exacerbated when associating with gangs" (p. 180).

Valdez's (2007) classification scheme is very useful, for no other gang research has identified distinguishable subgroups of girls who hang around boys actively involved in gangs. However, some researchers have used other terms to characterize them, including *associates* (Curry et al., 2002), *wannabes*, and youth who *kick it* (participate in gang social activities) (Garot, 2010). But Valdez's classification scheme is far more explicit than others and should prove very useful in distinguishing girls' levels or degrees of gang involvement for research, prevention, and intervention purposes.

Valdez (2007) emphasizes violent victimization as a predominant result of high-risk girls' exposure to gangs. Importantly, adolescent girls "are prey for male adolescents and older adults in a street culture that promotes hyper masculinity, sexual conquest, sexual aggression, and sexual objectification of women" (p. 111). Unfortunately, these girls view the gang life as an opportunity for them "to gain autonomy and independence, not only from family oppression, but also from cultural and class constraints" (p. 113). For girls in these circumstances, the gang is very likely to be viewed as a refuge, particularly for those who have been victimized at home. Paradoxically, these vulnerable girls are placing themselves at greater risk of violent victimization as a direct result of their association with gang members, including sexual and physical victimization by boyfriends, and also by other male gang members in the context of the gang such as at parties (pp. 114–128).

Risk Factors for Girls' Gang Joining

In the review that follows, we suggest how certain risk factors for delinquency and gang involvement may well apply to girls and boys alike, and underscore recent research which suggests that certain risk factors may be more influential for girls than for boys (Peterson, 2012; Peterson & Morgan, 2014). Although supporting research on this latter point is thin at present, evidence is accumulating. A brief summary of this research follows (for reviews of risk and protective factors for girls exposed to gangs, see also Petersen & Howell, 2013; Peterson, 2012).

Early Problem Behaviors. During childhood, certain risk factors for general delinquency may be elevated that render girls susceptible to gang involvement at a later point. A growing body of research identifies child delinquent girls with an early aggressive history (Pepler et al., 2010). "Some early risks have emerged as more characteristic of aggressive girls than boys, including estranged mother-daughter relationships, abuse, depression, eating disorders, social aggression, and early sexualized behaviors" (pp. 229–230)—some of which have been linked to gang participation. Hipwell and colleagues (2002) discovered a subgroup of Pittsburgh girls under age eight who displayed disruptive behaviors, particularly in the most disadvantaged neighborhood where gangs are most prevalent. In these neighborhoods, girls—just like boys—"are exposed to a greater number of risk factors, including exposure to different forms of community and family violence and an increased likelihood of affiliation with deviant peers" (Kroneman, Loeber, & Hipwell, 2004, p. 117).

A similar group of very young girls was discovered in Toronto based on measurements made with the Early Assessment Risk List for Girls (EARL-21G) (Augimeri, Walsh, Liddon, & Dassinger, 2011). This validated instrument revealed that more than half of the girls who had been referred for clinical treatment under age 12 had displayed aggressive behavior problems before age seven, tended to come from chaotic families with high levels of mother–daughter conflict, and had experienced multiple separations from their primary caregivers. Such early problem behaviors often lead to delinquency involvement, which, in turn, can increase the likelihood of gang membership.

Neighborhood Characteristics. In her research on a national sample of adolescents, K. Bell (2009) found that neighborhood disadvantage is an especially strong risk factor for gang joining among both girls and boys. In these neighborhoods, gangs fill a void created by weak social institutions (especially families and schools) and government (law enforcement and human services). In disorganized neighborhoods, gangs are virtually unfettered from forging their own wedges amid the concentrated poverty and accompanying social and physical disorder. S. Park, Morash, and Stevens (2010) and J. Miller (2013) underscore the reality that gang presence in neighborhoods is a key contextual factor, particularly where gangs have been institutionalized in neighborhoods. These dynamics are illuminated in Av. Valdez's (2007) research in which he discovered that girls' continuous exposure to high-risk and dangerous situations elevated them "beyond risk," and this circumstance virtually assured multiple negative outcomes, including physical fights, early onset of sexual behavior, substance use, violent victimization, and gang association. Antisocial neighborhoods such as this appear to have as much potency as a risk factor for girls' as for boys' gang joining (Gilman, Hill, Hawkins, et al., 2014).

Family Environments. Violent family environments have been consistently identified among antecedents of female gang involvement, including parental substance use, domestic violence, and physical and sexual abuse (Fleisher, 1998; J. Miller, 2001; Peterson, 2012). In vivid descriptions, Av. Valdez (2007) reported that girls' families and the West Side streets of San Antonio provided the major risk factors among gang-affiliated females. Drug and alcohol use, violent acts, and criminal behavior were "normalized" within the family context of the girls. Exposure to risky behaviors on the streets including delinquency, violence (particularly physical fights), substance use, and abusive sexual relations were common among the female gang associates. Many of these girls viewed the gang life as an opportunity for them "to gain autonomy and independence, not only from family oppression, but also from cultural and class constraints" (p. 113). Child abuse is common among girls who join gangs (Chesney-Lind, 2013). "Girls join gangs, at least in part, because they are suffering abuse at home, their families are deeply troubled, and they are searching for a surrogate family" (p. 123). In addition, living in a family with a gang member is a predictor of gang joining for girls and boys alike (Gilman, Hill, Hawkins, et al., 2014).

> "My mom was 21 when I was born and my dad was 15. Dad was in prison for murder when I was born. Dad was bad off, into drugs. He was deranged too." —Cara (in Fleisher, 1998, p. 61)

Negative Peers. Youth tend to develop friendships with those with whom they feel comfortable or with whom they have much in common. Associating with delinquent peers, called *peer* or *deviancy training* in modern-day terminology, has long been established as a risk factor for gang involvement (Hill et al., 1999), and this factor appears to be as potent for girls as for boys (Gilman, Hill, Hawkins, et al., 2014). Rejection by prosocial peers (being unpopular) is a key factor that pushes children into affiliations with delinquent groups and gangs (Howell & Egley, 2005b). Although peer relationships can be nuanced between genders in several respects, the negative effects of peers on delinquent behavior are remarkably similar for males and females (Weerman & Hoeve, 2012). Early dating also is a key risk factor for gang joining among girls (Fleisher, 1998; Thornberry, Krohn, et al., 2003).

School Factors. School-related problems—such as academic failure, low educational aspirations, negative labeling, and trouble at school—are a key risk factor for gang joining among girls and these may be more influential for them than for boys (Bjerregaard & Smith, 1993; Peterson, 2012; Thornberry, Krohn, et al., 2003). In addition, school safety concerns are a major factor leading to gang involvement among girls (K. Bell, 2009).

In sum, risk factors in these five widely recognized developmental domains can lead to gang joining for girls and boys alike. Moreover, risk factors for violence and gang joining appear to be similar across gender (Peterson & Carson, 2014). As is the case with boys, the presence of risk factors in multiple developmental domains increases the risk for girls (K. Bell, 2009; Gilman, Hill, Hawkins, et al., 2014; Thornberry, Krohn, et al., 2003). Other research strongly suggests that the cumulative effects of risk factors may be worse for girls than for boys, leading to multiple problem behaviors (Hipwell et al., 2002; Hipwell & Loeber, 2006). And girls also have higher levels of co-occurring problems than boys. These problems tend to begin emerging at very young ages. A major study of adolescent female offenders identified three high-risk profiles: (1) girls with criminal parents (very high risk); (2) victims of abuse (high risk); and (3) repeat offenders (high risk) (Van der Put et al., 2014).

We next turn to the issue of interventions for girls versus boys.

◈ Girls' Unique Treatment Needs and Implications for Prevention and Treatment

Recently, several scholars have discussed the evolution of terms that are commonly used to reference programs designed exclusively for girls or for both boys and girls (Hubbard & Matthews, 2008; Petersen & Howell, 2013; Peterson & Carson, 2014). New terminology is now widely promoted that simplifies discourse on this matter. The "female-specific" or "female-responsive" philosophy implies that girls have unique treatment needs, and the "what works" or "gender-neutral" philosophy implies that services are equally effective with girls and boys. The female-specific or female-responsive philosophy also suggests that programs for girls should be sensitive to unique treatment needs and also the context in which treatment is provided (e.g. the family context, to address mother–daughter relationships). Even though there is research support for both philosophies, Hubbard and Matthews (2008) insist the two approaches can be integrated to the greater benefit of girls. After highlighting girls' unique treatment needs, we provide examples of programs tailored specifically to girls and others that appear to benefit both genders.

In the past decade or more, research that has focused on the development and outcomes of girlhood aggression has flourished (Pepler et al., 2010). Also, much more is presently known about older females' mental health status and service needs from structured psychiatric assessments of multi-state samples on juvenile probation, in detention, and in juvenile correctional facilities (Wasserman, McReynolds, Schwalbe, Keating, & Jones, 2010). Although female gang members were not identified in these populations of juvenile offenders, the findings below regarding treatment needs likely apply to the relatively small proportion of girls among life-course persistent juvenile offenders who are actively involved in gangs.

- Antisocial females show more impairment[5] than antisocial males across a range of co-occurring social, health, or educational domains (McReynolds et al., 2008).

- Girls have higher levels of co-occurring problems than boys (McReynolds et al., 2008). First, girls' rates of anxiety and affective disorders[6] such as depression are higher than boys, and violent girls are more likely than other groups to have anxiety disorders (Wasserman et al., 2005; see also Obeidallah & Earls, 1999).

- Females are 10 times more likely to experience sexual assault than boys (McReynolds et al., 2010).

- Girls with substance abuse and affective disorders have higher delinquency recidivism rates than girls and boys with no disorder (McReynolds et al., 2010).

A national study of female-specific predictors of assaultive behavior in the late adolescence period (S. Park et al., 2010)[7] suggests several important targets for intervention (risk factors) and protective measures for "beyond risk" girls who associate with gangs and commit violent assaults themselves.[8] Early-age (before age 13) runaway (from home) girls reported significantly more assaults than other girls who did not display early problem behaviors. The more the gang presence (exposure), the more likely the girls assault others. Low hope for the future (as measured by expectations of arrest and victimization) also significantly predicted more assaults, while parental monitoring significantly predicted fewer assaults for girls. Additionally, for each year of school attended, girls' reports of assault were much lower, on average. Finally, girls who successfully adjusted benefitted from more parental monitoring and stronger ties to school and religious institutions. Regardless of the age group, interventions need to foster pro-social and relationship-based learning, and encourage the development of a positive gender identity and sense of agency (Hipwell & Loeber, 2006).

Recommended Female-Specific Services

In light of the above research, girls may be more responsive to cognitively based treatments (CBT)[9] than boys, particularly given that females often exhibit greater skills in perspective-taking and empathy (Pepler et al., 2010). This expectation has been confirmed in the application of CBT for young girls (ages 6 to 11) in the evidence-based Stop Now and Plan (SNAP®) Girls Connection (GC) (Augimeri et al., 2011). The program components are similar to the SNAP® Boys program, but there are important differences based on research and best practices for treating girls' aggression. In SNAP® Girls, for example, there is greater emphasis on relationship building. The SNAP® Girls therapeutic regimen showed significant positive changes on girls' problem behavior and parenting skills for the treatment versus the control groups, improved mother–daughter relations and bonding, less parental use of physical punishment and abuse of children (Augimeri et al., 2011), and good maintenance of treatment gains (Pepler et al., 2010). Owing to its demonstrated reduction of early problem behaviors and abusive parenting and associated childhood aggression, in the long term, the SNAP® Girls program should produce reductions in gang joining.

Because risk factors for girls' gang involvement span several domains of their lives, for optimal impact, gang prevention and intervention programs not only need to address multiple risk factors, but they also should address a number of risk factors in multiple segments of girls' lives. Chesney-Lind (2013) underscores the importance of addressing issues that are unique to girls and the contexts that can lead them to join a gang. These "strategies and programs include the need to prevent sexual abuse, strengthen family relationships, provide them with safety in their neighborhoods, help them avoid substance abuse and abusive boyfriends, and improve their skills to delay early sexual activity and parenthood" (p. 121).

Valdez and Petersen's San Antonio research on female affiliates (Petersen & Valdez, 2004; see also Av. Valdez, 2007) and also Peterson (2012) suggest that female violence prevention programs need to address these priorities: parental monitoring, running away from home, school connectedness, substance abuse, hopelessness, victimization, retaliatory violence, and gang exposure. Cultural contexts are particularly important (Chesney-Lind, 2013). In agreement with other research, Peterson and Carson (2014) note the importance of family context for girls, but they provide insights regarding how sex-specific content could improve low parental supervision for females, such as working intensively with caregivers on effective strategies, while working with girls to increase their connections with other adult figures to provide structure and accountability—and for males, decreasing impulsivity.

As Van der Put and colleauges (2014) noted, criminal parents place older girls at particularly high risk, and so they recommend therapy. This could be provided in such family-oriented programs as Brief Strategic Family Therapy (described below). Van der Put and colleagues also recommend an intensive treatment that focuses on multiple systems for girls who are victims of abuse, and further diagnostics to determine specific treatment needs for girls who are repeat offenders.

For girls in the juvenile justice system, the Voice Diagnostic Interview Schedule for Children would serve to identify their mental health and substance use treatment needs, as this assessment tool works equally well for girls and boys (McReynolds et al., 2010). In the context of community settings, Hubbard and Matthews (2008) recommend "strengths-based" supports, "a therapeutic model that allows girls to explore common problems in their lives and develop a sense of self-worth through intimate communication with others" (p. 238). More specifically, these experts support treatment approaches for girls that are (a) based on the interpersonal (relational) model and (b) trauma informed.

A female-specific program, *Movimiento Ascendencia* (Upward Movement) in Pueblo, Colorado,[10] was a promising program for Mexican American girls that operated in the early 1990s for the purposes of preventing them from joining gangs and reducing their gang involvement. Most of the girls served in this program were in need of prevention and intervention services. The average age for participants was 14; most of them were gang-involved and had experienced contact with the juvenile justice system.

Project activities centered around three main components: mediation or conflict resolution, social support, and cultural awareness. Williams, Curry, and Cohen (2002) report the program successfully provided a safe haven for girls in the target area, and that the program participants showed significant reduction of delinquency involvement and increases in school achievement. Wolf and Gutierrez (2012) identify several promising services that could meet girls' unique treatment needs, although none of these has been rigorously evaluated.

Chesney-Lind (2013) draws attention to the Female Intervention Team (FIT), which operates within the traditional probation structure of the Maryland Department of Juvenile Justice. The typical girl for whom FIT is tailored is a 16-year-old African American from a single-parent family who may be gang-involved. FIT focuses on girls' unique challenges (including family trauma) and builds on their need for positive interpersonal relationships. Services include family counseling (designed for 8- to 15-year-old girls, their parents, and, in some groups, grandparents) and a Rite of Passage program that gives older teens a positive introduction to womanhood and opportunities for community service.

A nongang program, Safe Dates, is an exemplary program for preventing dating violence that can help reduce girls' violent sexual victimizations, and would be equally valuable to girls at risk of violent victimization in the gang context. Geared to girls' and boys' interactions, the goals of this dual-gender program are to change adolescent dating violence norms, improve conflict-resolution skills for dating relationships, promote victims' and perpetrators' beliefs in the need for help and awareness of community resources for dating violence, promote help-seeking by victims and perpetrators, and improve peer help-giving skills. Foshee and colleagues (2005) found program effectiveness in the areas of psychological abuse perpetration, moderate physical violence perpetration, and sexual violence perpetration. Intended for middle and high school students, the Safe Dates program can stand alone or fit easily within health education, family, or general life-skills curriculums. It should be provided in communities with acknowledged gang activity.

Recommended Gender-Neutral Services

At this time, four gender-neutral programs have demonstrated effectiveness with gang-involved females; three were designed to prevent gang joining, and the remaining one, for intervention with girls and boys who are actively involved in San Antonio gangs. Although none of these programs was designed specifically for girls, they have demonstrated effectiveness with girls as well as boys. First, the Gang Resistance Education and Training (G.R.E.A.T.) program (Chapter 9) is the only program specifically focused on reducing gang membership that has been rigorously evaluated and proven effective, and no gender differences have been reported to date. Second, the Comprehensive Gang Program Model (Chapter 10) also appears to be effective for girls and boys alike. Third, the evidence-based ART program has shown positive results when tested with gang-involved youth in Brooklyn, New York. ART (Chapter 10) is designed to target youths with a history of serious aggression and other antisocial behavior.

Fourth, Brief Strategic Family Therapy (BSFT) is an evidence-based program for preventing, reducing, or treating adolescent behavior problems such as drug use, conduct problems, delinquency, sexually risky behavior, aggressive/violent behavior, and association with antisocial peers.[11] BSFT serves female and male children and adolescents between 8 and 17 years of age who display (or at risk for developing) these risky and harmful behavior problems. BSFT directly addresses symptoms of dysfunctional family patterns by promoting positive parenting, parental monitoring, effective parental discipline, and family cohesion. A modified version of BSFT, tailored to cultural values of Hispanic groups as well as contextual factors (frequent gang affiliation, high-crime neighborhoods), demonstrated effectiveness in reducing behavioral problems with gang members and was equally effective with girls and boys (Valdez, Cepeda, Parrish, Horowitz, & Kaplan, 2013)—and earlier, with aggressive bullying girls using the basic BSFT model (Nickel, Luley, Nickel, & Widermann, 2006).

Three other gender-neutral programs hold considerable promise for reducing delinquency and victimization among gang-involved girls. Zahn, Day, Mihalic, and Tichavsky's (2009) review of juvenile justice programs for girls identified two model programs that have produced comparable cross-gender outcomes, Multidimensional Treatment Foster Care (MTFC) and Multisystemic Therapy (MST). MTFC is an alternative to group or residential treatment, incarceration, or hospitalization for adolescents who have problems with chronic antisocial behavior, emotional disturbance, and delinquency, and this program has demonstrated effectiveness with girls as well as boys (Chamberlain, Leve, & DeGarmo, 2007; Leve & Chamberlain, 2007). This program holds excellent potential for effectiveness with gang-involved girls confined in residential juvenile correctional facilities.

Further research is quite likely to demonstrate the effectiveness of MST and Functional Family Therapy with girls who are involved in gangs. Research on the tailoring of these programs for gang members, including girls, is relayed in Chapter 10. In a study of the efficacy of MST with gang members, Boxer (2011) found lower treatment completion rates for gang members, not only when clients self-admitted gang membership but also when youths had strong gang associations. However, Boxer's research also revealed that girls are less likely to experience negative case closures than boys, suggesting that programs such as FFT and MST can be effective with gang-involved girls.

◈ Concluding Observations

Girls have been participants in U.S. gangs from the earliest point of recorded gang activity. Many years passed, however, before gang researchers took note of their active involvement. To be sure, the early research reduced their involvement to auxiliary roles with strong emphasis on subservience to males. But female gang studies undertaken in the late 1970s and 1980s moved research on female gangsters beyond these subservient and auxiliary roles. In time, girls would blend with boys in gangs and increase their criminal involvement and also their vulnerability for violent victimization.

Providing specialized prevention and treatment programs for girls and young women is a relatively new frontier. Evidence-based services for male gang members have a much longer history (Chapter 10). Many of those programs can be used advantageously with females. The challenge, however, is secondary prevention on behalf of girls, targeting services in a manner that insulates high-risk girls from gang involvement and personal victimization in gang-ridden cities. Both mothers and daughters in these areas underscore general safety concerns (Popkin, Leventhal, & Weismann, 2010). Girls begin experiencing sexual harassment and pressure from older boys and adult men during early adolescence, typically by ages 12 or 13 (Popkin, Leventhal, & Weismann, 2008). The protection of vulnerable girls is of utmost importance—especially as they move into the pubescent period.

A federal housing program aptly demonstrates this pressing need. In the large-scale Moving to Opportunity for Fair Housing Demonstration sponsored by the U.S. Housing and Urban Development agency, the life chances of very poor families with children were improved by enabling them to move out of the disadvantaged environments that contribute to undesirable outcomes (Popkin et al., 2008). Although boys' behaviors did not improve, both mothers and girls achieved a "dramatic reduction" in "female fear" (Popkin et al., 2010, p. 735). As for the girls, "compared with their counterparts still living in high-poverty neighborhoods, female experimental-group participants reported less harassment from men and boys, less pressure to engage in sexual behavior, and, as a result, said they were less fearful" (Popkin et al., 2008, p. 2). Experimental family girls reported significantly less psychological distress and anxiety and fewer problem behaviors than did girls in the control group families that did not move out. In addition, girls in the families that moved out experienced lower exposure to gangs and drug trafficking.

A community- or neighborhood-based strategy is required to preserve girls' healthy social and personal development without the necessity of moving out of established homesteads and away from family ties and friendship networks. Fleisher (1998) recommends supervised residential centers as the centerpiece of such a strategy. These centers, as Fleisher envisions them, would serve to shelter and protect girls, and link them with a variety of supports and services (including job training and placement), as well as help to ensure a healthy start for gang girls' children. Community safety issues must be addressed, of course, including curbing gang activity. Social and life skills training (Botvin, Griffin, & Nichols, 2006) should also be provided for girls to buffer them from negative influences and victimization. In short, these centers would serve as a one-stop resource for a variety of services and sources of assistance. Access to good quality education is also vital (Weber, 2010). "In totality, research on the quality of schooling available to girls in gang-saturated neighborhoods argues for school-based initiatives that support girls' resilience and promote their attachment to school" (Chesney-Lind, 2013, p. 127). Even schooling is a barrier for many gang-involved girls.

> "I ain't been to school in a long time and ain't so good in math. And anyways, I don't have no new clothes. I don't have sneakers; all the other kids are gonna laugh at me." —Cara (in Fleisher, 1998, p. 162)

At this juncture, no female-specific gang programs have proven effective, but three are very promising. Just one program has been tailored specifically to girls at risk of gang involvement, *Movimiento Ascendencia* (Upward Movement). This program has been shown to reduce girls' delinquency involvement and improve school achievement. Safe Dates, an exemplary program for preventing dating violence, also reduces girls' violent sexual victimizations and thus is a very promising program for reducing girls' violent victimization, and perhaps helping distance themselves from sexually exploitative males. Though not yet tested for prevention of gang joining, the SNAP® Girls Connection holds strong potential for this purpose because it is an evidence-based program that tempers early problem behaviors and aggression, while increasing child-mother bonding among very young girls. The SNAP® program is described in Chapter 9.

To date, four gender-neutral programs have demonstrated effectiveness with females who are either at risk of joining gangs or actively involved in gangs. The G.R.E.A.T. gang prevention program is discussed in Chapter 9, and the Comprehensive Gang Program Model is presented in Chapter 10. Both programs have been thoroughly evaluated and appear to be effective for girls and boys alike. Aggression Replacement Training has demonstrated effectiveness with girls as well as boys when tested with gang-involved youth in Brooklyn, New York. Last, Brief Strategic Family Therapy has demonstrated effectiveness with gang members and appears to be equally effective with girls and boys. Other evidence-based gender-neutral programs for reducing delinquency and gang involvement (Chapter 10) hold promise for girls.

DISCUSSION TOPICS

1. Why was gang research so slow to notice the active involvement of girls in gangs?

2. Explain the more serious criminal activity of modern-day female gangs. Do these factors also apply to male gangs?

3. Why does a mixture of males and females in gangs elevate the criminal involvement of the group as a whole?

4. Explain why female-specific programs are needed, and also why these are effective.

5. Class exercise: Develop a strategy for insulating girls from community conditions that lead to gang involvement and violent victimization.

RECOMMENDATIONS FOR FURTHER READING

Proliferation of Female Gangs in the 1980s

Brotherton, D. C. (1996). The contradictions of suppression: Notes from a study of approaches to gangs in three public high schools. *Urban Review, 28,* 95–117.

Fleisher, M. S. (1998). *Dead end kids: Gang girls and the boys they know.* Madison: University of Wisconsin.

Moore, J. W. (1991). *Going down to the barrio: Homeboys and homegirls in change.* Philadelphia: Temple University Press.

Moore, J. W., & Hagedorn, J. M. (1999). What happens to girls in the gang? In M. Chesney-Lind & J. Hagedorn (Eds.), *Female gangs in America: Essays on girls, gangs, and gender* (pp. 176–186). Chicago: Lake View Press.

Moore, J. W., & Hagedorn, J. M. (2001). *Female gangs* (Juvenile Justice Bulletin. Youth Gang Series). Washington, DC: U.S. Department of Justice, Office of Juvenile Justice and Delinquency Prevention.

Taylor, C. S. (1993). *Girls, gangs, women, drugs.* East Lansing: Michigan State University Press.

Early Sexual Victimization of Girls Who Affiliate With Gangs

Cepeda, A., & Valdez, A. (2003). Risk behaviors among young Mexican American gang associated females: Sexual relations, partying, substance use, and crime. *Journal of Adolescent Research, 18,* 90–106.

Joe, K. A., & Chesney-Lind, M. (1995). Just every mother's angel: An analysis of gender and ethnic variations in youth gang membership. *Gender & Society, 9,* 408–430.

Miller, J. A. (2001). *One of the guys: Girls, gangs and gender.* New York: Oxford University Press.

Moore, J. W. (1991). *Going down to the barrio: Homeboys and homegirls in change.* Philadelphia: Temple University Press.

Moore, J. W., & Hagedorn, J. M. (1996). What happens to girls in the gang? In C. R. Huff (Ed.), *Gangs in America* (2nd ed., pp. 205–218). Thousand Oaks, CA: Sage.

Schalet, A., Hunt, J., & Joe-Laidler, K. (2003). Respectability and autonomy: The articulation and meaning of sexuality among the girls in the gang. *Journal of Contemporary Ethnography, 32,* 108–143.

Valdez, Av. (2007). *Mexican American girls and gang violence: Beyond risk.* New York: Palgrave Macmillan.

Yoder, K. A., Whitbeck, L. B., & Hoyt, D. R. (2003). Gang involvement and membership among homeless and runaway youth. *Youth and Society, 34,* 441–467.

Level of Female Involvement and Seriousness of Crime

Adamshick, P. Z. (2010). The lived experience of girl-to-girl aggression in marginalized girls. *Qualitative Health Research, 20,* 541–555.

Batchelor, S. (2009). Girls, gangs and violence: Assessing the evidence. *Probation Journal, 56,* 399–414.

Bjerregaard, B. (2002). Operationalizing gang membership: The impact measurement on gender differences in gang self-identification and delinquent involvement. *Women and Criminal Justice, 13,* 79–100.

Erickson, P. G., Butters, J. E., Cousineau, M., Harrison, L., & Korf, D. (2006). Girls and weapons: An international study of the perpetration of violence. *Urban Health, 83,* 788–801.

Esbensen, F., Winfree, L. T., He, N., & Taylor, T. J. (2001). Youth gangs and definitional issues: When is a gang a gang, and why does it matter? *Crime and Delinquency, 47,* 105–130.

Haymoz, S., & Gatti, U. (2010). Girl members of deviant youth groups, offending behavior and victimisation: Results from the ISRD2 in Italy and Switzerland. *European Journal on Criminal Policy and Research, 16,* 167–182.

Jones, N. (2008). Working the "Code": On girls, gender, and inner-city violence. *Australian and New Zealand Journal of Criminology, 41,* 63–83.

Ness, C. D. (2004). Why girls fight: Female youth violence in the inner city. *The Annals of the American Academy of Political and Social Science, 595,* 32–48.

Peterson, D. (2012). Girlfriends, gun-holders, and ghetto-rats? Moving beyond narrow views of girls in gangs. In S. Miller, L. D. Leve, & P. K. Kerig (Eds.), *Delinquent girls: Contexts, relationships, and adaptation* (pp. 71–84). New York: Springer.

Gender-Mixed Gang Activity

Fleisher, M. S. (1998). *Dead end kids: Gang girls and the boys they know.* Madison: University of Wisconsin.

Miller, J. A. (2001). *One of the guys: Girls, gangs and gender.* New York: Oxford University Press.

Miller, J. A., & Brunson, R. (2000). Gender dynamics in youth gangs: A comparison of males' and females' accounts. *Justice Quarterly, 17,* 419–448.

Peterson, D. (2012). Girlfriends, gun-holders, and ghetto-rats? Moving beyond narrow views of girls in gangs. In S. Miller, L. D. Leve, & P. K. Kerig (Eds.), *Delinquent girls: Contexts, relationships, and adaptation* (pp. 71–84). New York: Springer.

Valdez, Av. (2007). *Mexican American girls and gang violence: Beyond risk.* New York: Palgrave Macmillan.

Re-Victimization

Fleisher, M. S. (1998). *Dead end kids: Gang girls and the boys they know.* Madison: University of Wisconsin.

Hunt, G., & Joe-Laidler, K. (2001). Situations of violence in the lives of girl gang members. *Health Care for Women International, 22,* 363–384.

Miller, J. A. (2001). *One of the guys: Girls, gangs and gender.* New York: Oxford University Press.

Miller, J. A. (2008). *Getting played: African American girls, urban inequality, and gendered violence.* New York: New York University Press.

Moore, J. W. (1991). *Going down to the barrio: Homeboys and homegirls in change.* Philadelphia: Temple University Press.

Moore, J. W. (1994). The *chola* life course: Chicana heroin users and the barrio gang. *International Journal of Addictions, 29,* 1115–1126.

Moore, J. W., & Hagedorn, J. M. (1996). What happens to girls in the gang? In C. R. Huff (Ed.), *Gangs in America* (2nd ed., pp. 205–218). Thousand Oaks, CA: Sage.

Moore, J. W., & Hagedorn, J. M. (1999). What happens to girls in the gang? In M. Chesney-Lind & J. Hagedorn (Eds.), *Female gangs in America: Essays on girls, gangs, and gender* (pp. 176–186). Chicago: Lake View Press.

Moore, J. W., & Hagedorn, J. M. (2001). *Female gangs* (Juvenile Justice Bulletin. Youth Gang Series). Washington, DC: U.S. Department of Justice, Office of Juvenile Justice and Delinquency Prevention.

Valdez, Av. (2007). *Mexican American girls and gang violence: Beyond risk.* New York: Palgrave Macmillan.

Risk Factors for Girls

Bell, K. E. (2009). Gender and gangs: A quantitative comparison. *Crime and Delinquency, 55,* 363–387.

Esbensen, F., Deschenes, E. P., & Winfree, L. T. (1999). Differences between gang girls and gang boys: Results from a multi-site survey. *Youth and Society, 31,* 27–53.

Esbensen, F., Peterson, D., Taylor, T. J., & Freng, A. (2010). *Youth violence: Sex and race differences in offending, victimization, and gang membership*. Philadelphia: Temple University Press.

Hill, K. G., Howell, J. C., Hawkins, J. D., & Battin-Pearson, S. R. (1999). Childhood risk factors for adolescent gang membership: Results from the Seattle social development project. *Journal of Research in Crime and Delinquency, 36*, 300–322.

Petersen, R. D., & Howell, J. C. (2013). Program approaches for girls in gangs: Female specific or gender neutral? *Criminal Justice Review, 38*, 491–509.

Peterson, D., & Morgan, K. A. (2014). Sex differences and the overlap in youths' risk factors for onset of violence and gang involvement. *Journal of Crime and Justice, 37*, 129–154.

Thornberry, T. P., Krohn, M. D., Lizotte, A. J., Smith, C. A., & Tobin, K. (2003). *Gangs and delinquency in developmental perspective*. New York: Cambridge University Press.

Valdez, Av. (2007). *Mexican American girls and gang violence: Beyond risk*. New York: Palgrave Macmillan.

Effective Services for At-Risk Females and Gang Members

Boxer, P. (2011). Negative peer involvement in Multisystemic Therapy for the treatment of youth problem behavior: Exploring outcome and process variables in "real-world" practice. *Journal of Clinical Child & Adolescent Psychology, 40*, 848–854.

Chesney-Lind, M. (2013). How can we prevent girls from joining gangs? In T. R. Simon, N. M. Ritter, & R. R. Mahendra (eds.), *Changing course: Preventing gang membership* (pp. 121-133). Washington, DC: U.S. Department of Justice, U.S. Department of Health and Human Services.

Curry, G. D. (1999). Responding to female gang involvement. In M. Chesney-Lind & J. Hagedorn (Eds.), *Female gangs in America: Essays on girls, gangs, and gender* (pp. 133–153). Chicago: Lake View Press.

Petersen, R. D., & Howell, J. C. (2013). Program approaches for girls in gangs: Female specific or gender neutral? *Criminal Justice Review, 38*, 491–509.

Peterson, D. (2012). Girlfriends, gun-holders, and ghetto-rats? Moving beyond narrow views of girls in gangs. In S. Miller, L. D. Leve, & P. K. Kerig (Eds.), *Delinquent girls: Contexts, relationships, and adaptation* (pp. 71–84). New York: Springer.

Peterson, D., & Morgan, K. A. (2014). Sex differences and the overlap in youths' risk factors for onset of violence and gang involvement. *Journal of Crime and Justice, 37*, 129-154.

Valdez, Av., Cepeda, A., Parrish, D., Horowitz, R., & Kaplan, C. (2013). An adapted Brief Strategic Family Therapy for gang-affiliated Mexican American adolescents. *Research on Social Work Practice, 23*, 383–396.

Williams, K., Curry, G. D., & Cohen, M. (2002). Gang prevention programs for female adolescents: An evaluation. In W. L. Reed & S. H. Decker (Eds.), *Responding to gangs: Evaluation and research* (pp. 225–263). Washington, DC: U.S. Department of Justice, National Institute of Justice.

Wolf, A. M., & Gutierrez, L. (2012). *It's about time: Prevention and intervention services for gang-affiliated girls*. Oakland, CA: National Council on Crime and Delinquency.

NOTES

1. Key fighting female auxiliary gangs of the late 1800s were the Lady Locusts, the Lady Barkers, the Lady Flashers, the Lady Truck Drivers, and the Lady Liberties of the Fourth Ward (Sante, 1991, p. 220).
2. See the National Youth Gang Survey online analysis: http://www.nationalgangcenter.gov/Survey-Analysis/Demographics#anchorgender
3. The students were in 15 public school systems in nine survey cities in 2002–2004. The numbers of Black and multiracial groups were too small to be valid.
4. To be eligible, the young women needed to be Mexican American, between 14 and 18 years of age, and know of a male in one of the 27 male gangs in Valdez's previous study on gang violence in San Antonio (see Petersen & Valdez, 2005).
5. Meaning cognitively deficient, and displays impulsive and externalizing behaviors (Vaughn, DeLisi, Beaver, & Wright, 2009).

6. Mental illnesses, which predominantly affect mood and also have an effect on thoughts, behaviors, and emotions, including mania (Hayes, McReynolds, & Wasserman, 2005).

7. Based on National Longitudinal Survey of Youth data, risk and protective factors were measured on a sub-sample of youths ages 12 and 13 years in 1997 and assaultive behaviors (how many times they assaulted or attacked someone) were measured in 2001 and 2002.

8. Each year from 1997 to 2001, respondents were asked (yes or no) about gang membership in the last year. Gang presence or exposure was measured by affirmative responses to questions about (a) how many years youth had lived in a neighborhood with gangs and (b) how many years they had friends or siblings who had been in gangs between 1997 and 2001. These two items were combined to form an index of gang presence in the youth's environment (S. Park et al., 2010, p. 319).

9. A form of psychotherapy that emphasizes the importance of thinking about how persons feel and behaviors that follow.

10. It should be noted that this program is no longer in operation.

11. National Registry of Effective Programs and Practices, accessible at http://www.nrepp.samhsa.gov/ViewIntervention .aspx?id=151

CHAPTER **7**

National Gang Problem Trends: 1996 to 2009

◈ Introduction

There is no uniform nationwide timeline of street gang emergence in the United States. As discussed in Chapter 1, each of the four major geographic regions saw uneven development of gangs in the history of this country. Serious gangs first emerged on the East Coast in the 1820s, followed by the Midwest (Chicago) and West (Los Angeles) regions a century later, and in the South after another half century. In the more recent era, gang activity in America appears to exhibit a more uniform pattern. The National Gang Center (NGC) has tracked U.S. gang activity since its first systematic National Youth Gang Survey (NYGS) in 1996. This is the first study in any country that surveys a nationally representative sample of authoritative respondents annually regarding the prevalence of gang activity.

This chapter first reviews patterns of gang emergence and the presence of gang activity in the United States over the past half century. Next, trends in U.S. cities' histories of gang activity are examined using a new analytical tool that groups cities with similar gang problems. The political, economic, demographic, cultural, and regional context of cities is then explored to highlight how local context helps to shape trends in gang activity. Finally, factors that contribute to the emergence, persistence, and decline of gang activity in U.S. cities are considered.

◈ An Overview of Nationwide Gang Activity in the Modern Era

Gang Growth From the 1960s to the 1990s

W. Miller (2001) combined data from several sources to reveal sharp increases among counties and cities that reported gang problems at any time between the 1970s, 1980s, and the early 1990s (Figure 7.1). Despite the limitations of these data, a large proportion of jurisdictions that experienced gang

Figure 7.1 Cumulative Numbers of Gang Cities in the United States, 1970–1995, by Decade

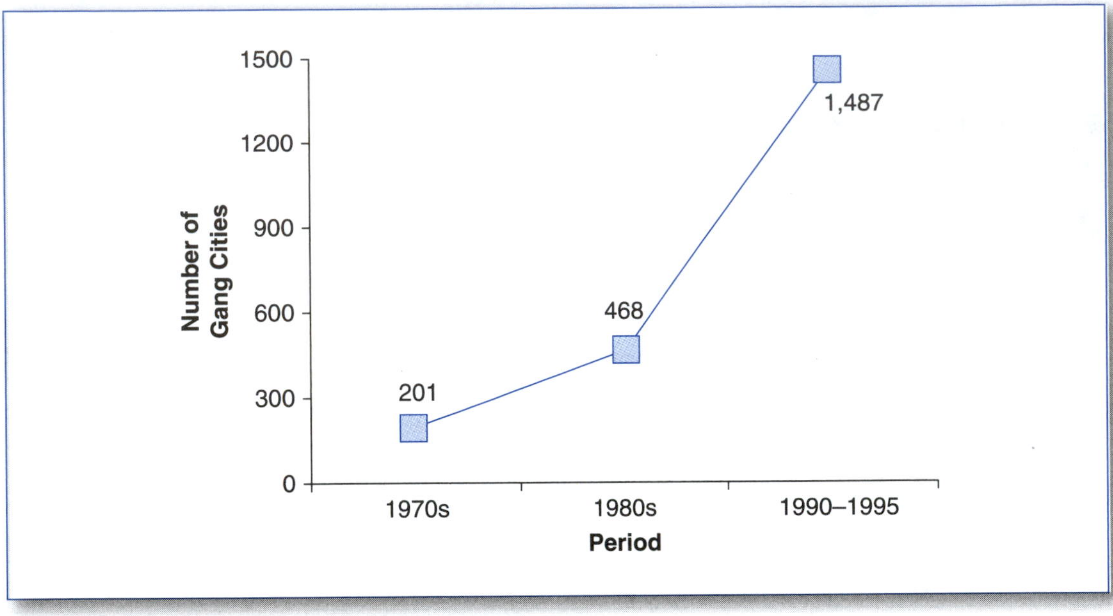

Source: W. Miller, 2001, p. 15.

activity in the mid-1990s said that their gang problem first emerged in the late 1980s and early 1990s, suggesting a sharp increase in the emergence of gangs in that period with a peak around the mid-1990s.

Given consistent growth of gang activity early in U.S. history, and evidence that gangs were present in almost 200 cities by the end of the 1970s, it is surprising that between 1967 and 1973, three major federal commissions,[1] each presenting comprehensive reviews of a wide range of major crime problems in the country, reached the following misleading conclusions (W. Miller, 1975, p. 75):

- Youth gangs are not now nor should they become a major object of concern in their own right.

- Youth gang violence is not a major crime problem in the United States.

- What gang violence does exist can fairly readily be diverted into "constructive" channels, primarily through provision of services by community-based agencies.

In a sharp contradiction of these assumptions, W. Miller (2001) summarizes his findings in the following manner:

Youth gang problems in the U.S. grew dramatically between the 1970s and the 1990s, with the prevalence of gangs reaching unprecedented levels. This growth was manifested by steep increases in the number of cities, counties, and states reporting gang problems. Increases in the number of gang localities were paralleled by increases in the proportions and populations of localities reporting gang problems. There was a shift in the location of regions containing larger numbers of gang cities, with the Old South showing the most dramatic increases. The size of gang problem localities also changed, with gang problems spreading to cities, towns, villages and counties smaller in size than at any time in the past. (p. 42)

Miller's (1982/1992) study also produced another very important conclusion regarding the locations of gangs.

More seriously criminal or violent gangs continued to be concentrated in slum or ghetto areas, but in many instances the actual locations of these districts shifted away from central or inner-city areas to outer-city or suburban communities outside city limits. [Yet] there was little evidence of any substantial increase in the proportions of middle-class youth involved in seriously criminal or violent gangs. (p. 78)

The assumption was that gangs were migrating outward from "gangland," from downtown areas of New York City, and from the transition zones where Thrasher found them in Chicago. Rather,

what has happened . . . is that slums or ghettos have shifted away from the inner city-to suburban outer-city, ring-city, or suburban areas—often to formerly middle- or working-class neighborhoods. Special concentration occurs in housing project areas. The gangs are still in the ghettos, but these are often at some remove from their traditional inner-city locations. (p. 76)

This important discovery is also reflected in national gang surveys begun in the mid-1990s, which are discussed in a later section of this chapter.

Explanations of Gang Growth in the 1980s and 1990s

A large influx of immigrant groups arrived in U.S. communities after the mid-1960s. The Immigration and Nationality Act of 1965 ended the national quotas on foreigners in the United States. Bankston (1998) notes this led to a shift in immigration to the states, from European origins to Central and South America and Asia. The new groups, according to W. Miller (2001), consisted largely of Asians (Cambodians, Filipinos, Koreans, Samoans, Thais, Vietnamese, and others) and Latin Americans (Colombians, Cubans, Dominicans, Ecuadorians, Mexicans, Panamanians, Puerto Ricans, and others). But not all of these groups have experienced similar problems in assimilation in America's communities. Bucerius (2010) contends those affected most "disproportionately originate from Mexico, Latin America and the Caribbean countries, including El Salvador, Guatemala, Haiti, the Dominican Republic, and the West Indies" (p. 235). By the late 1980s, according to Portes and Zhou (1993), the children of many American-born or Americanized parents among the new immigrants, dubbed "the new second generation," had reached adolescence. According to Rumbaut's Children of Immigrants Longitudinal Study, in 2005, children of post-1965 immigrants had grown to more than 30 million with a median age of eighteen (in Zhou, Lee, Vallejo, Tafora-Estrada, & Xiong, 2008, p. 37). Gang joining tends to commence with second-generation youth (Telles & Ortiz, 2008).

However, as W. Miller (2001) notes,

There is little consensus as to what has caused the striking growth in reported youth gang problems during the past 25 years. It is unlikely that a single cause played a dominant role; it is more likely that the growth was a product of a number of interacting influences. (p. 42)

Some of the most important influences track the stages of gang origins, expansions, and violence described in Chapter 4 (see also Howell, 2015). For example, the following influences have been suggested by W. Miller (2001, pp. 42–46) and others:

- Economic segregation—Indices of between-neighborhood economic inequality show fairly dramatic increases between the 1980s and 2000. Economic segregation of this kind can generate localized disadvantage that promotes family disorganization and low levels of social control. (Stages 1 & 2)

- Government policies—Permissive policies that followed the civil rights movement and urban riots of the 1960s allowed more ganging. In addition, the exodus of better educated and more prosperous city residents led to a reduction in the anti-gang influences that previous residents had provided in inner-city areas. (Stages 1 & 2)

- Gang names and alliances—In the 1980s, the pattern of adopting a common name and claiming a federated relationship with other gangs expanded enormously. The most prominent of these were the Los Angeles Crips and Bloods that originated in the 1960s. In succeeding years, hundreds of gangs adopted their names. Similar loose alliances of People and Folk "nations" formed in Chicago. (Stage 3)

- Migration—Those who also support the drug-trade explanation also particularly favor attributing the spread of gangs to migration of gangs themselves. (Stage 3)

- Gang subculture and the media—Contributions of the media to increased popularity of the gang culture is of central importance to recent youth gang growth in the United States from the mid-1970s onward. (Stage 3)

- Drugs—This popular explanation centers on the growth of the drug trade, and there is little doubt that this was one important factor in gang growth. However most gang involvement is at the street level, in individual sales, and not drug trafficking, according to law enforcement survey responses. (Stage 4)

The diffusion of gang culture may be one of the most important factors accounting for growth in reported youth gang problems in the 1980s and early 1990s, for reasons that W. Miller (2001) succinctly articulates:

The lifestyle and subculture of gangs are sufficiently colorful and dramatic to provide a basis for well-developed media images. For example, the Bloods/Crips feud, noted earlier, caught the attention of media reporters in the early 1990s and was widely publicized. Gang images have served for many decades as a marketable media product—in movies, novels, news features, and television drama—but the 1980s saw a significant change in how they were presented.

In the 1950s, the musical drama *West Side Story* portrayed gang life as seen through the eyes of adult middle-class writers and presented themes of honor, romantic love, and mild rebellion consistent with the values and perspectives of these writers. In the 1990s, the substance of gang life was communicated to national audiences through a new medium known as "gangsta rap." For the first time, this lifestyle was portrayed by youthful insiders, not adult outsiders. The character and values of gang life described by the rappers differed radically from the images of *West Side Story*. Language was rough and insistently obscene; women were prostitutes ("bitches," "ho's," and "sluts") to be used, beaten, and thrown away; and extreme violence and cruelty, the gang lifestyle, and craziness or insanity were glorified. Among the rappers' targets of hatred, scorn, and murder threats were police, especially black police (referred to as "house slaves" and "field hands"); other races and ethnic groups; society as a whole; and members of rival gangs.

The target audience for gangsta rap was adolescents at all social levels, with middle-class suburban youth constituting a substantial proportion of the market for rap recordings. The medium had its most direct appeal, however, for children and youth in ghetto and barrio communities, for whom it identified and clarified a set of values, sentiments, and attitudes about life conditions that were familiar to them. The obscene and bitterly iconoclastic gangsta rappers assumed heroic stature for thousands of potential gang members, replacing the drug dealer as a role model for many. Gangsta rap strengthened the desire of these youth to become part of a gang subculture that was portrayed by the rappers as a glamorous and rewarding lifestyle. (pp. 45–46)

Klein (2002) describes the result as a "general diffusion of street gang culture—the dress and ornamentation styles, the postures, and the argot of gang members—to the general youth population of the country" (p. 246). Now,

most young people in America recognize the look, the walk, and the talk of gang members. Many mimic it in part or in whole. Many try it out as a personal style. Play groups, break-dancing groups, taggers, and school peer groups experiment with gang life. (p. 246)

Gang culture is intertwined with the broader youth subculture. And youth culture, when emerging in disadvantaged contexts rife with criminal facilitators like guns and drugs, provides fertile ground for transforming youth gangs into violent street gangs (Howell, 2015).

◈ Nationally Reported Youth Gang Activity From the Mid-1990s

The Office of Juvenile Justice and Delinquency Prevention established the National Gang Center (NGC), formerly called the National Youth Gang Center, in 1994. Since 1996, the NGC has conducted an annual gang survey of a nationally representative sample of law enforcement agencies. The agencies included in the two nationally representative NYGS samples are detailed in Table 7.1.

Hereafter, *larger cities* refer to cities with populations of 50,000 or more, and *smaller cities* refer to cities, towns, and villages with populations between 2,500 and 49,999. Finally, *study population* refers to the entire group of jurisdictions that the current sample represents, that is, all jurisdictions served by county law enforcement agencies and all jurisdictions with populations of 2,500 or more served by city (e.g., municipal) police departments.

Table 7.1 National Youth Gang Survey Samples

1996–2001 NYGS Sample (Former Sample)	2002–Present NYGS Sample (Current Sample)
All police departments serving cities with populations of 25,000 or more (N = 1,216)	All police departments serving cities with populations of 50,000 or more (N = 624)
All suburban county police and sheriffs' departments (N = 661)	All suburban county police and sheriffs' departments (N = 739)
A randomly selected sample of police departments serving cities with populations between 2,500 and 24,999 (N = 398)	A randomly selected sample of police departments serving cities with populations between 2,500 and 49,999 (N = 543)
A randomly selected sample of rural county police and sheriffs' departments (N = 743)	A randomly selected sample of rural county police and sheriffs' departments (N = 492)

In the NYGS sample for 2002 to present, 63% of the agencies were also surveyed from 1996 to 2001, permitting an ongoing longitudinal assessment of gang problems in a large number of jurisdictions. The average annual survey response rate is approximately 85% for the entire sample, as well as within each area type. Of the respondents in the current sample, 99% have provided gang-related information in at least one survey year.

Survey recipients are asked to report information solely for *youth gangs*, defined as "a group of youths or young adults in your jurisdiction that you or other responsible persons in your agency or community are willing to identify as a 'gang.'" Motorcycle gangs, hate or ideology groups, prison gangs, and exclusively adult gangs are excluded from the survey. While the exclusion of these groups from the definition of youth gangs results in some loss of information about organized or semi-organized adult groups involved in illicit or illegal activities, restricting the definition in this way enables an investigation of long-term trends in the nature, prevalence, location, and violent activities of self-identified traditional youth gangs. Using this definition, the NYGS measures youth gang activity as an identified problem by interested community agents, specifically law enforcement officials.

Across survey years, questionnaire items have been designed to evaluate the soundness of this definitional approach. Respondents in the 1998 NYGS overwhelmingly defined gangs in terms of their involvement in criminal activity (National Youth Gang Center, 2000). Although some U.S. gang researchers have questioned the reliability and validity of information that law enforcement officers provide on gangs (J. Moore & Hagedorn, 2001; J. Sullivan, 2006), Decker and Pyrooz (2010b) and Katz and Fox (2011) proved the NYGS survey to have good reliability and validity in independent tests. *Reliability* refers to the extent to which results are consistent over time and an accurate representation of the total population under study. *Validity* refers to whether the research truly measures the phenomenon that it was intended to measure. Katz, Webb, and Schaefer (2000) suggest that law enforcement gang intelligence databases can provide a useful estimate of city gang activity. Pyrooz and colleagues (2010) note the police frequently interact with gangs and gang members, with ample opportunities to observe, document, and address emerging gang trends on the street.

Based on nationwide law enforcement reports in 2009, Egley and Howell (2011) estimate there were 28,100 gangs and 731,000 gang members throughout 3,500 jurisdictions in the United States.

Table 7.2 provides percentage changes in these key indicators of gang activity from 2002 to 2009. The number of jurisdictions with gang problems increased 21% from 2002 to 2009, and the estimated number of gangs increased 29% in the same period. The estimated number of gang members, which has averaged over 750,000 across survey years, decreased slightly from 2008 to 2009, but remains unchanged from the 2002 total. The prevalence rate of gang activity increased slightly from 2008 to 2009, to 34.5%, meaning that just over one in three localities reported gang activity in 2009 (Figure 7.2). Over the entire survey period, three trends are apparent in the level of gang activity: (1) a sharp decline

Table 7.2 Percentage Changes in Nationwide Gang Estimates from 2002 to 2009			
	2002–2009	**2005–2009**	**2008–2009**
Gang-problem jurisdictions	20.7	<1.0	5.1
Gangs	28.9	5.3	<1.0
Gang members	<1.0	−7.4	−5.6
Gang homicides (cities over 100,000 population only)	2.1	7.2	10.7

Source: Egley & Howell, 2011.

Figure 7.2 Prevalence of Gang Problems in Study Population, 1996 to 2009

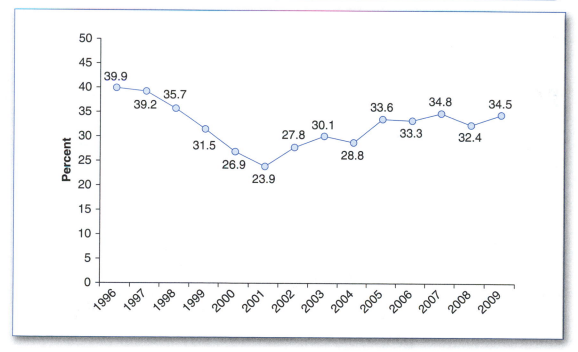

Source: National Gang Center.

throughout the late 1990s, (2) a sudden upturn beginning in 2001 and continuing until 2005, and (3) a relative leveling off thereafter.

Figure 7.3 shows the prevalence of gang activity within each the four NYGS subsamples: (1) police departments serving cities with populations of 50,000 or more, (2) suburban county police and sheriffs' departments, (3) police departments serving cities with populations between 2,500 and 49,999, and (4) rural county police and sheriffs' departments. Gang activity in all subsamples increased somewhat from 2002 to 2009. Each subsample follows a similar trend over time but at distinctly different levels. Larger cities consistently exhibit the highest prevalence rates of gang activity among the four groups, followed, in order, by suburban counties, smaller cities, and rural counties. The rates of reported gang activity in suburban counties are closest to rates for larger cities because of the relatively large populations in suburban counties (i.e., a higher capacity to sustain gang activity, Egley, Howell, & Major, 2006), the shifting of previous inner-city slums and ghettos to ring-city or suburban areas (W. Miller, 1982/1992), and the growing popularity of gang culture in these areas (W. Miller, 2001). Mirroring the overall prevalence trend, each of the subsamples shows uniform declines in the late 1990s, reaching a low point in 2001 and then steadily increasing before leveling off somewhat in recent years.

Figure 7.3   Reports of Gang Problems: 1996 to 2009, by Area Type

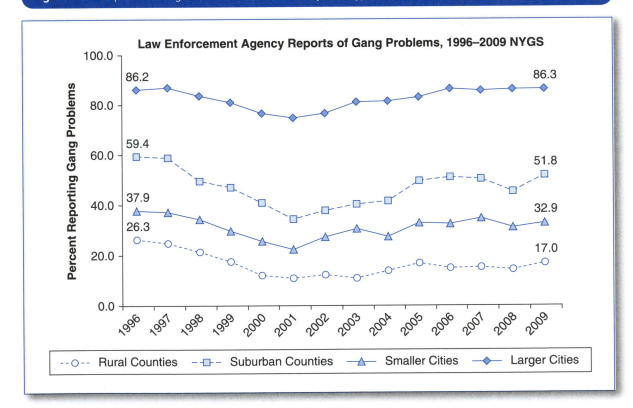

Source: National Gang Center.

Egley and Howell (2011) report the 2009 survey respondents also estimated year-to-year changes regarding other gang-related crimes and violence in their jurisdictions. For the gang-related offenses of robbery, aggravated assault, drug sales, and firearms use, most frequently reported by respondents was "no substantial change" (i.e., neither significant increase nor decrease) from 2008 to 2009 in the number of offenses committed. Among agencies reporting gang problems in 2009, half (49.8%) characterized their gang problems as "staying about the same," the highest percentage ever recorded in the NYGS. Agencies reporting a fluctuating pattern of gang activity over the past five years were more likely to characterize their gang problems as "getting worse" than were agencies consistently reporting gang activity.

The next section examines localities' histories of reported gang activity. For the first time, analysts are able to display groups of cities in terms of the consistency with which they report gang activity.

◈ Patterns in U.S. Localities' Histories of Gang Activity

Patterns of Gang Emergence

The oldest and very large gang problem cities were noted in Chapter 1 as New York City, Chicago, and Los Angeles. But do any cities in which gang activity emerged much later also display serious gang problems? To gain insight into the timing of the spread of gang problems across U.S. cities, the 2000 NYGS asked respondents for the approximate year when their current youth gang problem began, more simply referred to as *year of onset*. Figure 7.4 shows the cumulative percentage of cities by year of onset for each of four population groups.

Cities with very large population sizes (100,000 or more persons) experienced a much higher rate and earlier onset of gang activity than all other cities. Approximately one-third of these cities reported gang problems before 1985, and an additional 50% reported an onset of gang problems in the following 10-year period (i.e., from 1985 to the mid-1990s). These patterns are increasingly less pronounced across the remaining population groups, suggesting a cascading pattern of gang proliferation from the larger to the smaller populated cities and rural areas. This is also reflected in the average year of onset across population groups, which was 1985 for cities with populations of 100,000 and greater, 1988 for cities with populations of 50,000 to 100,000, 1990 for cities with populations of 25,000 to 49,999 and 1992 for cities with populations of less than 25,000 persons.

Gangs in newer gang problem jurisdictions are qualitatively different from traditional gangs in jurisdictions where gang problems began much earlier. Notably, gangs in the late-onset group commit fewer homicides (Egley, Howell, Curry, & O'Donnell, 2007). In localities that report onset of gang activity before 1990, 47% experienced gang homicides versus only 16% of localities that first reported gang activity in 2000 or later. In addition, 91% of localities in the former group reported gang-related firearm use, and 100% reported gang-related aggravated assaults, versus 65% and 74%, respectively, in the latter group. The before-1990 onset group also reported more gangs (7, on average) and gang members (178, on average) than localities in the latter group (4 gangs and 34 gang members, respectively).

The consistency of gang problems also varies directly with city size. Very large cities tend to have persistent[2] gang activity in comparison with small cities, which report gang activity sporadically. Uncertainty about gang presence is likely a main reason in these less populated areas.

In summary, NYGS data reveal a cascading pattern (of earlier to later onset) from the largest to the smallest localities and from urban to rural areas. A majority of cities, including those with populations

Figure 7.4   Patterns of Gang Emergence

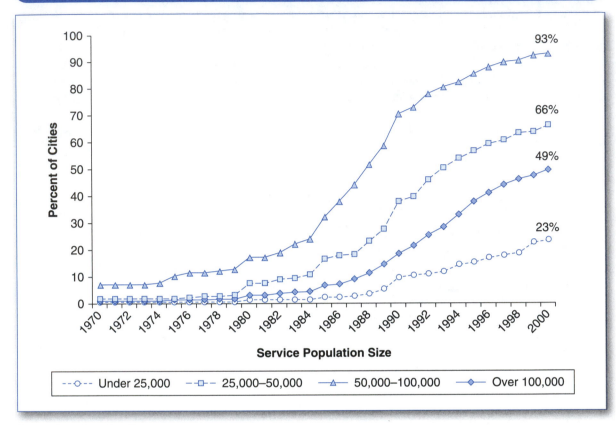

Source: Egley et al., 2006, p. 10.

greater than 100,000, reported the emergence of gang activity before 1996, which helps explain the peak in gang activity in the mid-1990s. The next section presents another view of cities' gang problem histories, grouping them according to similarities in their histories across more than a decade.

Presence of Gang Activity, 1996–2009

The analysis that follows is the first of its kind. *Trajectory modeling* has been widely used in the classification of individuals according to their pattern of offending over time (Lacourse et al., 2003; Piquero, 2008). In 2004, researchers began to apply this group-based trajectory method to model the criminal careers of geographic areas, like street segments and census tracts, to capture communities' trajectories across time and space (Griffiths & Chavez, 2004; Weisburd, Bushway, Lum, & Yang, 2004). This research, in turn, led Howell and colleagues (2011) to explore the possibility of modeling cities' gang problem histories. These analyses revealed that some cities in which officials say they have gang activity tend to report a consistent presence of gangs, while others experience no gang activity over time, rapid increases over time, rapid decreases, fluctuating presence of gang activity, or other more complex trends between 1996 and 2009. Trajectory models are used here to group jurisdictions that share similar trends in the outcome of interest (gang activity in this instance) and to graphically illustrate those patterns over the 14-year period.

The trajectory model in Figure 7.5 displays *trends in the presence of gang activity* across 1,517 jurisdictions—the number of U.S. localities surveyed every year in the NYGS between 1996 and 2009 (for samples, see Table 7.1). Of the total, 664 (43.8%) of the jurisdictions fall in the first trajectory (T1). This group exhibited a relatively lower prevalence of gang activity in 1996, which declined precipitously until 2001 before experiencing some growth that continued through 2009. By contrast, more than half of the jurisdictions (T2, $N = 853$; 56.2%) reported a near-chronic presence of gang activity across the time period. Thus, this trajectory model reveals that a small majority (56%) of all jurisdictions reporting gang activity have a persistent gang problem that, apart from the minor deviation in 2001, has remained virtually constant over time. In other words, just over half of all localities that reported gang activity across the 14 survey years experienced near-chronic gang activity.

Overall, the 14-year gang problem prevalence trend reported in the NYGS (Figure 7.2) shows two peaks in reported gang activity, in 1996, and in 2007–2009. This view of gang activity also suggests a sharp drop in the late 1990s and early 2000s. However, the trajectory analysis shows that more than half of the localities represented in Figure 7.2 rather consistently experienced gang problems across the 14 years. What primarily distinguishes those places reporting a consistent presence of gang activity (T2)

Figure 7.5   Trajectory Model: Presence of Gang Activity, 1996 Through 2009

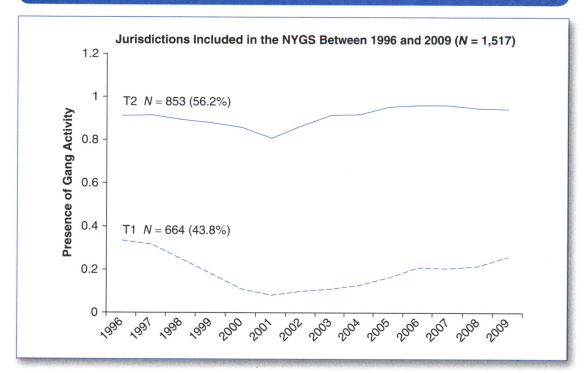

Source: Howell et al., 2011.

from those reporting a small and declining presence through the early 2000s (T1) is city size. The average population in 2000 of all near-chronic gang presence jurisdictions (T2) is 156,755 whereas it is only 42,905 among T1 jurisdictions. This means that cities reporting near-chronic gang presence between 1996 and 2009 are, on average, 3.65 times larger than those without chronic gang activity.

Table 7.3 shows the consistency of reported gang activity in cities with populations greater than 50,000 persons in the NYGS (referred to as *larger cities*). First, nearly 9 out of 10 (86.3%) cities reported gang activity in 2009. Second, almost 8 out of 10 (79.8%) of these cities consistently (each year) reported gang activity across at least a five-year window (between 2005 and 2009). In sharp contrast, fewer than 3 out of 10 (23.8%) smaller cities, towns, and villages consistently reported gang activity during the same period. Stated another way, persistent or stable gang activity is almost four times more likely to be found in larger cities.

These data and other prior NYGS analyses clearly demonstrate that gang activity—in terms of size of gang membership and the occurrence of gang violence—remains largely concentrated in the most populated areas in the United States (Egley et al., 2006; Egley, Howell, & Major, 2004; Howell, 2006). Therefore, the next analysis focuses only on jurisdictions with populations greater than 50,000. This permits an examination of larger cities with more persistent gang activity—where gang activity is not only more prevalent, but also more serious. For this reason, the next section begins to explore trends and patterns in the presence of gangs among cities with populations of at least 50,000 in the year 2000.

◈ Patterns of Gang Presence in Larger Cities

This exploratory research uses the 14 years of the NYGS. Figure 7.6 displays six identifiable groups in the analysis of a subgroup of 598 larger cities (cities with populations greater than 50,000 among those localities included in Figure 7.5). The most predominant group is the 418 cities in the trajectory group T5 (69.9% of the total sample), which reported a persistent and chronic gang problem over the 14-year period. Three groups of cities (T1, T2, and T3) showed increasing gang activity in the second half of the measurement period (Figure 7.6). The T1 group (25 cities; 4.2%) exhibited some minor increases in gang activity between 1996 and 2002 that escalates thereafter, but not to a chronic level. In both the T2 (4.8%; 29 cities) and T3 (9.2%; 55 cities) groups, gang activity escalates very sharply in the second half of the measurement period even though they had different experiences from 1996 to 2002. The T2 group showed virtually no presence of gang activity at the beginning of the survey period until 1998, and gang

Table 7.3 Law Enforcement Reports of Gang Activity, 2005 to 2009

Area Type	Gang Activity Reported in 2009	Gang Activity Consistently Reported, 2005–2009
Larger cities	86.3	79.8
Suburban counties	51.8	38.9
Smaller cities	32.9	23.8
Rural counties	17.0	11.0

Source: Egley & Howell, 2011, p. 2.

Figure 7.6   Trajectory Model: Presence of Gang Activity in Cities With Populations Greater Than 50,000

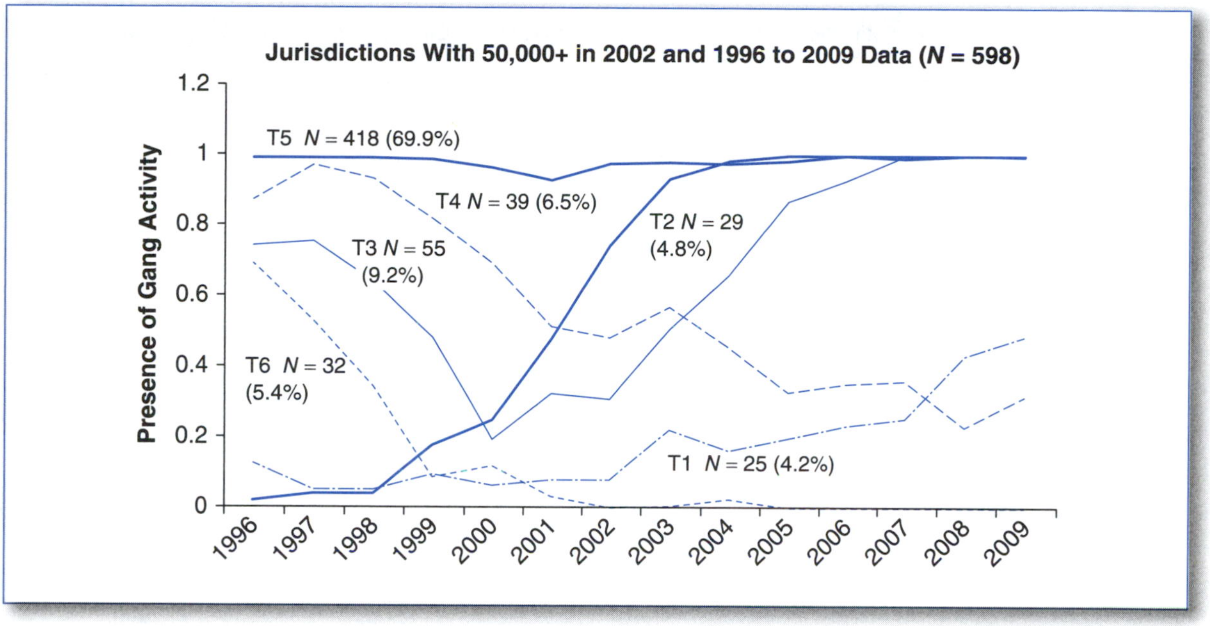

Source: Howell et al., 2011, p. 6.

activity rose sharply thereafter to near complete persistence from 2004 onward. Gang activity initially decreased in the T3 group of cities, and then sharply increased after 2002. The remaining two groups of cities (T4; 6.5%; 39 cities; and T6; 5.4%; 32 cities) reported decreasing gang activity almost entirely throughout the 14-year period.

In short, four main patterns are seen in the six groups of cities: first, no change (T5 group), second, increasing gang activity (T1 and T2 groups), third, decreasing gang activity (T4 and T6 groups), and fourth, a variable trend (T3 group). Seeing these distinctive patterns raises the question about the factors that might account for cities' various gang problem histories. Because of the novelty of this research, established explanations are not presently available for the trends observed here. Nonetheless, distinguishing larger cities by their trends in gang presence enables a preliminary exploration of differences in the political, economic, demographic, and cultural contexts of cities sharing the same patterns since the mid-1990s.

Political and Criminal Justice Context

To begin to disentangle whether and how local political context—and policies related to criminal justice processing, in particular—may be related to city gang trends, Table 7.4 provides mean differences in a host of local and state political factors that begin to distinguish those cities reporting chronic gang problems from cities with emerging, contracting, and variable presence of gangs between 1996 and 2009. While it cannot be definitively determined whether these relationships are a cause or a consequence

Table 7.4   Mean Differences in Political and Criminal Justice Context of Cities by Trajectory Group, 1996–2009

Political & Criminal Justice Policy Context	Chronic	Emerging	Contracting	Variable	p value	
Mean % of Republicans in the state legislature (2004)	55.93	45.35	49.50	54.08	.014	*
Mean state and local correctional expenditures per capita in state (2000; Census)	176.22	168.04	169.98	159.39	.007	**
Mean % of population institutionalized in fed. & state correctional institutions (2000)	0.71	0.62	0.70	0.66	.019	*
Mean budget of county or city prosecutors' offices per capita (2001; NPS)	23.32	19.33	20.91	15.32	.330	
Mean number of law enforcement officers per 100,000 in state (2005; UCR)	342.68	354.75	324.05	343.67	.065	ŧ
Mean institutional powers of governor score in 2000 (range 1–5; Beyle)	3.47	3.62	3.53	3.52	.021	*
Mean government ideology score (2000; Berry et al.)	48.94	47.07	44.52	42.09	.245	
Mean % of state legislative districts that are urban (1997)	31.48	27.44	27.53	29.87	.004	**
States have three strikes laws	.88	.93	.86	.80	.241	
States have death penalty	.87	.74	.72	.85	.003	**
States have state- funded indigent defense systems	.26	.57	.22	.43	.000	***

***$p<.000$; **$p<.01$; *$p<.05$; ŧ$p<.10$

Sources: U.S. Census Bureau, 2001; Unified Crime Reports [UCR], 2005; U.S. Dept. of Justice, Bureau of Justice Statistics, 2001; Beyle, 2012; Berry, Ringquist, Fording, & Hanson., 2010.

of city gang problems, many of these aspects of political and criminal justice context show significant group differences.[3] For example, the average state and local correctional expenditures in the year 2000 are significantly higher in chronic gang cities than in other cities (with an average of $176.22 per capita in chronic cities versus $168.04, $169.98, and $159.39 per capita in emerging, contracting, and variable cities, respectively). Chronic gang cities also tend to have more Republicans in the state legislature, larger statewide correctional populations, a non-significant but marginally more conservative average location of statewide elected officials on a liberal–conservative continuum (represented in a government ideology score reflecting the "policy mood" of the state), and a larger percentage of legislative districts in the state that are urban. Chronic and contracting gang cities also tend to be located in states that do not fund an organized indigent defense system relative to emerging gang cities (wherein approximately one quarter of all chronic and contracting gang cities are located in states with such a system compared to more than half of emerging and nearly half of variable gang cities).

Economic Context

Statewide and local Census data provide a snapshot of variations in the economic context of cities grouped according to distinctive gang presence trends in Table 7.5. It is noteworthy that the patterns of gang presence in larger cities are highly related to most economic measures. In terms of poverty, chronic gang cities tend to be located in states and counties with higher poverty levels, and the cities themselves tend have higher levels of poverty relative to cities characterized by the other gang presence trajectories. On average, chronic gang cities have the highest rates of poverty among African Americans and Hispanics, whereas contracting gang cities tend to have the lowest rates of poverty for both groups (for importance of economic inequality, see Schroeder, 2011). Emerging gang cities report higher average expenditures of social welfare and a lower average gross state product than do chronic gang cities, and contracting gang cities are associated with the highest average median household income. On the whole, city gang trends appear to be strongly related to economic conditions.

Demographic Context

Some aspects of racial and ethnic composition appear to be related to the presence of gang trends in large cities, although the patterns are not particularly strong. Chronic gang cities, on average, are located in both states and counties with marginally larger proportions of the population who are non-White, and chronic cities also have Hispanic populations that are proportionately twice as large as is typical of emerging, contracting, or variable gang cities (refer to Table 7.6). Citywide levels of racial heterogeneity are also related to trends in gang activity. Heterogeneity scores account for the number and size of groups in the local population and range from complete homogeneity (when every person in the population is member of the same group) to complete heterogeneity (when all racial groups comprise an equal size of the total population). In general, chronic gang cities are more racially heterogeneous than are emerging, contracting, and variable gang cities. On average, chronic and variable gang cities have a larger percentage of female-headed families with dependent children, greater residential mobility, and a larger proportion of the population who are young males than is generally the case for emerging and contracting gang cities. Chronic gang cities also show larger average proportions of the population who were born outside of the United States relative to the other cities, consistent with the notion that immigrant concentration influences local gang presence.

Cultural Context

Measuring the cultural context of places can be a difficult exercise involving the evaluation of shared norms, habits, ideologies, values, and orientations. It may be the case that the unique cultural codes of places either influence the emergence and/or persistence of gang activity *or* that gang presence affects the norms, values, and orientations of local residents. Said differently, culture may be both a cause and consequence of gang problems. Table 7.7 provides an initial exploration of some of the ways in which the cultural context of cities is related to their patterns of gang presence between 1996 and 2009. In general, chronic and contracting gang cities have higher average scores on two different punitiveness scales. B. Kutateladze (2011) developed a multidimensional punitiveness scale that distinguishes states

Table 7.5 Mean Differences in Economic Context of Cities by Trajectory Group, 1996–2009

Economic Context	Chronic	Emerging	Contracting	Variable	p value	
Mean % in poverty in state (2000)	12.33	11.40	12.16	11.40	.017	*
Mean % in poverty in county (2000)	12.21	11.67	10.64	10.34	.006	**
Mean % in poverty in city (2000)	14.35	11.15	10.64	12.13	.000	***
Mean % White in poverty in city (2000)	7.46	6.78	6.80	7.56	.450	
Mean % Black in poverty in city (2000)	21.51	18.39	15.13	18.55	.000	***
Mean % Hispanic in poverty in city (2000)	20.34	18.95	13.94	19.61	.000	***
Mean % female-headed households with children in poverty in city (2000)	38.05	33.03	29.11	34.82	.000	***
Mean expenditures on public welfare per 100,000 in state (2002)	88,221.45	101,873.80	89,801.18	86,758.55	.002	**
Mean gross state product in billions (2005)	687.39	467.42	540.79	404.41	.000	***
Mean % unemployed in city (2000)	4.19	3.49	3.37	3.81	.000	***
Mean % males 16+ in the labor force in city (2000)	71.45	72.58	72.98	73.54	.053	t
Mean % of males officially unemployed in city (2000)	4.58	3.93	3.73	4.16	.000	***
Mean % females 16+ in labor force in city (2000)	58.65	59.20	59.07	59.78	.551	
Mean % of females officially unemployed in city (2000)	3.83	3.09	3.04	3.54	.000	***
Average median household income in city (2000)	41,682.44	46,850.67	50,161.17	45,296.12	.000	***
Mean GINI index of income inequality in county (2000)	.45	.45	.44	.44	.262	

***p<.000; **p<.01; *p<.05; ᵗp<.10

Sources: Census 2000; U.S. Bureau of Economic Analysis, 2005.

Table 7.6   Mean Differences in Demographic Context of Cities by Trajectory Group, 1996–2009

Demographic Context	Chronic	Emerging	Contracting	Variable	p value	
Mean % non-White in state (2000)	25.76	23.36	23.70	22.02	.029	*
Mean % non-White in county (2000)	27.73	25.91	24.03	21.90	.015	*
Mean % Hispanic in city (2000)	19.16	7.71	6.76	8.93	.000	***
Mean % Black in city (2000)	14.58	12.94	11.46	15.01	.480	
Mean racial heterogeneity in city (2000)	.47	.33	.33	.36	.000	***
Mean % female headed families with children in city (2000)	13.44	11.44	10.49	12.36	.000	***
Mean % residentially mobile in city (2000)	52.00	46.12	48.34	50.85	.000	***
Mean % males 15 to 34 years old in city (2000)	15.88	14.26	14.80	15.77	.001	***
Mean % foreign born in city (2000)	15.70	10.46	11.65	9.91	.000	***

***$p<.000$; **$p<.01$; *$p<.05$

Source: Census 2000.

according to (a) political and symbolic punishment policies (such as the application of punitive sentencing like life without the possibility of parole or the death penalty, three strikes laws, sex offender registries, or felon disenfranchisement, among others); (b) incarceration punitiveness (including rates, flows, admissions, releases, and average terms, among others); (c) punitive punishing of "immorality" (including laws around age of consent, prostitution, gambling, and drunkenness, etc.); (d) punitive conditions of confinement (including prison overcrowding, access to medical care in prison, deaths of inmates, lawsuits filed, etc.); and (e) punitive treatment of juveniles in the justice system (including ages of court jurisdiction, transfer laws, incarceration rate, overcrowding, and juveniles in adult prisons, etc.). Kutateladze also calculated a scale of state punitiveness based on Tonry's (2001) six criteria including (1) incarceration rates, (2) the death penalty, (3) mandatory minimum sentences, (4) three strikes laws, (5) life-without-possibility-of-parole laws, and (6) average severity of sentences. Both chronic and contracting gang cities are located in states that have, on average, higher levels of punitiveness according to the Kutateladze and the Tonry punitiveness scales.

Perceptions about the proper role of the state are captured in political culture measures, such as the degree to which states can be defined as moralistic, traditionalistic, and individualistic. According to Elazar (1984), states with traditionalistic cultures are those in which government is charged with the maintenance of social order, often reflecting a contentment with the status quo, even if it tends to satisfy the interests of elites. Traditionalism does not distinguish cities with varied gang trends. However, the data illustrate that chronic gang cities are much more likely to be located in moralistic states and much less likely to be located in individualistic states, on average, than cities with other gang trends. By contrast, emerging gang cities are, on average,

Table 7.7   Mean Differences in Cultural Context of Cities by Trajectory Group, 1996–2009

Cultural Context	Chronic	Emerging	Contracting	Variable	*p* value	
Mean state located in the deep south	.15	.24	.18	.20	*.265*	
Mean % of state population who identify as evangelical Christians (2007; Pew Center)	24.25	21.67	25.90	24.20	*.175*	
Mean % state population preferring Starbucks over McDonalds (2008; Pew Center)	49.30	42.53	46.00	44.66	*.000*	***
Mean BK punitiveness score in state in 2009 (range 0–4; Kutateladze)	2.13	1.96	2.10	2.06	*.006*	**
Mean political and symbolic punitiveness scale	2.05	1.63	1.87	1.86	*.000*	***
Mean incarceration punitiveness scale	2.00	2.01	2.24	2.02	*.069*	t
Mean punishing immorality punitiveness scale	2.63	2.04	2.39	2.28	*.000*	***
Mean conditions of confinement punitiveness scale	1.88	1.90	1.73	1.96	*.028*	*
Mean juvenile justice punitiveness scale	2.06	2.22	2.27	2.16	*.001*	***
Mean Tonry punitiveness score in state in 2009 (range 0–4; Kutateladze)	2.14	1.68	2.16	1.93	*.000*	***
Mean state has a moralistic culture (1984; Elazar)	.46	.15	.38	.25	*.000*	***
Mean state has a traditionalistic culture (1984; Elazar)	.30	.30	.27	.36	*.669*	
Mean state has an individualistic culture (1984; Elazar)	.25	.56	.35	.38	*.000*	***

***p<.000; **p<.01; *p<.05; ᵗp<.10

Sources: Berry et al. (2010), Elazar (1984), Kutateladze (2011), and Pew Center (2009).

located in states that are individualistically oriented and not moralistic. This means that emerging gang cities are located in places in which the citizenry is more likely to support a utilitarian government that encourages private enterprise; conversely, chronic gang cities are in states in which the citizenry sees the government as a force for good charged with fostering a collective aims, even at the expense of individual interests.

Finally, researchers at the Pew Center (2009) asked a nationally representative sample of 2,260 adults whether they would prefer to live in a place with more Starbucks or McDonalds franchises. Preference for Starbucks is, on average, highest in chronic gang cities and lowest in emerging gang cities. According to this survey, preference for Starbucks over McDonalds is correlated with a host of demographic features like gender, age, income, region, race, religion, and political affiliation, indirectly suggesting that the social, demographic, and ideological contexts of chronic gang cities are distinctive from the contexts of emerging, contracting, and variable gang presence cities.

Modal Cities

This section provides a brief illustration of modal cities from various trajectories shown in Figure 7.6 to describe how political, economic, demographic, and cultural context vary across cities with distinctive gang presence trends. The modal cities selected here share many of the key political, economic, demographic, and cultural characteristics of the average chronic, emerging, contracting, and variable gang city, respectively. Consequently, these profiles provide a snapshot of larger urban contexts experiencing the four unique patterns of gang presence trends between 1996 and 2009.

Chronic Gang City: Modesto, California

Modesto, California may be considered an average city in the chronic gang group. In the year 2000, Modesto had a population of 188,856 (compared to a mean of 182,552 among all chronic gang cities). Like three quarters of chronic gang cities, Modesto is also located in a state without a state-funded indigent defense system, but with a relatively high score on the punitiveness scale and reflecting a moralistic stance toward government. Slightly more than 15% of residents in Modesto lived below the poverty line (which approximates the average of 14.4% in all chronic gang cities), slightly more than 6% of residents aged 16 and older were unemployed in Modesto in the year 2000 (compared to 4.2% in the average chronic gang city) and, like most chronic gang cities, Modesto is characterized by marginally greater racial heterogeneity (.51 compared to .47 in the average chronic city) than is found in cities without chronic gang problems. For these reasons, Modesto provides a suitable representation of a typical chronic gang city over the period.

While the police department in Modesto initiated a specialized unit (which has been variously referred to as the Gang Violence Suppression Unit, the Crime Reduction Task Force, the Street Terrorist Apprehension Team or, more recently, the Street Crimes Unit) to handle gang crime as early as the mid-1980s, persistent gang problems began to escalate as a function of increasing between-gang rivalries by the mid-2000s. Latino youth gangs dominate this area, although some Black and Asian gangs are known to operate in Modesto. According to an article in the *Modesto Bee*, those Latino gangs were generally affiliated with the Norteños, or northerners, in the mid- to late 1990s, but by the mid-2000s, growth in the street gang known as the Sureños, or southerners, was outpacing the Norteños (Herendeen, 2007). The Norteños, who identified themselves with the color red, could be easily distinguished from the Sureños, who favored blue. In addition to drug trafficking, violent crimes like robberies and homicides escalated as the rivalries between the gangs in Modesto intensified, leading police in both the metro area and the county (in the form of the 2004 County-wide Gang Intelligence Task Force) to direct resources specifically to gang suppression, investigation, prosecution, and prevention. Despite continuing efforts to maintain updated gang databases, ensure penalty enhancements in the prosecution of all gang-related violence, and support programs like G.R.E.A.T. (Gang Resistance Education and Training program) and Wake-Up (which involves a two-month series of classes for parents and juveniles in trouble with the law), Deputy District Attorney Thomas Brennan expressed concerns that "for every gang member I put in prison, there's two more taking his place" (Herendeen, 2007). To date, gang problems continue to plague residents in Modesto; for example, 10 Sureño gang members were charged with beating, stabbing, and shooting a 20-year-old man multiple times on Valentine's Day in 2013. The killing was premeditated by the group, who are accused of having driven around the city, flashing gang signs at prospective Norteño gang members, in search of a target (Guerra, 2013).

Emerging Gang City: Warwick, Rhode Island

Warwick, Rhode Island, shares many characteristics typical of emerging gang cities in the analysis. With a population of 85,808 in 2000, Warwick approximates the size of emerging gang cities (which average 78,105). Like other emerging cities, Warwick is located in a state that has a substantially smaller proportion of Republicans in the state legislature (15%), spends more money on public welfare ($132,399 per 100,000 in 2002), produces a reasonably low gross state product (43.62 billion in 2005), has a small foreign-born population (4.8%), and is located in a state that is both relatively non-punitive and characterized by an individualistic stance toward government. Law enforcement in Warwick also first reported gang problems in 2003 in the National Youth Gang Survey, despite having reported no gang activity between 1996 and 2002. Therefore, Warwick fits the profile of a typical emerging gang city in the United States.

Unlike the much larger city of Providence 12 miles to its north, the city of Warwick is not known for its gang problems. With the exception of an article published in *The Telegraph* newspaper on June 26, 1935, entitled "Witness Places Gang at Warwick: Rettich Brother-in-Law Testifies at Gang Trial," there are few reports of gang activity in Warwick and the Warwick Police Department does not have a specialized gang taskforce. Any street gang activity that does exist likely revolves around drug distribution activities. According to the 2003 National Drug Intelligence Center's report detailing an assessment of drug threats in Rhode Island, drug-related arrests are most likely to occur in the urbanized centers of the state including Warwick. The only international airport in Rhode Island is located in Warwick, and the city is also accessible to maritime vessels along the waterfront. Moreover, "Providence Police Department officials and Warwick law enforcement officials report that drug distributors in their jurisdictions commonly commit violent crimes to protect their turf, and drug abusers frequently commit crimes such as residential break-ins to support their drug addiction" (National Drug Intelligence Center, 2003, p. 4). The emergent nature of gang problems in Warwick is likely a function of the specific transportation avenues available in the city as well as a potential diffusion in youth gang problems from nearby Providence. Yet even law enforcement is reluctant to view youth crime as gang-related; for example, in a recent article from the March 11, 2014, edition of the *Warwick Daily News*, "Warwick police have played down suggestions of a youth gang forming in the town after four teens and one 12-year old were arrested for a weekend crime spree" ("Five Youths in Court").

Contracting Gang City: Newport Beach, California

Of the 71 cities composing the contracting gang trajectory, Newport Beach, California, can be considered an average contracting gang city. The population of Newport Beach (70,032 in 2000) fell just shy of the average city size of all contracting gang cities (at 74,475). Like most contracting gang cities, Newport Beach is located in a state with a slightly lower average number of law enforcement officers per 100,000 residents, a slightly higher average punitiveness score, and a moralistic stance toward government. The city also shares with other contracting gang cities a relatively low proportion of Hispanic residents in poverty (7.6%) and a relatively low proportion of families that are headed by a woman with dependent children (10.5%). While contracting cities tend to have higher than average median household incomes (at $50,161), Newport Beach is even more advantaged than most, with a median household income of $83,455. Nonetheless, Newport Beach shares most of the features of contracting gang cities and has reported a pattern of gang activity consistent with a declining gang problem. Specifically, law enforcement reported gang activity in 1997 and 1998, and again from 2001 through 2003, but no further gang problems thereafter. Newport Beach therefore represents a modal contracting gang city.

Newport Beach is one of the wealthier communities in Orange County, but these advantages have not always buffered it from gang activity. Some of this activity takes the form of violence between gangs heralding from other places in the county. Nonetheless, the local police department's Patrol Division maintains a Gang Suppression Unit, which has, in part, enabled the city to suppress gang activities that could otherwise spill over from nearby Santa Ana or Stanton. As early as 1993, the *Los Angeles Times* reported that police in Newport Beach were quick to acknowledge that its gang problem was small, with

> only 12 of the 15,000 gang members whom police have identified as living in Orange County resid[ing] in Newport Beach . . . [Yet] this coastal city [was] still a destination for thousands of tourists—including gang members—who flock[ed] to its beaches. (Wilgoren & Elston, 1993)

Thus, in 1993, the police began to track gang-related crimes, considered anti-ordinances, and formed a gang task force that was actively involved in stopping suspected gang members "whose clothes fit the profile" (Wilgoren & Elston, 1993). This aggressive strategy is considered by some Newport Beach residents to be excessive, but it may have worked. The Newport Beach police have not reported gang activity in the National Youth Gang Survey since 2003.

Variable Gang City: Asheville, North Carolina

Cities with variable gang problems between 1996 and 2009 tend to report gang activity at the beginning and the end of the periods, but few such problems in between. Asheville, North Carolina is an example of a typical variable gang city. Asheville's population in 2000 was 68,889, just shy of the average size of all variable gang cities (74,060). It is located in a state with relatively low correctional expenditures ($144 per capita in 2000) and a low gross state product ($350 billion in 2005), consistent with variable gang cities in general. Additionally, Asheville reported a small foreign-born population (5.2%) and scores below average on state punitiveness scales, like other variable gang cities. Reported gang activity in Asheville also followed the same trend as other variable gang cities between 1996 and 2009 with gang presence noted at the beginning and end of the period but not in the years between.

Since 1997, the government of North Carolina has been actively involved in documenting, tracking, and encouraging preventative efforts aimed at youth gang membership through the North Carolina Criminal Justice Analysis Center (NCCJAC) and the Governor's Crime Commission (NCGCC). The Asheville Mall instituted a curfew policy that required teenagers to be accompanied by a parent or guardian after 6:00 pm on Saturdays, that prohibited teens from wearing bandannas on the premises, and that prevented teens from congregating in groups greater than four, ostensibly to limit gang violence and unruly behavior in 1993 (Kipper & Ramey, 2012). This was some of the first early evidence that Asheville may harbor street gang problems. And while law enforcement reported some gang presence in Asheville between 1996 and 2000 in the National Youth Gang Survey, none was reported between 2001 and 2005. Yet from 2006 onward, Asheville witnessed another upswing in gang activity, largely located in and around the city's public housing developments (T. Moore, 2007). A few months later, reporters at the *Citizen-Times* were declaring that "gangs have shown quick growth . . . Asheville Police Chief Bill Hogan started talking publicly of an emerging gang problem after having said a little more than a year ago that the city had no significant problems with gangs" (Behsudi, 2007). Tagging, turf battles, drive-by shootings, and drug-selling activities were all attributable to increasing gang presence by 2007 and 2008, according to the police. In response, police used the North Carolina GangNET database more frequently, which, on the advice of the Attorney General's Office, allows law enforcement to include suspected or known gang members as young as 15 years of age in the statewide database. Standard forms for incident reports were reworked to include a "gang-related" check box, senior officers underwent gang identification and prevention training, the Asheville Police Department and school system implemented the G.R.E.A.T. program to promote prevention, police convened with officers from gang suppression units around the country to discuss investigation tactics, and two specialized officers were hired to man a new Gang Suppression Unit in 2008 (Behsudi, 2007; T. Moore, 2007; North Carolina Metropolitan Mayors Coalition, 2010). As these examples show, the city of Asheville represents an urban center struggling to deal with variable gang problems.

◈ Regional Variations in Gang Presence

Are there regional variations in gang presence trends? Table 7.8 shows that chronic stability is the typical experience for large cities in all census regions of the United States. However, less than half (44.6%) of the Northeastern cities report chronic gang activity, and more than one quarter (26.7%) of Northeastern cities are characterized as having an emerging gang problem between 1996 and 2009. By contrast, almost 90% of Western cities report chronic stability and a far smaller proportion are emerging (1.6%), contracting (6.5%), or variable (4.8%). Cities in the Midwest are unlikely to report emerging trends (5.6%), and much more likely to report contracting trends (19.7%). Finally, Southern cities are almost equally likely to report emerging (9.5%), contracting (11.2%), and variable (10.7%) patterns over the period. These findings suggest the possibility that the short-term natural histories of gang problems in cities across the United States vary by region.

◈ Explaining the Emergence, Persistence, and Decline of Gang Activity

Factors Affecting the Emergence of Gangs in New Cities

A number of factors may be associated with the emergence of gangs in new cities, including economic marginality, the migration of gang members from larger urban centers for the express purpose of enlarging their influence, and cultural diffusion. These factors draw from or share similarities to

Table 7.8 Cities with Chronic, Emerging, Contracting, and Variable Trends by Region, 1996–2009

	Chronic (T5)		Emerging (T1 & T2)		Contracting (T4 & T6)		Variable (T3)		Total
	n	%	N	%	N	%	N	%	N
All Cities	418	69.9	54	9.0	71	11.9	55	9.2	598
Cities in the Northeast	45	44.6	27	26.7	12	11.9	17	16.8	101
Cities in the Midwest	95	66.9	8	5.6	28	19.7	11	7.7	142
Cities in the South	116	68.6	16	9.5	19	11.2	18	10.7	169
Cities in the West	162	87.1	3	1.6	12	6.5	9	4.8	186

Stages 1 through 3 of Howell's model of gang emergence (see Chapter 4, this volume; Howell, 2015). Of these, gang migration has found the least support in the literature. Each factor is discussed in turn below.

Economic Marginality

Some of the earliest explanations for the emergence of gangs in major urban centers like New York, Chicago, or Los Angeles rested on social upheavals associated with urban change and economic conditions related to strain and marginalization. Socially disorganized communities are places with strong in- and out-migration flows, substantial economic instability, and elevated racial or ethnic heterogeneity, which undercut local efforts at socially controlling crime and violence (Sampson & Groves, 1989; Shaw & McKay, 1969). In these neighborhoods, collectivities of young people form gangs, each of which has a unique "tradition, unreflective internal structure, esprit de corps, solidarity, morale, group awareness, and attachment to a local territory" (Thrasher 1927/2000, p. 46). Collective struggles in the face of structural disadvantage thus set the stage for gang formation and, ultimately, the emergence of gangs and gang rivalries in cities. While there is some evidence to suggest that economic factors are less salient in the explanation of emerging gangs within rural areas (Wells & Weisheit, 2001), much of the literature shows that absolute and relative economic deprivation explain gang growth both across cities and between neighborhoods within cities (Hagedorn, 1988; Jankowski, 1991; Spergel, 1995).

Population Migration

Concern over the emergence of gangs in new cities has generally been attributed by law enforcement and the media to the movement of gang members to new locales. These migrants are viewed as threatening outsiders who are able to provide structural ties to groups in other parts of the country, franchise drug market opportunities, and import knowledge of gang customs from their past associations to local youth (Tapia, 2014). According to Maxson (1998), "reports of big-city gang members fanning out across the Nation seeking new markets for drug distribution have added fuel to concerns about gang proliferation and gang migration" (p. 1). Yet most of the major ethnographic studies conducted in cities with new or growing gang problems have failed to identify the migration of gang members from major cities as a proximate cause of gang proliferation (Decker & van Winkle, 1996; Hagedorn, 1988; Huff, 1989; Waldorf, 1993; Zevitz & Takata, 1992). Moreover, research by Maxson and colleagues (1996) shows that while law enforcement agencies in cities across the United States tended to report some migration of gang members into their locales in the 1990s, the vast majority of these jurisdictions acknowledged gang activity prior to the migration of gang members from other parts of the country, and 47% of cities in the study had fewer than 10 migrant gang members relocate in the year preceding the survey (Maxson, 1998; see also Klein & Maxson, 2006).

In general, gang member migrants are most likely to describe moving for family reasons, and equally likely to move to pursue employment opportunities, for court-ordered relocations, because of law enforcement crackdowns, or to paradoxically escape gang involvement than to enlarge drug distribution channels or to franchise the gangs with which they are affiliated (Maxson, 1998). Tapia (2014) recently showed that Latino gang members in the Midwest claim to have both direct and indirect ties to parent gangs outside of the city; however, he concedes that gang members may be overselling these connections in an effort to legitimize their status as the "real thing." There is little doubt, then, that population migration plays some role in the proliferation of gangs outside of major urban centers, but what is less clear is whether any of that migration reflects efforts to expand the influence, turf, or membership of criminal gangs to new and different areas of the country.

Cultural Diffusion

A third explanation for the emergence of gangs in new places, some of which have never harbored gangs in the past, is the potential for a diffusion of cultural symbols and iconic gang images portrayed in movies and specific music genres, like hip-hop and rap (Hagedorn, 2008; Maxson, 1998; van Gemert & Decker, 2008; Wells & Weisheit, 2001). Here, gangs in emerging gang cities simply "copycat" the rhetoric, rules, rituals, symbols, colors, hand signs, and gang names (Decker & Van Winkle, 1996; Tapia, 2014). Similarities between gang sets across places are a function of the emulation of popular culture lore regarding gangs, rather than an outgrowth of realized connections to nationally recognized outfits like the Bloods, Crips, People, Folks, or Latin Kings, for example. In this case, the transmission of culture is an imitative process enabled by broad influences across widely dispersed areas, without the necessity of direct contact between persons or groups (Cohen & Tita 1999). Cultural diffusion likely plays at least some role in the proliferation of gangs to new areas of the country.

Factors Affecting the Persistence of Gang Activity in Cities

Some key factors that may influence the persistence of gang activity—or chronic gang problems—in cities include, but are not limited to, continuing gang history or tradition, sustained economic deprivation, and the influence of returning prison gang inmates. Each of these, in addition to access to weapons and drug-trafficking operations, may contribute to the persistence of chronic and serious gang problems.

Gangs' Histories

Street gang histories and gang lore serve to perpetuate gang activity. Prominent gang names are often copied in distant cities, and this, along with glorification of gang life, past exploits, and acclaimed victorious battles, serves to bolster recruitment and member retention. This is particularly true in cities associated with established gang traditions.

IN FOCUS 7.1
REGIONAL TRENDS IN GANG ACTIVITY
AS VIEWED BY THE FBI AND POLICE AGENCIES

Not all sources agree on the most prominent gangs. The following documentation lists gang activity trends in large cities and states during the past few years compiled by the U.S. Federal Bureau of Investigation and state and local police agencies. This information suggests that gangs are often very adept in perpetuating gang culture.

Northeast region. New York City is no longer the epicenter of serious street gang activity in the Northeast as was the case in the early 1900s. Gradually, gang activity in this region expanded to include other East region and New England states, particularly Pennsylvania, New Jersey, and Connecticut (FBI, 2009). According to the FBI's intelligence reports, "The most significant gangs operating in the East Region are Crips, Latin Kings, MS-13, Ñeta, and United Blood Nation" (p. 16). "The most significant gangs operating in the New England Region are Hells Angels, Latin Kings, Outlaws, Tiny Rascal Gangster Crips, and UBN" (p. 17).

Central region. In the Midwest region, traditional Chicago gangs still have the strongest presence. According to the Chicago Crime Commission (2006), in 2008, the largest street gangs in Chicago include the Gangster Disciple Nation (GDN), Black Gangsters/New Breeds (BG), Latin Kings (LKs), Black P. Stone Nation, Vice Lords (VLs), the Four Corner Hustlers and the Maniac Latin Disciples (MLDs) (p. 11). The most recent chapter in Chicago gang history is the proliferation of gangs outside the city. By 2006, 19 gang turfs were scattered around Chicago, throughout Cook County (p. 119). Next, gangs began emerging in the larger region surrounding Chicago on the north, west, and south sides. The FBI (2009) includes other cities in this region that have extensive gang activity, particularly Cleveland, Detroit, Joliet, Kansas City, Minneapolis, Omaha, and St. Louis (p. 18).

Pacific region. Street gangs in Los Angeles remain legendary. This city is now said to be "the gang capital of the world" (Advancement Project, 2007, p. 1). The Los Angeles Police Department (2007) recently designated the 11 most notorious gangs in the city: 18th Street Westside (southwest area), 204th Street (Harbor area), Avenues (northeast area), Black P-Stones (southwest, Wilshire areas), Canoga Park Alabama (West Valley area), Grape Street Crips (southeast area), La Mirada Locos (Rampart, northeast areas), Mara Salvatrucha (Rampart, Hollywood, and Wilshire areas), Rollin 40s (southwest area), Rollin 30s Harlem Crips (southwest area), and Rolling 60s (77th St. area).

Southern region. The most significant gangs operating in the Southeast region (Deep South states) are said to be Crips, Gangster Disciples, Latin Kings, Sureños 13, and United Blood Nation (FBI, 2009). According to the FBI, the increased migration of Hispanic gangs into the region has contributed significantly to gang growth (p. 20). In the Southwest region (Texas, Oklahoma, New Mexico, Colorado, Utah, and Arizona), the most significant gangs are Barrio Azteca, Latin Kings, Mexikanemi, Tango Blast, and Texas Syndicate.

Sources: Chicago Crime Commission (2006); FBI (2009); Los Angeles Police Department (2007).

Local Economies

Alternatively, or additionally, chronic gang problems may thrive in cities independently of the conditions that precipitated gang formation to begin with (via prison gang influences or entrenched gang traditions, for example); yet gangs may also persist in response to enduring and severe economic deprivations. The analyses reported in Tables 7.4 through 7.7 show that chronic gang cities are places with elevated rates of male joblessness, low median household incomes, and high overall levels of poverty as well as elevated rates of poverty among African American and Hispanic populations more specifically. While these analyses are limited to the extent that they reflect state, city, or metropolitan features rather than local neighborhood contexts, they capture the kinds of obstacles that are found to hinder opportunities for social mobility among young males in the population, further serving to marginalize, demoralize, and isolate young men of color (Klein & Maxson, 2006). Some of these problems are influential in encouraging gang membership among both youth and young adults (Hagedorn, 1988, 2008; Rodríguez, 2001).

Returning Prison Gang Members

The most widely accepted definition of a *prison gang* is "an organization which operates within the prison system as a self-perpetuating criminally oriented entity, consisting of a select group of inmates who *have established an organized chain of command and are governed by an established code of conduct*" (Lyman, 1989, p. 48). This definition soon became outdated, however, as the term *prison gang* was expanded to encompass prison-based gangs with distinctive outside counterparts (sometimes called *prison street gangs*). The American Correctional Association (ACA) adopted in 1993 the more inclusive term *Security Threat Groups (STGs)*, defined as "two or more inmates, acting together, who pose a threat to the security or safety of staff/inmates, and/or to the orderly management of the facility/system" (ACA, 1993, p. 1). In time, STG virtually supplanted usage of prison gang terminology. This is owing to the expanded scope of prison gangs both inside and outside prisons, and to the growth of other adult criminal organizations that compromise management control of prisons that may also have counterparts outside prisons (Allender & Marcell, 2003).

In recent years, the issue of gang members returning from secure confinement has received greater attention, in part because of the growing numbers of inmates who are released annually. Sabol, Minton, and Harrison (2007) estimate that nearly 700,000 prison inmates arrive in communities throughout the United States each year. The proportion of these persons who are gang involved is unknown. A pioneering Illinois study has shed some light on this matter.

In Olson and Dooley's (2006) statewide study of more than 2,500 adult inmates released from Illinois prisons during 2000, nearly one-quarter of them were identified as gang members. Three-fourths (75%) of the gang members had a new arrest versus 63% of the nongang inmates in the follow-up period of almost two years. Gang members also were rearrested more quickly following release from prison, and were more likely to be arrested for violent and drug offenses than were nongang members. More than half (55%) of the gang members were readmitted to Illinois prisons within the two-year follow-up period, compared to 46% of the nongang members. Of those cited for a violation of the term of parole, gang members were more likely than nongang members to receive a violation on an arrest for a more serious offense (52% versus 42%, respectively). Similar findings emerged from Huebner, Varano, and Bynum's (2007) study of a sample of 322 young men aged 17 to 24 years released from prison in a Midwestern state: "As hypothesized, men who were involved in a gang or were drug dependent before entering prison had higher reconviction rates and recidivated more quickly than men who did not report involvement in gangs or drug use" (p. 208).

The return of gang members from prison to communities is a noticeable problem for approximately two-thirds of the gang problem jurisdictions nationwide (Egley et al., 2006). This is not a new issue, however. Of the agencies reporting the return of gang members from confinement in 2001, nearly two-thirds (63%) reported that returning members "somewhat" or "very much" contributed to an increase in violent crime among local gangs; 69% reported the same for drug trafficking. The impact of returning members is much greater on localities with more long-standing gang problems (Howell, 2006). In the view of law enforcement in the 2008 NYGS, returning gang inmates contribute rather evenly in the following ways, in descending order of importance: violent crime, drug trafficking, property crime, access to weapons, and dress and demeanor.

Factors Affecting the Decline of Gang Activity in Cities

A number of social and economic changes may help to explain the contraction of gang problems in certain U.S. cities. A few of these include the dramatic transformation of the delivery of public housing in the United States, as well as optimistic economic conditions. In effect, reversals on some of the features that encourage the entrenchment of gangs through Howell's (2015) stages can also help to explain gang de-escalation.

Transformation of Public Housing

As a consequence of the dismal state of affairs outlined in the 1992 *Final Report of the National Commission on Severely Depressed Public Housing*, the Department of Housing and Urban Development introduced the Housing Opportunities for People Everywhere (HOPE VI) program, which provided funds to revitalize and, where necessary, demolish severely distressed public housing developments that had markedly deteriorated after decades of institutional neglect and mismanagement (Popkin, Gwiasda, Olson, Rosenbaum, & Burton., 2000; Venkatesh, 2000). Cities like Chicago and Atlanta, once home to notorious violent and gang-ridden large-scale public housing complexes, underwent a dramatic transformation in the nature of housing assistance delivery, largely from project-based assistance to tenant-based Housing Choice Vouchers (Griffiths, 2014; Popkin, Rich, Hendey, Hayes, & Parilla, 2012). While these citywide transformation processes are recent enough to have precluded significant scholarly evaluation of the implications for gang disruption, preliminary studies of changing crime patterns in cities that have demolished most or all of their distressed public housing developments show a reduction in total crime in the immediate vicinity of the demolition in the short term (Rich, et al., 2010). Moreover, demolition provides at least some gang members with a prime opportunity for exit (Venkatesh, Çelimli, Miller, Murphy, & Turne, 2004). According to one study following Chicago's public housing transformation,

> on average, roughly 40% of the adolescents and young adults leave the gang immediately after relocation. Although the number of gang members who exit is high, over time, some members do eventually return to the gang. Indeed, 5% of those who exited will return to the gang one year after relocating; 26% will return after eighteen months. (p. 37)

While the potential exists for gang members residing in the former developments to relocate their activities to destination neighborhoods and even stimulate rivalries with gangs in their new communities

(Hagedorn & Rauch, 2007; Venkatesh et al., 2004), the elimination of gang turf—or set space—may both disrupt and undermine youth gang activities in the immediate area and throughout the city. Major shifts in the delivery of housing assistance in the United States may therefore have important consequences for fracturing, diminishing, or undercutting gang activities in urban centers in the long run.

Economic Advantage

The examination of local economic characteristics reported in Table 7.5 shows that contracting gang cities had, on average, median household incomes in excess of $50,000, a smaller proportion of city residents living below the poverty line, and a considerably lower proportion of impoverished female-headed households with dependent children than is typical in cities with more problematic gang patterns and trends. Moreover, the proportion of Hispanic and African American residents who are living below the poverty line is lowest in contracting gang cities. These characteristics suggest that increasing economic advantage and social opportunity may forestall gang activity over time in cities.

◈ Concluding Observations

Overall, two predominant gang trends are evident across the 14 years of the National Youth Gang Survey. First, there is remarkable stability in reported gang activity in larger cities. Few significant changes are seen in cities with populations greater than 50,000 persons (and adjacent suburban areas), where nearly two-thirds of all gangs and 8 out of 10 gang members are found. In addition, 8 out of 10 of these cities reported gang activity each year from 2005 to 2009. Second, gang activity is highly unstable in smaller cities, towns, villages, and rural counties. These localities have very small gangs, largely transitory gangs, few gang members, and little violence. To be sure, few gangs survive in these areas.

A closer examination of trends in larger cities shows that while 7 out of 10 cities with populations in excess of 50,000 report chronic gang problems between 1996 and 2009, some departures from this longer-term trend are apparent. In general, 9% of larger cities report increasing or variable trends, respectively, and 12% of cities reported a declining gang presence over the period. This variation in pattern means that not all larger cities uniformly experience gang activity and, moreover, that political, economic, demographic, cultural, or even regional differences may help to explain these variations. The data show that economic and cultural measures best distinguish cities following distinctive gang trends, with demographic and political factors playing a more minor role. Finally, chronic gang problems describe the largest proportion of cities in all regions, but larger cities in the West are most likely to characterize their gang problems as chronic. In general, cities in the Northeast are more likely to report emergent patterns than in other regions, and cities in the Midwest are most likely to report contracting gang activities compared to the rest of the country.

DISCUSSION TOPICS

1. Why do you suppose the presence of youth gang activity varies across cities of different sizes?

2. Which features of cities appear to best explain youth gang trends, and why should these factors matter?

3. How can prison gangs become involved in drug trafficking on the streets?

4. In what ways might social policies, like social welfare programs or the provision of housing assistance, influence the emergence, persistence, or decline of gang presence in places?

5. How can law enforcement use the patterns described in this chapter to fight gang activity in their jurisdictions?

RECOMMENDATIONS FOR FURTHER READING

Explanations of Gang Growth in the 1980s and 1990s

Alonso, A. A. (2004). Racialized identities and the formation of black gangs in Los Angeles. *Urban Geography, 25,* 658–674.

Chesney-Lind, M., & Hagedorn, J. (Eds.). (1999). *Female gangs in America.* Chicago: Lake View Press.

Cummings, S., & Monti, D. J. (Eds.). (1993). *Gangs: The origins and impact of contemporary youth gangs in the United States.* Albany: State University of New York Press.

Cureton, S. R. (2009). Something wicked this way comes: A historical account of Black gangsterism offers wisdom and warning for African American leadership. *Journal of Black Studies, 40,* 347–361.

Curry, G. D., Ball, R. A., & Decker, S. H. (1996). Estimating the national scope of gang crime from law enforcement data. In C.R.Huff (Ed.), *Gangs in America* (pp. 21–36). Thousand Oaks, CA: Sage Publications.

Klein, M. W. (1995). *The American street gang.* New York: Oxford University Press.

Miller, W. B. (1982/1992). *Crime by youth gangs and groups in the United States.* Washington, DC: U.S. Department of Justice, Office of Juvenile Justice and Delinquency Prevention.

Miller, W. B. (2001). *The growth of youth gang problems in the United States: 1970–1998.* Washington, DC: Office of Juvenile Justice and Delinquency Prevention.

Perkins, U. E. (1987). *Explosion of Chicago's Black street gangs: 1900 to the present.* Chicago: Third World Press.

Spergel, I. A. (1995). *The youth gang problem.* New York: Oxford University Press.

Vigil, J. D. (1988). *Barrio gangs: Street life and identity in Southern California.* Austin: University of Texas Press.

Vigil, J. D. (2002). *A rainbow of gangs: Street cultures in the mega-city.* Austin: University of Texas Press.

Vigil, J. D. (2007). *The projects: Gang and non-gang families in East Los Angeles.* Thousand Oaks, CA: Sage.

Prison Gangs

Camp, C. G., & Camp, G. M. (1988). *Management strategies for combating prison gang violence.* South Salem, NY: Criminal Justice Institute.

Camp, G. M, & Camp, C. G. (Eds.). (1985). *Prison gangs: Their extent, nature and impact on prisons.* Washington, DC: U.S. Department of Justice.

Daniels, S. (1987). Prison gangs: Confronting the threat. *Corrections Today, 66,* 126, 162.

Decker, S. H., Bynum, T., & Weisel, D.L. (1998). Gangs as organized crime groups: A tale of two cities. *Justice Quarterly, 15,* 395–423.

Early, P. (1991). *The hot house: Life inside Leavenworth Prison.* New York: Bantam Books.

Eckhart, D. (2001). Civil cases related to prison gangs: A survey of federal cases. *Corrections Management Quarterly, 5*(1), 60–65.

Fleisher, M. S. (1989). *Warehousing violence.* Newbury Park, CA: Sage.

Fleisher, M. S. (1995). *Beggars and thieves: Lives of urban street criminals.* Madison: University of Wisconsin Press.

Fleisher, M. S., & Decker, S. (2001). An overview of the challenge of prison gangs. *Corrections Management Quarterly, 5*(1), 1–9.

Fong, R. S., & Fogel, R. E. (1994–95, Winter). A comparative analysis of prison gang members, security threat group inmates and general population prisoners in the Texas Department of Corrections. *Journal of Gang Research, 2,* 1–12.

Gaes, G., Wallace, S., Gilman, E., Klein-Saffran, J., & Suppa, S. (2002). The influence of prison gang affiliation on violence and other prison misconduct. *The Prison Journal, 82,* 359–385.

Griffin, M. L., & Hepburn, J. R. (2006). The effect of gang affiliation on violent misconduct among inmates during the early years of confinement. *Criminal Justice and Behavior, 33,* 419–448.

Irwin, J. (1980). *Prisons in turmoil.* Boston: Little, Brown.

Jacobs, J. B. (1974). Street gangs behind bars. *Social Problems, 21,* 395–409.

Jacobs, J. B. (1977). *Stateville: The penitentiary in mass society.* Chicago: University of Chicago.

Jacobs, J. B. (2001). Focusing on prison gangs. *Corrections Management Quarterly, 5*(1), vi–vii.

Johnson, R. (1996). *Hard time: Understanding and reforming the prison.* Belmont, CA: Wadsworth.

Knox, G. W. (1998). *An introduction to gangs* (4th ed.). Peotone, IL: New Chicago Press.

Lane, M.P. (1989, July). Inmate gangs. *Corrections Today, 51,* 98–99.

Olson, D. E., & Dooley, B. (2006). Gang membership and community corrections populations: Characteristics and recidivism rates relative to other offenders. In J. F. Short & L. A. Hughes (Eds.), *Studying youth gangs* (pp. 193–202). Lanham, MD: AltaMira Press.

Pyrooz, D. C., Decker, S. H., & Fleisher, M. (2011). From the street to the prison, from the prison to the street: Understanding and responding to prison gangs. *Journal of Aggression, Conflict and Peace Research, 3,* 12–24.

Ralph, P., Hunter, J., Marquart, W., Cuvelier, J., & Merianos, D. (1996). Exploring the differences between gang and non-gang prisoners. In C. R. Huff (Ed.), *Gangs in America* (2nd ed., pp. 241–256). Thousand Oaks, CA: Sage.

Reiner, I. (1992). *Gangs, crime, and violence in Los Angeles.* Los Angeles: Office of the District Attorney of the County of Los Angeles.

Sanchez-Jankowski, M. S. (2003). Gangs and social change. *Theoretical Criminology, 7,* 191–216.

Schlosser, E. (1998). The prison-industrial complex. *The Atlantic Monthly* (December), 51–77.

Scott, G. (2004). "It's a sucker's outfit": How urban gangs enable and impede the integration of ex-convicts. *Ethnography, 5,* 107–140.

Shelden, R. G. (1991). A comparison of gang members and non-gang members in a prison setting. *The Prison Journal, 81*(2), 50–60.

Stevens, D. J. (1997, Summer). Origins and effects of prison drug gangs in North Carolina. *Journal of Gang Research, 4,* 23–35.

Toch, H. (2007). Sequestering gang members, burning witches, and subverting due process. *Criminal Justice and Behavior, 32,* 274–288.

Toch, H., & Adams, K. (1988). *Coping, maladaptation in prison.* New Brunswick, NJ: Transaction Publishing.

NOTES

1. President's Commission on Law Enforcement and Administration of Justice (1967); National Commission on the Causes and Prevention of Violence (Mulvihill & Tumin, 1969); National Advisory Commission on Criminal Justice Standards and Goals (1973).
2. The term *persistence* is used here to capture consistent gang presence on an annual basis; this is similar but not identical to the term *institutionalization*, which we used earlier to describe permanence of gangs in certain areas.
3. One-way analysis of variance (ANOVA) models are estimated to assess statistically significant group differences.

CHAPTER 8

Urban Gangs and Violence

◈ Introduction

Urban gang problems are examined in this chapter. The main focus here is on *serious violent gangs* in large cities. New research is presented that groups cities according to their experiences with serious gang violence over a 14-year period. Case studies of five cities' gang histories are reviewed to illustrate nationwide differences in serious violent gang problems. Both the correlates (features of gangs themselves) and the context (the local urban and regional environment) of serious gang violence are then examined. The chapter begins with research on the intensity of gang activity in urban areas.

Serious violent gangs have been characterized by a diverse set of criteria (see Serious Violent Gangs in the Further Reading section at the end of this chapter). Most notably, they are typically found in large cities and distinguished by a number of structural features, the first of which is the degree of organization (e.g., they have rules, meetings, and leadership roles, a large membership—at least 15 gangs and more than 200 members but with wide variations—and a multiple-year history). Second, these gangs are involved in violent crimes that physically harm victims, including homicide, aggravated assault, robbery, and nonlethal firearm injuries. These violent crimes frequently occur out of doors, on the streets, and in very small set spaces in neighborhoods with high violence rates. Moreover, such violent crimes likely involve multiple victims and suspects and have a contagious feature. Third, drug trafficking and firearm offenses are also very common. Fourth, these gangs tend to have both female and male members. Finally, cities experiencing serious gang violence tend to be socioeconomically disadvantaged, racially heterogeneous, and have a large foreign born population. They also tend to be located in more punitive states with larger correctional and prosecutorial budgets.

◈ The Intensity of Gangs in Cities

Patterns and Trends in the Number of Active Gangs in Cities

To begin to determine the intensity of the gang problem in local jurisdictions, the National Youth Gang Survey (NYGS) collects data on the number of active gangs, as well as an estimate of the number of gang members, in participating jurisdictions. Between 1996 and 2009, the average number of active gangs ranged from 16.73 (in 2005) to 23.33 (in 2001) across all jurisdictions. Not surprisingly, however, the size of the jurisdiction influences law enforcement's estimates of the number of gangs operating in their local areas. Figure 8.1 separates the very largest cities (more than 100,000 population) reporting to the NYGS between 1996 and 2009 from larger cities (50,000 to 99,999 population) and the remaining types of jurisdictions (including suburban counties, rural counties, and smaller cities with populations between 2,500 and 49,999). Three conclusions can be drawn from the pattern of gang intensity shown in these graphs. First, the very largest cities report the *greatest number* of distinct gangs, on average. This is not surprising, as cities like Chicago, Los Angeles, and New York have historically been home to many youth gangs. Second, *trends* in the average number of gangs reported by law enforcement vary by city size. For example, the number of gangs operating in smaller jurisdictions rose during some of the very same years that saw a decline among the largest cities (e.g., from 2003 to 2005). Finally, while it is difficult to directly compare trends in the number of gangs in cities with between 50,000 and 99,999 residents compared to "other" jurisdictions—given that other jurisdictions included counties with larger land masses and very small cities, resulting in dramatic differences in population density—cities between 50,000 and 99,999 actually report fewer, on average, annual number of gangs operating in the area than do these other jurisdictions.

Figure 8.1   Average Number of Gangs in the Jurisdiction by City Size

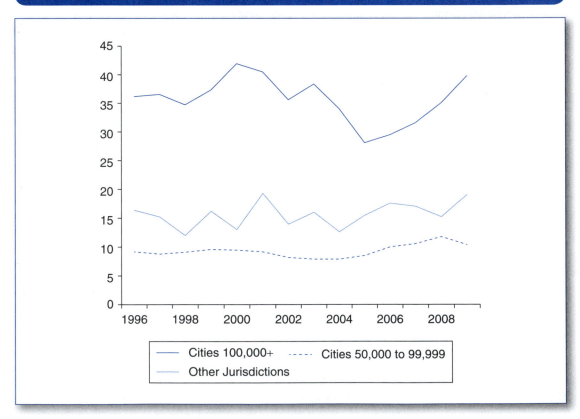

Patterns and Trends in the Number of Gang Members in Cities

Figure 8.2 shows that the very largest cities are home to the greatest number of active gang members as well. Again, this is to be expected given that the base population in these jurisdictions is large. In cities with populations in excess of 100,000 people, the average number of gang members known to law enforcement was quite volatile, ranging from 1,008 (in 2005) and 2,220 (in 2001). By contrast, law enforcement reported between 204 (in 1997) and 311 (in 2000) gang members, on average, in jurisdictions with populations ranging from 50,000 to 99,999, and the number of gang members typically reported in other kinds of jurisdictions ranged from 297 (in 2002) to 859 (in 2001). According to the graph, law enforcement estimates of the number of gang members in the very largest cities rose precipitously after a low in 2005, whereas the number of gang members operating in other jurisdictions continued to fall over the same period. In the next section, Howell, Egley and colleagues apply trajectory modeling to see if serious gang problem cities could be grouped on another dimension: violent crime involvement over the 14-year period.

◈ Serious Gang Problem Trends

The above analyses demonstrate that cities can be distinguished by their distinctively patterned intensity of gangs and gang members. With this in mind, the next step is to assess the relative seriousness

Figure 8.2 Average Number of Gang Members in the Jurisdiction by City Size

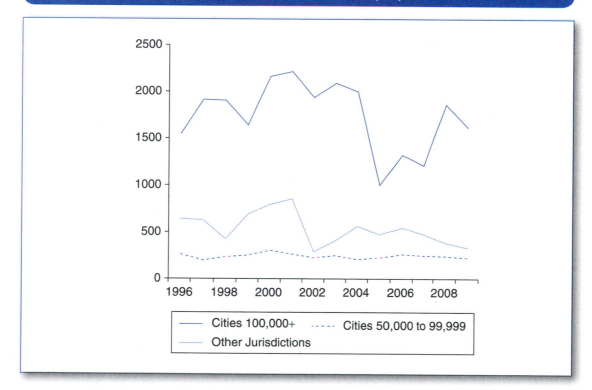

of gang activity among cities. For the purposes of this analysis, homicide is considered to be a primary indicator of serious gang violence.

Gang-Related Homicides and Serious Gang Activity

Homicides characterize serious gang problem cities more than any other factor, and gang-related homicides are heavily concentrated geographically in the United States. Most cities have no gang homicides, and those that do usually report very few of them from year to year in the NYGS (Egley et al., 2006). Rather, it is in a subset of larger cities (populations greater than 50,000) and adjacent suburban counties where the overwhelming majority (96%) of gang homicides occurred in 2009 (Table 8.1).

The trajectory analysis presented in Figure 8.3 examines trends in the proportion of all homicides that are gang related and, in contrast to the previous section, offers a more pointed investigation of *seriousness* of gang problems nationwide. Further, the analysis that follows is limited to the very largest cities, with populations in excess of 100,000 persons, and incorporates total annual homicide counts from the Federal Bureau of Investigation's Uniform Crime Report (UCR) data for all very large cities participating in the NYGS between 1996 and 2009. Recall that the largest cities in the nation are the cities with the greatest number of both gangs and gang members at every period. Overall, 247 cities met the criteria for inclusion. (Only two of the eligible cities were excluded from the analysis due to complete missing gang homicide data for the entire time period.) Proportional homicide rates—along which cities' patterns are aligned here—were determined by dividing the total number of gang homicides reported in the NYGS annually by the total number of homicides reported for the city in the UCR, multiplied by 100. This provides the percentage of all homicides that are gang related at each year for each jurisdiction.

The largest cluster of *very large cities* (with populations greater than 100,000) is seen in trajectory group T2 ($N = 105$; 42.5% of the total sample of 247 cities). This group of 105 cities experienced a steady rate of gang-related homicides over the 14-year period, wherein approximately 20% of annual homicides were gang related. The next largest group (T4; $N = 71$; 28.7%) experienced double the proportion of homicides that are gang-related, with approximately 40% of all homicides—or 4 in 10—gang-related over the same period. Another sizeable group, 55 very large cities (T1; 22.3%), averaged between 2% and 8% gang-related homicides over the 14-year period. The two remaining trajectory groups (T3; $N = 14$; 5.7% and T5; $N = 2$; 0.8%) experienced increases in annual gang-related homicides. Indeed, a cluster of

Table 8.1 Distribution of Gangs, Gang Members, and Gang Homicides by Area Type, 2009

	Gangs (%)	Gang Members (%)	Gang-Related Homicides (%)*
Larger cities (50,000+)	44.1	55.6	74.4
Suburban counties	21.4	23.3	22.1
Smaller cities	29.1	18.3	2.3
Rural counties	5.4	2.7	1.2

Note: Total reflects only homicides reported to NYGS, and is not a national total due to missing data and sampling design.

Source: Egley & Howell, 2010.

Figure 8.3 Trajectory Model: Percent of Gang-Related Homicides, Populations Greater Than 100,000

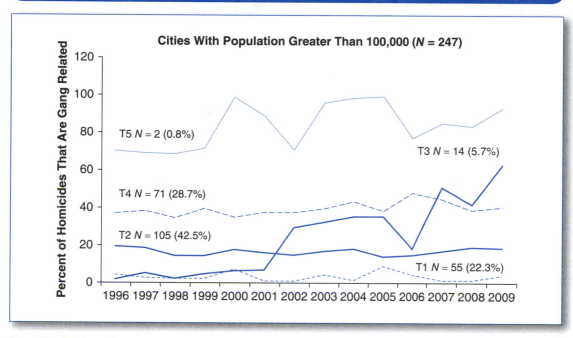

Source: Howell, Egley, et al., 2011, p. 7.

14 cities (T3) experienced a very sharp increase from 2001 to 2009, from only around 4% to more than 60% over this nine-year period. Finally, two very large cities (T5; Inglewood, California and Salinas, California) stand out for having started the 14-year period at nearly 70% of all lethal violence that was gang related. By 2009, however, almost all (more than 90%) of the homicides in these cities were believed to be gang related.

Three important observations can be made from this analysis of gang-related homicides as a proportion of the total number of homicides reported in the UCR for very large cities. Overall, nearly 8 out of 10 very large cities (78%; T2, T3, T4, and T5 combined) reported a consistently high level or increasing proportion of gang-related homicides over the 14-year period. Second, a remarkable degree of consistency in the rate of gang-related homicides across trajectory groups is observed (this stability is especially apparent for 71% of cities; T2 and T4). Third, *none* of the trajectory groups found in these cities displayed a pattern consistent with a decline in the prevalence of gang-related homicide between 1996 and 2009.

Regional Variation in Gang-Related Homicide Trends

Are some parts of the country more likely to experience elevated rates of gang violence? To begin to assess whether there are regional variations in the seriousness and rate of change of the gang violence problem, each of the 247 very large cities experiencing these varied levels and trends in the proportion of all homicides that are gang-related are mapped in Figure 8.4. A preliminary inspection suggests that

Figure 8.4 Map of Trajectories Reflecting Gang-Related Homicide Trends, Counties With Cities Having Populations Greater Than 100,000

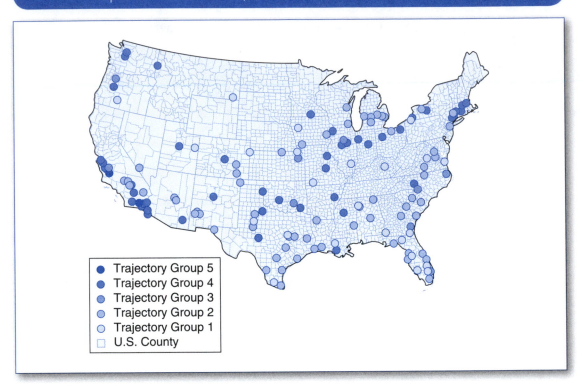

Source: Howell, Egley, et al., 2011, p. 8

T4 cities, or places where approximately 40% of all homicides are gang related over the period, are more typical in major urban centers located in the West, the Northeast, and parts of the Midwest. Cities characterized by T1, T2, or T3 trends appear more evenly spread across the United States, while the two T5 cities are located only in the West (California, more specifically).

Visual inspection of the map, alone, cannot confirm specific regional patterns. Therefore, Figure 8.5 further differentiates regional variations in serious gang violence trends. This graph shows the percentage of the very largest cities in each region (included in the NYGS) that can be characterized by the five gang violence trajectory patterns. More than half of these cities in the South and nearly half of these cities in the Midwest are T2 cities, whereas nearly half of these cities in the Northeast and the West are T4 cities. Overall, more than 85% of Southern cities are characterized by T1 or T2 trends, which generally show between zero and 20% gang-related homicide patterns that are relatively stable over the period. By contrast, nearly 1 in 10 very large cities in the Northeast show dramatic increases in the proportion of all homicides that are gang related between 2001 and 2009 (T3). The Northeast, the West, and to a lesser extent the Midwest all have their fair share of cities following a high and stable (T4) trend, whereas this pattern is quite uncommon in the South. Finally, both cities characterized by the most severe gang homicide problems—Salinas and Inglewood—are located in California, which constitute 2% of all of the very large jurisdictions in the West that participate in the NYGS.

Figure 8.5   Cumulative Percentage in Trajectory for Proportion of Homicides That Are Gang-Related, Populations Greater Than 100,000, by Region

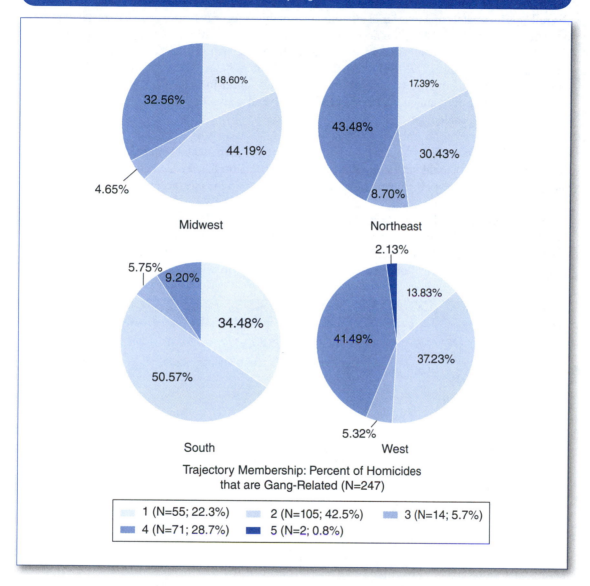

A Snapshot of Gang Homicide in the Largest Cities

The level of violence produced by gangs can be large. In the 167 NYGS cities that provided gang homicide data in 2009, Egley and Howell (2011) found that 110 (66%) cities reported a total of 1,017 gang homicides.[1] This total represents a 2% increase from 2002, a 7% increase from 2005, and an 11% increase from 2008 for these same cities (see Table 7.2 in Chapter 7).

Figure 8.6 shows the total percent of homicides that were gang related among cities with populations of 100,000 or more (for which homicide data were reported in 2009). Separate figures are presented for Chicago and Los Angeles because of their historically very large numbers of gang homicides. Overall, approximately one-quarter of all homicides in this category of cities were gang related in 2009. By comparison, one-half of the homicides in Los Angeles and one-third in Chicago were gang related.

Prior research has contrasted historical gang homicide patterns in Chicago and Los Angeles (Howell, 1999; Maxson, 1999). No other cities in the United States—or worldwide for that matter—come close to producing the volume of gang homicides found in these two cities. As discussed in Chapter 1, in each city, unique histories produced several waves of gang development that further exacerbated gang problems.

Aside from the prominence of Chicago and Los Angeles as gang homicide capitals, many other cities—particularly very large ones with populations greater than 100,000—have extremely high gang homicide rates and should not be ignored. As shown in Figure 8.3, 71 U.S. cities in this population category experienced very high gang homicide rates from 1996 to 2009, accounting for approximately 40% of all homicides (T4).

San Antonio researchers' analysis of 28 homicides that occurred in the course of their study yielded five distinct circumstances in which these occur and six different motives (Valdez et al., 2009). Key circumstances include drug-related disputes (typically an argument associated with drug transactions), gang disputes over a variety of gang-related issues, assaults in which victims are attacked without

Figure 8.6   Gang Homicide Prevalence, Cities With Populations Greater Than 100,000

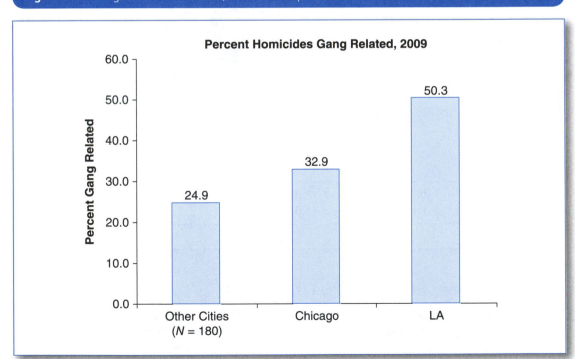

Source: Howell, Egley, et al. (2011)

notice, and *rolling out* (a gang exit rite that entails a physical beating by several gang members). Key motives include personal vendettas (feuds between victims and offenders), gang revenge or retaliation, gang rivalries, territorial trespassing, gang solidarity (camaraderie), and spontaneous retaliation (spur-of-the-moment retribution or defense).

◈ Case Studies of Gang Problems in Large Cities

The next sections feature case studies for a single city from each gang violence trend in Figure 8.3 (Abilene, Texas; St. Louis, Missouri; Springfield, Massachusetts; Pittsburgh, Pennsylvania; and Inglewood, California). Each of these cities is among larger cities in trajectory group T2 shown in Chapter 7 (Figure 7.5) that consistently experienced gang activities throughout the 14-year survey period from 1996 to 2009; however, each of these cities shows distinctive trends in the extent of their violence problem that is gang related (see Figure 8.3). Abilene, Texas, is in trajectory group one (T1) in Figure 8.3, a group that averages very little gang-related violence annually; in fact, law enforcement in Abilene reported that none of their homicides between 1996 and 2009 were gang-related. St. Louis, Missouri, represents a modal city in the second trajectory group (T2) shown in Figure 8.3 wherein, on average, 20% of their annual homicides are gang related. The relative stability of gang-related violence makes sense as several St. Louis gangs have a long history of violence and other criminal activity (Decker & Van Winkle, 1996; Rosenfeld et al., 1999). Springfield, Massachusetts, is in trajectory group three (T3) of Figure 8.3, which demonstrates a marked increase in serious gang violence especially after the year 2000. For example, after reporting that none of their homicides were gang related in the late 1990s, law enforcement in Springfield indicated that more than one-third (38%) of their homicides were gang related in 2000, more than half (56%) were gang related in 2005, and, by 2006, nearly three quarters were defined as such (71%). Pittsburgh, Pennsylvania, is in trajectory group four (T4; wherein, on average, 4 in 10 homicides are gang related annually). The city of Pittsburgh has a long history of gang involvement in drug trafficking and guns (R. A. Gordon et al., 2014). Finally, Inglewood, California—about 12 miles southeast of Los Angeles—is one of the two cities in which a large majority of the lethal violence that exists there is gang related (T5 in Figure 8.3); between 80% and 100% of all homicides in Inglewood are reportedly gang related in all but 2 of the 14 years over which data were collected. The city of Inglewood is known for its serious and violent gang problems; in fact, the movie *Boyz N The Hood*™ was filmed on location in Inglewood in 1991 (see Figure 8.7).

Abilene, Texas, Case Study

Abilene represents an example of a very large city with a very small gang violence problem. Unlike Fort Worth, Houston, and Corpus Christi, Abilene law enforcement reported virtually no street gang-related homicides between 1996 and 2009. This is not to say that gangs are absent in Abilene; indeed there is some evidence of a presence of Aryan, motorcycle, and prison gangs in the area, but gang-involved criminality appears to revolve largely around cocaine and methamphetamine trafficking by prison gang affiliates, rather than youth or street gang violence. As early as 1991, surveys conducted by the Attorney General's Office of police departments in Texas cities showed that Abilene had almost no problem with youth gang violence; the Abilene Police Department estimated that approximately five delinquent juvenile gangs or criminal street gangs, comprising 60–66 gang members in total, operated in the city in that survey (Morales, 1991). Standardizing to population size, Abilene is among the safest cities with respect

Figure 8.7   Boyz N The Hood™

Source: Getty Images.

to gang violence. Morales (1991) finds approximately 60 gang members and 4.7 gangs per 100,000 population, compared to El Paso, for example, which reports 670 gang members and 38.8 gangs per 100,000 residents.

At the beginning of the period under investigation, youth gang problems were viewed by Abilene law enforcement as difficult "to take seriously" (Eiserer, 1996). For example, police officer Leland Mitchell joked that, on entering a home on suspicion of marijuana, "he found four Bloods and four Crips playing a game of poker"; Chief Melvin Martin, police chief at the time, also argued that Abilene's gang problem was "almost nonexistent" relative to other similarly-sized cities in Texas (Eiserer, 1996). This was a marked improvement over the situation in the 1980s, when Abilene was believed to have up to 650 youth gang members. To stem the youth gang problem, the city of Abilene undertook a large-scale program to provide organized after-school and evening recreational activities to youth by building Boys and Girls Club gymnasiums near schools in high-crime areas (DeLattre, 1994). DeLattre attributes the dramatic decline in local youth gang problems to those recreational programs offered by the Boys and Girls Clubs and other police-initiated activities in Abilene between 1988 and 1993. These types of programs can reduce youth alienation and limit unstructured socializing time that might otherwise encourage the formation of youth conflict groups.

Latino prison gangs, some involving Abilene youth, have operated in the local area since the late 1970s. For example, the West Texas Tango gang merged with the Tango Blast Federation in 2004;

Tango Blast is classified as a Tier 1 gang by the Texas Department of Public Safety, meaning that it is among a small group of "organizations [that] pose the greatest gang threat to Texas due to their relationships with Mexican cartels, large membership numbers, high levels of transnational criminal activity, and organizational effectiveness" (Texas Department of Public Safety, 2013, p. 26). While loosely organized outside of prison and largely based in Austin, Fort Worth, Dallas, and Houston, some members of Tango Blast treat Abilene and other cities in north and west Texas area as their territory (Houston Intelligence Support Center, 2011). Indeed, in December of 2008, federal, state, and local law enforcement executed the arrests of a dozen members of the West Texas Puro Tango Blast prison gang for large-scale trafficking operations in Abilene and surrounding areas after a two-year intensive investigation (U.S. Department of Justice, 2008). In general, however, Abilene's gang problems are less a function of violent street gangs and more focused on organized drug trafficking or hate organizations.

St. Louis, Missouri, Case Study

St. Louis appears to be typical of very large cities with respect to the long-standing seriousness of its gang problem. In Figure 8.3, St. Louis is among the very large cities in the trajectory group T2 that consistently reported a high level of gang homicides (approximately 20% of total annual homicides, on average) during the 1996 to 2009 period.

In the following description of St. Louis gangs, Monti (1993) illustrates how gangs vary in their key characteristics depending on the degree to which their surrounding communities were well settled. In describing St. Louis communities as "less settled," "relatively settled," and "more settled," Monti refers to degrees of social disorganization, as indicated by racial/ethnic heterogeneity, rapid population movement, poverty, and unstable families and schools. His study of St. Louis gangs covered nearly a decade, beginning in 1984, corresponding with a period of accelerated gang growth across the city. These are based on his interviews of hundreds of male and female gang and nongang youths and other knowledgeable persons, including police officers (see Monti, 1991). The gangs Monti (1993) describes include only the "better-established groups composed largely, but not exclusively, of teenagers or young men in their twenties [and also] slightly older gangs that had established reputations for fierceness and, in most cases, a merchandising operation for illegal drugs" (p. 228). In particular, numerous nascent gangs comprised of younger children in north St. Louis and teenage gangs in south St. Louis are excluded.

Gang activity in north St. Louis. Known gangs located in the "less-settled" north St. Louis area numbered 19 in 1988—most of which had not been in existence long, typically only since 1984 (Monti, 1993). Most of the gangs in this area were still in the process of expanding and contracting, and only eight gangs had stable territories. Moreover, few of them had ties with other gangs. This introduces "brittleness" to gangs that makes them more vulnerable to outside attacks and seductions. Only Black males belonged to these gangs, but seven had female auxiliaries. Gang size varied enormously—but most had more than 30 members. These gangs were not particularly well organized. More than one leader was common and at least one person typically served as an "enforcer." Moreover, "the gangs had no strict hierarchy, or officer corps or formal rules for developing a 'gang policy,' and no set custom for initiating or removing members" (p. 233). Virtually all of the gangs in this area were described as "fighting gangs."

Gang activity in near north suburbs of St. Louis. Gangs in "relatively settled" communities (i.e., near north suburbs) of St. Louis numbered 14 in 1990 (Monti, 1993). The two largest gangs had more than 100 members and both maintained up to four age-graded sets that corresponded with the members' school status. Of these gangs, 12 had a fixed territory (three of which were female) and another gang, the Gangster Disciples, claimed a connection to the Chicago supergang of the same name. The remaining group was actually a drug gang. Criminal activities involving members of these gangs varied widely, although some patterned behavior was observed. Some junior high members began with burglaries and graduated into drug dealing. Others stole cars in auto theft rings. Some gangs were actively involved in drug distribution.

Gangs in this area were generally well established, such that children took their gang loyalties with themselves to schools. "There were children at every elementary school who were active gang members or serious about claiming some gang affiliation. Youngsters from all the municipalities were brought together at the junior and senior high schools" as a result of school desegregation plans (Monti, 1993, p. 242). Not surprising, "gang fights in city schools were more routine [in this area] and more likely to involve substantial violence" (p. 242). The "unsettled character" (i.e., poor school climate) of schools contributed to the seriousness of gang-related crime in and around the school, including drug and weapon use, intimidation, extortion, disruptiveness, and encroachment of nonstudents into the schools.

The early involvement of children in gangs in this area of St. Louis was noteworthy. "Children grew up knowing where they lived and the gang they eventually would join, if they chose to become a member" (Monti, 1993, p. 243). Even elementary school–aged children played at being a gang member. "While much of this play and imitative behavior had a game-like quality, the children took it seriously and appreciated the significance of what it meant to be a gang member" (p. 243). It was through role play such as "the wearing of colors, and flashing of signs that children explored the role of 'gang member' and identified themselves as potential recruits. The self-selection process continued at the junior and senior high schools" (p. 243).

Gang activity in central and south St. Louis. Gangs in "more-settled" areas (i.e., central and south St. Louis) were not as numerous as in the less-settled and relatively settled areas (Monti, 1993). This is attributable to two factors. First, part of this area, the central corridor, was very well settled and had only two gangs. Second, the gangs in the south St. Louis area were populated by Black youth from families that either lived in public housing projects or in relatively poor zones into which they had been relocated from housing developments downtown.

The principal established gangs in this area—the Thunder Katz, Peabody Boyz, Southside Posse, and South Side Gangsters—had fewer potential recruits, but the family and friendship ties among them were strong. Hence, these gangs were less vulnerable to outside attacks and seductions. Gangs in these areas were well integrated into the daily routines of the institutions and residents that shared the area with them; therefore, they seldom engaged in serious crimes or sustained criminal activities over a long period of time. In addition, these gangs did not exploit the vulnerability of the community; instead, they actually defended its integrity.

Springfield, Massachusetts, Case Study

Many of the cities characterized by the increasing youth gang violence trend (T3) in Figure 8.3 are places that, at least initially, are reluctant to acknowledge a gang problem in their local communities. This *denial* is a common reaction among law enforcement to initial signs of an emerging serious problem of gang-related violence (Huff, 1991). According to Huff, denial is followed by a second stage called *recognition* and a final stage characterized by *overreaction*. Tracking gang-related violence trends in city of Springfield, Massachusetts illustrates this pattern. In the 1990s, and early part of the 21st century, police denied or downplayed the role that organized gangs played in local violence; yet by 2006, law enforcement were beginning to admit that the city had seen a rising gang presence, reporting knowledge of more than 200 members across at least 10 gangs (Wagner, 2006). By 2006, the *Springfield News-Leader* reported that roughly half of all street gang members in the city were Bloods, although there was some evidence of activity by Crips, Black Gangster Disciples, Vice Lords, MS-13, Los Boricuas, and the Latin Kings. Yet the head of the Springfield Police Department's investigations division at the time, Major Steve Ijames, told the local newspaper,

> Let's talk about what overt behavior is consistent with the heavy influx of gang members. Street-corner drug-dealing. Dramatic spikes in violence. Lots of drive-by shootings. How prolific is that in this community? I think, statistically, the truth is it's very low. (in Wagner, 2006)

But during the same period, the county prosecutor's office was beginning to see an uptick in crimes committed by youthful gang members and had begun to argue for an aggressive strategy for dealing with street gang problems. This uptick soon morphed into an avalanche. Springfield became one of the most "dangerous cities in the United States" at the same time that gang presence in the city's North End surged (Weinberger, 2012). According to an article in the *New York Times*, the North End is an area of Springfield where "gang members and drug dealers cruised the streets on motor scooters carrying SKS semiautomatic rifles in broad daylight . . . [and] gunfire erupted almost daily" (Goode, 2012). The FBI, the Western Massachusetts Gang Task Force, and local law enforcement efforts were directed toward large-scale gang sweeps and major initiatives to combat the activities of "OG's" or "Old or Original Gangsters," who were responsible for recruiting youth into the gang to deal drugs and engaging in other criminal activities (Berry, 2009).

In response to this problem, Springfield adopted a unique program to combat gang crime and violence entitled the *Counter Criminal Continuum* (C^3) in 2009, which was said to draw heavily on counterinsurgency strategies employed by the military in Afghanistan and Iraq (Hibbard, Barbieri, Domnarksi, & Cutonne, 2014). Like community policing programs before it, C^3 relied on community involvement to generate collaborative strategies for targeting gang problems, including graffiti removal, dealing with complaints over the actions of negligent landlords, teacher and officer chaperoning of school children to bus stops, finding summer job opportunities for youth, and engaging "street leaders, residents who act as an informal intelligence network, [to] report suspicious activities to the authorities" (Goode, 2012). Borrowing from the Army Special Forces approach, C^3 is a two-pronged strategy focused on intelligence gathering and winning the trust of the local population (Weinberger, 2012). Collecting and analyzing data, including the social networks of gang members, has enabled Springfield police to disrupt gang activities by identifying the leaders and engaging in aggressive policing of those leaders, which then fractures the gang—a strategy consistent with the logic of Ceasefire and other violence-prevention programs across the country. While long-term evaluations of the C^3 approach are not yet available, early evidence is optimistic; for example, in the year following its formal implementation, crime declined by 62% (Weinberger, 2012), plummeting to its lowest violent crime rate in nearly three decades. Despite these relative successes, however, Springfield remained one of the 10 most dangerous cities under 200,000 in the United States in 2012 (Rizzo, 2013). View a *60 Minutes*™ segment on Springfield's law enforcement practices to combat gang drug and violence problems at http://www .cbsnews.com/news/counterinsurgency-cops-military-tactics-fight-street-crime-04-08-2013/

Pittsburgh, Pennsylvania, Case Study

Pittsburgh appears to be somewhat typical among very large cities (populations greater than 100,000) with respect to the long-standing seriousness of its gang problem. In Figure 8.3, Pittsburgh is among the very large cities in the trajectory group T4 that consistently reported a high level of gang homicides (approximately 40% of total annual homicides, on average) during the 1996 to 2009 period.

Having experienced onset of gang activity in 1991, Pittsburgh is considered a "late onset" city (Howell, Egley, et al., 2002). However, unlike other cities in that onset group that did not report a large problem with violent crimes before the end of the decade, Pittsburgh quickly developed a serious gang violence problem, as we shall see in the next section. Its gang activity developed in two stages, which are characterized here as onset of gang activity and recent gang activity.

Onset of gang activity in Pittsburgh. According to Tita (1999) and Cohen and Tita (1999), a surge in drug-related arrests (apparently driven by crack cocaine offenses) preceded the onset of gang activity in Pittsburgh. "Shots fired" calls (citizen-initiated emergency 911 calls to police) spontaneously increased in "a classic epidemic" during a pregang period (1990–1991) in census tracts[2] distributed widely throughout the city (Tita & Cohen, 2004, p. 195). Tita and Cohen observed that it was precisely in the high-violence communities that gangs emerged, which "was followed by a contagious spread of shots fired activity in gang tracts or tracts adjoining them," fueling an epidemic of gun violence or "contagious diffusion" to other areas (p. 195).

Violent urban street gangs, including sets (subgroups) of Black Crip and Blood gangs, began to take hold in Pittsburgh during the latter half of 1991, according to Tita and Cohen (2004). Gang emergence continued through 1993, and stabilized in 1994–1995 with no new gangs forming and no gangs desisting (Tita, Cohen, et al., 2005).

Perhaps largely attributable to the violent community context within which they formed, Tita and Ridgeway (2007) assert that "all of the gangs included in this [Pittsburgh] study share one thing in common: They are known to be violent" (p. 217), and Tita (1999) contends they have earned "respect" and fear from the community. Given the territorial and retaliatory natures of urban youth gang violence, it is reasonable to expect that gang-related violence would follow predictable spatial and temporal patterns. In short, Tita and Ridgeway (2007) state, "One might expect set space to serve as a sort of lightning rod for intergang violence" (p. 217). From the onset of gang activity in Pittsburgh, about two-thirds of all gang homicides were gang motivated (intergang disputes, initiation activities, or spontaneous drive-by killings).

Recent gang activity in Pittsburgh. Tita and colleagues' on-site study of Pittsburgh ended in 1995. This section summarizes the Pittsburgh Police Department's responses to the NYGS from 1996 onward. Beginning in 1996, with a well-publicized Federal Racketeer Influenced and Corrupt Organization Act indictment of a local street gang, which "had an enormous impact on all Pittsburgh gangs," "[g]angs and gang violence virtually disappeared from the streets of Pittsburgh" (p. 281). From 1996 to 1999, the number of gangs reported by the Pittsburgh Police Department dropped 77%, from 86 to just 20.

For several years thereafter, Pittsburgh police responses to the NYGS characterized the city's gang problem as somewhat stabilized but at a serious level, particularly in drug trafficking, aggravated assault, and firearm use. Law enforcement considered a majority of the gangs to be "drug gangs." The proportion of gang members that is Black has remained virtually unchanged over the 14-year period, averaging almost 86%. Gangs still were well established in certain areas of the city as at the beginning of the new millennium, with subgroups based on age, gender, and geographical area. Then the gang problem turned noticeably larger and more serious. In six out of nine years (2001 through 2009), Pittsburgh police said the city's gang problem was "getting worse" in three main respects.

First, law enforcement reported more gangs from the mid-2000s onward, which likely contributed to increased intergang conflicts and gang violence. While only 20 gangs were counted in 1999, an average of 36 was reported each year during 2001 to 2009, and this is a conservative estimate because Pittsburgh police count multiple sets as one gang. Although police had more difficulty estimating the number of gang members during the early part of this decade, during 2005 to 2008 an average of 869 gang members were reported each year. The few very large gangs were estimated to have between 95 and 200 members.

Second, gang members apparently remained in the gangs for multiple years. In the 1990s, police had estimated that 7 out of 10 gang members were juveniles. By 2008, this proportion had dropped to one-half, reflecting either more involvement of older gang members or aging of earlier members.

Third, inmates returning from prison may have reconnected with some of the gangs or joined outright as a result of relationships they formed in prison. Survey respondents said the returning inmates influenced local gang activity in important ways in the new decade, including drug trafficking, access to weapons, and violence itself. Three-fourths of these former inmates were estimated to be adults. From 2003 to 2006, the Pittsburgh Police Department reported more than 20 gang homicides each year along with increases in gang-aggravated assaults.

In sum, Pittsburgh's gang problem developed quickly and worsened measurably over time. Widespread drug dealing and gunplay preceded early gang emergence. Gangs emerged in the high-violence communities, followed by a contagious spread of shots fired activity in gang tracts or tracts adjoining them. Once the gangs developed a reputation for violence and earned respect for this, gang violence stabilized, but at a high level. Now, inmates returning from prison may well be refueling existing gangs.

Inglewood, California, Case Study

Inglewood has a long history of gang problems. Recent sources indicate that an Hispanic gang called Inglewood 13, as well as the Inglewood Family (an African American Blood set) and certain Crip sets, first emerged in the 1960s (Katz & Webb, 2003; Maxson, 1999). According to one senior officer in the Inglewood police department who was interviewed by Katz and Webb (2003),

> Well, I think here in Inglewood it was the just absolutely rapid quadrupling and tripling, just growth of gangs that seemed to explode in the late 70s and early 80s, and we just realized all of a sudden that not only did we have hundreds, we had thousands of gang members in the city, and probably hundreds of different gangs, and so [the gang unit] was born out of the necessity [in 1980] to understand the gangs, identify the gangs, identify the gang leaders, and stuff like that. It was specifically an intelligence gathering as opposed to an enforcement unit, and remains an intelligence gathering unit today. (p. 60)

Thus, it was in the 1980s that gang problems escalated for the city, when law enforcement began to see an intergenerational transmission of gang ties from parents to children and the expansion of street-level cocaine markets (Katz & Webb, 2003). Police-involved shootings also rose as gang violence worsened in the city, promoting the police department's gang unit to initiate a suppression-oriented approach to gang control (Katz & Webb, 2003; Lacey, 1990). The gang unit, in concert with various Anti-Crime Teams and other targeted policing units, instituted nighttime curfews and began actively patrolling gang hotspots in the early 1990s before launching community policing initiatives like organizing late-night basketball leagues and finding employment opportunities for specific gang members (Katz & Webb, 2003). The degree to which prevention and suppression activities were successful was a matter of some debate, but Inglewood's gang problem did not subside. By 1999, law enforcement reported that approximately 6.4% of city residents were active street gang members and that every neighborhood in Inglewood had been claimed by at least one gang (Katz & Webb, 2003).

While Inglewood gangs were involved to some degree in drug distribution, they were for the most part not organized or sophisticated criminal enterprises. Instead, local gang members were heavily involved in opportunistic and violent offending, and were responsible for a vast majority of all homicides in the city between 1996 and 2009. Some of these incidents of violence have stemmed from internal conflict among gangs who claim turf in Inglewood; among the eight most active gangs are five African American gangs including Black P Stone, Crinshaw Mafia Gangsters, Inglewood Family, Raymond Ave Crips, and Rollin 60s, and three Hispanic gangs including Inglewood 13, Lennox 13, and Tepus. Other incidents are a consequence of rivalries between gangs in Inglewood and outlying areas like Compton (in Los Angeles) and the tiny city of Westmont, which lies between Los Angeles and Inglewood. Just recently, Westmont was euphemistically called Death Valley given its extraordinarily high rate of lethal violence (Santa Cruz, 2014). The infiltration of gangs across all of Inglewood's neighborhoods and in proximate cities has contributed to the extraordinarily serious and sustained levels of gang violence over time.

◈ Contextual Characteristics That Contribute to Serious Gang Problems

These case studies illustrate an important point. Even though each of these cities has experienced some serious gang problem histories, their levels and trends in gang violence differ in key aspects that may have important implications for intervention. The main difference between St. Louis and Pittsburgh, for example, is that St. Louis has an older, more established gang problem with considerable diversity in various sectors of the city. In contrast, Pittsburgh has more homogeneous gangs with very extensive involvement in drug trafficking. Likewise, there are some similarities in the approaches to gang suppression undertaken by police in both Inglewood and Springfield as their respective gang problems became more serious and entrenched, yet Inglewood's problem with gang-related violence preceded Springfield's by at least two decades.

The economic and cultural context of these cities, access to crime facilitators, and drug-related factors provide important contextual influences on serious gang violence problems. This section identifies causes and correlates of serious street gang violence that largely track Stage 4 of Howell's (2015) model. A brief summary of important data and studies on each of these indicators follows.

Table 8.2 Contextual Characteristics of Modal Cities

	Abilene, TX	St. Louis, MO	Springfield, MA	Pittsburgh, PA	Inglewood, CA
Trajectory in Figure 8.3	T1	T2	T3	T4	T5
State and local correctional expenditures per capita in state (2000; BJS)	$180.00	$120.00	$125.00	$181.00	$212.00
Budget of county or city prosecutors' offices per capita (2001; NPS)	$9.80	$14.24	$14.83	$7.86	$24.17
% in poverty in city (2000)	15.4	24.6	23.1	20.4	22.5
% of males officially unemployed in city (2000)	5.7	7.7	5.8	6.5	7.0
% Hispanic in city (2000)	19.4	2.0	27.2	1.3	46.0
% black in city (2000)	8.8	51.2	21.0	27.1	47.1
Racial heterogeneity in city (2000)	.38	.55	.64	.47	.74
% female headed families with children in city (2000)	11.40	23.74	25.30	17.44	21.79
% foreign born in city (2000)	4.10	5.60	8.00	5.60	29.50
% of state population who identify as evangelical Christians (2007; Pew Center)	34	37	11	18	18
% state population preferring Starbucks over McDonalds (2008; Pew Center)	43.15	39.47	59.14	44.72	65.61
BK punitiveness score in state in 2009 (range 0–4; Kutateladze)	2.46	1.60	2.12	2.18	2.20

City Characteristics

Table 8.2 provides a summary of select contextual characteristics of the case study cities on each trajectory in Figure 8.3. Some of these results begin to disentangle contextual differences between places with unique patterns of serious gang violence. It is important to note that the cities above are selected purely for illustrative purposes, and there is likely much more within-group than between-group variation in some of these features of place. Importantly, however, variations in these demographic, economic, political, and cultural characteristics begin to paint a picture of the types of very large cities experiencing consistent gang presence, but hosting varied patterns of serious gang violence.

In general, Inglewood—which had inordinately high proportions of gang-related violence between 1996 and 2009—is located in a state and county with the highest levels of correctional expenditures and prosecutorial strength of all five cities. It is also characterized by a large African American and Hispanic population, reflected in absolute percentages as well as the index of racial heterogeneity. One-fifth to one-quarter of the population in each of these very large cities, irrespective of their gang violence trends, is living below the poverty line, with the exception of residents in Abilene, wherein a much lower proportion of residents are impoverished. The foreign-born population constitutes more than one-quarter of Inglewood's residents and 8% of residents in Springfield but only 4% to 5% of the populations of the remaining cities. In general, criminal justice strength, relatively disadvantaged socioeconomic conditions, and racial and ethnic heterogeneity appear greater in Inglewood than in the case study cities with less serious gang violence trends.

Availability of Crime Facilitators

Accessing Firearms

In general, guns are the weapon of choice for gang members who involve themselves in violence. This means that the availability of firearms should play some role in facilitating the violence perpetrated by local gangs. Because gang members often use illegal guns—either accessed through strawman[3] purchasers, through theft, or via illicit gun markets—rather than those acquired through legal channels, it is unlikely that state, county, or municipal gun control laws and ordinances will systematically influence serious gang violence trends (Murray, 1975). Nonetheless, *focused deterrence strategies*, like the "pulling levers" approach undertaken by the federal Project Safe Neighborhoods program, targets specific chronic offenders with high levels of criminal justice and social service intervention. Braga, Pierce, McDevitt, Bond, and Cronin (2008) describe the "pulling levers" approach as follows:

> In its simplest form, the approach consists of selecting an appropriate crime problem, such as youth homicide; convening an interagency working group of law-enforcement practitioners; conducting research to identify key offenders, groups, and behavior patterns; framing a response to offenders and groups of offenders that uses a varied menu of sanctions ("pulling levers") to stop them from continuing their violent behavior; focusing social services and community resources on targeted offenders and groups to match law-enforcement prevention efforts; and directly and repeatedly communicating with offenders to make them understand why they are receiving this special attention. (p. 134)

These targeted programs have been found to dramatically lower overall rates of gun-related violence, especially in Boston.

The Role of Firearms for Gang Members

Many gang studies show that the felt need for protection is the primary reason gang members own or carry an illegal gun (Esbensen, Deschenes, & Winfree, 1994). "It is therefore not surprising," explain Lizotte and colleagues (2000), "that when boys join gangs, the probability of carrying a hidden gun is substantially increased" (p. 829). Beginning in the 1970s, youth gangs were reported to have more weapons of greater lethality (W. Miller, 1982/1992). Stretesky and Pogrebin (2007) assert that gang-related gun violence can be understood in terms of self and identity that are heavily rooted in self-concepts of masculinity and reinforced by other gang members. Bjerregaard and Lizotte (1995) add that gangs are more likely to recruit adolescents who own a gun, and gang members are more than twice as likely as nongang members to own a gun for protection. "Gang members carry guns to protect themselves and their turf from rival gangs, who, in turn, must arm" (Lizotte et al., 2000, p. 830). Furthermore, C. Block and Block (1993) note that gun availability fuels gang violence. Lizotte and colleagues (2000) explain, "If one travels in a dangerous world of youth armed illegally and defensively with firearms, it only makes sense to carry a gun. Therefore, peer gun ownership for protection increases the probability of gun violence" (p. 830).

In the Rochester study cited here, during early adolescence, younger boys who are members of a gang have a higher probability of gun carrying. "In late adolescence, involvement in serious drug trafficking, independent of gang involvement, is a much stronger factor explaining hidden gun carrying"— typically after gang involvement has ended (Lizotte et al., 2000, p. 829). In this study and in the Pittsburgh longitudinal delinquency study referenced earlier in this chapter (R. A. Gordon et al., 2014), extensive involvement in drug sales and gun carrying typically come later in the life course, as discussed in Chapter 5.

Drug-Related Factors

Law enforcement views drug-related activity as the strongest factor influencing local gang violence (Figure 8.8). The Pittsburgh case study illustrates two ways in which gang involvement in illicit drug trafficking contributes to violence: first by their co-occurrence in communities, and second, by the direct involvement of gang members in trafficking. Among proposed explanations for the surge in youth violence and gang homicides in the late 1980s and early 1990s, Blumstein (1995a, 1995b, 1996) and Blumstein and Rosenfeld (1999) insist that the so-called crack cocaine epidemic is an important explanation, although the evidence is equivocal.

Another contributing factor to the sharp rise in drug-related arrests observed in the United States in the late 1980s and early 1990s was the "war on drugs" initiated by the Reagan administration (Howell, 2003b). To be sure, Howell and Decker (1999) conclude gang participation, drug trafficking, and violence occur together, and more so, according to Coughlin and Venkatesh (2003), in certain cities with more organized gangs, and where gangs are intermixed with drug trafficking groups. The Pittsburgh case study is an excellent illustration of this latter condition. In other words, these problems overlap considerably, but, as Decker (2007) notes, "Conflict between gangs accounts for more gang violence, including homicide, than does involvement in the drug trade" (p. 392).

Law enforcement officers themselves recognize the tangential and infrequent involvement of gangs in drug distribution. From the 1996 NYGS onward, Howell, Egley, and colleagues (2002) found only a minority of gang-problem jurisdictions report that gangs controlled a majority of the drug distribution in their jurisdiction. The bulk of the evidence from law enforcement, field studies, and youth surveys finds that most gangs lack key organizational characteristics to effectively manage drug distribution operations. Decker (2007) outlines specific criteria required for large-scale operations as follows, and few street gangs meet these criteria:

First, gangs must have an organizational structure with a hierarchy of leaders, roles, and rules. Second, gangs must have group goals that are widely shared by members. Third, gangs must promote stronger allegiance to the larger organization than to subgroups within it. Finally, gangs must possess the means to control and discipline their members to produce compliance with group goals. (p. 392)

Figure 8.8   Factors Influencing Local Gang Violence, National Youth Gang Survey, 2009

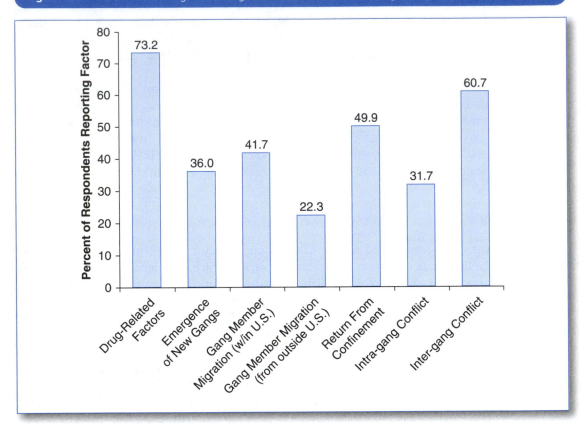

Source: National Youth Gang Center. (2000). 1998 National Youth Gang Survey. Washington, DC: U.S. Department of Justice, Office of Juvenile Justice and Delinquency Prevention.

In general, research supports a connection between drug-related offenses and lethal violence rates in multiple cities, but these are both considered potential outcomes of what Ousey and Lee (2004) call *preexisting social conditions*. These, alongside gang proliferation, mean that violence, gangs, and drug trafficking are often correlated across places, but gangs are not necessarily causally connected to elevated drug activity. Martinez, Rosenfeld, and Mares (2008) claim indicators of social disorganization (socioeconomic disadvantage and residential instability) predict drug activity, which, in turn, leads to higher levels of criminal violence (aggravated assault and robbery). Moreover, violence rates may be higher where gang problems are especially serious, and several studies of individuals' increased violence rates while involved in gangs suggest this possibility. Nevertheless, research shows that relatively unorganized gangs are not able to control local drug dealing operations very effectively.

At the individual level, Bjerregaard's (2010) research to date supports each of three potential connections among involvement in gangs, drugs, and violence. The first possibility is that gang membership promotes involvement in drugs and that both gang membership and drug involvement in turn increase violence. Second, drug involvement or violent behavior may precede gang membership. Third, gang membership, drug involvement, and violent behaviors all occur simultaneously and are simply manifestations of the same antecedent factors.

In a nationwide test of the relationships between individual gang membership, drug involvement, and violence in the National Longitudinal Survey of Youth, Bjerregaard (2010) found that gang membership influences drug involvement in teenagers, though less than anticipated. Misleading impressions of greater gang drug involvement are reported when the sequencing of gang, drug, and violence involvement is not separated in the analysis.[4] Across several longitudinal studies with high-risk, large-city samples, Krohn and Thornberry (2008) found drug use and involvement in drug sales increase with gang membership and decrease when youth leave gangs, but drug sales remain elevated in some sites. This excellent review of longitudinal studies also concludes that "the weight of the evidence suggests that street gangs do facilitate or elicit increased involvement in delinquency, violence and drugs" (p. 147) at the individual level.

Research in Pittsburgh supports that conclusion. For example, Loeber and colleagues (2008) found that in the youngest cohort, "drug dealing and gang membership in late childhood significantly increased the risk of violence in late adolescence and dealing and gun carrying in early adolescence significantly increased the risk of violence in late adolescence" (p. 163). In this study, "drug dealing, gang membership, and gun carrying were strongly related to serious violent offending over time . . . Gang members who carried guns had about three to five times the risk of later violence even with controls for violence" (p. 163).

This long-term and very comprehensive Pittsburgh study of child, adolescent, and young adult crime reveals that violence is most likely to occur where drug trafficking, gun ownership and use, and gang activity intersect (R. A. Gordon et al., 2014). The youngest cohort was ages 12–16 at the middle of the 1990s, the approximate peak of the crack cocaine epidemic in Pittsburgh that Tita, Cohen, and colleague (2005) amply documented. Furthermore, both gang activity and homicides in Pittsburgh escalated in the early 1990s in concert with the crack cocaine epidemic in the city, "peaking just prior to the middle of the decade, and then falling through the late 1990s" (p. 236). This confluence was seen in gang member crime patterns. R. A. Gordon and colleagues (2014) found that

> the evidence for particular forms of multitype delinquency is consistent with gangs using violence in instrumental ways, as a means to make money either by protecting drug territory or by supporting the acquisition and selling of stolen goods as well as drugs, at least in Pittsburgh in the 1990s. (p. 248)

In sum, at the individual level, gang involvement typically promotes participation in violence, drug use, and drug trafficking, and perhaps prolongs gang member involvement in drug sales. The Pittsburgh case study illustrates what criminologists call a *period effect*, when historical events serve to exacerbate criminal activity—in this particular case, gang involvement in drug trafficking at the peak of a crack cocaine epidemic in the city. But the sequencing can vary from one neighborhood or community to another, from one city to another, and from one cohort to another in the same city.

◈ Features of Gangs That Contribute to Serious Gang Problems

A number of features of gangs—including the number of gangs in cities, size of gang membership, level of gang organization and structure, the influence of prison gangs, possibilities for transnational gangs, group process, and cultural codes—are important indicators of serious gang problems in large cities. Indeed, the presence of these features provides some indication that places have reached Stage 5 of Howell's (2015) model. A brief summary of important data and studies on each of these indicators follows.

Number of Gangs

The number of gangs is a potent correlate of overall gang crime, particularly where multiple gangs are active in a restricted area. Approximately two-thirds of all gangs were located in cities with populations above 50,000 and adjacent suburban counties in 2009 (Table 8.1). Generally speaking, studies in Chicago (R. Block, 2000; C. Block & Block, 1993) and Los Angeles (Hutson et al., 1995) show that the number of gangs present in an area significantly relates to the area's overall level of violence and other crimes.[5] In the southeast area of Chicago, where three or four different named gangs were sometimes active in the same area, R. Block (2000) illustrates this point:

> The conflict between the Black Disciples and BGDN has resulted in many deaths in District 7, where all four major black gangs were active, and in the housing projects in District 2. The southeast area includes the former turf of the El Rukins (now renamed the Black P. Stone Nation) and the oldest Mexican neighborhood in Chicago, where the Latin Kings are active. (p. 378)

R. Block (2000) examined gang homicides in very small *grid squares*, consisting of 150 meters on a side, revealing that "the relationship between the number of gangs that are active in an area and the levels of assaults and drug-related incidents is remarkably high" (p. 379).[6] This research found that gangs do not necessarily need to be large to carry out a large number of homicides. In fact, the remaining street gangs other than the largest four Chicago gangs were responsible for more police-recorded offenses of any type than any one of the top four. Many of these smaller street gangs were relatively new in Chicago, predominantly Latino, and continuously fighting among themselves over limited turfs.

> "[How did you personally feel about fighting?] I loved it, loved it. I was one of the first ones in. I liked to throw blows… I put my life down for [my gang] many times, that's how I got shot—five times—and knifed." —Anonymous male member of the Hoya Maravilla gang (in J. Moore, 1991, pp. 61–62)

Number of Gang Members

Three findings about the number of gang members are important. First, gang members are far more prevalent within larger cities. Approximately 8 out of 10 gang members are located in cities with populations above 50,000 and adjacent suburban counties in 2009 (Table 8.1). Second, Egley and colleagues (2006) conclude that gang members are far more numerous in densely populated cities that report a persistent gang problem. Third, Decker and Pyrooz (2010b) found that in the largest cities both the number of gang members and number of gangs "are strong, positive, and significant" correlates of gang homicides (p. 369), but that the number of gang members is a much stronger correlate than the number of gangs (although both measures are statistically significant). This is understandable given that some law enforcement agencies count multiple sets as one gang while others enumerate only larger gangs.

Gang Structures and Conflicts

Gang Structure

Previous research has not always been clear on the correlation between gang structure and gang violence, largely because much of the research viewed gangs as either highly organized (resembling adult organized-crime groups) or unorganized. Thrasher (1927/2000) is widely recognized for his *natural history of the gang*, which accounts for how gangs develop and evolve from a play group to a full-fledged criminal gang. For instance, Thrasher observed that gangs in the embryonic stage may evolve into a more highly organized unit, from a "diffuse" gang to a "solidified" criminal gang, and eventually, possibly become a "conventionalized" (formalized) organization if it, for example, becomes an athletic club or a pleasure club of some sort. But as pointed out in Chapter 2, few highly formalized gangs have been found elsewhere. C. Taylor (In Focus 8.1) asserts that some gangs evolve into criminal organizations.

IN FOCUS 8.1
GANG TRANSFORMATIONS IN DETROIT

C. Taylor (1990b) identified three different motivational gang categories in Detroit: scavenger, territorial, and corporate. *Scavenger* gangs mainly consist of lower and underclass youths. They are urban survivors who prey on the weak and have no common bond except their impulsive behavior and need to belong. They engage in senseless, spontaneous crimes for fun. Leadership constantly changes (p. 105). Scavengers are also the social and violent gangs that Yablonsky (1959) identified, and the "42 Gang" of Chicago that Shaw and McKay (1942) studied.

Territorial gangs, Taylor (1990b) contends, evolve from scavenger gangs, when they define a territory and become more organized for a specific purpose. Someone assumes a leadership role, which is part of the process of organization. They actively defend their territory, the area of their "business." They become "rulers" of their turf, generally defined as neighborhood and ethnic boundaries, using physical violence as their only enforcement tool against invaders (pp. 107–108).

Corporate gangs are highly organized for the purpose of engaging in illegal money-making ventures. In Chicago, for a time, they served as "farm teams" for mafia organizations. They took on many of the characteristics of a business organization, motivated only by profit. They operated by rules and military-like discipline. Their membership came from all social classes (Taylor, 1990b).

Taylor (1990b) illustrates the transformation of a scavenger gang to a territorial gang, then to a corporate gang with the case of the 42 Gang in Chicago. Even as scavengers, they were considered one of the most vicious gangs in the United States at that time, once they staked a territory, grew, and

(Continued)

(Continued)

became more formal in their organization. Some of them graduated into the lower ranks of the Capone mob, although some of the mobsters thought the 42 Gang "too crazy" for organized crime work. Most of them eventually were maimed, killed, or imprisoned for murder, armed robbery, or rape.

The growth of the lucrative drug trade in the mid- to late 1980s redirected scavenger gangs into independent organizations in their own right in Detroit. Taylor (1990b) contends that the advent of the new era of drug use and trafficking gave new life and purpose to scavenger gangs. Without the Job Corps and other programs, they saw the drug business as a way out of poverty. These conditions combined to move Black youths for the very first time into "mainstream major crime." The Detroit scavenger gangs became part of organized crime in America. They became "imperialists" (p. 113). As Taylor put it, "The fact is that drugs have taken street gangs and given them the capability and power to become social institutions" (p. 114).

Source: C. Taylor, 1990a, 1990b, pp. 105–114. Reprinted with permission from SAGE Publications, Inc.

As research has become more sophisticated, the findings have become clearer. For example, Esbensen, Osgood, Taylor, Peterson, and Freng (2001) show that when gangs are even "somewhat organized" (i.e., have initiation rites and so on), members self-report involvement in more serious delinquent acts than other youths. In other research, a study of detained youths in three Arizona sites, Decker and colleagues (2008) found that "the more organized the gang, even at low levels of organization, the more likely it is that members will be involved in violent offenses, drug sales, and violent victimizations" (p. 169).

Egley and Howell (2010) associate other structural characteristics of gangs with gang violence. Using NYGS data, gangs that have subgroups based on age, gender, and geographic area or territory are associated with higher homicide levels. Among 2009 survey respondents, asked directly whether gangs in their jurisdiction have such subgroups, only 33% of localities that acknowledged gang activity reported none of these three subgroupings. Almost one-third (32%) reported one of the three subgroups, 18% reported any two of them, and 17% reported having all three subgroups. While the existence of any one of these subgroups predicted gang violence, odds ratios reached statistical significance with any two of the subgroups, and the odds ratio more than doubled from a condition in which only one subgroup was present to the presence of all three subgroups. This national research strongly suggests that the greater the organization of gangs into subgroups of some sort, the greater the likelihood of gang-related violence.

In sum, evidence is growing "that measures of gang membership and the number of gangs are . . . robust, whether reported by individual gang members or official agencies" (Decker & Pyrooz, 2010b, p. 371). And the number of gangs, the number of gang members, and the presence of gang subgroups predict gang homicide in very large cities.

Intergang Conflict

Numerous studies show that most intergang violence, including homicides, is commonly related to several circumstances (maintenance of set space, interpersonal "beefs," normative or order violations, surprise assaults, and drug-turf disputes) and a variety of motives (defending one's identity as a gang member, defense of the gang's honor and reputation, set space trespassing, gang revenge or retaliation, personal spontaneous retaliation) (Braga, 2004; Hughes & Short, 2005; Papachristos, 2009; Tita, Cohen, et al., 2005). Interestingly, the bulk of intergang violence is directed against others of the same racial/ethnic background, often in battles for prominence or turf disputes.

The most detailed information on dispute pretexts among gangs and gang members comes from two studies in which research teams observed thousands of gang members' daily behaviors over several years. In the first one, a Chicago study, Hughes and Short's (2005) analysis of Short's observations in the 1960s of more than 2,600 incidents involving members of 20 lower or working-class gangs over three years revealed valuable insights on typical dispute pretexts (In Focus 8.2). When outcomes were examined, those that precipitated violence per se were largely retaliations (55%), followed by identity attacks (36%), and normative or order violations (31%).

IN FOCUS 8.2
GANG DISPUTE PRETEXTS

1. *Norm violations* include "annoying" behavior, failure to fulfill an obligation, ignoring, causing, or contributing to another's loss, boasting, cheating, unacceptable demeanor, and taking and/or violating another person's property.

2. *Noncompliance with an order* is begrudging acquiescence or (implicit or explicit) refusal to comply with demands to engage in or to not engage in a certain behavior.

3. *Actions that suggest a need to defend others* are behaviors directed toward one party that elicit a verbal or physical sanction from one or more observers.

4. *Money or debts* involve failure to repay a financial loan upon collection by the lender.

5. *Unfair or rough play* includes actions that are inconsistent with the explicit or implicit rules governing participation in an organized athletic contest.

6. *Identity attack* is any direct attack on personal or gang identity—including accusations, insults, challenges, and physical violations that do not result in bodily harm—and degrading rejections and yelling.

7. *Concern regarding opposite sex relations* involves behaviors that are upsetting because of the challenge they represent to another party's claim to a romantic interest.

8. *Territory or neighborhood honor* include actions undertaken by one party that directly threaten another's claim to a particular territory.

9. *Racial concerns* involve physical or verbal actions undertaken by one party against another solely because of race.

10. *Fun or recreational incidents* include physical or verbal actions that lead to hostilities during leisure activities such as "playing the dozens" and less organized body punching and horsing around.

(Continued)

(Continued)

11. *Retaliation* is action undertaken by one party to avenge a previous attack or any other perceived or actual wrongdoing by the targeted party or a close associate.

12. *Rumors* include physical or verbal actions undertaken by one party to seek redress for negative information allegedly disseminated by the targeted party.

13. *Robbery* involves intimidating or violent actions undertaken by one party to acquire money or property from another.

14. *Misunderstanding* includes intended or actual actions directed at one or more persons who are mistakenly identified or accused of a wrongdoing that did not occur.

15. *General troublemaking* is physical or verbal harassment for no apparent reason.

16. *Other pretexts* include physical or verbal actions undertaken for other reasons, such as doing what someone else asked, indirectly harassing one person or group of persons by harming others, and preempting an anticipated attack.

Source: Hughes & Short, 2005, pp. 48–49.

Earlier, W. Miller's (1966) pioneering study of Boston gangs revealed the nature of gang-based retaliations. Over a two-year period of field observation of 200 members of seven violent gangs by field workers, approximately 54,000 behaviors and interpersonal sentiments were recorded. Although violent intergang conflicts were extremely rare, Miller found that "gang members fight to secure and defend their honor as males; to secure and defend the reputation of their local area and the honor of their women; and to show that an affront to their pride and dignity demands retaliation" (p. 112).

Prison Gangs

The Gypsy Jokers (actually a motorcycle club) were the first acknowledged prison gang, formed in the 1950s in Washington state prisons (Camp & Camp, 1985). Violent prison gangs grew in concert with the massive expansion of prison populations in the United States that began in the 1970s and continued for 30 years (Howell, 2015). By the end of the 1970s, bona fide prison gangs were prevalent in a dozen states. In a mid-1980s survey of all state and federal prisons, facility administrators in 33 states indicated that they had gangs in their prisons (Camp & Camp, 1985). Having been formed to provide protection inside prisons from rival street gang members, the prison gangs were "an extension of an identical organization imported from the streets" (Jacobs, 1974, p. 397). Two states stand out for sheer strength and statewide influence of their prison gangs: California and Illinois.

California has been dubbed the "mother" of major prison gangs because six major prison gangs were active in the state's prisons by 1984, and these without doubt contributed directly to the growth of gang activity throughout the state and to some extent in the West region. Gang suppression legislation, coupled with the state's indeterminate sentence provision, and its "Three Strikes and You're Out" law served to increase confinement of street gang members (Schlosser, 1998). In turn, growing conflicts and assaults between northern and southern California gang inmates led to the formation of *Sureños* and *Norteños* networks, and a rivalry that produced many gang wars, both in prisons and on the streets (National Alliance of Gang Investigators' Associations, 2009). Rival southern California Hispanic street gangs thus were enemies with anyone from northern California, and vice versa. In time, this rivalry would unite the respective clusters of gangs in jails and state prisons. By the mid-1990s, the California prison system was said to be full of warring gangs, members of the Crips, Bloods, Mexican Mafia, and Black Guerrilla Family, to name a few.

In Chicago, massive incarceration of gang members followed Mayor Daley's 1969 gang war. Prison administrators inadvertently strengthened the gangs by using them to help maintain control of prisons, thus allowing them "to consolidate, form alliances, and grow in number and strength" (Venkatesh, 2002, p. 133). The Illinois prison gangs were "reorganized at a level of sophistication that dwarfed the type of structures that had developed in the streets" (Perkins, 1987, p. 17). By the mid-1970s, Latino, African-American, and Caucasian gangs in Chicago and elsewhere across the state had merged into two major coalitions in Illinois prisons, the "People" and the "Folks" by inmates who were seeking protection through coalition building (Chicago Crime Commission, 2006). They soon took control of older inmate organizations by guile and targeted violence, and became the strongest force within the prisons. Once members were freed from prisons, they quickly moved to battle, overpower, and subsume the weaker street corner groups (Cureton, 2009). By the mid-1980s, Illinois had the largest number of gangs and gang members in prison of all U.S. states (Camp & Camp, 1985). Across Illinois, Department of Corrections officials estimated that some 5,300 inmates were active gang members in 1984, constituting 34% of all inmates (p. 134). Some of the Chicago gang leaders formed organizational networks both inside and outside prisons that linked inmates with others in jails and on the streets in illegal enterprises, creating what came to be called *webs, supergangs,* or *gang nations* (Venkatesh, 2002, p. 134). "But significantly, and unlike past inmate groups, the gangs maintained their ties to the streets" (Hagedorn, 2006, p. 203). People and Folk alliances accounted for the major street conflicts that took place in Chicago in the 1980s (Perkins, 1987). Under these coalitions, gang conflicts were far more serious because they involved multiple gangs on occasion.

In a 2009 survey of Directors of Security in the 53 U.S. prison systems (federal and state) systems, 19% of all inmates were classified as gang members, half of whom belonged to gangs prior to imprisonment. Nearly 12% of all inmates had been "validated" as gang members, and approximately one-quarter of all members were leaders or hard core members.[7] These criteria include, but are not limited to

- gang tattoos,

- correspondence to or from known gang members or correspondence containing references to gang activity,

- wearing gang colors,

- association with known gang members,

- possession of gang-related literature,

- possession of a photograph of known gang members, and

- identification by a fellow prisoner as a gang member.

"The principle behind the teardrop is to symbolize pain . . . Every time you go to prison, you get a teardrop, y'know, the teardrops you see going down from the corner of the eye." —Maniac (in Leap, 2012, pp. 108–109)

Once that classification has been made, the prisoner is "administratively segregated," meaning that he/she is housed separately from and receives different treatment than prisoners who have not been validated as gang members or associates. In the view of prison systems, the most important rationales for Security Threat Group (STG) or prison gang affiliation are: fear of other inmates/gangs (91%), sense of belonging (82%), personal status (70%), economic benefits (58%), and access to contraband (60%). Officials in 75% of the surveyed prison systems reported an increase in the membership of STG members over the preceding five years, as well as increased disruptive behavior (67%), more sophisticated operations (61%), and a history of violence (59%).

Transnational Gangs as a Version of Street Gangs

The prospect of "transnational" gangs, especially in Los Angeles, has heightened international security concerns (Franco, 2010). Four issues concerning these gangs are pertinent to our main focus in this chapter. First, are these the most dangerous gangs in Los Angeles? Second, do these gangs appreciably increase gang violence in other U.S. cities? Third, are these gangs an international security threat? Finally, do these gangs contribute significantly to the seriousness of gang violence along the U.S. Southwest–Mexico border?

Unfortunately, there is no single definition of a transnational gang. Franco (2010, pp. 1–2) cites one or more of the following characteristics in various definitions,

including (1) gangs that are criminally active and operational in more than one country; (2) gangs that are involved in criminal activities committed by gang members in one country that may be planned, directed, and controlled by gang leaders in another country; (3) gangs that tend to be mobile and adapt to new areas; and (4) the criminal activities of such gangs tend to be sophisticated and transcend national borders.

For a gang to be considered transnational, Franco suggests that it should have more than one of the preceding characteristics, and in most cases, so-called transnational gangs meet only the first criterion. Just two street gangs are referenced as potential transnational gangs: the 18th Street (*Mara Dieciocho*) Mexican American gang and Mara Salvatrucha (MS-13). These gangs have been characterized as "transnational" largely because members of these gangs have been reported in Central America and in the United States, and these gangs have a particular transnational migratory pattern between Los Angeles and Central America. Moreover, both gangs "have established gang cliques in El Salvador, Honduras, Guatemala, and Mexico that are modeled on, and perhaps linked to, U.S. MS-13 and M-18 gangs" (Franco, 2010, p. 2). Having originated in Los Angeles, M-13 gang members have been reported by law enforcement in cities in seven states (Franco, 2010). Two features of these gangs have fueled security concerns, first their enormous membership (Chapter 2), and second, their possible involvement in multi-national organized crime, particularly through connections with major drug cartels in Central America and Mexico.

The Los Angeles Police Department (LAPD) (2007) considers both MS-13 and 18th Street gangs to be among the most dangerous gangs in the city, and it publicly targeted these along with nine other gangs among the top 11 gangs targeted for suppression practices in 2007. A Los Angeles street gang expert (Alonso, 2008) points out that 18th Street is actually a collection of as many as 20 separate autonomous gang cliques operating under the same label with separate barrios in the San Fernando Valley surrounding Los Angeles. The LAPD listed just one such clique, Eighteenth Street Westside. Alonso also notes that the LAPD named three MS-13 cliques, one of which may not be particularly dangerous in his ongoing assessment.

Little gang violence has been associated with MS-13 and 18th Street gangs in other cities (FBI, 2011). Although the most recent FBI gang threat assessment (2011) asserts that MS-13 and 18th Street are among the Sureño gangs that are spreading most rapidly in the United States, these particular gangs were associated with extensive violence only in the Washington, DC, area (p. 17). This matter is disputed, however. The Washington Office on Latin America (WOLA) study revealed that 18th Street, at that time, did not "have a strong presence in the DC area, though small cliques may form and disband occasionally" (McGuire, 2007, p. 1), and that MS-13, the most well known of the two gangs that exist both in Central America and the United States, did have a notable presence in the Washington area. Moreover, neither gang appeared to be engaged in a systematic effort to become more involved in organized crime. "In contrast to the WOLA report, law enforcement officials point to evidence that the Washington DC area's gangs are indeed criminally active and may show signs of increasing criminal sophistication" (Franco, 2008, p. 8). Interestingly, neither 18th Street nor MS-13 is among the most prominent drug trafficking operations in the Southwest region (National Gang Intelligence Center, 2012), and neither of these gangs is said to present the highest level of threat in Texas prisons at this time (Joint Crime Information Center, 2014; Texas Fusion Center, 2013). Other reports have linked MS-13 with major drug cartels in Central America and Mexico (U.S. Government Accountability Office, 2010).

But are these gangs truly transnational or a "new urban insurgency" (Manwaring, 2009a, 2009b)? Experts on Central American and Mexican gangs question the elevation of these gangs to international-level security threats (Cruz, 2010; Hazen & Rodgers, 2014). MS-13 and 18th Street came to be discussed as possible transnational gangs because of their reputation in Los Angeles and cross-fertilization in Central America with local gangs (called *maras* in Spanish) in El Salvador, Honduras, and Guatemala. Central America *maras*, previously small territorial gangs, grew into large dangerous gangs in two phases (Cruz, 2014): first, from having been inculcated with gang culture and identity in Los Angeles, and second, from El Salvadorian *mano dura* (heavy handed) gang control policies and a "war on gangs" that brought overreliance on imprisonment, and inadvertently reconstituted the gangs into hierarchical structures. Briefly, the MS-13 and 18th Street gangs in Central America were not extensions of the Los Angeles–based gangs. As a result of intermittent back and forth migration, local *maras* adopted gang culture of the Los Angeles–based MS-13 and 18th Street gangs. Strictly speaking, the local *maras*, renamed MS-13 and 18th Street, were perhaps "trans-formed" rather than "transnational," yet they continued fighting one another, and with increasingly serious violence (Rogers & Hazen, 2014).

The El Salvadorian Mano Dura Act of 2003 permitted the detention and prosecution of suspected gang members under the newly classified felony of "illicit association." The new law had the unintended effect of strengthening local gangs. Confining large numbers of MS-13 and 18th Street gang members gave them the opportunity to reorganize themselves and recruit new members. At the same time, the El Salvadorian government declared war on these gangs, and this increased their resolve. "The *mano duro* blow seemed to have moved youth gangs toward a more criminalized type of violence" (Cruz, 2014, p. 136). Yet, expert analysts on Central American gang activity contend that neither the MS-13 nor the 18th Street gangs meet criteria for "transnational" status (for supporting information, see G. Jones, 2014; Rodgers & Hazen, 2014). In essence, "the transnational nature of the maras is more imagined than real, at least in the present" (Rodgers & Hazen, 2014, p. 4). Moreover, "groups that appear similar at first glance may be quite different on closer inspection" (p. 5). In March 2012, authorities in El Salvador facilitated a truce between MS-13 and the 18th Street gang (Thale, Bateman, & Goerdt, 2013). Other well-informed sources question the very existence of truly transnational street gangs (Hazen & Rodgers, 2014; Jones, 2013; McGuire, 2007; Seelke, 2012; United Nations Office on Drugs and Crime, 2007; Washington Office on Latin America, 2010). Nevertheless, the intermingling of these and other local gangs with international drug-trafficking organizations and transnational criminal organizations, which does occur in the Mexico and Central America corridor that extends into the Southwest United States, is a serious matter (Seele, Arnson, & Olson, 2013; Seelke, 2012; U.S. Agency for International Development, 2006). This situation bears close watch.

Violent Hot Spots and Gang Set Space

Violent hot spots and gang turf often co-occur, and these neighborhood places are said to have criminal *trajectories* in their own right (Griffiths & Chavez, 2004; Tita & Cohen, 2004). In Chicago in the mid-1990s, at the height of gang violence, R. Block (2000) explains,

> Even the largest street gangs were active only in limited areas. Police, community residents, and gang members perceived these activity areas, "turfs," differently. Some gangs are ephemeral. They may occupy a fixed area for only a few months. For other gangs, a core turf may exist for generations, [but overall, gang] boundaries are constantly shifting, are extremely tedious to map. (p. 369)

In the course of interviews with gang members, Tita, Cohen, and Engberg (2005) asked them to map places where they came together as a sociological group, that is, their set space. This study indicates that the location of gang set space is usually a very small geographic area, much smaller than neighborhoods or even census tracts. R. Block's (2000) study showed that multiple-gang activity was observed in just 4.5% of the total grid squares citywide ($N = 25,744$); however, "these squares accounted for 23.0% of the assaults and 44.3% of all drug-related incidents" (p. 379). Papachristos's (2009) Chicago study demonstrates that these homicidal patterns of gang conflict are extremely stable over time. "Gang members come and go, but their patterns of behavior create a network structure that persists and may very well provide the conduit through which gang values, norms, and culture are transmitted to future generations" (p. 119).

The earliest studies on gangs, like that undertaken by Thrasher (1927/2000), show that "boundary lines" and "borderlands" of gang turf—or the "interstitial areas"—are particularly vulnerable to elevated levels of violence as a means of defending and enlarging territory. Recent research on gangs and violent communities more broadly confirms this pattern (Anderson, 1999). For example, using sophisticated mathematical models, Brantingham and his colleagues (2012) show that the physical boundary equidistant between, and perpendicular to, the set spaces of two rival gangs has the greatest concentration of between-gang violence. This is exactly the outcome that would be expected in a competition between rival gangs for physical space.

Group Process

As discussed in Chapter 5, the typical gang is constantly in flux. As long as the gang is in an inactive state, that is, not attacked by a rival, even fringe members can keep it alive. Jankowski (1991) observed that the Los Angeles Mexican American gangs became violently active when the hardcore element grew in size or when an age cohort with a large hard-core membership moved into a central leadership position. "If the hard core is large, then the gang will be violently active, but if the hard core is small, then the gang will be violently inactive, regardless of the static structure" (p. 137). Cohesive gangs challenge more rival gangs and, in turn, are more frequently challenged themselves.

In prior research, Klein (1969) lists six key connections between group process and gang violence:

1. Gang process selectively crystallizes factors leading to violent behavior.

2. The gang legitimates displays of aggression.

3. Gang membership inadvertently leads to violence on behalf of the gang because this mistakenly appears to be expected.

4. The gang permits or reinforces the commission of violent acts.

5. The gang helps to draw attention to immediate as opposed to long-range consequences of activity.

6. The gang is a medium for the status-deprived member to seek peer group status. (pp. 1143–1144)

This is not to say that gangs routinely encourage their members to "get out and be violent" (p. 1144). Indeed, some gangs are not involved in violence at all, and in other cases the gang acts as a constraining force on its members, prohibiting or discouraging behavior which otherwise would result in discomfort for the group as a whole. "The gang more commonly does nothing so much as wonder what to do" (p. 1144). Spergel (1966) described this situation as follows: "A dozen youngsters suddenly find themselves walking down the street to a fight, and eight or ten or even all of them, individually, may be wondering why he is there" (p. 115).

The importance of group process in gangs and the implications of this for the violent character of many gangs, according to Decker (2007), cannot be overstated. Decker (1996) delineated a seven-step process to account for observed gang violence spurts—episodic gang conflicts that wax and wane and sometimes extend over a number of years (C. Block & Block, 1993). The process Decker (1996) observed in St. Louis begins with a loosely organized gang:

1. Loose bonds to the gang

2. Collective identification of threat from a rival gang (through rumors, symbolic shows of force, cruising, and mythic violence), reinforcing the centrality of violence that expands the number of participants and increases cohesion

3. A mobilizing event, possibly, but not necessarily, violence

4. Escalation of activity

5. Violent event

6. Rapid de-escalation

7. Retaliation (p. 262)

As Horowitz (1983) explains, "In seeking to protect and promote their reputation, gangs often engage in prolonged 'wars,' which are kept alive between larger fights by many small incidents and threats of violence" (p. 94). One gang may claim *precedence*, which means that the other group must challenge that gang if they want to retain their honor and reassert their reputation. "Whatever the 'purpose' of violence, it often leads to retaliation and revenge creating a feedback loop where each killing requires a new killing" (Decker & Van Winkle 1996, p. 186), often "spreading from one neighborhood to another and outliving the initial source of the problem" (Decker, 2007, p. 398).

Similarly, Papachristos (2009) found that murders spread in the neighborhood through a process of social contagion as gangs respond to threats from other gangs. Specific murders, particularly those in public view, have the intended effect of threatening the social status and ranking of groups within the neighborhood. Thus, to avoid subjugation themselves, other gangs "must constantly (re)establish their social status through displays of solidarity—in this case, acts of violence—which, in turn, merely strengthen these murder networks" (p. 76). Papachristos's findings "suggest that gangs are not groups of murderers per se, but rather embedded social networks in which violence ricochets back and forth . . . [and] what begins as a single murder soon generates a dozen more as it diffuses through these murder networks" (p. 76). These events become, in effect, "dominance contests" in which "violence spreads through a process of social contagion that is fueled by normative and behavioral precepts of the code of the street" (p. 81).

Culture and the Code of the Street

Some of the earliest studies on youth delinquency and youth gangs evoked cultural, or more precisely subcultural, values and orientations to explain in-group cohesion and shared motives, drives, and experiences (Bordua, 1961; Cloward & Ohlin, 1960; A. Cohen, 1955; Short, 1968). After a protracted movement away from cultural explanations, research by E. Anderson (1999) reinvigorated this tradition by the mid- to late 1990s. Based on his Philadelphia ethnographic research, Anderson coined the phrase *code of the street* as a set of informal rules or street culture governing interpersonal public behavior, particularly violence. At the heart of Anderson's code is the idea of respect. Youngsters on dangerous streets who follow the street code attempt to build reputations for themselves as commanding respect, or *juice*, thereby warding off potential attackers. One of the street code's most pervasive norms is that of *retribution*, stipulating that personal attacks (verbal or physical) must be avenged. This set of normative behavior was communicated interpersonally and in rap music (Kubrin, 2005).

Brezina, Agnew, Cullen, and Wright (2004) found some support for Anderson's basic thesis using national youth survey data. Stronger support has emerged from studies in Georgia and Iowa with neighborhood-level data that measured adolescents' adoption of Anderson's street code (E. Stewart, Schreck, & Simons, 2006; E. Stewart & Simons, 2010). This research found that, indeed, adolescents who follow the street culture have a higher probability of offending (see also Keith & Griffiths, 2014). Moreover, at the individual level, adoption of the street code "seems to aggravate the risk of victimization because most of the potential offenders are themselves operating by the street code" (Stewart et al., 2006, p. 448). At the neighborhood level, Stewart and Simons (2010) conclude,

> the positive effect of individual-level street code values on violent delinquency is increased when an adolescent lives in a neighborhood where the street culture is endorsed. This pattern of results adds to the growing literature that describes how neighborhood structural characteristics combined with deviant cultural and situational codes lead to the perpetuation of violence. (p. 592)

Stewart and fellow researchers' (2006) earlier study also drew attention to this cycle of violence: "As a consequence, the potential for relatively minor infractions to escalate into major violent encounters (e.g., lethal violence) increases, thereby leading to a cycle of violence in African American communities" (p. 449).

Despite the seeming relevance of cultural codes to group behavior and, more specifically, to the cultivation of antisocial or criminal youth gangs, however, very few studies have explicitly linked the code of the street to youth gang membership (but see Matsuda, Melde, Taylor, Freng, & Esbensen, 2013).

◈ Concluding Observations

An examination of gang presence histories in Chapter 7 showed that larger cities (50,000 residents or more) in the NYGS tended to report consistent gang presence at each year between 1996 and 2009. Yet this analysis did not differentiate the nature and seriousness of the gang violence problem. Therefore, this chapter reports on preliminary analyses of gang-related homicide trends in the very largest cities (with populations greater than 100,000) in the United States. These analyses revealed that more than 8 out of 10 very large cities reported a consistently high level or increasing proportion of gang-related homicides over the 14-year period. None of these cities evidenced a decreasing pattern.

The findings suggest that gang activity and its associated violence remains an important and significant component of the U.S. crime problem. While it has been reasonably assumed that gang-related violence would be following the overall dramatic declines in violent crime nationally, analyses reported in this chapter and by Howell, Egley, and associates (2011) provide overwhelming evidence to the contrary—that is, gang violence rates have continued at exceptional levels over the past decade *despite* the remarkable overall crime drop. Gang violence that is rather commonplace in very large cities seems largely unaffected by, if not independent from, other crime trends—with the possible exceptions of drug trafficking and firearm availability.

The number of gang members, number of gangs, and other structural characteristics are important indicators of serious gang activity in the largest cities. Research confirms that both the number of gangs and the number of gang members predict gang homicide, particularly where gang subgroupings exist, based on age, gender, and geographical area.

Several contextual factors inflame gang set space, including local socioeconomic characteristics of place, the availability of firearms, and patterns of drug trafficking or related activities. In addition, features of the gangs themselves, like the number of gangs or gang members, inmates returning from prison, intergang conflict, and transnational gang growth influence the seriousness of local gang violence problems. Moreover, set space (as originally noted in Chapter 3, where gang members most frequently hang out) serves as a sort of "lightning rod" for intergang violence (Tita & Ridgeway, 2007), which manifests even more dramatically in the interstitial areas between gang turf. Group processes, especially contagion, can enliven gang members and unify them in collective violence, and cultural codes may offer an explanation for shared values or orientations of members. At the individual level, gang involvement promotes or facilitates individual participation in violence, drug use, and drug trafficking, and perhaps prolongs gang member involvement in drug sales; importantly, these crimes can co-occur.

The influence of each of the indicators of serious gang activity and contextual factors associated with gang violence can vary from one neighborhood or community to another, from one city to another, and from one gang to another in the same city. Serious gaps in knowledge remain with respect to the role of prison gangs and the impacts of returning gang-involved inmates.

DISCUSSION TOPICS

1. Why do we find regional trends in gang violence?

2. Which factors facilitate gang violence, and how can we capitalize on this knowledge to reduce gang-related violence?

3. Why do gang problems become increasingly more serious in some cities and not in others?

4. What are some distinctive features of gangs in the city case studies?

5. What are the distinctions between transnational and transformed gangs?

RECOMMENDATIONS FOR FURTHER READING

Serious Violent Gangs

Braga, A. A., Kennedy, D. M., & Tita, G. E. (2002). New approaches to the strategic prevention of gang and group-involved violence. In C. R. Huff (Ed.), *Gangs in America III* (pp. 271–285). Thousand Oaks, CA: Sage.

Decker, S. H. (2007). Youth gangs and violent behavior. In D. J. Flannery, A. T. Vazsonyi, & I. D. Waldman (Eds.), *The Cambridge handbook of violent behavior and aggression* (pp. 388–402). Cambridge: Cambridge University Press.

Decker, S. H., Katz, C. M., & Webb, V. J. (2008). Understanding the black box of gang organization: Implications for involvement in violent crime, drug sales, and violent victimization. *Crime and Delinquency, 54,* 153–172.

Decker, S. H., & Pyrooz, D. C. (2010). On the validity and reliability of gang homicide: A comparison of disparate sources. *Homicide Studies, 14,* 359–376.

Egley, A. E., & Howell, J. C. (2012). *Highlights of the 2010 National Youth Gang Survey.* Washington, DC: Office of Juvenile Justice and Delinquency Prevention.

Griffiths, E., & Chavez, J. M. (2004). Communities, street guns and homicide trajectories in Chicago, 1980–1995: Merging methods for examining homicide trends across space and time. *Criminology, 42,* 941–975.

Howell, J. C. (1999). Youth gang homicides: A literature review. *Crime and Delinquency, 45,* 208–241.

Howell, J. C. (2006). *The impact of gangs on communities* (NYGC Bulletin No. 2). Tallahassee, FL: National Youth Gang Center.

Hutson, H. R., Anglin, D., Kyriacou, D. N., Hart, J., & Spears, K. (1995). The epidemic of gang-related homicides in Los Angeles County from 1979 through 1994. *Journal of the American Medical Association, 274,* 1031–1036.

Klein, M. W., & Maxson, C. L. (1989). Street gang violence. In M. E. Wolfgang, & N. A. Weiner (Eds.), *Violent crime, violent criminals* (pp. 198–234). Newbury Park, CA: Sage.

Lien, I.-J. (2005a). Criminal gangs and their connections: Metaphors, definitions, and structures. In S. H. Decker & F. M. Weerman (Eds.), *European street gangs and troublesome youth groups* (pp. 31–50). Lanham, MD: AltaMira Press.

Lien, I.-J. (2005b). The role of crime acts in constituting the gang's mentality. In S. H. Decker & F. M. Weerman (Eds.), *European street gangs and troublesome youth groups* (pp. 105–125). Lanham, MD: AltaMira Press.

Maxson, C. L. (1999). Gang homicide: A review and extension of the literature. In D. Smith & M. Zahn (Eds.), *Homicide: A sourcebook of social research* (pp. 197–220). Thousand Oaks, CA: Sage.

Maxson, C. L., Gordon, M. A., & Klein, M. W. (1985). Differences between gang and nongang homicides. *Criminology, 23*, 209–222.

Papachristos, A. V. (2009). Murder by structure: Dominance relations and the social structure of gang homicide. *American Journal of Sociology, 115*, 74–128.

Tita, G. E., & Abrahamse, A. (2004). Gang homicide in LA, 1981–2001. *Perspectives on Violence Prevention, 3*, 1–18.

Tita, G. E., & Abrahamse, A. (2010). *Homicide in California, 1981–2008: Measuring the impact of Los Angeles and gangs on overall homicide patterns.* Sacramento, CA: Governor's Office of Gang and Youth Violence Policy.

Tita, G. E., Cohen, J., & Engberg, J. (2005). An ecological study of the location of gang "set space." *Social Problems, 52*, 272–299.

Tita, G. E., & Ridgeway, G. (2007). The impact of gang formation on local patterns of crime. *Journal of Research in Crime and Delinquency, 44*, 208–237.

Crack Cocaine "Epidemic"

Brownstein, H. (1996). *The rise and fall of a violent crime wave: Crack cocaine and the social construction of a crime problem.* Guilderland, NY: Harrow and Heston.

Cockburn, A., & St. Clair, J. (1998). *Whiteout: The CIA, drugs and the press.* London: Verso.

Cork, D. (1999). Examining space-time interaction in city-level homicide data: Crack markets and the diffusion of guns among youth. *Journal of Quantitative Criminology, 15*, 379–406.

Golub, A., & Johnson, B. D. (1997). *Crack's decline: Some surprises among U.S. cities* (Research in Brief). Washington, DC: National Institute of Justice.

Grogger, J., & Willis, M. (1998). *The introduction of crack cocaine and the rise in urban crime rates* (National Bureau of Economic Research Working Paper No. W6353). Cambridge, MA: National Bureau of Economic Research.

Hartman, D. A., & Golub, A. (1999). The social construction of the crack epidemic in the print media. *Journal of Psychoactive Drugs, 31*, 423–433.

Reeves, J. L., & Campbell, R. (1994). *Cracked coverage: Television news, the anti-cocaine crusade, and the Reagan legacy.* Durham, NC: Duke University.

Sampson, R. J. (2008). Rethinking crime and immigration. *Contexts, 7*, 28–33.

Transformed or Transnational Gangs

Cruz, J. M. (2010). Central American *maras*: From youth street gangs to transnational protection rackets. *Global Crime, 11*, 379–398.

Cruz, J. M. (2014). *Maras* and the politics of violence in El Salvador. In J. M. Hazen & D. Rodgers (Eds.), *Global gangs: Street violence across the world* (pp. 123–146). Minneapolis: University of Minnesota.

Franco, C. (2010). *The MS-13 and 18th Street Gangs: Emerging transnational gang threats?* (CRS Report RL34233, updated January 22, 2010). Washington, DC: Congressional Research Service, Library of Congress.

Hagedorn, J. M. (2008). *A world of gangs: Armed young men and gangsta culture.* Minneapolis: University of Minnesota Press.

Hazen, J. M., & Rodgers, D. E. (Eds.). (2014). *Global gangs: Street violence across the world.* Minneapolis: University of Minnesota.

Jones, G. A. (2014). "Hecho en Mexico": Gangs identities, and the politics of public security. In J. M. Hazen & D. Rodgers (Eds.), *Global gangs: Street violence across the world* (pp. 255–280). Minneapolis: University of Minnesota.

Jütersonke, O., Muggah, R., & Rodgers, D. (2009). Gangs, urban violence, and security in Central America. *Security Dialogue, 40*(4–5), 373–397.

Moore, J. W. (1998). Understanding youth street gangs: Economic restructuring and the urban underclass. In M. W. Watts (Ed.), *Cross-cultural perspectives on youth and violence* (pp. 65–78). Stamford, CT: JAI.

Moore, J. W. (2007). Female gangs: Gender and globalization. In J. M. Hagedorn, *Gangs in the global city* (pp. 187–203). Chicago: University of Illinois Press.

Rodgers, D., & Hazen, J. M. (2014). Introduction: Gangs in a global and comparative perspective. In J.M. Hazen & D. Rodgers (Eds.), *Global gangs: Street violence across the world* (pp. 1–25). Minneapolis: University of Minnesota.

Seelke, C. R. (2014). *Gangs in Central America* (CRS Report for Congress RL34112). Washington, DC: Congressional Research Service, Library of Congress.

Vigil, J. D. (1988). *Barrio gangs: Street life and identity in Southern California.* Austin: University of Texas Press.

Vigil, J. D. (1990). Cholos and gangs: Culture change and street youth in Los Angeles. In C. R. Huff (Ed.), *Gangs in America* (pp. 116–128). Newbury Park, CA: Sage.

Vigil, J. D. (1998). *From Indians to Chicanos: The dynamics of Mexican-American culture* (2nd ed.). Prospect Heights, IL: Waveland.

Vigil, J. D. (2002). *A rainbow of gangs: Street cultures in the mega-city.* Austin: University of Texas Press.

Zilberg, E. (2011). *Space of detention: The making of a transnational gang crisis between Los Angeles and San Salvador.* Durham, NC: Duke University Press.

Studies on Gang Retaliations

Block, C. R., & Block, R. (1993). *Street gang crime in Chicago* (Research in Brief). Washington, DC: U.S. Department of Justice, National Institute of Justice.

Decker, S. H. (2007). Youth gangs and violent behavior. In D. J. Flannery, A. T. Vazsonyi, & I. D. Waldman (Eds.), *The Cambridge handbook of violent behavior and aggression* (pp. 388–402). Cambridge: Cambridge University Press.

Hughes, L. A. (2013). Group cohesiveness, gang member prestige, and delinquency and violence in Chicago, 1959–1962. *Criminology, 15,* 798–832.

Hughes, L. A., & Short, J. F. (2005). Disputes involving gang members: Micro-social contexts. *Criminology, 43,* 43–76.

Papachristos, A. V. (2009). Murder by structure: Dominance relations and the social structure of gang homicide. *American Journal of Sociology, 115,* 74–128.

Tita, G. E., Riley, K. J., & Greenwood, P. (2005). *Reducing gun violence: Operation Ceasefire in Los Angeles.* Washington, DC: National Institute of Justice.

Valdez, Av., Cepeda, A., & Kaplan, C. (2009). Homicidal events among Mexican American street gangs: A situational analysis. *Homicide Studies, 13,* 288–306.

Gang Features and Structure

Decker, S. H., & Pyrooz, D. C. (2010). On the validity and reliability of gang homicide: A comparison of disparate sources. *Homicide Studies, 14,* 359–376.

Esbensen, F., Winfree, L. T., He, N., & Taylor, T. J. (2001). Youth gangs and definitional issues: When is a gang a gang, and why does it matter? *Crime and Delinquency, 47,* 105–130.

Katz, C. M., Webb, V. J., & Schaefer, D. (2000). The validity of police gang intelligence lists: Examining differences in delinquency between documented gang members and non-documented delinquent youth. *Police Quarterly, 3,* 413–437.

Pyrooz, D. C., Fox, A. M., & Decker, S. H. (2010). Racial and ethnic heterogeneity, economic disadvantage, and gangs: A macro-level study of gang membership in urban America. *Justice Quarterly, 14,* 1–26.

Vigil, J. D. (1993). The established gang. In S. Cummings & D. J. Monti (Eds.), *Gangs: The origins and impact of contemporary youth gangs in the United States* (pp. 95–112). Albany: State University of New York Press.

NOTES

1. This analysis was reported in Egley and Howell (2011).
2. A census tract is considered to be a reasonable approximation of a "neighborhood" or a "community" (Griffiths & Chavez, 2004, p. 942).
3. Strawman gun purchasers are buyers who can legally obtain firearms according to local requirements, but do so on behalf of individuals who would be ineligible (Cook & Cole, 1996).
4. For example, see Bellair and McNulty (2009).
5. Studies in several established gang cities show that when multiple gangs are active within specific geographic areas, violent, drug, and property crime rates are higher—especially violent crimes, in Chicago (R. Block, 2000; Papachristos, 2009), St. Louis (Decker & Van Winkle, 1996; Monti, 1993), Boston (Braga, Papachristos, & Hureau, 2010), and Pittsburgh (Tita & Cohen, 2004; Tita, Cohen, et al., 2005; Tita & Ridgeway, 2007).
6. Squares with no gang activity had an average of 2.88 assaults. Those with one active gang averaged 13.5 assaults. Those squares with four gangs averaged 42.7 assaults in 1996 (R. Block, 2000, p. 379).
7. Though state prison systems may use a standard written definition of what constitutes a gang member, the process for actually proving that someone is a gang member, and the amount of proof required, can vary by state. California has been segregating suspected gang members since at least 1984, and other states have studied California in developing their own gang validation procedures (Columbia Human Rights Law Review, 2011, p. 864).

CHAPTER 9

What Works

Gang Prevention

◈ Introduction

This chapter provides information on evidence-based[1] programs and strategies for preventing gang involvement. Chapter 5 explained how delinquent behavior and gang involvement unfold over time as risk factors accumulate. The next three chapters provided information on girls in gangs (Chapter 6), the continuing presence of gangs across the United States (Chapter 7), and the greater seriousness of gang problems in very large cities (Chapter 8). Taken together, these four chapters strongly suggest that the prevention of gang activity is of paramount importance, the focus of this chapter. Chapter 10 focuses on integrating intervention and suppression programs and strategies with prevention, with particular emphasis on comprehensive frameworks for addressing gang problems.

The purposes for devoting an entire chapter to gang prevention are threefold. First, juvenile delinquency precedes gang involvement, which necessitates more expanded and system-wide strategies. Second, communities should integrate delinquency prevention and gang prevention strategies and programs, forming a continuum. Third, there are some complicated contexts that prevention programs and strategies must address, particularly the ambiguity that often arises when seeking to identify starter gangs and gang members, and distinguishing bullying behaviors in schools from gang activity.

The process of systematically assessing gang activity in schools and in the community is described in the first section of this chapter. The next section presents a framework for organizing delinquency prevention and early intervention programs and strategies. The final section provides information on promising and effective prevention programs.

◈ Gang Intervention: Risk-Focused, Data-Driven, and Research-Based Gang Prevention

The likelihood of successfully preventing gang activity is greater if community initiatives are data driven and research based. This approach involves first, determining the presence of research-based risk factors for gang membership (provided in Chapter 5) along with an assessment of the scope and nature of gang activity, and second, providing a continuum of evidence-based programs.

Community Assessments

Before launching an anti-gang initiative, a community should conduct a gang problem assessment to identify elevated risk factors that lead to child delinquency and gang involvement. To be successful, communities must define youth gangs, tailor programs and strategies to them, and identify and target the youth who are at greatest risk of joining (Howell, 2010a). Because every community has its own characteristics, each must agree on and take ownership of a specific definition that will guide its data collection and strategic planning. Chapter 3 presented a practical definition that should be considered as a guide for the assessment (Howell, 2013b):

- The group has five or more members.

- Members share an identity, typically linked to a name and often other symbols.

- Members view themselves as a gang, and are recognized by others as a gang.

- The group associates continuously, evidences some organization, and has some permanence.

- The group is involved in an elevated level of criminal activity.

Stakeholders in every community that conducts an assessment should agree on the definition that will guide its data collection and strategic planning. This definition will serve as a useful point of departure. It has been disseminated for this purpose by the U.S. Department of Justice and the U.S. Department of Health and Human Services (Simon et al., 2013).

As part of its Comprehensive Gang Program Model, the Office of Juvenile Justice and Delinquency Program (OJJDP) has published *A Guide to Assessing Your Community's Youth Gang Problem* (2009a), a user-friendly resource to assist communities that are prepared to conduct a gang-problem assessment. This guide simplifies the data-collection process, helping communities determine types and levels of gang activity, gang crime patterns, community perceptions of local gangs and gang activity, and gaps in community services for gang prevention. In Guilford County, North Carolina, a community organization, the Juvenile Crime Prevention Council (JCPC), conducted its first countywide assessment of gang activity using the OJJDP guide (Graves et al., 2010). The JCPC has used this excellent gang problem assessment as a basis for developing a continuum of prevention and intervention programs and strategies with guidance provided in the OJJDP (2009b) *Comprehensive Gang Model: Planning for Implementation.*

Ideally, the assessment should provide an understanding of the scope and seriousness of the gang problem within the city, community, or neighborhood. To help communities understand their unique gang situation, an assessment should answer these questions:

- Who is involved in gang-related activity, and what is the history of these gangs?
- What crimes are these individuals committing?
- When are these crimes committed?
- Where is gang-related activity primarily occurring?
- Why is the criminal activity happening (e.g., individual conflicts, gang feuds, gang members acting on their own)?

In addition to helping communities answer questions about gang emergence, OJJDP's Comprehensive Gang Model promotes a problem-solving approach to gang-related crime, asking communities to identify

- neighborhoods with many risk factors for gang involvement,
- schools and other community settings in which gangs are active,
- hot spots of gang crime,
- high-rate gang offenders, and
- violent gangs.

Although this may be cursory at the outset, it would be helpful if the assessment could provide at least preliminary information on the structure of the most active gangs. For prevention purposes, it is important to know age and gender composition, and the relative size of gangs. In less violent crime territories, social gangs or school-based gangs are also likely to be found, on which prevention and intervention strategies should be focused.

To assist with gang problem assessment, strategic planning and continuum building, the OJJDP Strategic Planning Tool (www.nationalgangcenter.gov/SPT/Programs/110) provides the following:

- A list of risk factors for delinquency and gang membership organized by age
- Data indicators (i.e., measures of risk factors)
- Data sources (from which relevant data can be retrieved)
- Hyperlinks connecting risk factors with effective programs that address them
- A "Community Resource Inventory," for community planning groups to record information on existing programs
- Information on promising and effective juvenile delinquency and gang programs
- Strategies that address specific risk factors for various age groups

Institutionalizing regular gang problem assessments is advisable in cities with populations greater than 50,000 persons. In late 2009, North Carolina became the first state to begin implementing a statewide gang prevention and intervention initiative, the Community-Based Youth Gang Violence Prevention Project (North Carolina Department of Juvenile Justice and Delinquency Prevention [DJJDP], 2009). It was based in part on a statewide assessment that revealed an elevated level of gang activity in schools (North Carolina DJJDP & Department of Public Instruction, 2008) and in the juvenile justice system across the state (M. Howell & Lassiter, 2011). In North Carolina, each county's Juvenile Crime Prevention Council is statutorily required to review annually the needs of juveniles who are at risk or who have been associated with gangs or gang activity (i.e., make an assessment), and respond with appropriate programs and strategies (S.L. 1998–202, § 143B-851).

Once community stakeholders have processed the assessment findings, the next step is to develop a strategic plan that identifies current program gaps and maps a continuum of prevention and intervention program services and sanctions. Prevention and intervention services should be directed to the neighborhoods, schools, and families from which gangs emanate. Before presenting the prevention and early intervention framework, it is important to consider two complicated contexts within the framework that prevention programs and strategies must address—starter gangs and bullying.

Starter Gangs

Rather than immediately joining serious, violent street gangs, most youth become involved in less criminal groups referred to here and earlier as *starter gangs*. The term intentionally underscores this important point: Prevention work needs to focus in particular on newly formed gangs along with at-risk youngsters in both neighborhood and school settings.

But how do the starter gangs form? As noted in Chapter 3, Huff (1989) specified three ways: (1) from conflict between adolescent groups at regularly scheduled competitive events that festers and grows; (2) from similar conflict that develops among young groups in public gathering places such as malls and on the streets, and other social gatherings; and (3) when a previously gang-involved youth moves into town. In addition, the youngest cliques in larger gangs might be considered starter gangs. Examples include the "peewee" and "wannabe" cliques in established gangs.

IN FOCUS 9.1
HOW THE SAN DIEGO DEL SOL GANG FORMED

One of the original members of Del Sol explained how he and a number of other boys formed their gang. In their teenage years, they began going to parties. Other youths at the parties would ask them, "Where are you from?" Such queries can be challenges or simple questions. However, when asked by members of other gangs, the questions are typically challenges. To avoid conflict, the reply "I'm not from anywhere" means the respondent does not claim a gang—at least not at the moment. It also is a way of losing some face and may result in being attacked anyway for being a punk (a weakling).

After being roughed up at several encounters, a group of Del Sol boys (named after a low-income housing development) decided that the next time they went to a party together, they would "carry" (bring weapons). If anyone asked them where they were from, they would reply *"Del Sol. Y que?"* The use of "Y que?" in the context of Mexican American gangs means, "And what are you going to do about it?" It is an unequivocal challenge. If they were attacked, they would bring out their weapons and fight back. After a number of encounters where challenges were made and answered, Del Sol became recognized as a gang.

Source: Sanders, 1994, p. 43.

Sanders's (1994) account of how a group came to be recognized as a gang and also to view themselves as a gang as a result of conflict is a common example. Other avenues to gang formation are also typical, of course. Starter gangs described in this chapter often form as a result of experimenting with gang culture and symbols. Others are formed in barrios in which belonging to a gang in one's neighborhood is expected (Vigil, 1988).

Child delinquents are more likely to participate in starter gangs than other children—or to initiate group formation themselves. Prior involvement in both delinquency and aggression increases this likelihood. Indeed, as Craig and colleagues (2002) suggest, the problem behaviors associated with becoming a gang member appear to emerge before age 10. The neighborhood context (e.g., lack of adult supervision and associating with older delinquents) elevates risk of gang exposure. Vigil (1993) delineates seven steps that are often involved in the gang joining process. These steps apply to children in the school setting, beginning in elementary school and unfolding as the child enters middle school. Vigil's steps presume that gangs already exist in and around the school. Vigil's seven steps to gang joining are as follows:

1.   In elementary school, children may have heard about gangs and are thus not surprised by them when they see these barrio groups in middle school. They already have heard about conflicts involving gangs in the barrio and at the schools that they soon will enter.

2.   Seeing these gangs at middle school for the first time validates their importance, and provides impetus for incoming children's own gang affirmation.

3.   At middle school, children commonly are coping "with the various groupings and cliques there that have carved out their social niches. Gangs are already evident at this level, and the school yard has its separate barrio gang hangouts where the youngsters gravitate" (p. 102).

4.   The most vulnerable children enter middle school with poor academic achievement, and their family strains and street exposure make matters worse. "As they become more and more involved in the oppositional subculture, they become increasingly disdainful of teachers and school officials—and in the process become budding dropouts" (p. 103).

5.   As intergroup conflicts increase in intensity and frequency, an individual's reputation spreads as a known and committed gang member. At middle school, ready-made friends and protectors await the uneasy child, some of whom are known to him, and he begins to gravitate to those who appear to provide some protection.

6.   The child or adolescent who joins the gang may feel compelled to do so, for to be isolated is to invite disaster. Faced with the prospect of belonging to nothing and no one, youngsters in this situation may feel that they *must* join the gang, "even though the requisites for membership are quite demanding and life threatening" (p. 104).

7.   Youths may first casually associate with a gang, perhaps a chance bonding. Walking home from school with friends, a child might stop along the way with older friends and perhaps engage in delinquency in the company of gang members with whom he had been hanging out. Mutual acceptance is followed by an initiation—a "baptism" into the gang—he is now committed to it.

Gang activity is not confined to the school grounds themselves, of course. It begins to escalate very early on school days, once students begin to gather in the neighborhood, at bus stops, or on the way to school, and gang-related violence peaks earlier in the day (Figure 9.1) on school days than on nonschool days and also earlier than other violent crimes involving juveniles (Wiebe, Meeker, & Vila, 1999). Modern-day school environments may give rise to gangs and more gang activity when student bonds to schools and teachers are broken by poor school climates characterized by zero-tolerance policies, less support for students in overcoming individual risk factors, harsh one-size-fits-all punishments, and elevated school suspension and expulsion rates.

The gang-forming process likely begins with a small group of rejected, aggressive children. Cairns and Cairns (1994) reason that aggressive and antisocial youths begin to affiliate with one another in childhood, while Kupersmidt, Coie, and Howell (2003), as well as Warr (2002) find this

Figure 9.1   Gang Offenses per Time of Day

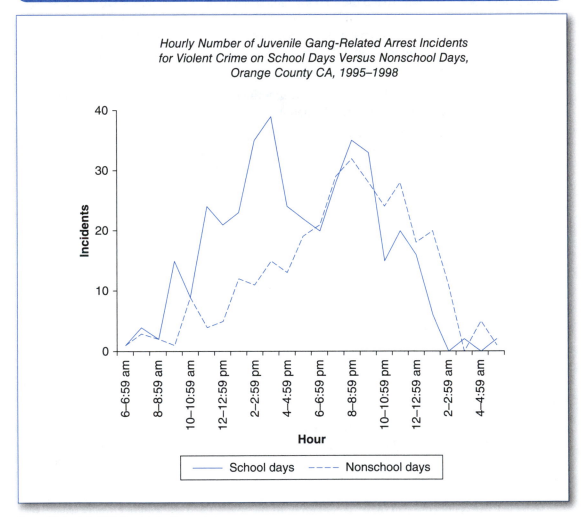

Source: Wiebe et al., 1999. Reprinted with permission.

pattern of aggressive friendships continues through adolescence. Fleisher (1995) notes an internal process characterizing rejected children: "The group behavior of rejected children follows the internal social processes that typify children's school playgroups. Boys and girls tacitly classify themselves into those who are rejected, neglected, accepted, aggressive, unpopular, disliked and liked, and so on" (p. 119). Social rejection by prosocial youths, according to Coie and Dodge (1998), may serve to channel rejected, aggressive children toward deviant peer groups.

Based on a French study, Debarbieux and Baya (2008) suggest that some starter gangs may emerge in "difficult" schools. This research identified current or future gang members among a small subgroup of "highly rebellious" students "who consider that everything is wrong with school and that teachers are awful, who commit aggression more often than others, who are punished repeatedly and more frequently than the others, and who have developed a feeling of hatred and rejection of everything that represents order" (p. 214). These students (ages 12 and older) most often attended the most "difficult" schools—those characterized by greater levels of student victimization, self-reported violence, poor student–teacher relations, and systems of punishment that pupils did not accept well. This core group (4% to 5% of all students) was responsible for most disorder and violence in 16 schools that were studied. This subgroup contained a significant proportion of gang members—up to 11% in the most "difficult" schools.

> This does not mean that they constitute a "group," or the beginnings of a gang. They could be isolated individuals although [many do] identify with each other and form a real group. If, initially, they were not considered gang members, their being on the margins of the school norms slowly leads them to identify themselves as a group. (p. 215)

It also is prudent to locate gang prevention programs in schools because student risk levels for multiple problem behaviors can be easily identified by widely accepted survey methods. A statewide Massachusetts Youth Risk Behavior Survey of high school students added the gang membership question to the Centers for Disease Controls' alternate year Youth Risk Behavior Survey. The research team (Gebo & Sullivan, 2014) took a unique approach. The risk categories were first created. Next, the authors looked at where gang members are found within the risk groups: Low Risk, Mental Health problems, Intensified (moderate) Risk, and High Risk. Less than 1% fell in the Low Risk and Mental Health groups, exactly 1% fell in the Intensified Risk group, and 21% fell in the High Risk group. This research substantiates the findings of the French study in showing that high-risk youth in schools often join gangs.

Ongoing association away from school is the next phase of gang development. A major consequence of estrangement in school (feelings of powerlessness, exclusion, and fear for one's safety) is what Hutchison and Kyle (1993) believe is a strong identification with the immediate peer group in the barrio who share the same feeling and experience. Fleisher (1998) adds that incipient members of the newly formed groups begin to display signs of involvement:

> Like the groups they left behind at school, rejected boys and girls adopt the equivalent of distinctive school clothing and colors, the insignia of membership. Members learn group cheers, rhymes, and folklore, wear group clothing, engage in rites of passage and intensification, uphold communal values (like school children's loyalty to their school) and they give themselves a name. (p. 119)

IN FOCUS 9.2
BEHAVIORS ASSOCIATED WITH JOINING A GANG

- Negative changes in behavior, such as

  o withdrawing from family;
  o declining school attendance, performance, or behavior;
  o staying out late without reason;
  o unusual desire for secrecy;
  o confrontational behavior, such as talking back, verbal abuse, name calling, and disrespect for parental authority;
  o sudden negative opinions about law enforcement or other adults in positions of authority (e.g., school officials or teachers); and
  o changes in attitude about school, church, or other normal activities or change in behavior in these activities

- Unusual interest in one or two particular colors of clothing or a particular logo
- Interest in gang-influenced music, videos, and movies
- Use and practice of hand signals to communicate with friends
- Peculiar drawings or gang symbols on schoolbooks, clothing, notebooks, or even walls
- Drastic changes in hair or dress style or having a group of friends who have the same hair or dress style
- Withdrawal from longtime friends and forming bonds with an entirely new group of friends
- Suspected drug use, such as alcohol, inhalants, and narcotics
- Presence of firearms, ammunition, or other weapons
- Nonaccidental physical injuries such as being beaten or injuries to hands and knuckles from fighting or a gang initiation
- Unexplained cash or goods, such as clothing or jewelry

Source: National Gang Center (n.d.).

Vigil (1993) asserts that regular group involvement in illegal activity is the next step toward gang formation. Exclusion from school may further facilitate crossing the tipping point toward gang formation, but as Thrasher (1927/2000) noted, the group does not become a gang until it begins to excite disapproval and opposition. Parents or neighbors may look on it with suspicion or hostility; the storekeepers or the cops may begin to chase it; contact is made with a rival or an enemy in a nearby gang; or some representative of the community steps in and tries to break it up. "This is the real beginning of the gang, for now it starts to draw itself more closely together" (p. 10). Klein (1995) identifies two "signposts" that indicate actual "tipping." The first one is a commitment to a criminal orientation or willingness to use violence. The second signpost is when the gang-to-be takes on a collective criminal orientation as a group, "a gang," that is set apart from other groups in the community. "Now the delinquent group has become a gang" (Fleisher, 1995, p. 119).

If gang activity is not curbed in its earliest stages, more serious gang activity can develop. Gangs are present in many schools in the United States. In a national sample of schools (G. Gottfredson & Gottfredson, 2001), 36% of principals reported gang problems in their surrounding *communities*, and 65% of principals in urban schools acknowledged community gang problems. These data are generally in agreement with student reports. The *National Survey of American Attitudes on Substance Abuse XV: Teens and Parents* (National Center on Addiction and Substance Abuse, 2010) found that 45% of high school students and 35% of middle school students say that there are gangs or students who consider themselves to be part of a gang in their schools. During the 2007–2008 school year, 43% of public high schools and 35% of middle schools experienced discipline problems related to gangs at least once (Robers et al., 2010).

Figure 9.2 illustrates the clustering of gangs in and around schools as indicated by the location of gang-related crimes in Guilford County, North Carolina. The spatial distribution of gang-related crimes in this figure illustrates the dual presence of young gangs inside schools and within a one-mile radius around schools in the community. Thus, other interventions need to be implemented in schools as well as in the surrounding community to address gang activity.

Bullying

Student bullying, as Lassiter and Perry (2009) suggest, is a potential contributor to gang joining in and around schools, particularly when it makes children feel unsafe. Bullying should not be disregarded;

Figure 9.2   Guilford County Schools and Gang-Related Incidents, January–December 2009

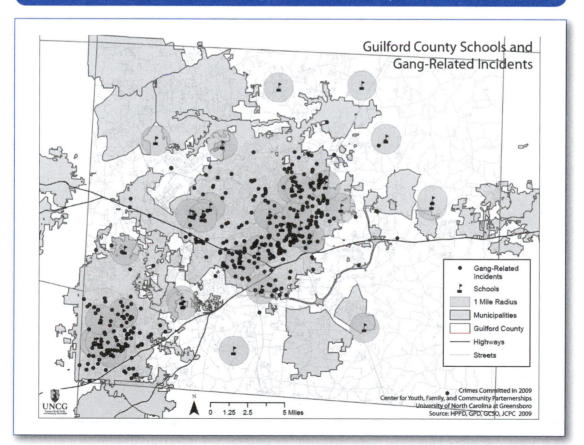

Source: Graves et al., 2010. Reprinted by permission of the illustrator, Kelly N. Graves.

this can be a serious problem in which children and adolescents use power through frequent acts of aggression to intimidate and control others, and make them feel powerless in their relationships (Pepler, Madsen, Levene, & Webster, 2004). During the 2007–2008 school year, Robers and fellow researchers (2010) found 44% of public high schools, 22% of middle schools, and 21% of primary schools experienced discipline problems related to student bullying at least once a week or daily. Larochette, Murphy, and Craig (2010) assert that most bullying at school appears to be racially motivated, and Mexican Americans and African Americans are the most common victims, depending on the location.

Interestingly, bullying behavior causes aggressive and violent behavior, rather than the other way around (Kim, Leventhal, Koh, Hubbard, & Boyce, 2006), although aggressive youth are actively involved, to be sure (N. White & Loeber, 2008). In this way, bullying may lead to more serious offenses (Figure 9.3), may encourage possible gang involvement, or is symptomatic of starter gangs. Early intervention in problem behaviors such as bullying is more likely to be successful than delaying action until physical violence occurs.

In a study involving 15 known gang problem schools across the United States, Carbone-Lopez, Esbensen, and Brick (2010) found that girls and boys are equally affected, and that boys were more

Figure 9.3   The Youth Violence Continuum

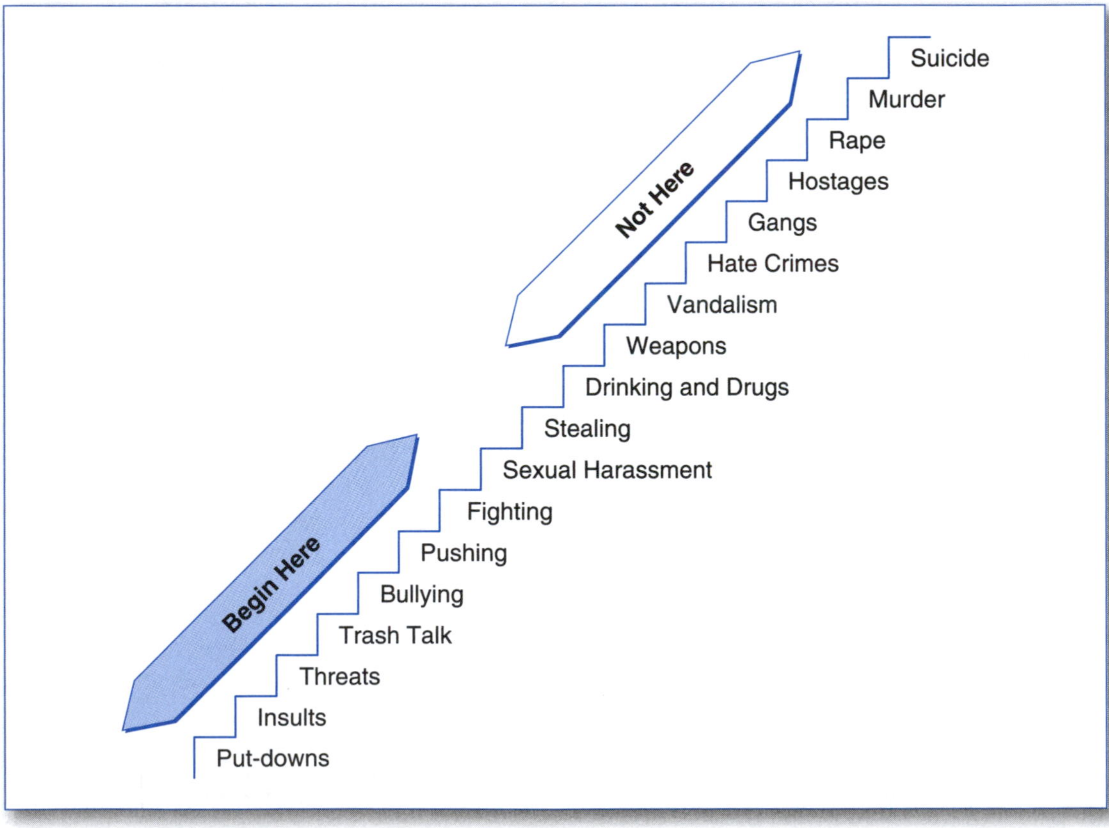

Source: Lassiter & Perry, 2009. Reprinted with permission.

likely to experience direct or physical forms of bullying while girls were more likely to report being teased or joked about. The research team recommended that "prevention and intervention efforts can be gender-neutral in their approach. In particular, efforts to reduce students' involvement in delinquent and criminal activity should also reduce their risk of being bullied at or en route to school" (p. 343).

Overall, school-based anti-bullying programs are effective, leading to an average decrease in bullying of 20% to 23% and in victimization of students by 17% to 20% (Ttofi & Farrington, 2011; see also Ferguson, Miguel, Kilburn, & Sanchez, 2007). Olweus, Limber, and Mihalic (1999) note that the highly regarded Bullying Prevention Program has demonstrated additional benefits including significant improvements in the "social climate" of the class, as reflected in students' reports of improved order and discipline, and reduced reports of general antisocial behavior, such as vandalism and fighting—outcomes which greatly enhance its practical benefits.

Yiu & Gottfredson (2014) find in a nationwide school-based study that community influences on individual gang involvement are largely mediated by school and personal variables. In particular, school safety and students' personal sense of safety emerged as important variables that predicted gang involvement. Controlling for school, community, and individual variables,

> individual fear and a safe school climate directly affect gang participation. The model-implied effect for individual fear is large and statistically significant, and the effect implied for the school climate variable is more modest in size and marginally statistically significant. (p. 637)

Moreover, there is good reason to believe that gangs, school disorder, and teaching quality are closely linked.

First and foremost, threats to school safety must be addressed. Osher, Dwyer, and Jackson (2004) recommend that threat assessment be considered a component of a comprehensive approach toward maintaining a safe school. Such an assessment can identify students who may need additional services as well as more general problems in the school environment, such as bullying, that merit broader attention. The Virginia model for student threat assessment (Cornell & Sheras, 2006) appears to have the most practical utility for this purpose. We propose below a continuum of evidence-based services that can span individual, family, peer, school, and community contexts.

◈ A Framework for Prevention and Early Intervention

Windows of opportunity for delinquency prevention and early intervention are shown in Figure 9.4. Because gang membership is presented as a pathway to serious and violent delinquency, delinquency prevention programs must work to target gang involvement. As explained in Chapter 5, the top section of the figure shows the major risk factor domains that influence youth: family, school, peer group, individual characteristics, and community. At birth—or beginning in the prenatal period for some infants—the biological family is the central influence on infants and children. During preschool, and especially in elementary school and onward, the array of risk factors expands as some children are exposed to negative influences outside the home (particularly school problems and delinquent peers). Family, school, and peer influences continue from childhood to young adulthood, although family influences gradually fade as friends become more important. In addition, individual characteristics and community factors can come into play at any point during childhood and adolescence. It is important to provide an array of prevention and intervention programs across the entire continuum that address each of the risk factor domains.

Figure 9.4   Windows of Opportunity for Delinquency Prevention and Early Intervention

Risk and Protective Factors				
Family	School	Peer Group	Individual Characteristics	Community
Age 3	Age 6	Age 9	Age 12	Age 15	Age 18
Conduct Problems	Elementary School Failure	Child Delinquency	Gang Member	Serious and Violent Delinquency
Prevention		Intervention		Suppression

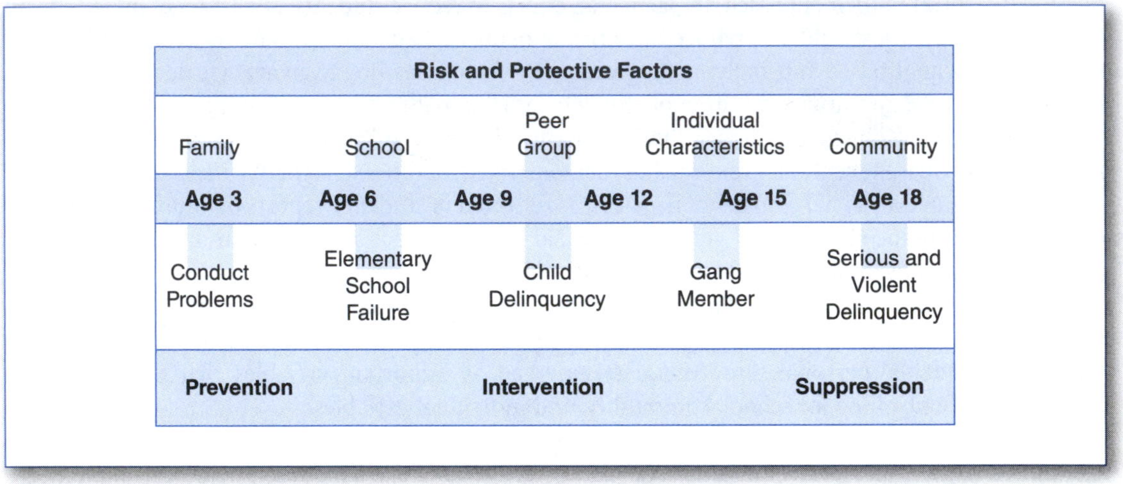

Source: Howell, 2009, p. 151.

The next section focuses on broad intervention strategies or methods of addressing gang involvement and the big picture of continuum building—in a manner that reduces risk across the multiple contexts. This is a useful framework for organizing community programs because it helps engage agency and community representatives in the collective enterprise of continuum building. Later in this chapter we recommend programs that address the specific problem behaviors in Figure 9.4. Readers are reminded that protective factors are not addressed in this chapter. As explained in Chapter 5, the research foundation on these is inadequate at this time.

◈ Building a Continuum of Effective Delinquency Prevention and Early Intervention Programs

A number of places have implemented processes of building countywide, citywide, or statewide continuums of delinquency prevention and early intervention programs. Implementing effective programs is not as simple as pulling a model program off the shelf (Howell et al., 2014). Three main approaches can be taken to translate the body of research evidence about effective programs into practice for everyday use by practitioners and policy makers, what commonly is called *evidence-based practice* (Howell et al., 2014). In each of these approaches, studies must meet very high standards of methodological quality. The first approach is to conduct an evaluation of each program and, if it is found ineffective, to use that evidence to improve or terminate it. This approach is cost prohibitive in statewide initiatives. The second approach is to draw on lists of model programs, with evidence of effectiveness, as certified by an authoritative source. A third approach is to implement a type of program that has been shown to be effective on average by a meta-analysis of many studies of that program type, but to do so in the manner that the research indicates will yield that average effect or better. The Campbell Collaboration is at the forefront of systematic reviews in criminology and criminal justice. Several of these reviews provide guidelines for juvenile justice programs.

IN FOCUS 9.3

REPOSITORIES OF RESEARCH-BASED DELINQUENCY PREVENTION PROGRAMS

- OJJDP Strategic Planning Tool: www.nationalgangcenter.gov/SPT/
- Model Programs Guide (Office of Juvenile Justice and Delinquency Prevention): http://www.ojjdp.gov/mpg/
- Blueprints for Violence Prevention: http://www.colorado.edu/cspv/blueprints/
- National Registry of Effective Programs and Practices (Substance Abuse and Mental Health Services Administration, U.S. Department of Health and Human Services): http://nrepp.samhsa.gov
- Exemplary and Promising Safe, Disciplined and Drug-Free Schools Programs (U.S. Department of Education): http://www2.ed.gov/admins/lead/safety/exemplary01/index.html
- What Works Clearinghouse, U.S. Department of Education (on educational interventions, some of which address youth violence and substance abuse prevention): http://ies.ed.gov/ncee/wwc/
- Campbell Collaboration (systematic reviews in criminology and criminal justice): http://www.campbellcollaboration.org/reviews_crime_justice/

A major caveat is in order. At present, we know relatively little about the effects of taking evidence-based programs to scale in public health and related areas of mental health, education, welfare, and criminal justice (Howell et al., 2014). For example, major shortcomings exist in achieving high fidelity with evidence-based substance abuse and violence prevention programs in community settings (Fagan, Hanson, Hawkins, & Arthur, 2008). In addition, in two national assessments, G. Gottfredson and Gottfredson (2001) and Hallfors and Godette (2002) found poor implementation for many delinquency and violence prevention programs that schools attempted to adopt. Transporting *exemplary*, *blueprint*, or otherwise *model programs* into everyday practice settings also has proved to be more difficult than originally assumed. There are many challenging issues associated with translating an evidence-based program into routine practice in a way that closely replicates the relevant circumstances of the original research. As a result, the desirable program effects on delinquency and subsequent offending found in the research studies often are attenuated when even carefully implemented model programs are scaled up for general application (Howell et al., 2014; Rhoades, Bumbarger, & Moore, 2012; Welsh, Sullivan, & Olds, 2010). Program adaptations to everyday settings are common in this process, and with that, additional slippage (Rhoades et al., 2012). The more advantageous route for stakeholders is a continuum-building strategy that strengthens existing programs and fills gaps with effective and promising programs.

Numerous research-based program options are available that communities should consider for inclusion in their continuum of delinquency prevention and early intervention programs. In Focus 9.3 contains links to key repositories of research-based delinquency prevention programs, including those mentioned in the subsequent sections. Because of the availability of these electronic databases, and the comprehensive information they contain on programs, individual programs need not be described in detail here. Readers are reminded that our main focus is on programs that prevent early development of juvenile delinquency and other problem behaviors. By addressing a variety of risk factors for gang involvement, these programs can make a contribution to preventing gang membership. Among the many effective delinquency prevention programs, attention is drawn here to those that stand out as holding considerable promise in the gang field as a result of having successfully targeted high-risk youth and families in high-risk settings. In addition, the reviewed programs often serve racial/ethnic minorities and girls.

The remainder of this chapter illustrates how effective delinquency prevention programs can be integrated with gang programs to form a continuum in accord with the Comprehensive Gang Prevention, Intervention, and Suppression Program Model presented in Chapter 10. Figure 9.5 illustrates a user-friendly way of viewing programs that should help program developers and managers grasp the interconnection of programs at these more targeted levels of intervention, which are organized by intervention levels.

Wyrick (2006) organizes this continuum in four levels. *Primary prevention* (also called *universal* prevention) targets the entire population (all youth and families and other members) in communities.[2] A key resource might be a one-stop community center that makes services accessible and visible to the entire community, including prenatal and infant care, afterschool activities, truancy and dropout prevention, and job training programs. *Secondary prevention* identifies young children (ages 7 to 14) at high risk and—drawing on the resources of schools, community-based organizations, and faith-based groups—intervenes with appropriate services before early problem behaviors turn into serious delinquency and gang involvement. *Intervention* targets active gang members and close associates, and involves aggressive outreach and program recruitment activity. Support services for gang-involved youth and their families help youth make positive choices. *Suppression* focuses on identifying the most dangerous gangs and weakens them by removing the most criminally active and influential gang members from the community. Figure 9.5 presents a model that is useful for planning a Comprehensive Gang Program Model Continuum of programs and strategies within the above continuum segments.

- Level 1 (at the top of the triangle) is composed of serious, chronic, and violent gang and nongang offenders. These offenders make up a relatively small portion of the population, but commit a disproportionately large share of illegal activity and are the main focus of targeted enforcement initiatives (gang suppression).

- Level 2 comprises gang-involved youth and their associates, who make up a relatively larger share of the population. These youth are involved in significant levels of illegal activity but are not necessarily in the highest offending category. Typically ranging in age from 12 to 24 years old, these adolescents and also older adults are candidates for gang intervention strategies and outreach.

- Level 3 is made up of high-risk youth—ages 7 to 17 who have already displayed signs of delinquency and an elevated risk for gang membership but are not yet gang involved. Most of these youth will not join gangs, but they represent a pool of prime candidates for future gang membership, appropriate targets for secondary prevention services, and early intervention measures.

- Level 4 represents all youth, families, and residents living in a community where gangs are present. Primary prevention services such as gang awareness education are needed at this level.

Figure 9.5   Focusing Anti-Gang Strategies

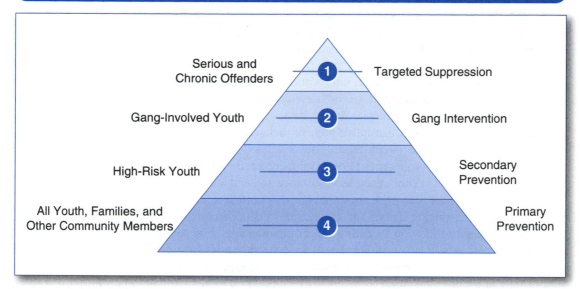

Serious and
Chronic Offenders   1   Targeted Suppression

Gang-Involved Youth   2   Gang Intervention

High-Risk Youth   3   Secondary
Prevention

All Youth, Families, and   4   Primary
Other Community Members   Prevention

Source: Adapted from Wyrick, 2006, p. 56.

We next supply key programs that communities should consider placing in local continuums within Levels 3 and 4. Effective programs for Levels 1 and 2 are presented in Chapter 10. Readers are advised that programs need not be specifically tailored to gang prevention to make a contribution toward this goal. As seen in Chapter 5, children on a trajectory of worsening antisocial behavior are more likely to join gangs during adolescence. To provide protection against this unwanted outcome, children and adolescents must be supported in healthy physical, social, mental, and emotional development. Readers are reminded that gender-specific programs for girls are discussed in Chapter 6.

Level 4. Programs for All Youth and Families and Other Community Members

Just one of the programs described here is tailored to preventing gang joining. In fact, specific youths are not targeted in this level of the recommended continuum. Wyrick (2006) provides several examples, including public awareness campaigns, one-stop centers that improve access to public services, school readiness training, school-based life skills programs, community clean up and lighting projects, and community organizing. The main goals of these programs are improved cognitive skills, school readiness, and social and emotional development.

Early childhood education is a linchpin for success in life (Weber, 2010). The Promise Academy Charter Middle School is an evidence-based middle school that serves predominately low-income, minority students in Harlem who are typically are two or three years behind grade level. This middle school is a project of Harlem Children's Zone that operates in a 97-block area in the Harlem neighborhood of New York, NY, that combines "no excuses" charter schools with communitywide initiatives to address some of the main problems that underprivileged children face every day, such as inadequate schools, high-crime neighborhoods, and health issues. The Promise Academy combines structural reforms with wraparound services to provide students with a comprehensive college preparatory program, and the school proved successful in boosting students' achievement in math and English/language arts in elementary school and math in middle school (Will & Fryer, 2010).

Although this has not been investigated, it is quite possible that the Promise Academy Charter Middle School is preventing some youth from joining a gang. In a comparable situation, the Montreal Preventive Treatment Program, an early intervention evidence-based program demonstrated an impact on gang involvement even though it was not developed with this purpose in mind. It was specifically designed to prevent antisocial behavior among boys, ages seven to nine, of low socioeconomic status who had previously displayed disruptive problem behavior in kindergarten. This program demonstrated that a combination of parent training and childhood skill development can steer children away from gangs. Tremblay and colleague's (1996) evaluation of the program showed both short- and long-term gains, including less delinquency, less substance use, and less gang involvement at age 15.

The Perry Preschool is an evidence-based preschool intellectual enrichment program. It has even proved effective in reducing serious and chronic delinquency in long-term follow-ups. This program provides high-quality education for disadvantaged children ages three to four to improve their capacity for future success in school and in life. The HighScope curriculum emphasizes an open approach to learning; children are active participants. The follow-up of experimental groups at age 27 showed that significantly fewer program group members than nonprogram group members were chronic offenders (Schweinhart et al., 2005). In addition, study subjects had fewer arrests at age 19, significantly fewer arrests for drug manufacturing and drug distribution offenses, and less involvement in serious fights, gang fights, causing injuries, and police contact. (For additional information, see the OJJDP Model Programs Guide, In Focus 9.3.)

PeaceBuilders is a schoolwide violence prevention program for elementary schools (K–5). This program attempts to create a positive school climate by developing positive relationships between students and school staff; directly teaching nonviolent attitudes, values, and beliefs; and providing incentives for young people to display these behaviors at school, in the community, and at home. PeaceBuilders introduces a common language to a school centered on six principles: Praise people; avoid put-downs; seek wise people as advisers and friends; notice and correct hurts we cause; right wrongs; and help others. Activities and rewards designed to teach and encourage these "peace-building" behaviors are woven into the school's everyday routine with the participation of all staff in the school, including teachers, classroom aides, administrators, librarians, nurses, playground monitors, and any others who regularly interact with students. Outcomes include improved social competence, more frequent positive and prosocial behavior, and reduced aggression (Flannery et al., 2003), and high-risk children reported more decreases in aggression and more increases in social competence in comparison to children at medium and low levels of risk (Vazsonyi, Belliston, & Flannery, 2004). (For additional information, see the National Registry of Effective Programs and Practices, In Focus 9.3.)

Gang Resistance Education and Training (G.R.E.A.T.) is a universal (for all students in a given school) evidence-based program for preventing gang joining. G.R.E.A.T. educates students about the dangers of gang involvement. In its approach, the G.R.E.A.T. lesson content places considerable emphasis on cognitive-behavioral training, social skills development, refusal skills training, and conflict resolution. However, the primary service is skills-based training. In a four-year follow-up, G.R.E.A.T. showed impressive results (Esbensen et al., 2011; Esbensen, Osgood, Peterson, Taylor, & Carson, 2013; Esbensen, Peterson, Taylor, & Osgood, 2012). In addition to improvements in several risk factors—such as having less anger, more use of refusal skills, and less risk-seeking among elementary and middle school students—the school-based curriculum generated positive attitudes toward police and less positive attitudes about gangs, and it reduced the odds of gang joining among racially/ethnically diverse groups of youth by 24%. It is noteworthy that these results held up over a 4-year follow-up.

Positive Behavioral Interventions and Supports (PBIS) framework (pbis.org) is a three-tiered promising model for instruction and intervention (Sugai & Simonsen, 2012). PBIS is based on the principle that academic and behavioral supports must be provided at a schoolwide level to address effectively the needs of all students in a school (referred to as Tier 1: core, universal instruction, and supports). Some students with identified needs receive supplemental or targeted instruction and intervention in Tier 2 (targeted, supplemental interventions and supports). Last, in Tier 3, intensive, individualized interventions and supports are provided for the relatively few students with the most severe needs, requiring intensive and individualized behavioral treatment and academic support. Although Kutash, Duchnowski, and Lynn (2006) note that results to date do not qualify PBIS as an evidence-based practice, PBIS is a promising framework with the potential of improving school climate and possibly linking those students with serious behavioral problems to needed services. Most experts in the field agree that PBIS is in its infancy, and the most promising results have been found when PBIS was implemented in conjunction with functional behavioral assessments of troubled students for serious behavioral problems. Nevertheless, given that the G.R.E.A.T. program has produced several beneficial outcomes that are called for in Tier 1 of the PBIS framework, "it could be incorporated within this framework in any school system to help achieve PBIS delinquency prevention goals and specifically where gang problems exist in the schools themselves and in the surrounding community to prevent gang joining" (Howell, 2013a, p. 414).

Unsafe schools present obstacles to realizing the potential benefits of G.R.E.A.T. and PBIS implementation. G. Gottfredson and colleagues (2005) state the first priority for bonding students to schools is a safe school. Safety and security derive from two conditions: (1) an orderly, predictable environment where school staff provide consistent, reliable supervision and discipline; and (2) a school climate where students feel connected to the school and supported by their teachers and other school staff. First and foremost, effective supervision and control of behavior in schools are required to provide safety (G. Gottfredson, 2013). "For instance, schools that create schoolwide practices for managing discipline that incorporate behavioral principles, have clear expectations for conduct, and enforce rules firmly and fairly have repeatedly been found to experience less disorder" (p. 90). An expert on gang-related school safety, Gottfredson underscores the importance of basing prevention activities in schools on an assessment of the specific nature of the problems that gangs present—not only in and around the school, but also in the surrounding community. School safety plans should be developed. A balance of structure and support requires, according to Lassiter and Perry (2009), an organized, schoolwide approach that is practiced by all school personnel. Arciaga and colleagues (2010) provide explicit guidance in developing these safety plans.

Interestingly, traditional school security measures (security guards, metal detectors, locker checks, and the like) do not appear to be solutions, in and of themselves, to gang and other disruptive problems at school (Howell & Lynch, 2000). Misguided school policies such as zero tolerance break the bond between students and their school and teachers because such blanket rules cannot be enforced evenly, especially when harsh punishments are attached to violations. When adolescents feel cared for by people at their school and feel like a part of their school, they are less likely to use substances, engage in violence, or initiate sexual activity at an early age. Students who feel connected to school also report higher levels of emotional well-being.

School systems are increasingly difficult to access with delinquency and gang services, in large part because of the resistance to acknowledging a gang problem, and the plethora of surrounding myths. The National Gang Center recommends the following school intervention strategies (Arciaga et al., 2010):

- Build a comprehensive framework for the integration of child and adolescent services that links the juvenile justice system with human service and other related agencies, including schools, child welfare services, mental health agencies, and social services.

- Create an infrastructure consisting of client information exchange, cross-agency client referrals, a networking protocol, interagency councils, and service integration.

- Target potential and current serious, violent, chronic gang-involved juvenile offenders for resource priority.

- Provide case management by a particular agency for case conferencing and to coordinate services for offenders and the families of gang youth.

- Provide mentoring of at-risk and gang youths, counseling, referral services, gang conflict mediation, and anti-gang programs at schools in the community.

- Provide close supervision and monitoring of gang-involved youth by agencies of the juvenile or criminal justice system and also by community-based agencies, schools, and grassroots groups.

- Provide intensive probation supervision linked with more structured behavioral or skill building and multimodal interventions.

- Provide direct placement and referral of youth for employment, training, education, and supervision.

- Provide alternatives to gang involvement, including remedial and enriched educational programs for gang youth with academic problems and vocational and apprentice training. (p. 4)

Level 3. Programs for High-Risk Youth

Project BUILD (Broader Urban Involvement and Leadership Development; now the BUILD Violence Intervention Curriculum) is a violence prevention curriculum designed to help youth in detention overcome problems they may face in their communities, such as gangs, crime, and drugs. BUILD staff provide counseling, community education, and work-readiness training through four major approaches:

- The Prevention Program is a 10-week, in-school program aimed at preventing youths from drug use and gang life.

- The Intervention Program solicits gang members from the street for participation in recreational activities and offers them drug abuse education, referrals, and counseling.

- The Community Resource Development Program involves adults who volunteer to develop mentoring relationships with gang members and to develop strong community bonds and retard gang development.

- The Rehabilitation Program intervenes with adjudicated youth in the Cook County Juvenile Temporary Detention Center to reduce recidivism.

An earlier version of this program consisted of an anti-gang curriculum that was taught to eighth-grade students in Chicago middle schools located in lower- and lower-middle-class areas with high levels of gang activity. Following completion of the curriculum component, youth from the classrooms considered to be at high risk for joining a gang were invited to participate in an after-school program. It provided recreational activities, job skills training workshops, educational assistance programs, and social activities. At-risk youth were identified by teachers and project staff using gang rosters compiled by detached street-gang workers on the basis of interviews with gang members. The program targeted both males and females who were detained at the Cook County Juvenile Temporary Detention Center in Chicago, Illinois, and who were enrolled in the school on the premises. The study conducted by Lurigio and colleagues (2000) found that youths who participated in Project BUILD had significantly lower rates of recidivism compared to non–Project BUILD youths. Among those students who participated in Project BUILD, 33% returned to detention within a year, compared with 57% of non–Project BUILD youths.

For very early intervention with high-risk youth, the combination of home visiting and parent training is the most effective approach when targeting high-risk families. The most widely recognized and evidence-based program, Nurse-Family Partnership (NFP), provides first-time, low-income mothers of any age with home visitation services from public health nurses. Nurse home visitors work with families in their homes during pregnancy and the first two years of the child's life. Importantly, involvement of other family members and people in the mother's social network is emphasized. For very young abused children, trauma-focused cognitive behavioral therapy (TF-CBT) is designed to help 3- to 18-year-olds and their parents overcome the negative effects of traumatic life events such as child sexual or physical abuse. Although this program has not been tested for gang prevention, it reduces delinquency, an important precursor to gang joining. (For additional information, see the OJJDP Model Programs Guide, In Focus 9.3.)

Schools And Families Educating Children (SAFEChildren) is a family-focused preventive intervention designed to increase academic achievement and decrease risk for later drug abuse and associated problems such as aggression, school failure, and low social competence. Initially targeting first-grade children and their high risk families living in inner-city Chicago neighborhoods, SAFEChildren has two components. The first component of this evidence-based program is a multiple-family group approach that focuses on parenting skills, family relationships, understanding and managing developmental and situational challenges, increasing parental support, skills and issues in engaging as a parent with the school, and managing issues such as neighborhood problems (e.g., violence). Families participate in 20 weekly sessions (2–2.5 hours each) led by a trained, professional family group leader. The second component is a reading tutoring program for the child. Among families designated as high risk, Tolan, Gorman-Smith, and Henry (2004) found improved parenting skills, and among children also assessed as high risk, there was a decrease over time in child aggression and hyperactivity in participants compared to controls. (For additional information, see the National Registry of Effective Programs and Practices, In Focus 9.3.)

Boys and Girls Clubs Gang Prevention Through Targeted Outreach (GPTTO) is a promising program for preventing gang involvement at the community level. The overall philosophy of the program is to give at-risk youths ages 6 to 18 what they seek through gang membership (e.g., supportive adults, challenging activities, and a place to belong) in an alternative, socially positive setting. Arbreton and McClanahan's (2002) evaluation concluded that more frequent GPTTO Club attendance is associated with the following positive outcomes: (1) delayed onset of one gang behavior (less likely to start wearing gang colors); (2) less contact with the juvenile justice system (less likely to be sentenced to a residential placement by the court); (3) fewer delinquent behaviors (less likely to steal and less likely to start smoking marijuana); (4) improved school outcomes (higher grades and greater valuing of doing well in school); and (5) more positive social relationships and productive use of out-of-school time (engaging in more positive afterschool activities and increased levels of positive peer and family relationships). (For additional information on these programs, see the National Gang Center's Strategic Planning Tool: https://www.nationalgangcenter.gov/SPT/Program-Matrix.)

A wide variety of substance abuse prevention programs is available in evidence-based program repositories listed in the In Focus 9.3 box. (See especially the National Registry of Effective Programs and Practices.) LifeSkills Training (LST) is a program that seeks to influence major social and psychological factors that promote the initiation and early use of substances. LifeSkills has distinct elementary (8 to 11 years old) and middle school (11 to 14 years old) curricula that are delivered in a series of classroom sessions over three years. The sessions use lecture, discussion, coaching, and practice to enhance students' self-esteem, feelings of self-efficacy, ability to make decisions, and ability to resist peer and media pressures by teaching drug resistance skills, personal self-management skills, and general social skills. (See also the OJJDP Model Programs Guide, In Focus 9.3.)

One prevention program for high-risk youth has reduced behavioral problems among gang members. Brief Strategic Family Therapy (BSFT) is an evidence-based intervention for troubled families that has proved effective with Mexican American families and other races and ethnicities (Robbins & Szapocznik, 2000). As noted in Chapter 6, a modified version of BSFT, taking into account cultural values of Hispanic groups as well as contextual factors, including frequent gang affiliation in high-crime neighborhoods characterized by low levels of education, multigenerational use of drugs, extensive criminality, and high incarceration rates in San Antonio, proved effective with gang-involved boys and girls (Av. Valdez et al., 2013). A total of 200 adolescents, with equal proportions of males and females, and their family caregivers were randomly assigned to either a treatment or a control condition. Three behavioral problems were addressed—conduct, impulsivity, and hyperactivity—in addition to drug/alcohol use. Along with BSFT family therapy, gang diversion training for the adolescents and gang awareness for the parents was provided by outreach workers. Outcomes were positive (Av. Valdez et al., 2013). In particular, alcohol use among adolescents in the BFST treatment group declined in a six-month period following the intervention, but not drug use. Parents' ratings of their child's three behavioral problems also improved. These are very encouraging findings, showing evidence of effectiveness of BSFT with gang-affiliated adolescents in a very high-risk environment. This is the first such test of the adaptation of an evidence-based delinquency program for gang members and their families. (See the National Registry of Effective Programs and Practices, In Focus 9.3.)

Effective programs and strategies for Levels 1 and 2 in the gang prevention, intervention, and suppression continuum are discussed in Chapter 10. We close this chapter with discussion of two key settings in which prevention opportunities are often lost, first in school settings involving school resource officers, and second, the exposure of children to violence in families and communities.

School Resource Officers

The role of school resource officers (SROs) in promoting school safety is not always clear. In a recent North Carolina study, Langberg, Fedders, and Kukorowski (2011) concluded that the presence of armed law enforcement officers in middle and high schools "is a misguided approach that is financially unsound and educationally imprudent. Research shows that alternative policies and programs are available to create more positive school environments and ensure student and teacher safety" (p. 13).

To address unwarranted court referrals of misbehaving students, Langberg and colleagues' (2011) comprehensive North Carolina SRO study made the following recommendations:

- Teachers and administrators should have readily available, high-quality alternatives to suspensions, arrests, and court referrals, such as mediation, community service, restitution, and mental health programs.

- All SROs, security investigators, and other security personnel should be required to undergo mandatory, intensive, ongoing trainings, including instruction on

  o legal standards for searches and seizures of students in schools,

  o positive behavior interventions and supports (PBIS),

  o adolescent development science,

  o working with students who have disabilities and other special needs,

  o cultural competency,

  o de-escalating student misbehavior without using physical force,

  o using safe restraint techniques, and

  o long-term consequences of court involvement and arrests.

- School administrators and school police should adhere to clear limitations reflecting the status of SROs as fully authorized and armed law enforcement personnel.

- SROs should be prohibited from carrying guns and Tasers on school campuses.

- Students who commit minor offenses in schools should not be routinely arrested and referred to court—only as a last resort.

- Clear, standardized, well-publicized complaint procedures should be established for students, parents, teachers, and administrators to use when SROs behave inappropriately.

- The public should have access to more complete, easy-to-understand data about SROs.

As a practical approach, the diversion of very low-risk cases can easily be accomplished by addressing excessive referrals to juvenile courts from schools (largely for disruptive behaviors at school that should have been addressed as disciplinary matters). These high-volume referrals are often made by SROs. This problem is addressed directly in the Georgia Clayton County Model (Teske & Huff, 2011). In a collaborative initiative with the School Superintendent and Chief of Police, a memorandum of understanding (MoU) titled the "School Referral Reduction Protocol" was executed to (1) reduce suspensions, expulsions, and arrests and (2) develop alternatives to suspension and arrests, including assessment and treatment measures for chronically disruptive students. The protocol identified misdemeanor offenses no longer eligible for referral to the juvenile court unless the student had exhausted a two-tier process that includes (1) warning on the first offense to student and parent, (2) referral to a conflict skills workshop on the second offense, and (3) referral to the court on the third offense. A second MoU created a multidisciplinary panel to serve as a single point of entry for all child service agencies, including schools, when referring children, youth, and families at risk for petition to the court. The panel, called the Clayton County Collaborative Child Study Team, meets regularly to assess the needs of students at risk for court referral and recommends an integrated services action plan to address the student's disruptive behavior. Following establishment of the School Referral Reduction Protocol, referrals to the court were reduced by 67%. By the end of the 2011–2012 school term, the number of students referred to the juvenile court for school offenses was reduced by 83%. It was apparent that once prohibited from making arrests, school officials more readily engaged students in resolving behavioral issues, and this approach led to greater reductions in referrals to juvenile court.

Child Exposure to Violence and Community Safety

Community safety is the responsibility of adults on behalf of children and adolescents of all ages. Flannery, Singer, Van Dulmen, Kretschmar, and Belliston (2007) report results of a large survey of exposure to violence among adolescents. Nearly 40% of boys and 50% of girls reported seeing someone being slapped, hit, or punched at home, and 1 in 10 of the girls said they had been beaten at home. Such exposure to violence is related to mental health problems, aggressive behavior, and higher levels of reported violence. Juvenile justice system, child welfare, school, and mental health systems that serve as portals for services for troubled youth should be better qualified to assess girls' and boys' problem behaviors that appear outside the norm and equipped with more practical assessment tools. Evidence-based treatments for specific mental health disorders have been identified and available for some time, including cognitive-behavioral therapy and other treatments for traumatic victimization, posttraumatic stress disorder, and other mental health disorders (Wasserman & Ko, 2003).

For aggressive children at risk of becoming serious and violent offenders and perhaps gang involved, the leading evidence-based program is the Stop Now and Plan (SNAP®) program (Augimeri, Walsh, & Slater, 2011). The SNAP model is recognized as "the most extensively developed, longest sustained, empirically based intervention specifically for pre-offender youth under the age of 12" (Augimeri et al., 2011, p. 127; see also Augimeri & Koegl, 2012). The target population served by these programs is children who are clinically assessed as engaging in above-average levels of aggressive, destructive, or other antisocial behaviors. Both models are fully manualized and in various stages of replication in Canada, the United States, and Europe (Augimeri et al., 2011). Also evidence-based, SNAP® Girls is a gender-sensitive cognitive-behavioral program for young aggressive girls and their parents (Pepler et al., 2010). Augimeri's team discovered that more than half of the child delinquent girls displayed aggressive behavior problems before age seven, that they tended to come from chaotic families with high levels of mother–daughter conflict, and that they experienced multiple separations from their primary caregivers (Augimeri et al. 2011). This program lowers aggressive, bullying, and delinquent behaviors in the short term, with good evidence that these effects can be sustained over the intermediate future. A SNAP® Youth Justice Model that is geared to active gang members is currently under development.

Several promising community-centered programs should be considered. Every community should have violence prevention programs, and specific services for children who are exposed to violence—and victims themselves—at a very young age in their homes, neighborhoods, and at school and going to and from school. Flannery and colleagues (2007) identify several program priorities:

- Mental health professionals should be placed in schools to immediately identify children who need services and deliver or coordinate them.

- Interventions must include families and peer groups.

- Prevention services must address risk and protection at multiple levels and across multiple systems.

- Prevention services must also give priority to development of positive coping skills, competencies, and problem-solving skills that will help children and adolescents deal effectively with high levels of exposure to violence and victimization. (p. 315)

Both Fleisher (1998) and Vigil (2010) recommend supervised residential centers for the purpose of insulating girls from violent community contexts. These centers, as Fleisher envisions them, would have three specific objectives: "(1) to shelter and protect girls; (2) to provide job training, and job placement; and (3) to ensure a healthy start for gang girls' children" (p. 219). In short, these centers would serve as a one-stop resource for a variety of services and sources of assistance. Victimized and "beyond risk" girls should receive mental health screening and assessment, and are likely to benefit from cognitive-behavioral therapy, treatment for traumatic victimization and posttraumatic stress disorder, and other mental health services; health screening, health education, and basic health services; substance abuse services; and a full spectrum of on-grounds experiential learning and educational services (Av. Valdez, 2007). To draw attention to services, P. Adler, Ovando, and Hocevar (1984) strongly recommend family-level interventions with Mexican American families. For access to families, they suggest *block therapy*, a technique for engaging families that are in most need of assistance. A local priest or clergyman could initially convene these groups. This would be a very practical starting point for families of all racial/ethnic backgrounds.

◈ Concluding Observations

Preventing youth from joining gangs is challenging, and most programs have not shown noteworthy results. Several factors contribute to this challenge. Many alienated youth seek a place where they are accepted socially and often find it in the streets. Most youth who join gangs experience many risk factors and family, school, and community problems. Joining a gang can be a natural process for youth in socially and economically deprived areas of large cities. The gang may already be there, in their neighborhood, and some of their friends and relatives may belong to it. Under these conditions, gangs' promises of protection may gradually envelop these vulnerable youth.

A major prevention problem is the lack of gang awareness in schools, among community leaders, and among parents. G. Gottfredson and Gottfredson's (2001) national study showed that, in the 10% of schools with the greatest student gang participation rates, only 18% of principals recognized that gangs were a problem in their schools. Fortunately, school resource officers and safe and drug-free school coordinators recognize gang activity more frequently. All school systems that suspect gang activity should immediately undertake a gang assessment as described earlier.

It is possible to prevent youth from joining gangs. The first level of prevention involves strengthening the core social institutions that have failed to meet their developmental needs. School climate environments need to be improved and student "connectedness" to schools must be strengthened. Students must remain "tethered" to the school, their families, and community institutions such as faith-based organizations to buffer them from gang attractions. This means the school suspension, expulsion, and dropout rates must be reduced. Zero-tolerance policies must be relaxed, and tempered by risk assessments. Interventions with youth at high risk for delinquency and gang involvement must be applied early in life. Effective afterschool and alternative education programs are imperative. Community violence prevention programs are necessary to reduce the level of community violence and personal victimization of vulnerable youth. Programs should target girls and boys and both White and minority youth.

Poor implementation of gang-related programs in schools is a significant problem (G. Gottfredson, 2013). For effective implementation, delinquency and crime reduction programs that target children and adolescents must adhere with high fidelity to the requirements of the original model and target high-risk offenders (Howell et al., 2014).

Because youth who join gangs typically experience multiple problems in multiple developmental domains that change over time, a continuum of age-graded strategies and programs is needed to prevent gang involvement. These strategies and programs need to target risk factors in family, school, and community contexts. The next chapter describes how to link prevention and early intervention programs with later interventions for gang-involved youth and gang-suppression strategies.

Statewide implementation of prevention programming also appears feasible, as suggested by progress in the implementation of the Comprehensive Gang Model in gang problem counties by the North Carolina Department of Juvenile Justice and Delinquency Prevention (M. Howell & Lassiter, 2011), and in Massachusetts, where the Executive Office of Public Safety and Security is providing large-scale funding for prevention and intervention programs that support the model statewide in large urban areas (Gebo & Bond, 2012).

DISCUSSION TOPICS

1. Class exercise: Pick one or more risk factors for gang involvement in Table 5.2 in each developmental domain, select a target age range, review the programs that are linked to it in the OJJDP Strategic Planning Tool, and build an ideal continuum of prevention and early intervention programs: https://www.nationalgangcenter.gov/SPT

2. What strategies and programs would you propose to reduce female gang involvement?

3. Would your strategies and programs work as well elsewhere, and for White and African American children and adolescents?

4. What about males? Would you use the same strategies and programs for them?

5. After a community builds and implements a continuum of programs and structures, how can effectiveness of the entire continuum be determined?

RECOMMENDATIONS FOR FURTHER READING

Gang Prevention Programs and Strategies

Esbensen, F., Osgood, D. W., Taylor, T. J., Peterson, D., & Freng, A. (2001). How great is G.R.E.A.T.? Results from a longitudinal quasi-experimental design. *Criminology and Public Policy, 1,* 87–118.

Howell, J. C. (2010). *Gang prevention: An overview of current research and programs* (Juvenile Justice Bulletin). Washington, DC: U.S. Department of Justice, Office of Juvenile Justice and Delinquency Prevention.

Howell, J. C. (2013). Why is gang membership prevention important? In T.R. Simon, N.M. Ritter, & R.R. Mahendra (eds.). *Changing Course: Preventing Gang Membership* (pp. 7–18). Washington, DC: National Center for Injury Prevention and Control, Centers for Disease Control and Prevention, U.S. Department of Health and Human Services, and National Institute of Justice, Office of Justice Programs, U.S. Department of Justice.

OJJDP Comprehensive Gang Program Model

National Gang Center. (2010). *Best practices to address community gang problems: OJJDP's Comprehensive Gang Model.* Washington, DC: Author. Retrieved from www.ncjrs.gov/pdffiles1/ojjdp/231200.pdf

Difficulties Associated With Moving Model Programs Into Everyday Practice

Barnoski, R. (2004). *Outcome evaluation of Washington State's research-based programs for juvenile offenders* (Document No. 04–01–1201). Olympia: Washington State Institute for Public Policy. Retrieved from http://www.wsipp.wa.gov/ReportFile/852

Dodge, K. A. (2001). The science of youth violence prevention: Progressing from developmental epidemiology to efficacy to effectiveness to public policy. *American Journal of Preventive Medicine, 20*(1S), 63–70.

Fagan, A. A., Hanson, K., Hawkins, J. D., & Arthur, M. W. (2008). Implementing effective community-based prevention programs in the community youth development study. *Youth Violence and Juvenile Justice, 6,* 256–278.

Gottfredson, G. D. (2013). What can schools do to help prevent gang joining? In T. R. Simon, N. M. Ritter, & R. R. Mahendra (Eds.), *Changing course: Preventing gang membership* (pp. 89–104). Washington, DC: U.S. Department of Justice, U.S. Department of Health and Human Services.

Howell, J. C., Lipsey, M. W., & Wilson, J. J. (2014). *A handbook for evidence-based juvenile justice systems.* Lanham, MD: Lexington Books.

Karoly, L. A., Greenwood, P. W., Everingham, S. S., Houbé, J., Kilburn, M. R., & Rydell, C. P. (1998). *Investing in our children.* Santa Monica, CA: RAND.

Welsh, B. C., Sullivan, C. J., & Olds, D. L. (2010). When early crime prevention goes to scale: A new look at the evidence. *Prevention Science, 11,* 115–125.

Strategies for Prevention and Early Intervention

Dodge, K. A. (2001). The science of youth violence prevention: Progressing from developmental epidemiology to efficacy to effectiveness to public policy. *American Journal of Preventive Medicine, 20*(1S), 63–70.

Howell, J. C. (2010a). *Gang prevention: An overview of current research and programs* (Juvenile Justice Bulletin). Washington, DC: U.S. Department of Justice, Office of Juvenile Justice and Delinquency Prevention.

Howell, J. C. (2010b). Lessons learned from gang program evaluations: Prevention, intervention, suppression, and comprehensive community approaches. In R. J. Chaskin (Ed.), *Youth gangs and community intervention: Research, practice, and evidence* (pp. 51–75). New York: Columbia University Press.

Karoly, L. A., Greenwood, P. W., Everingham, S. S., Houbé, J., Kilburn, M. R., & Rydell, C. P. (1998). *Investing in our children.* Santa Monica, CA: RAND.

Peterson, D., & Morgan, K. A. (2014). Sex differences and the overlap in youths' risk factors for onset of violence and gang involvement. *Journal of Crime and Justice, 37,* 129–154.

Welsh, B. C., & Farrington, D. P. (2006). *Preventing crime: What works for children, offenders, victims, and places.* Dordrecht, The Netherlands: Springer.

Welsh, B. C., & Farrington, D. P. (2007). Save children from a life of crime. *Criminology and Public Policy, 6,* 871–879.

Welsh, B. C., Sullivan, C. J., & Olds, D. L. (2010). When early crime prevention goes to scale: A new look at the evidence. *Prevention Science, 11,* 115–125.

Preschool Programs

For additional information, see the Model Programs Guide: http://www.ojjdp.gov/mpg/htm

School Entry Programs

For additional programs, see the OJJDP Strategic Planning Tool at www.nationalgangcenter.gov/SPT/Planning-Implementation/Strategies/0. (Note that the database includes program structures.)

School-Based Intervention

Gottfredson, G. D. (2013). What can schools do to help prevent gang joining? In T. R. Simon, N. M. Ritter, & R. R. Mahendra (Eds.), *Changing course: Preventing gang membership* (pp. 89–104). Washington, DC: U.S. Department of Justice, U.S. Department of Health and Human Services.

Wilson, S. J., & Lipsey, M. W. (2007). School-based interventions for aggressive and disruptive behavior: Update of a meta-analysis. *American Journal of Preventive Medicine, 33*(Supplement), S130–S143.

NOTES

1. See Chapter 10 for the criteria adopted by nine federal agencies to identify "evidence-based" programs. Those criteria also apply to the programs identified as evidence based in this chapter.

2. Prevention methods can be classified as universal, selected, or indicated. Universal programs are applied to a complete population; selective programs are applied to a high-risk subgroup of the population; and indicated programs are applied to identified cases such as offenders.

CHAPTER 10

What Works in a Comprehensive Gang Program Approach

◈ Introduction

Research-based gang intervention, suppression, and comprehensive programs are reviewed in this chapter. Unfortunately, the U.S. federal government has funded very few gang program evaluations, and only one gang research and development program, hence the literature in this area is somewhat thin, though growing steadily. At the present time, 13 evidence-based programs with a demonstrated gang impact have been identified. Three of these were presented in Chapter 9: the Gang Resistance Education and Training Program (Level 4), the gang-adapted version of Brief Strategic Family Therapy, and the Montreal Preventive Treatment Program (intervention programs for high-risk youth in Level 3). Other effective programs for Levels 1 and 2 of the Comprehensive Gang Program Model Continuum (Figure 9.5) are reviewed in this chapter.

Much like juvenile justice and other disciplines, the gang field is fixated on replicating *model* or *exemplary* programs. The model programs approach entails selecting a recommended program from a list of research-supported programs and implementing it locally, but fidelity to the program developer's specifications for how the program is to be delivered is required to expect comparable results (Howell et al., 2014). In this approach, the recommended programs are supported in program-by-program reviews of the research. It is important to recognize that a program need not be designed specifically to address gang crime to have positive gang crime reduction impacts. As noted in Chapter 9, the Montreal Preventive Treatment Program reduced gang involvement as a result of addressing precursor disruptive and delinquent behaviors, and another prevention program, Perry Preschool, reduced gang fights. A reentry program, Operation New Hope, another case in point, is reviewed in this chapter. What accounts for these welcomed outcomes? Two explanations are plausible. First, gang and nongang

237

offenders share common risk factors (Table 5.2), and second, gang involvement overlaps substantially with serious, violent, and chronic offending (Baglivio et al., 2014; Howell et al., 2014). Hence, early-adolescence programs targeting these common factors may reduce youths' likelihood of involvement in both gangs and violence (Peterson & Morgan, 2014).

◈ The Comprehensive, Community-Wide Gang Program Model

This chapter promotes a community-wide structure for organizing and integrating local gang programs. The original version of this model, known as the Comprehensive, Community-Wide Gang Prevention, Intervention, and Suppression Program (commonly called the Comprehensive Gang Program Model, for short), was based on a decade of research in a nationwide assessment of youth gang problems and experimental programming in Chicago led by the late Irving Spergel (see Howell, 2015, for Spergel's legacy). The Comprehensive Gang Program Model synthesized both research on programs and best practices for successfully combating gang problems.

◈ First Steps

The Comprehensive Gang Program Model incorporates five strategies: (1) organizational change and development, (2) community mobilization, (3) opportunities provision, (4) social intervention, and (5) suppression (Spergel, 1991, 1995, 2007). Figure 10.1 shows how these strategies address program targets in ongoing activities, and each of these was generated from research on program initiatives in the national assessment by Spergel and colleagues (1994). Brief descriptions of each of the five strategies follow.

1. *Organizational change and development:* Development and implementation of policies and procedures that result in the most effective use of available and potential resources, within and across agencies, to better address the gang problem. (Spergel, 1995, pp. 171–296)

2. *Community mobilization:* Involvement of local citizens, including former gang-involved youth, community groups, agencies, and coordination of programs and staff functions within and across agencies

3. *Social intervention:* Involving youth-serving agencies, schools, grassroots groups, faith-based organizations, police, and other juvenile/criminal justice organizations in "reaching out" to gang-involved youth and their families, and linking them with the conventional world and needed services

4. *Opportunities provision:* Development of a variety of specific education, training, and employment programs targeting gang-involved youth

5. *Suppression:* Formal and informal social control procedures, including close supervision and monitoring of gang-involved youth by agencies of the juvenile/criminal justice system and also by community-based agencies, schools, and grassroots groups

Communities that adopt the Comprehensive Gang Program Model will benefit from the simplified implementation process that the Office of Juvenile Justice and Delinquency Prevention (OJJDP, 2009b) has created. OJJDP synthesized the elements of the Comprehensive Gang Program Model into five steps:

Figure 10.1   Comprehensive Gang Program Model

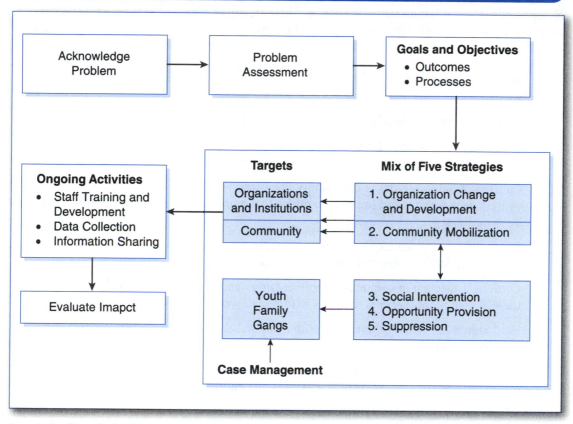

Source: National Gang Center, 2010.

1. The community and its leaders acknowledge the youth gang problem.

2. The community conducts an assessment of the nature and scope of the youth gang problem, leading to the identification of a target community or communities and population(s).

3. Through a steering committee, the community and its leaders set goals and objectives to address the identified problem(s).

4. The steering committee makes available relevant programs, strategies, services, tactics, and procedures consistent with the Comprehensive Gang Program Model's five strategies.

5. The steering committee evaluates the effectiveness of the response to the gang problem, reassesses the problem, and modifies approaches, as needed. (National Gang Center, 2010, p. 3)

The National Gang Center (2010) has refined these steps in several settings. A key to successfully combating youth gangs is to first mobilize the community. The reality is that communities respond to problems that their key leaders or stakeholders perceive to be important. The range of problems is broad, including natural disasters, public health problems, external threats, drugs, adult crime, juvenile delinquency, and gangs. In their literature review, Howell and Curry (2009) suggest several essential elements of successful community mobilization. These are organized in the sequence that follows. The sequence of steps suggested here assumes that the community has a low degree of organization to address such social problems.

- Recognize the current or potential gang problem as a major threat to community safety and security.

- Identify key neighborhood leaders in the community.

- Contact key neighborhood leaders, local agencies, and community groups to discuss their concerns and to inquire about their interest in a collective effort.

- Cultivate a natural leader, a community organizer, within the community. He or she must express deep feelings and impress on others that a problem exists and that something must be done about it.

- Ensure that the community leader or organizer urges the broadcast media to become involved in all aspects of the mobilization process as early as possible.

- Convene a meeting of community representatives and discuss emerging concerns. Think of these as community network meetings to formulate a cohesive plan.

- Hold numerous individual meetings with many stakeholders to seek their support and refine priority problems.

- Convene a second community-wide meeting. Think of this as a neighborhood involvement activity to heighten awareness of how community entities can interact to bring about a gang-free environment.

- Direct the community or agency leaders, with the aid of the community organizer, to begin to involve and solicit the support of a variety of local agencies or community groups, former gang influentials, and even selected gang youth to alert the community to the gang problem.

- Create or designate a formal community organization to act on behalf of the community group.

- Conduct an objective assessment of the potential gang problem.

- Set specific goals and objectives together with a timeline for their accomplishment. Seek to achieve small wins at the outset.

It is important to recognize that the sequencing of these steps may vary in different communities. For example, if a community already is well organized to deal with a variety of youth problems—often by an existing coalition of some sort—it would be advisable to take advantage of this existing infrastructure to address a gang problem. This situation would preclude the need to take several of the preliminary steps outlined here.

Community stakeholders should not begin thinking about programs and strategies for responding to gangs before they have assessed the community's own gang problem. Without the benefit of an empirical assessment, McCorkle and Miethe (2002) caution that community stakeholders run a high risk of being seriously mistaken about the nature of their gang problem. A common misstep is the assumption that local gangs, that in appearance may resemble distant Chicago or Los Angeles gangs (e.g., by hand signs, tattoos, or color of clothing), are equally dangerous. Every effort must be made in the assessment stage to discard preconceived notions because many of them are based on gang myths, as noted in Chapter 2. Guidelines for such an assessment were featured in Chapter 9.

Caution should be exercised in naming gangs in public products of the assessment. This can backfire in five ways, by (1) increasing the notoriety of gangs and individuals, further emboldening groups; (2) helping gangs recruit by giving youth the mistaken impression that the gang can provide protection; (3) fueling conflict between groups, sparking retaliation; (4) increasing cohesion of gangs by publicizing their criminal activity, enhancing their image as "baddest" in the community; and (5) provoking fear among citizens, further reducing public confidence in the justice system and creating a panic that can misdirect policy makers. Another cautionary note is the prospect of gang problem denial. Huff (1989, 1990) characterized the typical community's treatment of a gang problem as a three-stage process including denial, overreaction, and misidentification. Barrows and Huff (2009) observe that what typically happens after a period of denial, if a highly publicized violent gang crime occurs, is that policymakers implement a singular enforcement strategy, often with sole emphasis on suppression. Next, police may misidentify (i.e., over-identify) gang members and the underlying causes of gang membership, leading to ineffective responses.

An important point to underscore here is that communities should not wait for a tragic catalytic event to address gang activity. Sole reliance on law enforcement suppression strategies is typically the first response. Over the course of several years, communities then gradually embrace a more collaborative effort with community organizations and agencies. Success will come much more quickly in taking a balanced approach from the outset, one that is grounded in a careful assessment of gang activity.

◈ Comprehensive Gang Program Model Administrative Structure

The recommended administrative structure for implementing the Comprehensive Gang Program Model is shown in Figure 10.2, consisting of a steering committee, the lead agency, a project director, a research partner, and an intervention team (National Gang Center, 2010, pp. 5–24).

A steering committee oversees the gang project. These individuals are policy or decision makers from agencies and organizations that have an interest in or responsibility for addressing the community's gang problem. These representatives should not only set policy and oversee the overall direction of the gang project, but they should take responsibility for spearheading efforts in their own organizations to remove barriers to services and fill service gaps—an important form of organizational change. The steering committee should also develop effective criminal justice, school, and social agency procedures; and promote policies that will further the goals of the gang strategy. Ideally, this group oversees an assessment of the local gang problem and, using data obtained through the assessment, develops strategies to combat it.

The project coordinator or director is responsible for the day-to-day management of the project and reports directly to the steering committee.

Figure 10.2   OJJDP Comprehensive Gang Program Model Administrative Structure

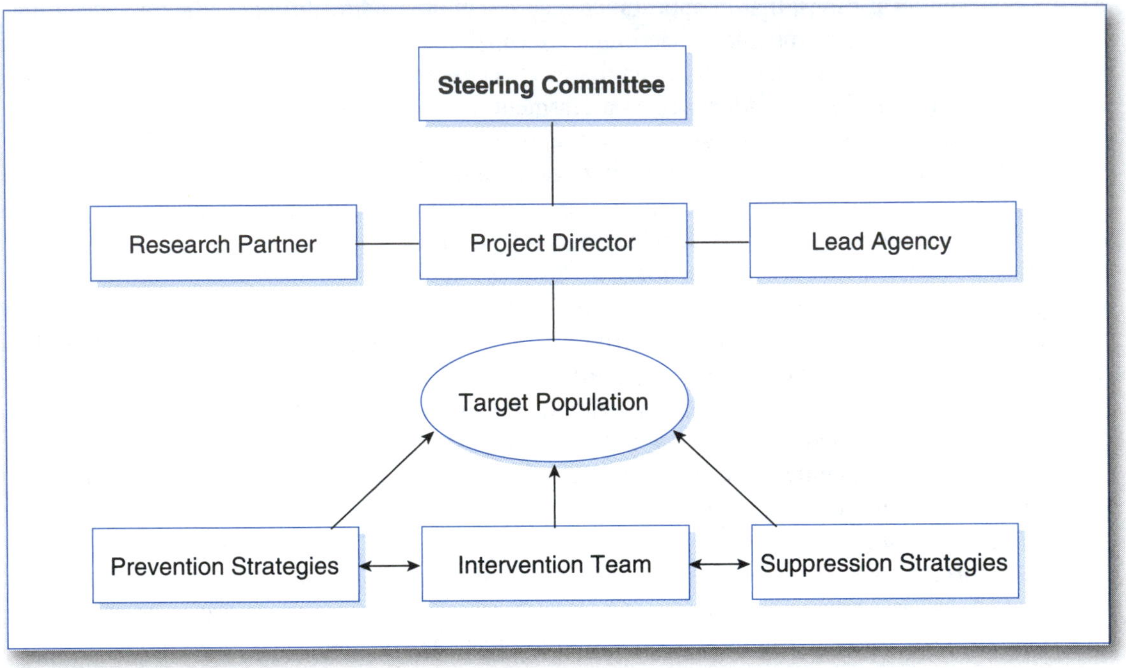

Source: National Gang Center, 2010.

Those persons in positions of responsibility for addressing the problem—representatives of police, schools, probation, youth agencies, grassroots organizations, government, and others—form the assessment team and participate in identifying the gang problem's scope, severity, and unique features.

An intervention team is an essential component of the Comprehensive Gang Program Model. At a minimum, the following key agencies that are crucial to an effective intervention team's success should be represented on the team (National Gang Center, 2010): law enforcement representatives involved in gang investigation and enforcement; juvenile and adult probation or parole officers who will have frequent contact with program clients; school officials who can access student educational data for program clients and leverage educational services; appropriate social service or mental health providers who can leverage services and provide outcome information to the team; a representative who can assist in preparing program clients for employment and find jobs for them; and outreach workers who can directly connect to program clients on the street, in their homes, or at school.

Because of the intensive work involved in helping youth negotiate their way around gangs in high-risk environments, and assisting others in extracting themselves from gangs, it goes without saying that "the outreach component of this model is critical to program success" (National Gang Center, 2010, p. 20). The outreach workers' primary role is to build relationships with program clients and with other gang-involved and at-risk youth in the community. These workers generally are the primary source of program referrals and they often play an active role in delivering services, working closely with community service providers. In addition, "outreach workers are the intervention team's eyes and ears on the street, giving the team perspective on the personal aspects of gang conflicts and violence and how these affect the team's clients" (p. 20). The outreach workers also should play an active role in the development and execution of comprehensive treatment plans in intervention teams. According to Pyrooz and colleagues (2014), accelerating the process of leaving a gang, or reducing the length of gang membership, is quite likely to reduce victimization and subsequent criminality. Research indicates that supportive peer and family networks, outreach workers, and services play an important part in the desistance process.

The NGC has developed a Strategic Planning Tool (SPT) (www.nationalgangcenter.gov/), introduced in Chapter 9, that communities can use to assess their youth violence and gang problem and employ in conjunction with the Comprehensive Gang Program Model to develop a continuum of prevention, intervention, and suppression programs and strategies. For prevention planning, this tool includes research-based risk factors and indicators to assist communities in conducting a risk and program needs assessment. The SPT contains a section (the Community Resource Inventory) within which community planning groups can record and maintain information on existing programs, which would help enormously in identifying and filling program gaps. It supports a problem-solving approach to gang-related crime by engaging communities in the identification of elevated risk factors for gang involvement in communities and schools, locations of gang activity, hotspots of gang crime, and high-rate gang offenders and violent gangs. The SPT also contains information on promising and effective juvenile delinquency and gang programs and strategies that address specific risk factors among various age groups. Resource materials that assist communities in developing an action plan to implement the Comprehensive Gang Program Model are available online at www.nationalgangcenter.gov/Comprehensive-Gang-Model/About.

◈ Implementing the Comprehensive Gang Program Model

The Comprehensive Gang Program Model aims to reduce gang involvement and gang crime at three levels: communities, gangs, and individuals. These are the specific priority goals:

1. Prevent and reduce gang involvement and thereby reduce related gang crime.

2. Reduce gang-related crimes committed by particular gangs.

3. Reduce youth gang crime and violence in targeted neighborhoods/communities.

Stated in terms of a continuum, *prevention* programs are needed to target youths at risk of gang involvement, to reduce the number of youths who join gangs; *intervention* programs and strategies are needed to provide sanctions and services for younger youths who are actively involved in gangs to separate them from gangs; and law enforcement *suppression* strategies are needed to target the most violent gangs and older, most criminally active gang members. Therefore, a balanced and integrated approach employing multiple strategies is most likely to be effective, and the research supports this approach (Spergel, 2007; Spergel et al., 2006).

Source: National Gang Center (2010).

> ## IN FOCUS 10.1
> ## HIGHLIGHTS OF GANG-RELATED LEGISLATION
>
> - All 50 states and the District of Columbia (DC) have enacted some form of legislation concerning gangs or gang-related activity.
> - 42 states and DC have legislation that defines *gang*.
> - 14 states have legislation that defines *gang member*.
> - 31 states define *gang crime/activity*.
> - 28 states have passed gang-prevention laws.
> - 30 states have laws that provide for enhanced penalties for gang-related criminal acts.
> - 14 states and DC have enacted anti-carjacking statutes.
> - More than half the states have laws against graffiti.
> - 26 states and DC have legislation on gangs and schools.
> - 12 states have enacted laws that deal with gang-related databases.
>
> *Source:* National Gang Center (2013b).

◈ Evidence-Based Gang Programs

Table 10.1 includes more specific information on the activities in each implementation phase and, based on experiences of other comprehensive projects, the approximate length of time it takes to complete the activities in each phase (National Gang Center, 2010). Each community's administrative structure and practices, community politics, and community readiness will dictate the actual length of each phase. Existing gang legislation also needs to be taken into account.

This section reviews effective gang-related intervention and suppression programs that have been identified since systematic reviews of gang programs began in 2005. Systematic reviews of gang programs were made a U.S. government executive branch priority at that time, and nine federal agencies were directed by the White House[1] to establish criteria for these reviews. Using this methodology, programs were scored on the following widely accepted scientific standards for judging program effectiveness:

- Conceptual Framework (theoretical base, program activities rationale, research base)

- Program Fidelity (adherence to original program operation guidelines, dosage, and program attrition)

- Evaluation Design (research design, sample size, group equivalence)

- Outcome Evidence (follow-up period, outcome differences, integrity of findings)

These are standard scientific criteria for judging program effectiveness, and these criteria continue to be widely used by most federal agencies. The OJJDP Strategic Planning Tool groups programs into

Table 10.1   Timeline for Implementing the Comprehensive Gang Program Model

Assessment and Planning (6–12 months)	Capacity Building (3–6 months)	Full Implementation (12–18 months)
Identify key stakeholders.	Complete the contract procurement process for program services.	Initiate program services.
Form a steering committee.	Develop program policies and procedures.	Initiate client referral process.
Establish gang definitions.	Advertise, hire, and train new staff to provide services.	Begin client intake process for prevention and intervention clients.
Hire a project coordinator.	Develop a client referral and recruitment process.	Begin conducting client reviews during intervention team meetings.
Solicit a research partner.	Select intervention team members.	Begin providing focused suppression efforts.
Conduct a comprehensive community assessment (including the Community Resource Inventory).	Conduct intervention team training.	Begin conducting community prevention activities.
	Provide gang-awareness training to project service providers.	Reach program caseload capacity.
	Develop a community resource referral and feedback process.	
	Develop a program referral process.	
	Train project partners on the project referral process.	
	Develop a data collection and analysis system.	

one of the following classifications (based on cumulative scores assigned to each section of the program rating tool):

Level 1 (Exemplary)—In general, when implemented with a high degree of fidelity, these programs demonstrate robust empirical findings using a reputable conceptual framework and an evaluation design of the highest quality (experimental). Programs in this category are designated exemplary or model programs and are considered very effective.

Level 2 (Effective)—In general, when implemented with sufficient fidelity, these programs demonstrate adequate empirical findings using a sound conceptual framework and an evaluation design of high quality (quasi-experimental).

Level 3 (Promising)—In general, when implemented with minimal fidelity, these programs demonstrate promising (although inconsistent) empirical findings using a reasonable conceptual framework and a very limited evaluation design (single group pre- and post-test) that requires causal confirmation using more appropriate experimental techniques. Only a few of these programs are reviewed here. (Interested readers should consult the Strategic Planning Tool.)

Level 4 (Ineffective)

Table 10.2 illustrates evidence-based programs that scored in the first two levels (i.e., Levels 1 and 2). When programs meet the aforementioned criteria for determining program effectiveness, these programs can rightly be considered "evidence based." Some rating systems use more stringent criteria to identify only "model programs." For example, this is the approach taken for the Blueprints for Violence Prevention (http://www.colorado.edu/cspv/index.html). However, this does not mean that no other programs are "effective" by traditional scientific criteria. The aforementioned criteria that nine federal agencies agreed on were intended to classify "effective" programs. However, other programs that do not meet these criteria could also be effective. A comprehensive meta-analytic study that included homegrown programs found that some of these other programs outperformed even "blueprint" programs on occasion (Howell et al., 2014, p. 69).

To provide the most valid results, an impact evaluation must use a control group of comparable juveniles who do not receive the program, preferably assigned randomly to program and no-program conditions. An evaluation of this sort for a specific program can provide credible evidence of effectiveness and, with positive results, that program can rightly claim to be evidence-based. (Howell & Lipsey, 2012, p. 18.)

Evidence-Based Gang Prevention Programs

None of the gang programs shown in Table 10.2 has been classified as a "model" program. Rather, evidence-based gang programs identified to date can only be classified generally as "effective," because crime reductions associated with these programs are not large, and only one of the programs used random assignment: Gang Resistance Education and Training (G.R.E.A.T.). Except in the prevention arena (the G.R.E.A.T. evaluation randomly assigned classrooms), random assignment is impractical in the gang field for public safety and moral (excessive risk to public safety) reasons. Three gang prevention programs are evidence based at this time: Gang Resistance Education and Training (L-1), Project BUILD (L-2), and the Montreal Preventive Treatment Program (L-1). Each of these programs was reviewed in Chapter 9. Because poor school climates may contribute to gang formation and emergence, programs that improve school climate are needed. An excellent evidence-based candidate was reviewed in Chapter 9, PeaceBuilders (for elementary and middle schools, K–8). We now turn to consideration of effective gang intervention and suppression programs.

Evidence-Based Gang Intervention Programs

Aggression Replacement Training (ART) (L-2) is a 10-week, 30-hour cognitive-behavioral program administered to groups of 8 to 12 juvenile offenders three times per week. ART has three main

Table 10.2 Effective Gang and Gang-Related Programs

Program Name	Rating*	Key References
Gang Resistance Education and Training	L-1	Esbensen et al., 2001; Esbensen et al., 2013
Montreal Preventive Treatment Program[y]	L-1	Tremblay et al., 1996
Project BUILD (Broader Urban Involvement and Leadership Development)	L-2	Lurigio et al., 2000
Aggression Replacement Training	L-2	Goldstein et al., 1998
Brief Strategic Family Therapy—gang-adapted	L-2	Av. Valdez et al., 2013
Aggressive Behavioral Control Program	L-2	Di Placido et al., 2006
Operation New Hope[y]	L-2	Josi & Sechrest, 1999
Hardcore Gang Investigations Unit	L-2	Dahmann, 1983,1995; Pyrooz et al., 2011
OJJDP Comprehensive Gang Prevention, Intervention, and Suppression Program Model	L-2	Spergel, 1986; Spergel et al., 2006; Spergel, 2007; Hayeslip & Cahill, 2009; Hodgkinson et al., 2009
Boston Midcity Project[x]	L-2	W. Miller, 1962; Hodgkinson et al., 2009
Cure Violence Chicago, Baltimore	L-2	Skogan et al., 2008; Ransford et al., 2010
Operation Ceasefire	L-2	Braga & Weisburd, 2012

[*]Legend: L-1=exemplary-effective program; L-2=effective program. Criteria for all program ratings are provided in the OJJDP Strategic Planning Tool (http://www.nationalgangcenter.gov/SPT/Planning-implementation/Review).

[x] This program is not in the OJJDP Model Program Guide or the OJJDP Strategic Planning Tool database because it no longer exists.

[y] These two programs did not purposefully target youth at risk of gang involvement or gang members; nevertheless, they demonstrated evidence of effectiveness, respectively, with these two target groups.

curriculum components: structured learning training, which teaches social skills; anger control training, which teaches youth a variety of ways to manage their anger; and moral education, which helps youth develop a higher level of moral reasoning.

ART has demonstrated effectiveness with both girls and boys in multiple settings and has shown positive results when tested with gang-involved youth in Brooklyn, New York (Goldstein, et al., 1998; Goldstein & Glick, 1994). More rigorous evaluations have assessed the effectiveness of ART as an intervention for incarcerated juvenile delinquents. In these studies, ART enhanced prosocial skill competency and overt prosocial behavior, reduced the level of rated impulsiveness, decreased the frequency and intensity of acting-out behaviors, and enhanced the participants' levels of moral reasoning. In a Washington State Institute for Public Policy study, Barnoski (2004) found that when ART is delivered competently, the program reduced felony recidivism and was found to be cost-effective. A rare asset of ART is that the program recruits the most violent gang members in the community. In sum, ART is an evidence-based juvenile justice program that has demonstrated evidence of effectiveness with gang members.

Another treatment program stands out for having reduced recidivism among imprisoned gang members. The Aggressive Behavioral Control Program (L-2) has demonstrated evidence of effectiveness in rehabilitation of young inmates in Canadian prisons (Di Placido, Simon, Witte, Gu, & Wong, 2006). Housed in the maximum-security Regional Psychiatric Centre, the program provides high-intensity, cognitive-behavioral therapy designed specifically for high-risk, high-need offenders, those who typically demonstrate low responsiveness to rehabilitative services. Prison gang inmates (average age 25) were included in the eligible target group and the evaluation demonstrated program effectiveness with them as well. The program also produced favorable cost benefits.

One correctional aftercare program has produced positive short-term effects for gang members: the Operation New Hope program (formerly called Lifeskills '95) (L-2), which was implemented in California's San Bernardino and Riverside counties. This program was designed for high-risk, chronic juvenile offenders released from the California Youth Authority. In addition to reintegrating these youths into communities, the New Hope program aimed to reduce their need for gang participation and affiliation as a support mechanism. An evaluation of the program's results found that participating youths were far less likely to have frequent associations with former gang associates than were members of the control group. In addition, youths assigned to the control group were about twice as likely as program participants to have been arrested, to be unemployed, and to have abused drugs or alcohol frequently since their release. The outcomes for this program suggest that some recidivism-reduction impact may be realized by giving special attention to gang members in reentry programming.

In addition to individualized case management of comprehensive reentry plans, probation, parole, and other staff working with returning gang-affiliated inmates must exercise special skills in steering them from gang life. The first challenge is separating them from prison gangs in which they had been members. Parolee safety and security of others is a major consideration. The prison gang mantra "blood in, blood out" is not an empty promise in many cases. At the same time, inmates' dependence on prison gangs and street gangs in the urban areas to which they return must be broken. To further complicate matters, family members with whom they are reunited may also be gang members. Identification and immediate engagement of returning gang-affiliated inmates in alternatives to gang life, like job training or employment, needed services, and a substitute support network are paramount.

To increase the validity of gang member classifications, juvenile correctional facilities, jails, and state prison systems should develop and establish a method for assessing and classifying individuals who are gang affiliated or gang involved, or who are at high risk of becoming gang involved, at the time of their intake and throughout their detention or incarceration. Training should be provided for institutional intake and classification staffs on how to identify, assess, and classify inmates who are at high risk of becoming gang affiliated or involved. Tailored to the prison context, the excellent criteria for the purpose of documenting active street gang members shown below (In Focus 10.2) could be modified for use in juvenile detention and correctional facilities. It also is important to create and maintain a complete electronic record or paper trail about gang-involved individuals to ensure that any significant new information about them is communicated to other key personnel and agencies throughout their incarceration, release to the community, community supervision, and discharge from supervision processes.

IN FOCUS 10.2
CRITERIA FOR IDENTIFYING A SECURITY THREAT GROUP MEMBER

1. Self-admission

2. Gang tattoo or branding

3. Possession of Security Threat Group (STG) paraphernalia (e.g., STG lessons, rules, oaths, etc.)

4. Information from an outside law enforcement agency

5. Information obtained during a Special Investigations Division investigation

6. Correspondence from other known STG members

7. Group gang photo

8. Other (e.g., active participation in STG-related activity)

Source: New Jersey Department of Corrections (American Probation and Parole Association and Institute for Intergovernmental Research, 2011).

Three promising juvenile delinquency programs are worthy of mention here. A correctional program developed for violent juvenile offenders also proved equally effective for rehabilitating gang members. The Wisconsin Mendota Juvenile Treatment Center (MJTC) provided cognitive–behavioral services to the most disturbed boys in the state's secure correctional facilities, both Aggression Replacement Training (Goldstein et al., 1998) and the "decompression" treatment model (Caldwell & Van Rybroek, 2001). Caldwell, Vitacco, and Van Rybroek (2006) found the MJTC youths had less than half the recidivism rates of the comparison group, and the program produced benefits of $7.18 for every dollar of costs. Given the effectiveness of Aggression Replacement Training, its use in the treatment regimen suggests that MJTC is likely to be effective with gang members.

A court-based nongang program also holds promise for the rehabilitation of gang members, the Multidisciplinary Team (MDT) Home Run program in San Bernardino County, California. The program's MDT resembles an intervention team recommended in the Comprehensive Gang Program Model. Four professionals make up each MDT: (1) a probation officer, (2) a licensed therapist, (3) a social worker, and (4) a public health nurse. Probation officers refer high-risk youthful offenders (including gang members) and their families. Each team provides intensive and comprehensive wraparound services for six months. Schram and Gaines's evaluation (2005) compared outcomes for randomly selected gang and nongang offenders from among all youths served in the MDT program. Both gang and nongang members reported improvements in school performance, family functioning, and decreases in alcohol and substance abuse, as well as delinquency involvement. Programs likely would be more effective with gang members if an outreach worker were added to the MDT to assist gang members in negotiating a path away from gangs. Outreach workers and school resource officers need to coordinate their efforts.

A North Carolina community-based residential program for high-risk juvenile offenders developed by Methodist Home for Children (MHC) has demonstrated effectiveness, according to Strom, Colwell, Dawes, and Hawkins (2010), in rehabilitating juvenile delinquents, including gang members, who were candidates for long-term confinement. Nearly one in five (19%) MHC youth were reported to be gang associates. The MHC therapeutic Model of Care incorporates both individual and family counseling in its multipurpose homes that provide residential services for youth referred through the state's Department of Juvenile Justice and Delinquency Prevention. This is a very promising program model for gang members that blends them into the treatment group but provides attentive services during reentry to avoid reengagement with hometown gangs.

Gang Suppression

Two targeted gang suppression strategies have proved effective: the Hardcore Gang Investigations Unit and Operation Ceasefire (Table 10.2). The Hardcore Gang Investigations Unit (L-2) (initially called Operation Hardcore) is a prosecutorial gang suppression program that was created by the Los Angeles District Attorney's Office in 1979 and is still operating today. Its distinctive features include reduced caseloads, additional investigative support, resources for assisting victims, and vertical prosecution—in which the prosecutor who files a case remains responsible for it throughout the prosecution process. In an independent evaluation of Operation Hardcore, Dahmann (1983, 1995) showed fewer dismissals; more convictions or adjudications, including more convictions or adjudications on the most serious charge; and a higher rate of state prison commitments or secure confinement dispositions for cases subject to the program compared to for cases undergoing the normal prosecutorial process. Further analysis (Pyrooz, Wolf, & Spohn, 2011) revealed that Operation Hardcore is an effective gang prosecution strategy because Hardcore cases were significantly less likely to be rejected; that is, gang-related homicide cases prosecuted by the specialized unit were more likely to advance to the next stage of adjudication.

Boston Operation Ceasefire (L-2) is a problem-oriented policing deterrence project that instituted a zero-tolerance policy for any law-breaking activity on the part of identified individuals, with the aim of reducing homicide (Kennedy, 2010). In Boston, high-rate violent offenders with histories of gang-related crimes (identified through a review of police arrest records in a problem analysis) were rounded up and notified in a community meeting that they were subject to long prison sentences for any subsequent law, probation, or parole violations. In these community meetings, federal, state, and local law enforcement authorities "were saying explicitly that violence would no longer be tolerated, and backing up that message by pulling every lever legally available when violence occurred" (Braga & Hureau, 2012, p. 134). Successful convictions that drew long federal sentences were widely publicized in the community to deter others. In various Ceasefire sites, a menu of "sticks" and "carrots" was offered to offenders. Sticks were a range of sanctions or "levers" used to encourage gang members to desist from violence by "retailing" the message to gang members that (1) all of them would be held accountable for violence committed by any one of them and that (2) violent crime would have consequences (long prison sentences). Services were offered as an alternative incentive to turn away from crime. These "carrots" can include job training and development, substance abuse treatment, and tattoo removal. A large reduction in the annual number of youth homicides was reported in Boston and significant decreases were noted in other cities, including

Indianapolis, Indiana; Los Angeles, California; Lowell, Massachusetts; Cincinnati, Ohio; and Stockton, California (Braga & Weisburd, 2012).

A formidable obstacle to reducing gang violence is the huge cache of guns that are readily available to gangs. Research shows that beginning in the 1970s, gangs' access to more lethal weapons grew (C. Block & Block, 1993; W. Miller, 1982/1992). Therefore, Ludwig (2005), along with Wellford, Pepper, and Petrie (2005), contend that "supernormal" reductions in gang firearm homicide are not on the horizon for the United States in the absence of effective access limitations, but Ludwig (2005) and McGarrell and associates (2009) find genuine reductions from strategic intervention in small geographical locations by coupling targeted patrols, gang units, and aggressive prosecution in areas where gangs account for a large share of gun violence; that is, in violent hotspots or gang set spaces. However, the most cost-effective strategy may well be intervention with "violence interrupters" in potential gang-related shootings with the Cure Violence model (described below), because Cohen, Piquero, and Jennings (2010) demonstrate enormous cost savings from successful interventions before criminal justice system, victim, and incarceration costs are incurred.

With this aim in mind, a distinctly different comprehensive community approach to preventing and reducing gang violence was formed in Chicago in 1999, named CeaseFire Chicago, later changed to Cure Violence (L-2). Cure Violence uses an evidence-based public health approach to reduce shootings and killings with highly trained street violence interrupters, outreach workers, public education campaigns, and community mobilization. It uniquely approaches violence as an infectious disease. "We're trying to interrupt the next event, the next transmission, the next violent activity" (founder Gary Slutkin, in Kotlowitz, 2008, p. 1). Cure Violence works to identify, engage, and promote change among those gang members most likely to be involved in shootings or killings; detect and interrupt events that could lead to violence or retaliation; and change norms about the acceptance and use of violence (Howell & Young, 2013).

Rather than aiming to directly change the behaviors of a large number of individuals, Cure Violence outreach workers concentrate on changing the behavior and risky activities of a small number of selected members of the community who have a high chance of either "being shot" or "being a shooter" in the immediate future (Howell & Young, 2013, p. 40). To stem the cycle of retaliatory violence, violence interrupters (mostly former gang members) work alone or in pairs mediating conflicts between gangs and high-risk individuals on the streets and in hospital emergency rooms. With reality therapy, they interject themselves into on-the-spot decision making by individuals at risk of shooting others, helping potential shooters weigh the likely disastrous, life-changing outcomes against perceived short-term gains. Long-term change agents (outreach workers) address key immediate causes of violence, including norms regarding violence, and serve as positive role models for young people, steering them to resources such as jobs or educational training and needed services.

An independent evaluation (Skogan, et. al., 2008) found significantly reduced homicides and shootings in six of the seven Cure Violence sites, in some of the most violent, gang-ridden communities in Chicago. A later research update found that the program worked to decrease violence with 40 of the most violent gangs in Chicago (Ransford, Kane, Metzger, Quintana, & Slutkin, 2010). An evaluation of a sister program in Baltimore (Webster, Whitehill, Vernick, & Curriero, 2013) drew similar conclusions. Cure Violence has been replicated in six Illinois cities outside Chicago, and in neighborhoods in Baltimore, Maryland; Kansas City, Missouri; New Orleans, Louisiana; New York City and other neighborhoods in New York; Philadelphia, Pennsylvania; and Puerto Rico (Howell & Young, 2013).

W. Miller's (1962) evaluation of a comprehensive Boston program is one of the most rigorous gang program evaluations ever conducted. (This program no longer exists.) For three years, project staff in the Midcity Project (established in Roxbury, Boston, in 1954) provided intensive services to 400 members of seven gangs. This "total community" project consisted of three major program components: community organization, family service, and gang work. The project aimed to open channels of access to legitimate opportunities, especially in the education and employment areas. The project plan was comprehensive and unusually well implemented. Nevertheless, Miller's (1962) evaluation reported only a "negligible impact" (p. 187). However, the actual impact was larger than Miller's statistical analysis suggested, based on Hodgkinson and colleagues' (2009) systematic review of comprehensive gang programs.

The Utility of Gang Intelligence Databases. Gang intelligence databases hold a great deal of potential as a tool for targeting chronic and violent gang offenders. In an Arizona study, Katz and colleagues (2000) compared the criminal histories of gang members and associates documented by the Mesa Police Department's Gang Unit with undocumented delinquent youth in the files of the Maricopa County Juvenile Probation Department. This comparison revealed that documented gang members and associates of gang members were significantly more criminally active than their undocumented delinquent counterparts. This research suggests that crime control benefits can accrue from maintaining accurate and useable intelligence information on chronic and violent gang offenders. However, Barrows and Huff (2009) and Caudill and colleagues (2014) caution that such databases can be misused, if unaffiliated persons are inadvertently entered into the intelligence system. Therefore, it is very important to ensure that definitions of gang membership are explicit and members are accurately classified. State and local agencies that receive federal funds to operate criminal intelligence systems must comply with specific regulations, including those in 28 CFR Part 23. Technical assistance reviews of criminal intelligence systems and their compliance with the regulations have been provided at no charge through funding from the U.S. Department of Justice, Bureau of Justice Assistance. These reviews should address special procedures for handling criminal intelligence information on juveniles. More frequent purging of the information on juveniles should also be considered, as suggested by research, presented in Chapter 3, which shows most adolescents who join a gang remain in it for less than one year. One process for protecting non gang juveniles is to "firewall" them in the criminal intelligence systems, restricting the dissemination of potentially incorrect information on their gang involvement. Barrows and Huff draw attention to the Minnesota guidelines for operating the State's GangNET intelligence system.

Intelligence-Led Policing. Evaluation research to date provides fairly robust evidence that hot spots policing is an effective crime prevention strategy (Braga, Papachristos, & Hureau, 2012). Greater benefits, however, may come from American intelligence-led policing (ILP). In recent years, ILP has proved to be an advanced technique for combating well-organized gangs. ILP "is executive implementation of the intelligence cycle to support proactive decision making for resource allocation and crime prevention . . . At its core, ILP helps leaders make informed decisions to address agency priorities" (Bureau of Justice Assistance, 2009, p. 4). The five key steps in implementing ILP are (1) an information collection plan; (2) analysis that connects data by linking incidents, activities, or criminal behaviors; (3) producing intelligence reports on the analysis results; (4) operational strategies that are based on the intelligence reports; and (5) an evaluation of the results. San Diego's anti-gang initiative that integrated law enforcement components is an excellent illustration of how ILP led to successful control of established gangs. The San Diego Police Department strategy is referred to as the "West Coast Offense" because it is a flexible, fast, and well-thought-out method of scoring high-profile arrests of gang leaders quickly and often. Gang-related violence, which accounts for around 35% of San Diego's homicides, declined dramatically. Additionally, a number of the most violent gang sets were deactivated.

The Evidence-Based Comprehensive Gang Program Model

In 1987, the OJJDP launched a Juvenile Gang Suppression and Intervention Research and Development Program. In the first phase, Spergel (1990) and also Spergel and Curry (1993) conducted a comprehensive national assessment of organized agency and community group responses to gang problems in the United States. It remains the only national assessment of efforts to combat gangs. In the second phase, the Comprehensive, Community-Wide Gang Program Model was developed (Spergel 1995; Spergel & Curry, 1993; Spergel et al. 1992, 1994) as the final product of the gang research and development program. In several tests and demonstrations of this model over the past 15 years, this program model has been called the Little Village Gang Violence Reduction Program; the Spergel Model; the Comprehensive Gang Program Model; the Comprehensive Gang Prevention, Intervention, and Suppression Program Model (L-2); and the Gang Reduction Program. Spergel's prototype gang program model was the Crisis Intervention Services Project (CRISP) that he implemented successfully in Chicago in the 1980s (Spergel, 1983). An international meta-analysis of comprehensive gang programs (Hodgkinson et al., 2009) found that this project produced the largest reduction in gang crime of all programs included in this systematic review.

In 1993, the initial version of the Comprehensive Gang Program Model was implemented in the Little Village neighborhood of Chicago, a low-income and working-class community that is approximately 90% Mexican American (Spergel, 2007). The Little Village Gang Violence Reduction Program targeted mainly older members (ages 17 to 24) of two of the area's most violent Mexican American gangs, the Latin Kings and the Two Six. The program targeted and provided services to individual gang members (rather than to the gangs as groups). Specifically, the Little Village program targeted more than 200 of the "shooters" (i.e., the influential members or leaders of the two gangs). As a whole, these two gangs accounted for about 75% of felony gang violence in the Little Village community. The process evaluation (Spergel et al., 2006) revealed that it was implemented with high fidelity on most "Program Implementation Characteristics" (Table 10.3), as indicated by the scored "Levels of Implementation" for the Chicago site.

The priority goal of the project was to reduce the extremely high level of gang violence among youth who were already involved in the two gangs; drug-related activity was not specifically targeted. The main goal was to be accomplished by a combination of outreach work, an intervention team, case management, youth services, and suppression. Virtually all of the outreach youth workers were former members of the two target gangs. Their program-related activities included crisis intervention, family and individual counseling and referrals for services, and surveillance and suppression activities. Altogether, Spergel (2007) observed a good balance of services and suppression.

Each of the intervention team members applied their own skills in providing services to project youth and supplying contacts for others. In due course, the team (mainly outreach youth workers, police, and probation officers) convened biweekly and exchanged information on violence that was occurring (or about to occur) in the community. Suppression contacts, made mainly by project police, reduced the youth's interest in and attachment to the gang. Services such as job placement reduced target youth's time spent with other gang members.

Spergel (2007) examined the effects of the Little Village project on the approximately 200 hardcore gang youth targeted for services during the period in which the program served them. The following are some key findings:

- Self-reports of criminal involvement showed that the program reduced serious violent and property crimes, and the frequency of various types of offenses including robbery, gang intimidations, and drive-by shootings.

- The program was more effective with older, more violent gang offenders than with younger, less violent offenders.

- Active gang involvement was reduced among project youth, mostly for older members, and this change was associated with less criminal activity.

- Most youth in both targeted gangs improved their educational and employment status during the program period.

- Employment was associated with a general reduction in youth's criminal activity, especially in regard to reductions in drug dealing.

Spergel (2007) next compared arrests among project youth versus two control groups: one that received minimal services, and the other that received no services from project workers. This comparison revealed the following:

- Program youth had significantly fewer total violent crime and drug arrests.

- The project had no significant effect on total arrests, property arrests, or other minor crime arrests.

Spergel (2007) also compared community-wide effects of the project on arrests in Little Village versus other nearby communities with high rates of gang crime. His analysis compared arrests in the periods before and during the program's implementation and revealed the following:

- The project was less effective in its overall impact on the behavior of the target gangs as a whole— that is, changing the entrenched pattern of gangbanging and gang crime among the target gangs—than in reducing crime among targeted members. Gang violence was on the upswing during the project period (1992 to 1997) in this general area of Chicago, one of the deadliest gang-violence areas of the city, but the increase in homicides and other serious violent gang crimes was lower among the Latin Kings and Two Six compared with the other Latino and African American gangs in the area.

- Similarly, the increase in serious violent gang crimes was lower in Little Village than in all other comparable communities. Residents and representatives of various organizations likewise perceived a significant reduction in overall gang crime and violence in Little Village during the program period.

Table 10.3   Program Implementation Characteristics: Degree of Importance and Levels of Implementation

Program Implementation Characteristics		Degree of Importance to Program Success[†]	Levels of Implementation by Project Site[‡]					
			Chicago	Mesa	Riverside	Bloomington-Normal	San Antonio	Tucson
Program Elements (Structure)	City/county leadership	***	2	4	4	1	1	1
	Steering committee	**	1	4	3	1	1	0
	Interagency street team/ coordination	***	4	4	3	0	0	0
	Grassroots involvement	*	3	1	1	0	1	0
	Social services: youth work, individual counseling, family treatment, and recreation	**	3	3	3	2	3	3
	Criminal justice participation	***	4	4	4	1	1	0
	School participation	**	1	3	3	3	2	0
	Employment and training	**	3	1	4	3	1	0
	Lead agency/ management/ commitment	***	4	4	4	0	0	0
Strategies	Social intervention: outreach and crisis intervention	**	4	3	3	1	1	0
	Community mobilization: interagency and grassroots	**	1	3	2	1	0	0

(Continued)

Table 10.3 (Continued)

Program Implementation Characteristics		Degree of Importance to Program Success[†]	Levels of Implementation by Project Site[‡]					
			Chicago	Mesa	Riverside	Bloomington-Normal	San Antonio	Tucson
	Provision of social opportunities: education, job, and culture	**	3	2	2	2	1	0
	Suppression	***	4	4	3	0	0	0
	Organizational change and development	***	2	4	4	0	0	0
Operating Principle	Targeting gang members/at-risk gang youth	***	4	2	3	1	3	3
	Balance of service	***	4	3	3	0	0	0
	Intensity of service	*	4	3	3	1	0	0
	Continuity of service	**	2	1	2	2	0	2

Source: Spergel et al., 2006, pp. 216–217; National Gang Center, 2010, Table A1, p. 43.

[†]Importance of characteristic to success: *** = extremely, ** = moderately, * = somewhat

[‡]Levels of implementation: 4 = excellent, 3 = good, 2 = fair, 1 = poor, 0 = none

In summary, the outcomes for the Little Village project are consistent for violent crimes across analyses at all three impact levels: (1) individual, (2) group (gang), and (3) community (especially in the views of residents). The evaluation suggested that a youth outreach (or social intervention) strategy may be more effective in reducing the violent behavior of younger, less violent, gang youth. A combined youth outreach and police suppression strategy might be more effective with older, more criminally active and violent gang youth, particularly with respect to drug-related crimes.

Interactive and collaborative project outreach worker efforts combining suppression, social support, and provision of social services were shown to be most effective in changing the criminal involvement of gang members. Larger program dosages (multiple providers and greater frequency and duration of services) proved to be important and were associated with reduced levels of arrests for violent crimes. Four types of services or sanctions predicted successful outcomes among program youth: (1) suppression (particularly by police), (2) job referrals by youth outreach workers, (3) school referrals (mainly by outreach youth workers), and (4) program dosage (contacts by all workers together).

The Six-Site Comprehensive Gang Program Model Evaluation

The Comprehensive Gang Program Model (CGPM) (L-2) has demonstrated effectiveness in multiple cities (Cahill & Hayeslip, 2010; Hayeslip & Cahill, 2009; Spergel, 2007; Spergel et al., 2006). Researchers looked at six cities in the initial evaluation of the model; they compared youth and neighborhoods that received CGPM programming with matched comparison groups of youth and neighborhoods that did not receive the programming (Spergel et al., 2006). They found that the program was implemented with high fidelity in three of six sites (Chicago, IL; Riverside, CA; and Mesa, AZ). In these three sites, there were statistically significant reductions in gang violence, and in two of these sites, there were statistically significant reductions in drug-related offenses when compared with the control groups of youth and neighborhoods (Spergel et al., 2006). (For a site-by-site summary of the degree of fidelity to the CGPM, see Table 10.3.)

At the successful sites, a key factor was length of time that clients were engaged in the program. When youth were in the program for two or more years, there were fewer arrests for all types of offenses. In general, arrest reductions were greater among older youth and females compared to younger youth and males. General deterrence effects (across the project area) were not as strong as the program effects for individual youth. Nevertheless, these three sites were somewhat successful in integrating police suppression with service-oriented strategies. In summary, the Spergel research team's (2006) evaluation indicates that, when properly implemented, a combination of intervention and suppression strategies was successful in reducing the gang problem.

An analysis of program strategy revealed that collaboration among outreach workers was more effective in reducing arrests, particularly for younger youth engaged, or about to be engaged, in violent behavior. Outreach (opportunities provision) contacts alone were especially effective in reducing drug-use and drug-selling arrests. However, the interaction of outreach and suppression strategies was more effective with chronic offenders and older youth than were outreach contacts alone, particularly for those youth with preprogram arrests for property crime. Overall, larger program dosages (multiple providers and greater frequency and duration of services) proved to be important and were associated with reduced levels of arrests for violent crimes.

Spergel's (2010b) later preliminary analysis across all six sites using the propensity-score matching statistical procedure to construct more exact treatment and control groups (nearly 900 youth) showed even more positive results in support of the comprehensive, community-wide approach. In the multivariate analyses, program youth, compared to equivalent non-served comparison youth, reduced their felony violence arrests by 60% in the inclusive six-site sample, and by 220% among youth who had violence arrests either in the preprogram or program period. Drug arrests were even more highly significantly reduced by program youth compared to non-served equivalent youth—3.4 times in the inclusive six-site sample. Older youth, 19 and older, did better than younger youth in reducing arrests for violence, but not drug arrests. Females generally did better than males in reducing arrests, except for drug arrests. There was little difference in changes in arrest patterns for youth of different racial/ethnic backgrounds. A very significant finding was that youth who were in the program longer did better than those who were in for shorter periods. Also very important, the comprehensive gang-program approach significantly hastened aging out of the gang structure and process.

In a later evaluation of the CGPM in four cities (Los Angeles, CA; Richmond, VA; Milwaukee, WI; and North Miami Beach, FL), researchers concluded that the model was successfully implemented in all four sites despite substantial variation in the nature of the sites' gang problems, albeit with varying impacts (Hayeslip & Cahill, 2009). The researchers also found that although results varied across outcomes, one or more indicators of crime reduction were seen.

The Los Angeles Gang Reduction Program (LA GRP) site is located in the Boyle Heights area, three miles east of downtown Los Angeles. This area is home to a large Latino immigrant population, predominantly from Mexico. Five major gangs inhabited the target area. The LA GRP program model included prevention, intervention, and suppression components. Overall, Hayeslip and Cahill (2009) found the LA GRP to achieve full and effective implementation. Findings revealed that shots-fired calls declined significantly post-implementation, as did violent gang crimes. The trends for all gang crimes were similar in the target area and the comparison area, although gang crimes decreased more in the target area after the implementation.

In sum, the CGPM has demonstrated evidence of its effectiveness in reducing gang violence when fully implemented with program fidelity. Although the research to date has been primarily on the intervention and suppression components, the CGPM holds promise for integrating prevention activities with intervention programs and suppression strategies. Research to date on the CGPM supports the following outcomes:

- A combined youth outreach and police suppression strategy appears to be more effective with older, more criminally active and violent gang youth, particularly with respect to drug-related crimes.

- Interactive and collaborative efforts, combining prevention, suppression, social support, and provision of social services, were shown to be most effective in changing criminal involvement of gang members.

- Larger service dosages (multiple providers and greater frequency and duration of services) were associated with reduced levels of arrests for violent crimes.

- Reductions were larger for older youth, 19 and older, than for younger youth in reducing violence arrests.

Multiple replications of the CGPM have provided insight into best practices (National Gang Center, 2010). Core elements crucial to successful implementation of the Model include the following:

- An effective Steering Committee convened by community leaders and policymakers to share responsibility for addressing local gang problems.

- A comprehensive assessment for the purpose of identifying three key target groups: (1) at-risk youth for prevention strategies, (2) gang-involved youth for intervention strategies, and (3) violent gangs and gang leaders for integrated intervention and suppression strategies. The assessment also inventories existing programs and services. This step is critical for successful integration of multiple strategies (National Gang Center, 2010).

- A multidisciplinary Intervention Team that manages cases for the coordinated delivery of targeted services to gang members who have been identified through screening criteria drawn from the assessment.

- Once the Intervention Team has been convened, street outreach workers play an active role in connecting gang members to necessary services. Outreach workers are not only the primary source of program referrals; they often play an active role in delivering services and working closely with community service providers. In addition, outreach workers are the Intervention Team's "eyes and ears" on the street, giving the team perspective on the personal aspects of gang conflicts and violence, and how these affect the team's clients (Arciaga & Gonzalez, 2012). Evaluations have substantiated that well-implemented outreach work is essential for success (Hayeslip & Cahill, 2009; Spergel et al., 2006; see also Howell, in press).

- A project coordinator who can serve as liaison between the Steering Committee and the Intervention Team. Sustained leadership is critical for long-term program success and to ensure the effectiveness of the program coordinator (Hayeslip & Cahill, 2009).

Compatibility of the Comprehensive Gang Program Model and Operation Ceasefire

Braga and Hureau (2012) make a strong case for integrating the CGPM and Operation Ceasefire. Their insights are compelling. First, both models are driven by strategic problem analysis. Second, both models employ suppression strategies in targeting high-rate offenders. In the Comprehensive Gang Program Model Continuum (Figure 9.5), this is Level 1. Operation Ceasefire relies on law enforcement and probation for control/restraint of active violent gang members; so does the CGPM. Third, both models call for social intervention and opportunity provision for less violent gang members. The main distinction is that the CGPM specifically calls for an intervention team with outreach services. But in a similar emphasis, Operation Ceasefire aims to increase its "preventive power by offering gang members any assistance they need: protection from their enemies, drug treatment, access to education and job training programs and the like" (Braga & Hureau, 2012, p. 144). Fourth, both models call for community mobilization strategies to promote community-wide engagement in carrying out the multi-component strategy that each of these models promotes, even though the particulars of the respective strategies may differ. The potential benefits of integrating these two evidence-based models in a jurisdiction seem very worthwhile, particularly given the prospect of producing a stronger continuum, with the CGPM giving priority to the lower and middle levels of the continuum, and Operation Ceasefire focused on the upper level.

On the Horizon

The Blueprints for Gang Prevention project at the University of Maryland is conducting a randomized controlled trial of a popular model program for rehabilitating juvenile delinquents, Functional Family Therapy (FFT), to ascertain its effectiveness in reducing gang involvement and delinquency among current gang members. This program promises to deliver positive results because family problems are widespread among gang members (Chapter 5). However, in the long term, effectiveness with gang members is likely to be attenuated, based on Boxer's (2011) findings on lower treatment completion rates for these often-intractable clients, and research showing routine loss of program fidelity when model programs are moved into everyday practice (Rhoades et al., 2012; Welsh et al., 2010). A major implication of this research is that outreach services should be linked with all gang intervention programs to boost program completions and also promote desistance from gangs. Gang members often suffer from multiple marginality—particularly alienation from families and schools—thus their everyday lives lack structure and generally are chaotic, causing them to miss treatment sessions, and continue to choose gang life over structured treatment. Frequent arrests—which are common for active gang members—also interfere with treatment completion (Boxer, 2011).

Because of its impressive track record with serious delinquents (Henggeler & Schoenwald, 2011), the Multisystemic Therapy (MST) program surely will prove to be effective in reducing delinquency with gang members—provided it is implemented with high fidelity. This is a reasonable expectation because MST views youths as being nested within a complex of interactive systems that encompass individual, family, and extra-familial (peer, school, neighborhood) factors (Henggeler, Schoenwald, Borduin, Rowland, & Cunningham, 2009). MST targets the specific factors in each youth's and family's ecology (family, peer, school, and neighborhood) that are contributing to antisocial behavior. As seen in Chapter 5, these are the main developmental domains that elevate youths' risk of joining a gang and remaining active. MST interventions are pragmatic and goal oriented, and they emphasize the development of family strengths. To accomplish the goal of family empowerment, MST also addresses identified barriers to effective parenting (e.g., parental drug abuse, parental mental health problems) and helps family members to build an indigenous social support network (e.g., with friends, extended family, neighbors, fellow church members). A study of the effectiveness of MST with gang members is under way, led by Paul Boxer, and it is quite likely to yield positive results for delinquency reduction and desistance from gang activity. Results of this evaluation of MST with gang members in eight states' juvenile justice systems who were routinely served in ongoing MST programs are forthcoming. Preliminary results (only on success of program completion to date) are very encouraging (Boxer, 2011).

Nevertheless, caution should be exercised when considering the replication of an "exemplary" or "model" program. As noted in Chapter 9, state and local agencies face many challenges in the course of moving highly regarded exemplary or model programs into routine practice with high fidelity. Howell and colleagues (2014) identify several obstacles that are common in everyday settings. First, the model program is likely to serve a more heterogeneous population than was used in the original studies. Second, the service infrastructure within which the model program must operate is likely to be weaker than that organized by the program developer when conducting the evaluation research. Third, well-trained service providers and sufficient funds for personnel and capital expenditures may not be available in everyday practice settings to fully meet the requirements of a model program. Generally speaking, anticipated outcomes often are attenuated when model programs are scaled up or rolled out for general application.

◆ Concluding Observations

There is good news herein about the availability of effective gang programs. The evidence base for gang programming has grown enormously in the past decade. At the turn of this century, there were no proven effective gang programs (Howell, 2000). Presently, at least a dozen programs have shown some evidence of effectiveness in reducing gang crime, and several nongang programs have also shown good potential for preventing or reducing gang-related activity (Table 10.2; see also Chapter 9). However, there are several important caveats. Most important, none of the rated-effective programs has shown dramatic effects; rather, most effects are modest. Some criminologists expect large impacts from gang programs, including Klein and Maxson (2006), but it is unrealistic to expect uniformly large crime reductions from programs that are working with active members of violent gangs. Across the board, recidivism reductions from juvenile delinquency programs are attenuated for juvenile samples with aggressive/violent histories (Lipsey, 2009). Moreover, desistance from gangs is delayed among "embedded" members (Pyrooz et al., 2013). It is encouraging, however, that four of the evidence-based gang programs were demonstrated to be effective in Chicago and Los Angeles (two in each city), indisputably the reigning capitals of gang violence. This is a major source of encouragement, particularly given that anti-gang program development is yet in its infancy. Just one gang research and development program has been undertaken, the CGPM. However, it has produced considerable evidence of effectiveness in several controlled studies, none of which was a site chosen by Spergel, the CGPM developer.

Communities that have gangs need to undertake a comprehensive assessment that begins with risk factors. The National Gang Center has developed an assessment protocol that any community can use to assess its gang problem. This protocol provides guidance on the associated gang prevention, intervention, and suppression continuum of programs and strategies that make sense for communities with varied gang problems. Resource materials that assist communities in developing an action plan to implement the CGPM are also available. Prevention programs are needed to target youth at risk of gang involvement, to reduce the number of youth who join gangs; intervention programs and strategies are needed to provide sanctions and services for younger youth who are actively involved, to separate them from gangs; and law enforcement suppression strategies are needed to target the most violent gangs and older, criminally active gang members. A balanced and integrated approach is most likely to be effective.

Another theme in the evidence-based gang programs reviewed here is the positive results from a number of multidisciplinary or comprehensive programs. The integration of strategies (e.g., provision of support to members in separating from gangs with suppression that discourages further involvement in gang crime) and services (multiple service providers and high dosage levels) has emerged as a predominant feature of effective gang programs. In addition, Hodgkinson and colleagues' (2009) systematic review of comprehensive gang programs suggests that the key features of effective programs are (a) case management (an intervention team), (b) community involvement in the planning and delivery of interventions, and (c) expertise sharing among involved agencies. Hodgkinson's team found that the higher quality programs that produced positive effects included one or more of the following mechanisms of change:

- A case management strategy for service provision that was personalized to individual offenders
- Community involvement in the planning and delivery of interventions
- Expertise sharing between agencies
- Provision of incentives to gang members to change their offending behavior, including educational opportunities, tattoo removal, and financial assistance (pp. 2–3)

Because of the tradition of thinking of "programs" as the only solution to crime problems, observers sometimes fail to recognize that the CGPM is a *program structure*, an organizational framework that guides users through a systematic data gathering, analysis, and strategic planning process, and provides an administrative framework for an organized community initiative that becomes a permanent component of local governance. Thus, successful implementation depends on community stakeholders' (a) acknowledgment that they possibly or actually have a gang problem and (b) a willingness to work together in solving it. Implementation failures are therefore shortcomings of community stakeholders, not inherent flaws in the framework. Granted, it is difficult to intervene effectively when gangs are entrenched in the cracks of society and require institutional and organizational modifications to reduce their impact. As of this writing, no shortcuts have been found in solving "the gang problem," which, in its most serious forms, is directly linked to fractures in social, cultural, educational, legal, and economic systems, many of which are referenced in Chapters 1 and 4. Therefore, the impact of a single program in these multifaceted contexts is expected to be minimal. Citywide and countywide initiatives are needed because gang members and other violent offenders often commit crimes outside their own neighborhoods. In addition, this model promotes organizational change, particularly in governmental agencies, and integration of multiple services provided by various agencies.

The OJJDP Strategic Planning Tool described earlier in this chapter identifies both evidence-based and promising gang programs, using scientific criteria for determining "effective" programs that nine federal agencies agreed upon (http://www.nationalgangcenter.gov/About/Strategic-Planning-Tool). Because of the dearth of well-researched gang programs, the SPT review process does not aim to identify exemplary programs. Two often-cited negative reviews of gang programs have two limitations in common: failure to include all of the available studies and unevenness in application of evidence-based criteria (Gravel, Bouchard, Descormiers, Wong, & Morselli, 2013; Klein & Maxson, 2006). Among the gang program reviews to date, Hodgkinson and colleagues' (2009) analysis is the most systematic and strongest methodologically, employing rigorous meta-analytic methods, and this study also is most comprehensive in coverage of controlled studies of comprehensive gang programs. Thus we suggest building on the foundation Hodgkinson and colleagues have established, to examine the effectiveness of the entire continuum of gang prevention, intervention, and suppression programs.

DISCUSSION TOPICS

1. How would you go about helping an active gang member negotiate his or her way out of a serious gang?

2. Why is law enforcement suppression sometimes effective when integrated with services?

3. If you were a state or federal program manager in charge of designing an anti-gang program, describe the key components you would require.

4. Revisit the Chapter 9 class exercise you carried out for prevention programs using the OJJDP Strategic Planning Tool (www.nationalgangcenter.gov/SPT) to build an ideal program continuum. Next, add intervention and suppression programs and strategies.

5. How would you go about tailoring your continuum of intervention and suppression programs and strategies to adolescent girls and young women?

RECOMMENDATIONS FOR FURTHER READING

Gang Intervention and Suppression Program Evaluations

Braga, A. A., & Hureau, D. M. (2012). Strategic problem analysis to guide comprehensive gang violence reduction strategies. In E.Gebo & B. J. Bond (Eds.), *Beyond suppression: Community strategies to reduce gang violence* (pp. 129–151). Lanham, MD: Lexington Books.

Braga, A. A., & Weisburd, D. L. (2012). The effects of focused deterrence strategies on crime: A systematic review and meta-analysis of the empirical evidence. *Journal of Research in Crime and Delinquency, 49,* 323–358.

Gravel, J., Bouchard, M., Descormiers, K., Wong, J. S., & Morselli, C. (2013). Keeping promises: A systematic review and a new classification of gang control strategies. *Journal of Criminal Justice, 41,* 228–242.

Hodgkinson J., Marshall, S., Berry, G., Reynolds, P., Newman, M., Burton, E., Dickson, K., & Anderson, J. (2009). *Reducing gang-related crime: A systematic review of "comprehensive" interventions. Summary report.* London: EPPI-Centre, Social Science Research Unit, Institute of Education, University of London.

Howell, J. C. (2000). *Youth gang programs and strategies.* Washington, DC: U.S. Department of Justice, Office of Juvenile Justice and Delinquency Prevention.

Howell, J. C. (2010). Lessons learned from gang program evaluations: Prevention, intervention, suppression, and comprehensive community approaches. In R. J. Chaskin (Ed.), *Youth gangs and community intervention: Research, practice, and evidence* (pp. 51–75). New York: Columbia University Press.

Howell, J. C. (in press). The legacy of Irving A. Spergel. In S. Decker & D.C. Pyrooz (Eds.), *The Wiley handbook of gangs.* Hoboken, NJ: John Wiley & Sons.

Klein, M. W., & Maxson, C. L. (2006). *Street gang patterns and policies.* New York: Oxford University Press.

OJJDP Comprehensive Gang Program Model Evaluations

Cahill, M., & Hayeslip, D. (2010). *Findings from the Evaluation of OJJDP's Gang Reduction Program* (Juvenile Justice Bulletin). Washington, DC: U.S. Department of Justice, Office of Juvenile Justice and Delinquency Prevention.

Hayeslip, D., & Cahill, M. (2009). *Community collaboratives addressing youth gangs: Final evaluation findings from the Gang Reduction Program.* Washington, DC: Urban Institute.

Howell, J. C. (in press). The legacy of Irving A. Spergel. In S. Decker & D.C. Pyrooz (Eds.), *The Wiley handbook of gangs.* Hoboken, NJ: John Wiley & Sons.

Spergel, I. A. (2007). *Reducing youth gang violence: The Little Village Gang Project in Chicago.* Lanham, MD: AltaMira Press.

Spergel, I. A. (2010). Community gang programs: Theory, models, and effectiveness. In R. J. Chaskin (Ed.), *Youth gangs and community intervention: Research, practice, and evidence* (pp. 222–248). New York: Columbia University Press.

Spergel, I. A., Wa, K. M., & Sosa, R. V. (2006). The comprehensive, community-wide, gang program model: Success and failure. In J. F. Short & L. A. Hughes (eds.), *Studying Youth Gangs* (pp. 203–224). Lanham, MD: AltaMira Press.

Risk Factors and Treatment Needs of Active Gang Members

Baglivio, M. T., Jackowski, K., Greenwald, M.A., and Howell, J.C. (2014). Serious, violent, and chronic juvenile offenders: A statewide analysis of prevalence and prediction of subsequent recidivism using risk and protective factors. *Criminology and Public Policy, 13,* 83–116.

Howell, J. C., Lipsey, M. W., & Wilson, J. J. (2014). *A handbook for evidence-based juvenile justice systems.* Lanham, MD: Lexington Books.

Howell, M. Q., & Lassiter, W. (2011). *Prevalence of gang-involved youth in NC.* Raleigh: North Carolina Department of Juvenile Justice and Delinquency Prevention.

Gun Availability and Gang Violence

Cook, P. J., & Ludwig, J. (2006). The social costs of gun ownership. *Journal of Public Economics, 90,* 379–391.

Lizotte, A. J., Tesoriero, J. M., Thornberry, T. P., & Krohn, M. D. (1994). Patterns of adolescent firearms ownership and use. *Justice Quarterly, 11,* 51–73.

Sheley, J. F., & Wright, J. D. (1993). *Gun acquisition and possession in selected juvenile samples* (Research in Brief). Washington, DC: National Institute of Justice and Office of Juvenile Justice and Delinquency Prevention.

Sheley, J. F., & Wright, J. D. (1995). *In the line of fire: Youth, guns and violence in urban America.* Hawthorne, NY: Aldine De Gruyter.

Watkins, A., Huebner, B., & Decker, S. (2008). Patterns of gun acquisition, carrying and use among juvenile and adult arrestees: Evidence from a high-crime city. *Justice Quarterly, 25,* 674–700.

Suppression

Braga, A. A., Pierce, G. L., McDevitt, J., Bond, B. J., & Cronin, S. (2008). The strategic prevention of gun violence among gang-involved offenders. *Justice Quarterly, 25,* 132–162.

Bynum, T. S., & Varano, S. P. (2003). The anti-gang initiative in Detroit: An aggressive enforcement approach to gangs. In S. H. Decker (Ed.), *Policing gangs and youth violence* (pp. 214–238). Belmont, CA: Wadsworth/Thompson Learning.

Kennedy, D. M. (2010). Taking criminology seriously: Narratives, norms, networks, and common ground. In R. J. Chaskin (Ed.), *Youth gangs and community intervention: Research, practice, and evidence* (pp. 206–221). New York: Columbia University Press.

Ludwig, J. (2005). Better gun enforcement, less crime. *Criminology and Public Policy, 4,* 677–716.

National Research Council. (2004). *Firearms and violence: A critical review.* Washington, DC: The National Academies Press.

Papachristos, A. V., Meares, T., & Fagan, J. (2005). *Attention felons: Evaluating Project Safe Neighborhoods in Chicago.* Chicago: The Law School, University of Chicago.

Rosenfeld, R., Fornango, R., and Baumer, E. (2005). Did Ceasefire, Compstat, and Exile reduce homicide? *Criminology and Public Policy, 4,* 419–449.

Utility of Gang Intelligence Databases

Barrows, J., & Huff, C. R. (2009). Gangs and public policy: Constructing and deconstructing gang databases. *Criminology and Public Policy, 8,* 675–703.

Bjerregaard, B. (2003). Anti-gang legislation and its potential impact: The promises and the pitfalls. *Criminal Justice Policy Review, 14,* 171–192.

Caudill, J. W., Trulson, C. R., Marquart, J. W., & DeLisi, M. (2014, June 27). On gang affiliation, gang databases, and prosecutorial outcomes. *Crime & Delinquency.* DOI: 10.1177/0011128714541203.

Project Safe Neighborhoods

Healy, G. (2002). *There goes the neighborhood: The Bush-Ashcroft plan to "help" localities fight gun crime* (Policy Analysis No. 440). Washington, DC: Heritage Foundation.

Katz, C. M., & Webb, V. J. (2006). *Policing gangs in America.* New York: Cambridge University Press.

Ludwig, J. (2005). Better gun enforcement, less crime. *Criminology and Public Policy, 4,* 677–716.

McGarrell, E. F., & Chermak, S. (2003). Problem solving to reduce gangs and drug-related violence in Indianapolis. In S. H. Decker (Ed.), *Policing gangs and youth violence* (pp. 77–101). Belmont, CA: Wadsworth/Thompson Learning.

McGarrell, E. F., Hipple, N. K., Corsaro, N., Bynum, T. S., Perez, H., Zimmermann, C. A., et al. (2009). *Project Safe Neighborhoods—A national program to reduce gun crime: Final project report.* Lansing: Michigan State University.

NOTE

1. The administration of President George W. Bush.

Glossary

Age blocks: Middle childhood, ages 7 to 9; late childhood, ages 10 to 12; early adolescence, ages 13 to 15; late adolescence, ages 16 to 19; early adulthood, ages 20 to 25 (Loeber et al., 2008).

Anglo: Early Americans largely of English heritage and English territories (including the Scotch and Irish), and also Dutch, German, Swedish, and Scandinavian peoples (Pincus & Ehrlich, 1999, pp. 223–228). Also, in contemporary usage, *Anglo* is used to distinguish Americans (non-Hispanics) from Mexican Americans, Hispanics, or Latinos (Telles & Ortiz, 2008).

Backup: "Having a network of friends to protect a person from attack, with force if necessary" (Sullivan, 2006, p. 25).

Barrio: A neighborhood in a Mexican community (Vigil, 1988); also Puerto Rican neighborhoods or communities, such as East Harlem, known as El Barrio (Bourgois, 2003).

Block gangs: When adolescents in a bona fide gang strongly identify with their street block which they represent (see also the definition for *represent*).

Chicano: "An identity that symbolized cultural and political autonomy for Mexican Americans rather than assimilation and acceptance as white," particularly in association with the Chicano movement (Telles & Ortiz, 2008, pp. 92–93). This term also is used "to reflect the multiple heritage experience of Mexicans in the U.S., comprised of Indian, Spanish, Mexican, and Anglo backgrounds" (Vigil, 1998, pp. 1, 251–255).

Cholo: Marginal; living in a period between dominant races or cultures; a subcultural style of dress, walk, talk, values, and norms that reflects the mixed nature of Mexican, American, and street experiences (Vigil, 1993).

Claim: To declare one's gang affiliation or membership; to represent a gang.

Dissed: Disrespected.

Drug-related dispute: An argument associated with drug transactions, use, or a combination (Valdez et al., 2009).

Gang retaliation or revenge: Retribution associated with specific gang incident (Valdez, et al., 2009).

Gang rivalry: An ongoing feud between two gangs (Valdez et al., 2009).

Gang solidarity: Expression of shared goals, norms, and aims among gang members (camaraderie) (Valdez et al., 2009).

Gang sweeps: Police teams are deployed to a specific area with the main objective of arresting gang members (Klein, 1995, 2004).

Gangsta: Gang member.

Gangsta rap: Music popularized in the early 1990s that extols the gang lifestyle (Ro, 1996).

Go down: To attack or declare war on another gang (Perkins, 1987).

Green light: A Mexican Mafia mechanism for enforcing "taxing" (extorting) a percentage of barrio gangs' street-level drug sales. If a barrio did not pay up, barrio members in prison would be threatened or killed—green lighted (Vigil, 2007, p. 69).

Heart: Courage (Perkins, 1987).

Heater: Gun (Perkins, 1987).

Hispanic: "This term is used particularly by federal and state bureaucracies to refer to persons who reside in the United States who were born in, or trace their ancestry back to, one of 23 Spanish-speaking nations" (Moore & Pinderhughes, 1993, p. xi). Many of these individuals prefer to use the term *Chicano, Latino,* or *Mexican American.*

Homeboy: A fellow gang member; also a friend in the neighborhood.

Hood: The neighborhood.

Hybrid gang culture: Gang culture characterized by a mixture of graffiti and symbols (that are copied from other gangs); less concern over turf or territory; members of mixed race or ethnicity; members may belong to more than one gang; members may switch from one gang to another (Starbuck et al., 2001).

Jap: To ambush or attack someone (Perkins, 1987).

Klika: Spanish word for clique, or cohort within the gang (Vigil, 1988).

Latino: See *Hispanic.*

Locality: The major types of named place units found in the United States including cities, suburban areas, and counties (W. Miller, 2001).

Loco: Generally unrestrained conduct (J. Moore, 1991).

Locos: Crazies; usually in the gang context; shorthand for *vatos locos* (Vigil, 1988).

Locura: "A mind-set complex that values crazy or unpredictable thinking and acting" (Vigil, 1988, p. 178).

Muy loco: Getting drunk, loaded with drugs, and fighting (J. Moore, 1991).

Nor, Norteño: Northern California gangs (Al Valdez, 2007).

Odds ratio: A measure of the strength of the relationship between two variables (i.e., the number of times more likely).

O.G: Original Gangster; long-time gang member.

Pachucos: A transitional form of gang that evolved out of the *palomilla* cohorting tradition (age-graded groupings), the youngest of which might be considered "boy gangs" (Bogardus, 1926); more generally, the *pachuco* (subcultural) lifestyle of early Mexican Americans (J. Moore, 1978; Vigil, 1988, 1990).

Packing: Carrying a firearm (Perkins, 1987).

Palomilla: A Mexican term for an age or sex cohort (Vigil, 1988).

Persistent gang problem: Consistent reports of gang problems across all survey years (Egley et al., 2004). See *variable gang problem.*

Piece: A weapon, usually a gun (Perkins, 1987).

To play the dozen: To speak disparagingly of another person's family (Perkins, 1987).

Punk: "A boy who won't fight; a boy with no gang affiliation" (Perkins, 1987).

Racketeering: "Patterns of craft governance found in trades like construction, laundry, and kosher foods, where unions and associations enforced standard prices and wages through strikes, boycotts, and violence" (Cohen, 2003, p. 576).

Rep: "Reputation, usually a fighting reputation" (Perkins, 1987, p. 77).

Represent: "To assert a social claim to a social group or a very specific local area, such as a city block or a housing project, with the clear implication that the members of the group or the youthful residents of the area would provide backup" (Sullivan, 2006, p. 26).

Rolled on: "When several girls ambush one girl or a large group ambushes a smaller group" (Ness, 2010, p. 71).

Rolling out: A gang exit rite that entails a physical beating by several gang members (Valdez et al., 2009).

Rumble: Gang fight.

Set tripping: An insult or a challenge, often the catalyst for gang-related violence (Arciaga, Sakamoto, & Jones, 2010).

Shorty: Younger gang member (Papachristos, 2001).

Square: "One who doesn't like gangs" (Perkins, 1987, p. 78).

Sur, Sureños: Southern California gangs (Al Valdez, 2007).

Throw down: Challenge another gang or gang member.

Trajectories (in criminology): The classification of individuals according to their pattern of offending over time (Lacourse et al., 2003; Piquero, 2008); also displays of communities' distinct crime and gang histories across time and space (Griffiths & Chavez, 2004; Tita et al.,

2005), and dimensions of cities' gang problem histories (Howell et al., 2011).

Turf: "A gang's own territory; also street or sidewalk" (Perkins, 1987).

V.L. (Vata Loca): Crazy dudette (female gangster) (Al Valdez, 2007).

V.L. (Vato Loco): Crazy dude (male gangster) (Al Valdez, 2007).

Variable gang problem: Reported gang activity in one or more years but not in every year (Egley et al., 2004). See *persistent gang problem.*

Vata loco: "Literally, crazy guy; refers to wild and violent behavior" (Vigil, 1988, p. 180).

Veterano: "Veteran; an older gang member who has been through it all and is now a role model for younger members" (Vigil, 1988, p. 180).

Walked into the gang: An informal initiation ritual for Mexican youth who have lived in the barrio most of their lives and grown up with others in street socialization. In these instances, the ritual "is a pro forma affair—a couple of punches by close friends and they are in" (Vigil, 2007, p. 58).

Warlord: "Prime minister of gang or one who plans strategy" (Perkins, 1987, p. 79).

Zip gun: "A homemade gun capable of firing a .22 caliber bullet, made with a car [radio] aerial and a wooden stock or cap pistol frame" (Perkins, 1987, p. 79).

References

Acuna, R. (1981). *Occupied America*. New York: Harper & Row.

Adamshick, P. Z. (2010). The lived experience of girl-to-girl aggression in marginalized girls. *Qualitative Health Research, 20,* 541–555.

Adamson, C. (1998). Tribute, turf, honor and the American street gang: Patterns of continuity and change since 1820. *Theoretical Criminology, 2,* 57–84.

Adamson, C. (2000). Defensive localism in white and black: A comparative history of European-American and African-American youth gangs. *Ethnic and Racial Studies, 23,* 272–298.

Adler, F. (1975a). The rise of the female crook. *Psychology Today, 9,* 42–46, 112–114.

Adler, F. (1975b). *Sisters in crime: The rise of the new female criminal*. New York: McGraw-Hill.

Adler, P., Ovando, C., & Hocevar, D. (1984). Family correlates of gang membership: An exploratory study of Mexican-American youth. *Hispanic Journal of Behavioral Sciences, 6,* 65–76.

Advancement Project. (2005). *Education on lockdown: The schoolhouse to jailhouse track*. Washington, DC: Author.

Advancement Project. (2007). *Citywide gang activity reduction strategy: Phase III report*. Los Angeles: Author.

Agnew, R. (2005). *Why do criminals offend? A general theory of crime and delinquency*. Los Angeles: Roxbury Publishing Company.

Allender, D. M., & Marcell, F. (2003, June). Career criminals, security threat groups, and prison gangs. *FBI Law Enforcement Bulletin, 72*(6), 8–12.

Alleyne, E., & Wood, J. L. (2012). Gang membership: The psychological evidence. In F. Esbensen & C. L. Maxson (Eds.), *Youth gangs in international perspective: Results from the Eurogang Program of Research* (pp. 151–168). New York: Springer.

Alleyne, E., & Wood, J. L. (2014). Gang involvement: Social and environmental factors. *Crime & Delinquency, 60,* 547–568.

Alonso, A. A. (2004). Racialized identities and the formation of black gangs in Los Angeles. *Urban Geography, 25,* 658–674.

Alonso, A. A. (2008). Los Angeles names top ten gangs. Retrieved June 20, 2014, from http://www.streetgangs.com/features/los-angeles-names-top-ten-gangs#sthash.jejSy8Wr.dpbs

Alvarez, A., & Bachman, R. (1997). Predicting the fear of assault at school and while going to and from school in an adolescent population. *Violence and Victims, 12,* 69–85.

American Correctional Association. (1993). *Gangs in correctional facilities: A national assessment*. Laurel, MD: American Correctional Association.

American Probation and Parole Association and Institute for Intergovernmental Research. (2011). *Guidelines to gang reentry*. Lexington, KY: Author. Available on compact disk from the APPA: appa@csg.org.

Anbinder, T. (2001). *Five points*. New York: Free Press.

Anderson, E. (1998). The social ecology of youth violence. *Crime and Justice, 24,* 65–104.

Anderson, E. (1999). *Code of the street: Decency, violence, and the moral life of the inner city*. New York: W. W. Norton.

Anderson, N. (1926). *The hobo*. Chicago: University of Chicago Press.

Arbreton, A. J. A., & McClanahan, W. (2002). Targeted outreach: Boys & Girls Clubs of America's approach to gang prevention and intervention. Philadelphia: Public/Private Ventures.

Arciaga, M. (2001). *Evolution of prominent youth subcultures in America*. Tallahassee, FL: Institute for Intergovernmental Research, National Gang Center.

Arciaga, M. (2007). *Multidisciplinary gang intervention teams* (NYGC Bulletin No. 3). Tallahassee, FL: National Youth Gang Center.

Arciaga, M., & Gonzalez, V. (2012). *Street outreach and the Comprehensive Gang Model* (NGC Bulletin No. 7). Tallahassee, FL: National Gang Center.

Arciaga, M., Sakamoto, W., & Jones, E. F. (2010). *Responding to gangs in the school setting* (NYGC Bulletin No. 5). Tallahassee, FL: Institute for Intergovernmental Research, National Gang Center.

Arnett, J. J. (2000). Emerging adulthood: A theory of development from the late teens through the twenties. *American Psychologist, 55,* 469–480.

Arredondo, G. F. (2004). Navigating ethno-racial currents: Mexicans in Chicago, 1919–1939. *Journal of Urban History, 30,* 399–427.

Asbury, H. (1927). *Gangs of New York: An informal history of the underworld.* New York: Knopf.

Atlanta Public Housing Authority. (2010). *Atlanta Housing Authority 15 Year Progress Report: 1995–2010.* Atlanta: Atlanta Public Housing Authority.

Augimeri, L. K., & Koegl, C. J. (2012). Raising the bar: Transforming knowledge to practice for children in conflict with the law. In R. Loeber & B. C. Welsh (Eds), *The Future of Criminology* (pp. 204–210). Oxford: Oxford University Press.

Augimeri, L. K., Walsh, M., Liddon, A. D., & Dassinger, C. R. (2011). From risk identification to risk management: A comprehensive strategy for young children engaged in antisocial behavior. In D. W. Springer & A. Roberts (Eds.), *Juvenile justice and delinquency* (pp. 117–140). Sudbury, MA: Jones & Bartlett.

Augimeri, L. K., Walsh, M. M., & Slater, N. (2011). Rolling out SNAP, an evidence-based intervention: A summary of implementation, evaluation and research. *International Journal of Child, Youth and Family Studies, 2,* 330–352.

Augustyn, M. B., Thornberry, T. P., & Krohn, M. D. (2014). Gang membership and pathways to maladaptive parenting. *Journal of Research on Adolescence, 24,* 252–267.

Auletta, K. (1982). *The underclass.* New York: Random House.

Baglivio, M. T., Jackowski, K., Greenwald, M. A., Howell, J. C. (2014). Serious, violent, and chronic juvenile offenders: A statewide analysis of prevalence and prediction of subsequent recidivism using risk and protective factors. *Criminology and Public Policy, 13,* 83–116.

Ball, R. A., & Curry, G. D. (1995). The logic of definition in criminology: Purposes and methods for defining "gangs." *Criminology, 33,* 225–245.

Bankston, C. L. (1998). Youth gangs and the new second generation: A review essay. *Aggression and Violent Behavior, 3,* 33–45.

Barnoski, R. (2004). *Outcome evaluation of Washington State's research-based programs for juvenile offenders* (Document No. 04-01-1201). Olympia: Washington State Institute for Public Policy. Retrieved from http://www.wsipp.wa.gov/ReportFile/852

Barrows, J., & Huff, C. R. (2009). Gangs and public policy: Constructing and deconstructing gang databases. *Criminology and Public Policy, 8,* 675–703.

Batchelor, S. (2009). Girls, gangs and violence: Assessing the evidence. *Probation Journal, 56,* 399–414.

Battin, S. R., Hill, K. G., Abbott, R. D., Catalano, R. F., & Hawkins, J. D. (1998). The contribution of gang membership to delinquency beyond delinquent friends. *Criminology, 36,* 93–115.

Battin-Pearson S. R., Thornberry, T. P., Hawkins, J. D., & Krohn, M. D. (1998). *Gang membership, delinquent peers, and delinquent behavior* (Juvenile Justice Bulletin. Youth Gang Series). Washington, DC: Office of Juvenile Justice and Delinquency Prevention.

Becker, H. S. (1999). The Chicago school, so-called. *Qualitative Sociology, 22,* 3–12.

Beckett, K., & Sasson, T. (2004). *The politics of injustice: Crime and punishment in America* (2nd ed.). Thousand Oaks, CA: Pine Forge Press.

Behsudi, A. (2007, October 3). Asheville gang violence increasing rapidly: Residents, police try to counteract new challenge. *The Citizen-Times.* Retrieved from http://www.national gangcenter.gov/Gang-Related-News?st=NC

Bell, J., & Lim, N. (2005). Young once, Indian forever: Youth gangs in Indian Country. *The American Indian Quarterly, 29,* 626–650.

Bell, K. E. (2009). Gender and gangs: A quantitative comparison. *Crime and Delinquency, 55,* 363–387.

Bellair, P. E., & McNulty, T. L. (2009). Gang membership, drug selling, and violence in neighborhood context. *Justice Quarterly, 26,* 644–669.

Benda, B. B., Corwyn, R. F., & Toombs, N. J. (2001). Recidivism among adolescent serious offenders: Prediction of entry into the correctional system for adults. *Criminal Justice and Behavior, 28,* 588–613.

Bendixen, M., Endresen, I. M., & Olweus, D. (2006). Joining and leaving gangs: Selection and facilitation effects on self-reported antisocial behaviour in early adolescence. *European Journal of Criminology, 3,* 85–114.

Bennett, W., DiIulio, J., & Waters, J. (1996). *Body count.* New York: Simon & Schuster.

Bernard, W. (1949). *Jailbait.* New York: Greenberg.

Bernard, T. (1992). *The cycle of juvenile justice.* New York: Oxford University Press.

Bernburg, J. G., Krohn, M. D., & Rivera, C. J. (2006). Official labeling, criminal embeddedness, and subsequent delinquency: A longitudinal test of labeling theory. *Journal of Research in Crime and Delinquency, 43,* 67–88.

Berry, S. (2009, October 8). 13 suspected gang members arrested in Springfield drug sweep. *MassLive.com.* Retrieved from http://www.masslive.com/news/index.ssf/2009/10/nine_suspected_gang_members_ar.html

Berry, W. D., Ringquist, E. J., Fording, R. C., & Hanson, R. L. (2010). Measuring citizen and government ideology in the U.S. states: A re-appraisal. *State Politics and Policy Quarterly, 10,* 117–135.

Best, J., & Hutchinson, M. M. (1996). The gang initiation rite as a motif in contemporary crime discourse. *Justice Quarterly, 13,* 383–404.

Beyle, T. L. (2012). *Gubernatorial power: The institutional power ratings for the 50 governors of the United States*. University of North Carolina at Chapel Hill. Retrieved from http://www.unc.edu/~beyle/gubnewpwr.html

Bingenheimer, J. B., Brennan, R. T., & Earls, F. J. (2005). Firearm violence exposure and serious violent behavior. *Science, 308,* 1323–1326.

Bjerregaard, B. (2002a). Operationalizing gang membership: The impact measurement on gender differences in gang self-identification and delinquent involvement. *Women and Criminal Justice, 13,* 79–100.

Bjerregaard, B. (2002b). Self-definitions of gang membership and involvement in delinquent activities. *Youth and Society, 34,* 31–54.

Bjerregaard, B. (2003). Anti-gang legislation and its potential impact: The promises and the pitfalls. *Criminal Justice Policy Review, 14,* 171–192.

Bjerregaard, B. (2010). Gang membership and drug involvement: Untangling the complex relationship. *Crime and Delinquency, 56,* 3–34.

Bjerregaard, B., & Lizotte, A. J. (1995). Gun ownership and gang membership. *Journal of Criminal Law and Criminology, 86,* 37–58.

Bjerregaard, B., & Smith, C. (1993). Gender differences in gang participation, delinquency, and substance use. *Journal of Quantitative Criminology, 9,* 329–355.

Block, C. R., & Block, R. (1993). *Street gang crime in Chicago* (Research in Brief). Washington, DC: U.S. Department of Justice, National Institute of Justice.

Block, C. R., Christakos, A., Jacob, A., & Przybylski, R. (1996). *Street gangs and crime: Patterns and trends in Chicago.* Chicago: Illinois Criminal Justice Information Authority.

Block, R. (2000). Gang activity and overall levels of crime: A new mapping tool for defining areas of gang activity using police records. *Journal of Quantitative Criminology, 16,* 369–383.

Blumstein, A. (1995a). Violence by young people: Why the deadly nexus? *National Institute of Justice Journal*(August), 1–9.

Blumstein, A. (1995b). Youth violence, guns, and the illicit-drug industry. *Journal of Criminal Law and Criminology, 86,* 10–36.

Blumstein, A. (1996). Youth violence, guns, and illicit drug markets. *Research Preview.* Washington, DC: U.S. Department of Justice, National Institute of Justice.

Blumstein, A. (2000). Disaggregating the violence trends. In A. Blumstein and J. Wallman (Eds.), *The* crime drop in America (pp. 13–41). New York City: Cambridge University Press.

Blumstein, A., & Rosenfeld, R. (1999). Trends in rates of violence in the U.S.A. *Studies on Crime and Prevention, 8,* 139–167.

Bogardus, E. S. (1926). *The city boy and his problems: A survey of boy life in Los Angeles*. Los Angeles: House of Ralston.

Bookin-Weiner, H., & Horowitz, R. (1983). The end of the gang: Fact or fiction? *Criminology, 21,* 585–602.

Bordua, D. J. (1961). Delinquent subcultures: Sociological interpretations of gang delinquency. *The Annals of the American Academy of Political and Social Sciences, 338,* 119–136.

Botvin, G. J., Griffin, K. W., & Nichols, T. R. (2006). Preventing youth violence and delinquency through a \universal school-based prevention approach. *Prevention Science, 7,* 403–408.

Bourgois, P. (2003). *In search of respect: Selling crack in El Barrio* (2nd ed.). New York: Cambridge University Press.

Bowker, L. H. (1978a). Gangs and prostitutes: Two cases of female crime. In L. H. Bowker (Ed.), *Women, crime, and the criminal justice system* (pp. 143–169). Lexington, MA: Lexington Books.

Bowker, L. H. (Ed.). (1978b). *Women, crime and the criminal justice system.* Lexington, MA: Lexington Books.

Bowker, L. H., & Klein, M. W. (1983). The etiology of female juvenile delinquency and gang membership: A test of psychological and social structural explanations. *Adolescence, 18,* 739–751.

Boxer, P. (2011). Negative peer involvement in Multisystemic Therapy for the treatment of youth problem behavior: Exploring outcome and process variables in "real-world" practice. *Journal of Clinical Child & Adolescent Psychology, 40,* 848–854.

Bradley, A., & DuBois, A. (Eds.). (2011). *The anthology of rap.* New Haven, CT: Yale University Press.

Braga, A. A. (2004). *Gun violence among serious young offenders* (Problem-oriented Guides for Police. Problem-Specific Guides Series No. 23). Washington, DC: Office of Community Oriented Policing Services.

Braga, A. A., & Hureau, D. M. (2012). Strategic problem analysis to guide comprehensive gang violence reduction strategies. In E. Gebo & B. J. Bond (Eds.), *Beyond suppression: Community strategies to reduce gang violence* (pp. 129–151). Lanham, MD: Lexington Books.

Braga, A. A., Kennedy, D. M., & Tita, G. E. (2002). New approaches to the strategic prevention of gang and group-involved violence. In C. R. Huff (Ed.), *Gangs in America III* (pp. 271–285). Thousand Oaks, CA: Sage.

Braga, A. A., Kennedy, D. M., Waring, E. J., & Piehl, A. M. (2001). Problem-oriented policing, deterrence, and youth violence: An evaluation of Boston's Operation Ceasefire. *Journal of Research in Crime and Delinquency, 38,* 195–225.

Braga, A. A., Papachristos, A. V., & Hureau, D. M. (2010). The concentration and stability of gun violence at micro places in Boston, 1980–2008. *Journal of Quantitative Criminology, 26,* 33–53.

Braga, A. A., Papachristos, A. V., & Hureau, D. M. (2012). The effects of hot spots policing on crime: An updated systematic review and meta-analysis. *Justice Quarterly*, iFirst:1–31.

Braga, A. A., & Pierce, G. L. (2005). Disrupting illegal firearms markets in Boston: The effects of Operation Ceasefire on the supply of new handguns to criminals. *Criminology and Public Policy, 4,* 717–748.

Braga, A. A., Pierce, G. L., McDevitt, J., Bond, B. J., & Cronin, S. (2008). The strategic prevention of gun violence among gang-involved offenders. *Justice Quarterly, 25,* 132–162.

Braga, A. A., & Weisburd, D. L. (2012). The effects of focused deterrence strategies on crime: A systematic review and meta-analysis of the empirical evidence. *Journal of Research in Crime and Delinquency, 49,* 323–358.

Brame, B., Nagin, D. S., & Tremblay, R. E. (2001). Developmental trajectories of physical aggression from school entry to late adolescence. *Journal of Child Psychology and Psychiatry and Allied Disciplines, 42,* 503–512.

Brantingham, P. J., Tita, G. E., Short, M. B., & Reid, S. (2012). The ecology of gang territorial boundaries. *Criminology, 50,* 851–885.

Brezina, T., Agnew, R., Cullen, F. T., & Wright, J. P. (2004). The code of the street: A quantitative assessment of Elijah Anderson's subculture of violence thesis and its contribution to youth violence research. *Youth Violence and Juvenile Justice, 2,* 303–328.

Broidy, L. M., Tremblay, R. E., Brame, B., Fergusson, D., Horwood, J. L., Laird, R., et al. (2003). Developmental trajectories of childhood disruptive behaviors and adolescent delinquency: A six-site, cross-national study. *Developmental Psychology, 39,* 222–245.

Brotherton, D. C. (1996). The contradictions of suppression: Notes from a study of approaches to gangs in three public high schools. *Urban Review, 28,* 95–117.

Brotherton, D. C., & Barrios, L. (2004). *The Almighty Latin King and Queen Nation: Street politics and the transformation of a New York City gang.* New York: Columbia University Press.

Brown, W. K. (1977). Black female gangs in Philadelphia. *International Journal of Offender Therapy and Comparative Criminology, 21,* 221–228.

Brown, W. K. (1999). Black female gangs in Philadelphia. In M. Chesney-Lind & J. Hagedorn (Eds.), *Female gangs in America: Essays on girls, gangs, and gender* (pp. 57–63). Chicago: Lake View Press.

Brownstein, H. (1996). The rise and fall of a violent crime wave: Crack cocaine and the social construction of a crime problem. Guilderland, NY: Harrow and Heston.

Brunson, R. K. (2007). "Police don't like Black people": African-American young men's accumulated police experiences. *Criminology & Public Policy, 6*(1), 71–102.

Bryant, D. (1989). *Communitywide responses crucial for dealing with youth gangs* (Juvenile Justice Bulletin). Washington, DC: U.S. Department of Justice, Office of Juvenile Justice and Delinquency Prevention.

Bucerius, S. M. (2010). Fostering academic opportunities to counteract social exclusion. In N. A. Frost, J. D. Freilich, & T. R. Clear (Eds.), *Contemporary issues in criminal justice policy: Policy proposals from the American Society of Criminology* (pp. 235–245). Belmont, CA: Wadsworth.

Bureau of Justice Assistance. (2009). *Navigating your agency's path to intelligence-led policing.* Washington, DC: U.S. Department of Justice, Bureau of Justice Assistance.

Burgess, E. W. (1925). The growth of the city: An introduction to a research project. In R. E. Park & E. W. Burgess (Eds.), *The city* (pp. 47–62). Chicago: University of Chicago Press.

Bursik, R. J., Jr., & Grasmick, H. G. (1993). *Neighborhoods and crime: The dimensions of effective community control.* New York: Lexington.

Bushway, S. D., Krohn, M. D., Lizotte, A. J., Phillips, M. D., & Schmidt, N. M. (2013). Are risky youth less protectable as they age? The dynamics of protection during adolescence and young adulthood. *Justice Quarterly, 30,* 84–116.

Bynum, T. S., & Varano, S. P. (2003). The anti-gang initiative in Detroit: An aggressive enforcement approach to gangs. In S. H. Decker (Ed.), *Policing gangs and youth violence* (pp. 214–238). Belmont, CA: Wadsworth/Thompson Learning.

Cahill, M., & Hayeslip, D. (2010). *Findings from the Evaluation of OJJDP's Gang Reduction Program* (Juvenile Justice Bulletin). Washington, DC: U.S. Department of Justice, Office of Juvenile Justice and Delinquency Prevention.

Cairns, R. B., & Cairns, B. D. (1994). *Lifelines and risks: Pathways of youth in our time.* New York: Cambridge University Press.

Caldwell, M. F., & Van Rybroek, G. (2001). Efficacy of a decompression treatment model in the clinical management of violent juvenile offenders. *International Journal of Offender Therapy and Comparative Criminology, 45,* 469–477.

Caldwell, M. F., Vitacco, M., & Van Rybroek, G. J. (2006). Are violent delinquents worth treating? A cost-benefit analysis. *Journal of Research in Crime and Delinquency, 43,* 148–168.

California Council on Criminal Justice. (1989). *Task force report on gangs and drugs.* Sacramento: California Council on Criminal Justice.

Camp, G. M, & C. G. Camp (Eds.). (1985). *Prison gangs: Their extent, nature and impact on prisons.* Washington, DC: U.S. Department of Justice.

Camp, C. G., & G. M. Camp. (1988). *Management strategies for combating prison gang violence.* South Salem, NY: Criminal Justice Institute.

Campbell, A. (1984/1991). *The girls in the gang: A report from New York City.* New York: Basil Blackwell.

Campbell, A. (1990). Female participation in gangs. In C. R. Huff (Ed.), *Gangs in America* (pp. 163–182). Newbury Park, CA: Sage.

Campbell, A. (1999). Self-definition by rejection: The case of gang girls. In M. Chesney-Lind & J. Hagedorn (Eds.), *Female gangs in America: Essays on girls, gangs, and gender* (pp. 100–117). Chicago: Lake View Press.

Carbone-Lopez, K., Esbensen, F., & Brick, B. T. (2010). Correlates and consequences of peer victimization: Gender differences in direct and indirect forms of bullying. *Youth Violence and Juvenile Justice, 8,* 332–350.

Carson, D. C., Peterson, D., & Esbensen, F. (2013). Youth gang desistance: An examination of the effect of different operational definitions of desistance on the motivations, methods, and consequences associated with leaving the gang. *Criminal Justice Review, 38,* 510–534.

Cartwright, D. S., Tomson, B., & Schwartz, H. (1975). *Gang delinquency.* Monterey, CA: Brooks/Cole.

Caspi, A., Lahey, B. B., & Moffitt, T. E. (2003). *The causes of conduct disorder and serious juvenile delinquency.* London: Guilford Press.

Catalano, R. F., & Hawkins, J. D. (1996). The social development model: A theory of antisocial behavior. In J. D. Hawkins (Ed.), *Delinquency and crime: Current theories* (pp. 149–197). New York: Cambridge University Press.

Caudill, J. W., Trulson, C. R., Marquart, J. W., & DeLisi, M. (2014, June 27). On gang affiliation, gang databases, and prosecutorial outcomes. *Crime & Delinquency*, DOI: 10.1177/0011128714541203.

Cavan, R. (1927). *Suicide.* Chicago: University of Chicago Press.

Cepeda, A., & Valdez, A. (2003). Risk behaviors among young Mexican American gang associated females: Sexual relations, partying, substance use, and crime. *Journal of Adolescent Research, 18,* 90–106.

Chamberlain, P., Leve, L. D., & DeGarmo, D. S. (2007). Multidimensional treatment Foster care for girls in the juvenile justice system: 2-year follow-up of a randomized clinical trial. *Journal of Consulting and Clinical Psychology, 75,* 187–193.

Chesney-Lind, M. (1993). Girls, gangs, and violence: Reinventing the liberated female crook. *Humanity and Society, 17,* 321–344.

Chesney-Lind, M. (1999). Girls, gangs, and violence: Reinventing the liberated female crook. In M. Chesney-Lind & J. Hagedorn (Eds.), *Female gangs in America: Essays on girls, gangs, and gender* (pp. 295–310). Chicago: Lake View Press.

Chesney-Lind, M. (2013). How can we prevent girls from joining gangs? In T. R. Simon, N. M. Ritter, & R. R. Mahendra (Eds.), *Changing course: Preventing gang membership* (pp. 121–133). Washington, DC: U.S. Department of Justice, U.S. Department of Health and Human Services.

Chesney-Lind, M., & Hagedorn, J. (Eds.). (1999). *Female gangs in America.* Chicago: Lake View Press.

Chicago Crime Commission. (1995). *Gangs: Public enemy number one, 75 years of fighting crime in Chicagoland.* Chicago: Author.

Chicago Crime Commission. (2006). *The Chicago Crime Commission gang book.* Chicago: Author.

Clarke, R. V. (1995). Situational crime prevention. In M. Tonry & D. Farrington (Eds.), *Building a safer society: Strategic approaches to crime prevention* (pp. 91–150). Chicago: University of Chicago Press.

Clear, T. R. (2009). *Imprisoning communities: How mass incarceration makes disadvantaged neighborhoods worse.* Oxford: Oxford University Press.

Cloward, R. A., & Ohlin, L. E. (1960). *Delinquency and opportunity: A theory of delinquent gangs.* New York: Free Press.

Cockburn, A., & St. Clair, J. (1998). *Whiteout: The CIA, drugs and the press.* London: Verso.

Cohen, A. K. (1955). *Delinquent boys: The culture of the gang.* Glencoe, IL: The Free Press.

Cohen, A. W. (2003). The racketeer's progress: Commerce, crime, and the law in Chicago, 1900-1940. *Journal of Urban History, 29,* 575–596.

Cohen, B. (1969). The delinquency of gangs and spontaneous groups. In T. Sellin & M. E. Wolfgang (Eds.), *Delinquency: Selected studies* (pp. 61–111). New York: John Wiley & Sons.

Cohen, J., & Tita, G. E. (1999). Spatial diffusion in homicide: Exploring a general method of detecting spatial diffusion processes. *Journal of Quantitative Criminology, 15,* 451–493.

Cohen, L. E., & Felson, M. (1979). Social change and crime rate trends: A routine activity approach. *American Sociological Review, 44,* 588–608.

Cohen, M. A., Piquero, A. R., & Jennings, W. G. (2010). Estimating the costs of bad outcomes for at-risk youth and the benefits of early childhood interventions to reduce them. *Criminal Justice Policy Review, 21,* 391–434.

Coid, J. W., Ullrich, S., Keers, R., Bebbington, P., & DeStavola, B. L. (2013). Gang membership, violence, and psychiatric morbidity. *American Journal of Psychiatry, 170,* 985–993.

Coie, J. D., & Dodge, K. A. (1998). The development of aggression and antisocial behavior. In N. Eisenberg (Ed.), *Handbook of child psychology. Vol. 3: Social, emotional, and personality development* (5th ed., pp. 779–861). New York: Wiley.

Coleman, J. S. (1988). Social capital in the creation of human capital. *American Journal of Sociology, 94,* 95–120.

Coleman, J. S. (1990). *Foundations of social theory.* Cambridge, MA: Harvard University Press.

Columbia Human Rights Law Review. (2011). Security classification and gang validation. Ch. 31 of *A jailhouse lawyer's manual* (9th ed.). New York: Columbia Human Rights Law Review.

Cook, P. J., & Cole, T. B. (1996). Strategic thinking about gun markets and violence. *JAMA, 275,* 1765–1767.

Cook, P. J., & Laub, J. H. (1998). The unprecedented epidemic of youth violence. In M. Tonry & M. H. Moore (Eds.), *Youth violence* (pp. 27–64). Chicago: University of Chicago Press.

Cook, P. J., & Ludwig, J. (2006). The social costs of gun ownership. *Journal of Public Economics, 90,* 379–391.

Cork, D. (1999). Examining space-time interaction in city-level homicide data: Crack markets and the diffusion of guns among youth. *Journal of Quantitative Criminology, 15,* 379–406.

Cornell, D., & Sheras, P. (2006). *Guidelines for responding to student threats of violence.* Longmont, CO: Sopris West.

Coughlin, B. C., & Venkatesh, S. A. (2003). The urban street gang after 1970. *Annual Review of Sociology, 29,* 41–64.

Covey, H. C. (2010). *Street gangs throughout the world.* Springfield, IL: Charles C Thomas.

Craig, W. M., Vitaro, F., Gagnon, C., & Tremblay, R. E. (2002). The road to gang membership: Characteristics of male gang and non-gang members from ages 10 to 14. *Social Development, 11,* 53–68.

Cressey, P. (1932). *The taxi dance hall.* Chicago: University of Chicago Press.

Cruz, J. M. (2010). Central American *maras:* From youth street gangs to transnational protection rackets. *Global Crime, 11,* 379–398.

Cruz, J. M. (2014). *Maras* and the politics of violence in El Salvador. In J. M. Hazen & D. Rodgers (Eds.), *Global gangs: Street violence across the world* (pp. 123–146). Minneapolis: University of Minnesota.

Cummings, L. L. (1994). Fighting by the rules: Women street fighters in Chihuahua, Mexico. *Sex Roles, 30,* 189–198.

Cummings, S. (1993). Anatomy of a wilding gang. In S. Cummings & D. J. Monti (Eds.), *Gangs* (pp. 49–74). Albany: State University of New York Press.

Cummings, S., & Monti, D. J. (Eds.). (1993). *Gangs: The origins and impact of contemporary youth gangs in the United States.* Albany: State University of New York Press.

Cureton, S. R. (2009). Something wicked this way comes: A historical account of Black gangsterism offers wisdom and warning for African American leadership. *Journal of Black Studies, 40,* 347–361.

Currie, E. (1998). *Crime and punishment in America.* New York: Henry Holt.

Curry, G. D. (1998). Female gang involvement. *Journal of Research on Crime and Delinquency, 35,* 100–118.

Curry, G. D. (1999). Responding to female gang involvement. In M. Chesney-Lind & J. Hagedorn (Eds.), *Female gangs in America: Essays on girls, gangs, and gender* (pp. 133–153). Chicago: Lake View Press.

Curry, G. D. (2000). Self-reported gang involvement and officially recorded delinquency. *Criminology, 38,* 1253–1274.

Curry, G. D., Ball, R. A., & Decker, S. H. (1996). Estimating the national scope of gang crime from law enforcement data. In C. R. Huff (Ed.), *Gangs in America* (pp. 21–36). Thousand Oaks, CA: Sage.

Curry, G. D., & Decker, S. H. (2003). *Confronting gangs: Crime and community* (2nd ed.). Los Angeles: Roxbury.

Curry, G. D., Decker, S. H., & Egley, A. Jr. (2002). Gang involvement and delinquency in a middle school population. *Justice Quarterly, 19,* 275–292.

Curry, G. D., & Spergel, I. A. (1988). Gang homicide, delinquency and community. *Criminology, 26,* 381–405.

Curry, G. D., & Spergel, I. A. (1992). Gang involvement and delinquency among Hispanic and African-American adolescent males. *Journal of Research in Crime and Delinquency, 29,* 273–291.

Dade County District Attorney (1988, May 11). *Dade County gangs:1987.* Final report of the Grand Jury, Circuit Court of the Eleventh Judicial Circuit of Florida in and for the County of Dade. Miami, FL: Dade County District Attorney.

Dahmann, J. (1983). Prosecutorial response to violent gang criminality: An evaluation of operation hardcore. Washington, DC: National Institute of Justice.

Dahmann, J. (1995). Operation Hardcore: A prosecutorial response to violent gang criminality. In M. A. Klein, C. L. Maxson, & J. Miller (Eds.), *The modern gang reader* (pp. 301–303). Los Angeles: Roxbury Publishing Company.

Daniels, S. (1987). Prison gangs: Confronting the threat. *Corrections Today, 49,* 66.

Davis, M. (2006). *City of quartz: Excavating the future in Los Angeles* (2nd ed.). New York: Verso.

Dawley, D. (1992). *A nation of lords: The autobiography of the vice lords* (2nd ed.). Prospect Heights, IL: Waveland Press.

Debarbieux, E., & Baya, C. (2008). An interactive construction of gangs and ethnicity: The role of school segregation in France. In F. van Gemert, D. Peterson, & I.-L. Lien (Eds.), *Street gangs, migration and ethnicity* (pp. 211–226). Portland, OR: Willan Publishing.

Decker, S. H. (1996). Deviant homicide: A new look at the role of motives and victim-offender relationships. *Journal of Research in Crime and Delinquency, 33,* 427–449.

Decker, S. H. (2007). Youth gangs and violent behavior. In D. J. Flannery, A. T. Vazsonyi, & I. D. Waldman (Eds.), *The Cambridge handbook of violent behavior and aggression* (pp. 388–402). Cambridge: Cambridge University Press.

Decker, S. H., Bynum, T., & Weisel, D. L. (1998). Gangs as organized crime groups: A tale of two cities. *Justice Quarterly, 15,* 395–423.

Decker, S. H., & Curry, G. D. (2000). Addressing key features of gang membership: Measuring the involvement of young members. *Journal of Criminal Justice, 28,* 473–482.

Decker, S. H., Katz, C. M., & Webb, V. J. (2008). Understanding the black box of gang organization: Implications for involvement in violent crime, drug sales, and violent victimization. *Crime and Delinquency, 54,* 153–172.

Decker, S. H., & Kempf-Leonard, K. (1991). Constructing gangs: The social definition of youth activities. *Criminal Justice Policy Review, 5,* 271–291.

Decker, S. H., & Pyrooz, D. C. (2010a). Gang violence worldwide: Context, culture, and country. *Small Arms Survey, 5,* 129–155.

Decker, S. H., & Pyrooz, D. C. (2010b). On the validity and reliability of gang homicide: A comparison of disparate sources. *Homicide Studies, 14,* 359–376.

Decker, S. H., Pyrooz, D. C., & Moule, R. K. (2014). Disengagement from gangs as role transitions. *Journal of Research on Adolescence, 24,* 268–283.

Decker, S. H., & Van Winkle, B. (1996). *Life in the gang: Family, friends, and violence.* New York: Cambridge University Press.

Decker, S. H., & Weerman, F. M. (Eds.). (2005). *European street gangs and troublesome youth groups.* Lanham, MD: AltaMira Press.

DeLattre, E. J. (1994). *Character and cops: Ethics in policing.* Lanham, MD: Rowman & Littlefield.

De Leon, A. (2001). *Ethnicity in the Sunbelt: Mexican Americans in Houston.* Houston: University of Houston Series in Mexican American Studies.

Deschenes, E. P., & Esbensen, F. (1999). Violence among girls: Does gang membership make a difference? In M. Chesney-Lind & J. Hagedorn (Eds.), *Female gangs in America: Essays on girls, gangs, and gender* (pp. 277–294). Chicago: Lake View Press.

Deuchar, R. (2009). *Gangs, marginalised youth and social capital.* Sterling, VA: Trentham Books.

Di Placido, C., Simon, T. L., Witte, T. D., Gu, D., & Wong, S. C. P. (2006). Treatment of gang members can reduce recidivism and institutional misconduct. *Law and Human Behavior, 30,* 93–114.

Diamond, A. J. (2001). Rethinking culture on the streets: Agency, masculinity, and style in the American city. *Journal of Urban History, 27,* 669–685.

Diamond, A. J. (2009). *Mean streets: Chicago youths and the everyday struggle for empowerment in the multiracial city, 1908–1969.* Berkeley: University of California Press.

DiIulio, J. J., Jr. (1995a). Arresting ideas. *Policy Review, 74,* 12–16.

DiIulio, J. J., Jr. (1995b, November 27). The coming of the super-predators. *Weekly Standard,* pp. 23–28.

DiIulio, J. J. (1997, June 11). Jail alone won't stop juvenile super-predators. *The Wall Street Journal,* p. A23.

Dimitriadis, G. (2006). The situation complex: Revisiting Frederic Thrasher's The Gang: A Study of 1,313 Gangs in Chicago. *Cultural Studies and Critical Methodologies, 6,* 335–353.

Dishion, T. J., Veronneau, M. H., & Myers, M. W. (2010). Cascading peer dynamics underlying the progression from problem behavior to violence in early to late adolescence. *Development and Psychopathology, 22,* 603–619.

Dmitrieva, J., Gibson, L., Steinberg, L., Piquero, A., & Fagan, J. (2014). Predictors and consequences of gang membership: Comparing gang members, gang leaders, and non-gang-affiliated adjudicated youth. *Journal of Research on Adolescence, 24,* 220–234.

Dodge, K. A. (2001). The science of youth violence prevention: Progressing from developmental epidemiology to efficacy to effectiveness to public policy. *American Journal of Preventive Medicine, 20*(1S), 63–70.

Durán, R. J. (2012). *Gang life in two cities: An insider's journey.* Chichester, NY: Columbia University Press.

Early, P. (1991). *The hot house: Life inside Leavenworth Prison.* New York: Bantam Books.

Eckhart, D. (2001). Civil cases related to prison gangs: A survey of federal cases. *Corrections Management Quarterly, 5*(1), 60–65.

Eddy, P., Sabogal, H., & Walden, S. (1988). *The cocaine wars.* New York: W. W. Norton.

Egley, A., Jr. (2005). *Highlights of the 2002–2003 National Youth Gang Surveys* (OJJDP Fact Sheet, June 2005–01). Washington, DC: U.S. Department of Justice, Office of Juvenile Justice and Delinquency Prevention.

Egley, A., Jr., & Howell, J. C. (2010). *Gang activity, subgroups, and crime.* Paper presented at the annual meeting of the American Society of Criminology, San Francisco, November.

Egley, A., Jr., & Howell, J. C. (2011). *Highlights of the 2009 National Youth Gang Survey.* Washington, DC: Office of Juvenile Justice and Delinquency Prevention.

Egley, A. E., & Howell, J. C. (2012). *Highlights of the 2010 National Youth Gang Survey.* Washington, DC: Office of Juvenile Justice and Delinquency Prevention.

Egley, A. Jr., & Howell, J. C. (2013). *Highlights of the 2011 National Youth Gang Survey.* Washington, DC: U.S. Department of Justice, Office of Juvenile Justice and Delinquency Prevention.

Egley, A., Jr., Howell, J. C., Curry, G. D., & O'Donnell, C. E. (2007). *Are the newer gangs different?* Paper presented at the annual meeting of the American Society of Criminology, Atlanta, November.

Egley, A., Jr., Howell, J. C., & Major, A. K. (2004). Recent patterns of gang problems in the United States: Results from the 1996–2002 National Youth Gang Survey. In F. Esbensen, S. G. Tibbetts, & L. Gaines (Eds.), *American youth gangs at the millennium* (pp. 90–108). Long Grove, IL: Waveland Press.

Egley, A., Jr. Howell, J. C., & Major, A. K. (2006). *National Youth Gang Survey: 1999–2001*. Washington, DC: U.S. Department of Justice, Office of Juvenile Justice and Delinquency Prevention.

Egley, A. E., O'Donnell, C. E., & Howell, J. C. (2009). *Over a decade of National Youth Gang Survey research: What have we learned?* Paper presented at the annual meeting of the American Society of Criminology, November. Philadelphia, PA.

Eiserer, T. (1996, October 6). Abilene gang situation different from big cities. *Abilene Reporter-News*. Retrieved from http://texnews.com/news/gangs100696.html

Eitle, D., Gunkel, S., & Gundy, K. V. (2004). Cumulative exposure to stressful life events and male gang membership. *Journal of Criminal Justice, 32,* 95–111.

Elazar, D. J. (1984). *American federalism: A view from the States* (3rd ed.). New York: Harper & Row.

Elder, G. H., Jr. (Ed.). (1985). *Life course dynamics: Trajectories and transitions, 1968–1980*. Ithaca, NY: Cornell University Press.

Elder, G. H. Jr. (1997). The life course and human development. In R. M. Lerner (Ed.), *Handbook of child psychology. Vol. 1: Theoretical models of human development* (pp. 939–991). New York: Wiley.

Erickson, P. G., Butters, J. E., Cousineau, M., Harrison, L., & Korf, D. (2006). Girls and weapons: An international study of the perpetration of violence. *Urban Health, 83,* 788–801.

Esbensen, F. (2000). *Preventing adolescent gang involvement: Risk factors and prevention strategies* (Juvenile Justice Bulletin. Youth Gang Series). Washington, DC: U.S. Department of Justice, Office of Justice Programs, Office of Juvenile Justice and Delinquency Prevention.

Esbensen, F., Brick, B. T., Melde, C., Tusinski, K., & Taylor, T. J. (2008). The role of race and ethnicity in gang membership. In F. V. Genert, D. Peterson, & I. Lien (Eds.), *Street gangs, migration and ethnicity* (pp. 117–139). Portland, OR: Willan.

Esbensen, F., & Carson, D. C. (2012). Who are the gangsters? An examination of the age, race/ethnicity, sex, and immigration status of self-reported gang members in a seven-city study of American youth. *Journal of Contemporary Criminal Justice, 28*(4), 465–481.

Esbensen, F., & Deschenes, E. P. (1998). A multi-site examination of gang membership: Does gender matter? *Criminology, 36,* 799–828.

Esbensen, F., Deschenes, E. P., & Winfree, L. T. (1999). Differences between gang girls and gang boys: Results from a multi-site survey. *Youth and Society, 31,* 27–53.

Esbensen, F., & Huizinga, D. (1993). Gangs, drugs, and delinquency in a survey of urban youth. *Criminology, 31,* 565–589.

Esbensen, F., Huizinga, D., & Weiher, A. W. (1993). Gang and non-gang youth: Differences in explanatory variables. *Journal of Contemporary Criminal Justice, 9,* 94–116.

Esbensen, F., & Lynskey, D. P. (2001). Youth gang members in a school survey. In M. W. Klein, H. Kerner, C. L. Maxson, & E. Weitekampf (Eds.), *The Eurogang paradox: Street gangs and youth groups in the U.S. and Europe* (pp. 93–113). Amsterdam: Kluwer Academic Publishers.

Esbensen, F., & Maxson, C. E. (2012). *Youth gangs in international perspective: Results from the Eurogang Program of Research*. New York: Springer.

Esbensen, F., Osgood, D. W., Peterson, D., Taylor, T. J., & Carson, D. C. (2013). Short and long term outcome results from a multi-site evaluation of the G.R.E.A.T. program. *Criminology & Public Policy, 12,* 375–411.

Esbensen, F., Osgood, D. W., Taylor, T. J., Peterson, D., & Freng, A. (2001). How great is G.R.E.A.T.? Results from a longitudinal quasi-experimental design. *Criminology and Public Policy, 1,* 87–118.

Esbensen, F., Peterson, D., Freng, A., & Taylor, T. J. (2002). Initiation of drug use, drug sales, and violent offending among a sample of gang and nongang youth. In C. R. Huff (Ed.), *Gangs in America III* (pp. 37–50). Thousand Oaks, CA: Sage.

Esbensen, F., Peterson, D., Taylor, T. J., & Freng, A. (2010). *Youth violence: Sex and race differences in offending, victimization, and gang membership*. Philadelphia: Temple University Press.

Esbensen, F., Peterson, D., Taylor, T. J., Freng, A., Osgood, D. W., Carson, D. C., & Matsuda, K. N. (2011). Evaluation and evolution of the Gang Resistance Education and Training (G.R.E.A.T.) program. *Journal of School Violence, 10,* 53–70.

Esbensen, F., Peterson, D., Taylor, & Osgood, D. W. (2012). Results from a multi-site evaluation of the G.R.E.A.T. Program. *Justice Quarterly, 29,* 125–151.

Esbensen, F., & Tusinski, K. (2007). Youth gangs in the print media. *Journal of Criminal Justice and Popular Culture, 14,* 21–38.

Esbensen, F., & Winfree, L. T. (1998). Race and gender differences between gang and non-gang youths: Results from a multi-site survey. *Justice Quarterly, 15,* 505–526.

Esbensen, F., Winfree, L. T., He, N., & Taylor, T. J. (2001). Youth gangs and definitional issues: When is a gang a gang, and why does it matter? *Crime and Delinquency, 47,* 105–130.

Fabelo, T., Thompson, M. D., Plotkin, J. D., Carmichael, D., Marchbanks, M. P., & Booth, E. A. (2011). *Breaking school rules: A statewide study of how school discipline relates to students' success and juvenile justice system involvement*. New York: Council of State Governments Justice Center.

Fagan, A. A., Hanson, K., Hawkins, J. D., & Arthur, M. W. (2008). Implementing effective community-based prevention programs in the community youth development study. *Youth Violence and Juvenile Justice, 6,* 256–278.

Fagan, J., & Chin, K. L. (1989). Initiation to crack: A tale of two epidemics. *Contemporary Drug Problems, 16,* 579–618.

Farrington, D. P. (2003). Developmental and life-course criminology: Key theoretical and empirical issues—the 2002 Sutherland Award Address. *Criminology, 41,* 221–255.

Farrington, D. P. (2005). *Integrated developmental and life-course theories of offending.* New Brunswick, NJ: Transaction Publishing.

Farrington, D. P. (2006). Building developmental and life-course theories of offending. In F. T. Cullen, J. P. Wright, & K. R. Blevins (Eds.), *Taking stock: The status of criminological theory* (pp. 335–364). New Brunswick, NJ: Transaction Publishing.

Farrington, D. P., Loeber, R., & Joliffe, D. (2008). The age-crime curve in reported offending. In R. Loeber, D. P. Farrington, M. Stouthamer-Loeber, H. R. White, & E. Wei, *Violence and serious theft: Development and prediction from childhood to adulthood* (pp. 77–104). New York: Routledge.

Federal Bureau of Investigation. (2008). *The MS-13 threat: A national assessment.* Washington, DC: U.S. Department of Justice, Federal Bureau of Investigation.

Federal Bureau of Investigation. (2009). *National gang threat assessment: 2009.* Washington, DC: U.S. Department of Justice, Federal Bureau of Investigation.

Federal Bureau of Investigation. (2011). *National gang threat assessment: 2011.* Washington, DC: U.S. Department of Justice, Federal Bureau of Investigation.

Felson, M. (2006). The street gang strategy. In M. Felson (Ed.), *Crime and nature* (pp. 305–324). Thousand Oaks, CA: Sage.

Felson, M., & Cohen, L. E. (1980). Human ecology and crime: A routine activity approach. *Human Ecology, 8,* 389–406.

Ferguson, C. J., Miguel, C. S., Kilburn, J. C., & Sanchez, P. (2007). The effectiveness of school-based anti-bullying programs: A meta-analytic review. *Criminal Justice Review, 32,* 4001–4414.

Fernandez, M. E. (1998). An urban myth sees the light again. *The Washington Post,* p. B2.

Fishman, L. T. (1995). The Vice Queens: An ethnographic study of Black female gang behavior. In M. W. Klein, C. L. Maxson, & J. Miller (Eds.), *Modern gang reader* (pp. 83–92). Los Angeles: Roxbury.

Fishman, L. T. (1999). Black female gang behavior: An historical and ethnographic perspective. In M. Chesney-Lind & J. Hagedorn (Eds.), *Female gangs in America: Essays on girls, gangs, and gender* (pp. 64–84). Chicago: Lake View Press.

Fishman, M. (1978). Crime waves as ideology. *Social Problems, 25,* 531–543.

Five youths in court over night crime spree. (2014, March 11). *Warwick Daily News.* Retrieved from http://www.warwick-dailynews.com.au/news/five-youths-in-court-over-night-crime-spree/2194482/

Flannery, D. J., Alexander T., Vazsonyi, A. K. Liau, S. G., Pcowell, K. E., Atha, H., Vesterdal, W., & Embry, D. D. (2003). Initial behavior outcomes for the PeaceBuilders universal school-based violence prevention program. *Developmental Psychology, 39,* 292–308.

Flannery, D. J., Singer, M. I., Van Dulmen, M., Kretschmar, J. M., & Belliston, L. M. (2007). Exposure to violence, mental health, and violent behavior. In D. Flannery, A. Vazonsyi, & I. Waldman (Eds.), *Cambridge handbook of violent behavior* (pp. 306–321). Cambridge: Cambridge University Press.

Flannery, D. J., Vazsonyi, A. T., & Waldman, I. D. (2007). *Cambridge handbook of violent behavior.* Cambridge: Cambridge University Press.

Fleisher, M. S. (1989). *Warehousing violence.* Newbury Park, CA: Sage.

Fleisher, M. S. (1995). *Beggars and thieves: Lives of urban street criminals.* Madison: University of Wisconsin Press.

Fleisher, M. S. (1998). *Dead end kids: Gang girls and the boys they know.* Madison: University of Wisconsin Press.

Fleisher, M. S. (2002). Doing field research on diverse gangs: Interpreting youth gangs as social networks. In C. R. Huff (Ed.), *Gangs in America* (3rd ed., pp. 199–217). Thousand Oaks, CA: Sage.

Fleisher, M. S. (2006a). *Societal and correctional context of prison gangs.* Cleveland, OH: Case Western Reserve University, Mandel School of Applied Social Sciences.

Fleisher, M. S. (2006b). Youth gang social dynamics and social network analysis: Applying degree centrality measures to assess the nature of gang boundaries. In J. F. Short & L. A. Hughes (Eds.), *Studying youth gangs* (pp. 86–99). Lanham, MD: AltaMira Press.

Fleisher, M. S., & Decker, S. (2001). An overview of the challenge of prison gangs. *Corrections Management Quarterly, 5,* 1–9.

Fong, R. S., & Fogel, R. E. (1994–95, Winter). A comparative analysis of prison gang members, security threat group inmates and general population prisoners in the Texas Department of Corrections. *Journal of Gang Research, 2,* 1–12.

Foshee, V. A., Bauman, K. E., Ennett, S. T., Suchindran, C., Benefield, T., & Linder, G. F. (2005). Assessing the effects of the dating violence prevention program "Safe Dates" using random coefficient regression modeling. *Prevention Science, 6,* 245–257.

Franco, C. (2008). *Youth gangs: Background, legislation, and issues* (CRS Report RL33400, updated January 25, 2008). Washington, DC: Congressional Research Service, Library of Congress.

Franco, C. (2010). *The MS-13 and 18th Street Gangs: Emerging transnational gang threats?* (CRS Report RL34233). Washington, DC: Congressional Research Service, Library of Congress. Updated January 22, 2010.

Freng, A., & Esbensen, F. (2007). Race and gang affiliation: An example of multiple marginality. *Justice Quarterly, 24,* 600–628.

Freng, A., & Taylor, T. J. (2013). Race and ethnicity: What are their roles in gang membership? In T. R. Simon, N. M. Ritter, & R. R. Mahendra (Eds.), *Changing course: Preventing gang membership* (pp. 135–149). Washington, DC: U.S. Department of Justice, U.S. Department of Health and Human Services.

Gaes, G., Wallace, S., Gilman, E., Klein-Saffran, J., & Suppa, S. (2002). The influence of prison gang affiliation on violence and other prison misconduct. *The Prison Journal, 82,* 359–385.

Gannon, T. M. (1967). Dimensions of current gang delinquency. *Journal of Research in Crime and Delinquency, 4,* 119–131.

Garot, R. (2010). *Who you claim: Performing gang identity in school and on the streets.* New York: New York University Press.

Gatti, U., Tremblay, R. E., Vitaro, F., & McDuff, P. (2005). Youth gangs, delinquency and drug use: A test of selection, facilitation, and enhancement hypotheses. *Journal of Child Psychology and Psychiatry, 46,* 1178–1190.

Gebo, E., & Bond, B. J. E. (2012). *Beyond suppression: Community strategies to reduce gang violence.* Lanham, MD: Lexington Books.

Gebo, E., & Sullivan, C. J. (2014). A statewide comparison of gang and non-gang youth in public high schools. *Youth Violence and Juvenile Justice, 12,* 191–208.

Geis, G. (2002). Ganging up on gangs: Anti-loitering and public nuisance laws. In C.R. Huff (Ed.), *Gangs in America III* (pp. 257–270). Thousand Oaks, CA: Sage.

Gilfoyle, T. J. (2003). Scorsese's *Gangs of New York*: Why myth matters. *Journal of Urban History, 29,* 620–630.

Gilman, A. B., Hill, K. G., & Hawkins, J. D. (2014). The long-term consequences of adolescent gang membership on adult functioning. *American Journal of Public Health, 104,* 938–945.

Gilman, A. B., Hill, K. G., Hawkins, J. D., Howell, J. C., & Kosterman, R. (2014). The developmental dynamics of joining a gang in adolescence: Patterns and predictors of gang membership. *Journal of Research on Adolescence, 24,* 204–219.

Giordano, P. C. (1978). Girls, guys, and gangs: The changing social context of female delinquency. *Journal of Criminal Law and Criminology, 69,* 126–132.

Glesmann, C., Krisberg, B., & Marchionna, S. (2009). *Youth in gangs: Who is at risk? Focus.* Oakland, CA: National Council on Crime and Delinquency.

Goldman, L., Giles, H., & Hogg, M. A. (2014). Going to extremes: Social identity and communication processes associated with gang membership. *Group Processes & Intergroup Relations, 1,* 1–20.

Goldstein, A. P., & Glick, B. (1994). *The prosocial gang: Implementing Aggression Replacement Training.* Thousand Oaks, CA: Sage.

Goldstein, A. P., Glick, B., & Gibbs, J. C. (1998). *Aggression Replacement Training: A comprehensive intervention for aggressive youth* (Rev. ed.). Champaign, IL: Research Press.

Golub, A., & Johnson, B. D. (1997). *Crack's decline: Some surprises among U.S. cities* (Research in Brief). Washington, DC: National Institute of Justice.

Goode, E. (2012, April 30). With green beret tactics, combating gang warfare. *New York Times.* Retrieved from http://www.nytimes.com/2012/05/01/us/springfield-mass-fights-crime-using-green-beret-tactics.html?pagewanted=all&_r=0

Gordon, R. A., Lahey, B. B., Kawai, E., Loeber, R., Stouthamer-Loeber, M., & Farrington, D. P. (2004). Antisocial behavior and youth gang membership: Selection and socialization. *Criminology, 42,* 55–88.

Gordon, R. A., Rowe, H. L., Pardini, D., Loeber, R., White, H. R., & Farrington, D. (2014). Serious delinquency and gang participation: Combining and specializing in drug selling, theft and violence. *Journal of Research on Adolescence, 24,* 235–251.

Gordon, R. M. (1994). *Incarcerating gang members in British Columbia: A preliminary study.* Victoria, BC: Ministry of the Attorney General.

Gorman-Smith, D., & Loeber, R. (2005). Are developmental pathways in disruptive behaviors the same for girls and boys? *Journal of Child and Family Studies, 14,* 15–27.

Gottfredson, D. C., Cross, A., & Soule, D. A. (2007). Distinguishing characteristics of effective and ineffective after-school programs to prevent delinquency and victimization. *Criminology and Public Policy, 6,* 289–318.

Gottfredson, G. D. (2013). What can schools do to help prevent gang joining? In T. R. Simon, N. M. Ritter, & R. R. Mahendra (Eds.), *Changing course: Preventing gang membership* (pp. 89–104). Washington, DC: U.S. Department of Justice, U.S. Department of Health and Human Services.

Gottfredson, G. D., & Gottfredson, D. C. (2001). *Gang problems and gang programs in a national sample of schools.* Ellicott City, MD: Gottfredson Associates.

Gottfredson, G. D., Gottfredson, D. C., Payne, A. A., & Gottfredson, N. C. (2005). School climate predictors of disorder: Results from a national study of delinquency prevention in schools. *Journal of Research in Crime and Delinquency, 42,* 412–444.

Gravel, J., Bouchard, M., Descormiers, K., Wong, J. S., & Morselli, C. (2013). Keeping promises: A systematic review and a new classification of gang control strategies. *Journal of Criminal Justice, 41,* 228–242.

Graves, K. N., Ireland, A., Benson, J., DiLuca, K., Chiu, K., Johnston, K., Dunn, L., McCoy, S., & Sechrist, S. (2010). *Guilford County gang assessment: OJJDP Comprehensive Gang Assessment Model.* Greensboro, NC: Center for Youth, Family, and Community Partnerships, University of North Carolina at Greensboro.

Griffin, M. L., & Hepburn, J. R. (2006). The effect of gang affiliation on violent misconduct among inmates during the early years of confinement. *Criminal Justice and Behavior, 33,* 419–448.

Griffiths, E. (2014). Public housing and crime patterns. In G. Bruinsma & D. Weisburd (Eds.), *Encyclopedia of criminology and criminal justice* (pp. 4143–4152). New York: Springer.

Griffiths, E., & Chavez, J. M. (2004). Communities, street guns and homicide trajectories in Chicago, 1980–1995: Merging methods for examining homicide trends across space and time. *Criminology, 42,* 941–975.

Grogger, J., & Willis, M. (1998). *The introduction of crack cocaine and the rise in urban crime rates* (National Bureau of Economic Research Working Paper No. W6353). Cambridge, MA: National Bureau of Economic Research.

Guerra, P. (2013, February 25). Modesto killing likely to go before a grand jury. *Modesto Bee.* Retrieved from http://www.mod bee.com/2013/02/25/2593689/not-guilty-pleas-in-gang -related.html

Gugliotta, G., & Leen, J. (1989). *Kings of cocaine.* New York: Simon & Schuster.

Gurr, T. R. (1989). *Violence in America.* Newbury Park, CA: Sage.

Hagedorn, J. M. (1988). *People and folks: Gangs, crime and the underclass in a Rustbelt city.* Chicago: Lake View Press.

Hagedorn, J. M. (1994). Homeboys, dope fiends, legits, and new jacks. *Criminology, 32,* 197–217.

Hagedorn, J. M. (1998). Gang violence in the postindustrial era. In M. Tonry & M. H. Moore (Eds.), *Youth violence* (pp. 365–420). Chicago: University of Chicago.

Hagedorn, J. M. (2006). Race, not space: A revisionist history of gangs in Chicago. *Journal of African American History, 91,* 194–208.

Hagedorn, J. M. (2008). *A world of gangs: Armed young men and gangsta culture.* Minneapolis: University of Minnesota Press.

Hagedorn, J. M., & Rauch, B. (2007). Housing, gangs, and homicide: What we can learn from Chicago. *Urban Affairs Review, 42,* 435–456.

Hallfors, D., & Godette, D. (2002). Will the "Principles of Effectiveness" improve prevention practice? Early findings from a diffusion study. *Health Education Research, 17,* 461–470.

Hallsworth, S., & Young, T. (2008). Gang talk and gang talkers: A critique. *Crime Media Culture, 42,* 175–195.

Hardman, D. G. (1967). Historical perspectives of gang research. *Journal of Research in Crime and Delinquency, 4,* 5–26.

Hardman, D. G. (1969). Small town gangs. *Journal of Criminal Law, Criminology and Police Science, 60,* 173–181.

Hare, R. D., Hart, S. D., & Harpur, T. J. (1991). Psychopathy and the *DSM-IV* criteria for antisocial personality disorder. *Journal of Abnormal Psychology, 100,* 391–398.

Harris, M. C. (1988). *Cholas: Latino girls and gangs.* New York: AMS Press.

Harrison, L. E. (1999). How cultural values shape economic success. In F. L. Pincus and H. J. Ehrlich (Eds.) *Race and Ethnic Conflict* (pp. 97–109). Boulder, CO: Westview Press.

Hartman, D. A., & Golub, A. (1999). The social construction of the crack epidemic in the print media. *Journal of Psychoactive Drugs, 31,* 423–433.

Haskins, J. (1974). *Street gangs: Yesterday and today.* Wayne, PA: Hastings Books.

Haviland, A. M., & Nagin, D. S. (2005). Causal inferences with group-based trajectory models. *Psychometrika, 70,* 1–22.

Haviland, A. M., Nagin, D. S., Rosenbaum, P. R., & Tremblay, R. E. (2008). Combining group-based trajectory modeling and propensity score matching for causal inferences in nonexperimental longitudinal data. *Developmental Psychology, 44,* 422–436.

Hawkins, D. F. (2011). Things fall apart: Revisiting race and ethnic differences in criminal violence amidst a crime drop. *Race and Justice, 1,* 3–48.

Hawkins, J. D. (Ed.). (1996). *Delinquency and crime: Current theories.* New York: Cambridge University Press.

Hayden, T. (2005). *Street wars: Gangs and the future of violence.* New York: New Press.

Hayes, M., McReynolds, L. S., & Wasserman, G. A. (2005). Paper and Voice MAYSI-2: Format comparability and concordance with the Voice DISC-IV. *Assessment, 12,* 395–403.

Hayeslip, D. W. Jr. (1989). *Local-level drug enforcement: New strategies* (Research in Action No. 213). Washington, DC: U.S. Department of Justice, National Institute of Justice.

Hayeslip, D., & Cahill, M. (2009). *Community collaboratives addressing youth gangs: Final evaluation findings from the Gang Reduction Program.* Washington, DC: Urban Institute.

Haymoz, S., & Gatti, U. (2010). Girl members of deviant youth groups, offending behavior and victimisation: Results from the ISRD2 in Italy and Switzerland. *European Journal on Criminal Policy and Research, 16,* 167–182.

Haynie, D. L., Steffensmeier, D., & Bell, K. E. (2007). Gender and serious violence: Untangling the role of friendship sex composition and peer violence. *Youth Violence and Juvenile Justice, 5,* 235–253.

Hazen, J. M., & Rodgers, D. E. (Eds.). (2014). *Global gangs: Street violence across the world.* Minneapolis: University of Minnesota.

Healy, G. (2002). There goes the neighborhood: The Bush-Ashcroft plan to "help" localities fight gun crime (Policy Analysis No. 440). Washington, DC: Heritage Foundation.

Hemphill, S. A., Toumborou, J. W., Herrenkohl, T. L., McMorris, B. J., & Catalano, R. F. (2006). The effect of school suspensions and arrests on subsequent adolescent behavior in Australia and the United States. *Journal of Adolescent Health, 39,* 736–744.

Henggeler, S. W., & Schoenwald, S. K. (2011). Evidence-based interventions for juvenile offenders and juvenile justice policies that support them. *Social Policy Report, 25,* 3–26.

Henggeler, S. W., Schoenwald, S. K., Borduin, C. M., Rowland, M. D., & Cunningham, P. B. (2009). *Multisystemic treatment of antisocial behavior in children and adolescents* (2nd ed.). New York: Guilford Press.

Herendeen, S. (2007, September 20). Gangs thriving in Modesto: Experts expose lifestyle myths, urge teens' families to step up. *Modesto Bee.* Retrieved from http://www.modbee.com/2007/09/20/72474/gangs-thriving-in-modesto.html

Hibbard, B. G., Barbieri, J., Domnarski, M., & Cutone, M. (2014). Counter criminal continuum (C3) policing in Springfield, Massachusetts: A collaborative effort between city and state police to reduce gang violence. *The Police Chief: The Professional Voice of Law Enforcement, 78,* 30–36.

Hill, K. G., Chung, I. J., Guo, J., & Hawkins, J. D. (2002). *The impact of gang membership on adolescent violence trajectories.* Paper presented at the International Society for Research on Aggression, XV World Meeting, Montreal, Canada, July.

Hill, K. G., Howell, J. C., Hawkins, J. D., & Battin-Pearson, S. R. (1999). Childhood risk factors for adolescent gang membership: Results from the Seattle Social Development Project. *Journal of Research in Crime and Delinquency, 36,* 300–322.

Hill, K. G., Lui, C., & Hawkins, J. D. (2001). *Early precursors of gang membership: A study of Seattle youth* (Juvenile Justice Bulletin. Youth Gang Series). Washington, DC: U.S. Department of Justice, Office of Juvenile Justice and Delinquency Prevention.

Hipp, J. R., Tita, G. E., & Boggess, L. N. (2009). Intergroup and intragroup violence: Is violent crime an expression of group conflict or social disorganization? *Criminology, 47,* 521–564.

Hipwell, A. E., Keenan, K., Bean, T., Loeber, R., & Stouthamer-Loeber, M. (2008). Reciprocal influences between girls' behavioral and emotional problems and caregiver mood and parenting style: A six-year prospective analysis. *Journal of Abnormal Child Psychology, 36,* 663–677.

Hipwell, A. E., & Loeber, R. (2006). Do we know which interventions are effective for disruptive and delinquent girls? *Clinical Child and Family Psychology Review, 9,* 221–255.

Hipwell, A. E., Loeber, R., Stouthamer-Loeber, M., Keenan, K., White, H. R., & Kroneman, L. (2002). Characteristics of girls with early onset of disruptive and antisocial behavior. *Criminal Behaviour and Mental Health, 12,* 99–118.

Hipwell, A. E., Pardini, D. A., Loeber, R., Sembower, M. A., Keenan, K., & Stouthamer-Loeber, M. (2007). Callous-unemotional behaviors in young girls: Shared and unique effects relative to conduct problems. *Journal of Clinical Child and Adolescent Psychology, 36,* 293–304.

Hipwell, A. E., White, H. R., Loeber, R., Stouthamer-Loeber, M., Chung, T., & Sembower, M. (2005). Young girls' expectancies about the effects of alcohol, future intentions and patterns of use. *Journal of Studies on Alcohol, 66,* 630–639.

Hodgkinson, J., Marshall, S., Berry, G., Reynolds, P., Newman, M., Burton, E., Dickson, K., & Anderson, J. (2009). *Reducing gang-related crime: A systematic review of "comprehensive" interventions: Summary report.* London: EPPI-Centre, Social Science Research Unit, Institute of Education, University of London.

Horowitz, R. (1983). Honor and the American dream: Culture and identity in a Chicano community. New Brunswick, NJ: Rutgers University Press.

Horowitz, R. (1990). Sociological perspectives on gangs: Conflicting definitions and concepts. In R. Huff (Ed.), *Gangs in America* (pp. 37–54). Newbury Park, CA: Sage.

Houston Intelligence Support Center. (2011). *Houston high-intensity drug trafficking area gang threat assessment: 2011.* Houston, TX: Author.

Howell, J. C. (1998). *Youth gangs: An overview* (Juvenile Justice Bulletin. Youth Gang Series). Washington, DC: U.S. Department of Justice, Office of Juvenile Justice and Delinquency Prevention.

Howell, J. C. (1999). Youth gang homicides: A literature review. *Crime and Delinquency, 45,* 208–241.

Howell, J. C. (2000). *Youth gang programs and strategies.* Washington, DC: U.S. Department of Justice, Office of Juvenile Justice and Delinquency Prevention.

Howell, J. C. (2003a). Diffusing research into practice using the Comprehensive Strategy for Serious, Violent, and Chronic Juvenile Offenders. *Youth Violence and Juvenile Justice: An Interdisciplinary Journal, 1,* 219–245.

Howell, J. C. (2003b). *Preventing and reducing juvenile delinquency: A comprehensive framework.* Thousand Oaks, CA: Sage.

Howell, J. C. (2006). *The impact of gangs on communities* (NYGC Bulletin No. 2). Tallahassee, FL: National Youth Gang Center.

Howell, J. C. (2007). Menacing or mimicking? Realities of youth gangs. *The Juvenile and Family Court Journal, 58,* 9–20.

Howell, J. C. (2009). *Preventing and* reducing juvenile delinquency: A comprehensive framework (2nd ed.). Thousand Oaks, CA: Sage.

Howell, J. C. (2010a). *Gang prevention: An overview of current research and programs* (Juvenile Justice Bulletin). Washington, DC: U.S. Department of Justice, Office of Juvenile Justice and Delinquency Prevention.

Howell, J. C. (2010b). Lessons learned from gang program evaluations: Prevention, intervention, suppression, and comprehensive community approaches. In R. J. Chaskin (Ed.), *Youth gangs and community intervention: Research, practice, and evidence* (pp. 51–75). New York: Columbia University Press.

Howell, J. C. (2013a). GREAT results: Implications for PBIS in schools. *Criminology and Public Policy, 12,* 413–420.

Howell, J. C. (2013b). Why is gang membership prevention important? In T. R. Simon, N. M. Ritter, & R. R. Mahendra (Eds.), *Changing course: Preventing gang membership* (pp. 7–18). Washington, DC: National Center for Injury Prevention and Control, Centers for Disease Control and Prevention, U.S. Department of Health and Human Services, and National Institute of Justice, Office of Justice Programs, U.S. Department of Justice.

Howell, J. C. (in press). The legacy of Irving A. Spergel. In S. Decker & D.C. Pyrooz (Eds.), *The Wiley Handbook of Gangs.* Hoboken, NJ: John Wiley & Sons.

Howell, J. C. (2015). *The history of street gangs in the United States.* Lanham, MD: Lexington Books.

Howell, J. C., & Curry, G. D. (2009). *Mobilizing communities to address gang problems* (NYGC Bulletin No. 4). Tallahassee, FL: National Youth Gang Center.

Howell, J. C., & Decker, S. H. (1999). *The youth gangs, drugs, and violence connection* (Juvenile Justice Bulletin. Youth Gang Series). Washington, DC: Office of Juvenile Justice and Delinquency Prevention.

Howell, J. C., & Egley, A., Jr. (2005a). *Gangs in small towns and rural counties* (NYGC Bulletin No. 1). Tallahassee, FL: National Youth Gang Center.

Howell, J. C., & Egley, A., Jr. (2005b). Moving risk factors into developmental theories of gang membership. *Youth Violence and Juvenile Justice, 3,* 334–354.

Howell, J. C., Egley, A., Jr., & Gleason, D. K. (2002). Modern day youth gangs. *Juvenile Justice Bulletin. Youth Gang Series.* Washington, DC: U.S. Department of Justice, Office of Juvenile Justice and Delinquency Prevention.

Howell, J. C., Egley, A., Jr., Tita, G., & Griffiths, E. (2011). *U.S. gang problem trends and seriousness.* Tallahassee, FL: Institute for Intergovernmental Research, National Gang Center.

Howell, J. C., & Gleason, D. K. (1999). *Youth gang drug trafficking* (Juvenile Justice Bulletin. Youth Gang Series). Washington, DC: U.S. Department of Justice, Office of Juvenile Justice and Delinquency Prevention.

Howell, J. C., Lipsey, M. W., & Wilson, J. J. (2014). *A handbook for evidence-based juvenile justice systems.* Lanham, MD: Lexington Books.

Howell, J. C., & Lynch, J. (2000). *Youth gangs in schools* (Juvenile Justice Bulletin. Youth Gang Series). Washington, DC: U.S. Department of Justice, Office of Juvenile Justice and Delinquency Prevention.

Howell, J. C., & Moore, J. P. (2010). *History of street gangs in the United States* (National Gang Center Bulletin No. 4). Tallahassee, FL: Institute for Intergovernmental Research, National Gang Center.

Howell, J. C., Moore, J. P., & Egley, A., Jr. (2002). The changing boundaries of youth gangs. In C. R. Huff (Ed.), *Gangs in America* (3rd ed., pp. 3–18). Thousand Oaks, CA: Sage.

Howell, J. C., & Young, M. A. (2013). What works to curb U.S. street gang violence? *The Criminologist, 38*(1), 39–43.

Howell, M. Q., & Lassiter, W. (2011). *Prevalence of gang-involved youth in NC.* Raleigh: North Carolina Department of Juvenile Justice and Delinquency Prevention.

Hoyt, F. C. (1920). Gang in embryo. *Scribners Magazine, 68,* 146–154.

Hubbard, D. J., & Matthews, B. (2008). Reconciling the differences between the "gender responsive" and the "what works" literature to improve services for girls. *Crime and Delinquency, 54,* 225–258.

Huebner, B. M., Varano, S. P., & Bynum, T. S. (2007). Gangs, guns, and drugs: Recidivism among serious, young offenders. *Criminology & Public Policy, 6,* 187–221.

Huff, C. R. (1989). Youth gangs and public policy. *Crime and Delinquency, 35,* 524–537.

Huff, C. R. (1990). Denial, overreaction, and misidentification: A postscript on public policy. C. R. Huff (Ed.), *Gangs in America* (pp. 310–317). Newbury Park, CA: Sage.

Huff, C. R. (1991). Denial, overreaction, and misidentification: A postscript on public policy. In C. R. Huff (Ed.), *Gangs in America* (pp. 310–317). Newbury Park, CA: Sage.

Huff, C. R. (1993). Gangs in the United States. In A. Goldstein & C. R. Huff (Eds.), *The gang intervention handbook* (pp. 3–20). Champaign, IL: Research Press.

Huff, C. R. (1996). The criminal behavior of gang members and non-gang at-risk youth. In C. R. Huff (Ed.), *Gangs in America* (2nd ed., pp. 75–102). Thousand Oaks, CA: Sage.

Huff, C. R. (1998). *Comparing the criminal behavior of youth gangs and at-risk youth. Research in Brief.* Washington, DC: U.S. Department of Justice, Office of Justice Programs, National Institute of Justice.

Hughes, L. A. (2005). Studying youth gangs: Alternative methods and conclusions. *Journal of Contemporary Criminal Justice, 21,* 98–119.

Hughes, L. A. (2006). Studying youth gangs: The importance of context. In J. F. Short & L. A. Hughes (Eds.), *Studying youth gangs* (pp. 37–46). Lanham, MD: AltaMira Press.

Hughes, L. A. (2007). Youth street gangs. In M. P. McShane & F. P. Williams, III (Eds.), *Youth violence and juvenile delinquency. Vol. 1: Juvenile offenders and victims* (pp. 41–60). Westport, CT: Praeger.

Hughes, L. A. (2013). Group cohesiveness, gang member prestige, and delinquency and violence in Chicago, 1959–1962. *Criminology, 15,* 798–832.

Hughes, L. A., & Short, J. F. (2005). Disputes involving gang members: Micro-social contexts. *Criminology, 43,* 43–76.

Huizinga, D. (2010). *Who are the long-term gang members?* Paper presented at the annual meeting of the American Society of Criminology, San Francisco, November.

Huizinga, D., & Lovegrove, P. (2009). *Summary of important risk factors for gang membership.* Boulder, CO: Institute for Behavioral Research.

Hunt, G., & Joe-Laidler, K. (2001). Situations of violence in the lives of girl gang members. *Health Care for Women International, 22,* 363–384.

Hutchison, R. (1993). Blazon nouveau: Gang graffiti in the barrios of Los Angeles and Chicago. In S. Cummings & D. J. Monti (Eds.), *Gangs* (pp. 137–171). Albany: State University of New York Press.

Hutchison, R., & Kyle, C. (1993). Hispanic street gangs in the Chicago Public Schools. In S. Cummings & D. J. Monti (Eds.), *Gangs* (pp. 113–136). Albany: State University of New York Press.

Hutson, H. R., Anglin, D., Kyriacou, D. N., Hart, J., & Spears, K. (1995). The epidemic of gang-related homicides in Los Angeles County from 1979 through 1994. *Journal of the American Medical Association, 274,* 1031–1036.

Irwin, J. (1980). *Prisons in turmoil.* Boston: Little, Brown.

Jackson, P. I. (1991). Crime, youth gangs, and urban transition: The social dislocations of postindustrial economic development. *Justice Quarterly, 8,* 379–397.

Jackson, P. G., & Rudman, C. (1993). Moral panic and the response to gangs in California. In S. Cummings & D. Monti (Eds.), *Gangs* (pp. 257–275). Albany: State University of New York Press.

Jacobs, J. B. (1974). Street gangs behind bars. *Social Problems, 21,* 395–409.

Jacobs, J. B. (1977). *Stateville: The penitentiary in mass society.* Chicago: University of Chicago Press.

Jacobs, J. B. (2001). Focusing on prison gangs. *Corrections Management Quarterly, 5*(1), vi–vii.

Jankowski, M. S. (1991). *Islands in the street: Gangs in American urban society.* Berkeley: University of California Press.

Joe, K. A. (1994). The new criminal conspiracy? Asian gangs and organized crime in San Francisco. *Journal of Research in Crime and Delinquency, 31,* 390–394.

Joe, K. A., & Chesney-Lind, M. (1995). Just every mother's angel: An analysis of gender and ethnic variations in youth gang membership. *Gender & Society, 9,* 408–430.

Johnson, K. (2006, July 13). Police tie jump in crime to juveniles: Gangs, guns, add up to increased violence. *USA Today,* pp. A1, A3.

Johnson, R. (1996). Hard time: Understanding and reforming the prison. Belmont, CA: Wadsworth.

Johnstone, J. W. (1981). Youth gangs and black suburbs. *Pacific Sociological Review, 24,* 355–375.

Joint Crime Information Center. (2014). *Texas gang threat assessment: A state intelligence estimate.* Austin: Texas Department of Public Safety, Intelligence & Counterterrorism Division.

Jones, G. A. (2014). "Hecho en Mexico": Gangs identities, and the politics of public security. In J. M. Hazen & D. Rodgers (Eds.), *Global gangs: Street violence across the world* (pp. 255–280). Minneapolis: University of Minnesota.

Jones, N. (2008). Working the "Code": On girls, gender, and inner-city violence. *Australian and New Zealand Journal of Criminology, 41,* 63–83.

Josi, D., & Sechrest, D. K. (1999). A pragmatic approach to parole aftercare: Evaluation of a community reintegration program for high-risk youthful offenders. *Justice Quarterly, 16*(1), 51–80.

Justice Policy Institute. (2000). *The punishing decade: Prison and jail estimates at the millennium.* Washington, DC: Justice Policy Institute.

Jütersonke, O., Muggah, R., & Rodgers, D. (2009). Gangs, urban violence, and security in Central America. *Security Dialogue, 40*(4–5), 373–397.

Kalb, L. M., & Loeber, R. (2003). Child disobedience and noncompliance: A review. *Pediatrics, 111,* 641–652.

Kaplan, H. B., & Damphouse, K. R. (1997). Negative social sanctions, self-derogation, and deviant behavior: Main and interactive effects in longitudinal perspective. *Deviant Behavior, 18,* 1–26.

Karoly, L. A., Greenwood, P. W., Everingham, S. S., Houbé, J., Kilburn, M. R., & Rydell, C. P. (1998). *Investing in our children.* Santa Monica, CA: RAND.

Katz, C. M., & Fox, A. (2011). *The reliability of NYGS data.* Paper presented at the annual meeting of the American Society of Criminology, Washington, DC, November.

Katz, C. M., & Schnebly, S. M. (2011). Neighborhood variation in gang member concentration. *Crime and Delinquency, 57,* 377–407.

Katz, C. M., & Webb, V. J. (2003). *Police response to gangs: A multi-site study*. Washington, DC: National Institute of Justice. Retrieved from http://cops.usdoj.gov/files/ric/CDROMs/GangCrime/pubs/PoliceResponsetoGangs.pdf

Katz, C. M., & Webb, V. J. (2006). *Policing gangs in America*. New York: Cambridge University Press.

Katz, C. M., Webb, V. J., & Schaefer, D. (2000). The validity of police gang intelligence lists: Examining differences in delinquency between documented gang members and non-documented delinquent youth. *Police Quarterly, 3*, 413–437.

Katz, J., & Jackson-Jacobs, C. (2004). The criminologists' gang. In C. Sumner (Ed.), *The Blackwell companion to criminology* (pp. 91–124). Malden, MA: Blackwell.

Keenan, K. (2001). Uncovering preschool precursor problem behaviors. In R. Loeber & D. P. Farrington (Eds.), *Child delinquents: Development, intervention, and service needs* (pp. 117–134). Thousand Oaks, CA: Sage.

Keiser, R. L. (1969). *The Vice Lords: Warriors of the street*. New York: Holt, Rinehart & Winston.

Keith, S., & Griffiths, E. (2014). Urban code or urban legend: Endorsement of the street code Among delinquent youth in urban, suburban, and rural Georgia. *Race & Justice, 4*(3), 270–298.

Kelley, B. T., Loeber, R., Keenan, K., & DeLamatre, M. (1997). Developmental pathways in boys' disruptive and delinquent behavior. *Juvenile Justice Bulletin*. Washington, DC: Office of Juvenile Justice and Delinquency Prevention.

Kennedy, D. M. (2010). Taking criminology seriously: Narratives, norms, networks, and common ground. In R. J. Chaskin (Ed.), *Youth gangs and community intervention: Research, practice, and evidence* (pp. 206–221). New York: Columbia University Press.

Kennedy, D. M., & Braga, A. A. (1998). Homicide in Minneapolis. *Homicide Studies, 2*(3), 263–290.

Kennedy, D. M., Piehl, A. M., & Braga, A. A. (1996). Youth violence in Boston: Gun markets, serious youth offenders, and a use-reduction strategy. *Law and Contemporary Problems, 59*(Special Issue), 147–196.

Kent, D. R., Donaldson, S. I., Wyrick, P. A., & Smith, P. J. (2000). Evaluating criminal justice programs designed to reduce crime by targeting repeat gang offenders. *Evaluation and Program Planning, 23*, 115–124.

Kim, Y. S., Leventhal, B. L., Koh, Y.-J., Hubbard, A., & Boyce, W. T. (2006). School bullying and youth violence. *Archives of General Psychiatry, 63*, 1035–1041.

Kingston, B., Huizinga, D., & Elliott, D. S. (2009). A test of social disorganization theory in high-risk urban neighborhoods. *Youth & Society, 41*, 53–79.

Kipper, B., & Ramey, B. (2012). *NO COLORS: 100 ways to stop gangs from taking away our communities*. New York: Morgan James.

Klein, M. W. (1969). Violence in American juvenile gangs. In D. J. Mulvihill & M. M. Tumin (Eds.), *Crimes of violence* (pp. 1427–1460). Washington, DC: National Commission on the Causes and Prevention of Violence.

Klein, M. W. (1971). *Street gangs and street workers*. Englewood Cliffs, NJ: Prentice Hall.

Klein, M. W. (1995). *The American street gang*. New York: Oxford University Press.

Klein, M. W. (2002). Street gangs: A cross-national perspective. In C. R. Huff (Ed.), *Gangs in America III* (pp. 237–254). Thousand Oaks, CA: Sage.

Klein, M. W. (2004). *Gang cop: The words and ways of Officer Paco Domingo*. Walnut Creek, CA: AltaMira Press.

Klein, M. W., & Maxson, C. L. (1989). Street gang violence. In M. E. Wolfgang, & N. A. Weiner (Eds.), *Violent crime, violent criminals* (pp. 198–234). Newbury Park, CA: Sage.

Klein, M. W., & Maxson, C. L. (1994). Gangs and cocaine trafficking. In D. MacKenzie & C. Uchida (Eds.), *Drugs and crime: Evaluating public policy initiatives* (pp. 42–58). Thousand Oaks, CA: Sage.

Klein, M. W., & Maxson, C. L. (2006). *Street gang patterns and policies*. New York: Oxford University Press.

Klein, M. W., Maxson, C. L., & Cunningham, L. C. (1991). Crack, street gangs, and violence. *Criminology, 29*, 623–650.

Knox, G. W. (1998). *An introduction to gangs* (4th ed.). Peotone, IL: New Chicago Press.

Kontos, L., Brotherton, D., & Barrios, L. (2003). *Gangs and society: Alternative perspectives*. New York: Columbia University Press.

Kotlowitz, A. (1992). *There are no children here: The story of two boys growing up in the other America*. New York: Anchor Books.

Kotlowitz, A. (2008, May 4). Blocking the transmission of violence. *New York Times Magazine*, 1–9.

Krohn, M. D., Lizotte, A. J., Bushway, S. D., Schmidt, N. M., & Phillips, M. D. (2014). Shelter during the storm: A search for factors that protect at-risk adolescents from violence. *Crime & Delinquency, 60*, 379–401.

Krohn, M. D., Schmidt, N. M., Lizotte, A. J., & Baldwin, J. M. (2011). The impact of multiple marginality on gang membership and delinquent behavior for Hispanic, African American, and White male adolescents. *Journal of Contemporary Criminal Justice, 27*, 18–42.

Krohn, M. D., & Thornberry, T. P. (2008). Longitudinal perspectives on adolescent street gangs. In A. Liberman (Ed.), *The long view of crime: A synthesis of longitudinal research* (pp. 128–160). New York: Springer.

Krohn, M. D., Thornberry, T. P., Rivera, C., & Le Blanc, M. (2001). Later careers of very young offenders. In R. Loeber & D. P. Farrington (Eds.), *Child delinquents: Development, intervention, and service needs* (pp. 67–94). Thousand Oaks, CA: Sage.

Krohn, M. D., Ward, J. T., Thornberry, T. P., Lizotte, A., & Chu, R. (2011). The cascading effects of adolescent gang involvement across the life course. *Criminology, 49,* 991–1028.

Kroneman, L., Loeber, R., & Hipwell, A. E. (2004). Is neighborhood context differently related to externalizing problems and delinquency for girls compared with boys? *Clinical Child and Family Psychology Review, 7,* 109–122.

Kubrin, C. E. (2005). Gangstas, thugs, and hustlas: Identity and the code of the street in rap music. *Social Problems, 52,* 360–378.

Kupersmidt, J. B., Coie, J. D., & Howell, J. C. (2003). Building resilience in children exposed to negative peer influences. In K. I. Maton, C. J. Schellenbach, B. J. Leadbeater, C. J. Schellenbach, & A. L. Solarz (Eds.), *Investing in children, youth, families and communities: Strengths-based research and policy* (pp. 251–268). Washington, DC: American Psychological Association.

Kutash, K., Duchnowski, A. J., & Lynn, N. (2006). *School-based mental health: An empirical guide for decision-makers.* Tampa: University of South Florida, The Louis de la Parte Florida Mental Health Institute, Department of Child & Family Studies, Research and Training Center for Children's Mental Health.

Kutateladze, B. (2011). Measuring state punitiveness in the United States. *Punitivity: International Developments, 8,* 151–179.

Lacey, M. (1990, January 18). Police report 50% jump in Inglewood murders: Crime: Drugs, gang violence blamed for increase: Figures make 1989 second deadliest year in city's history. *Los Angeles Times.* Retrieved from http://articles.latimes.com/1990-01-18/news/we-110_1_inglewood-police-department

Lacourse, E., Nagin, D. S., Tremblay, R. E., Vitaro, F., & Claes, M. (2003). Developmental trajectories of boys' delinquent group membership and facilitation of violent behaviors during adolescence. *Development and Psychopathology, 15,* 183–197.

Lacourse, E., Nagin, D. S., Vitaro, F., Cote, S., Arseneault, L., & Tremblay, R. E. (2006). Prediction of early-onset deviant peer group affiliation. *Archives of General Psychiatry, 63,* 562–568.

Lahey, B. B., Gordon, R. A., Loeber, R., Stouthamer-Loeber, M., & Farrington, D. P. (1999). Boys who join gangs: A prospective study of predictors of first gang entry. *Journal of Abnormal Child Psychology, 27,* 261–276.

Lane, J., & Meeker, J. W. (2000). Subcultural diversity and the fear of crime and gangs. *Crime and Delinquency, 46,* 497–521.

Lane, J., & Meeker, J. W. (2003). Women's and men's fear of gang crimes: Sexual and nonsexual assault as perceptually contemporaneous offenses. *Justice Quarterly, 20,* 337–371.

Lane, M. P. (1989, July). Inmate gangs. *Corrections Today, 51,* 98–99.

Larochette, A., Murphy, A. N., & Craig, W. M. (2010). Racial bullying and victimization in Canadian school-aged children: Individual and school level effects. *School Psychology International, 31,* 389–408.

Lassiter, W. L., & Perry, D. C. (2009). Preventing violence and crime in America's schools: From put-downs to lock-downs. Santa Barbara, CA: Praeger.

Le Blanc, M. (1993). Prevention of adolescent delinquency, an integrative multilayered control theory based perspective. In D. P. Farrington, R. J. Sampson, & P. O. H. Widstrom (Eds.), *Integrating individual and ecological aspects of crime* (pp. 279–322). Stockholm: National Council for Crime Prevention.

Le Blanc, M., & Lanctot, N. (1998). Social and psychological characteristics of gang members according to the gang structure and its subcultural and ethnic makeup. *Journal of Gang Research, 5,* 15–28.

Le Blanc, M., & Loeber, R. (1998). Developmental criminology updated. In M. Tonry (Ed.), *Crime and justice: An annual review of research* (Vol. 23, pp. 115–198). Chicago: University of Chicago Press.

Leap, J. (2012). Jumped in: What gangs taught me about violence, drugs, love, and redemption. Boston: Beacon Press.

Leinwald, D. (2007, March 1). DEA busts ring accused of sending tons of drugs to US. *USA Today,* p. A11.

Leinwald, D. (2000, February 25). LAPD, neighborhood shaken. *USA Today,* p. 3A.

Langberg, J., Fedders, B., & Kukorowski, D. (2011). *Law enforcement officers in Wake County schools: The human, educational, and financial costs.* Durham, NC: Advocates for Children's Services.

Lerman, P., & Pottick, K. J. (1995). The parents' perspective: Delinquency, aggression, and mental health. Chur, Switzerland: Harwood.

Leve, L. D., & Chamberlain, P. (2007). A randomized evaluation of multidimensional treatment foster care: Effects on school attendance and homework completion in juvenile justice girls. *Research on Social Work Practice, 17,* 657–663.

Levitt, S. D., & Venkatesh, S. A. (2001). Growing up in the projects: The economic lives of a cohort of men who came of age in Chicago public housing. *American Economic Review, 91,* 79–84.

Li, X., Stanton, B., Pack, R., Harris, C., Cottrell, L., & Burns, J. (2002). Risk and protective factors associated with gang involvement among urban African American adolescents. *Youth and Society, 34,* 172–194.

Lien, I.-J. (2005a). Criminal gangs and their connections: Metaphors, definitions, and structures. In S. H. Decker & F. M. Weerman (Eds.), *European street gangs and troublesome youth groups* (pp. 31–50). Lanham, MD: AltaMira Press.

Lien, I.-J. (2005b). The role of crime acts in constituting the gang's mentality. In S. H. Decker & F. M. Weerman (Eds.), *European street gangs and troublesome youth groups* (pp. 105–125). Lanham, MD: AltaMira Press.

Lipsey, M. W. (1995). What do we learn from 400 research studies on the effectiveness of treatment with juvenile delinquents? In J. McGuire (Ed.), *What works? Reducing reoffending* (pp. 63–78). New York: John Wiley.

Lipsey, M. W. (2009). The primary factors that characterize effective interventions with juvenile offenders: A meta-analytic overview. *Victims and Offenders, 4,* 124–147.

Lipsey, M. W., & Chapman, G. (2011). *Standardized Program Evaluation Protocol (SPEP): A user's guide.* Nashville, TN: Peabody Research Institute, Vanderbilt University.

Lipsey, M. W., & Howell, J. C. (2012). A broader view of evidence-based programs reveals more options for state juvenile justice systems. *Criminology and Public Policy, 11,* 515–523.

Lizotte, A. J., Howard, G. J., Krohn, M. D., & Thornberry, T. P. (1997). Patterns of illegal gun carrying among young urban males. *Valparaiso University Law Review, 31,* 375–393.

Lizotte, A. J., Krohn, M. D., Howell, J. C., Tobin, K., & Howard, G. J. (2000). Factors influencing gun carrying among young urban males over the adolescent-young adult life course. *Criminology, 38,* 811–834.

Lizotte, A. J., Tesoriero, J. M., Thornberry, T. P., & Krohn, M. D. (1994). Patterns of adolescent firearms ownership and use. *Justice Quarterly, 11,* 51–73.

Lobo, A. P., Flores, R. J. O., & Salvo, J. J. (2002). The impact of Hispanic growth on the racial/ethnic composition of New York City neighborhoods. *Urban Affairs Review, 37,* 703–727.

Loeber, R. (1990). Development and risk factors of juvenile antisocial behavior and delinquency. *Clinical Psycahology Review, 10,* 1–41.

Loeber, R. (1996). Developmental continuity, change, and pathways in male juvenile problem behaviors and delinquency. In J. D. Hawkins (Ed.), *Delinquency and crime: Current theories* (pp. 1–27). New York: Cambridge University Press.

Loeber, R., Burke, J. D., & Pardini, D. A. (2009). Development and etiology of disruptive and delinquent behavior. *Annual Review of Clinical Psychology, 5,* 291–310.

Loeber, R., & Farrington, D. P. (Eds.). (1998). *Serious and violent juvenile offenders: Risk factors and successful interventions.* Thousand Oaks, CA: Sage.

Loeber, R., & Farrington, D. P. (Eds.). (2001). *Child delinquents: Development, interventions, and service needs.* Thousand Oaks, CA: Sage.

Loeber, R., & Farrington, D. P. (2011). *Who will kill and who will be killed? Development of young homicide offenders and victims.* New York: Springer.

Loeber, R., Farrington, D. P., Howell, J. C., & Hoeve, M. (2012). Overview, conclusions and key recommendations. In R. Loeber & D. P. Farrington (Eds.). *From juvenile delinquency to adult crime* (pp. 315–383). New York: Oxford University Press.

Loeber, R., Farrington, D. P., Stouthamer-Loeber, M., White, H. R., & Wei, E. (2008). *Violence and serious theft: Development and prediction from childhood to adulthood.* New York: Routledge.

Loeber, R., Farrington, D. P., Stouthamer-Loeber, M., Moffitt, T. E., Caspi, A., White, H. R., Wei, E. H., & Beyers, J. M. (2003). The development of male offending: Key findings from fourteen years of the Pittsburgh Youth Study. In T. P. Thornberry & M. D. Krohn (Eds.), *Taking stock of delinquency: An overview of findings from contemporary longitudinal studies* (pp. 93–136). New York: Kluwer Academic/Plenum Publishers.

Loeber, R., Keenan, K., & Zhang, Q. (1997). Boys' experimentation and persistence in developmental pathways toward serious delinquency. *Journal of Child and Family Studies, 6,* 321–357.

Loeber, R., Slot, W., & Stouthamer-Loeber, M. (2007). A cumulative, three-dimensional, development model of serious delinquency. In P.-O. Wikstrom & R. Sampson (Eds.), *The explanation of crime: Context, mechanisms and development series* (pp. 153–194). Cambridge: Cambridge University Press.

Loeber, R., Wei, E., Stouthamer-Loeber, M., Huizinga, D., & Thornberry, T. P. (1999). Behavioral antecedents to serious and violent offending: Joint analyses from the Denver Youth Survey, Pittsburgh Youth Study and the Rochester Youth Development Study. *Studies on Crime and Crime Prevention, 8,* 245–263.

Lombardo, R. M. (1994). The social organization of organized crime in Chicago. *Journal of Contemporary Criminal Justice, 10,* 290–313.

Lombardo, R. M. (2002). The Black Hand: Terror by letter in Chicago. *Journal of Contemporary Criminal Justice, 18,* 394–409.

Lopez, D. A., & Brummett, P.O. (2003). Gang membership and acculturation: ARSMA-II and choloization. *Crime and Delinquency, 49,* 627–642.

Lopez, E. M., Wishard, A., Gallimore, R., & Rivera, W. (2006). Latino high school students' perception of gangs and crews. *Journal of Adolescent Research, 21,* 299–318.

Lopoo, L. M., & Western, B. (2005). Incarceration and the formation and stability of marital unions. *Journal of Marriage and the Family, 67*(3), 721–734.

Los Angeles Police Department. (2007). *2007 Gang Enforcement Initiatives.* Los Angeles: Author.

Ludwig, J. (2005). Better gun enforcement, less crime. *Criminology and Public Policy, 4,* 677–716.

Lurigio, A. J., Bensinger, G. D., & Thompson, S. R. (2000). *A process and outcome evaluation of Project BUILD: Years 5 and 6.* Unpublished Report. Chicago: Loyola University.

Lyman, M. D. (1989). *Gangland: Drug trafficking by organized criminals.* Springfield, IL: Charles C Thomas.

Lyons, W., & Drew, J. (2006). *Punishing schools: Fear and citizenship in American public education.* Ann Arbor: University of Michigan Press.

Macleod, J. F., Groves, P. G., & Farrington, D. P. (2012). *Explaining criminal careers.* Oxford: Oxford University Press.

Major, A. K., Egley, A., Jr., Howell, J. C., Mendenhall, B., & Armstrong, T. (2004). Youth gangs in Indian Country. *Juvenile Justice Bulletin.* Washington, DC: U.S. Department of Justice, Office of Juvenile Justice and Delinquency Prevention.

Manwaring, M. G. (2009a). *A "new" dynamic in the western hemisphere security environment: The Mexican Zetas and other private armies.* Carlisle, PA: Strategic Studies Institute, U.S Army College. Retrieved from www.StrategicStudiesInstitute.army.mil

Manwaring, M. G. (2009b). *State and nonstate associated gangs: Credible "midwives of new social orders."* Carlisle, PA: Strategic Studies Institute, U.S Army College. Retrieved from www.StrategicStudiesInstitute.army.mil

Mares, D. (2010). Social disorganization and gang homicides in Chicago: A neighborhood level comparison of disaggregated homicides. *Youth Violence and Juvenile Justice, 8,* 38–57.

Marks, C. (1985). Black labor migration: 1910–1920. *Critical Sociology, 12,* 5–24.

Martinez, R., Rodriguez, J., & Rodriguez, L. (1998). *East Side stories: Gang life in East L.A.* New York: PowerHouse.

Martinez, R., Rosenfeld, R., & Mares, D. (2008). Social disorganization, drug market activity, and neighborhood violent crime. *Urban Affairs Review, 43,* 846–874.

Matsuda, K. N., Esbensen, F., & Carson, D. C. (2012). Putting the "gang" in "Eurogang": Characteristics of delinquent youth groups by different definitional approaches. In F. Esbensen & C. L. Maxson (Eds.), *Youth gangs in international perspective: Results from the Eurogang Program of Research* (pp. 17–33). New York: Springer.

Matsuda, K. N., Melde, C., Taylor, T. J., Freng, A., & Esbensen, F.-A. (2013). Gang membership and adherence to the "code of the street." *Justice Quarterly, 30*(3), 1–29.

Maxson, C. L. (1998). *Gang members on the move* (Juvenile Justice Bulletin. Youth Gang Series). Washington, DC: Office of Juvenile Justice and Delinquency Prevention.

Maxson, C. L. (1999). Gang homicide: A review and extension of the literature. In D. Smith & M. Zahn (Eds.), *Homicide: A sourcebook of social research* (pp. 197–220). Thousand Oaks, CA: Sage.

Maxson, C. L., Gordon, M. A., & Klein, M. W. (1985). Differences between gang and nongang homicides. *Criminology, 23,* 209–222.

Maxson, C. L., & Klein, M. W. (1990). Street gang violence: Twice as great, or half as great? In C.R. Huff (Ed.), *Gangs in America* (pp. 71–100). Newbury Park, CA: Sage.

Maxson, C. L., Woods, K., & Klein, M. W. (1996). Street gang migration: How big a threat? *National Institute of Justice Journal, 230* (February), 26–31.

Maxson, C. L., Whitlock, M., & Klein, M. W. (1998). Vulnerability to street gang membership: Implications for prevention. *Social Service Review, 72*(1), 70–91.

McCorkle, R. C., & Miethe, T. D. (2002). *Panic: The social construction of the street gang problem.* Upper Saddle River, NJ: Prentice Hall.

McGarrell, E. F., & Chermak, S. (2003). Problem solving to reduce gangs and drug-related violence in Indianapolis. In S. H. Decker (Ed.), *Policing gangs and youth violence* (pp. 77–101). Belmont, CA: Wadsworth/Thompson Learning.

McGarrell, E. F., Hipple, N. K., Corsaro, N., Bynum, T. S., Perez, H., Zimmermann, C. A., & Garmo, M. (2009). *Project Safe Neighborhoods—A national program to reduce gun crime: Final project report.* Lansing: Michigan State University.

McGuire, C. (2007). *Central American youth gangs in the Washington D.C. area.* Washington, DC: Washington Office on Latin America.

McReynolds, L. S., Schwalbe, C. S., & Wasserman, G. A. (2010). The contribution of psychiatric disorder to juvenile recidivism. *Criminal Justice and Behavior, 37,* 204–216.

McReynolds, L. S., Wasserman, G. A., DeComo, R. E., John, R., Keating, J. M., & Nolen, S. (2008). Psychiatric disorder in a juvenile assessment center. *Crime and Delinquency, 54,* 313–334.

McWilliams, C. (1943, June). Zoot-suit riots. *New Republic, 108,* 818–820.

McWilliams, C. (1948/1990). *North from Mexico: The Spanish-speaking people of the United States* (Rev. ed.). New York: Greenwood.

Melde, C. (2009). Lifestyle, rational choice, and adolescent fear: A test of a risk-assessment framework. *Criminology, 47,* 781–812.

Melde, C., & Esbensen, F. (2011). Gang membership as a turning point in the life course. *Criminology, 49,* 513–552.

Melde, C., & Rennison, C. M. (2008). The effect of gang perpetrated crime on the likelihood of victim injury. *American Journal of Criminal Justice, 33,* 234–251.

Melde, C., Taylor, T. J., & Esbensen, F. (2009). "I got your back": An examination of the protective function of gang membership in adolescence. *Criminology, 47,* 565–594.

Miethe, T. D., & McCorkle, R. C. (1997). Gang membership and criminal processing: A test of the "master status" concept. *Justice Quarterly, 14,* 407–427.

Miller, B. J. (2008). The struggle over redevelopment at Cabrini-Green, 1989–2004. *Journal of Urban History, 34,* 944–960.

Miller, J. A. (2001). *One of the guys: Girls, gangs and gender.* New York: Oxford University Press.

Miller, J. A. (2008). *Getting played: African American girls, urban inequality, and gendered violence.* New York: New York University Press.

Miller, J. A. (2013). Getting into gangs. In C. L. Maxson, A. Egley, J. A. Miller, & M. A. Klein (Eds). *The modern gang reader* (4th ed., pp. 86–102). New York: Oxford University Press.

Miller, J. A., & Brunson, R. (2000). Gender dynamics in youth gangs: A comparison of males' and females' accounts. *Justice Quarterly, 17,* 419–448.

Miller, J. A., & Decker, S. H. (2001). Young women and gang violence: Gender, street offending, and violent victimization in gangs. *Justice Quarterly, 18,* 601–626.

Miller, W. B. (1958). Lower class culture as a generating milieu of gang delinquency. *Journal of Social Issues, 14,* 5–19.

Miller, W. B. (1962). The impact of a "total community" delinquency control project. *Social Problems, 10,* 168–191.

Miller, W. B. (1966). Violent crimes in city gangs. *The Annals of the American Academy of Political and Social Science, 364,* 96–112.

Miller, W. B. (1966/2011). *City gangs.* Phoenix, AZ: Arizona State University.

Miller, W. B. (1973). Race, sex, and gangs: The Molls. *Trans-Action, 11*(1), 32–35.

Miller, W. B. (1974a). American youth gangs: Fact and fantasy. In L. Rainwater (Ed.), *Deviance and liberty: A survey of modern perspectives on deviant behavior* (pp. 262–273). Chicago: Aldine.

Miller, W. B. (1974b). American youth gangs: Past and present. In A. Blumberg (Ed.), *Current perspectives on criminal behavior* (pp. 210–239). New York: Knopf.

Miller, W. B. (1975). *Violence by youth gangs and youth groups as a crime problem in major American cities.* Washington, DC: U.S. Department of Justice, Office of Juvenile Justice and Delinquency Prevention.

Miller, W. B. (1982/1992). *Crime by youth gangs and groups in the United States.* Washington, DC: U.S. Department of Justice, Office of Juvenile Justice and Delinquency Prevention.

Miller, W. B. (2001). *The growth of youth gang problems in the United States: 1970–1998.* Washington, DC: Office of Juvenile Justice and Delinquency Prevention.

Miller, W. B., Geertz, H., & Cutter, H. S. G. (1962). Aggression in a boys' street-corner group. *Psychiatry, 24,* 283–298.

Moffitt, T. E. (1993). Adolescence-limited and life-course-persistent antisocial behavior: A developmental taxonomy. *Psychological Review, 100,* 674–701.

Monti, D. J. (1991). The practice of gang research. *Sociological Practice Review, 1,* 29–39.

Monti, D. J. (1993). Gangs in more- and less-settled communities. In S. Cummings & D. J. Monti (Eds.), *Gangs: The origins and impact of contemporary youth gangs in the United States* (pp. 219–253). Albany: State University of New York Press.

Moore, J. W. (1978). *Homeboys: Gangs, drugs and prison in the barrios of Los Angeles.* Philadelphia: Temple University Press.

Moore, J. W. (1988). Introduction: Gangs and the underclass: A comparative perspective. In J. M. Hagedorn, *People and Folks* (pp. 3–17). Chicago: Lake View Press.

Moore, J. W. (1991). *Going down to the barrio: Homeboys and homegirls in change.* Philadelphia: Temple University Press.

Moore, J. W. (1993). Gangs, drugs, and violence. In S. Cummings & D. J. Monti (Eds.), *Gangs* (pp. 27–46). Albany: State University of New York Press.

Moore, J. W. (1994). The *chola* life course: Chicana heroin users and the barrio gang. *International Journal of Addictions, 29,* 1115–1126.

Moore, J. W. (1998). Understanding youth street gangs: Economic restructuring and the urban underclass. In M. W. Watts (Ed.), *Cross-cultural perspectives on youth and violence* (pp. 65–78). Stamford, CT: JAI.

Moore, J. W. (2007a). Female gangs: Gender and globalization. In J. M. Hagedorn (Ed.), *Gangs in the global city* (pp. 187–203). Chicago: University of Illinois Press.

Moore, J. W. (2007b). Foreword. In A. Valdez, *Mexican American girls and gang violence: Beyond risk* (pp. ix–xii). New York: Palgrave Macmillan.

Moore, J. W., & Hagedorn, J. M. (1996). What happens to girls in the gang? In C. R. Huff (Ed.), *Gangs in America* (2nd ed., pp. 205–218). Thousand Oaks, CA: Sage.

Moore, J. W., & Hagedorn, J. M. (1999). What happens to girls in the gang? In M. Chesney-Lind & J. Hagedorn (Eds.), *Female gangs in America: Essays on girls, gangs, and gender* (pp. 176–186). Chicago: Lake View Press.

Moore, J. W., & Hagedorn, J. M. (2001). *Female gangs* (Juvenile Justice Bulletin. Youth Gang Series). Washington, DC: U.S. Department of Justice, Office of Juvenile Justice and Delinquency Prevention.

Moore, J. W., & Long, J. M. (1987). *Final report: Youth culture vs. individual factors in adult drug use.* Los Angeles: Community Systems Research.

Moore, J. W., & Pinderhughes, R. (1993). Introduction. In J. W. Moore & R. Pinderhughes (Eds.), *In the barrios: Latinos and the underclass debate* (pp. xi–xxxix). New York: Russell Sage Foundation.

Moore, J. W., & Vigil, D. (1993). Barrios in transition. In J. W. Moore & R. Pinderhughes (Eds.), *In the barrios: Latinos and the underclass debate* (pp. 27–49). New York: Russell Sage Foundation.

Moore, J. W., Vigil, D., & Garcia, R. (1983). Residence and territoriality in Chicano gangs. *Social Problems, 31,* 182–194.

Moore, T. J. (2007, March 10). Bangin'. . . in Asheville? *The Urban News.* Retrieved from http://theurbannews.com/our-town/2007/bangin-in-asheville/

Morales, D. (1991). *Gangs in Texas cities: Background, survey results, state level policy options.* Washington, DC: U.S. Department of Justice, National Institute of Justice. Retrieved from https://www.ncjrs.gov/pdffiles1/Digitization/137580NCJRS.pdf

Morash, M. (1983). Gangs, groups, and delinquency. *British Journal of Criminology, 23,* 309–335.

Morenoff, J. D., Sampson, R. J., & Raudenbush, S. W. (2001). Neighborhood inequality, collective efficacy, and the spatial dynamics of urban violence. *Criminology, 39*(3), 517–559.

Mulvihill, D. J., & Tumin, M. M. (Eds.). (1969). *Crimes of violence.* Washington, DC: U.S. Government Printing Office.

Murray, D. R. (1975). Hanguns, gun control laws and firearm violence. *Social Problems, 23,* 81–93.

National Advisory Commission on Criminal Justice Standards and Goals. (1973). *A national strategy to reduce crime.* Washington, DC: U.S. Government Printing Office

National Alliance of Gang Investigators' Associations. (2005). *National gang threat assessment: 2005.* Washington, DC: Bureau of Justice Assistance, U.S. Department of Justice.

National Alliance of Gang Investigators' Associations. (2009). *Quick guide to gangs.* Washington, DC: Bureau of Justice Assistance, U.S. Department of Justice.

National Center on Addiction and Substance Abuse. (2010). *National Survey of American Attitudes on Substance Abuse XV: Teens and parents, 2010.* New York: Author.

National Drug Intelligence Center. (2003). *Rhode Island: Drug threat assessment.* Washington, DC: U.S. Department of Justice.

National Drug Intelligence Center. (2008). *National drug threat assessment: 2009.* Washington, DC: U.S. Department of Justice, National Drug Intelligence Center.

National Gang Center. (n.d.) *Parents' guide to gangs.* Tallahassee, FL: Author. Retrieved from http://www.nationalgangcenter.gov/Content/Documents/Parents-Guide-to-Gangs.pdf

National Gang Center. (2010). *Best practices to address community gang problems: OJJDP's Comprehensive Gang Model.* Washington, DC: Author. Retrieved from www.ncjrs.gov/pdffiles1/ojjdp/231200.pdf

National Gang Center. (2013a). *Federal and state definitions of the terms "gang," "gang crime," and "gang member."* Tallahassee, FL: Institute for Intergovernmental Research, National Gang Center.

National Gang Center. (2013b). Highlights of gang-related legislation: December, 2013. Tallahassee, FL: Institute for Intergovernmental Research, National Gang Center. Retrieved from http://www.national gangcenter.gov/Legislation/Highlights

National Gang Intelligence Center. (2012). *National Gang Threat Assessment: 2011.* Washington, DC: Federal Bureau of Investigation, U.S. Department of Justice.

National Research Council. (2004). *Firearms and violence: A critical review.* Washington, DC: The National Academies Press.

National Youth Gang Center. (2000). *1998 National Youth Gang Survey.* Washington, DC: U.S. Department of Justice, Office of Juvenile Justice and Delinquency Prevention.

Needle, J., & Stapleton, W. V. (1983). *Police handling of youth gangs.* Washington, DC: U.S. Department of Justice, Office of Juvenile

Ness, C. D. (2004). Why girls fight: Female youth violence in the inner city. *The Annals of the American Academy of Political and Social Science, 595,* 32–48.

Ness, C. D. (2010). *Why girls fight: Female youth violence in the inner city.* New York: New York University Press.

Nickel, M., Luley, J., Nickel, C., & Widermann, C. (2006). Bullying girls—changes after Brief Strategic Family Therapy: A randomized, prospective, controlled trial with one-year follow-up. *Psychotherapy and Psychosomatics, 75,* 47–55.

North Carolina Department of Juvenile Justice and Delinquency Prevention. (2009). *Request for proposals: Community-based youth gang violence prevention grant project.* Raleigh: Author.

North Carolina Department of Juvenile Justice and Delinquency Prevention & Department of Public Instruction. (2008). *School violence/gang activity study* (S.L. 2008-56). Raleigh: Author.

North Carolina Metropolitan Mayors Coalition. (2010). *Anti-gang summary by city.* Retrieved from http://ncmetromayors.com/files/2010/12/Updated-10-City-Anti-Gang-Summary-North-Carolina-Metropolitan-2.pdf

Obeidallah, D. A., & Earls, F. J. (1999). Adolescent girls: The role of depression in the development of delinquency. *Research Preview.* Washington, DC: U.S. Department of Justice, National Institute of Justice.

Oehme, C. G. (1997). Gangs, groups and crime: Perceptions and responses of community organizations. Durham, NC: Carolina Academic Press.

Office of Juvenile Justice and Delinquency Prevention. (2009a). *OJJDP Comprehensive Gang Model: A guide to assessing a community's youth gang problems.* Washington, DC: U.S. Department of Justice, Office of Juvenile Justice and Delinquency Prevention. Retrieved from www.nationalgang center.gov/Content/Documents/Assessment-Guide/ Assessment-Guide.pdf

Office of Juvenile Justice and Delinquency Prevention. (2009b). *OJJDP Comprehensive Gang Model: Planning for implementation.* Washington, DC: U.S. Department of Justice, Office of Juvenile Justice and Delinquency Prevention. Retrieved from www.nationalgangcenter.gov/Content/Documents/ Implementation-Manual/Implementation-Manual.pdf

Olson, D. E., & Dooley, B. (2006). Gang membership and community corrections populations: Characteristics and recidivism rates relative to other offenders. In J. F. Short & L. A. Hughes (Eds.), *Studying youth gangs* (pp. 193–202). Lanham, MD: AltaMira Press.

Olweus, D., Limber, S., & Mihalic, S. F. (1999). *Blueprints for violence prevention, book nine: Bullying prevention program.* Boulder, CO: Center for the Study and Prevention of Violence.

Osher, D., Dwyer, K., & Jackson, S. (2004). *Safe, supportive and successful schools: Step by step.* Longmont, CO: Sopris West.

Ousey, G. O., & Lee, M. R. (2004). Investigating the connections between race, illicit drug markets, and lethal violence, 1984–1997. *Journal of Research in Crime and Delinquency, 41,* 352–383.

Pager, D. (2003). The mark of a criminal record. *American Journal of Sociology, 108*(5), 937–975.

Papachristos, A. V. (2001). *A.D., after the Disciples: The neighborhood impact of federal gang prosecution.* Peotone, IL: New Chicago Schools Press.

Papachristos, A. V. (2004). *Gangs in the global city: The impact of globalization on post-industrial street gangs.* Paper presented at the Workshop on the Sociology and Cultures of Globalization. Chicago: University of Chicago, Department of Sociology.

Papachristos, A. V. (2005a). Gang world. *Foreign Policy, 147*(March–April), 48–55.

Papachristos, A. V. (2005b). Interpreting inkblots: Deciphering and doing something about modern street gangs. *Criminology & Public Policy, 4,* 643–651.

Papachristos, A. V. (2009). Murder by structure: Dominance relations and the social structure of gang homicide. *American Journal of Sociology, 115,* 74–128.

Papachristos, A. V., Hureau, D. M., & Braga, A. A. (2013). The corner and the crew: The influence of geography and social networks on gang violence. *American Sociological Review, 18,* 417–447.

Papachristos, A. V., & Kirk, D. S. (2006). Neighborhood effects on street gang behavior. In J. F. Short & L. A. Hughes (Eds.), *Studying youth gangs* (pp. 63–84). Lanham, MD: AltaMira Press.

Papachristos, A. V., Meares, T., & Fagan, J. (2005). *Attention felons: Evaluating Project Safe Neighborhoods in Chicago.* Chicago: The Law School, University of Chicago.

Park, R. E. (1921). Sociology and the social sciences: The social organism and the collective mind. *The American Journal of Sociology, 27*(1), 1–21.

Park, R. E. (1936a). Human ecology. *The American Journal of Sociology, 42*(July), 1–15.

Park, R. E. (1936b). Succession: An ecological concept. *American Sociological Review, 1*(April), 171–179.

Park, R. E., & Burgess, E. W. (1921). *Introduction to the science of sociology.* Chicago: University of Chicago Press.

Park, R. E., & Burgess, E. W. (Eds.). (1925). *The city.* Chicago: University of Chicago Press.

Park, S., Morash, M., & Stevens, T. (2010). Gender differences in predictors of assaultive behavior in late adolescence. *Youth Violence and Juvenile Justice, 8,* 314–331.

Pastor, M. Jr., Sadd, J., & Hipp, J. (2001). Which came first? Toxic facilities, minority move-in, and environmental justice. *Journal of Urban Affairs, 23,* 1–21.

Patterson, G. R., Capaldi, D., & Bank, L. (1991). An early starter model for predicting delinquency. In D. J. Pepler & K. H. Rubin (Eds.), *The development and treatment of childhood aggression* (pp. 139–168). Hillsdale, NJ: Lawrence Erlbaum.

Paz, O. (1961/1990). *The labryinth of solitude.* London: Penguin.

Pepler, D. J., Madsen, K., Levene, K., & Webster, C. (2004). *The development and treatment of girlhood aggression.* Hillsdale, NJ: Lawrence Erlbaum.

Pepler, D. J., Walsh, M., Yuile, A., Levene, K. Jiang, D., Vaughan, & A., Webber, J. (2010). Bridging the gender gap: Interventions with aggressive girls and their parents. *Prevention Science, 11,* 229–238.

Perkins, U. E. (1987). *Explosion of Chicago's Black street gangs: 1900 to the present.* Chicago: Third World Press.

Petersen, R. D. (2004). Definitions of a gang and impacts on public policy. In R. D. Petersen (Ed.), *Understanding contemporary gangs in America* (pp. 19–34). Upper Saddle River, NJ: Pearson Prentice Hall.

Petersen, R. D., & Howell, J. C. (2013). Program approaches for girls in gangs: Female specific or gender neutral? *Criminal Justice Review, 38,* 491–509.

Petersen, R. D., & Valdez, A. (2004). Intimate partner violence among Hispanic females. *Journal of Ethnicity in Criminal Justice, 2,* 67–89.

Petersen, R. D., & Valdez, A. (2005). Using snowball-based methods in hidden populations to generate a randomized community sample. *Youth Violence and Juvenile Justice, 3,* 151–167.

Peterson, D. (2012). Girlfriends, gun-holders, and ghetto-rats? Moving beyond narrow views of girls in gangs. In S. Miller, L. D. Leve, & P. K. Kerig (Eds.), *Delinquent girls: Contexts, relationships, and adaptation* (pp. 71–84). New York: Springer.

Peterson, D., & Carson, D. C. (2012). The sex composition of groups and youths' delinquency: A comparison of gang and nongang peer groups. In F. Esbensen & C. L. Maxson (Eds.), *Youth gangs in international perspective: Results from the Eurogang Program of Research* (pp. 189–210). New York: Springer.

Peterson, D., Miller, J., & Esbensen, F. (2001). The impact of sex composition on gangs and gang delinquency. *Criminology, 39,* 411–439.

Peterson, D., & Morgan, K. A. (2014). Sex differences and the overlap in youths' risk factors for onset of violence and gang involvement. *Journal of Crime and Justice, 37,* 129–154.

Peterson, D., Taylor, T. J., & Esbensen, F. (2004). Gang membership and violent victimization. *Justice Quarterly, 21,* 793–815.

Peterson, R. D., & Krivo, L. J. (2009). Segregated spatial locations, race-ethnic composition, and neighborhood violent crime. *The Annals of the American Academy of Political and Social Science, 623,* 93–107.

Peterson, R. D., & Krivo, L. J. (2010). *Divergent social worlds: Neighborhood crime and the racial-spatial divide.* New York: Russell Sage Foundation.

Pew Center. (2009, February 10). McDonald's and Starbucks: 43% Yin, 35% Yang. *Pew Research: Social & Demographic Trends.* Retrieved from http://www.pewsocialtrends.org/2009/02/10/mcdonalds-and-starbucks-43-yin-35-yang/

Pincus, F. L., & Ehrlich, H. J. (1999). Immigration. In F. L. Pincus & H. J. Ehrlich (Eds.), *Race and ethnic conflict* (pp. 223–228). Boulder, CO: Westview Press.

Piquero, A. R. (2008). Taking stock of developmental trajectories of criminal activity over the life course. In A. Liberman (Ed.), *The long view of crime: A synthesis of longitudinal research* (pp. 23–78). New York: Springer.

Pitts, J. (2008). Reluctant gangsters: The changing face of youth crime. Devon, UK: Willan Publishing.

Pizarro, J. M., & McGloin, J. M. (2006). Explaining gang homicides in Newark, New Jersey: Collective behavior or social disorganization? *Journal of Criminal Justice, 34,* 195–207.

Pogarsky, G., Lizotte, A. J., & Thornberry, T. P. (2003). The delinquency of children born to young mothers: Results from the Rochester Youth Development Study. *Criminology, 41,* 1249–1286.

Popkin, S. J., Gwiasda, V. E., Olson, L. M., Rosenbaum, D. P., & Burton, L. (2000). *The hidden war: Crime and the tragedy of public housing in Chicago.* New Brunswick, NJ: Rutgers University Press.

Popkin, S. J., Leventhal, T., & Weismann, G. (2008). *Girls in the 'hood: The importance of feeling safe* (Brief No. 1). Washington, DC: The Urban Institute.

Popkin, S. J., Leventhal, T., & Weismann, G. (2010). Girls in the 'hood: How safety affects the life chances of low-income girls. *Urban Affairs Review, 45,* 715–744.

Popkin, S. J., Rich, M. J., Hendey, L., Hayes, C., & Parilla, J. (2012). Public housing transformation and crime: Making the case for responsible relocation. *Cityscape, 14,* 137–160.

Portes, A., & Rumbaut, R. G. (2005). Introduction: The second generation and the Children of Immigrants Longitudinal Study. *Ethnic and Racial Studies, 28,* 983–999.

Portes, A., & Zhou, M. (1993). The new second generation: Segmented assimilation and its variants. *The Annals of the American Academy of Political and Social Sciences, 530,* 74–96.

Pratt, T. C., & Cullen, F. T. (2005). Assessing macro-level predictors and theories of crime: A meta-analysis. In M. Tonry (Ed.), *Crime and justice: A review of research* (Vol. 32, pp. 373–450). Chicago: University of Chicago Press.

President's Commission on Law Enforcement and Administration of Justice. (1967). *The challenge of crime in a free society.* Washington, DC: U.S. Government Printing.

Puffer, J. A. (1912). *The boy and his gang.* Boston: Houghton Mifflin.

Pyrooz, D. C. (2014a). From colors and guns to caps and gowns: The effects of gang membership on educational attainment. *Journal of Research in Crime and Delinquency, 51,* 56–87.

Pyrooz, D. C. (2014b). "From your first cigarette to your last dying day": The patterning of gang membership in the life-course. *Journal of Quantitative Criminology, 30,* 349–372.

Pyrooz, D. C., Decker, S. H., & Fleisher, M. (2011). From the street to the prison, from the prison to the street: Understanding and responding to prison gangs. *Journal of Aggression, Conflict and Peace Research, 3,* 12–24.

Pyrooz, D. C., Decker, S. H., & Webb, V. J. (2014). The ties that bind: Desistance from gangs. *Crime and Delinquency, 60,* 491–516.

Pyrooz, D. C., Fox, A. M., & Decker, S. H. (2010). Racial and ethnic heterogeneity, economic disadvantage, and gangs: A macro-level study of gang membership in urban America. *Justice Quarterly, 14,* 1–26.

Pyrooz, D. C., Fox, A. M., Katz, C. M., & Decker, S. H. (2012). Gang organization, offending, and victimization: A cross-national analysis. In F. Esbensen & C.L. Maxson (Eds.), *Youth gangs in international perspective: Results from the Eurogang Program of Research* (pp. 85–105). New York: Springer.

Pyrooz, D. C., Sweeten, G., & Piquero, A. R. (2013). Continuity and change in gang membership and gang embeddedness. *Journal of Research in Crime and Delinquency, 50,* 239–271.

Pyrooz, D. C., Wolf, S. E., & Spohn, C. (2011). Gang-related homicide charging decisions: The implementation of a specialized prosecution unit in Los Angeles. *Criminal Justice Policy Review, 22,* 3–26.

Quicker, J. C. (1983a). *Homegirls: Characterizing Chicano gangs.* San Pedro, CA: International University Press.

Quicker, J. C. (1983b). *Seven decades of gangs.* Sacramento, CA: California Commission on Crime Control and Violence Prevention.

Quinn, E. (2005). *Nuthin' but a "g" thang: The culture and commerce of gangster rap.* New York: Columbia University Press.

Ralph, P., Hunter, J., Marquart, W., Cuvelier, J., & Merianos, D. (1996). Exploring the differences between gang and non-gang prisoners. In C. R. Huff (Ed.), *Gangs in America* (2nd ed., pp. 241–256). Thousand Oaks, CA: Sage.

Ransford, C., Kane, C., Metzger, T., Quintana, E., & Slutkin, G. (2010). An examination of the role of CeaseFire, the Chicago police, Project Safe Neighborhoods, and displacement in the reduction in homicide in Chicago in 2004. In R. J. Chaskin (Ed.), *Youth gangs and community intervention: Research, practice, and evidence* (pp. 76–108). New York: Columbia University Press.

Reckless, W. C., Dinitz, S., & Murray, E. (1956). Self-concept as an insulator against delinquency. *American Sociological Review, 21,* 744–746.

Redfield, R. (1941). *Folk culture of Yucatan.* Chicago: University of Chicago Press.

Reeves, J. L., & Campbell, R. (1994). Cracked coverage: Television news, the anti-cocaine crusade, and the Reagan legacy. Durham, NC: Duke University Press.

Rennison, C. M., & Melde, C. (2009). Exploring the use of victim surveys to study gang crime: Prospects and possibilities. *Criminal Justice Review, 34,* 489–514.

Resnick, M. D., Ireland, M., & Borowsky, I. (2004). Youth violence perpetration: What protects? What predicts? Findings from the National Longitudinal Study of Adolescent Health. *Journal of Adolescent Health, 35,* 424.e1–424.e10.

Rhoades, B. L., Bumbarger, B. K., & Moore, J. E. (2012). The role of a state-level prevention support system in promoting high-quality implementation and sustainability of evidence-based programs. *American Journal of Community Psychology, 50,* 386–401.

Rich, M., Owens, M. L., Griffiths, E., Haspel, M., Hill, K., Smith, A., & Stigers, K. (2010). *McDaniel-Glenn evaluation: Final report.* Retrieved from http://oucp.emory.edu/our_work/research/mg.html

Riis, J. A. (1892). *Children of the poor.* New York: Charles Scribner's Sons.

Riis, J. A. (1902/1969). *The battle with the slum.* Montclair, NJ: Paterson Smith.

Rizzo, K. (2013, November 25). Crime in America: Top 10 most dangerous cities under 200,000. *LawStreetMedia.com.* Retrieved from http://lawstreetmedia.com/blogs/crime/10-dangerous-small/

Ro, R. (1996). *Gangsta: Merchandizing the rhymes of violence.* New York: St. Martin's Press.

Robbins, M. S., & Szapocznik, J. (2000). *Brief strategic family therapy* (Juvenile Justice Bulletin). Washington, DC: U.S. Department of Justice, Office of Juvenile Justice and Delinquency Prevention.

Robers, S., Zhang, J., & Truman. (2012). *Indicators of school crime and safety, 2011* (NCES 2012-002/ NCJ 236021). Washington, DC: U.S. Department of Justice, National Center for Education Statistics, Bureau of Justice Statistics.

Rodgers, D., & Hazen, J. M. (2014). Introduction: Gangs in a global and comparative perspective. In J. M. Hazen & D. Rodgers (Eds.), *Global gangs: Street violence across the world* (pp. 1–25). Minneapolis: University of Minnesota.

Rodríguez, L. (2001). *Hearts and hands: Creating community in violent times.* New York: Seven Stories Press.

Rosenfeld, R., Bray, T. M., & Egley, A., Jr. (1999). Facilitating violence: A comparison of gang-motivated, gang-affiliated, and nongang youth homicides. *Journal of Quantitative Criminology, 15,* 495–515.

Rosenfeld, R., Fornango, R., & Baumer, E. (2005). Did Ceasefire, Compstat, and Exile reduce homicide? *Criminology and Public Policy, 4,* 419–449.

Rubel, A. J. (1965). The Mexican American palomilla. *Anthropological Linguistics, 4,* 29–97.

Sabol, W. J., Minton, T. D., & Harrison, P. M. (2007). *Prison and jail inmates at midyear 2006* (Bureau of Justice Statistics Bulletin). Washington, DC: U.S. Department of Justice, Bureau of Justice Statistics.

Sampson, R. J. (2002). The community. In J. Petersilia & J. Q. Wilson (Eds.), *Crime: Public policies for crime control* (pp. 225–252). Oakland, CA: Institute for Contemporary Studies Press.

Sampson, R. J. (2008). Rethinking crime and immigration. *Contexts, 7,* 28–33.

Sampson, R. J., & Graif, C. (2009). Neighborhood social capital as differential social organization: Resident and leadership dimensions. *American Behavioral Scientist, 52,* 1579–1605.

Sampson, R. J., & Groves, B. W. (1989). Community structure and crime: Testing social-disorganization theory. *American Journal of Sociology, 94,* 774–802.

Sampson, R. J., & Laub, J. H. (1993). *Crime in the making: Pathways and turning points through life.* Cambridge, MA: Harvard University Press.

Sampson, R. J., & Laub, J. H. (1997). A life-course theory of cumulative disadvantage and the stability of delinquency. In T. P. Thornberry (Ed.), *Developmental theories of crime and delinquency* (pp. 133–161). New Brunswick, NJ: Transaction Publishing.

Sampson, R. J., & Laub, J. H. (2005). A life-course view of the development of crime. *The Annals of the American Academy of Political and Social Science, 602,* 12–45.

Sampson, R. J., Morenoff, J. D., & Gannon-Rowley, T. (2002). Assessing "neighborhood effects": Social processes and new directions in research. *Annual Review of Sociology, 28,* 443–478.

Sampson, R. J., Raudenbush, S. W., & Earls, F. (1997). Neighborhoods and violent crime: A multilevel study of collective efficacy. *Science, 277,* 918–924.

Sanchez-Jankowski, M. S. (1991). *Islands in the street: Gangs and American urban society.* Berkeley: University of California Press.

Sanchez-Jankowski, M. S. (2003). Gangs and social change. *Theoretical Criminology, 7,* 191–216.

Sanders, W. B. (1994). *Gangbangs and drive-bys: Grounded culture and juvenile gang violence.* New York: Aldine de Gruyter.

Santa Cruz, N. (2014, January 19). South Vermont Avenue: L.A. county's "death valley": Tiny Westmont has highest homicide rate in the country. *Los Angeles Times.* Retrieved from http://homicide.latimes.com/post/westmont-homicides/

Sante, L. (1991). *Low life: Lures and snares of old New York.* New York: Vintage Books.

Sarnecki, J. (2001). *Delinquent networks: Youth co-offending in Stockholm.* Cambridge: Cambridge University Press.

Saunders, B. (2011, February 12). The upshot might be no hoax. *The News and Observer,* p. B1.

Schalet, A., Hunt, J., & Joe-Laidler, K. (2003). Respectability and autonomy: The articulation and meaning of sexuality among the girls in the gang. *Journal of Contemporary Ethnography, 32,* 108–143.

Schlosser, E. (1998). The prison-industrial complex. *The Atlantic Monthly* (December), pp. 51–77.

Schneider, E. C. (1999). Vampires, dragons, and Egyptian kings: Youth gangs in postwar New York. Princeton, NJ: Princeton University Press.

Schram, P. J., & Gaines, L. K. (2005). Examining delinquent non-gang members and delinquent gang members: A comparison of juvenile probationers at intake and outcomes. *Youth Violence and Juvenile Justice, 3,* 99–115.

Schroeder, M. B. (2011). Economic inequality, economic segregation, and political participation. Retrieved from ProQuest Dissertations and Theses. (Accession Order No. AAT 304510362)

Schweinhart, L. J., Montie, J., Xiang, Z., Barnett, W. S., Belfield, C. R., & Nores, M. (2005). *Lifetime effects: The High/Scope Perry Preschool study through age 40.* Ypsilanti, MI: The High/Scope Press.

Scott, J. H. (1904–05). Social instinct and its development in boy life. *Association Seminar, 13* (June–July), 257–270, 285–308, 355–358, 365–379.

Seele, A., Arnson, C. J., & Olson, E. L. (2013). *Crime and violence in Mexico and Central America: An evolving but incomplete US policy response.* Washington, DC: Migration Policy Institute.

Seelke, C. (2012). *Gangs in Central America* (CRS Report RL34112). Washington, DC: Congressional Research Service, Library of Congress.

Seelke, C. R. (2014). *Gangs in Central America* (CRS Report for Congress RL34112). Washington, DC: Congressional Research Service, Library of Congress.

Shaw, C. R. (1930). *The jack roller.* Chicago: University of Chicago Press.

Shaw, C. R., & McKay, H. D. (1931). Social factors in juvenile delinquency: A study of the community, the family, and the gang in relation to delinquent behavior. In *National Commission on Law Observance and Enforcement, Report on the causes of crime* (Vol. 2, No. 13, Ch. 6). Washington, DC: U.S. Government Printing Office.

Shaw, C. R., & McKay, H. D. (1942). *Juvenile delinquency and urban areas.* Chicago: University of Chicago Press.

Shaw, C. R., & McKay, H. D. (1969). *Juvenile delinquency and urban areas* (2nd ed.). Chicago: University of Chicago Press.

Shaw, C. R., Zorbaugh, F. M., McKay, H. D., & Cottrell, L. S. (1929). *Delinquency areas.* Chicago: University of Chicago Press.

Shelden, R. G. (1991). A comparison of gang members and non-gang members in a prison setting. *The Prison Journal, 81*(2), 50–60.

Sheldon, H. D. (1898). The institutional activities of American children. *The American Journal of Psychology, 9,* 424–448.

Sheley, J. F., & Wright, J. D. (1993). *Gun acquisition and possession in selected juvenile samples* (Research in Brief). Washington, DC: National Institute of Justice and Office of Juvenile Justice and Delinquency Prevention.

Sheley, J. F., & Wright, J. D. (1995). *In the line of fire: Youth, guns and violence in urban America.* Hawthorne, NY: Aldine De Gruyter.

Short, J. F., Jr. (1968). *Gang delinquency and delinquent subcultures.* Oxford: Harper & Row.

Short, J. F., Jr. (1996). *Gangs and adolescent violence.* Boulder: Center for the Study of Prevention of Violence, University of Colorado.

Short, J. F., Jr. (1998). The level of explanation problem revisited—The American Society of Criminology 1997 Presidential Address. *Criminology, 36,* 3–36.

Short, J. F., Jr. (2006). Why study gangs? An intellectual journey. In J. F. Short & L. A. Hughes (Eds.), *Studying youth gangs* (pp. 1–14). Lanham, MD: AltaMira Press.

Short, J. F., Jr., & Hughes, L. A. (2006a). Moving gang research forward. In J. F. Short & L. A. Hughes (Eds.), *Studying youth gangs* (pp. 225–238). Lanham, MD: AltaMira Press.

Short, J. F., Jr., & Hughes, L. A. (Eds.). (2006b). *Studying youth gangs.* Lanham, MD: AltaMira Press.

Short, J. F., Jr., & Hughes, L. A. (2009). Urban ethnography and research integrity: Empirical and theoretical dimensions. *Ethnography, 10,* 397–415.

Short, J. F., Jr., & Hughes, L. A. (2010). Promoting research integrity in community-based intervention research. In R. J. Chaskin (Ed.), *Youth gangs and community intervention: Research, practice, and evidence* (pp. 127–151). New York: Columbia University Press.

Short, J. F., Jr., & Strodtbeck, F. L. (1965/1974). *Group process and gang delinquency.* Chicago: University of Chicago Press.

Simon, T. R., Ritter, N. M., & Mahendra, R. R. E. (2013). *Changing course: Preventing gang membership* (NCJ 239234). Washington, DC: National Center for Injury Prevention and Control, Centers for Disease Control and Prevention, U.S. Department of Health and Human Services, and National Institute of Justice, Office of Justice Programs, U.S. Department of Justice.

Skiba, R. J., & Peterson, R. (1999). The dark side of zero tolerance: Can punishment lead to safe schools? *Phi Delta Kappan, 80,* 372–376.

Skogan, W. G., Hartnett, S. M., Bump, N., & Dubois, J. (2008). *Evaluation of CeaseFire-Chicago.* Final Report to the National Institute of Justice. Chicago, IL: Northwestern University. Retrieved from http://www.ncjrs.gov/pdffiles1/nij/grants/227181.pdf

Skolnick, J. H. (1989). *Gang organization and migration.* Sacramento, CA: Office of the Attorney General of the State of California.

Skolnick, J. H. (1990). The social structure of street drug dealing. *American Journal of Police, 9,* 1–41.

Snyder, H. N., & Sickmund, M. (2006). *Juvenile offenders and victims: 2006 national report.* Washington, DC: Office of Juvenile Justice and Delinquency Prevention.

Spaulding, C. B. (1948). Cliques, gangs, and networks. *Sociology and Social Research, 32,* 928–937.

Spergel, I. A. (1964). *Racketville, Slumtown and Haulberg: An exploratory study of delinquent subcultures.* Chicago: University of Chicago Press.

Spergel, I. A. (1966). *Street gang work: Theory and practice.* Reading, MA: Addison-Wesley.

Spergel, I. A. (1984). Violent gangs in Chicago, IL: In search of social policy. *Social Service Review, 58,* 199–226.

Spergel, I. A. (1986). The violent youth gang in Chicago, IL: A local community approach. *Social Service Review, 60,* 94–131.

Spergel, I. A. (1990). Youth gangs: Continuity and change. In M. Tonry & N. Morris (Eds.), *Crime and justice: A review of research* (Vol. 12, pp. 171–275). Chicago: University of Chicago.

Spergel, I. A. (1991). *Youth gangs: Problem and response.* Washington, DC: U.S. Department of Justice, Office of Justice Programs, Office of Juvenile Justice and Delinquency Prevention.

Spergel, I. A. (1995). *The youth gang problem: A community approach.* New York: Oxford University Press.

Spergel, I. A. (2007). Reducing youth gang violence: The Little Village Gang Project in Chicago. Lanham, MD: AltaMira Press.

Spergel, I. A. (1995). *The youth gang problem.* New York: Oxford University Press.

Spergel, I. A. (2007). Reducing youth gang violence: The Little Village Gang Project in Chicago. Lanham, MD: AltaMira Press.

Spergel, I. A. (2010a). Community gang programs: Theory, models, and effectiveness. In R. J. Chaskin (Ed.), *Youth gangs and community intervention: Research, practice, and evidence* (pp. 222–248). New York: Columbia University Press.

Spergel, I. A. (2010b). *A comprehensive, community-wide approach to the youth gang problem.* Paper presented at the 2010 Canada–U.S. Gang Summit, Toronto, March.

Spergel, I. A., & Bobrowski, L. (1989). Minutes from the Law Enforcement Youth Gang Definitional Conference: September 25, 1989. Rockville, MD: Juvenile Justice Clearinghouse.

Spergel, I. A., Chance, R., Ehrensaft, C., Regulus, T., Kane, C., & Laseter, R. (1992). *Technical assistance manuals: National gang suppression and intervention program.* Chicago: University of Chicago, School of Social Service Administration.

Spergel, I. A., Chance, R., Ehrensaft, C., Regulus, T., Kane, C., Laseter, R., Alexander, A., & Oh, S. (1994). *Gang suppression and intervention: Community models.* Washington, DC: U.S. Department of Justice, Office of Juvenile Justice and Delinquency Prevention.

Spergel, I. A., & Curry, G. D. (1993). The National Youth Gang Survey: A research and development process. In A. Goldstein & C. R. Huff (Eds.), *The gang intervention handbook* (pp. 359–400). Champaign, IL: Research Press.

Spergel, I. A., Wa, K. M., & Sosa, R. V. (2006). The comprehensive, community-wide, gang program model: Success and failure. In J. F. Short & L. A. Hughes (Eds.), *Studying youth gangs* (pp. 203–224). Lanham, MD: AltaMira Press.

St. Cyr, J. L. (2003). The folk devil reacts: Gangs and moral panic. *Criminal Justice Review, 28,* 26–45.

Starbuck, D., Howell, J. C., & Lindquist, D. J. (2001). *Into the millennium: Hybrids and other modern gangs* (Juvenile Justice Bulletin. Youth Gang Series). Washington, DC: U.S. Department of Justice, Office of Juvenile Justice and Delinquency Prevention.

Stevens, D. J. (1997, Summer). Origins and effects of prison drug gangs in North Carolina. *Journal of Gang Research, 4,* 23–35.

Stewart, E. A., Schreck, C. J., & Simons, R. L. (2006). "I ain't gonna let no one disrespect me": Does the code of the street reduce or increase violent victimization among African American adolescents? *Journal of Research in Crime and Delinquency, 43,* 427–458.

Stewart, E. A., & Simons, R. L. (2010). Race, code of the street, and violent delinquency: A multilevel investigation of neighborhood street culture and individual norms of violence. *Criminology, 48,* 569–605.

Stouthamer-Loeber, M., Loeber, R., Stallings, R., & Lacourse, E. (2008). Desistance from and persistence in offending. In R. Loeber, D. P. Farrington, M. Stouthamer-Loeber, et al. (Eds.), *Violence and serious theft: Development and prediction from childhood to adulthood* (pp. 269–306). New York: Routledge.

Stouthamer-Loeber, M., Loeber, R., Wei, E., Farrington, D. P., & Wikstrom, P. H. (2002). Risk and promotive effects in the explanation of persistent serious delinquency in boys. *Journal of Consulting and Clinical Psychology, 70,* 111–123.

Stretesky, P. B., & Pogrebin, M. R. (2007). Gang-related gun violence: Socialization, identity, and self. *Journal of Contemporary Ethnography, 36,* 85–114.

Strom, K. J., Colwell, A., Dawes, D., & Hawkins, S. (2010). *Evaluation of the Methodist Home for Children's value-based therapeutic environment model.* Research Triangle Park, NC: Research Triangle Institute.

Sugai, G., & Simonsen, B. (2012). *Positive behavioral interventions and supports: History, defining features, and misconceptions.* Storrs, CT: Center for Positive Behavioral Interventions and Supports, University of Connecticut.

Sullivan, J. P. (2006). Maras morphing: Revisiting third generation gangs. *Global Crime, 7*(3–4), 487–504.

Sullivan, M. L. (1993). Puerto Ricans in Sunset Park, Brooklyn: Poverty amidst ethnic and economic diversity. In J. W. Moore & R. Pinderhughes (Eds.), *In the barrios: Latinos and the underclass debate* (pp. 1–25). New York: Russell Sage Foundation.

Sullivan, M. L. (2005). Maybe we shouldn't study "gangs": Does reification obscure youth violence? *Journal of Contemporary Criminal Justice, 21,* 170–190.

Sullivan, M. L. (2006). Are "gang" studies dangerous? Youth violence, local context, and the problem of reification. In

J. F. Short & L. A. Hughes (Eds.), *Studying youth gangs* (pp. 15–36). Lanham, MD: AltaMira Press.

Sundt, J. L., Castellano, T. C., & Briggs, C. S. (2008). The sociopolitical context of prison violence and its control: A case study of supermax and its effect in Illinois. *The Prison Journal, 88,* 94–122.

Suttles, G. D. (1968). *The social order of the slum: Ethnicity and territory in the inner city.* Chicago: University of Chicago Press.

Sweeten, G., Pyrooz, D. C., & Piquero, A. R. (2013). Disengaging from gangs and desistance from crime. *Justice Quarterly, 30,* 469–500.

Tapia, M. (2014). Latino street gang emergence in the Midwest: Strategic franchising or natural migration? *Crime & Delinquency, 60,* 592–618.

Taylor, C. S. (1990a). *Dangerous society.* East Lansing: Michigan State University Press.

Taylor, C. S. (1990b). Gang imperialism. In C. R. Huff (Ed.), *Gangs in America* (pp. 103–115). Newbury Park, CA: Sage.

Taylor, C. S. (1993). *Girls, gangs, women, drugs.* East Lansing: Michigan State University Press.

Taylor, T. J. (2008). The boulevard ain't safe for your kids . . . Youth gang membership and violent victimization. *Journal of Contemporary Criminal Justice, 24,* 125–136.

Taylor, T. J., Freng, A., Esbensen, F., & Peterson, D. (2008). Youth gang membership and serious violent victimization: The importance of lifestyles and routine activities. *Journal of Interpersonal Violence, 23,* 1441–1464.

Telles, E. E., & Ortiz, V. (2008). *Generations of exclusion.* New York: Russell Sage Foundation.

Teske, S. C., & Huff, J. B. (2011). When did making adults mad become a crime? The court's role in dismantling the school-to-prison pipeline. *Juvenile and Family Justice Today,* Winter, 14–17.

Texas Department of Public Safety. (2013). *Texas public safety threat overview.* Retrieved from http://www.txdps.state.tx.us/director_staff/media_and_communications/threatoverview.pdf

Texas Fusion Center. (2013). *Texas gang threat assessment: 2012.* Austin, TX: Texas Fusion Center, Intelligence & Counterterrorism Division, Texas Department of Public Safety.

Thale, G., Bateman, J., & Goerdt, A. (2013). One year into the gang truce in El Salvador: Can the Funes administration turn the fragile truce into sustainable public policy? Washington, DC: Washington Office on Latin America. Retrieved from http://www.wola.org/commentary/one_year_into_the_gang_truce_in_el_salvador

Thomas, W. I. (1923). *The unadjusted girl.* Boston: Little, Brown.

Thomas, W. I., & Znaniecki, F. (1927). *The Polish peasant in Europe and America.* New York: Alfred A. Knopf.

Thompson, C., Young, R. L., & Burns, R. (2000). Representing gangs in the news: Media constructions of criminal gangs. *Sociological Spectrum, 20,* 409–432.

Thornberry, T. P. (1987). Toward an interactional theory of delinquency. *Criminology, 25*(4), 863–891.

Thornberry, T. P. (Ed.). (1997). *Developmental theories of crime and delinquency.* New Brunswick, NJ: Transaction Publishing.

Thornberry, T. P. (1998). Membership in youth gangs and involvement in serious and violent offending. In R. Loeber & D. P. Farrington (Eds.), *Serious and violent juvenile offenders: Risk factors and successful interventions* (pp. 147–166). Thousand Oaks, CA: Sage.

Thornberry, T. P. (2005). Explaining multiple patterns of offending across the life course and across generations. *The Annals of the American Academy of Political and Social Science, 602,* 156–195.

Thornberry, T. P., & Krohn, M. D. (2001). The development of delinquency: An interactional perspective. In S. O. White (Ed.), *Handbook of youth and justice* (pp. 289–305). New York: Plenum.

Thornberry, T. P., & Krohn, M. D. (2005). Applying interactional theory to the explanation of continuity and change in antisocial behavior. In D. P. Farrington (Ed.), *Integrated developmental and life-course theories of offending* (pp. 183–210). New Brunswick, NJ: Transaction Publishing.

Thornberry, T. P., Krohn, M. D., Lizotte, A. J., Smith, C. A., & Tobin, K. (2003). *Gangs and delinquency in developmental perspective.* New York: Cambridge University Press.

Thornberry, T. P., Lizotte, A. J., Krohn, M. D., Smith, C. A., & Porter, P. K. (2003). Causes and consequences of delinquency: Findings from the Rochester Youth Development Study. In T. P. Thornberry & M. D. Krohn (Eds.), *Taking stock of delinquency: An overview of findings from contemporary longitudinal studies* (pp. 11–46). New York: Kluwer Academic/Plenum Publishers.

Thrasher, F. M. (1927/2000). *The gang: A study of 1,313 gangs in Chicago.* Chicago: New Chicago School Press.

Tita, G. E. (1999). *An ecological study of violent urban street gangs and their crime.* Unpublished dissertation. Pittsburgh, PA: Carnegie Mellon University.

Tita, G. E., & Abrahamse, A. (2004). Gang homicide in LA, 1981–2001. *Perspectives on Violence Prevention, 3,* 1–18.

Tita, G. E., & Abrahamse, A. (2010). Homicide in California, 1981–2008: Measuring the impact of Los Angeles and gangs on overall homicide patterns. Sacramento, CA: Governor's Office of Gang and Youth Violence Policy.

Tita, G. E., & Cohen, J. (2004). Measuring spatial diffusion of shots fired activity across city neighborhoods. In M. F. Goodchild & D. G. Janelle (Eds.), *Spatially integrated social science* (pp. 171–204). New York: Oxford University Press.

Tita, G. E., Cohen, J., & Engberg, J. (2005). An ecological study of the location of gang "set space." *Social Problems, 52,* 272–299.

Tita, G. E., & Griffiths, E. (2005). Traveling to violence: The case for a mobility-based spatial typology of homicide. *Journal of Research in Crime and Delinquency, 42,* 275–308.

Tita, G. E., & Ridgeway, G. (2007). The impact of gang formation on local patterns of crime. *Journal of Research in Crime and Delinquency, 44,* 208–237.

Tita, G. E., Riley, K. J., & Greenwood, P. (2003). From Boston to Boyle Heights: The process and prospects of a "pulling levers" strategy in a Los Angeles barrio. In S. H. Decker (Ed.), *Policing gangs and youth violence* (pp. 102–130). Belmont, CA: Wadsworth/Thompson Learning.

Tita, G. E., Riley, K. J., & Greenwood, P. (2005). *Reducing gun violence: Operation Ceasefire in Los Angeles.* Washington, DC: National Institute of Justice.

Tita, G. E., Riley, K. J., Ridgeway, G., Grammich, C., Abrahamse, A., & Greenwood, P. W. (2003). *Reducing gun violence: Results from an intervention in East Los Angeles.* Santa Monica, CA: RAND.

Tobin, K. (2008). *Gangs: An individual and group perspective.* Upper Saddle River, NJ: Prentice Hall.

Toch, H. (2007). Sequestering gang members, burning witches, and subverting due process. *Criminal Justice and Behavior, 32,* 274–288.

Toch, H., & Adams, K. (1988). *Coping, maladaptation in prison.* New Brunswick, NJ: Transaction Publishing.

Tolan, P. H., & Gorman-Smith, D. (1998). Development of serious and violent offending careers. In R. Loeber & D. P. Farrington (Eds.), *Serious and violent juvenile offenders: Risk factors and successful interventions* (pp. 68–85). Thousand Oaks, CA: Sage.

Tolan, P. H., Gorman-Smith, D., & Henry, D. (2004). Supporting families in a high-risk setting: Proximal effects of the SAFEChildren Preventive Intervention. *Journal of Consulting and Clinical Psychology, 72*(5), 855–869.

Tonry, M. (Ed.). 2001. *Penal reform in overcrowded times.* New York: Oxford University Press.

Tonry, M. (2009). Explanations of American punishment policies: A national history. *Punishment and Society, 11,* 377–394.

Tremblay, R. E., Masse, L., Pagani, L., & Vitaro, F. (1996). From childhood physical aggression to adolescent maladjustment: The Montreal Prevention Experiment. In R. D. Peters & R. J. McMahon (Eds.), *Preventing childhood disorders, substance abuse, and delinquency* (pp. 268–298). Thousand Oaks, CA: Sage.

Ttofi, M. M., & Farrington, D. P. (2011). Effectiveness of programs to reduce school bullying: A Systematic and meta-analytic review. *Journal of Experimental Criminology, 7*(1), 27–56.

Tuttle, W. M. (1996). *Race riot: Chicago in the Red Summer of 1919*. Chicago: University of Chicago Press.

Uniform Crime Reports. 2005. *Crime in the United States 2005. Table 77: Full-time Law Enforcement Employees by State, 2005.*

United Nations Office on Drugs and Crime. (2007). *Crime and development in Central America: Caught in the crossfire*. New York: Author.

United States Attorney General. (1989). *Drug trafficking: A report to the President of the United States*. Washington, DC: U.S. Department of Justice

U.S. Agency for International Development. (2006). *Central America and Mexico gang assessment*. Washington, DC: Bureau for Latin American and Caribbean Affairs, U.S. Agency for International Development.

U.S. Bureau of Economic Analysis. (2005). Gross Domestic Product (GDP) by State, 2006. http://www.bea.gov/newsreleases/regional/gdp_state/2007/gsp0607.htm

U.S. Census Bureau. (2001). Census 2000 Summary File 1. Population in Group Quarters: Institutionalized Population: Correctional Institutions.

U.S. Department of Justice. (2008, December 5). *Arrests dismantle cocaine and methamphetamine trafficking organization in Abilene, Texas*. Retrieved from http://www.justice.gov/usao/txn/PressRel08/valdiviez_etal_tango%20blast_indict_abilene_pr.html

U.S. Department of Justice, Bureau of Justice Statistics. (2002). *National Prosecutors Survey, 2001* [Computer file]. Conducted by the National Opinion Research Center. ICPSR ed. Ann Arbor, MI: Inter-university Consortium for Political and Social Research.

U.S. General Accounting Office. (1989). *Nontraditional organized crime*. Washington, DC: U.S. Government Printing Office.

U.S. General Accounting Office. (1996). *Violent crime: Federal law enforcement assistance in fighting Los Angeles gang violence*. Washington, DC: U.S. Government Printing Office.

U.S. Government Accountability Office. (2010). *Combating gangs: Federal agencies have implemented a Central American gang strategy, but could strengthen oversight and measurement of efforts*. Washington, DC: U.S. Government Accountability Office.

Valdez, Al. (2007). *Gangs: A guide to understanding street gangs* (5th ed.). San Clemente, CA: LawTech.

Valdez, Al, & Enriquez, R. (2011). *Urban street terrorism: The Mexican Mafia and the Surenos*. Santa Ana, CA: Police and Fire.

Valdez, Av. (2003). Toward a typology of contemporary Mexican American youth gangs. In L. Kontos, D. Brotherton, & L. Barrios (Eds.), *Gangs and society: Alternative perspectives* (pp. 12–40). New York: Columbia University Press.

Valdez, Av. (2007). *Mexican American girls and gang violence: Beyond risk*. New York: Palgrave Macmillan.

Valdez, Av., Cepeda, A., & Kaplan, C. (2009). Homicidal events among Mexican American street gangs: A situational analysis. *Homicide Studies, 13*, 288–306.

Valdez, Av., Cepeda, A., Parrish, D., Horowitz, R., & Kaplan, C. (2013). An adapted Brief Strategic Family Therapy for gang-affiliated Mexican American adolescents. *Research on Social Work Practice, 23*, 383–396.

Valdez, Av., Kaplan, C. D., & Codina, E. (2000). Psychopathy among Mexican American gang members: A comparative study. *International Journal of Offender Therapy and Comparative Criminology, 44*, 46–58.

Valdez, Av., & Sifaneck, S. J. (2004). "Getting high and getting by": Dimensions of drug selling behaviors among Mexican gang members in south Texas. *Journal of Research in Crime and Delinquency, 41*(1), 82–105.

Van der Put, C. E., Deković, M., Hoeve, M., G. J. J. M. Stams, van der Laan, P. H., & Langewouters, F. E. M. (2014). Risk Assessment of girls: Are there any sex differences in risk factors for re-offending and in risk profiles? *Crime and Delinquency, 60*, 1033–1056.

van Gemert, F., & Decker, S. (2008). Migrant groups and gang activity: A contrast between Europe and the USA. In F. van Gemert, D. Peterson, & I.-L. Lien (Eds.), *Street gangs, migration and ethnicity* (pp. 15–30). Portland, OR: Willan Publishing.

van Gemert, F., Peterson, D., & Lien, I.-L. (Eds.). (2008). *Street gangs, migration and ethnicity*. Portland, OR: Willan Publishing.

Vazsonyi, A. T., Belliston, L. M., & Flannery, D. J. (2004). Evaluation of a school-based, universal violence prevention program: Low-, medium- and high-risk children. *Youth Violence and Juvenile Justice, 2*, 185–206.

Vaughn, M. G., DeLisi, M., Beaver, K. M., & Wright, J. P. (2009). Identification of latent classes of behavioral risk based on early childhood manifestations of self-control. *Youth Violence and Juvenile Justice, 7*, 16–31.

Veal, R. T. (1919). *Classified bibliography of boy life and organized work with boys*. New York: Association Press.

Venkatesh, S. A. (1996). The gang and the community. In C. R. Huff (Ed.), *Gangs in America* (2nd ed., pp. 241–256). Thousand Oaks, CA: Sage.

Venkatesh, S. A. (2000). *American project: The rise and fall of a modern ghetto*. Cambridge, MA: Harvard University Press.

Venkatesh, S. A. (2002). *American project: The rise and fall of a modern ghetto* (2nd ed.). Cambridge, MA: Harvard University Press.

Venkatesh, S. A. (2008). *Gang leader for a day: A rogue sociologist takes to the streets*. New York: Penguin Press.

Venkatesh, S. A., Çelimli, I., Miller, D., Murphy, A., & Turne, B. (2004). *Chicago public housing transformation: A research report.* Working Paper. Columbia University: Center for Urban Research and Policy. Retrieved from http://www.columbia.edu/cu/curp/publications2/PH_Transformation_Report.pdf

Vericker, T., Pergamit, M., Macomber, J., & Kuehn, D. (2009). *Vulnerable youth and the transition to adulthood: Second-generation Latinos connecting to school and work* (ASPE Research Brief, July). Washington, DC: Office of Human Services Policy, U.S. Department of Education.

Vigil, J. D. (1988). Barrio gangs: Street life and identity in Southern California. Austin: University of Texas Press.

Vigil, J. D. (1990). Cholos and gangs: Culture change and street youth in Los Angeles. In C. R. Huff (Ed.), *Gangs in America* (pp. 116–128). Newbury Park, CA: Sage.

Vigil, J. D. (1993). The established gang. In S. Cummings & D. J. Monti (Eds.), *Gangs: The origins and impact of contemporary youth gangs in the United States* (pp. 95–112). Albany: State University of New York Press.

Vigil, J. D. (1998). From Indians to Chicanos: The dynamics of Mexican-American culture (2nd ed.). Prospect Heights, IL: Waveland.

Vigil, J. D. (2002). *A rainbow of gangs: Street cultures in the mega-city.* Austin: University of Texas Press.

Vigil, J. D. (2004). Street baptism: Chicano gang initiation. In F. Esbensen, S. G. Tibbetts, & L. Gaines (Eds.), *American youth gangs at the millennium* (pp. 218–228). Long Grove, IL: Waveland Press.

Vigil, J. D. (2006). A multiple marginality framework of gangs. In A. Egley, C. L. Maxson, J. Miller, & M. W. Klein (Eds.), *The modern gang reader* (3rd ed., pp. 20–29). Los Angeles: Roxbury.

Vigil, J. D. (2007). *The projects: Gang and non-gang families in East Los Angeles.* Thousand Oaks, CA: Sage.

Vigil, J. D. (2008). Mexican migrants in gangs: A second-generation history. In F. van Gemert, D. Peterson, & I.-L. Lien (Eds.), *Street gangs, migration and ethnicity* (pp. 49–62). Portland, OR: Willan Publishing.

Vigil, J. D. (2010a). *Gang redux: A balanced anti-gang strategy.* Long Grove, IL: Waveland Press.

Vigil, J. D. (2010b). Multiple marginality and human development: Applying research insights for gang prevention and intervention. In R. J. Chaskin (Ed.), *Youth Gangs and Community Intervention: Research, Practice, and Evidence* (pp. 155–174). New York: Columbia University Press.

Vigil, J. D. (2014). Cholo! The migratory origins of Chicano gangs in Los Angeles. In J. M. Hazen & D. Rodgers (Eds.), *Global gangs: Street violence across the world* (pp. 49–64). Minneapolis: University of Minnesota.

Vigil, J. D., & Long, J. M. (1990). Emic and etic perspectives on gang culture. In C. R. Huff (Ed.), *Gangs in America* (pp. 55–70). Newbury Park, CA: Sage.

Voogd, J. (2008). *Race riots and resistance: The Red Summer of 1919.* New York: Peter Lang Publishing, Inc.

Wacquant, L. (2001). Deadly symbiosis: When ghetto and prison meet and mesh. *Punishment & Society, 3*(1), 95–133.

Wacquant, L. (2007). Urban outcasts: A comparative sociology of advanced marginality. Cambridge: Polity Press.

Wagner, M. (2006, February 19). Do we have a gang problem? Police admit Springfield is home to hundreds of gang members, but they say a presence doesn't equal a problem: Some residents say police hide behind semantics as gangs poison neighborhoods with drugs, violence and crime. *Springfield News-Leader.* Retrieved from http://archive.news-leader.com/article/20060219/NEWS01/602190383/Do-we-gang-problem-

Wakefield, S., & Wildeman, C. (2013). *Children of the prison boom: Mass incarceration and the future of American inequality.* Oxford: Oxford University Press.

Waldorf, D. (1993). When the Crips invaded San Francisco—gang migration. *Journal of Gang Research, 1,* 11–16.

Waldorf, D., & Lauderback, D. (1993). *Gang drug sales in San Francisco: Organized or freelance?* Alameda, CA: Institute for Scientific Analysis.

Walker-Barnes, C. J., & Mason, C. A. (2001). Ethnic differences in the effect of parenting on gang involvement and gang delinquency: A longitudinal, hierarchical linear modeling perspective. *Child Development, 72,* 1814–1831.

Walker, M. L., & Schmidt, L. M. (1996). Gang reduction efforts by the Task Force on Violent Crime in Cleveland, Ohio. In C. R. Huff (Ed.), *Gangs in America* (2nd ed., pp. 263–269). Thousand Oaks, CA: Sage.

Warr, M. (1996). Organization and instigation in delinquent groups. *Criminology, 34,* 11–37.

Warr, M. (2002). *Companions in crime: The social aspects of criminal conduct.* New York: Cambridge University Press.

Washington Office on Latin America. (2010). *Executive summary: Transnational youth gangs in Central America, Mexico and the United States.* Washington, DC: Author.

Wasserman, G. A., & Ko, S. J. (2003). *Columbia guidelines for child and adolescent mental health referral.* New York: Columbia University Department of Child and Adolescent Psychiatry, Center for the Promotion of Mental Health in Juvenile Justice.

Wasserman, G. A., McReynolds, L. S., Ko, S. J., Katz, L. M., & Carpenter, J. (2005). Gender differences in psychiatric disorders at juvenile probation intake. *American Journal of Public Health, 95,* 131–137.

Wasserman, G. A., McReynolds, L. S., Schwalbe, C. S., Keating, J. M., & Jones, S. A. (2010). Psychiatric disorder, comorbidity,

and suicidal behavior in juvenile justice youth. *Criminal Justice and Behavior, 37,* 1361–1376.

Wasserman, G. A., & Seracini, A. M. (2001). Family risk factors and interventions. In R. Loeber & D. P. Farrington (Eds.), *Child delinquents: Development, interventions, and service needs* (pp. 165–189). Thousand Oaks, CA: Sage.

Waters, T. (1999). *Crime and immigrant youth.* Thousand Oaks, CA: Sage.

Watkins, A., Huebner, B., & Decker, S. (2008). Patterns of gun acquisition, carrying and use among juvenile and adult arrestees: Evidence from a high-crime city. *Justice Quarterly, 25,* 674–700.

Weber, K. (Ed.). (2010). *Waiting for "superman."* New York: Perseus Books Group.

Webster, D. W., Whitehill, J. M., Vernick, J. S., & Curriero, F. C. (2013). Effects of Baltimore's *Safe Streets* program on gun violence: A replication of Chicago's CeaseFire Program. *Journal of Urban Health, 90,* 27–40.

Weerman, F. M., & Hoeve, M. (2012). Peers and delinquency among girls and boys: Are sex differences in delinquency explained by peer factors? *European Journal of Criminology, 9,* 228–244.

Weinberger, S. (2012). A data-driven war on crime: Scientific tools inform a unique combination of military tactics and police work. *Nature, 484,* 16–17.

Weisburd, D., Bushway, S., Lum, C., & Yang, S. (2004). Trajectories of crime at places: A longitudinal study of street segments on the city of Seattle. *Criminology, 42,* 283–321.

Weisel, D. L. (2002a). *Contemporary gangs: An organizational analysis.* New York: LFB Scholarly Publishing.

Weisel, D. L. (2002b). The evolution of street gangs: An examination of form and variation. In W. Reed & S. Decker (Eds.), *Responding to gangs: Evaluation and research* (pp. 25–65). Washington, DC: U.S. Department of Justice, National Institute of Justice.

Weisel, D. L. (2004). *Graffiti* (Problem-Oriented Guides for Police. Guide No. 9). Washington, DC: Office of Community Oriented Policing Services.

Weisel, D. L., & Howell, J. C. (2007). Comprehensive gang assessment: A report to the Durham Police Department and Durham County Sheriff's Office. Durham, NC: Durham Police Department.

Welch, M., Price, E. A., & Yankey, N. (2002). Moral panic over youth violence: Wilding and the manufacture of menace in the media. *Youth & Society, 34,* 3–30.

Wellford, C., Pepper, J. V., & Petrie, C. (2005). *Firearms and violence: A critical review.* Washington, DC: National Academies Press.

Wells, L. E., & Weisheit, R. A. (2001). Gang problems in nonmetropolitan areas: A longitudinal assessment. *Justice Quarterly, 18,* 791–823.

Welsh, B. C., & Farrington, D. P. (2006). Evidence-based crime prevention. In B. C. Welsh & D. P. Farrington (Eds.), *Preventing crime: What works for children, offenders, victims, and places* (pp. 1–17). Dordrecht, The Netherlands: Springer.

Welsh, B. C., & Farrington, D. P. (2007). Save children from a life of crime. *Criminology and Public Policy, 6,* 871–879.

Welsh, B. C., Sullivan, C. J., & Olds, D. L. (2010). When early crime prevention goes to scale: A new look at the evidence. *Prevention Science, 11,* 115–125.

West, C. (1993). *Race matters.* Boston: Beacon.

White, N. A., & Loeber, R. (2008). Bullying and special education as predictors of serious delinquency. *Journal of Research in Crime and Delinquency, 45,* 380–397.

White, R. (2008). Disputed definitions and fluid identities: The limitations of social profiling in relation to ethnic youth gangs. *Youth Justice, 8,* 149–161.

Whyte, W. F. (1943a). Social organization in the slums. *The American Sociological Review, 8,* 34–39.

Whyte, W. F. (1943b). *Street corner society: The social structure of an Italian slum.* Chicago: University of Chicago Press.

Wiebe, D. J. (1998). *Targeting and gang crime: Assessing the impacts of a multi-agency suppression strategy in Orange County, California.* Paper presented at the annual meeting of the American Society of Criminology, Washington, DC, November.

Wiebe, D. J., Meeker, J. W., & Vila, B. (1999). *Hourly trends of gang crime incidents, 1995–1998.* University of California, Irvine: Focused Research Group on Gangs.

Wiist, W. H., Jackson, R. H., & Jackson, K. W. (1996). Peer and community leader education to prevent youth violence. *American Journal of Preventive Medicine,* Suppl., *12*(5), 60.

Wikstrom, P. H., & Treiber, K. (2009). Violence as situational action. *International Journal of Conflict and Violence, 3,* 75–96.

Wilgoren, J., & Elston, B. (1993, April 29). Newport Beach moves to head off gang problems: Crime: Affluent community's rates of graffiti and teen violence are 'miniscule' compared to other areas, but city has shaped aggressive strategy: Some residents say police overreact. *The Los Angeles Times.* Retrieved from http://articles.latimes.com/1993-04-29/news/mn-28509_1_newport-beach

Will, D., & Fryer, R.G., Jr. (2010). *Are high-quality schools enough to increase achievement among the poor? Evidence from the Harlem Children's Zone.* Cambridge, MA: The Kennedy School, Harvard University. Retrieved from http://scholar.harvard.edu/files/fryer/files/hcz_nov_2010.pdf

Williams, K., Curry, G. D., & Cohen, M. (2002). Gang prevention programs for female adolescents: An evaluation. In W. L. Reed & S. H. Decker (Eds.), *Responding to gangs: Evaluation and research* (pp. 225–263). Washington, DC: U.S. Department of Justice, National Institute of Justice.

Wilson, J. Q. (1995). Crime and public policy. In J. Q. Wilson & J. Petersilia (Eds.), *Crime* (pp. 489–507). San Francisco: ICS Press.

Wilson, S. J., & Lipsey, M. W. (2007). School-based interventions for aggressive and disruptive behavior: Update of a meta-analysis. *American Journal of Preventive Medicine, 33*(Supplement), S130–S143.

Wilson, W. J. (1987). *The truly disadvantaged: The inner city, the underclass, and public policy.* Chicago: University of Chicago Press.

Wilson, W. J. (1999). Societal changes and vulnerable neighborhoods. In F. L. Pincus & H. J. Ehrlich (Eds.), *Race and ethnic conflict* (pp. 110–119). Boulder, CO: Westview Press.

Winfree, L. T., Fuller, K., Vigil, T., & Mays, G. L. (1992). The definition and measurement of "gang status": Policy implications for juvenile justice. *Juvenile and Family Court Journal, 43,* 29–38.

Winterdyk, J., & Ruddell, R. (2010). Managing prison gangs: Results from a survey of U.S. prison systems. *Journal of Criminal Justice, 38,* 730–736.

Wirth, L. (1928). *The ghetto.* Chicago: University of Chicago Press.

Witness Places Gang at Warwick: Rettich Brother-in-Law Testifies at Gang Trial. (1935, June 26). *The Telegraph.* Available at http://news.google.com/newspapers?nid=2209&dat=19350626&id=Rvo_AAAAIBAJ&sjid=m6QMAAAAIBAJ&pg=6706,6144748

Wolf, A. M., & Gutierrez, L. (2012). *It's about time: Prevention and intervention services for gang-affiliated girls.* Oakland, CA: National Council on Crime and Delinquency.

Wolfgang, M. E., & Ferracuti, F. (1967). *The subculture of violence: Towards an integrated theory in criminology.* London: Tavistock Publications.

Wood, J., & Alleyne, E. (2010). Street gang theory and research: Where are we now and where do we go from here? *Aggression and Violent Behavior, 15,* 100–111.

Woodward, C. V. (1951). *Origins of the new south, 1877–1913.* Baton Rouge: Louisiana State University Press.

Wyrick, P. A. (2006). Gang prevention: How to make the "front end" of your anti-gang effort work. *United States Attorneys' Bulletin, 54,* 52–60.

Yablonsky, L. (1959). The delinquent gang as a near-group. *Social Problems, 7,* 108–117.

Yablonsky, L. (1967). *The violent gang* (Rev. ed.). New York: Penguin.

Yiu, H. L., & Gottfredson, G. D. (2014). Gang participation. *Crime & Delinquency, 60,* 619–642.

Yoder, K. A., Whitbeck, L. B., & Hoyt, D. R. (2003). Gang involvement and membership among homeless and runaway youth. *Youth and Society, 34,* 441–467.

Zahn, M. A., Day, J. C., Mihalic, S. F., & Tichavsky, L. (2009). Determining what works for girls in the juvenile justice system: A summary of evaluation evidence. *Crime and Delinquency, 55,* 266–293.

Zatz, M. S. (1987). Chicano youth gangs and crime: The creation of moral panic. *Contemporary Crises, 11,* 129–158.

Zatz, M. S., & Portillos, E. L. (2000). Voices from the barrio: Chicano/a gangs, families, and communities. *Criminology, 38,* 369–401.

Zevitz, R. G., & Takata, S. R. (1992). Metropolitan gang influence and the emergence of group delinquency in a regional community. *Journal of Criminal Justice, 20,* 93–106.

Zhou, M., Lee, J., Vallejo, J. A., Tafora-Estrada, R., & Xiong, Y. S. (2008). Success attained, deterred, and denied: Divergent pathways to social mobility in Los Angeles's new second generation. *The Annals of the American Academy of Political and Social Science, 620,* 37–61.

Zilberg, E. (2011). *Space of detention: The making of a transnational gang crisis between Los Angeles and San Salvador.* Durham, NC: Duke University Press.

Zorbaugh, H. (1929). *Gold coast and slum.* Chicago: University of Chicago Press.

Index

Rap music, 83–84

Raudenbush, S. W., 91(n)

Raymond Ave Crips, 188

Reaction formation theory, 74 (table)

Reckless, W. C., 101

Recreational incidents, 197

Recruiting, 32–33, 185, 224, 241

Recruitment myth, 32–33

Reentry plans (prison gang members), 248

Regional cell model, prison gangs, 50–51

Regional trends, 167

Relatives:

    female, of gang members, 131

    in Valdez typology, 131

    See also Brief Strategic Family Therapy

        (BSFT); Family risk factors

Reliability, of survey, 148

Reno, Nevada, 25

Rep, 85, 266

Represent, 267

Research-based gang prevention, 212–221

Research-based programs, 223–224

Residential centers, supervised, 233

Resistance identities, 84

Retaliation, 16, 181, 197, 198, 204, 241

Retribution, 181, 204

Revenge, 181, 197, 204

Ricky Ross, 83

Ridgeway, G., 30, 48, 186

Riley, K. J., 30, 48

RIP (Rest in Peace), 56

Risk factors for gang involvement:

    about, 103–104, 107–110 (table)

    community or neighborhood factors, 112

    early adolescent stage, 105 (figure), 111–114

    family risk factors, 112, 130

    girls and, 129–131

    individual risk factors, 113–114

    later childhood stage, 105 (figure), 111

    peer risk factors, 113, 130

    preschool stage, 105 (figure), 106

    school entry stage, 105 (figure), 106, 110–111

    school risk factors, 112–113

Rite of Passage program, 136

Ritual, 53–54, 56

Ritual-associated myths, 31–32

Rivalry, gang, 265

Robbery, 198

Robert Taylor Homes (RTH), 6–7

Rochester, New York, 63, 64

Rochester Youth Development Study:

    firearm possession and use, 191

    life-course—persistent and adolescence-limited

        offenders, 96

    onset of juvenile offending, 96

    protective factors, 115

    young girls, 126

Rolled on, 127, 267

Rollin 30s Harlem Crips, 167

Rollin 40s, 167

Rollin 60s, 167, 188

Rolling out, 181, 267

Romantic interests, 103

Rosenfeld, R., 36

Routine activities/opportunity theory, 74 (table), 86–87

RTH. *See* Robert Taylor Homes (RTH)

Rumble, 267

Rumors, 198

Running away, 95 (figure), 96, 135

Rural areas, 64

SAFEChildren. *See* Schools And Families Educating

    Children (SAFEChildren)

Safe Dates, 136

Safety, community, 232

Salvadorian gangs, 66

Sampson, R. J., 79, 88, 91(n), 96–97

San Antonio:

    barrio-territorial gangs, 52

    Brief Strategic Family Therapy (BSFT), 230

    early gang formation, 12–13

    family risk factors, 132

    female affiliates, 135

    first problems in, 13

    gang association *versus* membership, 103

    gang romantic interests, 103

    girls' gang association, 103

    homicides, 180

    prevention program characteristics, 255–266 (table)

    sociopath study, 114

    Southern gang history, 12–13

    study of girls, 129–131

    Valdez' four gang types, 51–52

Sanders, W. B., 53, 102–103

San Diego:

    formation of the Del Sol gang, 214

    gangs with low levels of organization, 25

    Mexican American gangs, 102–103

San Francisco, 11, 25

Sante, L., 1

About the Authors

Dr. James C. (Buddy) Howell is a Senior Research Associate with the National Gang Center, in Tallahassee, Florida, where he has worked for 19 years. He formerly worked at the U.S. Department of Justice for 23 years, mostly as director of research and program development in the Office of Juvenile Justice and Delinquency Prevention. He has published 50 works on youth and street gangs, and a similar number on juvenile justice and delinquency prevention, and seven books on both topics. His gang publication topics include street gang history; gang homicides; drug trafficking; gangs in schools; hybrid gangs; myths about gangs; risk factors; gang problem trends; gang history in the United States; and what works in preventing gang activity, combating gangs, and reducing gang crime. He is very active in helping states and localities reform their juvenile justice systems and use evidence-based programs, and in working with these entities to address youth gang problems in a balanced approach.

Dr. Elizabeth Griffiths is an Associate Professor in the School of Criminal Justice at Rutgers University-Newark. After completing her Ph.D. in Sociology at the University of Toronto, she joined the faculty of the Department of Sociology at Emory University before moving to Rutgers in 2011. She is also a former predoctoral fellow of the National Consortium on Violence Research and a former Junior Fellow of the Centre of Criminology at the University of Toronto. Her research spans multiple substantive and methodological areas, including communities and crime, spatial diffusion of violence, temporal trends in homicide, the emergence of gangs in places, the transformation of public housing, youth crime and the code of the street, the efficacy of drug-free zones, and victimization risk, among others.

⑤SAGE researchmethods

The essential online tool for researchers from the world's leading methods publisher

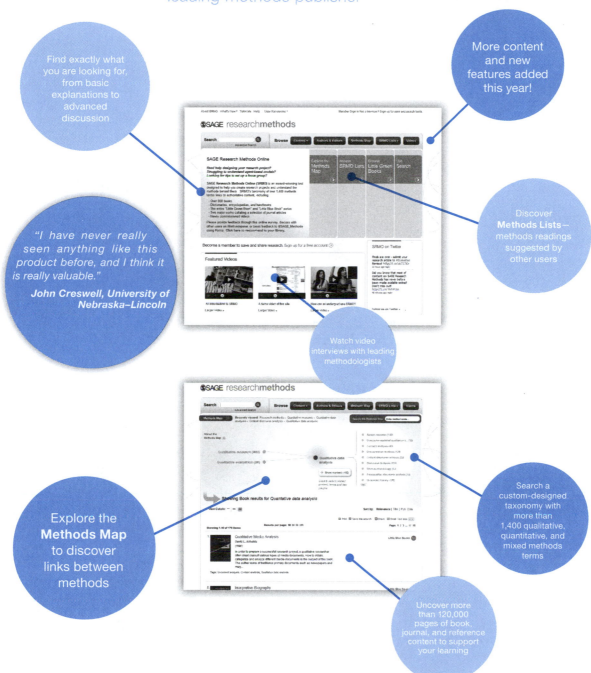

Find exactly what you are looking for, from basic explanations to advanced discussion

More content and new features added this year!

"I have never really seen anything like this product before, and I think it is really valuable."

John Creswell, University of Nebraska–Lincoln

Discover **Methods Lists**— methods readings suggested by other users

Watch video interviews with leading methodologists

Explore the **Methods Map** to discover links between methods

Search a custom-designed taxonomy with more than 1,400 qualitative, quantitative, and mixed methods terms

Uncover more than 120,000 pages of book, journal, and reference content to support your learning

Find out more at
www.sageresearchmethods.com